G U

IRELAND

Travel Publications

Irl. Ang 1

Note to readers

To help you plan your trip, look at the itineraries shown on the map on the inside of the rear cover of the book and read the chapter entitled "Practical information".

More detailed itineraries are shown on larger-scale maps in the main text of the guide. The symbol ■ indicates possible overnight stops. After each description of a town or itinerary, there is a "Making the most of..." section (eg "Making the most of Dublin"); this provides practical details about the place: access, useful addresses, accommodation, restaurants, leisure, shopping, etc. Hotels and places to eat are ranked by price (in pounds and euros as appropriate) to help you manage your budget. Bear in mind that living costs vary constantly and that opening times are subject to modification, and that the practical information given in the guide may have changed since publication.

Michelin Travel Publications
Published in 2001

◄NEOS►

N ew – In the NEOS guides emphasis is placed on the discovery and enjoyment of a new destination through meeting the people, tasting the food and absorbing the exotic atmosphere. In addition to recommendations on which sights to see, we give details on the most suitable places to stay and eat, on what to look out for in traditional markets and where to go in search of the hidden character of the region, its crafts and its dancing rhythms. For those keen to explore places on foot, we provide guidelines and useful addresses in order to help organise walks to suit all tastes.

E xpert – The NEOS guides are written by people who have travelled in the country and researched the sites before recommending them by the allocation of stars. Accommodation and restaurants are similarly recommended by a 🐢 on the grounds of quality and value for money. Cartographers have drawn easy-to-use maps with clearly marked itineraries, as well as detailed plans of towns, archaeological sites and large museums.

O pen to all cultures, the NEOS guides provide an insight into the daily lives of the local people. In a world that is becoming ever more accessible, it is vital that religious practices, regional etiquette, traditional customs and languages be understood and respected by all travellers. Equipped with this knowledge, visitors can seek to share and enjoy with confidence the best of the local cuisine, musical harmonies and the skills involved in the production of arts and crafts.

S ensitive to the atmosphere and heritage of a foreign land, the NEOS guides encourage travellers to see, hear, smell and feel a country, through words and images. Take inspiration from the enthusiasm of our experienced travel writers and make this a journey full of discovery and enchantment.

B. Brillion/MICHELIN

B. Brillion/MICHELIN

THE REPUBLIC OF IRELAND

NORTHERN IRELAND

Setting the scene

The monastic site
at Glendalough

THE EMERALD ISLE

Ireland covers an area of 84 421sq km, which makes it roughly a third the size of Great Britain. Around 5.4 million people live here, 1.7 million of them in the North. The shape and relatively small size of the island – maximum distance north-south 483km, east-west 275km – means that nowhere is one very far from the sea. But short distances do not necessarily mean short travelling times; roads are often narrow and winding, some stretches carry a lot of traffic, and signposting can be vague. But Ireland, perhaps more than anywhere, is not a country to hurry through!

The face of the land

Despite the country's small size, it has an extraordinary diversity of landscapes, thanks to a long and varied geological history.

Fire and water form the land

Ireland's oldest rocks date from the Paleozoic era (570-245 million years ago). Among them are the granite making up the **Wicklow** and **Blackstair Mountains** in the southeast and parts of **Donegal** in the northwest. But the most commonly-occurring rock is Carboniferous limestone, the foundation over which the rivers in the centre of the country wind their sinuous course.

The imprint of the volcanoes – Ireland's mountains were formed during the continental folding of around 280 million years ago, modified subsequently by volcanic activity at the beginning of the Tertiary era. Despite their relatively low height, which rarely exceeds 800m, they are real mountains, and each range has its own particular personality. Some massifs and individual mountains have a very distinctive character indeed, among them the volcano-like shape of Errigal Mountain in Donegal. The most extensive uplands are the Wicklow Mountains to the south of Dublin, while the country's highest point is in the Iveragh Peninsula in southwestern Killarney, where **Carrantuohill** (1 038m) is the only summit to exceed 1 000m.

The mark of the glaciers – The appearance of today's landscape is largely the work of the glaciers, which only retreated about 10 000 years ago, after having held the country in a grip of ice for more than a million years. The ice eroded the ancient mountain ranges, gouging out corries and lakes, and depositing sheets of clay, sand and gravel, such as those forming the plain of the **Curragh** to the west of Dublin. **Drumlins** too were formed by the retreat of the ice, and these low, whaleback-shaped hills often determine the character of a whole landscape; they are particularly prominent in Ulster, where the islands in Strangford Lough show the presence of a drumlin "swarm".

Coasts wild and tame

Ireland's hills, plains and mountains meet the country's 3 172km of coastline in a variety of different ways. In places, rivers have carved out broad estuaries, while elsewhere there are **fjords** and other **inlets** running far inland, especially along the **west coast**. There are many stretches of spectacular cliffs; the south face of **Slieve League** in Donegal drops almost 600m into the sea, while the **Cliffs of Moher** in Co Clare, though lower, are equally impressive.

The **east coast** is gentler. Here, a quiet countryside of wooded hills and undulating farmland often reaches the sea in lines of low limestone cliffs and long sandy beaches. In the **north**, the coastline becomes more dramatic. In **Co Antrim**, basalt uplands cut by deep glens fall steeply to the sea, while the famous **Giant's Causeway** is made up of massed columns of hard basalt.

Pervasive peatlands

The appearance and ecology of much of the Irish landscape is determined by the presence of vast deposits of peat, or **"turf"** as it is known locally.

The typical Irish bog consists of a thick layer of spongy brown matter, which, when dried, can be used as a fuel of reasonable quality and has a characteristic, much appreciated smell. Peat is formed through the gradual decomposition of mosses and other plant material accumulating over thousands of years in damp conditions. Despite the identical way in which the peat is formed, different types of bog are distinguished depending on whether they belong to mountains, plains or woodland. The main difference is between **raised bog**, or climatic bog, developing from grasslands in areas of high rainfall in the west, and **blanket bog**, or topographical bog consisting mostly of decayed mosses, which is characteristic of the drier midlands.

The boglands in the centre of the country can reach a thickness of 12m, and it is this type of peat which lends itself to exploitation on an industrial scale. In the past, peat was extracted by hand, using a range of traditional tools, but in modern times the process has been mechanised. Peat is sold in the form of briquettes for use in domestic fires, and is burnt in power stations, supplying about 14% of the country's electricity. It is also used in horticulture and in the chemical industry.

Peat in the service of archaeology – The acidity of bogs means that many relics of the past have been preserved in them. These range from skeletons of giant Ice Age deer and mummified human corpses to Neolithic boats and a multitude of everyday items from many periods. Many of these treasures are prized items in the country's museums, while "bog fir" (pine wood thousands of years old) is used creatively by cabinetmakers.

Waters of Erin

The abundant rainfall falling on this greenest of lands feeds an important network of rivers totalling some 26 000km in length. Irish waterways became significant communication routes very early in the country's history, and were of great use to the Vikings in their incursions.

Watercourses – Ireland's longest river is the **Shannon** (370km), which drains much of the centre of the country and is navigable for much of its course. It widens out to form Lough Ree and Lough Derg, both very popular for pleasure craft as well as forming useful reservoirs capable of accommodating excess water in times of flood. In the 17C and 18C, the **Grand Canal** was dug, linking the Shannon to Dublin and the east coast, and opening up much of the country to inland navigation. A number of rivers of lesser importance than the Shannon, the **Blackwater**, the **Nore**, the **Suir**, the **Barrow** and the **Slaney**, originate in the centre of the country and converge towards the south coast; here they meet the sea in a series of drowned valleys, long inlets reaching far inland. Waterford Harbour, fed by the Three Sisters of Suir, Barrow and Nore, is the most impressive of these inlets.

A land of lakes – Lakes and loughs cover a total of 1 450sqkm of the country. The largest of them is **Lough Neagh** in Northern Ireland; vast but shallow, and teeming with eels, it occupies an area of 400sqkm. The reed-beds and flat farmland around its shores are unspectacular, in contrast to the forests and uplands framing **Lough Erne**, the largest of the countless bodies of water making up the Fermanagh lakeland. A unique feature of the Irish landscape is the **turlough** (or *turloch*), a temporary lake filling and emptying according to fluctuations in the water table. Artificial water bodies have their place too, ranging from the ornamental lakes laid out to enhance their parklands by 18C Anglo-Irish grandees to the upland reservoirs ensuring Dublin's water supply.

Four seasons in one day

Ireland has an **oceanic climate**, tempered by the influence of the **Gulf Stream** washing its western shores. Average temperatures fluctuate between 4°C and 7°C in the coldest months of January and February, and between 14°C and 16°C in the warmest months of July and August. Except in the high mountains, where temperatures sometimes fall below zero, it is rarely very cold.

Ireland enjoys abundant **precipitation** the whole year. April is the driest month, and maximum average sunshine occurs in May and June, with between 5hr30min and 6hr30min daily. Because of the winds blowing in from the Atlantic, the weather can change several times in the course of a single day, with a perfect blue sky giving way to a leaden cover of cloud in a matter of hours, if not minutes. Rare is the day without rain, and no traveller should be without their raincoat, anorak or umbrella (*see page 80*).

Majestic nature

Trees thrive in the Irish climate, and everywhere large and majestic specimens can be seen flourishing in the favourable environment. Nevertheless, some exposed areas in the west are almost treeless, and overall Ireland has the smallest amount of woodland cover of any European country, a mere 4% of its area.

Massive deforestation

Ireland was originally covered by vast forests of **oak**, the tree which has given its name to places like Kildare (*Cill Dara* = church of the oak wood) or Londonderry (*Doire* = oak grove). The clearing of woodland for agriculture took a dramatic turn in the 18C, when huge numbers of trees were felled for industrial purposes and ship-building, as well as to deprive rebels and insurgents of their traditional lurking places. Further felling took place in the late 19C, when estates were broken up to provide smallholdings. Since independence, a determined policy of reafforestation has been pursued, mostly using exotic conifers but also native deciduous trees, in the reclamation of worked-out peat bogs.

Parks and gardens

The country is rich in parklands, many of which form the basis of today's state-run Forest Parks, with an extraordinarily varied heritage of native and exotic trees.

Among the most striking natives are the **Common** or **English oak**, the **yew**, **holly** and **hawthorn**.

Much planted in graveyards, the distinctive **Irish yew**, with its vertical branches, was found originally at Florence Court in Co Fermanagh.

In the 18C, the Anglo-Irish gentry introduced an ever-widening range of exotics, some of which, like **beech** and **chestnut**, naturalised easily and became virtual natives. Parklands were laid out on the picturesque lines fashionable in England, taking particular advantage of the already striking natural scenery in areas such as Wicklow and Killarney. The benign influence of the Gulf Stream encouraged the planting of species such as **rhododendrons**, **tree-fuchsias**, **palm-trees**, **eucalyptus** and the ever-present **yucca**.

In the 19C, Victorian taste prevailed, with a love of the bright colours which new developments in horticultural technology could provide. As part of the British Empire, Ireland experienced cosmopolitan trends; **Japanese** gardens were one influence, and gardens were laid out on particular themes. In the end, though, the influence of English styles of gardening seems dominant, with Irish gardeners just as much in love as their neighbours with informal arrangements of plants drawn from all quarters of the globe, naturalistic in appearance but often with a strong underlying order and pattern.

Liberated exotics

Some plant species have acclimatised so well to Irish conditions that they have spread widely. Fuchsias grow in hedgerows and rhododendrons are pervasive. Adding their distinctive dashes of colour to the landscape are the native **gorse**, **broom**, **bracken** and **heather**, and, of course, the **shamrock**, its place in Irish life assured by St Patrick's use of it to explain the nature of the Holy Trinity.

Animal life

Sheep may seem to be the dominant species of animal in Ireland, but the country's wildlife is more varied than might be supposed, a fact easily confirmed by a visit to Dublin's fine Natural History Museum (*see page 114*). The giant deer of the Ice Age, their remains perfectly preserved in peat bogs, may have disappeared, but their remote offspring still populate the country's forests, and they are a not uncommon sight along the roadside. By contrast, there are no snakes in Ireland; contrary to legend, this is not because St Patrick got rid of them, but because there never were any.

H. Choimel/MICHELIN

Migrants and natives

Ireland has an exceptionally rich bird-life, thanks to its strategic location on **migration routes**. In autumn and winter, **waders** and **web-footed birds** on their way south from the Arctic pause to seek sustenance from the rich feeding-grounds of the marshes along the Irish coast, many of which are designated bird sanctuaries. In summer, there is a chance of glimpsing the **puffin** which nests in the cliffs in the southern part of the country. Other species to watch out for, preferably with the help of a good pair of binoculars, include black **cormorants**, long-necked **gannets**, shrieking **guillemots** and the strange **shelduck**, which nests in old rabbit burrows or in the shelter of boulders.

Creatures of the sea

Sometimes visible on offshore rocks or at the foot of a cliff are families of **grey** or **common seals**. Seals are a protected species, and tend to shun the proximity of humans, disappearing beneath the surface of the water as soon as people approach. The places where they are found are almost certain to abound in fish, their only food. The waters off the Irish coast are rich in fish. Close in are shoals of **herring**, as well as **sardine**, **pollack**, **skate**, **shark** and **bass**, plus **crabs** and **lobsters**, nearly all of which go for export.

The Irish are not particularly fond of fish, but nevertheless have gone in for fish-farming in a big way; **salmon** and **sea trout** are reared in quantity in the Galway area. This success story has to be measured against concerns that interbreeding between farmed and wild fish reduces the resistance to disease of the latter. Despite this, people come from far and wide to tickle trout and catch other fish in lakes and rivers which are still among the least polluted in Europe.

Ten millenia of history

Dates	Events
Mesolithic (8000-4000 BC)	The first humans settle in Ireland.
Neolithic (4000-2500 BC)	Dolmen and passage-grave culture (Boyne Valley).
Bronze Age (2500-500 BC)	Extraction of gold and use in jewellery.
Iron Age (from 500BC)	Arrival of the first Celts.

Middle Ages

432-61	St Patrick converts Ireland to Christianity.
6C-11C	Monastic period, creation of the Book of Kells; Viking invasions, foundation of Dublin.
1014	Vikings defeated at the Battle of Clontarf.
1169	Strongbow at the head of an Anglo-Norman army.
12C-16C	Anglo-Norman supremacy and castle building.

From Henry VIII to the Penal Laws

1539	Dissolution of the monasteries.
1541	Henry VIII proclaimed King of Ireland.
1607	Flight of the Earls; start of the Jacobean Plantation.
1642	Confederation of Kilkenny, an alliance between the native Irish and the Old English.
1649	Cromwell lands in Ireland and rapidly subjugates the country.
1688-89	Siege of Londonderry.
1690	James II defeated by William of Orange at the Battle of the Boyne.
1695	Promulgation of the Penal Laws.

From the Georgian era to the Great Famine

1714-1830	Reign of the four Georges; growth of Dublin and its enhancement with great public buildings.
1798	Rebellion of the United Irishmen.
1800	The Act of Union; creation of the United Kingdom and dissolution of the Irish Parliament.
1829	Roman Catholic Emancipation Act.
1848	Abortive Young Ireland uprising.
1845-49	The Great Famine kills one million Irish people.
1850-1930	More than 4 million Irish emigrate to North America.

Modern times

1858	Foundation of the Irish Republican Brotherhood.
1881	First Land Act.
1905	Foundation of Sinn Féin.
1914	Home Rule Bill signed by George V.
1916	Easter Rising.
1919-21	The "War of Independence", guerilla warfare between the IRA and British forces.
1921-23	Anglo-Irish Treaty partitioning Ireland. Civil War and creation of the Free State.
1932-48	Ireland led by Éamon de Valera.
1939-45	Ireland remains neutral in the Second World War.
1949	Proclamation of the Republic. Ireland quits the Commonwealth.
1971-94	Provisional IRA unleashes campaign of violence to force British withdrawal from Northern Ireland.
1972	"Bloody Sunday" in Derry.
1973	Both the Republic of Ireland and the United Kingdom join the European Economic Community.
1990	Mary Robinson elected President.
1994	First IRA cease-fire.
1998	10 April 1998 Good Friday Agreement signed. Northern Ireland Assembly meets for the first time.

DIVIDED NATION

It might seem inevitable that the inhabitants of an island, its borders neatly defined by the sea, would consider themselves a nation without too much need for reflection. And yet the idea of an Irish nation, in the modern sense of the word, is quite recent. At the end of the 19C, those Irish people who hoped to shake off British domination forged themselves an identity based on Catholicism and the Celtic heritage. Bearing in mind the great variety of influences the island has been subjected to, that the Celts themselves were just one lot of invaders among several others, and that Protestants are just as Irish as Catholics, this vision seems a little lacking. Nor does it measure up to the ideals of the pioneer republican Wolfe Tone, who promoted the notion of Irishness in place of Catholicism or Protestantism, and Ireland remains a nation divided into two.

From prehistory to the Celts (8000 BC to 5C AD)

Ireland was settled relatively late compared to the rest of Europe. People only began to move here at the end of the Ice Age about 8 000 to 10 000 years ago, mostly from Scotland.

Prehistoric people

Very little is known about the **Mesolithic** inhabitants of Ireland. Traces of them are limited to a few stone tools and encampments like those on Mount Sandel in Co Londonderry. These earliest Irish were not of Celtic stock – Celtic tribespeople only arrived in Ireland some 7 500 years later.

In the 4th millennium BC, a race of mysterious invaders arrived, members of a civilisation far more advanced than that of the native inhabitants. A recent study of the blood groups of people in western Ireland revealed that their ancestors may well have originated in the Middle East. Wherever their origin, the newcomers were farmers who used polished stone implements and practised a cult of the dead; the deceased were buried beneath **dolmens** and in **passage graves** like those in the Boyne Valley (*see page 155*).

Around 2500 BC, the **Bronze Age** reached an advanced cultural level in Ireland, evidence of which can be seen in the sumptuous gold jewellery exhibited in Dublin's National Museum (*see page 115*).

The coming of the Celts

A people of Asiatic origin who had settled in Central Europe, the Celts came to Ireland in a series of invasions between the 5C BC and the beginning of the Christian era. Around 250 BC they introduced the horse, the wheel and the working of iron. The Celts were divided into numerous tribes and nations, the main one being known as the **Gaels**. Their conquest of the country was gradual, only being completed in the 5C AD. By this time they were organised into two powerful kingdoms: the Eoganacht in the south and the Connachta in the north. The latter were under the domination of the strong and well-organised clan of the Uí Néill, later known as the O'Neills, who reigned from their hilltop at Tara in Co Meath. The division of the country into four large provinces dates from this time: **Connacht** in the west, **Ulster** in the north, **Leinster** in the east and southeast, and **Munster** in the southwest.

In the north as well as in the south, the country was broken up into a number of little kingdoms called **Tuatha**, which spent their time fighting each other. Sharing power with the petty kings were the **Brehons**, a druid-like caste, who combined the roles of judges, poets and sorcerers. There were no towns, and Ireland remained beyond the influence of Roman civilisation, despite the existence of trading links with the continent and with romanised Britain.

Thanks to St Patrick, something of the heritage of Roman civilisation was brought to Ireland through the medium of Christianity.

The age of monasticism

Early Irish Christianity was characterised by the foundation of a great number of monasteries and by its coexistence for a lengthy period with pre-Christian Celtic practices and the druidic Brehon Law.

Irish monasticism flourished up to the 8C, leaving a heritage of buildings like the remains at Glendalough in the Wicklow Mountains, founded by **St Kevin** at the beginning of the 7C, or those at Kells in Co Meath. It was at Kells that one of the greatest treasures of European monasticism, the Book of Kells, was written and gloriously illuminated *(see page 112)*.

This was a period in which the message of Christianity was propagated by Irish monks throughout a Europe suffering a succession of barbarian invasions. Missionaries like **St Brendan**, **St Columba** and St Furcy left their native land to establish monasteries all over the continent. Among their most important foundations were the abbeys of Lagny and Luxeuil in

P Thébault/MICHELIN

St Patrick

France, St Gallen in Switzerland and Würzburg in Germany. In Ireland itself, the monasteries were at the centre of a thriving intellectual and artistic life with many great achievements to its credit like the Book of Kells and the Book of Armagh.

The founder of Irish Christianity

Born somewhere in western Britain, the young Patrick was kidnapped by Irish pirates who sold him into slavery. He spent six years in Ireland, before escaping and returning home. He was converted to Christianity, and eventually became a bishop, leaving once more for Ireland on a mission to convert its inhabitants. Landing near Downpatrick in Ulster in the year 432, he explained the nature of Christianity to the local rulers by using the shamrock as a symbol of the Holy Trinity. Following a journey to Rome in 444, he came back to Ireland and founded the cathedral and archbishopric of Armagh. As related in his own writings and in traditional tales, he led a life very much like that of a druid, albeit an exceptionally powerful one, able to demonstrate the superiority of his God by the performance of miracles and all kinds of other exploits.

Viking invaders

The Vikings began to settle along the coasts of Ireland towards the end of the 8C. From their coastal bases they sailed inland along the rivers, meeting only feeble resistance from the peaceful Irish as they ransacked the monasteries and carried off their treasures. It was in reaction to such Viking raids that **round towers** *(see page 29)* were built in many places. But the Vikings were not merely bloodstained plunderers. They founded most of today's coastal towns (Dublin, Wexford, Waterford, Cork and Limerick). For their part, the Irish rulers frequently allied themselves with the Vikings in their conflicts with rival kingdoms. Traditional Celtic society was undermined, a process that ended in the domination of the whole of the country by King **BrianBorú**. In 1014, he emerged victorious, at the **Battle of Clontarf** near Dublin, over his former Viking allies. However, he died before being able to unite his subject kingdoms, which soon reverted to their familiar, quarrelsome habits.

The coming of the Anglo-Normans
In the 10C and at the beginning of the 11C, Ireland was the scene of constant feuding among its petty kings. As had happened in Viking times, one of them decided to ally himself with a foreign power in order to overcome his rivals. As a result of a bout of wife-stealing, the king of Leinster, **Diarmuid** (or Dermot) **McMurrough**, had been ousted from his throne. He seems to have had few inhibitions about appealing to **Henry II** of England to help him recover it. The Norman rulers of England had already considered the idea of acquiring territory in Ireland, but Henry was loath to commit himself too deeply, despite having been encouraged in such an enterprise by the Pope. The task of invading Ireland was entrusted to the Earl of Pembroke, **Richard de Clare**, popularly known as **Strongbow**. The Earl's men first set foot in Ireland at Baginbun on the southwestern tip of Co Wexford in 1169. Anglo-Norman military superiority soon made itself felt; all of Leinster was reconquered for Dermot, but when he died, the ambitious Strongbow declared himself lord of the province. This was too much for Henry, who came to Ireland in his turn, extracting not only a humiliating declaration of loyalty from Strongbow but receiving the submission of most of the Irish rulers too.

The age of the Anglo-Irish barons
Within the space of a few generations, almost the whole of Ireland had become a possession of the Anglo-Norman crown, and was divided up into baronies. Only Donegal and a part of present-day Co Tyrone remained in the hands of the native O'Donnells and O'Neills. As for Dublin, the city was totally Anglo-Norman in character. However, during the course of the 14C, there occurred what has come to be known as the Gaelic Recovery. Resentment of the English grew, and between 1315 and 1318 the native chieftains attempted, unsuccessfully, to re-conquer part of the island with the help of a force of Scottish mercenaries, the so-called Gallowglasses (*gallóglach* = foreign warrior), led by the brother of Robert the Bruce.

More Irish than the Irish – For their part, some of the Anglo-Norman families like the **Butlers** of Ormonde and the **Fitzgeralds** of Kildare had assimilated with the native Irish and adopted their ways to such an extent that the English crown took fright. In an attempt to maintain the distinction between Anglo-Normans and Irish, the **Statutes of Kilkenny** were promulgated, forbidding the English to indulge in such Celtic pastimes as hurling and bareback riding or using the Gaelic language *(see page 214)*. By the beginning of the 15C, the Fitzgeralds had become the most powerful family in the country, reigning over almost the whole of Ireland. With the right to levy their own taxes, they enjoyed almost complete independence from the English crown.

The Reformation (16C-17C)

Anglicans and Old English
The arrival of **Henry VIII** on the throne of England marked the end of the power and influence of the Fitzgeralds. Henry proclaimed himself head of the Church of England and set about putting his possessions in order. He had the Earl of Kildare thrown into the Tower of London (where he died in 1536), and ordered the execution of five of his brothers and his son.

King of Ireland – In 1541, in order to bind Church and state institutions more closely to the monarchy, Ireland was raised to the constitutional status of a kingdom, with Henry as king. The Dissolution of the monasteries was extended to Ireland, and the local rulers formally submitted their lands to the monarch, who graciously returned them with the proviso that they were now subject to English law. Henry's daughters **Mary** and **Elizabeth** showed themselves equally ruthless in pursuing English interests. All attempts at rebellion were firmly squashed, and in the 1560s and 1570s a first state-backed plantation of English settlers was carried out in Munster.

Patriotic response – These policies engendered a strong reaction, not only on the part of the native Irish but also among the descendants of the Anglo-Normans, now known as the Old English, most of whom had remained true to their Catholic faith. With their support, the powerful **Hugh O'Neill**, Earl of Tyrone, raised an army in Ulster and began a rising which dragged on for nine years. But despite initial successes, O'Neill's forces were insufficient, and he then made the mistake of calling on the Catholic **Philip II** of Spain for help. A Spanish force was landed at Kinsale in Co Cork but was defeated by **Lord Mountjoy**'s army in 1601, a victory signalling the end of Gaelic Ireland.

Plantation

After Kinsale, English law was extended to the whole of Ireland. O'Neill had been pardoned, but came to see that he and his kind had no place in this new dispensation. In 1607, he and a number of like-minded lords together with their families and retainers embarked on ships in Lough Swilly, never to return. This episode, called **The Flight of the Earls**, left the native, Catholic population of Ulster defenceless in the face of the English desire for domination. The Earls' lands were confiscated and redistributed to Protestant settlers from England and Scotland. This marked the beginnings of the Ulster **Plantation**, a process with consequences which are still felt all too keenly today. Taking possession of the best land and founding towns such as **Londonderry**, the Protestant settlers imported a way of life into the North which was quite alien to the native Irish. Rejected and dispossessed, the latter nursed a hatred for the newcomers and all they represented which in its turn engendered an enduring siege mentality among the settlers.

Cromwell the pitiless (1599-1658)

A country gentleman from Huntingdonshire, Cromwell was an astute politician and a ruthless and capable commander. Having just won a civil war, had the king's head cut off and sent England's peers packing, he turned his attention to Ireland and dealt with its problems in a characteristically brisk manner. Drogheda was the first town to fall to his men; there followed a systematic massacre of the garrison, the clergy and many of the inhabitants, most of whom were probably of English descent. The tactics of terror had the desired effect; on hearing of the slaughter, the garrisons of Dundalk and Trim took to their heels. Wexford's garrison, a contingent of Old English Royalist troops, was made of stouter stuff, and put up a spirited resistance. To no avail; the town was taken by storm, and another massacre ensued. The spirit of resistance was broken, and Cromwell was able to return to England after only a few months, leaving subordinate commanders to complete his grisly work.

The Confederation of Kilkenny

By the beginning of the 17C the Reformation had split into several streams, and Ireland as well as England was to become the scene of conflict between Anglicans and other Protestants, mainly Presbyterians. Attempts by **Charles I** to move towards an absolute form of monarchy with Anglicanism as the state religion precipitated the Civil War in England and had repercussions in Ireland. In 1642 the Irish and the Old English Catholics founded the **Confederation of Kilkenny** to defend their religion and their political rights. A year previously, the Catholics of the North had risen in revolt, committing atrocities against the settlers on a scale horrific enough in itself, but which lost nothing in the telling back in England. But all this was as nothing compared with the impact on Ireland of **Oliver Cromwell**. Not over-concerned with the subtle differences between Irish and Old English Catholics, Cromwell came to Ireland in 1649 determined to avenge the massacres of 1641 and stamp out all resistance to the authority of his government. Once conquest had been achieved, he set about dispossessing Catholic landowners of their property and redistributing it among his soldiers or to a new wave of settlers from England. Catholics were permitted to own property beyond the Shannon, but to the east of the river, on what was the best land, the only landowners were Protestants.

AKG Paris

William of Orange by Friedrich Pecht

Kings in conflict

Cromwell's death in 1658 and the Restoration of the monarchy in the person of **Charles II** ushered in a period of religious tolerance. The new sovereign was no doubt mindful of the fate suffered by his father through an excess of religious zeal. When in 1685 he was succeeded by his brother, **James II**, Irish Catholics began to hope that their losses might be made good. The hope was short-lived. James was ousted in a palace revolution, and his daughter Mary, together with her Dutch husband William III (William of Orange), enthroned in his place. James fled to Ireland, where he assembled a Catholic army. On 18 April 1689, his forces began the **Siege of Londonderry** but were unable to take the town (*see page 454*). In June 1690, William III landed at Carrickfergus and marched his army of Danes, Dutch, Germans, Huguenots, Italians, Norwegians, Poles and Swiss, plus English and Irish Protestants to the Boyne valley. Here he met James's army, which was somewhat smaller and less varied in composition but nevertheless contained many Frenchmen and a number of English Jacobites. The **Battle of the Boyne** lasted for most of 1 July. It ended in the rout of the Jacobite army, a victory which is triumphantly celebrated every year by the Orange Order, not on 1 July but, because of changes in the calendar, on the 12th.

The Anglo-Irish Ascendancy (late 17C-18C)

The defeat of King James and his Catholic army at the battle of the Boyne was followed a year later by the siege of Limerick, where the Irish army under the leadership of Patrick Sarsfield made a last stand. An honourable surrender was negotiated; under the provisions of the **Treaty of Limerick**, Catholics were guaranteed their property and the right to practise their religion freely, while Sarsfield and 11 000 of his followers (the "Wild Geese") were allowed to go into exile. Many of them made distinguished military careers in Continental armies. However, the English Parliament failed to ratify the treaty, and in 1695, the repressive **Penal Laws** were passed, imposing intolerable conditions on the education, property rights, and freedom of worship of Catholics. Presbyterians, considered as heretics, were persecuted too, and many left for America. The way was open for the Anglican elite, known as the **Ascendancy**, to lord it over the subjugated island.

Peace and prosperity

By the second half of the 18C, Ireland had known an exceptionally long period of peace. Relations between adherents of the different religions were eased, and under the reigns of the four Georges the island's economy prospered. Major works of urban improvement were carried out in Dublin, and the country's **Georgian architecture** became a model of its kind.

Revolutionary influences from France

The French Revolution inspired Ireland's Presbyterians to dream of freeing themselves from Anglican domination, and the formation in 1791 of the association known as the **United Irishmen** took place in Belfast, not Dublin. It was essentially a Protestant, not a Catholic project, led by the lawyer **Theobald Wolfe Tone**, who declared that he wished "to substitute the common name of Irishman for that of Catholic or Protestant". Tone fled to France in 1796, where he persuaded the authorities to come to the help of the revolution planned by the United Irishmen. Tempted by the prospect of attacking England by her back door, the French sent an expeditionary force. But the timing was faulty; arriving in Bantry Bay in the middle of December, the fleet was battered by storms. All its attempts to land the troops were frustrated and it was forced to sail away *(see panel, page 274)*.

Nevertheless, set on the idea of a republic, the United Irishman continued with their preparations, building up a revolutionary force composed of Catholic peasants as well as Protestants. Ruthless measures were taken by the authorities to infiltrate and disarm it, and when the rebellion broke out in 1798 it was easily defeated, though not before the insurgents had taken possession of a number of important towns such as Wexford. In June, the **Battle of Vinegar Hill** took place near Enniscorthy, Co Wexford. The rebels and those that had taken refuge with them were overcome, and many were massacred after the battle. Wolfe Tone himself landed from a French ship on the shores of Lough Swilly in October, but was almost immediately recognised and arrested. Condemned to death, he committed suicide in prison.

Daniel O'Connell by G Mulvany

National Gallery of Ireland, Dublin

The era of Catholic nationalism (1st half of 19C)

The Church counters republicanism

One reason for the failure of republicanism at this time was the attitude of the Roman Catholic Church, which felt its authority threatened all over Europe. Far from aiding the struggle for freedom, the Church helped ensure that Irishmen of whatever religion were to remain under Britain's domination for the whole of the 19C.

Union and emancipation

In 1800, the Dublin Parliament signed itself out of existence by passing the **Act of Union**, which created the United Kingdom and centralised power still further in London. Ireland's representatives, Protestant to a man, now met at Westminster, where they were of course a permanent minority in Parliament. For their part, politically aware Catholics now shifted their allegiance away from republicanism to the interests of their co-religionists, now identified with the Irish nation.

Daniel O'Connell – The lawyer Daniel O'Connell launched himself whole-heartedly into the struggle for Catholic rights. A former member of the yeomanry which had helped suppress the insurrection of 1798, he was no republican but an advocate of the political emancipation of the country's Catholics. His defeat of the Protestant candidate in an 1828 by-election covered him in glory in the eyes of his fellow-Catholics. A year later, Parliament passed the Roman Catholic Emancipation Act conceding the right of Catholics to enter Parliament.

Young Ireland – The 1830s were marked by much rural unrest. Secret societies, often virulently anti-Protestant, fought against the compulsory payment of tithes to the Anglican Church of Ireland and harked back to a supposed "Golden Age" of rural prosperity and equality. O'Connell attempted to channel such unrest by giving the priesthood a political role. However, faced with the extreme conservatism of many of the clergy, the Catholic middle classes began to desert the Church and O'Connell for the movement known as Young Ireland. Pervaded by the liberal, revolutionary ideas current all over the Europe of the 1840s, they launched an uprising in 1848 which conspicuously failed to generate popular support and was easily suppressed.

From Famine to revolt (second half of the 19C)

The Great Famine

By the time of Daniel O'Connell's death in 1847, Ireland was already in the grip of the worst famine in its history.

The potato – The potato had been introduced into the country in the 17C and had become the basic food of all Irish countryfolk except for those in the north, where agriculture was much more diversified. This meant that Catholics would be more affected by any failure of the potato crop than Protestants. This total dependence on the potato became catastrophic when **potato blight** made its appearance in 1845. In this first year of the Famine, many people managed to survive on their meagre savings, but the real impact of the blight was to be felt in the years that followed.

Official indifference – The Conservative government was reluctant to intervene, believing that politics should not interfere with the workings of the market. A number of attempts were made to provide relief work for the starving, notably by the construction of roads and by the building of field boundaries, the so-called **famine walls** which are still a feature of the countryside. But Ireland, which had had more than 8 million inhabitants in 1841, had lost almost a third of its population ten years later, through deaths by starvation and disease and by a massive **emigration** to North America.

The Irish in America

Between 1850 and 1930, over four million Irish men, women and children emigrated to America. Famine, misery and oppression were the principal factors behind this massive exodus. Irish-Americans developed into a compact and self-aware community, eminently capable of welcoming subsequent migrants from the homeland and helping them find work. The Irish did of course have one great advantage over most of the other immigrants to America from Europe – they spoke English, enabling them to jump a generation in the process of integration. Over the years, particularly in great cities like Boston and Chicago, the Irish played leading roles in public administration, their influence culminating in the 1960 election of President John Fitzgerald Kennedy.

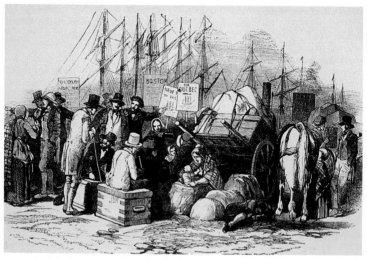

The road to exile

Bold Fenian men

In 1858, a New York Irishman, John O'Mahony founded the **Irish Republican Brotherhood**, which, in contrast to the conservative policy of O'Connell, went back to the republican ideals of 1798 and the Young Ireland movement.

The militants of the new movement called themselves Fenians, in memory of the legendary Celtic warriors known as the Fianna. Radical republicans, influenced by socialist ideas and partisans of the armed struggle, they attempted to rouse the Catholic masses, but met with the opposition of the Church in the person of Paul Cullen, the first Irish Cardinal, who was determined to keep the country free from the infection of any social or democratic revolution.

Industrialisation in the North, misery in the South – By the 1850s the Protestants of the North had long forgotten their 1798 dreams of independence. Ulster had hardly been affected by the Famine and was now in the throes of the Industrial Revolution, making it one of the wealthiest provinces of the United Kingdom.

Despite the grim working conditions of the time, Belfast's Catholic and Protestant proletariat were enjoying a prosperity in vivid contrast to the misery and stagnation of Dublin and the South.

Parnell and Home Rule

The idea of **Home Rule** within the framework of the United Kingdom was launched by Isaac Butt, a Protestant lawyer from Donegal. And it was another Protestant, **Charles Stewart Parnell**, who succeeded in creating an alliance between the advocates of Home Rule, a group of Fenians, and the proponents of agricultural reform.

Agricultural reform – In 1881, after further rural unrest and much violence, Parliament passed the first **Land Act**, giving tenants some elementary rights and encouraging the emergence of a class of Catholic smallholders.

Unionist opposition – Parnell's success in promoting land reform gave heart to the supporters of Home Rule. In 1885, his **Irish Parliamentary Party** sent 85 Members of Parliament to Westminster, and a year later Liberal Prime Minister **Gladstone** introduced the first Home Rule Bill. But Parliament rejected the Bill, and Gladstone resigned. Though Parnell was able to gain the support of the Catholic Church, the prospect of an autonomous, Catholic-dominated Ireland was not acceptable to Unionist Protestants. Denouncing Home Rule as "Rome Rule", they created the **Irish Unionist Party**, with MPs hostile to any form of autonomy. Poor Parnell found himself ensnared in a divorce scandal; forced to resign, he died shortly afterwards (*see page 178*).

The road to independence (late 19C – 1949)

Far from being laid to rest with the death of Parnell, the spectre of Home Rule continued to haunt British political life. Moreover, the last years of the 19C were marked by an astonishing revival of Gaelic culture.

Gaelic revival and revived Unionism

The **Gaelic League** was created in 1893 with the aim of reviving Irish as a spoken and literary language, at the same time as WB Yeats was promoting an authentic national literature and drama. A key component of the movement was the Abbey Theatre, which opened its doors in 1904 (*see page 66*). Parallel to this were the activities of the **Gaelic Athletic Association (GAA)** (*see panel, page 68*), which sponsored traditional sports such as hurling and Gaelic football, and was particularly well represented in rural areas.

Home Rule postponed – An end to Britain's "Irish problem" seemed in sight when the House of Commons passed a third Home Rule Bill in 1912. As ever, the House of Lords was implacably opposed to Home Rule, but their power to block legislation had now been limited to a period of two years, and the Bill would have become law anyway in late 1914. However, a more formidable opponent than the Lords now made itself felt. Resistance to the Bill by the Protestants of Ulster was total; under the leadership of the Dublin barrister **Sir Edward Carson**, tens of thousands of men drilled and armed themselves under the slogan, "Ulster will fight, and Ulster will be right". An incident at the British army's Curragh base cast doubt on the officer corps' reliability if ordered to put down an armed rising in Ulster against Home Rule. At the same time a Catholic militia, the **Irish Volunteers**, was formed in the South. Civil war seemed inevitable, and was only averted by the outbreak of the First World War; the implementation of Home Rule would now have to wait.

The Easter Rising

Ireland in the First World War – Irishmen of all political persuasions flocked to the colours, hoping that demonstrative loyalty to the British Crown would stand them in good stead when hostilities were over. The Irish Volunteers were divided on the issue, some hoping to conserve their strength in order to ensure that there would be no postwar British backsliding on the promise of Home Rule. The most militant nationalists, the Irish Republican Brotherhood, later to become the IRA, secretly prepared an uprising which would be carried out using arms and ammunition supplied by Germany.

Victory in defeat – The Rising began on **Easter Monday 1916**. As a military operation it was doomed from the start. One of its leaders, Sir Roger Casement, who had been negotiating with the German government, was disillusioned with the help offered and wanted the insurrection postponed. Landed from a German submarine on the Co Kerry coast, he was arrested almost immediately, and the German vessel bringing arms was intercepted by the Royal Navy. The planning of the Rising had been carried out in such secrecy that many potential participants were quite unaware of what they should do, and in the end, what had been intended as a national insurrection was limited to the city of Dublin. There were initial successes. The British authorities were taken almost completely by surprise, and many officers of the Dublin garrison were at the races. The insurgents occupied several public buildings and strategic locations, and the Republic was proclaimed by the poet Patrick Pearse from the steps of the General Post Office. But they were hopelessly outnumbered and outgunned, and after five days of bitter fighting, they surrendered, spat on by the public as they were marched through the streets of a devastated city. Opinion changed swiftly, however; the summary execution of the ringleaders – the badly wounded James Connolly had to be tied upright to a chair before being shot – provoked a wave of disgust, turning nationalist Irish feeling against compromise with Britain.

War and Partition

The elections held in late 1918 proved that Home Rule was dead. The moderate nationalists who had hoped for autonomy within the United Kingdom were replaced by members of the more radical **Sinn Féin** *("Ourselves alone")*. Under the leadership of Éamon de Valera, and scorning to take their seats in the British parliament, they met in Dublin as the **Dáil Éireann** (Assembly of Ireland) and declared the country independent.

IRA and Black and Tans – In 1919, the IRA began guerrilla warfare against the British under the charismatic leadership of **Michael Collins**. The war dragged on for two years, with atrocities committed by both sides. The IRA dealt with traitors and informers with the utmost ruthlessness, while the British auxiliaries known as the **Black and Tans** (because of their khaki trousers and dark green jackets) were their equals in (often indiscriminate) savagery. Hostilities were brought to an end by the signing of the **Anglo-Irish Treaty** in 1921. This gave southern Ireland – the **Free State** – independence within the Commonwealth, while the six predominantly Protestant counties of Ulster (Northern Ireland) remained within the United Kingdom. While this was just about acceptable to a majority of members of the Dáil, many nationalists were bitterly disappointed, and de Valera himself resigned.

Irish against Irish – There now broke out a savage **civil war** between supporters and opponents of the Treaty. Michael Collins, now commander of the Free State army, was assassinated by followers of de Valera. Fighting in Dublin left a number of public buildings severely damaged. Superior organisation, the introduction of measures like internment, the use of artillery supplied by the British, and the imposition of the death penalty for possession of arms, gave the advantage to the Free State government, while their adversaries, including the majority of the IRA, were riven by factionalism. In April 1923, after nearly a year of fighting, the IRA called a cease-fire, though no formal end to the conflict was ever negotiated.

The de Valera era – Standing aside from the government of the Free State, de Valera reorganised his supporters into a new party, **Fianna Fáil** *("Warriors of Ireland")*, whose elected representatives at first refused to take their places in a Dáil which still swore an oath to King George V. But eventually, in 1932, Fianna Fáil won a general election, and in 1933 de Valera became president of the Executive Council. His republican-minded but very conservative regime gave the Catholic church a "special position" in the nation's life, continued to claim the North as an integral part of Ireland, and despite some initiatives, failed to address the country's many social problems. In 1938, Britain handed back the "Treaty Ports" which it had retained for purposes of naval defence in 1921. With popular support, de Valera steadfastly maintained Irish neutrality during the Second World War, despite turning a blind eye to some Allied activities which might have compromised it.

Modern Ireland

The ever-present question of the North

See also page 432.

See also page 432.

Since 1937 the official name of the country had been Éire. In 1949 the **Republic of Ireland** was declared and all formal ties with Britain and the Commonwealth were severed. But the country remained poor and somewhat isolated, in contrast to the North, which had undergone a wartime boom in industry and employment.

R Holzbachova, P Bénet/MICHELIN

1916 recruiting poster

THE CALL TO ARMS

DAVID ALLEN & SONS LTD
40 Gt Brunswick St
DUBLIN
(Copyright)

IRISHMEN
DONT YOU HEAR IT?

B. Sigu/CORBIS SYGMA

David Trimble and John Hume receiving the Nobel Peace Prize.

A two-speed society – Still considering themselves the "loyal Irish" under threat from the Catholic Republic to the south, the majority Protestants of the North maintained from the start of the province's existence a regime which discriminated in matters of employment, housing and political representation against its 40% Catholic minority. And while many of the demands of the Civil Rights movement of the late 1960s were granted, this was not enough to satisfy the IRA, which resumed its interrupted campaign of violence in pursuit of a revolutionary solution to "the problem of the North".

A low profile in Dublin – The population of the Republic was torn between a natural sympathy for the nationalist cause and revulsion at the terror tactics of the **Provisional IRA**. The Dublin government had little room for manoeuvre, and tended to keep a low profile during the whole period of "the Troubles". It was also the case that over the same period, the Republic underwent such dramatic changes that the question of reunification no longer featured so strongly in the population's concerns.

Liberalism on all fronts

The Republic's entry into the **European Economic Community** in 1973 was an event of great significance. The country which had quit the Commonwealth after the Second World War now found itself a member of the same free-trade organisation as the United Kingdom, including of course Northern Ireland. The lowering of trade barriers was complemented by an opening of minds. The Catholic Church found itself challenged by the aspirations of feminists and the young, particularly with regard to social issues. Those articles of the Republic's constitution which placed Ireland under the protection of the Holy Trinity were removed, and, while many people remain devoutly religious, the idea has taken hold that religion is a matter for personal choice and not necessarily an irreducible part of the Irish identity. Liberalisation was accelerated by the election of a woman, **Mary Robinson**, as head of state (*see panel, page 34*). Homosexuality was decriminalised in 1993, and divorce was legalised following a referendum in 1995, though an earlier referendum in 1983 had rejected a more liberal approach to abortion. At the same time, dynamic financial and industrial policies and membership of the European Union helped Ireland modernise its economy and enjoy an astonishing rate of growth well above the European average.

ART AND ARCHITECTURE

The history of Irish art is intimately bound up with the religious and other beliefs of its people. It begins with the enigmatic signs carved by Neolithic artists on the stonework of their burial places, and continues after the Celtic conquest with a wealth of decorative art and manuscript illumination testifying to the fervour of Christian faith. And even though Irish artists have not always been able to make manifest their cultural identity, their creations have invariably been in harmony with the singular beauty of their country's landscapes.

Prehistoric builders and craftsmen

Lonely cabins and fortified camps

The fact that Ireland was peopled relatively late compared with the continent of Europe means that there are no cave paintings here. The country's first inhabitants, about 8 000 to 10 000 years ago, were hunter-gatherers living in **clocháns**, built of corbelled dry-stone and often called beehive huts because of their shape *(see illustration, page 310)*.

With the development of herding, people began to build fortified enclosures called **cashels** or **raths**, in which people and cattle could be secure. This form of settlement represents the prototype of the Irish village and explains why so many place-names incorporate the root *rath*. These fortified places were sometimes built on a considerable scale and seem to have functioned as places of worship and sacrifice; examples include the **ring forts** at Navan, near Armagh and Dún Aengus and Dún Chonchúir on the Aran Islands.

Many people lived on **crannógs**, artificial islands built on stilts in lakes and linked to each other by underground passageways hollowed out in the lake-bed. Some crannógs were lived in right up to the 17C *(see photo page 190)*.

Megaliths

As the Neolithic period gave way to the Bronze Age (3000-2000 BC), an advanced form of Megalithic architecture developed in the shape of the imposing **passage graves** of Newgrange, Knowth and Dowth in the Boyne Valley. With a covering of soil, these funerary structures were contemporary with the pyramids of Egypt, and appear in the landscape as grass-covered mounds of varying size known as **tumuli** or **cairns**. Inside, one or more burial chambers are related to a passageway or corridor containing the mortal remains of high-ranking people and their families.

The smaller tombs known as **dolmens** were also originally covered with soil, and were the resting-places of people of lower rank. In time, the earth covering was eroded away, leaving only the basic structure, which normally consists of a huge capstone supported on massive stone uprights.

The true function of the circles of standing stones called **cromlechs** is still unknown, though their layout suggests that many of them may have served as a form of calendar or as a sacrificial site. On occasion, as at Newgrange, the stones are decorated with geometric motifs of uncertain significance, though some experts believe that they are symbolic maps of the living-space of the associated community.

Goldsmiths

The Bronze Age (3000-2000 BC) was a period of great creativity as far as **weaponry** (javelins, swords, knives and shields) and **gold jewellery** were concerned. The period was characterised by mastery of the goldsmith's art, featuring techniques passed on later to the Celtic invaders who came to Ireland in the Iron Age.

Y Arthus-Bertrand/ALTITUDE/HOA QUI

The ringfort of Dún Chonchúir on the Aran Islands

Celtic tradition in the service of God
From Celts to Christians (5C BC-12C AD)

The Celts (*see page 46*) worshipped in the open air and re-used the sacred sites of their predecessors. They were notably deficient in building skills, in contrast to their expertise in the decorative arts.

Celtic ornamentation

The successive waves of Celts who settled in Ireland from around the 4C BC brought with them well-developed techniques of **metal-working**, particularly of bronze and gold, but also of iron. Craftsmen fashioned items for everyday use such as cauldrons, chains and finely-honed swords, as well as more intricate objects like buckles for belts and clasps and brooches for fastening clothes. Such work was often boldly designed and decorated with **geometric patterns**, usually incorporating the flowing lines and interlacing which also feature on stonework and sculpture. This type of decoration is characteristic of the **La Tène** culture, named after a site in Switzerland which was a principal focus of Celtic civilisation (4C-5C BC).

With the spread of Christianity from the 5C onwards, Irish artists went back to the art of the Celts to express this new vision of the world. As the Dublin National Museum's "Treasure" reveals (*see page 115*), the arts and crafts of Celtic Ireland were put into the service of Irish Christianity for several centuries. The 8C Tara Brooch and the 10C Shrine of St Patrick's Bell are regarded as being among the supreme achievements of the Celtic decorative arts tradition.

The architecture of early Christianity

The first Christian churches were timber structures, which, in the rare event of their not having been burnt down by the Vikings, eventually succumbed to the depredations of time, like all other structures of the period. Stone only began to be used in building in the 8C. Most **monasteries** were raised on the site of a saint's or hermit's burial place, a popular location for subsequent interments, and without exception Ireland's ruined monasteries are all surrounded by a cemetery.

Ogham stones

Between the 4C and the 7C, the Celts developed an unusual form of writing, consisting of a series of straight lines inscribed around a central line, often on the vertical face of a (pre-Celtic) standing stone. Each group of lines corresponded to a letter in the Latin alphabet. The term Ogham (or Ogam) is associated with Ogma, the Celtic god of eloquence and the legendary inventor of this alphabet. Ogham stones are usually found at the entrance to a tomb, and the inscriptions state the identity of the deceased.

Another feature of the early monastery was the **round tower** *(illustration page 36)*, built between the late 10C and the 12C. The towers with their conical cap served several purposes, functioning as bell-towers, look-outs, grain-stores and refuges in case of attack. Their height varies between 15m-20m, and they usually have a number of narrow windows on the top floor facing the cardinal points, with a single opening on each of the lower floors. The doorway is usually 3m above ground, reached by a ladder which could be raised and used to climb up to the other floors. This arrangement also gave some protection against attackers, though the Vikings usually made short work of such a feeble obstacle. The round towers at Kildare and Kilkenny are among the finest that have survived.

Stone churches only made their appearance from the 11C onwards. They were usually modest in scale but of massive appearance, often provided with a belfry and with few openings in their walls. The walls themselves were built without mortar and roofs were frequently **corbelled**, a type of construction nicely exemplified by St Kevin's Church at Glendalough and by St Gallus's Oratory *(illustration page 36)*. While the interior of such churches was left entirely undecorated, **high crosses** were often erected nearby. Decorated with geometric patterns or richly carved in bas-relief with Biblical scenes, they were used by the monks to explain the sacred texts to their illiterate congregations. Some crosses, like the one at Monasterboice, are as much as 7m high. Most feature the cross within a ring, the significance of which has not been established with any clarity.

The technique of manuscript

The four Trinity College manuscripts were the work of 9C monks who were masters of sophisticated techniques. The books were kept in a leather case and were written on vellum using a goose quill. The illumination was produced using a brush made from pine-marten bristles, while colours were made from a variety of animal, vegetable and mineral pigments. Lead oxide and cochineal yielded red, Cornish azurite blue, arsenic yellow, malachite green and lapis-lazuli dark blue. Colours were fixed using egg-white. Few of these materials were available in Ireland, and some had to be imported from very far away; the only known source of lapis-lazuli in the Middle Ages was a mine in Afghanistan!

The art of the illuminator

The monks who illuminated the Gospels gave free rein to their imagination. Manuscripts like the **Book of Kells** at Trinity College *(see page 112)* are exuberantly decorated with **interlacing** in vivid colours. Geometric patterning is enhanced by the addition of the figures of animals, notably the snakes and dragons typical of **Scandinavian art**.

Anglo-Norman art (12C-16C)

On their arrival in Ireland at the end of the 11C, the Normans usually erected their strongholds on sites which had already been used by the Celts, and in some cases by the country's Neolithic inhabitants. A number of places, like Drogheda's Millmount, have thus played a defensive role almost since the beginning of human settlement in the country.

From defence to domesticity

To begin with, Anglo-Norman castles were timber structures erected atop an artificial mound called a **motte**, linked by a stairway to a bailey, a stockaded enclosure protecting stables and other domestic buildings. From the 13C onwards, these fairly primitive arrangements gave way to more formidable stone **fortresses**, the most impressive of which are at Trim in Co Meath and Carrickfergus on Belfast Lough. The keep was surrounded by a high curtain wall sometimes with more than one gatehouse and a barbican with a drawbridge. As time went on, these castles lost much of their military significance, and many local lords contented themselves with fortified houses, which were primarily residences but were still provided with an array of defensive features like **murder holes** and **battlements**. Some of these buildings like Blarney Castle were still imposing structures, while at others, like Ormond Castle at Carrick-on-Suir, the priorities of defence have clearly given way to considerations of domestic comfort. By the end of the 17C, this tendency had become the norm.

Cathedrals and abbeys

The Irish Romanesque – The Romanesque style made its appearance in Ireland at a time when it was already giving way to the Gothic on the continent of Europe. Cormac's Chapel on the Rock of Cashel is one of the very few edifices of the period to have resisted the ravages of time and is the earliest example of Irish Romanesque architecture. It consists of a transept and nave profusely decorated with carvings of **human heads** and **animal motifs** as well as dogtooth moulding. The exterior decoration of Romanesque churches concentrated on the doorways; the finest example is at Clonfert (*see illustration, page 37*). Here, the door is surrounded by several arches carved with abstract patterns and animal motifs and is surmounted by a tall triangular gable with blind arcading and triangular patterning. The whole surface is a "riot of ornamentation... calling to mind the Celtic artist's horror of empty spaces" (Peter Harbison).

Gothic architecture – Only a hundred years or so separates the beginnings of Romanesque and the arrival of the Gothic style in Ireland. Brought here by the Anglo-Normans, it was strongly influenced by the **Early English** style typified by tall lancet windows. Good examples can be seen in the south transept of Dublin's St Patrick's Cathedral and in the chancel of the ruined Inch Abbey on Strangford Lough. Most Gothic churches have a battlemented tower, often topped by a **steeple**.

Built from the late 12C onwards, abbeys were also subject to the influence of English architecture, but in plan they followed their Continental prototypes, like the **Benedictine** layout of central rectangular cloister around which were grouped church, chapter house, refectory and sacristy. One of the most splendid examples of this pattern is the cloister at Jerpoint Abbey Co Kilkenny, which also has fine carvings of saints, knights and ladies in a typically Irish style. Just as in England, the Dissolution spelled the end of monastic life in Ireland, and most of the country's abbeys fell into ruin. Functioning abbeys, like Holy Cross near Cashel or Duiske Abbey at Graiguenamanagh near New Ross, mostly date from the early 20C.

Fortified towns

Until the arrival of the Vikings, Ireland had no towns, and people lived in cabins built of timber or cob and with roofs of thatch. Little more than large villages clustering around a castle, the earliest towns (Dublin, Cork, Waterford, Wexford and Drogheda) were founded by the Vikings before being fortified by the Normans. Most of these town fortifications have disappeared, but fragments remain in the south of the country, notably at Wexford and Youghal. All towns at this time possessed a **tholsel** (**custom house**), usually consisting of a gateway and several upper floors topped by a belfry. Subsequently, as at Kilkenny, the thosel became the town hall. In Ulster, the earliest towns made their appearance in the late 16C, at the time of the Plantation and the arrival of English and Scottish settlers. They consisted of **timber-framed buildings** lining streets converging on a star-shaped central square called the **Diamond**. Londonderry is the finest example of this kind of town-planning, and the city has also kept the line of walls which completely surrounds the old town.

England as model (17C-19C)

After the Battle of the Boyne, Protestant hegemony was assured, and the Anglo-Irish Ascendancy set out to express its domination of Irish life and the Irish landscape by a programme of fine building which lasted from 1690 into the 1800s. While many native Irish languished in endemic misery, the rents squeezed from them were used to grace the countryside with sumptuous residences in styles derived from the Italian Renaissance. Dublin too was largely rebuilt in Georgian style and adorned with palatial public buildings, and was widely regarded as the British Empire's second finest city.

Noble homes

With the villas of Palladio as his inspiration, the Italian architect **Alessandro Galilei** introduced Ireland to **Palladian architecture** in 1722 with his designs for Castletown House. The emphasis was on harmony and equilibrium between the

The Rock of Cashel

Y Travert/DIAF

F. Baume / MICHELIN

Dublin's Custom House

various parts of the building, the central block being linked to flanking pavilions by means of curved colonnades. Twenty years later the architect **Richard Castle** made the most complete statement of the Palladian style when he placed the mansion at Russborough in a landscape of lakes and mountains. The interiors of these aristocratic residences were no less sophisticated than their external appearance. Elegantly worked and often gilded **stucco** and **plasterwork** gave these country seats the supremely urbane look of great palaces. At Castle Coole near Enniskillen or Emo Court in Co Laois, sumptuous plasterwork combines with marble chimneypieces and grand staircases to make a setting of the utmost luxuriousness for the life led by the Ascendancy. The privileged Anglo-Irish elite was at its pinnacle of power and prosperity during the second half of the 18C, and its members recorded their confidence, wealth and satisfaction by having their portraits painted by prominent English and Irish artists, whose works adorn many a great house like Malahide near Dublin.

Malahide illustrates to perfection the fashionable **neo-Gothic** style which took hold from about 1760 onwards. Rather than build completely new residences, many owners of old castles employed architects like **Francis Johnston** who abandoned Classical rigour for **neo-Tudor** or **Scottish Baronial** Romantic fantasy. It was possible for a country house to have a Classical façade on one side, and neo-Gothic on the other. More frequently, though, buildings were completely redesigned in medieval or Renaissance style, a trend which lasted to the end of the 19C.

At the same time there arose a fashion for **gardens** extravagantly planted with exotic species brought from all over the Empire. Mount Stewart in Ulster is an outstanding example.

Georgian urbanism

In the course of the 18C, Dublin, which up to then had been little more than an untidy agglomeration of unplanned streets and buildings, became a real capital city. Under the reign of the four Georges, the town experienced unprecedented prosperity

and underwent a fundamental transformation. New streets and whole districts of elegant and comfortable terraced dwellings were laid out, mostly in the southern part of the city. Of three or more storeys, built in red or grey brick and with high windows and doorways with fanlights and sometimes with columned porticoes, these typically Georgian houses also graced other Irish towns, but it was above all in Dublin that they set the tone. Some of the finest are to be found in Merrion Square.

At the same time, Dublin set out to provide itself with an array of splendid public buildings in neo-Classical style. While **Edward Pearce**'s Parliament Building (now the Bank of Ireland) is still a Palladian structure, **neo-Classicism** became the order of the day under the leadership of **James Gandon**, who designed the Custom House, the Four Courts and King's Inns, all fronted (and backed) by an Ionic portico surmounted by a pediment.

New buildings for Catholic worship

The Penal Laws of 1695 had placed the practice of Catholicism under severe restrictions. Public worship was forbidden, and virtually all present-day Catholic churches were built after the passing of the Roman Catholic Emancipation Act in 1829. Together with the Protestant churches built in the same period, many were in the **Gothic Revival** style promoted by the English Catholic architect **Augustus Welby Pugin**. Usually provided with a soaring steeple, most of these edifices are very similar, with pointed windows and interiors filled with sculpture in a more Classical style. The best known churches of this kind are Dublin's two Church of Ireland cathedrals and St Finbar's Cathedral in Cork. Catholic churches of the period are characterised by more exuberantly decorated interiors, often featuring brilliantly coloured glass **mosaics** inspired by English Symbolism.

Towards an architectural revival

Many of Dublin's public buildings were badly damaged during the Easter Uprising, the 1919-21 fight for independence, and in the Civil War. Some of them had to wait until the 1980s before being fully restored.

For Ireland in general and Dublin in particular, the late 19C and early 20C was a barren time for art and architecture, far removed from mainstream European movements like Art Nouveau and Art Deco. Belfast was something of an exception, using its industrial wealth to deck itself out in monumental public buildings like the **neo-Renaissance** City Hall completed in 1906. Suburban expansion in Belfast was on the British model, with working-class **terraced** streets giving way to loosely structured, lower-density middle-class housing further out. Dublin followed the same pattern about a generation later.

Given the endemic poverty of the country over the course of the last century and the troubles which have afflicted it, it is perhaps not surprising that Ireland has only recently begun to participate fully in the artistic and architectural currents of the wider world. Dublin is now something of a showcase for a kind of Irish **Modernism**, notably in the regenerated area of Smithfield Village.

Painting and the search for identity

From the illuminated manuscripts of the Middle Ages to the 20C, it is difficult to discern the expression of a characteristic Irish style in painting. The collections of Dublin's National Gallery show that Irish artists between the 17C and 19C all followed British models. Many of them were portrait painters working for the Anglo-Irish Ascendancy, and apart from the work of **James Peacock** who painted fairground and market scenes, there is very little depiction of the common people. However, at the beginning of the 20C, as part of the wish to revive Gaelic roots, **Jack B Yeats**, brother of WB Yeats, painted typically Irish scenes, as in the National Gallery's *Liffey Swim* (*see page 114*).

Among other 20C painters, Belfast-born **John Lavery** painted numerous portraits and landscapes in a post-Impressionist style. Throughout his long life, **Roderic O'Connor** participated productively in many of the movements of modern art; many of his works are on show at the Hugh Lane Gallery, Dublin's major collection of 20C painting.

Glossary of architectural terms

Apse	Rounded or polygonal end of church or chapel.
Barbican	Fortified outwork protecting a bridge or gateway.
Bas-relief	Sculpture in which the main forms project slightly from the background.
Bailey	Outer stockaded or walled courtyard of castle.
Bastion	Projecting work in a fortification making it possible to fire on attackers from the side.
Cairn	Celtic mound of varying size.
Cashel	Fortified enclosure.
Capital	Crowning feature of column or pillar.
Chapter house	Building used as meeting place for a monastic community.
Classical	Architectural style inspired by Greek and Roman building.
Clochán	Primitive dwellings with drystone walls in beehive shape. Also called beehive huts.
Corbelling	Construction technique using inward-leaning drystone walls.
Corinthian	Classical Order of architecture characterised by capitals in the form of an acanthus leaf.
Crannóg	Artificial island built on stilts over a lake.
Cromlech	Stone circle.
Dolmen	Megalithic structure formed by a flat capstone supported on upright stones.
Doric	The earliest and simplest of the Classical Orders of architecture.
Early English	The earliest style of Gothic architecture in England, characterised by tall, slim lancet windows.
Effigy	Representation of a figure in a recumbent pose, usually on a tomb.
Gothic	Style of architecture which followed the Romanesque style in the 12C, characterised by ribbed vaults and pointed arches.
Ionic	Classical Order of architecture characterised by capitals ornamented with spiral projections.
Lancet	Tall, slim pointed windows characteristic of Early English architecture.
Machicolation	Row of openings beneath a projecting parapet allowing missiles to be dropped on an attacker.
Megalith	Massive stone forming part of a prehistoric monument.
Motte	Artificial mound supporting a Norman timber fortification.
Nave	The main part of a church between doorway and choir.
Palladian	Architectural style initiated by the Italian Renaissance architect Andrea Palladio, characterised by colonnades linking the different parts of a building.
Passage grave	Neolithic burial place with a stone-built corridor and burial chamber, covered with soil.
Rococo	Elaborate 18C style of decoration making profuse use of asymmetrical and shell-like forms.
Romanesque	Architectural style of the 10C-12C using massive walls and piers and rounded arches.
Stucco	Another name for plasterwork.
Transept	In a church with a plan in the form of a cross, the arms of the building at right angles to the nave.
Tumulus	Another name for an artificial mound, usually a burial place.

Early christian architecture

Round tower

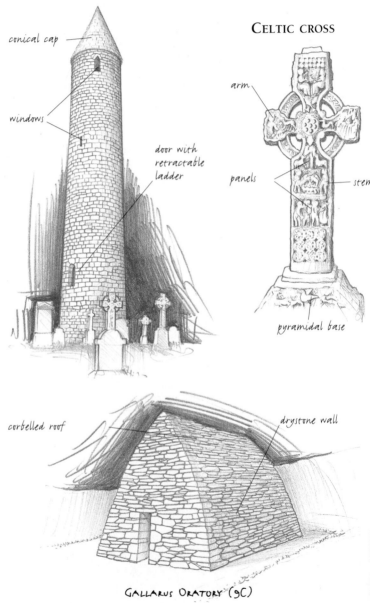

conical cap

windows

door with retractable ladder

Celtic cross

arm

panels

stem

pyramidal base

corbelled roof

drystone wall

Gallarus Oratory (9C)

H. Choimet/MICHELIN

ANGLO-NORMAN ARCHITECTURE

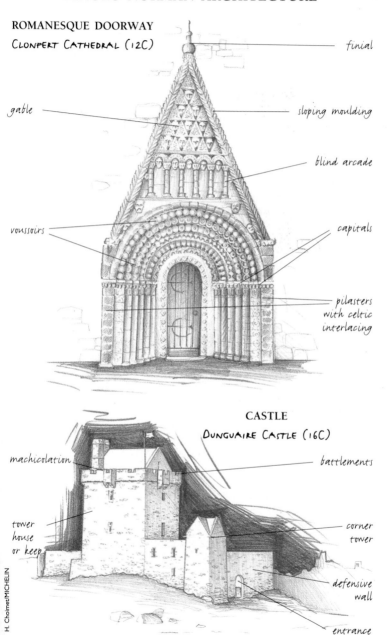

ROMANESQUE DOORWAY
Clonfert Cathedral (12C)

finial

gable

sloping moulding

blind arcade

voussoirs

capitals

pilasters
with celtic
interlacing

CASTLE
Dunguaire Castle (16C)

machicolation

battlements

tower
house
or keep

corner
tower

defensive
wall

entrance

H. Choimet/MICHELIN

IRELAND TODAY

The most important defining feature of contemporary Ireland remains its division into the **26 Counties** making up the Republic and the **Six Counties** of the province of Northern Ireland. After direct rule from Westminster for nearly three decades, Northern Ireland, often incorrectly referred to as Ulster (three of Ulster's historic counties, Donegal, Monaghan and Cavan are part of the Republic), now has its own Assembly, which has met only intermittently since the 1998 Easter Agreement because of the continuing dispute over IRA decommissioning *(see page 432)*.

An evolving democracy

The political life of the Republic is regulated by the **1937 Constitution**, which was drawn up at a time when Catholicism played a far more prominent part in national life than it does today. In 1972, after a referendum had been held, the article of the constitution giving the Catholic Church a "special position" wa s abolished, and after another referendum in 1995 the ban on divorce was lifted. Nevertheless, Ireland remains a country where there is **no formal separation of Church and State**. In practice, this means that the Church still plays a very significant role in education – 70 % of schools are confessional – and in social provision and health care. But the process of secularisation has speeded up in recent years, and most political parties nowadays are wedded to the idea of freedom of conscience in religious matters.

Parliamentary democracy

Ireland's **Parliament** (Oireachtas) consists of a **lower house**, the Dáil Éireann with 166 members, *teachtaí dála* or TDs, and an upper chamber, the Seanad (Senate) Éireann with 60 senators. The third element in the country's constitutional structure is the head of state, the **President** (Uachtarán na hÉireann). Every citizen over the age of 18 can vote in Dáil and Senate elections and can be a candidate when over the age of 21. TDs and senators are elected by a system of proportional representation, with one member representing on average about 40 000 inhabitants. Legislation is prepared in English and Gaelic, with the Gaelic version prevailing in cases of doubt. Any citizen over the age of 35 can be a presidential candidate. The president is elected by universal adult suffrage and has a mandate of seven years, renewable once only. Guardian of the constitution and head of the armed forces, the president nominates the government on the advice of parliament and can call a referendum. Following the term served by **Mary Robinson**, elected in 1990, another woman, **Mary McAleese**, has been President since 1997.

The president chooses the head of the executive, the Taoiseach, normally proposed by the majority party. The leader of Fianna Fáil, Bertie Ahern, has headed a coalition government since 1997.

Party fortunes

All inhabitants of Ireland, whatever their nationality, may vote in local elections, but only EU citizens may vote in European elections and only Irish citizens and UK subjects resident in the Republic are allowed to vote in Irish national elections.

Six parties are normally represented in the Dáil: Fianna Fáil, Fine Gael, Labour, Progressive Democrats, Democratic Left and the Green Party. The two main parties, Fianna Fáil and Fine Gael, emerged from the historic split in Sinn Féin between supporters and opponents of the 1921 Anglo-Irish Treaty.

The majority parties – Founded in 1926 by Eamon de Valera, **Fianna Fáil** *("Warriors of Destiny")* was made up of those who rejected the Treaty and Partition. A conservative-minded party, it governed the country several times between 1932 and 1994, and in the European Parliament forms part of the Democratic Alliance group of parties. It has alternated in government with the other main party, **Fine Gael**, which accepted Partition, if only as a temporary measure preceding eventual reunification. It was founded in 1933 as the successor to the pro-Treaty Cumann na nGaedheal party which had been heavily defeated by Fianna Fáil in a general election. It now occupies the centre ground of politics, and formed a government in 1994. It belongs to the Christian Democratic group of parties in the European Parliament.

Minor parties – The Irish political landscape includes a number of small parties which have occasionally taken part in coalition governments. This has been the case with the **Labour Party** created by James Connolly, Jim Larkin and William O'Brien at a trade union congress in Clonmel in 1912. The Labour Party belongs to the Socialist group of parties in Strasbourg and is affiliated to the Socialist International. The **Progressive Democrats**, founded in 1985 by Desmond O'Malley, was founded as a result of a split in Fianna Fáil, but neverthe-less formed a coalition with that party between 1989 and 1991 and again from 1997. Its leader, Mary Harney, is the first woman to lead a political party in Ireland.

Created in 1992, the **Democratic Left** is the only party represented in both parts of Ireland, helping to form a coalition with Fine Gael in December 1994.

The **Green Party** came into existence in 1982 through the fusion of a number of different movements and organisations. Its first TD was elected in 1989 and two representatives were sent to the European Parliament in 1994. The Greens have no leader, and the posts of party officials are rotated annually.

Mary Robinson

A. Gyori/SYGMA

Mary Robinson

On 7 November 1990, a date of considerable symbolic significance for the Republic of Ireland, the presidency of the country was filled by a female lawyer known for her liberal views on women's rights, on homosexuality and on minorities such as travellers. Though she failed to make further progress on the issue of abortion, Mary Robinson succeeded in getting parliamentary approval for a new divorce law, despite strong opposition from the Roman Catholic Church. In the course of her mandate, this dynamic woman has kept her popularity while energetically promoting civil liberties. Her human qualities and her legal competence have gained international recognition. Since 1997 Mary Robinson has played a leading role in the UN Commission for Human Rights.

The Celtic Tiger's great leap forward

With an annual growth rate of 8% since 1994 and an unemployment rate of 5%, the Irish economy is the most dynamic in the Western world. The country's spectacular progress has been compared to that of the nations of Southeast Asia some 15 years ago, and has led to the Republic being called "The Celtic Tiger". All the old clichés about Ireland have been turned on their head. While the Irish once went abroad to work, there is now a **labour shortage**, and foreign interests are competing to invest in the country. The historic poverty of the Irish State has given way to a **budgetary surplus** which is the envy of other European countries, and in 1999 Ireland allowed itself the luxury of cutting taxes by 3%. In the same year, the country exported software products which in terms of relative value were worth 10% more than those exported by the USA. Ireland's GDP per head is now higher than that of Canada.

This economic miracle cannot be explained by the exploitation of the country's natural resources. Ireland has no sources of energy apart from the peat which provides 14% of its electricity, and no mineral reserves other than lead and zinc, of which it is one of the main European producers.

The traditional sector slows down

Although undergoing modernisation, **agriculture** still employs almost 15% of the working population but only accounts for 10% of gross domestic product. Thanks to its grasslands, the best in Europe, Ireland has roughly twice as many **sheep** (8 million) as people. There are almost as many **cattle**, and Irish racehorses from the Kildare area are much sought after by breeders from all over the world.

The main crops are **sugarbeet**, **barley**, **oats**, **wheat** and of course **potatoes**, still a staple of the Irish diet.

The output of the **fishing industry** has increased seven-fold since the 1980s, almost the whole of it destined for export. More recently, catches have declined because of the quotas imposed by the EU. By contrast, Ireland has been in the forefront of **fish farming**, with production centred on the Galway area, where salmon is raised for smoking.

Industries old and new

Ireland's **manufacturing industry** has, paradoxically, benefited from its previous backwardness. While Northern Ireland's prosperity was originally based on the textiles and the heavy industries created during the Industrial Revolution, these activities became something of a handicap during the restructuring which began in the 1970s. By contrast, the South had no such dinosaurs to deal with, and was able to make a direct entry into the era of **hi-tech industry**. This ability to start from scratch without a backlog of rust-belt problems is one of the reasons for the country's current prosperity. Activities like **pharmaceuticals** and **electronics** now employ something like a quarter of the working population. From the early 1980s, firms specialising in **information technology** began to set up in Ireland, making use of very advantageous financial and other incentives and benefiting from a relatively cheap and under-unionised workforce. At the same time, **service industries** have been the most dynamic sector of the economy, accounting for 65% of GNP while employing 55% of the working population. An important factor in this success story is the high educational level of the workforce and its adaptability.

A European orientation

EU subsidies have played a role in Ireland's recent economic growth, as have financial incentives designed to attract foreign investment. Together with Greece, Spain and Portugal, Ireland has been eligible for the aid targeted at Europe's less favoured regions intended to help them catch up with the richer countries of the Union.

Between 1993 and 1997, Ireland received about IR£650 million of subsidies for modernisation of its public transport and highway infrastructure. At the same time, the country benefited from IR£2 billion in structural funds for agricultural support, modernisation of industry and services, and general improvements to the standard of living of its population.

A fiscal paradise

It would be wrong to conclude that Ireland owes its prosperity entirely to EU aid. Since the middle of the 1970s, successive governments have followed extremely liberal policies designed to attract **foreign firms** here. Free zones, easy repatriation of profits, and low taxes have encouraged 1 200 foreign firms, three-quarters of them from the US, to bring their operations to Ireland in the last six years, creating 300 000 new jobs, mostly in the **information** and **hi-tech** sectors. At the same time the country has earned a reputation for being a fiscal paradise for **off-shore** companies locating here, while writers choosing to "exile" themselves in Ireland are not liable to income tax.

The coin has two sides

The Irish state has benefited considerably from the effects of this economic boom, its revenue increasing to the extent that it has launched a IR£340 million public investment programme to be completed in 2006. Everything would seem to be for the best in all possible Irish worlds, but there is of course another side to the coin. The government's restrictive **incomes policy** based on a social contract is now creaking at the seams. In 1999, the public sector was affected by a whole series of strikes; discontent is rife among nurses, salaried transport workers, teachers and police, who have not only failed to benefit from growth but have been adversely affected by the rise in the cost of urban housing – Dublin house prices rose more than 37 % between 1997 and 1999 – obliging many people to undertake ever longer commuting journeys.

At the same time, the private sector has suffered from a severe **labour shortage**, which is particularly noticeable in the hotel and tourism industries. Experts estimate that by 2007 Ireland will need an additional 200 000 immigrant workers. But a country which historically was an exporter of people has had great difficulty in coming to terms with resident foreigners, especially if they are not well off. **Racism** exists, and is becoming more openly expressed, especially with regard to Dublin's small black community.

Understanding the political situation

6 Counties	The 6 counties which make up Northern Ireland, often wrongly termed "Ulster".
26 Counties	The 26 counties which make up the Republic of Ireland.
Bloody Sunday	Sunday, 31 January 1972, when an initially peaceful civil rights march in Derry degenerated into rioting and led to an attack on unarmed civilians by soldiers of the Parachute Regiment in which thirteen were shot dead. Following this, the Stormont Parliament was suspended and direct rule from London imposed.
The Crown	The British government.
Dáil Eireann	The parliament of the Republic of Ireland.
Decommissioning	The disarmament of paramilitary groups: this remains the major stumbling block to full implementation of the Good Friday Agreement.
Downing Street Declaration	The joint agreement made in 1993 by the British Prime Minister and the Taoiseach of the Republic of Ireland in which it was stated that the British government had no selfish, strategic, or economic interest in Northern Ireland and that the Irish government accepted that the democratic right of self-determination by the people of Ireland as a whole must be achieved and exercised with and subject to the agreement and consent of a majority of the people of Northern Ireland.
Éire	The Gaelic term for Ireland and the official name for the 26 counties from 1937 until 1949.
Free State	Name given to the independent part of Ireland between 1922-37.
Garda Síochána	Police force of the Republic of Ireland.
Gerrymandering	The redrawing of electoral boundary lines in order to control election results.
Good Friday Agreement	The agreement reached on 10 April 1998 by all the major political parties providing for the establishment of devolved government in Northern Ireland.
HM Prison Maze ("The Maze")	The largest prison in Northern Ireland, it held the bulk of paramilitary prisoners, from all sides of the conflict.
House of Commons	The lower chamber of the British parliament.
INLA	Irish National Liberation Army: an extreme terrorist splinter group of the IRA.
IRA	Irish Republican Army. The Provisional IRA is the largest republican paramilitary organisation.
Long Kesh	Another name for the Maze Prison. The largest prison in Northern Ireland, it held the bulk of paramilitary prisoners, from all sides of the conflict.
Loyalist	Alternative term for Unionist, often applied to paramilitary groupings.
Nationalist	Term applied to that part of the population of Northern Ireland aspiring to a united Ireland.
Orange Order	Unionist political organisation in Northern Ireland, organised around Lodges in the same way as Freemasons. Orange Order marches take place in July each year to commemorate the victory of the Protestant William of Orange over the Catholic James II and are often a source of conflict.
Republicanism	Historically, the movement associated with the struggle for complete independence from Great Britain. Used more recently to define the more intransigent forms of Irish nationalism.

RUC	Royal Ulster Constabulary: the Northern Ireland police force.
SDLP	Social Democratic and Labour Party: the principal nationalist political party in Northern Ireland; moderate and opposed to violence.
Sinn Féin	"Ourselves Alone". Republican party devoted to establishing a united Ireland; widely regarded as the political wing of the IRA.
Stormont	Site of the parliament of Northern Ireland, on the eastern outskirts of Belfast.
Taoiseach	The Prime Minister of the Republic of Ireland.
Ulster	One of the four provinces of Ireland (along with Connaught, Munster and Leinster), comprising the 6 counties of Northern Ireland and 3 counties of the Republic.
Unionism	Movement in favour of the union of Northern Ireland with Great Britain.
United Kingdom	The union of Great Britain and Ireland created by the Act of Union of 1800 which abolished the parliament in Dublin and centralised government in Westminster. Since independence, the union of Great Britain and Northern Ireland.
UUP	Ulster Unionist Party: the principal moderate unionist party in Northern Ireland, led since 1995 by David Trimble.

Meeting the people

Faithful friends

THE MIXING OF THE RACES

Clichés tend to have a long life. The clichés about the Irish more than most. So the women are all beautiful, with pale skins and ruddy cheeks and a piercing gaze, the men brick-complexioned, full of stories and fond of a pint. So much for stereotypes. The reality is quite different. Invaded over the millenia by people of highly varied origin, Ireland has a population of infinite physical variety, the result of a slow and very thorough process of marrying and mixing.

The island's population totals 5.4 million; of that, 3.7 million live in the Republic. The birth rate in the South is 19 per 1 000 and dropping, in the North 14 per 1 000. The population is a youthful one, more than half of it under the age of 25, but it is growing older, not least because of the decline in the birth rate in parallel with the decline in the influence of the Roman Catholic Church. Even so, this birth rate is the highest in Europe. The distribution of population is uneven; more than half the people live in urban areas, the remainder dispersed thinly over the countryside.

Origins

In prehistoric times, Ireland's first inhabitants, who had come here from Scotland, were hunter-gatherers. Then, in the Neolithic period, they scattered **megaliths**, standing stones, dolmens and stone circles over the land, all linked to their cult of the dead. They built rudimentary dwellings, grew crops and raised pigs, goats and sheep, well before other European peoples. During the Bronze Age, their mastery of metal-working enabled them to create superb objects, including massive pieces of gold jewellery.

Celts

The population began to take on a more fixed character with the arrival of successive waves of Celtic settlers. Bold warriors on horseback, the Celts brought with them from their wanderings around Europe not only iron-working skills and fine weaponry, but also an art which had been forged from many and diverse influences.

A refined society – Celtic society had an egalitarian character. People were organised in agricultural communities which practised a lifestyle of some sophistication, as is evident in their utensils and their **jewellery**. They were tall in stature, blond and with pale complexions, at least according to descriptions of them by the historians of Antiquity. They were familiar with wine, mead, had culinary skills and knew how to brew beer and make butter, leavened bread and vinegar, and had extensive trading relations with other peoples.

Fertile spirituality – The spiritual contribution of this proud and warlike people to the life of Ireland was an outstanding one. Their **cult of heroism** was the inspiration of much of the culture, mystique and above all, the **legends** of Ireland. The Celts had a special relationship with **Nature**, the setting for their sanctuaries and rituals and the symbol of their gods and goddesses. They worshipped the land and the sky, water, trees, mountains and animals. But more than anything else, they venerated legendary heroes, mythical warriors of extreme courage and utter invincibility, as well as savage and bloody gods. Their vision of death as a transition to a world existing in parallel to the material world accounts for their great courage in battle.

The power of the druids – The druids were the intellectual elite of Celtic society, fulfilling the role of judges and spiritual leaders (but only after completing a 20-year training). Their erudition and eloquence enabled them to transmit a culture which was strictly oral, organise ceremonies and funerary rituals, and help their communities relate to the forces of Nature. The depth of their influence was such that their heritage was far from effaced by Ireland's conversion to Christianity from the 4C onwards; the Irish continued to live in close-knit communities based on the idea of the family and the important role of women, on the law, art and a love of legends and poetry.

Vikings and Anglo-Normans

A further wave of invaders came to Ireland in the Middle Ages in the shape of the Vikings from Denmark, who quickly settled here and were integrated into Celtic society.

By contrast, the arrival of the Normans marked a turning-point of great significance, the introduction of colonisation. From their kingdom in England, the Normans imported continental influences; French became the country's official language, and the distinctive forms and practices of Celtic Christianity with its borrowings from paganism and ancient ritual were thoroughly **romanised**. But despite endless disputes and rivalries, the Anglo-Normans, often referred to as the Old English, took on many of the characteristics of the native Irish, much to the discomfiture of the authorities back in England.

In the 16C and 17C, as the Reformation progressed, the English state strengthened its grip on Ireland by encouraging settlers from England, Wales and Scotland to take over lands often confiscated from those proprietors considered disloyal. Disloyalty was identified with **Catholicism**, loyalty with **Protestantism**, in its Anglican form the official state religion. Some of the most bitter opponents of English government were the Old English themselves, many of whom put aside their differences with their native Irish neighbours in a common fight for their faith. Successive waves of settlers, some of them former soldiers paid with confiscated land rather than funds from a perennially hard-up Exchequer, came to Ireland, often appropriating the best land and paying little heed to the claims of the native Irish. Among the most numerous of these new Irish were Presbyterians from Scotland, who mainly settled in Ulster. Their dour and orderly ways contrasted with those of their free-spirited and garrulous neighbours, adding to their other more substantial resentments.

Huguenots and Spaniards

At the same time, another wave of Protestants arrived. These were the Huguenots, fleeing from Catholic persecution in France. They tended to settle in towns, bringing with them new ideas about commerce and industry and giving a definite boost to the country's economy. Catholic Spain tried on several occasions to interfere with England's plans for Ireland, and a certain number of Spaniards never returned home. Could those dark-eyed, sallow-complexioned western Irish types be their descendants?

Into exile

The Irish diaspora...

There are more Irish outside Ireland today than in the country itself. In the 19C and early 20C the principal destinations for emigrants were successively **Canada**, the **United States**, **Great Britain**, and to a lesser extent, **Australia**.

Roots retained – The Irish diaspora is distinct from others in that it has kept much of its culture and traditions; a St Patrick's Day procession in New York is enough to convince any sceptic of the truth of this statement. People of Irish descent tend to cultivate an intense nostalgia for the old country, which finds an outlet in the **genealogical centres** gracing many a town and village. The frequently difficult quest for family roots has become a veritable industry, attracting thousands of people of Irish origin, mostly from America, to try and trace their origins. Many a ballad was composed on the far side of the Atlantic by exiles evoking the cares and sorrows of their far-off homeland. More recent emigrants are less bothered by such concerns, tending to return home happily once they have made their fortune abroad. They add their bit to the country's growing diversity.

Travelling people

Despite their uncertain origins – quite distinct from those of the Romanis of continental Europe – Ireland's tinkers and travellers have a way of life very much like that of European gypsies. Of Catholic faith, they are probably the descendants of people evicted from their homes at the time of the Famine, and are used to living on the margins of society. Their access to education, housing and employment is problematic, and if they do choose to settle, they usually find themselves in the poorest type of accommodation. Many of them stay put for the winter, then set off on their wanderings as the weather improves. Councils are not keen on providing them with sites, and even if they do, it is not uncommon for the sites to be destroyed by the local inhabitants. The favourite places for travellers to settle for a while is along the verge of the highway or in lay-bys.

Homecomings – More recently, the younger generation which has spent time abroad working or studying, has tended to return home, encouraged to do so by a government in need of skilled manpower. The flourishing economy means that it is easy for such people to find jobs to match their talents. And the many foreign firms that have been attracted to the country have brought with them some of their own staff from America, Germany, France and elsewhere, helping to make Dublin in particular a more cosmopolitan city.

...and newcomers

From an ethnic point of view, Ireland is a very one-dimensional place. In the past, immigration was limited to settlers from England, Wales and Scotland, and has been associated with religious and ethnic conflict.

Prejudice and segregation – Because of a restrictive policy on immigration, there are few non-Europeans resident in Ireland. Prospective immigrants, other than citizens of EU countries, must prove that they have a job which cannot be filled by a native. This policy may change as a result of the shortage of skilled labour which has

Latins of the north?

C Legrand/MICHELIN

developed with increasing prosperity, but many Irish still look askew at non-European immigrants. Blacks, Arabs, and Asian people are present in very limited numbers, mostly performing menial jobs or working in restaurants and fast food outlets. Most legal immigrants have come from **India** and **Pakistan**, but more and more illegal immigrants have been attracted by the opportunities available. A smaller number of people have arrived from EU countries, as employees of foreign firms, as small-business people, artists and writers (who benefit from a favourable tax regime) or as pensioners. Their presence in villages and small towns tends to be a great source of curiosity among local people and their integration into local communities is not always problem-free.

Between 20 000 and 25 000 **travellers** or **tinkers** live in Ireland (*see panel opposite*). Many of them deal in scrap-metal or are rag-and-bone men, others are itinerant knife-grinders or repair pots and pans.

Northern Latins?

With their expansive and passionate character, their mysticism tempered by a very Mediterranean fatalism, their love of drama and their undeniable machismo, the Irish have often been thought of as a Latin people somehow transposed to the north-western edge of Europe. The phenomenon is explained in a variety of ways: Celtic ancestry, sensitivity, passions honed on a difficult history and the profound influence of the Catholic Church are among them.

Love of the dramatic – The irresistible charm of the Irish lies not only in their infinite kindness, but in their casual and joking manner, and the sudden way in which an upsurge of lyricism or emotion can colour the easy banter after a pint or two. It's no use looking for logic here; there's little rationality or consistency an abundance of fantasy and sentiment. There is too an insatiable curiosity about other people which can sometimes go too far, a sense of the tragic which can make a mountain out of a molehill, and a passion for introspection which never tires of exorcising the abuses of the past.

A new scrutiny – For some time now, Ireland has been undergoing profound change. Hitherto sacrosanct values in politics and religion are being questioned. The influence of the clergy on public and private life is endlessly debated in the media. Scandals are exposed on a daily basis, in politics and business as well as in the Church, and public figures held up for scrutiny and judgement. The media have had a field day, feeding and encouraging the public's love of gossip.

The art of conversation – Laughing, joking, taking the mickey, striking up acquaintance, lamenting how everything is going to the dogs, setting the world to rights, squeezing the last drop of juice out of every scandal ...maybe this is the most important thing for any visitor to Ireland to participate in: conversation, Irish style!

DAILY LIFE

A land lost in the mists of the past, its roads travelled by gaily painted caravans and tired donkeys pulling wobbly little carts, cloth-capped turf cutters heading for the pub, merry fiddlers making pretty red-heads dance to their tunes; this is the kind of sentimental image still sustained by the tourist industry. But daily life in Ireland, an astonishing mixture of tradition and pragmatism, is full of surprises. Photogenic groups of girls in white dresses still wend their way to Communion, but there are also plenty of sharp-suited computer wizards, while psychedelic artists and hard rock specialists coexist with grim-faced farmers and village violinists. The pub and the church are still the two focal points of life; people come together in the pub not only to drink, talk and make music, but to mark important events in life, like the wake after a burial. And the church is there, as it always has been, with its crucifixes, its saints, and its Blessed Virgin.

SLIDE FILE

Traditional music session

Women in Ireland

The place of women in Irish society has long been full of paradoxes. In the past, despite a lack of rights, and left behind by social progress, women nevertheless formed the backbone of families and communities. It has often been said of the Irishman that he only left the authority of his mother for that of his wife.

Women at home

Women's role was for many years limited to the domestic sphere and the family. The Church's proscription of contraception and the consequent multiple births prevented women from taking up most forms of professional activity other than **charity work**. But in the home their rule was unchallenged. Even after **contraception** had been legalised, many doctors continued to refuse to prescribe the pill to unmarried women. Family planning advice was usually in the hands of Church bodies, which encouraged procreation rather than contraception.

Women of the 1990s

Any real change to women's status had to wait until the 1990s. With the election of **Mary Robinson** as President in 1990, partly on the votes of minorities and the under-privileged, a period of transformation began. Even though sexuality remains a somewhat taboo subject, young Irishwomen have begun to enjoy a freedom comparable to that of their sisters in the rest of Europe. In the 1983 referendum, people

Desperately seeking someone

Irish countrymen tend to marry at a much more advanced age than anywhere else in Europe. Small farms do not produce enough revenue to support the numerous offspring of the traditional farming family. Most siblings would leave the land and look for work and marital opportunities in town or abroad, leaving the oldest son to work with his father and eventually take over the farm. By then he would most likely be 40 or older, without ever having had the time or the means to look for a partner. In parts of the thinly populated west, the proportion of unmarried men to women is still of the order of 20 to one. Lisdoonvarna in Co Clare is famous for its Matchmaking Festival (see page 344), when matchmakers do their best to introduce compatible partners to one another.

voted against the legalisation of **abortion** and the position remains the same today. A first referendum on **divorce** took place in 1986, when the "Noes" carried the day, but this result was overturned by a second poll in 1995, albeit by the slimmest of majorities (9 000). There were Catholic moves to invalidate the vote, and divorce only became legal in 1997. Since marriages are held in church a paradoxical situation has arisen; after a (fully legal) divorce, it is impossible to remarry except by doing so in another country, or by annulment by the Church of the first marriage.

School

Schooling is still run on a confessional basis, even though more and more voices have been raised against a system which has given rise to all kinds of abuses and scandals in the recent past.

Educational segregation

Catholics and Protestants have their own educational establishments and their own teachers, and children from different communities rarely mix. Until recently, it was very difficult for a teacher to find employment in a school of a different confession from their own. Even though there is a trend towards secularisation, there are still very many priests and nuns in the teaching profession, and, with the vast majority of the Republic's schools being Catholic, the Church's influence remains strong.

In the North, segregation is even more pronounced, since Protestants and Catholics tend to live in different areas. Despite efforts made to the contrary, fewer than 10 % of children attend multi-confessional schools, and teaching remains very marked by religion. For Catholics, this situation is linked to discrimination in employment and other areas,

C Legrand/MICHELIN

Schoolgirls

51

Uniformity at school

As in Britain, as the start of the school year approaches in August, clothes shops and department stores stock up with school uniforms. Most schools still insist on their pupils dressing in a standard way which identifies them as belonging to that particular establishment. Trousers for girls are frowned upon, but teenage girls show great ingenuity in adapting the uniform to demonstrate their individuality. Skirts may be de rigueur, but they can be worn daringly short, and shoes, which can be any colour you like as long as it's black, can have platform soles of astonishing thickness. The idea of course is to put everyone on the same footing, and the compulsory wearing of uniforms means that parents can buy one set of clothes for the school year and then not have to think any more about what their offspring are going to wear.

since employers can immediately tell what community a job-seeker comes from because of the school they attended.

The curriculum

In the Republic, boys and girls begin school at the age of 4-and-a-half and usually attend single-sex establishments for the whole of their schooling. Primary and secondary education is free and is compulsory until the age of 16. The school day begins at 9am and ends between 3pm and 4pm according to the age of the pupils, with a lunch break of an hour. Secondary schooling ends with a Leaving Certificate, and higher education is at university or institutes of technology. In Northern Ireland, the British model prevails, with GCSEs taken at 16 and Advanced Levels at 18, followed by university or some other establishment of higher education for those qualified.

The Irish at home

Irish houses are not really very different from British ones. The traditional long and low cottages with their roofs of thatch or corrugated iron have largely given way to run-of-the-mill modern bungalows and houses, often with a touch of the neo-Georgian or Deep South Classical about them. There is a surprising number of very large new residences, thanks to the economic boom and ready access to mortgages and loans. This kind of extravagant building harks back to a long-standing respect for property and to the tradition of large families, even though the latter hardly exist any more.

Around the hearth

In towns there are hardly any blocks of flats, and most council housing is in the form of small houses and gardens, each with its shed. The buildings lining village streets are often painted in traditional bright colours, with real rainbow effects in the case of shop-fronts. People do not seem to mind being visible from the street and curtains are rarely drawn. The main room in the home is still the **kitchen**. Central heating was a rarity until recently, and the kitchen was often the only room to be heated, usually with a coal or peat fire (*see page 11*). Members of the family gather here on their return from school or work and the kettle is permanently on the boil ready to make a nice cup of tea. Most meals are eaten here too. The kitchen is for family only, the **living room** being used when there are guests or perhaps for watching television, though the TV set is often in the kitchen, which remains the cosiest room in the house, especially when filled with the delightful scent of a turf fire.

Among the fields

Traditional houses are becoming more and more rare, even though some people have begun to build in the old style. There are two types of traditional farmstead: the prosperous farmer's classic single-storey building with a doorway, a little porch and five windows, and the more modest labourer's cottage or cabin, which in its simplest form consists of a door flanked by a single window on either side. Sometimes longer but always close to the ground, it would originally have had a thatched roof. With greater prosperity, damp, expensive thatch has given way to slate or, in poorer places, to corrugated iron. In the northwest, thatching has come back into favour, especially with tourists who long to stay in a picture-postcard holiday cottage. In Donegal and in other places close to the sea, the thatch is covered with netting to protect it from the ravages of the constant wind, with knots fixed to pegs at regular intervals along the top of the wall. In all cases, window-openings are tiny because of the severity of the climate. Houses turn their backs to the prevailing wind and sites are often chosen to maximise shelter. The dark interior consists of small rooms opening off the centrally-placed kitchen. Good examples of such vernacular buildings can be seen in a number of Folk Parks.

Thatching

TRACING ANCESTORS

The organisations listed below can assist in tracing Irish ancestors; some charge fees.

Republic of Ireland

Co Cavan
: **Cavan Genealogy Centre**, Cana House, Farnham Street, Cavan, Co Cavan, ☎ 049 436 1094, canahous@iol.ie, www.irishroots.net/cavan.htm Open Monday-Friday, 9.30am-4.30pm.

Co Clare
: **Clare Heritage Centre**, Church Street, Corofin, Co Clare, ☎ 065 683 7955, clareheritage@eircom.net, www.clareroots.com Open mid March-October, daily, 10am-6pm; otherwise, Monday-Friday, 9am-5pm. Admission charge. Extensive genealogical records making it possible to trace people who emigrated from Clare in the last century; in the aftermath of the Great Famine between 1851 and 1871 at least 100 000 people left the region.

Co Cork
: **Cork Archives Institute**, South Main Street, Cork, Co Cork, ☎ 0214 427 7809, cai@indigo.ie, www.corkcorp.ie Open Tuesday-Friday, 10am-1pm, 2.30pm-5pm by appointment only. Copious material consisting of family and private papers, some of potential genealogical interest, and chiefly of historical records relating to business, local government and trade union activities.

Co Donegal
: **Donegal Ancestry**, The Quay, Ramelton, Co Donegal, ☎ 074 51266, Fax 074 71702, donances@indigo.ie, www.indigo.ie/~donances Open all year, Monday-Friday, 9.30am-4.30pm (-3.30pm, Friday).

Co Dublin
: **National Library of Ireland**, Kildare Street, Dublin 2, ☎ 01 603 0022, Fax 01 676 6690, www.nli.ie Open Monday-Friday, 10am-4.45pm, Saturday, 10am-12.30pm. No postal queries.

Office of the Registrar General, Joyce House, 11 / 13 Lombard Street East, Dublin 2, ☎ 01 671 1000, Fax 01 635 4440, www.groireland.ie Open Monday-Friday, 9.30am-12.30pm, 2.15pm-4.30pm.

National Archives, Bishop Street, Dublin 8, ☎ 01 407 2300, Fax 01 407 2333, mail@nationalarchives.ie, www.nationalarchives.ie Open Monday-Friday, 10am-5pm

Co Leitrim
: **Leitrim Genealogy Centre**, County Library, Ballinamore, Co Leitrim, ☎ 078 44012, Fax 078 44425, leitrimgenealogy@eircom.net, www.irishroots.net/Leitrim.htm Open Monday-Friday, 10am-1pm and 2-5pm.

Co Limerick
: **Irish Palatine Heritage Centre**, Rathkeale, Co Limerick, ☎ 069 63511; Fax 069 63511; ipass@tinet.ie Open May-September, Monday-Saturday, 10am-midday and 2-5pm, Sunday, 2-6pm. Admission charge. Genealogical service for tracing Palatine ancestors.

Co Offaly
and Co Laois
: **Offaly and Laois** Family History Research Centre, Bury Quay, Tullamore, Co Offaly, ☎ 0506 21421, Fax 0506 21421, ohas@iol.ie, www.offalyhistory.com Open Monday-Friday, 9am-1pm and 2-4pm. Public Reading Room: Open 10am-4pm.

Co Roscommon
: **County Roscommon Heritage and Genealogy Society**, Church Street, Strokestown, Co Roscommon, ☎ 078 33380. Genealogical research service.

Co Tipperary	**Genealogical Service** Excel Heritage Centre, Tipperary, ☎ 062 52725, thu@iol.ie, www.iol.ie/~thu; Clans Office, James Street, Co Tipperary. Open Monday-Friday, 9am-5pm.
	Brú Ború Cultural Centre, Rock of Cashel, Co Tipperary, ☎ 062 61122, Fax 062 62700. Genealogy and Celtic Studies Centre.
	North Tipperary Genealogical Service, Nenagh District Heritage Centre, The Gate House, Kickham Street, Nenagh, Co Tipperary, ☎ 067 33850, Fax 067 33586. Open Monday-Friday, except bank holidays, 9.30am-5pm,
	Roscrea Heritage Centre, Castle Street, Roscrea, Co Tipperary, ☎ 0505 21850 / 21689, heritage@roscrea.net, www.elyocarroll.com/roscas.html Open April-October, 10am-6pm. Computerised genealogical service.
Co Waterford	**Waterford Heritage Genealogy Centre**, St Patrick's Church, Jenkin's Lane, Waterford, ☎ 051 876123, Fax 051 850645, mnoc@iol.ie, www.iol.ie/~mnoc Open all year, Monday-Friday, 9am-5pm(-2pm, Friday).
Co Westmeath	**Dún na Sí**, Knockdanney, Moate, Co Westmeath, ☎ 0902 81183, Fax 0902 81661, dunnasimoate@tinet.ie, www.core.ie/midlands/projects/mullingar/dunnasi/ Open all year, Monday-Friday 10am-4pm (-3pm Friday). Genealogy Research Centre for Co Westmeath.
Co Wicklow	**Wicklow Family Heritage Centre**, Wicklow's Historic Gaol, Wicklow Town, County Wicklow, ☎ 0404 20126, Fax 0404 61612, wfh@tinet.ie, www.wicklow.ie Open all year, Monday-Friday 9am-5pm (-4pm Friday).

Northern Ireland

Co Antrim	**General Register Office**, Oxford House, 49-55 Chichester Street, Belfast BT1 4HL, ☎ 028 9025 2000, Fax 028 9025 2120, www.nisra.gov.uk/gro
	Ulster Historical Foundation, 12 College Square East, Belfast BT1 6DD, ☎ 028 9033 2288, Fax 028 9023 9885, enquiry@uhf.org.uk, www.ancestryireland.com On-line database of Ulster family records.
Co Armagh	**Armagh Ancestry**, 42 English Street, Armagh, BT61 7BA, ☎ 028 3752 1802, Fax 028 3751 0033, ancestry@acdc.btinternet.com, www.armagh.co.uk Open all year, Monday-Saturday, 9am-5pm,
Co Derry	County Derry or Londonderry Genealogy Centre, Heritage Library, 14 Bishop Street, Derry, BT48 6PW, ☎ 028 7126 9792/ 71361661, Fax 028 7136 0921, ancestors@irelandmail.com, www.irishroots.net/Derry.htm
Co Fermanagh	**Roslea Heritage Centre**, Monaghan Road, Roslea, Co Fermanagh, ☎ 028 6775 1750. Open April-September, Monday-Friday, 10am-4pm, weekends and rest of year by appointment; October-March, Monday-Friday, 9am-5pm. £2, 50p (child).
Co Tyrone	**Heritage World**, Pomeroy Road, Donaghmore, BT70 3HG, ☎ / Fax 028 8776 1306, wok@heritagewld.com, www.heritagewld.com Open all year, Monday-Friday, 9am-1pm and 2pm-5pm. Extensive computerised archives enabling people to discover the path to their Irish roots.

Other sources of information

www.irishroots.net The website of the Irish Family History Foundation.

www.goireland.com/Genealogy The genealogy page of the Irish Tourism Service's website.

www.ireland.com/ancestor This site claims to have the largest collection of Irish genealogy links on the internet.

Association of Professional Genealogists in Ireland, 30 Harlech Crescent, Clonskeagh, Dublin 14, http://indigo.ie/~apgi/ Regulatory body for genealogy in Ireland.

Video: ***Searching for your ancestors in Ireland – A Professional Guide*** Shorway Video Ltd, ☎ 0507 25155, shorway@iol.iw, www.iftn.ie/production/shorway

Clan Gatherings

There are 243 Irish clans which hold annual clan gatherings on ancestral sites. Information is available from **Clans of Ireland**, Dr Margaret Tierney, Grange Clare, Kilmeague, Neath, Co Kildare.

THE IRISH ABROAD

What has been called the "Irish Diaspora" is a very real phenomenon, with millions of people of Irish descent living in countries other than Ireland, and far outnumbering those who have stayed "at home".

Early emigrants – Irish interest in the wider world began far earlier than the great periods of emigration in modern times. As the Roman Empire began to collapse in the late 3C, sea-borne Irish raiders terrorised western Britain, eventually founding petty and relatively short-lived kingdoms in Wales and Scotland. The Isle of Man took its name from the Irish deity Manannan, and Irish domination of the island lasted for many centuries. A different kind of expansion took place from the 6C onwards, when Irish monks set out to evangelise Britain and the continent of Europe (*see page 16*), some of them travelling to the edges of Christendom in Mecklenburg and on the Danube. They established a reputation, not only as effective missionaries and church leaders, but also as scholars, and for several centuries learned Irishmen were sought after by rulers such as Charlemagne, who staffed his palace schools with them.

Enforced exile – However, in the later Middle Ages, Ireland tended to look inward rather than outward. It was only when English determination to impose its own norms on its Irish possessions became intolerable, that new waves of Irish began to quit their country. In 1607, although pardoned for their role in a rebellion, many of the local rulers of Ulster stole away secretly in an episode known as the Flight of the Earls (*see page 18*), thereafter living on Papal pensions in Rome. At the end of the 17C, the defeat of James II led to the emigration of many thousands of Irish Catholics, many of them military men, the Wild Geese (*see page 20*), some of whom served with distinction in the armies of continental rulers. The tide of emigration swelled during the 18C, though most of those leaving the country were not Catholics, but Ulster Scots, descendants of the Presbyterians who had received lands during the Plantation of Ulster the previous century. As well as being discriminated against in an Ireland dominated by the Anglican Ascendancy, they had also suffered a series of

Revellers at the New York St Patrick's Day parade.

bad harvests. Their destination was America, where they have had an influence out of all proportion to their numbers; over a quarter of the Presidents of the United States have had Scotch-Irish blood in their veins.

The flood-gates open – In the 19C, the rising tide of emigration became a flood. The Napoleonic wars had brought modest agricultural prosperity, but this turned to depression with the ending of the conflict in 1815. In the following decades some 20 000 people left Ireland every year, most of them Catholics from the south and west, most of them sailing to America, often via Canada. The Great Famine pushed the numbers still higher, to an annual total of up to 100 000 fleeing misery and deprivation.

The Irish in America... – It has been calculated that a total of between five and six million people quit Ireland for the United States. They were not always made to feel welcome there; a strain of aversion to Roman Catholicism persisted for many years, and in addition, the sufferings endured before and during the voyage left many immigrants in a poor state of health. But they had the advantage of speaking the language, and the Irish mark on America was profound, economically, socially, and politically; they showed themselves masters of politics at state level, often controlling cities like New York, Boston and Chicago. In 1960, city boss Richard Daly of Chicago played a key role in securing the Democratic nomination for the first President of Irish Catholic descent, JF Kennedy. Subsequent presidents have been happy to claim a similar origin (Ronald Reagan, Bill Clinton). Although completely assimilated, many Irish Americans retain a sentimental attachment to the old country, and many have supported its struggle for independence. Five million dollars were raised by De Valera in the course of a tour of the USA undertaken in 1919. And while the American government has done much to promote reconciliation between Catholic and Protestant in Northern Ireland, certain organisations based in the US have provided weaponry and generous funding for the IRA.

...in Canada and Australia... – Many Irish emigrants to North America arrived in Quebec. Many moved on to the United States, but a good number stayed on in Canada, forming an even more significant component of the nation's population than in the USA. At the time of Confederation in 1867, the Irish were the largest English-speaking group (40 %). By the end of the 20C, perhaps some 5 million Canadians could claim Irish descent. Irish emigration to Australia has yielded a similar total in that country. In the early days of the colony, about a quarter of the population was Irish, many of them transported as convicts, but including a fair number of jailers and officials as well. More Irish made their way to Australia during the gold rush of the 1850s. The "larrikin" strain in Australian life is often associated with Irishness, as is a tendency to egalitarianism or to rebellion, exemplified in the figure of bushranger and bank robber Ned Kelly. Modern Australia prides itself on what it calls its Anglo-Celtic heritage, and has produced notable figures of Irish descent such as former prime minister Paul Keating.

...and in Britain – Not surprisingly, a kind of British-Irish symbiosis existed from an early date, with Irish people coming to England for a variety of reasons. Labourers crossed the Irish Sea for seasonal work, and Irish soldiers served with distinction in the army and navy from at least the 18C. Britain's Industrial Revolution drew in manpower from an over-populated, rural Ireland. By the middle of the 19C, there were some 750 000 Irish-born people in Britain, most of them in cities like Manchester and Liverpool, Newcastle, Glasgow and Edinburgh, and of course, London. Without the labour of Irish navvies, Britain's railways could not have been built. But mutual antipathy was common; the immigrants had little wish to become assimilated, and preferred to form their own distinct communities, often centred on a Roman Catholic church. As the 21C begins, the number of British with some sort of Irish ancestry is considerable; even that seemingly most English of all prime ministers, Margaret Thatcher, is descended from an Irish washerwoman who emigrated to England from Kenmare in 1811.

In 1990, President Mary Robinson claimed, with justification, that 70 million people world-wide were at least partially of Irish descent; an extraordinary figure, especially when compared with the modest population of the island itself.

RELIGION

There has been a tendency to reduce Ireland's political problems to a straightforward question of religious differences. But the history of the island since Independence and Partition shows clearly that religion can disguise fundamental political and social problems and issues. In the Republic, around 95% of the population are Catholics, while in the North there are just over 40% Catholics to slightly fewer than 60% Protestants. The birth rate among Catholics is higher than in the Protestant community, who foresee with trepidation a situation in which they will no longer form the majority.

Yesterday's religions...

The pagan heritage

According to legend, Ireland was converted to Christianity in the 5C, at a time when this Celtic land with its many divinities was under the spiritual leadership of the druids. Although soon won over to the idea of Christianity, the Irish kept many of their rituals; pilgrimages were made to ancient sacred sites, magic springs were converted into sacred wells, festivals were held whose origins went back to long-established celebrations and wishes were made accompanied by all sorts of offerings. In addition, Irish monastic life was led according to its own rule, which was more flexible than that laid down by Rome, and was strongly influenced by Celtic laws and customs. In addition, women played a more prominent role in religious life. These distinct traditions gradually weakened, especially when the Benedictine rule was brought to Ireland by the Anglo-Normans.

An instrument of political resistance

For hundreds of years, being a Catholic was virtually synonymous with resistance to English domination, while adherence to Protestantism, certainly in its Anglican form, was a guarantee of loyalty to the Crown. From its very beginnings, the Republic sought legitimacy in close co-operation with the Catholic Church, putting it in charge of almost everything in the social sphere and in education. Despite an increasing lack of interest in the Church on the part of the young, Ireland is still a deeply Catholic country, its traditions very much alive. In the Republic, where the Protestant minority has shrunk steadily since Independence, there are no religious conflicts of any significance. The opposite is, of course, the case in the North.

...and today's

Everyday piety

The Irish landscape proclaims the importance of religion almost everywhere, with crucifixes or statues of the Virgin Mary at crossroads, on hilltops and in village squares. Statuettes of Jesus, Mary and **St Patrick** are on sale in every gift shop. Passers-by frequently make the sign of the Cross in front of a church, and there is a good turn-out for Mass even on weekdays. Mass is held up to five or six times during the day. In towns, these traditions are tending to disappear, but in the country, many houses still have their little stoup in the wall duly filled with holy water. In Catholic areas, a picture of the Pope usually occupies a prominent place. Many churches have a well-used tap supplying holy water. People taking part in popular pilgrimages like the one up **Croagh Patrick** (*see page 382*) are careful to recite the prescribed prayers along the way.

Sacred spring on tap

Religion

C Legrand / MICHELIN

Everyday piety

Even if his role has diminished, the priest remains an important figure in family life – many families number priests among their members. Nevertheless, the Irish Church has had to face up to a serious crisis in numbers, with many clergy having left the country to serve as missionaries in the Third World.

Exorcising the stains of the past

Little by little, Ireland is casting off the tutelage of the clergy, more obviously so in towns and in popular tourist areas, though in the countryside, Catholic traditions are very much alive, and priests and nuns are respected figures. But the media has fastened on to the numerous scandals in which church people have been involved and which for a long time were kept under wraps. The press and TV have reported cases of paedophilia, violence in children's homes, adulterous affairs involving bishops, and abuses of power on the part of priests and nuns in convents and boarding schools. Dragging these scandals into the bright light of public debate has shaken the nation. Some incidents have been particularly poignant, like the pathetic affair of the Magdalen Laundries in convents run by the Sisters of Charity. Unprecedented attacks have been made on the clergy on radio and TV and in the press, almost as if a whole generation was wanting to settle accounts.

Marriage and death

Religious ceremonies nevertheless remain at the heart of Irish life, especially when family events are concerned. The first important ceremony in a person's life is the **first communion**. In May, children dressed in their best clothes take the first communion in the course of group ceremonies. Like participants in a miniature wedding, they form long lines in front of the church. For little girls it is an opportunity to choose a pretty dress, perhaps a mini-skirt with plenty of lace decoration, ribbons and polyester flowers.

As far as **marriage** is concerned, only a church wedding has legal validity and it is what nearly everyone wants, even though more and more young couples are living together before walking up the aisle. A wedding is very much a family affair, with the bridal dress and veil being the object of much attention. The stag night and hen night are important institutions, though nowadays boys and girls tend to get together towards the end of the evening.

Funeral services are of even greater importance, a chance for the whole community to come together in the way it always has. In the village, notice of death and details of the service are generally posted in the pub. Local radio sometimes broadcasts a list of the recently deceased, together with times of the placing of the body in the coffin, the removal of the coffin, the funeral Mass, and the burial. With the immediate family in attendance, relatives and friends come and pay their respects and offer condolences. Usually a big crowd assembles when the body is placed in the coffin and when it is removed. The coffin is followed on foot, often with farmers in their Sunday best bringing up the rear on their tractors. There is nothing particularly mournful about the cortege – except for the immediate family – and people chat freely with no false show of sadness. At the cemetery, the coffin disappears beneath heaps of flowers and other more weatherproof offerings like wreaths made from synthetic materials, pious statuettes in giant "snowballs", poetic verses inscribed on marble. People then proceed to the family residence where a substantial buffet is likely to be waiting. Or the reception might be held in the pub, where most of the guests will end up anyway.

The Magdalen Laundries

The Church was largely responsible for a whole network of institutions designed to deal with unmarried girls who became pregnant. Such young women were rather cruelly referred to as "Magdalens", a reference to the fallen woman forgiven by Jesus. Kept away from public view in convents, they were employed on a large scale as laundresses. The children born to them were taken away for adoption or placed in orphanages. Rejected by their families, some girls spent their whole lives in these institutions, which operated well into the 1980s. The treatment of the subject in a number of TV documentaries aroused bitter controversy.

MUSIC

It is not by chance that Ireland chose the **harp** as its emblem and put it on all its coins. An integral part of popular culture, music is ever-present wherever one goes in the country. The global success of the show *Riverdance* inspired by traditional dance revealed the attachment of the Irish to this heritage as well as its universal appeal. But in spite of the popularity of traditional music among visitors to the country, Ireland is the scene of considerable musical innovation, putting it at the forefront of the international scene. The fame of rock groups like the Boomtown Rats, **U2**, the Cranberries, the Pogues and singers like **Van Morrison** is evidence of the good state of health of Irish rock music.

Pubs and music

In Ireland music is a spontaneous art form, created above all in the country's pubs. Visitors are very likely to hear a pub session of some quality, and it is quite possible to catch famous groups performing in such relatively humble surroundings.

Trad music is usually made by several musicians interpreting a particular tune or a song. Most play by ear, adding their own interpretation to the piece, which is why a tune can sound quite different from one place to another. Some groups, especially out of season or in the villages, will invite other musicians to come and join them for a tune or two. The audience often joins in singing along with the better known songs.

Trad should be distinguished from folk, the former (played by people like Planxty or De Dannan) dance-orientated, the latter influenced by ballads and by American traditions (the perfect example is Christy Moore). Different again is the *sean-nós*, a rather nasal type of song derived from English and Scottish traditions and much used in rebel ballads.

Dancing is of course accompanied by music. **Set dancing** is carried on to the sound of a **céilí** band. The steps are laid down, though not always carried out, with great precision, and involve round dances as well as couples dancing together and frequently changing partners. Set dancing is taught to children in school and is practised on a fiercely competitive basis and at frequent sessions in the villages.

Musical instruments – All kinds of instruments are used at a *fleadh*, a traditional dance meeting. Most groups have a guitar or banjo, a concertina or accordion plus a set of spoons. But the basic instruments are the fiddle, the tin whistle, and the bodhrán (a big tambourine played with a stick or with the hand). The uilleann pipes have a special place in Irish hearts, as they were used in the past to stir warriors into acts of bravery and strike fear into the enemy. Not lending itself to strong rhythms and drinking songs, the harp does not feature in this kind of music.

The strength of tradition

The wretched conditions of rural life, the pain of exile and the country's troubled political history have all contributed to the repertoire. Music, song and dance have been an important way of expressing ever-present misery. Whether poignant and nostalgic recitative or frantic jig, music reflects all moods and states of mind. The words of songs reflect the struggle against the English, sordid prison conditions, rebel exploits and the sadness of emigrants. The recent rebirth of traditional music and its appeal to an international public dates from the 1960s and 1970s with groups like the **Chieftains**, the Dubliners, the Clancy Brothers, Planxty, Bothy Band, Clannad, the Fureys, the Wolfe Tones and Christy Moore. Some of these groups like the Bothy Band have disbanded, others like Clannad have changed their style (in their case to a kind of New Age rock), but all of them have been responsible for some of the great classics of popular music.

MUSICAL INSTRUMENTS

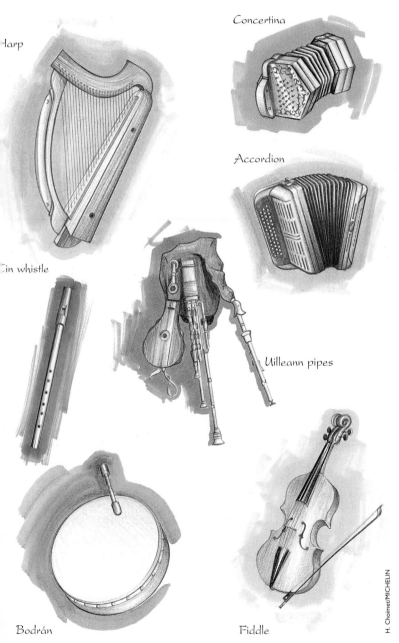

Harp

Concertina

Accordion

Tin whistle

Uilleann pipes

Bodrán

Fiddle

A galaxy of styles – Fans distinguish between several types of music. Songs for drinking to are perhaps the most compelling; sung by a group like the **Wolfe Tones** they guarantee a convivial evening. The **Fureys** excel at ballads, songs of exile and love, with a guitar and flute accompaniment. With their folk-inspired style, the **Bothy Band**, the Chieftans and **Clannad** – at their best – are not to be missed. The Dubliners and the Clancy Brothers are beginning to date now, although the former are still very popular with visitors from abroad. Representative, really authentic offerings come from **De Dannan** (their 1999 double CD is a marvel) as well as from the accordion of **Sharon Shannon**, one of the stalwarts of traditional music. **Christy Moore** sings songs with the power to move all hearts, and produces albums full of poetry and emotion in the folk tradition.

Women have come more and more to the forefront, with **Mary Black**, and more recently, heavenly-voiced **Eleanor Shanley**, **Enya** from Donegal, **Dolores Keane**, Frances Black and Loreena McKennitt well to the fore.

A fusion of styles – For several years now, a new and dynamic generation of young artists has revisited the traditional repertoire and enriched it with rhythms from elsewhere. These tasty cocktails are not much liked by purists but have their own appeal. They include the work of **Melanie O'Reilly**, whose album *House of the Dolphins* is a real treat, as well as **Kila** and her CD *Tóg É Go Bog É*, a stunning blend of African and Celtic rhythms. Taking the mixing process even further, **Afro Celt Sound System** has been a great success, particularly with younger fans. Visitors to Ireland should be on the look-out for new and less well-known groups and individuals, like the harpist **Laoise Kelly**, **Martin Hayes** or **Damp in the Attic** from Co Clare, or **Joe Bourke** from Connemara, whose superb album *Amara* employs the talents of some of the best Irish musicians to produce a wonderfully harmonious sound.

The rock and pop scene

The fantastic success of Irish rock groups like U2 or the Cranberries illustrates the vitality of Ireland's musical scene, but should not blind anyone to the incredible number of younger groups who draw their inspiration from these roots. Rock makes an excellent vehicle for articulating the dissatisfaction and rebellion which has long haunted Irish youth. Drawing on all kinds of international influences, they have composed a universal kind of music, blending folk, blues, rock and trad. The most famous group is of course U2 from Dublin. The music of the Irish but London-based **Pogues** is more based on the heritage of traditional music, like that of **Sinéad O'Connor**, the **Cranberries** and the **Corrs**. In the pubs of Dublin and Cork (a big centre for rock music nowadays) a thousand other groups thrive in the wake of big names like these. On the pop scene, the commercial success of boybands such as Boyzone and Westlife is testament to the continued exportability of Irish music.

Literature and cinema

See also page 99.

Even though English is the language of the arts in Ireland, both literature and the cinema have kept a personality which is very much their own and quite independent of British or American influences.

A love of words

Modern Ireland is proud to have been the birthplace of some of the greatest writers in the English language including no fewer than four winners of the Nobel Prize for Literature: **WB Yeats** (1923), **George Bernard Shaw** (1925), **Samuel Beckett** (1969) and **Seamus Heaney** (1995).

A land of legend

From the Celtic period onward, the inhabitants of Ireland have loved legends and epic stories. Though transmitted orally, these myths, dwelling essentially on the exploits of heroes, were finally written down and their themes taken up by modern poets, the greatest of them being WB Yeats. Initially, the epics were recounted by bards who fulfilled the role of official poets, with close connections to the chieftains of a clan. The history of the island before the coming of the Vikings is related in four great cycles. The Mythological Cycle tells of the deeds of the Tuatha Dé Danann, a race of heroic demi-gods from the era of the stone circles. Another tribe, the Fir Bolg, were the enemies of the Tuatha Dé Danann, and forced them to leave for the world beyond. In the most famous of these epics, the **Ulster Cycle**, the central hero, **Cuchulainn**, defends Ulster from its enemies, including the powerful Queen Maeve. The fantastic exploits of Cuchulainn exemplify the courage and high level of culture of the Celts. The Ossianic Cycle relates the adventures of this warrior and his comrades, their struggle in aid of the oppressed and their taste for great sporting feats (they were the inventors of Gaelic football!). The Cycle of the Kings is a mixture of heroic fiction and actual fact.

A language apart

The Irish have long been talented storytellers, poets and writers. In more recent times, a few have chosen to write in Gaelic, but most expressed themselves in English, using it in such a way as to add to the canon of work in that language in an original and inimitable way. Among the greatest of them was **Jonathan Swift** (1667-1745). Swift's world-wide fame was due to *Gulliver's Travels*, but he was also a writer of biting and effective satire such as *A Modest Proposal*, a pamphlet arguing that Ireland could be saved

James Joyce and other Dubliners

J Brun/EXPLORER

from poverty by eating children, which can be read as an attack on both English rule and Irish indolence. **Thomas Moore** (1779-1852) was fascinated by the Irish past, expressed in lyrical form in *Let Erin Remember the Days of Old*. **Oscar Wilde** (1854-1900) conquered the fin-de-siecle society of London with the wit of such plays as *The Importance of Being Earnest* and *A Perfect Husband*, but fell victim to scandal. In the hands of Irish writers, the English language often became clear, simple and vivid, familiar and sometimes insolent, often obeying the underlying structures and feeling of the Gaelic heritage. This extravagance and virtuosity contributed greatly to the reputation of Irish writing for intellectual agility. One of the great heroes of this literary revolution, **James Joyce** (1882-1941), contributed to the upheaval in the technique of writing. His subversive characters attracted the attention of the censor, with whom he remained locked in lifelong combat. Another of these writers, **John Millington Synge** (1871-1909), succeeded in expressing the torment of the Irish soul in English, while at the same time retaining grammatical forms inherited from Gaelic, notably in plays like *The Playboy of the Western World*. Among the other great talents making their contribution to the astonishing achievements of Irish literature in the 20C were **Sean O'Casey** (1880-1964), who brought working-class Dublin to vivid life, **Liam O'Flaherty** (1896-1984) and his passionate historical chronicles, the poet **Patrick Kavanagh** (1906-67), whose long poem *The Great Hunger* was a savage indictment of the deadliness of rural life, **Frank O'Connor** (1903-66) an outstanding writer of short stories shot with irony, **Flann O'Brien** (1912-66), experimental novelist and journalist, and **Brendan Behan** (1923-64), ex-Borstal boy, great drinker and exceptionally talented playwright.

Among the poets, **WB Yeats** (1865-1935) breathed new life into the Celtic imagination and its sagas. **Seamus Heaney** (1939-) testifies in his poems to his deep attachment to his roots in the landscape of Ulster.

The modern Irish theatre was founded by Yeats and his friend Lady Gregory when they established Dublin's **Abbey Theatre** in 1904. Staged here were the plays which have become the mainstays of the national repertoire, by writers such as JM Synge and Sean O'Casey. Early performances were frequently the occasion for spirited and occasionally violent polemics between writers, critics and the public. Modern Irish theatre has kept this audacious tradition alive, and there are regular productions of the work of the current generation of dramatists.

A new generation

The traditions established in the early part of the 20C have been maintained and renewed by succeeding generations. The most famous is undoubtedly **John McGahern** (1934-), whose *The Dark*, the harrowing story of a family adrift, caused a great scandal in 1965. After many a fight with the censor, the author withdrew to a kind of internal exile in Co Leitrim, where he continues to write short stories and novels in a powerful and uncompromising style. **Patrick McCabe** (1955-) writes in a dark and cynical manner which led to the short-listing of his *Butcher Boy* for the Booker Prize. The much-vaunted Booker has been won by **Roddy Doyle** (1958-) with his *Paddy Clarke Ha Ha Ha*; he also gained many plaudits for his trilogy *The Commitments*, *The Snapper*, and *The Van*, which depicts the bitter-sweet reality of suburban life and was subsequently adapted for the cinema. Women writers have come more and more to the forefront. **Edna O'Brien** (1930-), famous above all for her *Country Girls* trilogy, described the grim reality of women's lives with great wit and candour. Her example was followed by **Jennifer Johnston** (1930-) and **Julia O'Faolain** (1932-). Among the younger generation of writers, **Joseph O'Connor** (1963-), **Colm Toibín** (1955-), **Robert Macliam Wilson** (1964-) also play the game of realism with a sensibility tinged with black humour. Finally, the fame of **Frank McCourt** is unchallenged. Born in New York in 1930, he spent his childhood in Limerick, the setting for his acclaimed *Angela's Ashes (see page 322)*. Ironically most Irish writers are first published in Britain, since a form of censorship much influenced by the Church still exists.

Irish cinema

The great subject of Irish film is the country itself, its history and landscape, an inspiration for film-makers not just from Ireland but from all over the world. Many of their films have become classics of their kind.

Inspiring Ireland

The most celebrated of all films made in or about Ireland by foreign directors is probably *The Quiet Man* (1952) by the great John Ford. It tells the story of the relationship between an Irish-American returning to the old country (John Wayne) and a young Irishwoman (Maureen O'Hara). Filmed at Cong in Co Mayo, it features one of Hollywood's most stirring fight sequences. In *Man of Aran* (1934), Robert Flaherty used a sober semi-documentary style to evoke the harsh life of the Aran islanders. Set in the gorgeous scenery of the Dingle Peninsula, David Lean's *Ryan's Daughter* (1970) starred Robert Mitchum and Sarah Miles and told the story of an adulterous affair between a British officer and an Irish girl at the time of the First World War. **The Mauve Taxi** (1976), directed by the Frenchman Yves Boisset, was based on a novel by Michel Déon, a fellow-countryman resident in Ireland, and featured Charlotte Rampling and Philippe Noiret, as well as the countryside of Connemara, Cork and Kerry. In 1987, John Huston, who was of Irish descent and had spent part of his life in the west of Ireland, successfully adapted James Joyce's *Dubliners* for the screen. The Irish landscape has proved itself a splendid background for many a film ostensibly set elsewhere, including **Excalibur, The Spy Who Came In From The Cold, Barry Lyndon** and **Braveheart**. The government's financial incentives have helped promote this kind of activity, which has also contributed to a growing interest in Irish subjects and has served as a stimulant to the local film industry.

The emergence of a home-grown cinema

The government has also encouraged the making of films by Irish producers and directors. **Jim Sheridan** made a substantial contribution to the development of the Irish film with his poignant *My Left Foot* (1989). A year later came *The Field*, a sombre account of a doomed love affair, murder, and the quest for roots, set against a background of a passionate feeling for the land and filmed in the bleak landscapes of Connemara. Sheridan's more recent successes have included *In the Name of the Father* (1993) and *The Boxer* (1998).

The thriller *The Crying Game* (1992) by Neil Jordan was inspired by Frank O'Connor's short story which is one of the classics of 20C Irish literature. It depicts the confrontation between the IRA and the British army and the beginning of a friendship between two men on opposite sides of the divide. Jordan's blockbuster *Michael Collins* (1996) also dealt with the fraught Anglo-Irish relationship, tracing the role in the struggle for independence of this heroic figure, from the Easter Uprising to his assassination at the hands of his fellow-countrymen. The leading role was played with great sensitivity by Liam Neeson.

During the whole of this period, **Ken Loach** also made fine films such as *Hidden Agenda* (1990), *Land and Freedom* (1995) and *Carla's Song* (1997), though his work does not necessarily deal with Irish subjects.

The theme of Ireland's entry into the modern world has been the inspiration of several films based on novels by young writers. The best known are adaptations of works by Roddy Doyle, including *The Commitments* (1991) by the English director Alan Parker, *The Snapper* (1993) and *The Van* (1996) by Stephen Frears, which depict Dublin low life with a mixture of sensitivity and black humour. Inspired by an extremely popular novel by Maeve Binchy, *Circle of Friends* (1995) gives an insight into teenage life in the Ireland of the 1950s. More recently, *Waking Ned* (1999) pokes fun at some of the Irish stereotypes exemplified by a bunch of disreputable old rustics.

Enthusiasm for the cinema is also expressed in the blossoming of film festivals. The most important is the **Dublin Film Festival**, held annually in March. This attracts huge crowds, but the festivals held in Cork, Limerick and Galway are equally popular in their own way and are evidence of the healthy state of Irish cinema.

SPORT

Sport is a serious matter in Ireland. All the main international sports are played. Both **soccer** and **rugby** are followed passionately, and **golf** is extremely popular, with some of the world's finest courses. But perhaps most interesting of all are the country's own national sports.

Hurling

This is the most typically Gaelic of Ireland's national games, its origin lost in the mists of time. Celtic legend has many accounts of epic matches. An extremely fast sport, hurling is played by two teams each of 15 members who use the long curved stick called a hurley or *camán*, and a cork and leather ball called a *sliotar*. The pitch is 150m long and 80m wide with a goal and goalie at each end. The goal posts resemble those used in rugby. Three points are won if the ball passes beneath the bar, one if it goes above. The ball can be handled and carried for not more than four paces as long as it has been caught in the air or lifted from the ground by the hurley. A match lasts an hour, 30min for each half (35min for championship semi-finals and finals). Sometimes seeming violent and chaotic, hurling attracts passionate support in every village, especially in the south. **Camogie** (hurling for women) has the same rules apart from a few details (teams only have 12 players, the pitch is smaller, a match has two halves of 25min each, the goals have two bars and no physical contact is allowed).

Gaelic football

Gaelic football is played with a soccer-type ball by two teams of 15 players. As in hurling, a player can handle the ball and keep it for four paces but can only propel it with a punch or kick, not throw it. As the ball can be handled once it has been kicked, it is normal to see players dribbling the ball down the pitch now with their foot, now by hand. The pitch and goals are the same as for hurling. A major event in the nation's calendar, the championship final takes place every September at Dublin's Croke Park and attracts huge crowds. The traditional finalists are Cork or Kerry and Dublin.

Road bowling

This is a popular country sport, practised on rural roads. A metal ball has to be propelled down a predetermined section of road about 800m long without leaving the highway. Bends and potholes are the places where the real action takes place. Road bowling is particularly popular in the south and in Co Limerick and Co Armagh.

Horse racing

Ireland has a complex and passionate relationship with the horse. For the farmer, the horse has long been a companion and indispensable work-mate. Tinkers too have treated the horse as a comrade, taming the wildest of beasts with soft words. To appreciate this relationship, it is only necessary to visit the Ballymun area in Dublin and observe the friendly intimacy that exists between young children and their mounts. But above all, the Irish horse is the result of first-class breeding, the best in Europe, with its centre in Co Kildare *(see page 166)*. Irish horses are most prized for their performance in **hurdling** and **steeplechase**. During the season, there is one event after another, with all social classes deeply involved. The spectacle is an even more colourful one than its equivalent in Britain.

Hurling

Greyhound racing

The raising and training of greyhounds could be seen as a less costly equivalent of horse breeding, with whole families getting involved in breeding and racing one or more dogs. Racing takes places two or three nights a week. Races follow one another at regular intervals of 15min, each one only lasting a few minutes and accompanied by noisy encouragement. Betting usually only involves modest sums, meaning that the whole family can take part, including the children. The dogs frequently keep going even when the mechanical hare they have been chasing has stopped.

Greyhound racing in Cork

R. Holzbachova/P. Béner/MICHELIN

FESTIVALS AND HOLIDAYS

Most of Ireland's numerous festivals centre on music, dance and poetry. The most popular traditional festivities, like St Patrick's Day and Halloween have unfortunately become very commercialised, but are still a good excuse for a celebration, usually involving dancing and a measure of drinking.

St Patrick's Day

This is of course Ireland's national day, held every year on **17 March**. Even though Christianity had already begun to spread throughout the country by St Patrick's time, his contribution was decisive, and he is honoured with parades and celebrations of all kinds everywhere in Ireland and wherever Irish folk have settled. St Patrick's Day in Dublin easily eclipses the celebrations held elsewhere in the country. All good Catholics attend Mass, many of them wearing a **shamrock** buttonhole, a custom going back to the 16C. Commercialisation is steadily extending the scale of the event, though nowhere in Ireland does it come anywhere near the extent of New York's St Patrick's Day. The customary green leprechaun headgear also has its origin on the far side of the Atlantic.

Halloween

This is another excuse for dressing up and having fun. On the eve of **31 October**, the Day of the Dead (the Celts celebrated all their festivals on the eve of the day), children go from door to door chanting "trick or treat", the refusal of a gift of sweets being met with some form of diabolical revenge. The origin of Halloween goes back to the Celtic rituals of *samhain*, which celebrated the dead and the coming of winter, the moment when the boundary between the Here and Now and the Beyond ceased to exist, and the dead returned to haunt the living. In the old days, a candle would be placed in a window to help the deceased to find their way home, and a fire lit to warm them. This is another festival which is increasing in popularity, as in the rest of Europe. Commercialisation makes the most of it for weeks in advance, filling the shops with merchandise largely imported from the United States, but there is still plenty of spontaneity about the celebrations in a number of places, notably Derry.

Marching

Every year, on **12 July**, Ulster Protestants remember the victory of William of Orange in 1690 over Catholic James II. But the marching season begins long before, at Easter, and continues to August, with the biggest march of all, in Belfast, reserved for 12 July. Over the province as a whole there is a total of some 2 000 parades. The bowler-hatted and sash wearing marchers are accompanied by a pipe band and the enormous lambeg drums, originally brought from the Netherlands with William III's army, their noise intended to strike terror into the hearts of any enemy. With their triumphalist overtones, and sometimes bloody controversy about their routing through Catholic residential areas, the marches have been marred by their association with sectarian violence, even though the great majority of them are perfectly peaceful. As a kind of counterblast to the Orange parades, the Hibernian Order holds its own marches, its members wearing green sashes.

Music festivals

One of the outcomes of the extraordinary international success of Irish music has been an increase in the number of music festivals. The most important is the **All-Ireland Fleadh**, which functions as a kind of finale to all the local festivals and competitions. It is held every year in August in a different town in the west of the country, in an atmosphere which can only be described as... indescribable. Many of the other festivals have an excellent reputation, among them those held at Ballyshannon (Co Donegal), Miltown Malbay (Co Clare), Baltimore (West Cork), Cork (jazz), Castlebar (rock) and Galway.

February

All Ireland Dancing Championship (Ennis)
Early February. National traditional dance competition.

March

Dublin Film Festival
Ten days in early March. International films shown in a variety of venues.

St Patrick's Day
17 March. Only Dublin has a major parade, elsewhere this is primarily a religious festival.

Celtic Spring Festival
Three-week-long theatre, rock and Gaelic language festival held around St Patrick's Day, terminating with a parade. (Derry)

World Irish Dancing Championship (Dublin)
Late March. World championship of traditional Irish dance.

April

World Irish Dancing Championship (Cork)
World championship of traditional Irish dance.

Galway Poetry and Literature Festival
Public readings of poetry, debates, plays.

Panceltic Week (Tralee)
Celtic (Irish, Scottish, Welsh, Galician, Breton) music festival.

Football Cup (Dublin)
Gaelic Football All-Ireland Final.

May

Heineken Green Energy Music Festival
First weekend in May. Festival of international rock, jazz, blues and traditional music in Temple Bar.

Cuckoo Fleagh (Kinvarra)
First weekend in May. Traditional music (see page 342).

The Fiddle Fair (Baltimore, Co Cork)
Ten days in early May (see page 264).

Galway Early Music Festival
Mid-May. Three day traditional music festival.

Bantry Mussel Fair (Co Cork)
Mid-May. Traditional music and much consumption of mussels.

Fleadh Nua (Ennis, Co Clare)
Late May / early June. Traditional music and dance festival, most of which takes place in pubs and on the street.

Sligo Arts Festival
Late May / early June. Drama, poetry, music.

June

Writers Week (Listowel, Co Kerry)
Early June. Week-long festival of literature and poetry.

Bloomsday (Dublin)
16 June. Literary tour in the footsteps of James Joyce's Leopold Bloom.

Irish Derby (Kildare)
Late June. Curragh racecourse. Ireland's premier racing event.

Fleadh Amhrán agus Rince (Ballycastle, Co Antrim)
Late June. Festival of traditional song and dance.

AIB Music Festival in Great Irish Houses
Ten day festival of classical concerts in country houses.

July

Willie Clancy Summer School (Milltown Malbay, Co Clare)
First week in July. Traditional music.

Orange Marches
12 July.

South Sligo Summer School (Tubbercurry, Co Sligo)
Traditional music.

Galway Arts Festival	Late July. Lively festival with traditional music, literary events, drama, celebrations of all kinds.
Galway Races	Third or fourth week in July.
Croach Patrick Pilgrimage (Westport, Co Mayo)	Last Sunday in the month *(see page 382)*.

August

Ballyshannon Folk and Traditional Music Festival (Co Donegal)	Early August. One of the best of its kind.
Puck Fair (Killorglin)	Second week in August *(see page 291)*.
Dublin Horse Show	Second week in August. The most prestigious event of its kind.
Kilkenny Arts Festival	Mid-August. Classical and traditional music, theatre, literary events.
Rose of Tralee Festival & Tralee Races (Co Kerry)	Last weekend in August *(see page 305)*.
Connemara Pony Show (Clifden)	Important and highly picturesque horse fair, plus traditional music.
All Ireland Fleadh	A major traditional music and dance festival held each year in a different town.
Letterkenny International Folk Festival (Co Donegal)	Mid-August.

September

Lisdoonvarna Matchmaking Festival (Co Clare)	First week in September. Big get-together for lonely hearts, with music and dancing in pubs.
Sligo Literary Festival	Mid-September. Theatre, poetry, literary events.
Clifden Arts Week	Last week in September. Traditional music, readings, dance...
Westport Arts Festival	Last week in September. Readings, plays, concerts and a very picturesque horse fair.
Galway Oyster Festival	Last weekend in the month. Music and dancing in the pubs, large-scale oyster-eating.
Hurling Cup Final (Dublin)	
All-Ireland Ploughing Championship	Usually held in Co Cork. Major rural event.

October

Ballinasloe Horse Fair (Co Galway)	One of the country's main horse and cattle fairs, a lively event.
Wexford Opera Festival	Last fortnight of the month.
Cork Jazz Festival	Late October.

November

Belfast Festival	Drama, music and film in the Queen's University area.

Festivals and holidays

THE GAELIC LANGUAGE

The Gaelic language

While English is universally used in Ireland, **Gaelic** is a symbol of Irish identity and is promoted in the Republic, where all official documents must be in both languages. English is the only official language in Northern Ireland, though since the Good Friday Agreement, some concessions have been made regarding the use of Gaelic.

Deep roots

Gaelic is one of the family of **Indo-European languages** and, like Breton, Cornish, Welsh, Manx and Scots Gaelic, belongs to its Celtic branch. Of these, it is closest to Manx, now a dead language, and Scots Gaelic. The earliest known writings in a Celtic language were in Gaelic, and Gaelic illuminated manuscripts like the **Book of Kells** (*see page 112*) are a supreme achievement of the genre, not least because of the lovely alphabet used. For practical reasons of daily use and ease of reading, this alphabet was abandoned in the 1960s, and Roman letters introduced instead. Gaelic is a guttural language, with a trilled "r" and complex rules of pronunciation which are not easy for the outsider to master! Many letters are mute, while others are pronounced in various ways according to their position. For example, "bh" is often pronounced as "v" (the name Siobhàn is pronounced "Shevawn", "gh" corresponds to a lightly aspirated "h" as in Callaghan (*see Glossary, page 100.*)

Official status

Even though it is classed as having official precedence over English in the Republic, Gaelic is only spoken fluently by a small minority of the population. Between 30 000 and 40 000 people speak it as their maternal language or use it in daily life, out of a population of around 5.4 million. But since it is a compulsory subject in primary school, around a quarter to a third of the population can use it to some extent.

The Gaeltacht – Those parts of the country where Gaelic is in everyday use are called "gaeltacht". Gaelic-speaking areas are scattered all over Ireland, though the biggest concentration is in the west (Counties Cork, Kerry, Galway, Mayo and Donegal). Here, the road signs are in Gaelic, as are official communications and local radio programmes, sometimes to the confusion of monoglot English-speakers, especially when it comes to finding one's way!

From rejection to respect – The revival of Gaelic formed part of the awakening national consciousness in the 19C. Hitherto it had been thought of as an uncouth language of the peasantry, but now nationally aware intellectuals and middle-class people desired to show off their commitment to Celtic culture. Writers and dramatists considered it their duty to revive the old legends and customs, like Yeats in poetry and Synge in his plays and essays. The universities strove to stitch together the severed threads of cultural continuity by codifying the rules of the written language and giving the ancient writings the respect due to them. After independence, Gaelic became a compulsory exam subject in schools, while continuing to play virtually no part in daily life.

Gaelic today – Paradoxically, the official promotion of Gaelic has meant that it has ceased to be a dream, and for many young people it is felt as something of a burden. This has been countered by organising the teaching and learning of the language in a more relaxed way, and the summer schools run by cultural organisations in the Gaeltacht still attract lots of enthusiastic participants. In Northern Ireland by contrast, Gaelic is still thought of as the language of rebellion, and for a long time (until 1992) was not taught in schools and no road signs in Gaelic were allowed. When Sinn Féin leader Gerry Adams delivered his first speech in the new Northern Ireland Assembly, he made a point of using Gaelic.

Bilingual nameplate

CeARNÓᵹ
RUAÐRÍ MIC EASUMAIN
ROGER CASEMENT
SQUARE

THE CUISINE OF IRELAND

Irish cooking owes its reputation less to sophisticated preparation and more to the quality, abundance and freshness of its ingredients. Lamb, wild salmon, and other types of seafood are its great pride, and the wholesome food served in pubs includes stews in which the meat has been well and truly tenderised by a long period of marination. Wine is readily available, but perhaps the best accompaniment is a "glass" (of beer), or even a whiskey.

Solid nourishment
Quantity as well as quality is an indispensable part of any Irish meal, from breakfast onwards (see page 92).

The potato – Little more needs to be said about the role of the potato in Irish history (see page 21), though when supplemented by milk it supplied the poor with a highly nutritious diet. It still forms an important part of many meals, and can even be a meal in itself; Donegal's speciality, **boxty**, is a kind of pancake made from potatoes grated and boiled and sometimes stuffed. In colcannon, now served only rarely, potatoes are pureed together with cabbage, onion, milk and butter; in the past it was eaten on Fridays and days of fasting and above all at Halloween. On this occasion it included a ring, a dice and a button; the person who found the ring would be married within the year, while the button signified eternal bachelorhood and the dice a similar prospect of spinsterhood.

Seaweed – In the past, seaweed was used in coastal areas as a gelling agent. For example, the seaweed called carragheen moss replaced gelatine in desserts and gave body to stews. Sloke or sea spinach accompanied fish dishes or pork, its large flat leaves turning green when cooked. Red seaweed or dulse was used as a vegetable or dried before eating, or chewed like chewing gum, its salty taste going well with caramel.

Meat – Despite the proliferation of international restaurants and their sophisticated menus, there is still nothing to beat a good **Irish stew**, made from mutton, onions, carrots and potatoes and cooked at a low heat. Equally nourishing is **bacon and cabbage**, a country dish consisting of boiled ham served with cabbage and potatoes. Coddle is a slowly cooked mixture of potatoes, onions, ham and sausages, and another satisfying dish is beef casserole in stout, usually served with carrots, and, of course, potatoes.

Fish – Ingredients may be fresh, portions generous, but recipes are often nothing out of the ordinary. Until very recently, the range of fish and seafood was very limited, and often only served on Fridays. **Lobster**, crab claws, prawns and **oysters** are almost always ultra-fresh and best eaten with a straightforward accompaniment of garlic and herb butter. **Salmon** when smoked is the best in the world, and is also eaten as gravlax, or grilled or poached. Smoked salmon sandwiches are a real treat.

Some traditional foods – **Soda bread** is made from wholemeal flour, buttermilk and bicarbonate of soda, and goes very well with fish or **cheeses** such as Gubbeen, Cashel Blue, Cooleeney and Carrigbyrne. **Black pudding** often appears at breakfast-time. The best known is **drisheen**, a Co Cork speciality made from mutton. Pig's trotters or **crubeens** are cooked slowly in stock and much appreciated.

Desserts – Irish crumbles are good, whether made from rhubarb or apple. **Porter cake** is made from stout, dried fruit and spices, and is very filling.

Thirst-quenchers
No account of Irish gastronomy would be complete without mentioning the country's favourite beverages, from ubiquitous tea to stout and whiskey.

Beer – **Guinness** has become as much a symbol of Ireland as the tricolour or the harp. It is brewed in Dublin (see page 126), and connoisseurs reckon that it is best drunk on draught in that city or nearby, since it is supposed not to travel well. This may come as something of a surprise to Guinness enthusiasts around the world, but it is a test that every visitor should undertake and draw their own conclusions; it is certainly different from the product brewed in other countries. Guinness is not the country's only stout; its great rival, **Murphy's**, comes from Cork, and has its equally passionate adherents. Stout really is the thing to drink in Ireland, but for lovers of bitter, **Smithwick's** of Kilkenny brew a passable beverage, as do **Caffrey's** of Belfast. Like the British, the Irish have taken to lager in a big way, and one of the best-selling brands is Harp, brewed by Guinness but

Irish cuisine

Irish moonshine

Poteen is the name given to illicit spirits distilled at home or in some secret still tucked away in the countryside. The tradition goes back to the 17C, when stiff taxes were levied on – mostly imported – spirits and the Irish set about making their own, usually from potatoes. The tradition was strongest along the western coasts, from West Cork to Donegal, with stills hidden at the back of caves or in some remote bog. The latter location had the advantage that the men from the Revenue might become enmired in the course of their investigations. To some extent, poteen became a symbol of resistance to authority on the part of people who were no strangers to rebellion, nor to strong drink for that matter. The making of poteen is still illegal and still practised, the product usually guaranteeing the desired effect, though possibly at the expense of rotting the brain.

as about as different from their classic dark and heavy product as could be imagined. The microbrewery movement has taken off to some extent in Ireland, and real ale enthusiasts are likely to make interesting discoveries along the way.

Whiskey – Irish whiskey is associated with three places: Dublin **(Jameson's)**, Cork **(Midleton, Paddy's)** and **Bushmills** in Ulster. Note that "whiskey" by definition is Irish or American, whereas "whisky" without the "e" is either Scottish or Canadian. With or without an "e", the word whiskey comes from the Gaelic *uisce beatha* meaning "water of life". It seems to have met with favour among the invading Anglo-Normans, who called it *fuisce* which gradually merged into the present-day term. Elizabeth I is supposed to have had a taste for it.

The main distinction of Irish whiskey is that it is distilled three times, each distillation yielding a purer liquid than the previous one. The product is then matured in old sherry or Bourbon casks for between 3 and 15 years.

Even those who shrink at drinking whiskey neat will probably appreciate it in **Irish coffee**. This usually consists of a double measure of spirits, a good dollop of cream, plenty of brown sugar, and of course some strong coffee. It is served in a glass, with the cream remaining on the top and the liquid drunk through it. A "hot whiskey" with sugar, cloves, cinnamon and lemon makes a fine restorative after a long walk on a cold day.

Whiskey-based liqueurs include Bailey's, made from a secret recipe including cream, and Irish Mist, incorporating honey and heather.

Practical information

Outside the pub

BEFORE LEAVING

• **Local time**
Ireland is on Greenwich Mean Time (GMT) in winter and on GMT plus one hour in summer.

• **Telephoning to Ireland**
To telephone to the Republic of Ireland from the UK or elsewhere abroad, dial 00 353 followed by the area code minus its 0. To telephone to Northern Ireland from outside the UK, dial 00 44 followed by the area code minus the initial 0.

• **When to go**
The best time to visit Ireland is in **May** or **June**, when the light is at its best and the rhododendrons are in flower. Rain should be expected at any time of the year. It falls in many forms. Violent showers clear the air and bring out all the different shades of green in the landscape. "Soft" weather can last for days on end, with a round-the-clock drizzle not much thicker than a fog. Visitors should not be discouraged; every kind of weather has its own magic, and eventually it will change. The Irish reckon that the sun shines on them every day, even if it isn't for very long! **July** and **August** are the busiest months, and in parts of the south and west there can be traffic jams and finding somewhere to stay can be problematic. At these times it is a good idea to book in advance. The same applies to holiday weekends (*see pages 72-73*). Even in mid-summer, it is rarely really warm enough to lie around on the beach all day. In autumn, the landscape is at its most colourful, and **October** is the driest month of this time of the year. The rainiest time is between November and March, but winters are generally very mild. The coldest month is February, the driest April. The average temperature in Dublin varies between 2°C and 8°C in January, and between 11°C and 19°C in July. The temperature rarely falls below 0°C and only infrequently exceeds 25°C.

• **What to take**
Clothes
Even in mid-summer, some sort of wind- and waterproof jacket or anorak is vital. Rather than bring along an umbrella which may not stand up to a high wind, rely on a hood or cap. Even in July, evenings are likely to be cool, making **woollens** a necessity. The temperature varies from one B&B to another, and proper pyjamas can be a boon. Anyone who intends to go walking at all should have stout and waterproof shoes or boots. With the exception of Dublin, Ireland is still an overwhelmingly rural country, and, other than in luxury hotels, comfortable, casual clothes are all that is necessary. It is a great advantage in this damp country if they are easily washable as well! One very useful garment is the type of plastic poncho which takes up very little room, and which can keep the rain off your rucksack while walking or cycling.

Other items
Visitors from the UK to the Republic should remember that the Irish punt is by no means equivalent to the pound sterling, and that high-seeming prices may not seem so terrible after all once they have been converted. The Republic is in the euro-zone, and most prices are given in euros as well as in punts. Outside major centres it may be difficult to find a particular type of **photographic film**, particularly slide film, so it is a good idea to stock up in advance. Midges are active between June and August, especially in the evening, and a good **mosquito repellent** is invaluable. Electricity is supplied at 230 volts AC with flat 3-pin sockets like the UK model; US and other appliances are likely to require an adaptor.

• A trip for everyone
Travellers with children
The Irish are very fond of children and often over-tolerant of their behaviour. B&Bs can usually provide cots or folding beds. It should be borne in mind that small children can be particularly sensitive to midge-bites, and a mosquito net could prove useful as well as an insect repellent.

Women travellers
Ireland is not a dangerous country for women travelling on their own. The Irish tend to admire independently-minded women; this can take the form of somewhat laboured humour which is rarely really offensive. A woman on her own in a pub may well be offered a drink with no motive beyond genuine curiosity or friendliness. She should exercise her own judgement and take each case on its merits. Some caution is in order at pub closing time and in certain parts of Dublin and the larger towns.

Gay couples
Homosexual acts were only decriminalised in Ireland in 1993, and gays and lesbians still attract a degree of intolerance, especially in country areas. Openly gay couples should not be surprised if a B&B is claimed to be fully booked when it clearly isn't. **Gay Switchboard** Dublin, ☎ 01 872 10 55. **Lesbian and Gay Line**, Cork, ☎ 021 271 10 87.

Senior citizens
Older people usually meet with a special welcome and most Irish people will put themselves to a lot of trouble to help them in case of difficulty.

Disabled travellers
There is relatively little formal provision for the disabled, but plenty of goodwill. It is unusual for B&B's to have any special facilities, but this is often made up for by general helpfulness. But footpaths can be stony, access to beaches difficult, and pavements crowded. The Irish Tourist Board publishes a helpful brochure giving details of accommodation with facilities for the disabled.

Pets
There are no restrictions on bringing pets from the UK to Ireland. Check in advance whether hotels or B&Bs accept pets.

• Address Book
Tourist information
For Republic of Ireland
United Kingdom – Irish Tourist Board, 150 New Bond Street, London W1S 2AQ, ☎ 0800 039 7000, Fax 020 7493 9065; 53 Castle Street, Belfast, ☎ 01232 327 888, Fax 01232 240 201.
Australia – 5th Level, 36 Carrington Street, Sydney, NSW 2000, ☎ 02 9299 6177, Fax 02 9299 6323.
Canada – See under United States.
Ireland – Baggot Street Bridge, Dublin 2, ☎ 01850 230 330, Fax 066 979 2035 (callers within Republic of Ireland only).
United States – 345 Park Avenue, New York, NY 10154, ☎ 212 418 0800, Fax 212 379 9052.

For Northern Ireland
United Kingdom – St Anne Court, 59 North Street, Belfast BT1 1NB, ☎ 01232 231 221. 24 Haymarket, London SW1Y 4DG, ☎ 020 7766 9920, Fax 020 7766 9929.
Ireland – 16 Nassau Street, Dublin 2, ☎ 01 679 1977.
United States – 551 5th Avenue, Suite 701, New York, NY 10176, ☎ 212 922 0101, Fax 212 922 099.

Irish Embassies

United Kingdom – 17 Grosvenor Place, London SW1X 7HR, ☎ 020 7235 2171, Fax 020 7245 6961.
Australia – 20 Arkana Street, Yarraluma, Canberra, ACT 2600, ☎ 026 27 33 022, Fax 026 27 33 741.
Canada – Suite 1105, 130 Albert Street, Ottawa, Ontario, KIP SG4, ☎ 613 22 36 281, Fax 613 23 35 835.
United States – 2234 Massachusetts Avenue NW, Washington DC 20008, ☎ 202 462 3939, Fax 202 232 5993.

Web sites

Irish Tourist Board – www.ireland.travel.ie (full information on the country and how to get there).
Northern Ireland – www.gb.ni-tourism.com
www.city.net/countries/ireland (information on particular towns and regions).
www.irishtimes.com (website of the Irish daily).

• Documents required

ID, visas

All visitors (except UK subjects) entering Ireland must have a valid national **passport**. A booklet *Your Trip Abroad* gives US citizens much useful information for travelling abroad. It is obtainable from: Superintendent of Documents, PO Box 371954, Pittsburgh, PA 15250-7954, ☎ 202 512 1800.

Customs

Visitors entering Ireland from EU countries do not need to declare goods purchased in EU countries provided all taxes have been paid on them at the time of purchase. There are of course no longer any duty-free concessions between EU member countries. For people entering from non-EU countries, the duty-free allowances include: 200 cigarettes or 100 cigarillos or 50 cigars, 1 litre of spirits and 2 litres of wine, 250cc of toilet water and 50cc of perfume and other goods to the value of €180. People entering from non-EU countries may wish to register articles of value before leaving if they want to avoid the risk of having to pay duty on their return.

Vaccinations

No inoculations are necessary.

Driver's licence

EU nationals need a valid national driving licence, people from non-EU countries an **international driving licence**. The vehicle log-book and a nationality plate are also required. Insurance cover is compulsory, though a Green Card is no longer strictly necessary. Check with your insurer before leaving.

• Local currency

Cash

From 1 January 2001, the euro will be the official currency of the Republic of Ireland. The pound sterling remains the official currency of Northern Ireland. At the time of writing, GB£1 = €1.50. The euro is divided into 100 cents. There are notes denominated in 5, 10, 20, 50, 100, 200 and 500 euros and there are 8 euro coins denominated in 1 and 2 euros, 1, 2, 5, 10, 20 and 50 cents. In Northern Ireland there are notes to the value of £5, £10, £20, £50 and £100, with coins to the value of 5p, 10p, 20p, 50p, £1 and £2.

Currency exchange

There are facilities for changing money on ferries, in airports, at tourist offices and many shops and hotels. The rate of commission varies widely and should be checked before making a transaction.

Travellers' cheques

Travellers' cheques are accepted in most hotels and shops used to tourists (again, check the rate of exchange). Some form of ID is usually required. Getting travellers' cheques in euros will avoid commission charges.

Credit cards

The easiest way to obtain local currency is with a credit card or cash card at a cash machine. Since a flat fee is payable, it makes sense not to withdraw small amounts. Cash machines are common in towns, but rare in country areas, especially in the west. Visitors should ensure that they always have enough cash on them for daily purchases. Most petrol stations and many shops accept international credit cards like Visa or MasterCard. Buying a holiday with a credit card may include medical or other insurance; check at an early stage of planning a visit.

• Spending money

Any preconceptions about Ireland being a cheap place for a holiday can be forgotten. The Republic is expensive and Northern Ireland slightly more so. Costs can be kept down to about **€30 per person** a day by staying in youth hostels (€11-15 a night), lunching in a pub (€6-8), and using the hostel kitchen to prepare an evening meal (say €6-9), and travelling by bus.

The following costs are also **per person**, assuming a couple sharing a double room and cost of car hire.

By staying in basic B&Bs (€27 minimum), eating in pubs or cafes at lunchtime and ordinary restaurants in the evening (around €15), daily costs will be around **€70**. By spending about **€120** per day it is possible to stay in superior B&Bs or middling hotels, eat in restaurants at midday and in the evening, and have an occasional gourmet meal.

An additional sum should be allowed for visits to museums, country houses and the like (*see page 86*).

• Booking in advance

Bed and breakfast establishments are much in demand in summer and it is advisable to **book in advance** for June, July and August, as well as at holiday weekends. Dublin is busy all year round and reservations for accommodation should be made a good month in advance at all times. Car hire is best arranged in advance too, especially for visitors arriving by air.

• Insurance

Travel insurance is usually included in the price of a package holiday though you are not obliged to take it as part of the package and can usually buy it cheaper elsewhere. Independent travellers paying for their travel by credit card may also be provided with insurance cover. Check before booking.

GETTING THERE

There is a wide choice of alternative ways of getting to Ireland from Britain, with ferries linking different ports on both sides of the Irish Sea and numerous links by air. From Europe, the most convenient means of travel is by air, though there are direct ferries from France in summer. There are direct air services to Ireland from the United States.

• By air

Both the Republic and Northern Ireland are linked to cities in Britain by frequent scheduled flights. Fares vary considerably according to the time of year and day of the week and are subject to frequent change. Travel agents should be able to provide reliable information about the best bargains, but it is always worthwhile checking the travel supplements of major newspapers. There are direct air services to Ireland from major European cities and from the United States. Visitors from other parts of the world will probably find it most convenient to travel via London.

Scheduled flights (some only operated in summer)

Aer Lingus, ☎ 0845 9737 747, www.aerlingus.com Flights to Dublin from Birmingham, Bristol, Edinburgh, Glasgow, Leeds Bradford, London City, London Heathrow, London Gatwick, Manchester and Newcastle; to Cork from Birmingham and London Heathrow; to Shannon from London Heathrow.

Air Wales, ☎ 0870 0133 151, www.trrravel.com Flights to Cork from Cardiff.

British Airways, ☎ 0845 773 3377, www.britishairways.com Flights to Belfast International from Aberdeen, Birmingham, Cardiff, Glasgow, London Heathrow and Manchester; to Belfast City from Edinburgh, Glasgow, Liverpool, Manchester, Newcastle, Sheffield and Southampton; to Cork from Bristol, Glasgow, London Gatwick, Manchester and Plymouth; to Dublin from Cardiff, Sheffield and Southampton; to City of Derry from Glasgow and Manchester; to Dublin from London Gatwick; to Knock from Manchester; to Shannon from London Gatwick and Manchester; to Waterford from London Stansted and Manchester.

British European, ☎ 0870 5676 676, www.british-european.com Flights to Belfast City from Birmingham, Blackpool, Bristol, Exeter, Isle of Man, Leeds Bradford, London City, London Gatwick and London Stansted; to Dublin from Exeter; to Shannon from Birmingham and Glasgow; to Cork from Birmingham, Edinburgh, Exeter and Glasgow.

British Midland, ☎ 0870 6070 555, www.britishmidland.com Flights to Belfast International from East Midlands and London Heathrow; to Dublin from East Midlands and London Heathrow.

Celtic Airways, ☎ 01752 766 111. Flights to Cork from Plymouth.

Comed, ☎ 01253 402 661, www.blackpoolairport.com Flights to Belfast City and Dublin from Blackpool; to Belfast City from Isle of Man.

EasyJet, www.easyjet.com Flights to Belfast International from Liverpool and London Luton.

Gill Airways, ☎ 0191 2146 666, www.gill-airways.com Flights to Belfast City from Newcastle.

Keenair, ☎ 0151 4480 606. Flights to Cork from Liverpool.

Manx Airlines Ltd, ☎ 0845 7256 256. www.manx-airlines.com Flights to Dublin from Isle of Man.

Ryanair, ☎ 0870 1569 569, www.ryanair.com Flights to Dublin from Birmingham, Bournemouth, Bristol, Cardiff, Glasgow Prestwick, Leeds Bradford, Liverpool, London Gatwick, London Stansted, London Luton, Manchester and Teeside; to City of Derry from London Stansted; to Cork from London Stansted; to Kerry from London Stansted; to Knock from London Stansted.

Virgin Express, ☎ 020 7744 0004, www.virgin-express.com Flights to Shannon from London Gatwick.

• By ferry

Frequent drive-on / drive-off ferry services connect British ports with a number of destinations in the Republic and with Belfast and Larne in Northern Ireland. Fares vary considerably according to season, day of the week and time of day. Journey times have been considerably reduced by the introduction of catamarans and other high-speed craft. Most ports in both Britain and Ireland have a rail connection and some combined rail and ferry tickets are available: National Rail Enquiries, ☎ 0845 748 4950; Stenaline Rail / Ferry Reservations, ☎ 0870 5455 455. Coach services are operated between many British cities and destinations in Ireland: Eurolines, 52 Grosvenor Gardens, London SW1, ☎ 0870 514 3219.

F. Baume/MICHELIN

Irish Ferries, ☎ 0870 5 17 17 17, www.irishferries.ie Crossings from Holyhead to Dublin (Ferryport) by Dublin Swift (1hr49min) and by conventional ferry (3hr15min); from Pembroke to Rosslare by conventional ferry (3hr45min)

Stena Line, ☎ 0870 5 70 70 70, www.stenaline.co.uk Crossings from Fishguard to Rosslare by Lynx fastcraft (99min) and conventional ferry (3hr30min); from Holyhead to Dublin (Ferryport) by conventional ferry (3hr45min); to Dun Laoghaire (for Dublin) by fastcraft (99min); from Stranraer to Belfast by fastcraft (1hr45min) and conventional ferry (3hr15min) and to Larne by conventional ferry (2hr10min).

Norse Merchant Ferries, ☎ 0870 600 4321, www.norsemerchant.com Crossings from Liverpool to Dublin by conventional ferry (7hr30min). To Belfast (8hr30min) by conventional ferry ☎ 0151 944 1010.

P & O Irish Sea, ☎ 0870 242 4777, www.poirishsea.com Crossings from Liverpool to Dublin by conventional ferry (8hr); from Cairnryan to Larne by fastcraft (1hr) and conventional ferry 1hr45min); from Fleetwood to Larne by conventional ferry (8hr).

Sea Cat / Isle of Man Steam Packet Co Ltd, ☎ 08705 523 523, www.steampacket.com Crossings from Isle of Man to Dublin by fastcraft (2hr45min); from Liverpool to Dublin by fastcraft (3hr45min); from Heysham to Belfast by fastcraft (3hr45min); from Troon to Belfast by fastcraft (2hr30min).

Swansea Cork Ferries, ☎ 01792 456 116, www.swansea-cork.ie Crossings from Swansea to Cork (10hr).

From France, **Irish Ferries** operates a seasonal ferry service between Cherbourg or Roscoff and Rosslare (16hr-18hr) and **Brittany Ferries** links Roscoff and Cork (14hr).

THE BASICS

• **Address book**

Tourist information

Dublin – Dublin Tourist Centre, Suffolk Street, Dublin 2, ☎ 1850 230 330 (local call), ☎ 01 605 77 00 for information or ☎ 1800 668 668 to book accommodation (toll-free in Ireland). Summer: 8.30am-8pm; Sunday 10.30am-2pm; rest of year: 9am-5pm; closed Sunday, www.visit.ie/dublin
Northern Ireland Tourist Board, 16 Nassau Street, Dublin 2, ☎ 01 679 19 77. 9.15am-5.30pm weekdays, 10am-5pm Saturday.

Belfast – Northern Ireland Tourist Board, St Anne's Court, 59 North Street, ☎ 028 902 312 21. September-June: Monday 9.30am-5.15pm, Tuesday-Saturday 9am-5.15pm; July-August: 9am-7pm, Sunday 12pm-4pm. Belfast Welcome Centre, 47 Donegall Square, ☎ 028 902 466 09.

Embassies

United Kingdom – 29 Merrion Road, Dublin 4, ☎ 01 269 5211, Fax 01 205 3885.
Australia – Fitzwilton House (2nd floor), Wilton Terrace, Dublin 2.
Canada – Canada House, 65 St Stephen's Green, Dublin 2, ☎ 01 478 1988.
United States – 42 Elgin Road, Ballsbridge, Dublin 4, ☎ 01 668 8777.

• **Opening and closing times**

Banks

Banks open between 10am-4pm Monday-Friday, with slightly later closing at 5pm on Thursday. Most are closed on Saturday and Sunday. In larger towns and at airports there are usually bureaux de change open at the weekend. Banks in Ulster are generally open 9.30am-3.30pm Monday-Friday.

Post offices
Post offices open between 9am-5.30pm Monday-Friday and until 12.30pm on Saturday. In smaller places, the post office usually forms part of another shop.

Shops
Most shops open between 9am-5.30pm or 6pm Monday-Saturday, with late-night opening Thursday. Some department stores and shopping centres in larger towns open Sunday afternoon. Small general stores selling newspapers, cigarettes, sweets, telephone cards and parking discs often stay open until late in the evening.

Offices
Normally 9am-5pm Monday-Friday.

Pubs
Pubs are open 10.30am-11.30pm Monday-Saturday, 12.30pm-2pm and 4pm-11pm Sunday, with closing time 30min earlier in winter. Pub-restaurants may stay open longer and hours are extended for festivals.

In Cork, Cobh and Galway, consumption of alcohol in public places other than pubs and restaurants is prohibited.

Restaurants
Restaurants tend to close early, and it may be difficult to find somewhere to eat after 9pm except in larger towns.

• Museums, monuments and archaeological sites

Opening times
Opening times vary considerably, though as a general rule places are open 9.30am-5.30pm, sometimes later in summer. Many sites and establishments close between November-March. Official opening hours are given of places described in this guide, but they may not be strictly adhered to, especially when a site is manned by volunteers.

Admission charges
Entry fees can be quite high, but generally range between £2-£5 / €2.50-€6.30. There are reductions for students and for families. Anyone planning to visit more than a limited number of historic sites (including gardens) in the Republic should obtain the **Heritage Card** from Dúchas (Department of Arts, Heritage, Gaeltacht and the Islands) sites or national museums, price €19 for adults, €12.60 for senior citizens, €7.60 for students and €45.50 for families. The card is valid for one year and gives free admission to all Dúchas sites, identified by the name **Heritage Site**.

• Mail
Postage stamps are available from some shops as well as post offices. Irish stamps must be used in the Republic, British stamps in Northern Ireland. Post restante mail should be addressed as follows: name of recipient / Post Restante / main Post Office / town / county / Ireland.

• Telephone
The white and blue telephone boxes of **Eircom** can be found all over the Republic. Most now require phone cards, but there are still many accepting coins. Off-peak rates are charged between 6pm-8am and at weekends.

F. Baume/MICHELIN

Other telecom firms have public telephones in the larger towns but they are rare elsewhere. Phone cards are on sale at general stores. Making a call from a hotel or B&B is likely to be much more expensive than from a public telephone.

Phone cards bought in the Republic are not valid in Northern Ireland. Some public telephones in Belfast accept credit cards (Visa or MasterCard).

Mobile telephones can be used in most parts of Ireland. Check with the provider.

International calls

Codes – *To call Ireland from abroad, see page 80.*

To make an international call from the Republic or from Northern Ireland, dial 00 + country code + area code (less initial 0) + subscriber number.

The country code for Britain is 44, for Australia 61, for Canada and the United States 1. To call a Northern Ireland number from the Republic, dial 08. To call the Republic from Northern Ireland, dial 00 353.

Local calls

Codes –

Local calls are charged at the rate of €0.25 for three minutes.

Belfast 028	Galway 091	Sligo 071
Clifden 095	Kilkenny 056	Tralee 066
Cork 0214	Killarney 064	Waterford 051
Drogheda 041	Limerick 061	
Dublin 01	Londonderry / Derry 028	

Useful numbers

Directory Enquiries – In the Republic, dial 1190 for a local number, 1198 for an international number. In Northern Ireland, dial 192 for local numbers, 153 for international numbers. No charge is made for enquiries made from public telephones in Ireland.

Changes to telephone numbers

Changes to telephone numbers have been carried out recently in both the Republic and Northern Ireland. Numbers can be checked on web sites: in the Republic, www.goldenpages.ie; in the North, www.number-change.bt.com – click on "number-changer" and enter the number to be checked.

• Internet

Ireland is quite net-minded, and there are numerous cyber-cafes, even on the west coast. Many of them stay open until late in the evening and on Sunday. Charges are around €1.26 for 10min or €1.90 for 15min.

• Public Holidays

See the list of Festivals and Holidays on pages 72-73.

1 January	New Year (Republic and Northern Ireland)
17 March	St Patrick's Day (Republic; unofficial holiday, Northern Ireland)
March-April	Good Friday (Republic)
	Easter Monday (Republic and Northern Ireland)
First Monday in May	May Day
Last Monday in May	May Bank Holiday (Northern Ireland)
First Monday in June	June Bank Holiday (Republic)
12 July	Orange Day (Northern Ireland)
First Monday in August	August Bank Holiday (Republic)
Last Monday in August	August Bank Holiday (Northern Ireland)
Last Monday in October	October Bank Holiday (Republic)
25 and 26 December	Christmas Day and Boxing Day (Republic and Northern Ireland)

GETTING AROUND

• By car

Rental

Many airlines and travel agencies offer packages which include car hire. Numerous car rental firms operate in Ireland, with offices or desks in many towns and at airports. Reckon on around €228 to €305 per week, according to the season, for a category A vehicle (eg Opel Corsa or Ford Fiesta). Some companies give a discount for paying by credit card. Drivers should be **over 23 years** old and less than 70 and have had a driving licence for more than two years. A **national driving licence** is sufficient, though citizens of non-EU countries may want to obtain an international driving permit before travelling. Hiring a small car rather than a large limousine makes sense in Ireland; as well as the obvious fuel benefits, the narrow and often winding roads make high speeds impossible. Think carefully about whether all the additional insurance cover offered is really necessary, but make sure that the names of all drivers are shown on the rental agreement. Before driving from the Republic into Northern Ireland, check that this is covered by the insurance. Make sure that the hire company does not charge for fuel if the vehicle has been returned with a full tank.

Road network

Relatively few roads are really congested, and driving in Ireland can be a real pleasure for anyone not in a hurry. However, minor roads are often narrow and winding and the surface can leave a lot to be desired. This is true of some main roads as well. Local driving habits can be rather casual and erratic, and in remoter areas a lookout needs to be kept for non-motorised road users such as pushcarts, horse-drawn vehicles and cattle. There are few stretches of motorway, and main roads are usually two-lane, often with a hard shoulder which slower vehicles use when ready to be overtaken, but which can be poorly surfaced and end unpredictably. Journey times are likely to be longer than elsewhere in Western Europe, except in Northern Ireland where the road network is generally of a high standard.

Road signs

In the Republic, distances are given in miles on white signs, in kilometres on green signs, in theory at least. Away from main roads, distances given can be approximate or even contradictory, and many lanes are not signposted at all. A good **road map** or **atlas** is essential. In the Gaeltacht, signs may be in Gaelic only, and elsewhere there may be different versions of the same place name.

Highway code

As in Britain, driving is on the **left**, overtaking on the right. In the Republic, front seat belts must be worn, in Northern Ireland rear passengers too must belt up. No children under 12 years of age are allowed to travel in the front passenger seat. Speed limits in the Republic are 40kph (25mph) in built-up areas, 100kph (55mph) elsewhere. In the North there are as in the rest of the UK, 50kph (30mph) in built-up areas, 96kph (60mph) outside town and 113kph (70mph) on motorways. Traditional Irish courtesy on the roads is beginning to disappear with the growth of traffic, particularly in and around Dublin and Limerick, where jams are frequent. But using the horn is still regarded as something of an aggressive act, and road manners are generally far better than in the rest of Europe.

Fuel

All types of fuel are widely available at prices comparable to those in other European countries, though in the Republic diesel is much cheaper than in the UK.

Parking

A single yellow line along the edge of the road indicates that parking is restricted, a double line that it is forbidden at all times. Parking is regulated in a number of places by **parking discs**, obtainable from newsagents and other shops.

In emergencies

The police should be contacted in case of serious accidents, ☎ 999.

The Green Card provided by car insurers usually includes a form to complete in case of accident.

Automobile Association (AA)

Ireland – 23 Suffolk Street, Dublin 2, ☎ 01 283 3555.

UK – Fanum House, Basing View, Basingstoke, Hants, RG21 2EA, ☎ 0990 448 866 (switchboard), ☎ 0800 444 999 (joining & membership renewal).

Royal Automobile Club (RAC) –

Ireland – New Mount House, 22-24 Lower Mount Street, Dublin 2, ☎ 01 676 0113.

UK – RAC House, 1 Forest Road, Feltham, TW13 7RR, ☎ 020 8917 2500 (Head Office), ☎ 0906 834 7333 (travel information); ☎ 0990 722 722 (Customer Services).

• By taxi

Taxis only have meters in the larger towns. Elsewhere, agree on a fare beforehand, especially if travelling outside town.

• By train

The Republic has a much reduced rail network serving most of the principal towns. Speeds are slow, rarely exceeding 90kph, except in the case of the express service between Belfast and Dublin. Most lines radiate from Dublin and the only real cross-country line links Ennis and Limerick with Waterford and Rosslare Harbour. The national company is Irish Rail (Iarnród Éireann), ☎ 01 836 33 33, www.irishrail.ie The nationalised network in the North, run by NIR (Northern Ireland Railways), is even more limited. Anyone intending to travel a lot by rail in Ireland should consider purchasing an **Irish Rover** ticket, which allows unlimited journeys (in Northern Ireland as well as the Republic) for five (not necessarily consecutive) days during a 15-day period for around €100. The **Irish Explorer** ticket allows unlimited journeys by both train and bus for 8 (not necessarily consecutive) days over a period of 15 days for around €130. Full-time students are eligible to buy a **Travelsave Stamp**; used in conjuction with a student card, this gives a 50% reduction on rail fares and 15% off coach fares. It can be obtained at any USIT offices, including those in London (52 Grosvenor Gardens, London SW1W 0AG, ☎ 020 7730 7285) and Dublin (19/21 Aston Quay, O'Connell Bridge, Dublin 2, ☎ 01 602 1600), as well as at the Bus Éireann Travel Centre, Central Bus Station, Store Street, Dublin 1.

• By bus

The bus and coach network is extensive, reaching all parts of the island, and is the best way of getting around Ireland other than by car. The national companies are **Bus Éireann** in the Republic and **Ulsterbus** in the North. The Expressway Bus Timetable giving details of all long-distance services is available at bus stations and tourist offices. Frequency of services falls off sharply out of season, sometimes to as little as one bus a week. As well as the national network, there are other services run by small private companies which are often less expensive and faster, especially in the west (*details in the "Making the most of..." sections of the guide*). In Donegal, this is the only way of getting to many villages for travellers without a car. But Bus Éireann offers an interesting deal in the form of the **Irish Rambler** ticket, which gives 8 days of travel for around €87 and 15 days for around €130. The **Irish Explorer** ticket (*see above*) combining road and rail travel is also a good buy.

In general, buses are comfortable and less expensive than the train, there are stops en route, and bus stations are always close to town centres. By way of comparison, a Dublin-Cork return ticket costs around €40 by train and €21.50 by bus, a Dublin-Galway return €31.5 by train and €12.50 by bus.

• Domestic flights

There are scheduled flights linking Dublin with Cork, Shannon, Galway, Sligo, Kerry Airport (Farranfore) and Carrickfinn (Donegal) – **Aer Lingus**, ☎ 01 705 3333. A private firm flies between Galway and the Aran Islands – **Aer Arann**, ☎ 091 593 034.

• Hitch-hiking

Hitching is relatively easy in the Republic, and is widely practised by locals as well as visitors. Drivers are often happy to pick up a hitch-hiker for the sake of having some interesting conversation. The main problem, especially in remoter areas, is the lack of traffic. Hitching is probably safer than in most other countries, but there is always some element of risk. Drivers in the North may be reluctant to pick up one or more male hitch-hikers.

• Cycling

Rented bicycles may be old and in less than perfect condition, and anyone planning to cycle long distances should bring their own machine. Bear in mind the likely condition of roads, the undulating and occasionally mountainous nature of the terrain, and the constant wind which can seem to blow from all directions at once! Erratic behaviour on the part of other road users is also to be reckoned with, and cyclists need to watch out for motorists coming round corners in the middle of the road or overtaking with little room to spare. Footpaths are mostly unsuitable for cyclists because of their frequently muddy condition. Taking a bike by train or bus is not usually a problem, though a charge is normally made. Bicycles are carried free on ferries to the islands.

• Walking

Walking is becoming more and more popular in Ireland, though the long-distance footpath network is not particularly well developed *(see "Sports and pastimes" page 92)*.

• Caravanning

It is possible to hire a traditional caravan, but the reality is rather different from the picture postcard image. Because of the growth of motor traffic, horse-drawn caravans have been confined to certain routes, which are far from being the most picturesque. Fifteen kilometres a day is the maximum distance possible even without stopping very much, and looking after the horse is not a responsibility to be taken lightly. The cost will be around €750 per week (for 4 people), plus about €8 a night for parking, which is only allowed at specified points, plus compulsory insurance. Some travel agencies will arrange hire of a caravan of this kind together with the flight. The Irish Tourist Board publishes a relevant brochure.

F. Baume/MICHELIN

• Cruising

One way of exploring some of the Republic's pleasant but less spectacular scenery is by river cruiser. No special permit or licence is necessary *(see "Making the most of the Shannon Valley", page 336)*. The Tourist Board publishes a brochure setting out the various itineraries possible. A popular tour links Dublin to Limerick via the Grand Canal and the Shannon. **Shannon Erne Waterway Promotions Ltd**, Ballinamore, Co Leitrim, ☎ 078 44 855.

BED AND BOARD

• Where to stay

Most visitors to Ireland prefer to stay in bed and breakfast establishments. As well as being relatively inexpensive, it can be a good way of getting to know local people and picking up hints on what to do in the area.

Youth hostels

Youth hostels are the least expensive form of accommodation. Cleanliness and comfort vary considerably from one establishment to another. Staying in official hostels (50 in the Republic, 6 in the North) requires an **international membership card**, but many hostels ignore this or simply charge a small supplement. It is possible to join the local hostelling associations on the spot: for the Republic, **An Óige**, 61 Mountjoy Street, Dublin 7, ☎ 01 830 4555; Northern Ireland, **Hostelling International Northern Ireland**, 22 Donegall Road, Belfast BT12 5JN, ☎ 028 90 324 733. There is an increasing number of private hostels which require no membership. Many of them offer excellent accommodation and a good range of facilities: **Independent Holiday Hostels**, ☎ 01 836 4700, www.hostels-ireland.com

In towns, **Budget accommodation** is on the increase too, usually arranged in rooms with 1, 2 or 4 beds.

Camping

Because of the climate, camping in Ireland is only recommended for real enthusiasts. Away from the official campsites (www.camping-ireland.ie), farmers are usually quite happy for people to camp on their land if permission is asked.

Bed & breakfast

Bed and breakfast establishments vary considerably in comfort, location and style of establishment. With the boom in tourism, some have become more like small hotels and are perhaps rather more impersonal than they used to be. But most are the epitome of conviviality, and staying in them is to experience Ireland and the Irish at first hand. **Advance booking** is absolutely necessary in summer and at other holiday times, especially for anyone with a particular area or establishment in mind. This is particularly true for Dublin and the south and west coasts. Many establishments now have rooms with en suite facilities, though there are still plenty of – usually cheaper – standard rooms. Local tourist offices usually have lists of B&Bs and will make reservations for a small fee. Anyone planning to arrive after 6pm should make it clear at the time of booking. Turning up after 10pm is not really acceptable. Establishments approved by **Bord Fáilte** are indicated by a green shamrock symbol and arranged by category (Friendly Homes, Town & Country Homes, Irish Farmhouse Holidays). Such places normally meet certain standards of comfort, facilities and cost. Lists are available from tourist offices for between €2.50-€3.20, with illustrations in the case of Irish Farmhouses and Town & Country Homes. An independent association, **Family Homes of Ireland**, is identified by two hands holding a heart, and includes a growing number of B&Bs which are sometimes less expensive than those approved by Bord Fáilte (list available from member establishments or ☎ 091 552 000 / 552 634, www.family-home.ie). Farmhouse B&Bs are usually just that; working farms, where the décor may not be sophisticated but the welcome is likely to be a warm one. Most B&Bs are closed between October and March.

F. Baume/MICHELIN

Guesthouses and country houses

Half-way between a B&B and a hotel, these have more rooms and are more expensive than B&Bs, often justifiably so because of their charm and level of comfort and facilities. Some are historic buildings or delightful manor houses and may be as expensive as a luxury hotel. They are listed in a number of publications (Friendly Homes of Ireland, The Hidden Ireland, Ireland's Blue Book) available from Bord Fáilte.

Hotels

Hotels are fine for anyone who doesn't mind an international and impersonal atmosphere. But they are expensive and also tend to be patronised by tour groups. Their one great advantage is that they are often in a convenient town centre location and have restaurants and bars (though the latter can rarely compete with a pub for atmosphere). A number of top-class luxury hotels are in castles and great country houses.

• Costs

In the Republic of Ireland the rates charged by most bed and breakfast establishments are regulated by Bord Fáilte. Rates are calculated per person sharing a double room with breakfast included. Single travellers are usually charged a supplement of between €2.50-€6.30. Prices are slightly lower out of season in country areas. Accommodation is not cheap in Ireland, and allowance should be made for this when working out costs – it is difficult to find a double room for less than £30-£35 in the north and €46-€53 in the Republic.

The costs given in this guide are per person in the case of youth hostels and similar establishments, and for all other accommodation per person sharing a double room with breakfast included.

• Eating out

Sumptuous breakfasts mean that light lunches can be the order of the day. High tea or dinner is often served quite early, leaving the rest of the evening free.

Breakfast

The **Irish breakfast** is very much on the same lines as the traditional British breakfast, with plenty of protein in the form of bacon, egg, and sausages, plus fruit juice and cereals, and toast and marmalade, served with coffee or tea. Health awareness is growing, however, and more and more establishments are offering lighter alternatives, such as fish, or a continental breakfast.

Pub lunch

Restaurant lunches can be expensive, and at midday it makes sense to have a pub lunch. Lots of pubs offer soups, toasted sandwiches and other snacks, or a more substantial bacon and cabbage or Irish stew. The carvery lunch served in hotel bars as well as pubs can be more substantial still.

Evening meal

Restaurant prices tend to rise considerably in the evenings. One strategy is to eat early; some establishments only starting charging more after 7pm or 8pm-8.30pm in pubs. Midday and evening menus can be identical except for the price, though portions tend to be more generous at dinner time. Alcoholic drinks, particularly wines, are rather expensive in the Republic.

SPORTS AND PASTIMES

• Outdoors

Walking

Ireland abounds in superb walking country. It should be noted that many of the recommended walks are on tarmac roads and that some unsurfaced footpaths may be impassable in rainy weather. Anyone planning a walk lasting several days should make sure they have somewhere to stay at the end of each day by booking accommodation in advance. **South West Walks**, 40 Ash Street, Tralee, Co Kerry, ☎ 066 28 733, are a specialist agency running 8 to 11 day walks for groups all over Ireland, including the North.

Numerous guides with full descriptions of walks can be found in bookshops, though the maps in them are usually inadequate. They need to be supplemented by the excellent 1:50 000 scale **Discovery Series** of maps published by the Ordnance Survey of Ireland. The western parts of the Republic have the best walks, including the Beara Way, the Kerry Way and Burren Way. The publication **Walking Ireland, the Waymarked Walks**, lists waymarked footpaths with details of distances, access and accommodation and gives map references.

The Ulster Way, at 930km long, is one of Europe's finest long-distance footpaths. Extremely well-signposted and maintained, it runs right around Northern Ireland. The most comprehensive introduction and handbook to it is **The Ulster Way, a Guide to the Route and its Facilities** by Paddy Dillon. Another useful publication is **The Ulster Way, Accommodation for Walkers**, published by the Northern Ireland Tourist Board, which gives detailed information about where to stay en route.

Mountain biking

Mountain bike tours are organised by a number of travel operators. Bord Fáilte publish a useful booklet called **Cycling in Ireland**. The mountain bikes offered for hire are often in a pitiable condition and unlikely to be suitable for a lengthy or demanding trip. Enthusiasts are advised to bring their own machines.

Riding

There are plenty of riding centres in both the north and the Republic hiring mounts by the half day from around £50 / €75, or trips of several days for around £350 / €530 per week. A number of travel operators offer riding holidays, while **Horse Riding Ireland** has four centres distributed around the country (details from the National Tourist Office – *see "Before leaving" page 80*).

Golf

There are golf courses all over Ireland, some in superb settings. Golfers need to kit themselves out for wind and rain. Clubhouses are usually unpretentious and convivial. The brochure **Golfing in Ireland** published by Bord Fáilte gives comprehensive details of all clubs.

Angling

Fishing for salmon and trout in **rivers** and **lakes** is strictly controlled and can only be done with a permit (around €35 valid for a season). Permits are available from the various Fisheries Boards, angling equipment shops, and from some hotels in popular fishing spots. The brochure *Game Angling* published by Bord Fáilte gives useful information. Sea angling can be shore-based, offshore, or deep-sea. Full details are given in the brochure *Sea Angling* published by Bord Fáilte (*see also the "Making the most of..." sections in the guide*).

Hunting

The season lasts from September to the end of January, with some variations according to species (rabbit and wood pigeon can be shot all year). Most hunting is purely recreational and is subject to strict regulation. Anyone wanting to bring sporting guns with them to Ireland should apply two months before travelling. Details from Bord Fáilte and the **National Parks and Wildlife Service**, 7 Ely Place, Dublin 2, ☎ 01 661 31 11.

• The sea

Scuba-diving and **sailing** are both practised in Ireland (*see the "Making the most of..." sections in the guide*), but on the whole the Irish prefer land-based pursuits. It needs to be borne in mind that the sea is frequently rough and cold and the weather unpredictable.

• Spectator sports

See page 68.

Gaelic football and hurling

There are Gaelic football and hurling teams in every school and town. Regional and national championship matches are usually sold out well in advance; this is particularly true of the finals held in Dublin, when tickets and accommodation both need booking weeks if not months beforehand.

Greyhound racing

This is another extremely popular national sport, with racing carried on several nights a week in many places *(see the "Making the most of..." sections in the guide)*.

Horse racing

Racing is in every Irish person's blood, and there are racecourses all over the island. The most popular events include the Irish Grand National at Fairyhouse, Co Meath on Easter Monday and the 3-day meeting at Punchestown, Co Kildare in the last week in April. Others are held in Killarney in May, at the Curragh in June, Killarney again in July, Tramore and Tralee in August, Galway and Listowel in September, and Leopardstown and Limerick in December.

• Night life

Theatre

There is theatre of a high standard in several places. Modern and classic plays are performed at the famous **Abbey Theatre** in Dublin (Abbey Street, ☎ 01 878 7222), and at the **Gate Theatre** (Parnell Square East, ☎ 01 874 4045, while the **Olympia Theatre** (72 Dame Street, ☎ 01 677 7744) stages more popular performances such as musicals. Tralee has the **National Folk Theatre of Ireland** (☎ 066 23055) which evokes the traditional way of life in music, song, dance and mime, while Galway has the **Irish Theatre** (☎ 091 562 024). The **Belltable Arts Theatre** in Limerick (☎ 061 319 866) hosts a variety of theatre productions. In the North, the **Arts Theatre** in Belfast (☎ 028 9023 9450) puts on mostly mainstream productions.

Pubs

A visitor to Ireland would need real determination to avoid the convivial Irish pub, the centre of much social life, and one of the best places to meet local people and listen to good music *(see page 62)*.

Discotheques

In the larger towns, discos and clubs take up where the pubs leave off, around midnight.

SHOPPING

• Things to buy

Clothes

Woollens – Famous Irish sweaters are on sale everywhere. Prices and quality should always be checked carefully. Remember that *hand loomed* is still machine-made and not the same as *hand knitted*, and check the material used; the big Aran sweaters are normally made from pure Irish wool. Garments also come in cotton, linen, and silk. For a sweater to age well, the stitch needs to be close, and the garment to fit well; it will stretch in use. Loose and floppy stitching is not a good sign; it usually means that big needles have been used in order to economise on wool, and the sweater is likely to lose its shape quickly. Reckon on between €122 and €152 for a hand-knitted sweater, between €30 and €76 for a machine-made item.

Cloth – Irish tweeds are a popular buy with visitors from abroad. The most famous are from Donegal, made on hand-operated looms. A good quality tweed has a dry and rather rough feel and loses creases instantly. It costs between €21 and €30 per metre, slightly less by the yard, which is still used in smaller shops. The weavers' studios all over the country offer hand-made cloth, often in very original designs.

F. Baume/MICHELIN

Tailored clothes – Tweed and tartan form the basis for most tailoring. The cut of suits and the material used is classic and hard-wearing and unlikely ever to go out of fashion. Men's suits cost from €136 upwards, women's rather more. The best-known tailors are Magee of Donegal and Avoca Handweavers in Co Wicklow. Both also have a good range of stylish tartan skirts, as well as waxed jackets and coats. Younger designers spurn traditional materials like wool and linen in favour of very international clothes.

Headgear – Irish tweed caps are available in a wonderful variety of colours and cloths (from around €17), as are hats, scarves and shawls (from around €12).

Jewellery

Largely inspired by Celtic art, **silver jewellery** is inexpensive and often beautifully designed. There are classic Claddagh rings (*see page 362*) as well as pendants and brooches. A growing number of craftspeople are making elegant **gold jewellery** on the same lines and at a reasonable price. There is a wealth of **costume jewellery**, some of it inspired by classic Celtic pieces like the Tara brooch: reckon on between €7 and €15. Finally, green **Connemara marble** set in silver is used in many different kinds of jewellery in classic shapes and styles.

Crafts

Rugs – Tweed and mohair rugs are available in various sizes and in a limited range of patterns in natural or bright colours. At between €45-€152 they are good value.

Lace and linen – **Ulster linen** is famous for its fine quality. It is used for bed and table linen and for tea towels and handkerchiefs. **Irish lace** is another tradition that is very much alive. Place-mats, cushion-covers and all sorts of other little items make good and inexpensive presents from €3 upwards.

Pottery – The number of craft potteries is steadily growing all across the country. They turn out simply made everyday items in restrained colours. Some designers produce whole collections which are on sale in superior souvenir shops.

Porcelain – Ireland's most famous porcelain is Belleek in the North (*see page 443*), characterised by basketwork, flowers and interlacing. Other less prestigious porcelain comes from Ballyshannon in Donegal.

Crystal – Waterford glass is of course world-famous, but there are other types of Irish crystal too. There are glassworks at Galway, Kilkenny, Tipperary and in Tyrone. Souvenir shops usually have a selection.

Celtic crafts – The Celtic heritage has been the inspiration for a whole range of crafts, some of dubious quality. Fine work can be seen on sale next to merchandise of a decidedly inferior standard. Some things made out of rushes like traditional good-luck charms can be rather appealing. A number of younger designers make stone objects which draw freely on the great motifs of traditional iconography. Finally, a growing band of painters and graphic artists are producing fine prints, the very best of which capture the mystic essence of the Irish landscape.

Shopping

Music

Recordings – Recordings of famous groups are no cheaper in the Republic than in the UK, but it can be fun tracking down the work of less well-known musicians which may not be available elsewhere. Record shops invariably have recordings made by local performers, and assistants are usually more than happy to advise *(see page 62)*.

Musical instruments – Tin whistles are sold everywhere, as are factory-made *bodhráns*. The best places to find hand-made instruments are in Dublin, Roundstone in Connemara, and Galway.

Food

Spirits – Spirits are generally expensive. There may be bargains aboard the ferry and at the airport.

Smoked salmon – Smoked salmon can be dispatched abroad. Reckon on €15 per kg upwards.

Farmhouse cheese – Individual farmhouse cheeses are acquiring a good reputation. They can be bought from the producer or in good delicatessens.

Where to shop

Traditional crafts, souvenirs and gifts are probably best bought in souvenir shops. But be ready to compare prices and do not hesitate to mention it if the same article is on sale elsewhere at a lower price – a reduction may be made. Department stores in towns have a range of traditional items, possibly at higher prices than in souvenir shops. Food and drink purchases are best made in supermarkets or delicatessens. Smoked salmon can be bought directly from the producer *(see the "Making the most of..." sections in the guide)* or at good fishmongers.

HEALTH AND SAFETY

• Precautions

No special precautions are necessary before visiting Ireland. No inoculations are required and no special hazards need to be taken into account. The high level of precipitation and frequent windy conditions mean that it may often feel colder than indicated by the actual temperature, so a sweater or similar warm garment is necessary in all seasons, as is good rainwear. In summer, the menace of midges can be combatted by use of an insect repellent.

• Health

EU nationals visiting either part of Ireland are entitled to free medical treatment under reciprocal arrangements. They should obtain **Form E111** before departure, complete it, and present it when requiring any form of treatment. In principle this applies in the Republic to UK nationals as well, but in practice it is not usually necessary. Nationals of non-EU countries should ensure that they have comprehensive medical insurance.

• Chemists and pharmacies

Non-prescription medicines are freely available in supermarkets. Minor medical problems can often be solved by a pharmacist, who can advise whether or not a doctor should be consulted.

• Emergencies

In both the Republic and Northern Ireland, dial 999 for any emergency service, stating whether it is police, fire brigade or ambulance that is required.

• Border controls
The border between the Republic and Northern Ireland is not always clearly identified and may not be visible at all. There are occasional checks on vehicles and passengers, though far fewer than before the Good Friday Agreement.

• Electricity
Current is at 220 volts. Plugs are normally 3 pin in the UK, and an adaptor will be necessary to run electrical appliances from European countries and elsewhere.

• Laundry
There are laundrettes in all towns in Ireland, some offering a full service, including ironing. Many hostels have a laundrette or at least a washing machine. A few B&Bs will also wash clothes for a charge.

• Newspapers
The Republic has several national daily papers, including the famous *Irish Times* and the *Irish Independent*. The national tabloid is the *Star*. Many people read a town or regional daily, full of interesting snippets about the locality and what's on. British papers are available on the same day in many places, other international papers only in the larger towns if at all. British papers are available at most places in Northern Ireland, while the province's most widely read paper is the *Belfast Telegraph*, which comes out in the afternoon.

• Public toilets
Usually free in the Republic, where facilities for men and women may be identified in Gaelic (*Mná* = women, *Fir* = men), with mostly pay-toilets in the North. Most petrol stations have toilets for the use of customers, though the key may have to be asked for.

• Radio and television
In the Republic, national television and radio is provided by RTE (*Radio Telefís Éireann*), with three TV channels, including a channel broadcasting in Gaelic, and three radio stations, again including one for Gaelic-speakers. These are supplemented by an array of local radio stations. British terrestial TV channels can usually be picked up, as they can in the North, where Ulster TV is the local independent station.

• Thefts
Petty crime is on the increase in Dublin and some other large towns, but no more than the normal precautions are necessary. Care should be taken when parking a vehicle, and no items should be left visible in the car, even in a supervised car park. Expensive cameras should not be flaunted in certain parts of Dublin in the evening. Cash is best carried in an inside pocket, and not all in one place. People staying in hostels should secure their backpacks and keep valuables with them.

• Tipping / gratuities
Tipping is not widespread in Ireland, and in hotels any service charge is included in the bill. If service is not included in a restaurant bill, the normal amount to leave is around 10%.

• Units of measurement
Both Imperial and metric measurements are used in the Republic and in Northern Ireland; fuel for example is dispensed in litres, but beer in pints.

Distances in this guide are given in kilometres. As a rule of thumb, one kilometre is five-eighths of a mile: 5 miles is therefore about 8 kilometres, 10 miles is about 16 kilometres and 20 miles is about 32 kilometres.

Consult the table below for other useful metric equivalents:

Degrees Celsius	35°	30°	25°	20°	15°	10°	5°	0°	-5°	-10°
Degrees Fahrenheit	95°	86°	77°	68°	59°	50°	41°	32°	23°	15°

1 centimetre (cm) = 0.4 inch
1 metre (m) = 3.3 feet
1 metre (m) = 1.09 yards
1 litre = 1.06 quart
1 litre = 0.22 gallon
1 kilogram (kg) = 2.2 pounds

• **Weather forecasts**
Comprehensive weather forecasts appear in the press, and on radio and TV.

LOOK AND LEARN

• **General**
ARDAGH John, *Ireland and the Irish: Portrait of a Changing Society*, Penguin 1995. Comprehensive survey of Ireland in transition.
FLETCHER Martin, *Silver Linings*, Nicholson 2000. Times reporter's unsentimental look at the people and landscape of Northern Ireland.
WATERS John, *An Intelligent Person's Guide to Modern Ireland*, Duckworth 1997.

• **History**
ADAMSON Ian, *The Identity of Ulster*, Pretani Press 1982.
BECKET JC, *The Making of Modern Ireland 1603-1923*, Faber & Faber 1966. Excellent, compact introduction to the history of Ireland over the last few centuries.
CAHILL Thomas, *How the Irish Saved Civilisation*, Doubleday 1997.
CONNOLLY SJ (Ed), *The Oxford Companion to Irish History*, OUP 1998. Comprehensive reference work.
COOGAN Tim Pat, *The Troubles, Ireland's Ordeal 1969-1995*, Hutchinson. Popular account of recent events as they affected both North and South by former Irish Press editor.
COOGAN Tim Pat, *Wherever Green is Worn: The Story of the Irish Diaspora*, Hutchinson 2000. Celebration of the Irish world-wide.
De PAOR Liam, *The Peoples of Ireland*, Hutchinson 1986. Social, cultural and political life from prehistory to recent times.
ELLIOTT Marianne, *The Catholics of Ulster*, Penguin 2000. Authoritative and absorbing account of the often harsh history of Northern Ireland's Catholic community.
FOSTER Roy, *The Oxford Illustrated History of Ireland*, OUP 1998. Beautiful pictures from a wide variety of sources and authoritative text.
KEE Robert, *Ireland, A History*, Abacus 1995. Well-illustrated account, brief on early history, fascinating and much fuller on recent events.
McCONVILLE Michael, *From Ascendancy to Oblivion, the Story of the Anglo-Irish*, Quartet Books 1986. The entertainingly-told story of the rise and fall of the Anglo-Irish ascendancy.
NEVILLE Peter, *A Traveller's History of Ireland*, Windrush 1992. First-rate, concise paperback, one of an established series.
RAFFERTY Joseph (Ed), *The Celts*, Mercier Press, Dublin 1988.

SIMMS George Otto, **Brendan the Navigator**, O'Brien Press 1990. Mysteries and marvels encountered by the saintly sailor in the course of his epic voyage.

STEWART ATQ, **The Narrow Ground, Aspects of Ulster 1609-1969**, Faber & Faber 1977. Unionist view of Ulster history.

WOODHAM-SMITH Cecil, **The Great Hunger**, Penguin 1988. Classic history of the Famine.

• Landscape and building

AALEN FHA, WHELAN K and STOUT M (Eds), **Atlas of the Irish Rural Landscape**, Cork University Press. Lavish and sumptuously illustrated description of the Irish landscape heritage.

KIELY B, **The Aerofilms Book of Ireland from the Air**, Weidenfeld and Nicolson 1985. Bird's-eye view of Ireland.

MITCHELL Frank, **The Irish Landscape**, Collins 1976.

MITCHELL Frank (Ed), **The Book of the Irish Countryside**, Blackstaff 1987.

ORME AR, **The World's Landscapes: Ireland**, Longman 1970.

ROTHERY Sean, **A Field Guide to the Buildings of Ireland**, Lilliput 1997. Well-illustrated description of the country's minor buildings.

TREVOR W, **A Writer's Ireland: Landscape in Literature**, Thames and Hudson 1984. Irish novelist's lovingly observed literary tour.

WHITTOW JB, **Geology and Scenery in Ireland**, Penguin 1975. The country's skeleton laid bare.

• Mythology

DANAHER Kevin, **Folk Tales of the Irish Countryside**, Mercier 1988.

SMYTH Daragh, **A Guide to Irish Mythology**, Irish Academic Press 1988.

YEATS WB (Ed), **Fairy and Folk Tales of Ireland**, Colin Smythe 1973.

• Literature

See page 65.

DOYLE Roddy, **Paddy Clarke Ha Ha Ha**, Vintage 1994. Dublin life as seen by a 10-year old. Booker Prize winner 1993.

HEANEY Seamus, **Opened Ground: Poems 1966-1996**, Faber and Faber 1998. Selection of poems by the winner of the 1996 Nobel Prize for Literature.

JOYCE James, **Dubliners**, Penguin 1999; **Portrait of the Artist as a Young Man**, Penguin 1999; **Ulysses**, Penguin 2000; **Finnegan's Wake**, Faber and Faber 1975.

McCABE Patrick, **The Butcher Boy**, Picador 1993. The realities of country life uncovered as a young man descends into madness.

McCOURT Frank, **Angela's Ashes**, 1997. Forlorn Limerick childhood recalled.

McGAHERN John, **The Dark**, Faber and Faber 2000; **Amongst Women**, Faber and Faber 1991; **The Barracks**, Faber and Faber 2000; **Collected Stories**, Faber and Faber 1992.

MADDERN Deirdre, **The Birds of the Innocent Wood**, Faber and Faber 1989.

O'BRIEN Edna, **The Country Girls Trilogy**, Penguin 1988. Rollicking misadventures of escaped convent girls.

O'CROHAN Tomás, **The Islandman**, OUP 1978. English translation of Gaelic account of traditional life.

SAYERS Peig, **Peig**, Edco. Essential for an understanding of rural life in the Gaeltacht that was.

SYNGE JM, **The Aran Islands**, Penguin 1992. The classic account of traditional island life.

WELCH Robert (Ed), **The Oxford Companion to Irish Literature**, OUP 1996.

WILSON Robert McLiam Wilson, **Ripley Bogle**, Minerva 1997; **Eureka Street**, Vintage 1999. Funny, no-holds-barred accounts of Belfast life.

• Music

See page 62.
A very basic introduction to traditional music would include:
Clannad, *The Collection* or *Clannad in Concert*.
De Dannan, *How the West was Won*.
The Bothy Band, *Old Hag You Have Killed Me*.
Altan, *Another Sky*.
Christy Moore, *Collection Part 2*.
Plus albums by the Wolfe Tones, The Chieftans and The Fureys.

• Films

See page 67.
Films worth seeing (or seeing again): *Man of Aran* (1934), *The Quiet Man* (1952), *Ryan's Daughter* (1970), *Dubliners* (1987), *The Crying Game* (1992), *Michael Collins* (1996), and the adaptation of Roddy Doyle's trilogy, *The Commitments*, *The Van* and *The Snapper*.

GLOSSARY

There is no such thing as a monoglot Gaelic speaker, but some signposts are in Gaelic, some Gaelic terms have entered the English language. And local people usually appreciate some attempt to address them in their own language, however rudimentary.

Everyday expresssions

Dia duit	Good morning	Sláinte	Cheers
Fáilte	Welcome	Craic	Good conversation in convivial setting

Signs and notices

An lár	Town centre	Garda / Gardaí	Police
Banc	Bank	Leithreas	Toilets
Bealach amach	Exit	Mná	Women
Bealach isteach	Entrance	Fir	Men
Dúnta	Closed	Oifig an Phoist	Post office
Oscailte	Open		

Institutions

Bord Fáilte	National Tourist Board	Iarnród Éireann	Irish Railways
Bus Éireann	National bus company	Sinn Féin	Political party ("ourselves alone")
Dáil	Parliament		
Éire	Ireland	Taoiseach	Prime Minister
Fianna Fáil	Political party	TD	
Fine Gael	Political party	(Teachta Dála)	Member of Parliament
Gaeltacht	Irish-speaking district		
Garda / Gardaí (plural)	Police		

Place names and landscape features

Baile (Bally)	Town	Doire (Derry)	Oak grove
Bán (Bawn)	Castle enclosure	Innis	Island
Beann (Ben)	Peak	Cill / Kil / Kill	Early church or chapel, monastic site
Caiseal (Cashel)	Castle, fortified enclosure	Cnoc (Knock)	Hill
Crannóg	Artificial island	Loch / Lough	Lake or loch
Curach (Curragh)	Small fishing boat made of hide stretched over wooden frame	Rath	Ringfort
		Sliabh (Slieve)	Mountain
		Tholsel	Town Hall or market house

REPUBLIC OF IRELAND

Official name: Republic of Ireland
Area: 70 282sqkm
Population: around 3 700 000
Capital: Dublin
Currency: euro (€)

Exploring the Republic of Ireland

Passage East

The Japanese Garden, Powerscourt

D Faure/DIAF

DUBLIN
AND AROUND

Divided by the Liffey, Co Dublin is home to almost a third of the country's population even though it is Ireland's smallest county. Colonised in turn by Vikings and Normans, this ancient Celtic homeland prospered in the 18C, when Dublin became the second city of the British Isles. But the subsequent problems associated with the long march to independence meant that for many years it was unable to progress at the same pace as other European capitals.

Today's Dublin has certainly joined the modern world; a showcase for an Ireland newly prosperous, but which has kept its multi-faceted and complex soul. While some parts of town move to the rhythm of fashionable pubs known for their music as much as for their beer, this is still Europe's only capital city where a horse market is held at the foot of an ultra-modern hotel. And beyond the busy streets of the city centre and its elegant Georgian quarters there are miles and miles of red-brick housing of the utmost banality. Further out still, however, the picture changes completely. Here is a region of great charm, deeply provincial. To the north of Dublin Bay, nestling at the foot of a hill, is the little harbour town of Howth, seemingly impervious to the siren song of modernity. To the south, the coast from Dun Laoghaire to Bray is lined with sandy beaches bordered by a sea which, given a splash of sunlight, turns turquoise and takes on a look of the Riviera, an impression in no way hindered by the profusion of yuccas and other exotic plants growing in the luxuriant gardens of exquisite Victorian villas.

DUBLIN★★★
(BAILE ÁTHA CLIATH)
Capital of the Republic of Ireland – Pop 953 000
County town of Co Dublin
See plan I (built-up area) page 128 and plan II (centre) page 110

Not to be missed
A tour of the Temple Bar pubs.
The Book of Kells in Trinity College.
Celtic treasures in the National Museum.
Smithfield horse market.

And remember...
Dublin is best explored on foot;
allow a minimum of at least two days to get to know the essentials.
Book accommodation several weeks in advance whatever the season.
Avoid the Christmas / New Year period, when most hotels,
restaurants and museums are closed.

Haughty and proletarian, Catholic and Anglican, Celtic behind a Classical façade, Dublin rejoices in the paradoxes of its complex identity. Cutting the city in two, the Liffey accentuates the differences between the densely populated north and the refined south, its former Britishness far from forgotten. In becoming, rather belatedly, the capital of the Republic of Ireland in 1949, Dublin may have affirmed its Celtic identity without however completely effacing the influence of the Crown. The city's heart beats to the tune of *Molly Malone*. As heady as the foam atop a properly drawn pint of Guinness, Dublin life cocks a snook at the grey skies of everyday and gets its own back on the miseries and injustices of the past. The city is a place which deserves to be explored, not just visited. It's worth remembering that one of Joyce's heroes bore the name of Daedalus, creator of a labyrinth. Good humour will help the Dublin explorer find their way around this labyrinthine and mischievous city, its features always twisted in a grin, its eye ever ready with a wink.

The aristocratic Custom House peers at its proud reflection in the sombre waters of the Liffey, while the austere façade of Trinity College contrasts with the extraordinary opulence of its illuminated manuscripts. Not far away, the fabulous Neolithic treasures of the National Museum could almost make one forget the terrible sufferings of the past. That painful past does indeed seem far away in the noisy watering-holes of Temple Bar, where a young generation can be found joyously celebrating their country's new-found prosperity.

A tumultuous thousand years

From Dyfflin to Dublin – The foundation of Dublin goes back to the year of grace 988. At that time, the little harbour settlement already established by the Vikings some way upstream from the mouth of the Liffey was called Dyfflin, from the Celtic *Dubh Linn*, a reference to the black pool on the site of the present castle. But, like most things in Irish history, it was not quite as straightforward as that; the place had another Celtic name, *Baile Átha Cliath*, the "settlement by the hurdle ford". The two centuries of Viking domination were marked by constant conflict between Nordic pagans and native Celts who had converted to Christianity 500 years previously. This period was brought to an end in 1014 by the victory of the Celtic king, **Brian Ború**, at the Battle of Clontarf to the northwest of Dublin. Less than two hundred years later, the Normans arrived and began fortifying the town and building a castle.

Dublin and around

English domination – During the reign of Henry II, Dublin gradually took on the character of an English city. Its inhabitants rarely ventured beyond its walls for fear of being massacred by the natives, who had retreated into the **Wicklow Mountains**. From here, for more than 400 years, they launched repeated, but unsuccessful attempts to reconquer the city.

In the 17C, Cromwell took possession of Dublin, now an important trading centre. The city flourished even more in the following century, leaving a heritage of fine public buildings like the Custom House and the Four Courts, as well as the sumptuous residences erected by a prosperous middle class during the reigns of George II and George III.

Decline and renaissance – At the end of the 18C, the largely autonomous Irish Parliament had its seat in Dublin, by now Great Britain's second largest city. But in 1800, the **Act of Union** creating the United Kingdom ushered in a period of decline. Peasants fleeing miserable conditions in the countryside flooded into the city and were herded into slums. The very worst times came between 1847-1852, when the **Famine** brought about massive emigration to America, British relief measures proved woefully inadequate, and Dublin seemed the capital of a nation almost on the point of disappearance. Misery was intensified for many by the conditions brought about by the Industrial Revolution. Travellers' tales from the end of the 19C describe Dublin's proletariat as one of the wretchedest in Europe, ravaged by crime, prostitution and alcoholism. Not surprising, then, that Irish nationalism took on something of the character of a moral crusade.

Pride recovered – In the early years of the 20C, Dublin intellectuals set out to restore dignity to their fellow countrymen. The renaissance of the Gaelic language and the creation of the **Abbey Theatre** by William Butler Yeats and Lady Gregory were as much about national pride as about cultural progress. The long general strike of 1913, then the 1916 Uprising made Dublin the capital of resistance and of Irish nationalism. Independence in 1922 was followed by civil war, leaving the city much diminished. British rule was over, but in its place came that particularly stifling Roman Catholic conservatism which caused intellectuals like Joyce and Beckett to flee the country. It was only in 1973, with the entry of Ireland into the **European Community**, that Dublin at last began to open up to the outside world. Nowadays, with half its population aged under 30, and thanks to bold economic measures, this dynamic capital city has become a financial centre of great importance as well as one of Europe's favourite tourist destinations.

Dublin districts

Spread out around its bay, Dublin concentrates its main places of interest to visitors in a relatively restricted area on the south bank of the Liffey. Here are Trinity College, the trendy **Temple Bar** area (Plan II D3), the National Museum and National Gallery, all within a few minutes walk of one another. In the same part of the city is the pedestrian precinct of **Grafton Street** (Plan II D3-D4) with its numerous shops, as well as parks like **St Stephen's Green** (Plan II D4-F4) and **Merrion Square** (Plan II F4), offering a green refuge in the very heart of the city. To the south, foreign embassies have installed themselves in the fine Georgian residences of the smart **Ballsbridge** area (Plan II F4). Then a few kilometres from the city centre towards the southern end of Dublin Bay is the harbour of **Dún Laoghaire** (see plan page 132) where the ferries from England dock. The **north bank** developed later than the south and is less extensive. This is working-class Dublin, though here too is **O'Connell Street** (Plan II D1-D2), the focal point of several shopping streets. Relief from the bustle of the city centre can be found in **Phoenix Park** (Plan I A2-B2), the city's largest open space, located on the northwestern outskirts, or in the residential area of **Clontarf** (Plan I F1) facing the sea and the bird sanctuary of **North Bull Island** (from Plan I F1).

Dublin

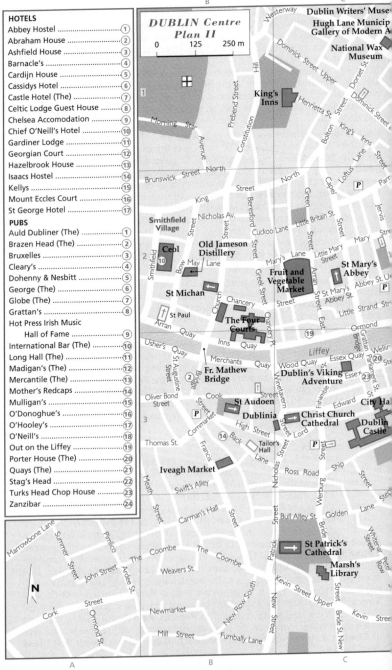

HOTELS

PUBS

DUBLIN Centre Plan II

0   125   250 m

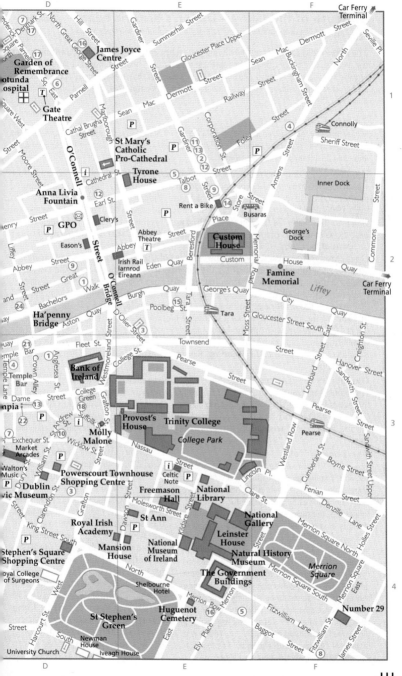

South of the Liffey – Dublin's historic heart** (Plan II)
Allow a day and a half on foot including museum visits

The core of old Dublin had hardly altered in appearance since Georgian times, until the return of prosperity in the early 1990s which brought about major changes. Nowadays the area around Trinity College buzzes with activity, as shoppers, students and tourists all go about their business. At night, Temple Bar in particular is as busy as in the daytime.

Trinity College** (E3)

Main entrance on College Green. October-May: 9.30am-5pm; Sunday 12.30pm-4.30pm; June-September: 9.30am-4.30pm. Admission charge – combined ticket for the Book of Kells and the Old Library. Allow 1hr30min).

Founded in 1592 in the reign of Elizabeth I, this stronghold of Anglo-Saxon culture was one of the great symbols of English dominance in Ireland. Admission was limited to Protestants up until 1873, and no woman could study here whatever her faith until 1903. For its part, the Catholic church forbade the faithful to register here until well into the 1960s. Of the roughly 8 000 students enrolled today, some may perhaps become as famous as predecessors like **Jonathan Swift**, **Oscar Wilde**, **Bram Stoker** or **Samuel Beckett**.

Once through the austere façade, the hubbub of the street is soon forgotten in this series of quiet quadrangles lined for the most part with buildings from the 18C date, most of the original structures having disappeared. Beyond Front Square is **Parliament Square** with its little **chapel** *(on the left)*, open to all faiths since 1972. Over the lawns of **Library Square** rises the **Campanile**, 30m high and completed in 1852 on the presumed site of a medieval monastery. At the end of the courtyard, the red-brick **Rubrics** (from the Latin *rubrica* = red ochre) are the University's oldest remaining buildings, dating from the end of the 17C. Signs pointing to the *Book of Kells* lead visitors round the **Reading Room**, a small neo-Classical structure like a Greek temple.

Old Library★★ – This imposing 65m-long building dating from the first half of the 18C houses one of the three most important libraries in the British Isles. Ever since the Act of Union of 1800 it has received a copy of everything published in the British Commonwealth, and now has some three million volumes on its shelves. On the ground floor, the **Turning Darkness into Light**★★ exhibition is devoted to the origins of manuscripts and the art of illumination in Ireland *(see page 29)*, using explanatory panels and large-scale enlargements of illuminated pages. Then comes the **Treasury**, where, protected from the light, are the original copies of the **Book of Dimma**★★, the **Book of Armagh**★★, the **Book of Durrow**★, and above all, the **Book of Kells**★★★, famous for the end-paper of the Gospel of St Matthew with its fantastic overall patterning of symbolic interlaced animals. On the Library's upper floor is the **Long Room**★★, a majestically proportioned vaulted gallery 65m long, with **shelves**★ holding some 200 000 venerable volumes. To

The Book of Kells

The most famous of the four manuscripts on show at Trinity has an astonishing history. This copy of the four Gospels is supposed to have been the work of St Columcille (St Columba), founder of the monastery on Iona. After a particularly savage Viking raid, the monks fled to Kells in Co Meath to the northwest of Dublin. In 1007, the book disappeared in the course of another raid, but miraculously reappeared three months later. In 1016, Kells was burnt down, but the manuscript was saved once more. Similar adventures occurred on a further dozen occasions. In 1653 the book was sent to Dublin for safe keeping during Cromwell's campaigns. Finally, in 1661, the Bishop of Meath presented it to Trinity College, together with the Book of Durrow.

Dublin and around

The Long Room at Trinity College

either side of the Long Room's central space are 18C marble busts of the great philosophers and writers. On the right-hand side is an **Irish harp**, which, so the story has it, once belonged to Brian Ború, victor over the Danes at the Battle of Clontarf in 1014. The harp has featured prominently on coins and banknotes, but alas for authenticity, it dates from the 15C and so cannot have been the property of the great Celtic warrior.

Facing the Library, in the Arts and Social Science Building, is the **Dublin Experience** (*20 May-29 September: hourly between 10am-5pm. Admission charge*), a multi-media show devoted to the history of the city.

At the southeast corner of Fellows' Square is the garden surrounding **Provost's House** (*not open to the public, but can be seen from Grafton Street*), one of the finest Georgian residences in Dublin.

From Trinity College to Merrion Square (D3)

The Classical edifice facing Trinity College was built at the beginning of the 18C to house the Irish Parliament, then later altered by **James Gandon**, the architect of the Four Courts and the Custom House. On 2 August 1800, a day of ill omen for the future of the country, Parliament put an end to its sovereignty by passing the Act of Union making Ireland an integral part of the United Kingdom. A year later, the building was sold and became the **Bank of Ireland**∗(*Admission to the former House of Lords during banking hours, or guided tour Tuesday at 10.30am, 11.30am and 1.45pm*), a role it still fulfils. The former House of Commons is now the banking hall, with a magnificent **ceiling** with lion-head ornamentation. The old House of Lords is preserved more or less in its original state, and features a superb coffered ceiling and fine 17C **tapestries**.

Go south down Grafton Street.

At the corner of Suffolk Street stands the statue of Molly Malone, the Dublin beauty who wheeled her wheelbarrow down streets broad and narrow, selling her Cockles and mussels *Alive, alive, oh!*

Go along Nassau Street with its shops and, on the left, the railings of College Park, and continue as far as Merrion Square.

F. Baume/MICHELIN

Around Merrion Square★ (F1)

Dublin's most elegant square is lined with fine **Georgian houses** from the end of the 18C. Of equal height and harmonious proportions, they have particularly fine doorways, with copper canopies and lovely semi-circular fanlights.

In summer, the **gardens** in the square are a carefully tended jungle of luxuriant vegetation with many exotics. **Sculptures** are placed along the pathways, one of them representing **Oscar Wilde** *(in the northwest corner)*; it is made from 40 different kinds of stone from different parts of the world.

Anyone wanting to get an idea of what went on behind the elegant Georgian façades should visit **No 291 Fitzwilliam Street** *(10am-5pm; Sunday 2pm-5pm; closed Monday. Admission charge)*. The fully-furnished interior gives a very complete idea of the lifestyle of an upper middle-class family at the beginning of the 19C, and an audio-visual show tells the story of the house and the surrounding district.

A good address

Merrion Square is associated with many a famous name. Oscar Wilde lived at No 1, Daniel O'Connell at No 58, WB Yeats at No 82 and the writer of sensational novels Sheridan Le Fanu at No 70. The British Embassy occupied No 29 until it was burnt down by an angry mob in 1972 following the events of Bloody Sunday in Londonderry.

To the southwest of Merrion Square, the **Government Buildings** *(guided tour in groups of limited size, Saturday 10.30am-3.30pm. Tickets from the National Gallery)* are easily identified because of their police guard. Begun in 1904 to house the Royal College of Science, the neo-Classical buildings were completed in 1922 and are now used as committee and conference rooms for the Government and as offices for the *Taoiseach.*

Museum district★ (E3-E4)

While in the Merrion Square area, visitors should at the very least take a quick look at the remarkable collection of stuffed animals in the **Natural History Museum**★ *(10am-5pm; Sunday 2pm-5pm; closed Monday. Free admission)*. The entrance to this beautiful museum, whose collections must rival those of Noah's Ark, is guarded by the huge skeletons of a giant **moose** and a giant **deer**. These creatures lived some 10 000 years ago; their remains were found in bogs, hence their blackened colour and their exceptional state of preservation.

The **National Gallery**★★ *(10am-5.30pm; Thursday 10am-8.30pm; Sunday 2pm-5pm. Free admission)* has one of the finest painting collections in Europe. A controversial new block housing information services and visitor facilities is currently being added to the gallery, and opening times and visiting conditions may change on its completion.

To the left of the entrance is the **Shaw Room**, dedicated to George Bernard Shaw, born in Dublin in 1856, beyond it the **Yeats Museum**, opened in 1999 to honour Jack B Yeats (1871-1957) the artist brother of WB Yeats. His **Liffey Swim**★ is one of his best-known pictures in the gallery, painted in 1923 and depicting this once extremely popular race which is still held every year in the first or second week of September.

Rooms I to VI are devoted to Irish painting of the 18C and 19C, which was subject to the same influences as British art of the period, being affected in particular by the **Symbolism** which was very much in vogue towards the end of the 19C *(the best examples are hung in Room V)*. The north wing has works by British landscape painters and portraitists like **Gainsborough**, **Hogarth** and **Reynolds**, as well as more recent canvases like the best known portrait of **James Joyce**, painted by Jacques Blanche in the 1930s.

The gallery also has a representative collection of European art, exhibited on the upper floor. There are works by Uccello, Mantegna and Caravaggio, Rembrandt, Vermeer and Franz Hals, El Greco, Velasquez, Goya, Claude, Chardin and Géricault, and there are a number of fine works by the Impressionists.

Turn right out of the National Gallery into Upper West Merrion Street, then left again into Clare Street and continue as far as Kildare Street.

Once a rendezvous for the Anglo-Irish gentry, the **Kildare Street Club** is famous for its sumptuous interior décor. Outside, sculptures at the foot of the columns depict monkeys playing billiards and a bear practising the violin. The building is now the home of the Alliance Française.

Also in Kildare Street is the Royal College of Medicine and the **National Library*** *(Monday-Wednesday 10am-9pm; Thursday-Friday 10am-5pm; Saturday 10am-1pm; closed Sunday. Admission charge. Heritage Site)*. The Library's rotunda echoes that of the National Museum. It is worthwhile climbing the monumental staircase of Connemara marble in order to look into the **Reading Room**, where researchers and students can be seen at work beneath the magnificent **semicircular ceiling*** in various shades of green, divided up by stucco pilasters.

Set back from the National Gallery and the National Museum is the Classical outline of **Leinster House**. Built in the first half of the 18C as the residence of the Duke of Leinster, the building now serves as the seat of Ireland's **Parliament** (Oirechtas), consisting of the **Dáil**, the lower house, with 160 elected members, the Teachtaí Dála or TDs, and the **Seanad**, with 60 members *(advance booking necessary to watch debates, ☎ 01 678 9911)*.

The **National Museum of Ireland**** *(10am-5pm; Sunday 2pm-5pm. Free admission)* has fascinating collections devoted to Neolithic and Celtic civilisation, and its Treasury has an array of all kinds of artefacts giving a comprehensive overview of early Irish art and culture.

The ground floor has exhibits illustrating the beginnings of human settlement in Ireland. There are brooches, buckles and pendants and many other **precious objects***** in gold, recovered from tombs and other hiding places, a truly sumptuous collection dating from between around 2000 BC and 700 BC. A number of items owe their excellent state of preservation having lain in bogs, and together give an idea of the way of life of the country's inhabitants around 2 000 to 3 000 years ago; they include a 20m long **dugout*** from Galway. An array of **weaponry*** of Bronze and Iron Age date shows that the first Irish people attached great importance to decoration. They also practised human sacrifice; the **mummified body*** of a man found in a bog at Gallagh reveals that he died by strangulation, a frequent practice in the whole of northern Europe.

The collections in the **Treasury**** demonstrate the evolution of Irish secular and religious art. The first Celts arrived in Ireland around 650 BC, but it is only about 300 years later that the first interlaced motifs appear which are so characteristic of Celtic art. They are related to the La Tène culture of Central Europe, where such motifs first appeared. The superb **Tara brooch**** is a fine late example, and many

Dublin

Celtic gold

Apart from its religious significance for them, gold no doubt served the Celts as a currency and means of exchange. In order to recover the precious metal which can be found in most Irish rivers, they used techniques identical to those in the rest of Europe. Sheepskins were soaked in the stream in order to catch tiny particles of gold; the skins were dried, then burnt, the gold being left among the cinders. The most important discoveries of hoards of gold were at Tara (see page 156) and at Mooghaun near Ennis. Here, navvies working on a new railway line discovered a fabulous treasure, which they hastened to melt down. Those Mooghaun items now in the National Museum were saved thanks to the intervention of a knowledgeable local.

National Museum of Ireland, Dublin

The Tara Broach

religious artefacts exhibit the same kind of ornamentation. A high point of achievement in the art of the goldsmith can be seen in the 12C **Shrine of St Patrick's Bell**. The first floor is mostly devoted to the Viking period, showing them to have been more interested in the art of warfare than in any arts or crafts. Their reputation for cruelty seems well earned when borne witness to by the **slave's collar** displayed in the same showcase as a **skull** with traces of several vicious blows. However, the Viking occupation did not completely suppress the expression of Christian belief. The **Cross of Cong★** dating from the 12C and enclosing a fragment of the True Cross is evidence of the richness of medieval Celtic art. One room has a collection of Egyptian antiquities, among them some lovely portraits.

Back down on the ground floor (*by the cafeteria*), the history of modern Ireland is dealt with by an exhibition entitled **The Road to Independence**, with weapons from the 1916 Uprising, IRA uniforms, and the first typewriter with Gaelic lettering.

From Kildare Street, go back up elegant Molesworth Street and stop at **Freemason's Hall** (*10am-5pm. Closed weekends. Free admission*), seat of the Grand Lodge of Ireland. This astonishing building combines most of the styles familiar to Victorian architects and for good measure adds some Masonic symbolism. By the time it was built, in 1869, Irish Freemasonry had become an almost exclusively Protestant affair, regularly denounced from Catholic pulpits, though in its early days it attracted adherents from all denominations.

Leave Molesworth Street by turning left into Dawson Street towards St Stephen's Green.

On the left rises the neo-Romanesque façade of **St Ann's Church**. In the 18C, well-off members of the congregation would leave loaves of bread for the poor around the altar, and the custom has persisted, albeit in symbolic form. The church frequently hosts excellent lunchtime concerts.

Further on is the **Royal Irish Academy**, a Georgian building housing an important library. The elegant **Mansion House** from the beginning of the 18C is the official residence of the Lord Mayor of the city. It was here, in 1919, that the first modern Irish parliament proclaimed the country's independence.

On Merrion Row, just beyond the **Shelbourne Hotel**, one of Dublin's most prestigious establishments, railings protect the **Huguenot Cemetery**, the resting-place of the descendants of Protestants who fled France to escape religious persecution in the late-17C, and who contributed much to the country's economic development.

Around St Stephen's Green★ (D4-E4)

This 10-hectare open space is very popular with office workers who eat their picnic lunches here on fine days, but it is also an asset to the city as a whole. Its present appearance dates from the late-19C, when the brewery magnate **Arthur Guinness** obtained permission to convert what had been common land into a public park. Among the amenities are **fountains**, an artificial lake, **statues** of James Joyce, Jack B Yeats and other celebrities, as well as a **blind garden**, with the names of plants spelt out in Braille.

Facing the northwestern corner of the Green is **St Stephen's Green Shopping Centre** with an extraordinary façade with wrought iron decoration. Beyond is pedestrianised **Grafton Street**★, one of the city's busiest shopping streets. A good place to halt awhile is **Bewley's Oriental Café** with its delightful Art Nouveau décor (*see "Making the most of Dublin"*). Other purchases can be made close by, in the **Powerscourt Townhouse Shopping Centre**, an elegant shopping gallery inserted into the inner courtyard of an 18C residence (*reached through Johnson Court, a passageway halfway between St Stephen's Green and Trinity College*).

No 58 South William Street (*to the rear of Powerscourt Townhouse Shopping Centre*) is the home of the **Dublin Civic Museum** (D3) (*10am-6pm; Sunday 11am-2pm; closed Monday. Free admission*). The museum has an extraordinary array of bric-a-brac and other objects, all in some way related to the history of the city and its celebrities. As well as a collection of shop signs, there is the famous **Head of Nelson** (*see panel page 123*).

Go back up South William Street, then along Trinity Street towards the Liffey.

Temple Bar★ (D3)

To the west of Trinity College, between the Liffey and Dame Street, this lively part of town got its name from Sir William Temple, the university Provost, who owned land hereabouts in the late-17C including a riverside walk called The Bar. At one time it seemed that this run-down area of small shops and warehouses was going to be wiped off the map to make way for a huge new bus station. But in the early 1990s it was saved by a radical change in public opinion, not least because of the involvement of the rock group U2. The city council put its weight behind rehabilitation of the area, and nowadays it stands out as a model of urban regeneration, with cultural centres, discotheques, pubs, fashionable places to eat, all attracting an enthusiastic clientele, especially at weekends, when the level of noise and crowding reaches its peak. In the daytime, however, it's a great place for a relaxing and fascinating stroll. Narrow streets lead down to the quayside and the **Ha'penny Bridge** (D2), a charming pedestrian bridge built in 1816 which has become one of the symbols of the city. It is also known as the Liffey Bridge. The Ha'penny refers to the toll levied whenever someone crossed the bridge, a practice which continued right up to the early 20C.

Return to **Dame Street** (D3), one of the city's main thoroughfares, lined with Victorian buildings. On the corner of Sycamore Street stands the **Olympia Theatre**, Dublin's oldest (1879) remaining theatre, many of its contemporary rivals having fallen victim to fire.

On the far side of the street, next to a splendid example of a Victorian Baroque bank, is the main entrance to Dublin Castle.

From the Castle to St Patrick's Cathedral

Dublin Castle★★ (C3) – *Guided tour of the State Apartments and the Powder Tower undercroft: 10am-7pm; weekends and public holidays 2pm-5pm. Times subject to alteration at short notice due to official events. Admission charge. Heritage Site.*

Little remains of the Norman stronghold built on the site of a Viking encampment by King John in 1204, the present buildings dating mostly from the 18C and 19C. The residence of the representatives of the British Crown from the Middle Ages until 1922, the building is now used for official ceremonies.

Beyond the porch *(on the right-hand side of the courtyard used for parking)* are the **State Apartments★★**. Opulent French furnishings and monumental chandeliers of Irish crystal set the tone of these grandiose interiors charged with history. One room served as a prison for the Socialist leader James Connolly, wounded in the course of the Easter Rising in 1916. In 1998 the Northern Ireland peace accords were signed in the **State Drawing Room**. In the adjacent room stands a superb octagonal marquetry **table★**, the creation of which occupied a prisoner for seven years. Presidential investitures take place in **St Patrick's Hall**, a former ballroom hung with the 22 banners of the ancient Order of the Knights of St Patrick.

The **Powder Tower★** rises above the remains of the Norman castle which were excavated during the 1980s. The excavations can be studied from a stairway; one feature which becomes evident is a portion of the castle moat, 12m deep and 20m across. Analysis of the materials used in the construction of the Viking walls revealed that their mortar was made from horsehair, egg-white and bull's blood.

Outside the Castle, it is worth glancing into the interior of **City Hall** (C3). Built between 1769 and 1779, it is a harmonious Classical structure with a cupola, and originally served as the Royal Exchange.

Before visiting Christ Church Cathedral, go along into Parliament Street towards the Liffey and turn left into Essex Street.

Halfway between a guided history tour and Disneyworld, **Dublin's Viking Adventure** (C3) *(Tuesday-Saturday 10am-4.30pm. Admission charge)* takes visitors on a trip aboard a Viking longship back to the time when these northern warriors descended on Dublin's predecessor Dyfflin. Actors play the role of people from the past, and a Viking village produces authentically ancient-smelling odours.

Return to Lord Edward Street (the continuation of Dame Street).

Christ Church Cathedral★★ (C3) *(10am-5pm. Admission charge)*, the Anglican cathedral of the Diocese of Dublin, was for many years the place of worship of the Anglo-Irish Establishment. A stone church was built here in 1172 on the orders of the Norman Richard de Clare, Earl of Pembroke, nicknamed "Strongbow", on the site of a wooden church of 1038. Additions and alterations were made in medieval times and later, and in the 18C and early 19C shops and taverns occupied the ancient cloisters. The present cathedral, a mixture of Romanesque and Early English styles, dates mostly from 1871-78, though the north wall of the nave has survived from the original building.

The south transept contains the remarkable tiered **tomb of the Earl of Kildare★**, who died in 1734. His effigy is extraordinarily realistic, and the sorrow obviously felt by his mourning widow in no way detracts from her charms. The **Strongbow monument** *(in the south aisle)* served for centuries as a meeting place for signing contracts of all kinds, and the wear and tear on the Earl's effigy can be explained by the vigour of past financial negotiations. The 12C **crypt** houses a small museum, with odds and ends including not just old stones but also a pillory and the mummified remains of a cat and a rat which were discovered in a pipe of the grand organ.

A covered passageway linking the Cathedral to Synod Hall leads across Winetavern Street.

A rainy day on Grafton Street

Once the central meeting-place of Ireland's Anglican clergy, **Synod Hall** now houses **Dublinia** (C3) *(April-September: 10am-5pm; October-March: 11am-4pm; Sunday 10am-4.30pm. Admission charge)*. An audio-guide helps visitors find their way around the Dublin of the Middle Ages, illustrated by life-like tableaux. Somewhat less hi-tech but a vital source of information for archaeologists are the deposits accumulated on the banks of the Liffey which, when interpreted, reveal much about the daily life of Vikings and Normans. From Synod Hall visitors can climb to the top of **St Michael's Tower**, but the view from behind the rather grubby windows is hardly worth the effort.

In a garden laid out on the site of the old town walls on the High Street stands **St Audeon's Church** (B3) *(weekends only: 2.30pm-5pm)*. This is Dublin's oldest parish church, founded by the Normans in 1190. It is Protestant, but next to it is a Catholic church dedicated to the same saint, a 7C bishop of Rouen.

Go along Cornmarket, a bustling street with pavements more or less taken over by florists and greengrocers. Then turn left into **Francis Street** (B3-B4), a long street given over almost completely to **antique shops**, which despite their deliberate air of neglect nevertheless charge exorbitant prices. But anyone interested in antiques will still find it worthwhile to have at least a look at the variety of merchandise on offer. By Dean Swift Square is **Iveagh Market**, a red-brick covered market unfortunately no longer in use. The splendid oriental heads on the keystones of the arcades are particularly striking.

At the end of Francis Street turn left into Dean Street, then left again into Patrick Street.

St Patrick's Cathedral⋆⋆ (C4) – *May-October: 9am-6pm; Saturday 9am-5pm; Sunday 10am-11am / 12.45pm-3pm; November-April: 9am-6pm; Saturday 9am-4pm; Sunday 10.30am-11am / 12.45pm-3pm. Admission charge. Buses nos 50, 50A, 54, 54A, 56A from the city centre.*

A little way south of the centre, Dublin's second Anglican cathedral once stood among a slum district, which was demolished at the beginning of the 20C. Here too, the Guinness family had a hand in things, helping to finance the fine red-brick buildings to the north of **St Patrick's Park**. At the far end of this open space is the **writers' wall** honouring the country's great literary figures.

The Cathedral was built on the site of the spring where Ireland's patron saint is supposed to have baptised some of his first converts, an event recalled by a **plaque** *(to the left of the park entrance)*. Like Christ Church Cathedral, St Patrick's was begun in the 12C, but nothing remains of the original building, rebuilt several times over in the course of the centuries – the present structure dates essentially from the 1860s. To the right, behind a column near the southwest entrance, a copper plaque marks the modest **tomb of Jonathan Swift**, Dean here between 1713 and 1743, laid to rest together with his companion Stella. His **death-mask**, along with his **moveable pulpit** and various personal effects are on display in the north transept. Beyond the baptistery stands the imposing **Boyle Monument**, consisting of a group of 16 polychrome statues representing members of the family of the great Earl of Cork, erected by him in 1632 in memory of Lady Katherine, his second wife. Opposite the entrance, on the other side of the nave, is the **door** from the old chapter house with its legendary hole. The story goes that the feuding Earls of Kildare and Ormonde pursued their quarrel into the Cathedral; Ormonde barricaded himself in the chapter house, whereupon Kildare cut a hole in the door, and put his arm through, inviting Ormonde to shake hands in a gesture of reconciliation. This gave the English language the phrase "chancing one's arm".

The Cathedral has numerous **commemorative monuments** recalling the centuries-long service of Irishmen in the British army. In the choir, where Handel's *Messiah* was first performed, hang the **banners** of the Knights of the Order of St Patrick, an order founded by George III to honour the Anglo-Irish nobility.

From the Cathedral, a narrow road on the left leads to **Marsh's Library★** (C4) *(Monday, Wednesday, Thursday and Friday 10am-12.45pm / 2pm-5pm; Saturday 10.30am-12pm; closed Tuesday and Sunday. Admission charge)*. Founded in 1701 by Archbishop **Narcissus Marsh**, this is the country's oldest public library, with 25 000 precious volumes, its mission was to bring culture to the people of Ireland, at least to those who could read. To protect the books, readers were shut into alcoves and the books themselves were attached by chains to the wall to further discourage theft.

City centre north★ (Plan II)
Allow a day

On conquering Dublin in 1170 the Normans forced the Vikings across the Liffey to the north, where they established the settlement of Oxmanstown. While the south bank of the river underwent a continuous process of urban development, the north was only urbanised in the 18C, when the city's most famous neo-Classical public edifices – Four Courts, Custom House and King's Inns – were built here. But it is well worthwhile straying from the classic tourist trail around the north of the city centre to explore its busy pedestrianised streets, its shopping centres and its traditional Moore Street market. Also not to be missed is Smithfield Village, a new development laid out on the site of the old Jameson Distillery and the venue for the horse market held on the first Sunday of the month.

Around the Custom House
There is a fine view from the south bank of the Liffey of the dome and colonnaded façade of the **Custom House★★** (E2). Completed in 1791 by James Gandon after a construction period lasting 12 years, Dublin's most remarkable neo-Classical building almost disappeared from the scene after catching fire during the Civil War in May 1921. More recently, an ambitious restoration programme has returned it to its former glory. The building now houses the administrative offices of the **High Court**. The **Custom House Visitor Centre** *(Mid-March-November: 10am-5pm; weekends 2pm-5pm; November-mid-March: same hours but closed Monday, Tuesday and Sunday. Admission charge)* beneath the dome describes Gandon's life and work as well as the events of 1921.

On the riverbank, close to the docks, are the six bronze figures of the **Famine Memorial** (F2). Placed here in 1997, this moving monument pays tribute to the memory of the many who perished in the Great Famine.

To the west of the Custom House, on the corner of Abbey Street Lower and Marlborough Street, the modern building of the **Abbey Theatre** (E2) is not much to look at. Founded in 1904, the theatre played an important part in the revival of Irish culture. Associated with it were such writers as **WB Yeats**, **Sean O'Casey**, **Lady Augusta Gregory** and **JM Synge**. Some of the plays first performed here received a hostile reception, like Synge's *Playboy of the Western World*.

In Marlborough Street, **St Mary's Pro-Cathedral** (D1) is the central Roman Catholic place of worship in a city dominated by not one, but two Protestant cathedrals, Christ Church and St Patrick's. The term "Pro", an abbreviation for "provisional", reflects the possibly unfounded hope that Christ Church may one day become a Catholic establishment. Just opposite the Pro-Cathedral is **Tyrone House** (E2), built in 1742 and now the home of the Ministry of Education.

Around O'Connell Street (D1-D2)
Known then as Gardener's Mall, O'Connell Street was the focal point of fashionable Dublin in the 18C, with a central promenade featuring fine trees and an array of statuary. Nowadays Georgian elegance has mostly been replaced by fast food outlets and

neon lighting, but the generous dimensions of the street remain intact. At the end of the 19C the street was renamed in honour of **Daniel O'Connell**, the lawyer and politician largely responsible for the passing of the Catholic Emancipation Act in 1829. He is honoured here with an allegorical monument by the bridge over the Liffey which also bears his name, and which has the additional distinction of almost being broader than it is long.

Built between 1815-18 in neo-Classical style with a monumental portico, the **General Post Office** occupies a whole block at the junction of O'Connell Street with Henry Street. For Dubliners, their post office is more important as a symbol than as a public building. At the time of the Easter Uprising, the "Provisional Government of the Irish Republic" made the GPO's **main hall** its headquarters, and it was from here that the trade union leader **James Connolly** and the nationalist **Patrick Pearse** proclaimed the Republic and the country's independence. The building caught fire during the fighting of 1916 and was only reopened to the public in 1929. Inside, a series of pictures recalls these historic events, and there is also a sculpture in bronze of the death of **Cuchulainn**, the mythical Celtic hero who was a symbol of Irish popular resistance.

At right angles to O'Connell Street by the Post Office is **Henry Street**, traffic-free and lined with shops, many of which remain open on Sunday. Take the second turning on the right into **Moore Street**, one of the city's most popular thoroughfares, with a daily **market** with stalls selling vegetables, fish and clothing. The continuation of Moore Street on the far side of O'Connell Street is **Earl Street**, with its statue of **James Joyce** appearing to emerge from **Madigan's** (*see "Making the most of Dublin"*). Beneath the wide-brimmed hat, Joyce's features seem even more enigmatic than ever.

Back in O'Connell Street, in the central reservation by the junction with Cathedral Street, is a more modern piece of public sculpture in the shape of the **Anna Livia Fountain**, whose figure of a young woman in the water has been unkindly nick-

O'Connell Bridge

G Biudzin/MICHELIN

named "the floozie in the jacuzzi". The sculpture was installed here at the time of Dublin's millennium celebrations in 1988, and represents the allegorical figure invented by Joyce to symbolise the Liffey.

Further along O'Connell Street at the junction with Parnell Street is the memorial to **Charles Stewart Parnell**, the man of destiny as glorious as he was controversial *(see page 179).*

(see page 179).

The junction of O'Connell Street with Henry Street and North Earl Street has always been considered the very centre of Dublin, and it was here that the imposing Nelson's Column stood, a replica of the one in London's Trafalgar Square. Erected in 1809, it was hollow inside, and a spiral staircase led to a viewing platform at the top. In 1966 this symbol of British power and military might was blown up by the IRA to mark in their inimitable way the 50th anniversary of the Easter Uprising. Column and statue were destroyed, but not lost for good. A few weeks later, two "authentic" heads of Nelson could be seen in two different antique shops. The real one – but is it really – is on display at the Dublin Civic Museum (see page 117).

Around Parnell Square (D1)

Founded in the middle of the 18C at a time when infant mortality had reached horrifying proportions, the **Rotunda Hospital** still functions as a maternity hospital. In Classical style, the building incorporates a **Baroque chapel** *(open to the public)*, richly decorated with gilded stuccowork. Expectant fathers can often be found in the pub opposite, which goes by the name of "the waiting room".

Nearby is one of the city's most celebrated theatres, the **Gate Theatre**, established at the same time as the Rotunda in the hope that its performances would help finance the work of the hospital. From its beginnings in 1929, the Gate's repertory company aimed to put on plays less narrowly "Irish" than the Abbey Theatre. It was here that **Orson Welles** first carried a spear.

Behind the Rotunda Hospital, the **Garden of Remembrance** was laid out in 1966 to honour the memory of the victims of the Easter Uprising.

On the north side of the square, the **Dublin Writers' Museum**★★ *(10am-5pm; Sunday and public holidays 11am-5pm; June-August: closes 6pm weekdays. Admission charge)* is housed in the former residence of Lord Farnham, one of the great Anglo-Irish magnates of the 18C. In 1891 the building passed into the ownership of the Jameson family, distillers of the famous whiskey, and their stained glass coat of arms features in a number of the windows. With few documents at its disposal, the museum nevertheless succeeds by means of an audio-tour in evoking the importance of the writers of Dublin in particular and Ireland in general in the context of the world's literary heritage. Visitors will be surprised to find no mention of contemporary writers such as the Nobel Prize winner Seamus Heaney. It seems that the museum has been very careful not to ruffle any literary feathers by only dealing with writers who are safely dead. However, today's leading lights need not be unduly bothered; their association has its headquarters – the **Irish Writers' Centre** – right next door.

Anyone at all interested in painting will want to visit the **Hugh Lane Gallery of Modern Art**★★ *(9.30am-6pm; Friday-Saturday 9.30am-5pm; Sunday 11am-5pm; closed Monday; open to 8pm Thursday April-August. Free admission. Free chamber music and contemporary music concerts Sunday afternoon).* Designed by Sir William Chambers for James Caulfield, first Earl of Charlemont, **Charlemont House** is the home of the art collection of Sir Hugh Lane, who perished in the sinking of the *Lusitania (see page 258)* and whose chief enthusiasm was for the French Impressionists. French works form the core of the collection, and include major pictures by **Manet** and **Degas**, the famous *Waterloo Bridge* by **Monet**, a self-portrait by **Courbet**, canvases by **Bonnard**, **Vlaminck**, and **Rouault**, as well as a fascinating sketch of **Millet's** *Gleaners*. Modern Irish painters are strongly represented as well. **Roderic**

Dublin

Local Nobels

No other city of the size of Dublin can pride itself on having been the birthplace of so many winners of the Nobel Prize for Literature: WB Yeats in 1923, George Bernard Shaw in 1925, Samuel Beckett in 1969, and Seamus Heaney in 1995. Four winners in a place of less than a million inhabitants – as many as in the whole of Russia! But then Dublin seems always to have been blessed with writers of the highest calibre, from Jonathan Swift to Oscar Wilde, from Joyce to Beckett, able to transmute the genius of the place into universal significance. That this was often done in exile from a country where prejudice has often stifled free expression could be said to enhance rather than diminish their achievement.

O'Connor (1860-1940) is without doubt the most interesting figure. He benefited from an exceptionally long artistic career, in the course of which he became familiar with the main currents in modern art. During his prolonged stay in France, he painted at Pont-Aven with Gauguin and was instrumental in building bridges between the art of France and the British Isles. Other Irish paintings of note include the atmospheric *Lakeside Cottage* by Paul Henry, and the dramatic reconstruction of a Fenian attack, *The Rescue of the Prison Van at Manchester*, by Maurice MacGonical.

The cube-like building at the corner of Dorset Street and Granby Row *(the continuation of Parnell Square West)* houses the **National Wax Museum** (C1) *(10am-5.30pm; Sunday 1pm-6pm. Admission charge)*. The museum concentrates on the great figures of Irish history as well as on pop stars, and there is also a small chamber of horrors.

Go back to the Writers' Museum, turn into Denmark Street, then right into North Great George's Street, a quiet road lined with Georgian residences.

Die-hard Joyce fans will appreciate the **James Joyce Centre** *(June-August: 9.30am-5pm; Sunday and public holidays 11am-5pm; September-May: 9.30am-5pm; Sunday and public holidays 12.30pm-5pm. Admission charge)*, housed in an 18C building (No 35) which in the early 1900s was the home of the dancing-master Denis J Maggini, a dandyish figure who makes several appearances in *Ulysses*. An audio-visual show evokes the Dublin of Joyce's time, but the Centre is best known for what is indubitably the city's wackiest event, **Bloomsday★★**.

West of O'Connell Street

Set in gardens to the west of Parnell Square between Bolton Street and Constitution Street, **King's Inns★** (C1) *(not open to the public)* was built to plans by **James Gandon** in 1818. Another of the city's great neo-Classical public buildings, it still serves its original purpose as lodgings and offices for the legal profession.

Beyond the entrance to King's Inns is **Henrietta Street** (C1), one of Dublin's oldest remaining Georgian streets. Many of the columned porticoes could definitely do with a face-lift.

From Henrietta Street turn into Bolton Street then Capel Street. A right turn leads to St Mary's Abbey, another right turn into Meetinghouse Lane.

Little remains of the Cistercian abbey founded here in 1139. **St Mary's Abbey** (C2) *(mid-June-mid-September: Wednesday and Sunday 10am-5pm. Admission charge. Heritage Site)* has only kept part of its vaulted **chapter house** where the monks used to assemble after Matins. A small exhibition here tells the story of the abbey.

To the rear of the abbey is the city's **Fruit and Vegetable Market** (C2), built in red and yellow brick in Victorian neo-Classical style.

Take any of the streets leading down to Ormond Quay.

The quayside is lined with the premises of Dublin's countless solicitors. The financial encouragement given by the Government to foreign firms setting up in Ireland has done no harm at all to this sector of the legal profession, the only body able to deal with the mountain of paperwork involved.

Close by, the great colonnaded **dome** of the city's law courts rises above Inns Quay. Built between 1785 and 1802 by **James Gandon**, the architect also responsible for the Custom House and King's Inns, the **Four Courts*** (B2-B3) are so called because the building used to house the original four courts of Chancery, Common Pleas, King's Bench and Exchequer. Badly damaged during the Civil War of 1922, the courts were subsequently restored, though bullet holes can still be seen in some of the columns of the portico. It is well worthwhile looking into the majestic **main hall** beneath the dome, where lawyers and clients earnestly discuss current cases.

A very special day
16 June 1904 corresponds to the day of Leopold Bloom's Dublin Odyssey. Every year at around this time, the James Joyce Centre stages a whole series of light-hearted events aimed at making Joyce's work more accessible. Things begin with a mock burial at Glasnevin Cemetery, continue with a boat trip on the Liffey, a "Ulysses" bus tour and a "Bloomsday afternoon tour", a not entirely serious pilgrimage around the principal places mentioned in the novel. For those unable to be in Dublin at this time, the Centre and the tourist office have put together a fascinating "Ulysses Map of Dublin" showing all the places featured in the book. On the ground, they are identified by a copper plaque quoting the relevant lines from the novel.

At the western end of the Four Courts the **Father Mathew Bridge** (B3) spans the Liffey at the point where the first crossing was built, the famous **Baile Átha Cliath** (*see above*). The 19C bridge is named after a priest – also honoured with a statue in O'Connell Street – who was a passionate campaigner against the evils of alcohol (*see page 216*).

From the end of the bridge go down Church Street as far as **St Michan's Church*** (B2) (*10am-12.45pm; Closed Sunday. Admission charge*), the oldest church on the north bank, founded by the Danes in 1095. The present grey stone structure dates from 1685. Handel is supposed to have composed his Messiah on the church's monumental **organ**, but the church's main interest for visitors lies in its **crypt**. The mummified corpses here owe their state of preservation, not, as is often asserted, to fumes from the nearby whiskey distillery, but to the character of the subsoil.

Go north up Church Street and take the first turning on the left.

Smithfield Village (B2)

The modern buildings surrounding the monumental chimney of Jameson's distillery are part of a redevelopment programme begun in the 1990s intended to regenerate this old warehouse district.

The Jameson family made whiskey here from 1780 until 1972, but the famous product, like most other brands of Irish whiskey, is now distilled at Midleton near Cork, and the **Old Jameson Distillery**** (*daily 9.30am-6pm, last tour 5pm. Admission charge*) has been turned into a museum. Visitors can see a film, enjoy a series of lifelike tableaux illustrating the different stages of whiskey production from malting floor to still. The whole experience is expertly conveyed and most enjoyable, not least because of the pervasive and pleasant odours throughout, to say nothing of the final sampling of the product.

The rehabilitation of the surrounding area is likely to take several more years. Already completed are several shops, a luxury hotel with a glass façade, and **Ceol, The Traditional Irish Music Centre**** (*9.30am-6pm; Sunday 10.30am-6pm. Admission charge. Live music in the restaurant hall Thursday, Friday and Saturday at 9pm and Sunday 12.30pm-2pm. Free admission*). The Centre demonstrates how contemporary Irish musicians are attempting to blend tradition and modernity. Visitors may at first be disconcerted by the use of interactive techniques and electronic systems which seem to have little to do with a kind of music more usually

Dublin

Their kingdom for a horse

Smithfield is the location of Dublin's most unusual market. On the first Sunday of the month, the only horse fair still held in a European capital takes place at the foot of one of the city's most modern hotels. Traders and buyers mingle in a pungent atmosphere of horse sweat and droppings. Children from Dublin's less favoured estates are among the keenest clients, on the look-out for a steed that will be their companion, their means of locomotion, and their badge of status in the group. It's quite something to see them confidently bargaining with all the swagger of an adult, taking possession of their new mount, then riding off proudly bareback.

associated with the smoky interiors of dimly-lit pubs with a peat fire smouldering away in a corner. But despite this somewhat cold atmosphere it is easy to appreciate the intense musicological effort going on here; music from every part of Ireland is represented, with its particular traditions, performers and instruments (all of which can be experienced by children in their own interactive section). One of the most exciting things is the 18-minute **film***, which uses a panoramic screen and all kinds of special effects. The audience is taken on a dizzy flight around Ireland, and literally plunged into the lively musical atmosphere of pubs from different counties; people emerge smiling, their heads buzzing with the sound of accordions, fiddles and harps.

The southern suburbs (Plan I)
On foot or by bus

Hop along to the Hop Store

There's little chance of visitors losing their way in the St James' Gate area; all they have to do is follow their noses and the smell of hops, which gradually gets stronger as the Guinness brewery gets closer.

Guinness Hop Store (C3) – *Buses 51B and 78A from Aston Quay and bus 123 from O'Connell Street. April-September: 9.30am-5pm; Sunday and public holidays 10.30am-4.30pm; October-March: 9.30am-4pm; Sunday and public holidays 12pm-4pm. Admission charge includes tasting.* Part of the brewery's old hop store has been converted into a museum entirely devoted to Ireland's most famous beer. There are examples of Guinness's famous posters, a full explanation of how the dark brew is made, and a tasting, as well as a souvenir shop full of promotional material in the form of pens, T-shirts, watches, ties and so on...

Kilmainham

In the middle of a pleasant park near Heuston Station (*buses 24, 79 and 90 from Aston Quay*), **Kilmainham Royal Hospital** (B2-B3) was built at the end of the 17C to accommodate wounded and retired soldiers, and is the largest building of its era in Ireland. It was commissioned by James Butler, first Duke of Ormond, who had been inspired by Les Invalides in Paris while in exile there. The

Dublin's black brew

Arthur Guinness began brewing on the banks of the Liffey in 1759, but the quality and colour of his beer had nothing to do with the dark waters of Dublin's river. He called his product porter, after a London beer made with roasted, unmalted barley and much in favour among the metropolis's market porters. Nowadays Guinness and similar beers are known as stouts rather than porters. Other stouts are brewed in Ireland, but Guinness is easily the most popular, not just here but world-wide, with a high proportion of the product going for export, though it is brewed abroad as well. Keen drinkers argue interminably about whether Guinness is better bottled or on draught, and whether the unpasteurised Irish version is superior to the pasteurised product brewed in London. Guinness not only make Guinness, they are also responsible for a drink – Harp lager – utterly unlike the dark and hoppy brew with a creamy head and intense and satisfying taste for which the firm is best known.

chapel has been restored in an exemplary manner, while parts of the rest of the complex have been converted to house the **Irish Museum of Modern Art** *(Tuesday-Saturday 10am-3.30pm; Sunday and public holidays 12pm-5.30pm. Free admission)*. The museum is best known for its retrospective exhibitions of the works of contemporary artists. The permanent collection is of less interest, though there are some fine works by the Hungarian-born pioneer of op-art, **Vasarely**.

To the west of the Royal Hospital on Inchicore Road (Buses 51, 51B, 78A and 79) stands **Kilmainham Gaol**★ (B3) *(April-September: daily 9.30am-6pm, last tour 4.45pm; October-March: Monday-Friday 9.30am-5pm, last tour 4pm; Sunday 10am-6pm, last tour 4.45pm. Admission charge. Heritage Site)*. Completed in 1792, the old prison at Kilmainham is intimately linked with the struggle for independence, and many an Irish patriot spent time behind its walls. The last of them was **Éamon de Valera** before he became independent Ireland's prime minister and later president. The gaol closed in the 1920s, was restored in the 1960s and is now a museum of itself, with many mementoes of the nationalist and independence movement.

There are plenty of reminders of the severe penalties meted out for trivial offences, such as several years incarceration or transportation to Australia for stealing a piece of bread or similar item. During the Famine people would commit such crimes in the hope of being imprisoned here and of having at least something to eat. Kilmainham was a place of execution: in the year 1850, there was a total of 9 052 hangings, almost 25 a day. It was here too that some of the participants in the Easter Rising met their end, among them **Joseph Plunkett**, who was allowed to marry Grace Gifford in the prison chapel a matter of hours before his execution. **James Connolly** was so badly wounded in the fighting that he had to be bound to a chair to make a satisfactory target for the firing squad.

By the Grand Canal

The former synagogue in Portobello is now the **Irish Jewish Museum** (C3) *(3-4 Walworth Road, near Victoria Street. Buses 16, 16A, 19 and 19A. May-September: Tuesday, Thursday and Sunday 11am-3pm; October-April: Sunday only 10.30am-2.30pm)*. This fascinating little museum was opened in 1985 by the President of Israel, Chaim Herzog, Belfast-born and a one-time resident of Dublin. It has displays and mementoes relating to the long history of Ireland's small Jewish community, present in the country since the 11C. One of its most illustrious members was Robert Briscoe (1914-69), Lord Mayor of Dublin in the 1960s.

Joyce's Jewish hero
If the Jews have a long history in Ireland, so does anti-Semitism, always latent in traditional Catholic culture. Reacting against the stifling Roman Catholicism of his youth, James Joyce centred "Ulysses" around the character of Leopold Bloom. Making his hero a Jew gave him a certain neutrality in an Ireland torn at the time by civil war, and it may also be relevant that Joyce maintained close relations with Jews throughout his life.

North of the Liffey (Plan I)
On foot or by bus

Phoenix Park area

The last of the barracks to be evacuated by the British in 1922 is now the **National Museum of Ireland Collins Barracks**★ (B2-C2) *(Benburb Street. Buses 25, 25A, 66, 67 and 90. Tuesday-Saturday: 10am-5pm; Sunday 2pm-5pm. Free admission)*. Once named the Royal Barracks, the complex now bears the name of the general who directed the struggle against the British between 1919-21. Part of the National Museum, it is mostly devoted to **arts and crafts**. The collections are very diverse, sometimes confusingly so. They include 18C dinner services, Ancient Greek vases, Bavarian beer mugs and Chinese miniatures, as well as fine examples of the Irish

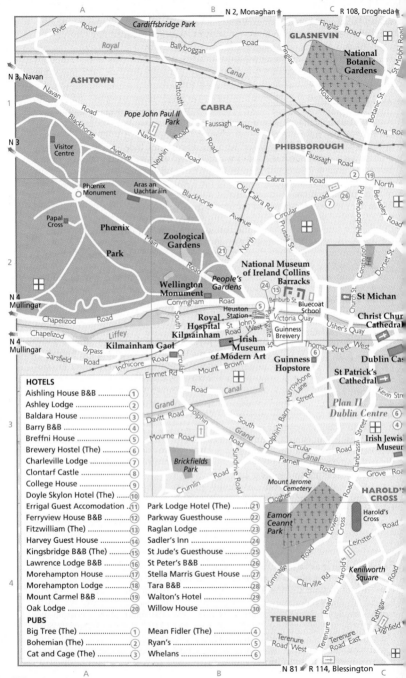

Cardiffsbridge Park

River Road

GLASNEVIN

Royal

Ballyboggan

Road

National
Botanic
Gardens

Canal

ASHTOWN

N 3, Navan

Navan

Road

CABRA

Pope John Paul II Park

Faussagh Avenue

PHIBSBOROUGH

N 3

Blackhorse

Navan

Road

Nephin

Road

Ratoath

Faussagh Road

Visitor
Centre

Avenue

Road

Old Cabra Rd

Cabra

Road

North

Berkeley Road

Phœnix
Monument

Aras an
Uachtaráin

Blackhorse

Circular

North

Phibsborough Rd

Papal
Cross

Phœnix

Zoological
Gardens

Avenue

Prussia St.

Constitution Hill

Dorset St.

N 4
Mullingar

Park

Main

Road

Wellington
Monument

People's
Gardens

National Museum
of Ireland Collins
Barracks

Benburb St.

St Michan

Church St.

Chapelizod

Conyngham   Road

Road

Heuston
Station

Bluecoat
School

St John's

Christ Church
Cathedral

N 4
Mullingar

Chapelizod

Liffey

South

Royal
Hospital
Kilmainham

Road

West

Gate

Victoria Quay

Usher's Quay

Sarsfield

Bypass

Kilmainham Gaol

Inchicore   Road

Circular

St John's
Road

Irish
Museum
of Modern Art

Guinness
Brewery

Thomas   Street   West

Dublin Cas

Road

Emmet Rd

Mount   Brown

Guinness
Hopstore

St Patrick's
Cathedral

Marrowbone   Lane

Kevin Stre

Grand

Canal

Plan II
Dublin Centre   6

Davitt   Road

Dolphin

South   Grand

Mourne   Road

Road

Circular

Clanbrassil   Street

Irish Jewish
Museum

Brickfields
Park

Sundrive   Road

Canal

Parnell   Road

Crumlin

Road

Grove   Rd

Mount Jerome
Cemetery

Clogher

HAROLD'S
CROSS

Eamon
Ceannt
Park

Harold's
Cross

Kimmage

Lower   Cross   Road

Clarville Rd

Harold's

Leinster   Road

Kenilworth
Square

TERENURE

Terenure   Road   West

Terenure   Road   East

Clarville   Rd

Rathgar

Highfield

HOTELS

Aishling House B&B	①
Ashley Lodge	②
Baldara House	③
Barry B&B	④
Breffni House	⑤
Brewery Hostel (The)	⑥
Charleville Lodge	⑦
Clontarf Castle	⑧
College House	⑨
Doyle Skylon Hotel (The)	⑩
Errigal Guest Accomodation	⑪
Ferryview House B&B	⑫
Fitzwilliam (The)	⑬
Harvey Guest House	⑭
Kingsbridge B&B (The)	⑮
Lawrence Lodge B&B	⑯
Morehampton House	⑰
Morehampton Lodge	⑱
Mount Carmel B&B	⑲
Oak Lodge	⑳

Park Lodge Hotel (The)	㉑
Parkway Guesthouse	㉒
Raglan Lodge	㉓
Sadler's Inn	㉔
St Jude's Guesthouse	㉕
St Peter's B&B	㉖
Stella Marris Guest House	㉗
Tara B&B	㉘
Walton's Hotel	㉙
Willow House	㉚

PUBS

Big Tree (The)	①
Bohemian (The)	②
Cat and Cage (The)	③

Mean Fidler (The)	④
Ryan's	⑤
Whelans	⑥

North Bull
Island
R 105
Howth

Collins   Road

KILLESTER

Casino
Marino

Clontarf
Golf Course

Griffith   Avenue

Farm Rd

⑤ ㉚
⑩ ③
⑨
⑪ ③

DRUMCONDRA

Griffith

Avenue

MARINO

Howth

St Anne's
Park

Vernon   Av.

Castle   Avenue

Vernon   Avenue

⑧

Clonliffe   Road

Richmond   Road

Drumcondra

Fairview

Fairview Park

Clontarf

Road

⑯
㉘
①

St Lawrence Road

CLONTARF

⑫④   Clontarf   Road

Royal

Road

George

Mountjoy
Square

North Strand Road

Canal

East

Wall

Alfie Byrne

Road

Suir

N

Gardiner St.

Connolly

Seville Place

Sheriff   Street

Easy Road

Tolka   Quay

Alexandra   Road

Custom House

House   Quay

North Wall   Quay

Alexandra Bassin

Tara

City   Quay

Liffey

East Wall Road

Holyhead
Liverpool

Pearse

Ringsend   Road

Ringsend
Park

Pigeon   House   Road

nity
llege

Merrion
Square

Macken   Street

Waterways
Visitors
Centre

Shelbourne
Park

RINGSEND

ephen's
n

St.

Baggot St.
Lower

Fitzwilliam

Bath   Avenue

Sean Moore
Park

Beach   Road

Irishtown
Nature Park

gh St.
dens

⑬

i

Leeson St. Lower

Haddington

Pembroke Rd

Northumberland

Shelbourne Rd

Claremont Rd

SANDYMOUNT

Park

Strand

DUBLIN

and
and Parade   Leeson St. Upper

Raglan   Rd

㉓

Clyde   Rd

nelagh

Road

THMINES

⑳

Pembroke

㉕⑰

②

Morehampton

Herbert Park

BALLSBRIDGE

⑱

Herbert
Park

Anglesea   Road

Merrion   Road

Shrewsbury Rd

BAY

DONNYBROOK

Sandford Rd

Eglinton Road

Ailesbury   Road

Merrion   Road

Palmerston Road

ston Park

Milltown

Clonskeagh

Stillorgan

Nutley   Lane

Elm Park

DUBLIN
Built-up area
Plan I

0   0,5   1 km

Road

Dodder

University
College Dublin
U

silversmith's art; silver has been extracted in quantity from the Wicklow Mountains and the Tipperary area since the Middle Ages. On the second floor, the furniture collections include fine Victorian items, among them examples of the Killarney style, recognisable by motifs carved in holly, maple, oak and other native woods.

Beyond Collins Barracks is a vast area of dreary housing estates. Seemingly untouched by the country's rising prosperity, they nevertheless enjoy an attractive setting in the neighbourhood of Phoenix Park.

From Collins Barracks, the nearest entrance to Phoenix Park is 10min away on foot along Infirmary Road. Buses 10, 25 and 26 from the city centre.

Laid out in the 18C, **Phoenix Park★** (A2-B2) is the largest urban park in Europe, covering an area of 700 hectares. Its name comes from the Gaelic *"fionn uisce"* ("clear waters"), and the park still has a number of ponds, a habitat for waterfowl and a particularly fierce breed of duck. In 1979 Pope John Paul II celebrated Mass here in the presence of a million of the faithful.

A wonderful place to relax on fine days, the park also has an array of sports and recreational facilities, including cricket pitches and children's play areas. Here too is the official residence of the Irish President as well as the American Embassy. The 60m obelisk of the **Wellington Monument** is visible from far away; it took 40 years to complete this memorial to the victor of Waterloo.

The southeastern corner of the park is occupied by **Dublin Zoo** (*Summer: 9.30am-6pm; Sunday 10.30am-6pm; Winter: 9.30am-4pm; Sunday 10.30am-5pm. Admission charge*), one of the world's first establishments of its kind. Little different from other zoos, it has one special distinction; a former resident, a lion, provided the roar which was such a memorable curtain-raiser to MGM movies.

Marino

Around 3km from the city centre, near Malahide Road. Buses 20A, 20B, 27, 27A, 27B, 42 and 42C.

Casino Marino★ (E1) (*February-April and November: Wednesday-Sunday 12pm-4pm; May and October: daily 10am-5pm; June-September: daily 9.30am-6.30pm. Admission charge. Heritage Site*) is a fine example of 18C Palladian architecture, a folly which formed part of a vast project designed by the architect **William Chambers** for the Earl of Charlemont. This liberal-minded nobleman built himself a palace and gardens not just for his own pleasure but also for that of his contemporaries, who were invited to roam freely over the whole estate. The delightful little pavilion resembles a Greek temple and contains items of furniture of rare delicacy.

North Bull Island (from F1)

5.5km northeast of the city centre. Take the DART towards Howth, get off at Raheny and cross the bridge at the end of Watermill Road. Buses 30 (via Dollymount), 29A, 29B, 31, 32, 32A and 32B. By car, go along Clontarf Road towards Howth and take the second bridge on the right by St Anne's Park.
Allow 2hr for a tour of the island on foot.

Also known as **Dollymount Island**, the island stretches for 5km, bounded to the east by a line of sandy beaches, which are popular with swimmers when weather permits. Most of the island is occupied by a golf course, but it is also an important **bird sanctuary**, one of the most species-rich in Europe. Winter is the best time for a visit; countless wading birds pause here during their migratory passage. In order to get information about the island's wildlife and environment, call at the little yellow house in the middle of the island, which has a **Visitors' Interpretive Centre** (*Monday-Friday 10.15am-1pm / 1.30pm-4.30pm, closes 1.30pm Friday; weekends 10am-1pm / 1.30pm-5.30pm*).

Excursions from Dublin
By car, bus or DART

Dún Laoghaire*

12km from Dublin city centre. For directions, see "Making the most of Dún Laoghaire". Allow a day. At the southern end of Dublin Bay, the formerly independent communities of Monkstown, Dalkey, Sandycove and Dún Laoghaire have been amalgamated to form the Borough of Dún Laoghaire. With its ferry terminal, the port here is an important gateway to Ireland for visitors coming from Britain, but few linger here for very long. This is despite the fact that Dún Laoghaire is not lacking in either charm or interest. There are plenty of pretty Victorian villas and gardens as well as the Martello tower featured in Ulysses, the castle at Dalkey, and the seafront, which in summer has just a tinge of the Riviera about it. And should Dublin's hotels be full, quite likely at certain times of the year, there are plenty of places to stay here.

The **National Maritime Museum** (*Easter-May and October: Sunday and public holidays 1pm-5pm; May-September: Tuesday-Sunday and public holiday Mondays 1pm-5pm. Admission charge*) is housed in the Mariners' Church of 1823, close to Moran Park. Among the collections evoking the country's maritime heritage and the evolution of the art of navigation is a fine array of model ships, a French longboat captured during an attempted landing in Bantry Bay in 1796 (*see panel page 274*), and a chart from the German submarine from which Sir Roger Casement was landed in 1916.

James Joyce Tower and Museum* (*April-end October: 10am-1pm / 2pm-5pm; Sunday and public holidays 2pm-6pm. Admission charge*). The museum is located in the Martello tower rising over the little bay at Sandycove (1km south of Dún Laoghaire), one of a number built along this stretch of coast for fear of a French invasion in 1804. It is here that the first chapter of Ulysses opens, and in 1962, Joyce's editor, Sylvia Beach decided that it would be a suitable place to exhibit his correspondence, photographs, manuscripts and other personal items. There is a first edition of Ulysses illustrated by Matisse, who seems not to have read the book since the drawings depict incidents not from Joyce, but from Homer. From the top of the tower there is a panoramic **view** of Dublin Bay and the Howth peninsula.

At the foot of the tower, a stairway leads down through the rocks to **Forty Foot Pool**, a sort of natural swimming pool once the exclusive preserve of male nudists. Times changed, and eventually ladies were admitted, but nowadays there are no nudists here at all. The little bay nearby is a favourite spot for swimmers too.

To the south of Sandycove, 3km away, the busy township of **Dalkey** once boasted no fewer than 7 castles. Three still stand, dating from the 15C and 16C. **Bulloch Castle** (*not open to the public*) dominates the little fishing harbour just north of Dalkey; **Archbold's Castle** is now the Town Hall, and **Goat Castle** houses the **Dalkey Heritage Centre** (*Tuesday-Friday 9.30am-5pm; weekends and public holidays 11am-5pm. Admission charge*). This little museum has excellent exhibits on local history; the

Joyce at Sandycove

In 1904, Joyce, then 22 years old, was just beginning his career as a writer, when he was invited to stay in the Martello tower at Sandycove by the fashionable poet Oliver St John Gogarthy. Gogarthy wanted to get a closer look at the young man who had attacked him savagely in a newspaper article. Joyce's stay was even more memorable than it might otherwise have been; in the middle of the night, another guest, an Anglo-Irish gentleman by the name of Trench loosed off a shot from his revolver at the panther which had featured in his nightmare. Joyce decided on the spot to quit this curious company, and before the month was out, had left Ireland altogether.

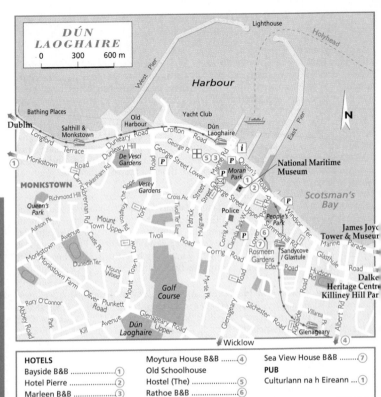

name Goat Castle is a play on the name of the family who once resided here, the Chevers (*chèvre* = goat in French). From the battlements there is a fine all-round view of Dalkey in its setting.

On the northwestern edge of Dalkey, **Killiney Hill Park** is a pleasant place for a stroll. One of the signposted footpaths leads from the car park to an 18C obelisk, from where there is an unbeatable **view*** over the whole of Dublin Bay, from Howth in the north to Bray in the south.

It would be a pity to leave Dalkey without enjoying the splendid **panorama**** from Vico Road, which winds like a corniche along the steep hillside south of the town. When the sun shines, visitors could almost be excused for thinking they had suddenly been transported to the Riviera, such is the abundance of rhododendrons and yuccas, to say nothing of the turquoise waters of the bay.

The Howth peninsula*

Allow a day for a tour around the whole of the peninsula. Howth has no tourist information centre, but there is a useful panel with a plan of the area opposite the St Lawrence Hotel on the left coming out of the DART station.

Dominated by the **Ben of Howth** (171m), the peninsula closes off Dublin Bay to the north, about 12km from the city. The town has a fishing harbour (turn left out of the station) lined with restaurants and popular with city-dwellers who flock here at the weekend to enjoy the music in the numerous pubs. In the past, Howth's harbour was one of the most important along this coast. It was here in July 1914 that Asgard, the yacht belonging to Erskine Childers, author of The Riddle of the Sands, landed with a cargo of weapons and ammunition destined for the Irish Volunteers. Howth also had an important abbey; **St Mary's Abbey** (keys from the address at the entrance) is now in ruins, but its walls still rise over the houses climbing up from the harbour (another entrance by the graveyard).

Go back the way you came, continue past the DART station and turn left towards the Deer Park Hotel. After 100m turn right.

The **National Transport Museum** (June-September: daily 10am-6pm; Saturday 2pm-6pm; October-May: weekends and public holidays 2pm-5.30pm. Admission charge) consists of a group of sheds housing several dozen old vehicles, spanning transport history from the stagecoach via the double-decker bus to the armoured car.

On the way towards the Deer Park Hotel, on the right, is **Howth Castle**, dating from the 16C and in a good state of preservation (not open to the public).

Carry on for a further 1km to the car park of the Deer Park Hotel. Then go round the hotel to the right and follow the track to the foot of the hill.

The **rhododendrons** rapidly invading the area were planted in the 19C by the owners of Howth Castle. At flowering time in May and June they are a sensational sight. A stairway leads to the heights from where there is a unique **view**** over the whole of Dublin Bay. From here it is possible to go right round the peninsula along a cliff-top path.

Several hundred metres from the harbour, the tiny island of **Ireland's Eye** (boats from Howth's East Pier, operated by Frank Doyle & Sons, ☎ 01 831 42 00 or mobile 0876 78211) was inhabited by monks in the 8C, as evidenced by the ruins of **St Nessan's Church**. The island served later as an observation post, thanks to its **Martello tower**. Nowadays it is a bird sanctuary with a lovely sandy beach.

Malahide Castle**

17km north of the city centre via the N1 and the R106 from Swords. Bus 42 from Talbot Street. From Dublin there is also a Dublin Bus excursion along the coast to the north which takes in Malahide. Train from Connolly Street or Pearse Station. Park open all year 10am-dusk. Guided tours of the Castle: 10am-12.30pm / 2.15pm-4.45pm; Sunday 2.15pm-5.45pm. Admission charge for Castle, Botanical Garden and Model Railway Museum.

Built in the 12C and in the ownership of the Talbot family until 1976, the **Castle**** was rebuilt and added to several times, notably by James Gandon, the architect of the Four Courts and Custom House in Dublin (see above). The remarkably well-preserved interior contains fine **furniture** of the 17C and 18C, as well as a **portrait gallery** and paintings by British and Irish masters. In summer, the **Botanical Garden** has a striking variety of exotic plants from Chile, Tasmania and New Zealand.

The **Fry Model Railway Museum**, set up in some of the outbuildings, is also worth a visit. Cyril Fry, a former railway engineer, took 38 years to build this extraordinary model railway with a total track length of 4 kilometres.

Newbridge House*

At Donabate, 20km north of Dublin via the N1 and the R126. April-September: Tuesday-Saturday 10am-1pm / 2pm-5pm; weekends and public holidays 2pm-6pm. October-March: weekends and public holidays 2pm-5pm. Admission charge. Guided tour.

This elegant Georgian residence, set in lovely parkland, was built in 1740 for Charles Cobb, the Anglican Archbishop of Dublin. The interior has kept a good part of its original furniture as well as fine Rococo **stuccowork**. The outbuildings have been laid out as a **museum of rural life**, with reconstructions of a carpenter's shop, a blacksmith's forge, and a cartwright's workshop.

Castletown House***

At Celbridge, 22km west of Dublin. Turn left beyond Lucan, at the beginning of the M4. Eight buses daily from Dublin to Celbridge (3 on Sunday). April-September: 10am-6pm; Saturday 11am-6pm; Sunday and public holidays 2pm-6pm; October: Monday-Friday 10am-5pm; closed Saturday; Sunday and public holidays 2pm-5pm; November-March: Sunday and public holidays 2pm-5pm. Admission charge.

One of the finest examples of Palladian architecture in Europe, Castletown was built for William Conolly (1662-1729), Speaker of the Irish House of Commons. Son of a Donegal inn-keeper, Conolly became the richest man in Ireland thanks to clever speculation with the lands confiscated from Catholics after the victory of William of Orange in 1690. Some of the design work was given to an Italian, Alessandro Galilei, the first architect to build in the Palladian style in Ireland. The interior decoration was completed 30 years later by Conolly's great-nephew, though the guiding hand in the design of the **green drawing room**, the **dining room** and the extremely elegant **long gallery** in Pompeian style was Mrs Conolly's.

Conolly's Folly, a 40m-high obelisk mounted on two tiers of arches, was erected by Mrs Conolly not only as a memorial to her husband, but also in order to give employment to local people during the famine of winter 1739.

Dublin and around

Making the most of Dublin

COMING AND GOING

By plane – Dublin International Airport (from Plan I D1), ☎ 01 814 11 11, 10km north of the centre, via N1 and M1 and motorway E1. There is a taxi stand in front of the arrivals hall; reckon on around €15 to the city centre, journey time 20-30min. Shuttle bus to Heuston Station via the Busáras bus station in Store Street near Connolly Station: Monday-Saturday 6.40am-11pm; Sunday 7.10am-11pm. City buses 33, 41, 41A, 41B and 41C (€1.65, exact fare only) run in both directions 6am-11.30pm (journey time 45min).
Flight information: ☎ 01 886 67 05.
Luggage and passenger assistance ☎ 01 814 46 33, Fax 01 814 49 42. *Police and lost property* ☎ 01 814 44 81.
Left luggage, in the car park passageway (6am-10pm): ☎ 01 814 46 33.

By train – Iarnród Éireann / Irish Rail links Dublin with principal towns in the Republic and with Belfast. Trains from **Heuston Station** (Plan I B2) run to Cork, Tralee, Limerick, Ennis, Galway, Westport, Ballina, Kildare and Waterford. Trains from Connolly Station (Plan II F1) serve Sligo, Drogheda and Belfast, Maynooth, Wexford and Rosslare.

Information and reservations: **Iarnród Éireann**, 35 Abbey Street (Plan II, D2-E2), ☎ 01 836 62 22; Monday-Friday 9.15am-5pm; Saturday 9am-1pm. UK ferry tickets as well as rail tickets. Internet rail timetable: www.irishrail.ie

By bus – Bus Éireann has a dense network of services covering parts of the North as well as the Republic (*see "Making the most of…" for particular areas*). The **Busáras** bus station is close to Connolly Station, Store Street (Plan II E2-F2), ☎ 01 836 61 11. Reductions for students aged 16 and over with student ID validated by USIT (Union of Students of Ireland). Information: ☎ 01 703 25 75.

By boat – Irish Ferries boats dock at the terminal at the mouth of the Liffey (Plan I F2), 10mins from Custom House (buses 53 and 53A).
Stena-Sealink ferries dock at Dún Laoghaire, 8km south of the city centre. DART or buses 7, 7A and 8.

GETTING AROUND

Visitors are strongly advised not to try and get around the city by car. Parking spaces are limited and the rules are rigidly enforced. Releasing a clamped vehicle costs €126. Theft from cars is widespread, by day as well as by night; nothing should be left visible inside a vehicle, and it is best to make use of a secure car park (list available from the tourist information centre). The centre of Dublin is relatively compact and it is easy to get around on foot. Pay careful attention to house numbers, which are not always in logical sequence. Even numbers can be in ascending order on one side of a street, odd numbers in descending order on the other side; thus a street with 100 buildings in it can have No 1 facing No 99.

By bus – Shank's pony apart, buses are the best way of exploring the city, especially from the upper deck. Buses heading for the centre show "An Lár" on the indicator panel. Tickets cost between €0.70 and €1.58 according to the distance travelled. Fares are paid into a slot machine using the exact money; drivers cannot give change. Details of reduced fares and special offers from **Dublin Bus**, 59 Upper O'Connell Street (Plan II D1), Monday-Friday 9am-5pm, ☎ 01 873 42 22. Last buses 11.30pm. Night buses run 12am-2pm from Westmoreland Street and College Green near Trinity College.

By train – The most useful line is **DART** (Dublin Area Rapid Transit) which runs for 40km along the coast from Howth in the north to Bray in the south, calling at three stations in the city centre, **Connolly Station** (Plan II F1), **Tara Street** (Plan II E2), and **Pearse Station** (Plan II F3).

By taxi – There are not many taxi ranks in the centre and finding a cab after 11pm at the weekend is not always easy. There are often taxis in **Foster Place** (Plan II D3), to the rear of the Bank of Ireland. Fares are based on metered mileage, with an extra charge for luggage. Tips are appreciated though not compulsory.

Car hire – A complete list of car rental agencies is available from **Car Rental Council of Ireland**, 5 Upper Pembroke Street (near St Stephen's Green), Dublin 2, ☎ 01 676 16 90, Fax 01 661 92 13. Favourable rates can sometimes be obtained from: **Access Car Rentals**, ☎ 01 844 48 48, Fax 01 844 48 47. This company does not have a desk at the airport, but cars can be picked up there if arranged in advance; **Thrifty**, 33 Bachelors Walk (Plan II D2), ☎ 01 872 64 01, Fax 01 972 93 08; **National Car Rental**, Dublin Airport, ☎ 01 844 41 62.

The major international firms also have desks at the airport: **Avis**, Dublin Airport, ☎ 01 605 75 00; **Budget**, Dublin Airport, ☎ 01 844 51 50; **Hertz**, Dublin Airport, ☎ 01 844 54 66.

Bicycle hire – Recommended accessories include helmet, robust bicycle lock, and rainproof clothing. The main bike hire operations include: **Rent a Bike**, 56 Lower Gardiner Street (Plan II E2), close to Connolly Station, ☎ 01 874 42 47; **Harding**, 30 Bachelors Walk (Plan II D2), close to O'-Connell Street, ☎ 01 873 24 55; **Dublin Bike Tours**, ☎ 01 679 08 99, Fax 01 661 19 73, organises guided bicycle tours around Dublin (3hr) for €15 per person. Starting point in front of Christ Church Cathedral: daily 1 April-31 October 9.45am and 1.45pm. There is also a special tour for early birds at 6am, stopping for breakfast at the Fruit Market. Advance booking essential.

ADDRESS BOOK

Tourist information – **Dublin Tourism Information Centre**, Suffolk Street (Plan II D3), is housed in St Andrew's Church, close to Trinity College, ☎ 01 605 77 00. Summer: 8.30am-8pm; Sunday 10.30am-2pm. Rest of year: 9am-5pm, closed Sunday. General information on Dublin, hotel reservations, sale of public transport tickets and city tours, maps and guides for the whole of Ireland. A branch at 12 O'Connell Street (Plan II D1-D2), ☎ 01 878 80 53. Another branch in the airport arrivals hall, ☎ 01 605 77 55. Daily 8am-10pm. General information plus hotel or B&B reservations (€1.27 commission and 10% of the charge, remainder payable at hotel).

The head office of Ireland's national tourism organisation, **Bord Fáilte**, is on Baggot Street Bridge (Plan I D3) southeast of St Stephen's Green near the Grand Canal, ☎ 01 602 40 00.

Northern Ireland Tourist Board, 16 Nassau Street (Plan II E3), Monday-Friday 9.15am-5.30pm; Saturday 10am-5pm, ☎ 01 679 19 77, Fax 01 677 15 87. Tourist information for the North.

Banks / Currency exchange – There are cash machines in the arrival and departure halls at the airport. Bureau de change at the bank in the departure hall (daily 6am-8pm). Bureaux de change in banks, major hotels, at the Tourism Information Centre and (on Sunday as well) at the General Post Office. Another bureau de change is on Westmoreland Street (Plan II D3) near Trinity College: Monday-Saturday 9am-9pm, Sunday 10am-7pm.

Post Office / Telephone – Coin and card-operated phone boxes on many street corners and at post offices. Phone cards obtainable at post offices, general stores and newsagents.

Calls can be made at reduced rates at the **International Call Shop**, 46 Temple Bar (Plan II D3), ☎ 01 679 60 77. Monday-Wednesday 10am-11pm; Thursday-Sunday 10am-12am. Calls can be made from the shop or by using a prepaid card from any public phone box. UK (including Northern Ireland) €0.19 per minute, USA €0.23 per minute. It could be worthwhile laying in a stock of these cards before setting off on a tour of the country.

Internet – Cyberbase, 13 Cathedral Street (Plan II D2), close to the tourist office on O'Connell Street, ☎ 01 878 78 98, Monday-Friday 9am-11pm; weekends 10am-10pm. **Cyberia Café**, Temple Lane South (Plan II D3), close to Barnacle's Hostel, Temple Bar. Open 7 days a week.

Medical service – All emergencies, ☎ 999 or 112.

Mater Misercordia Hospital, Eccles Street (Plan I C2), ☎ 01 830 11 22 (buses 10, 22, 38 and 120); **Meath Hospital**, Heytesbury Street (Plan I C3),

☎ 01 453 65 55 / 453 60 00 (buses 16, 16A, 19, 19A, 22, 22A and 55); **Beaumont Hospital**, Beaumont Road, Dublin 9, ☎ 01 837 99 74/837 99 66, for all poisoning cases. Women's health, **Dublin Well Woman Centre**, 73 Lower Lesson Street (Plan I D3), ☎ 01 661 00 83 / 661 00 86.

O'Connell's Pharmacy, 55 Lower O'Connell Street (Plan II D2), ☎ 01 873 04 27. Monday-Saturday 8.30am-10pm; Sunday 10am-10pm.

Embassies – Australia, Fitzwilton House. Wilton Terrace, Dublin 2, ☎ 01 676 15 17.

Canada, 65 / 68 St Stephen's Green South, Dublin 2, ☎ 01 478 19 88.

Great Britain, 31-33 Merrion Road, Dublin 4, ☎ 01 205 37 00.

United States, 43 Elgin Road, Dublin 4, ☎ 01 668 87 77.

Airlines – The main airlines have offices at the airport. **Aer Lingus**, ☎ 01 886 88 88 / 705 22 22, Fax 01 705 38 32; **Ryanair**, ☎ 01 609 78 00.

Safety – Police, ☎ 999. Tourist police at the upper end of O'Connell Street (Plan II D1) close to Dublin Bus, ☎ 01 872 54 44.

Loss or theft of travel documents or money, contact **Tourist Victim Support**, Parliament Street (Plan II C3), ☎ 01 679 86 73, who will help with formalities in difficult cases. Dublin is far from being a dangerous city, though drug-related crime is increasing, particularly in the area between O'Connell Street and Lower Gardiner Street.

WHERE TO STAY

Accommodation is in short supply in Dublin and has not kept pace with the steep rise in the number of visitors, least of all at weekends and in summer. Furthermore, hotels and B&Bs are not cheap and often fully booked. Whatever type of accommodation travellers are looking for, they are strongly advised to book several weeks in advance. In case of difficulty, it is easier to find somewhere to stay north of the Liffey or in the suburbs.

• **Around Temple Bar** (Plan II D3)

Under €13

⌂ **Ashfield House**, 19-20 D'Olier Street, ☎ 01 679 77 34, Fax 01 679 08 52, ashfield@indigo.ie – 104 beds `CC` A good place to stay right in the city centre near Trinity College and Temple Bar. Dormitories with 6-10 beds and 10 double or triple rooms with shower. Continental breakfast included in price. Cooking and laundry facilities. Book at least one month in advance in summer.

Barnacle's, 1 Cecilia Street, ☎ 01 671 62 77, Fax 01 671 65 91 – 92 beds `CC` Fluorescent green dormitories and 10 double and triple bedrooms with shower and WC. Pleasant lounge, continental breakfast included in price. Friendly reception. Book at least a month in advance.

Abbey Hostel, 29 Bachelors Walk, Dublin 1, ☎ 01 878 807 00, Fax 01 878 07 19, info@abbey-hostel.ie – 130 beds. Private youth hostel, slightly more expensive than the competition, but good location north of the Liffey near O'Connell Bridge and opposite the Temple Bar area. Dormitories with 4 to 6 beds with showers and WC on the landing, plus some double rooms with own facilities. Cafeteria, cooking and barbecue facilities and bicycle hire. Book in advance May-September.

Between €75-90

Kellys, 36-37 South Great George Street, ☎ 01 677 92 77 / 677 96 88, Fax 01 671 32 16 – 27rm ⌂ `TV` `CC` Old and partly renovated hotel, one of the few family-run hotels in central Dublin. Level of comfort no more than reasonable, but excellent location and friendly reception.

• **Near Merrion Square** (Plan II F4)

Between €75-115

The Fitzwilliam, 41 Upper Fitzwilliam Street, Dublin 2, ☎ 01 662 51 55 / 660 04 88, Fax 01 676 74 88 – 13rm ⌂ 𝄞 ✕ `TV` `CC` In the heart of Georgian Dublin, in a late-18C building, this delightful small hotel has quiet, comfortable and tastefully furnished rooms, as well as a restaurant – **Le Mangetout** – with a good reputation (see below).

• **Ballsbridge** (Plan I D-E3)

This refined residential district close to Herbert Park consists of buildings dating from the early years of the last century standing in well-planted gardens. A number of embassies are located here, as well as plenty of B&Bs and guesthouses. Buses 10, 46A and 46B from the city centre.

Under €13

Morehampton House, 78 Morehampton Road, ☎ 01 668 88 66, Fax 01 668 87 94 – 90 beds and 5rm `CC` This is the only hostel in the area, a favourite with young visitors from abroad. The dormitories with 4-16 beds are bright, spacious, well-kept and non-smoking and have their own facilities. Continental breakfast included in the price. Cooking facilities.

Between €50-65

Oak Lodge, 4 Pembroke Park, ☎ 01 660 60 96, Fax 01 668 17 21 – 3rm ⌂ `TV` In a quiet street of red-brick houses with attractive gardens, this little B&B has spacious and tastefully furnished rooms. Good value for this area.

Between €65-90

St Jude's Guesthouse, 17 Pembroke Park, ☎ 01 668 09 28 / 668 09 28 – 7rm ⌂ `TV` `CC` Classically decorated rooms in a red-brick detached house. Family atmosphere and warm welcome.

Ashley Lodge, 4 Herbert Park, ☎ 01 668 30 04, Fax 01 667 26 75 – 5rm ⌂ 𝄞 `TV` `CC` Mr David McKeogh lets comfortable and soberly decorated rooms. The ones facing Morehampton Road tend to be noisy.

Between €90-100

⌂ **Morehampton Lodge**, 113 Morehampton Road, Donnybrook, ☎ 01 282 74 99, Fax 01 283 75 95 – 18rm ⌂ 𝄞 `TV` `CC` Huge and comfortable rooms overlooking the gardens of a lovely house dating from around 1900. All rooms have a fridge, hairdryer and iron. Off-street parking.

Between €100-130

⌂ **Raglan Lodge**, 10 Raglan Road, ☎ 01 660 66 97, Fax 01 660 67 81 – 7rm ⌂ `TV` `CC` Indubitably one of Dublin's finest B&Bs, a large Victorian house with immense and opulently decorated rooms overlooking a park open to residents only. The sumptuous Irish breakfast is served on fine porcelain in the elegant dining room.

• **Custom House area** (Plan II E2)
The advantage of staying in this area is its proximity to O'Connell Street, the bus station and Connolly Station. The hotels and B&Bs tend to fill up quickly, especially at weekends. Because demand outstrips supply, that legendary Irish hospitality is less in evidence here than elsewhere.

Under €13
Cardijn House, 15 Talbot Street, ☎ 01 878 84 84 / 878 86 18 / 874 17 20 (after 6pm), Fax 01 878 80 91 – 45 beds. Easily the least expensive place in Dublin for those who enjoy community life and crowds. Dormitories with 4-12 beds with separate showers and WC. Basic accommodation, cursory reception, and midnight curfew. Continental breakfast included.

Isaacs Hostel, 2-5 Frenchmans Lane, ☎ 01 855 56 60, Fax 01 855 56 64, hostel@isaacs.ie – 280 beds ✗ CC
Cheerful backpackers' hangout. Young clientele, but all are welcome. Accommodation in dormitories with 4, 6 or 12 beds, with showers and WC on the landing, plus some double and single rooms with own shower. Facilities include Internet, cafeteria, safes, bike storage, bureau de change, left luggage and kitchen.

Abraham House, 82-83 Lower Gardiner Street, ☎ 01 855 06 00, abraham@indigo.ie – 200 beds. One of Dublin's largest hostels, mediocre level of comfort and generally not particularly appetising.

Chelsea Accommodation, 61-62 Lower Gardiner Street, ☎ 01 855 00 35 – 70 beds. Dormitories and double rooms, a few steps from the bus station. Minimal comfort and cleanliness, for use in cases of dire necessity only.

Between €65-90
Gardiner Lodge, 87 Lower Gardiner Street, ☎ 01 836 52 29, Fax 01 836 32 79 – 15rm ⌂ ♪ TV CC This small Georgian hotel is one of the most appealing in

this part of town, with a good level of comfort and rooms attractively furnished with antiques. Prices rise considerably at the weekend and in summer.

Georgian Court, 77-79 Lower Gardiner Street, ☎ 01 855 78 72, Fax 01 855 57 15 – 45rm ⌂ TV CC Dating from 1802, this old house has rooms without any special charm but are well-kept. Below-standard breakfast. Rates vary according to season and day of the week.

Hazelbrook House, 85 Lower Gardiner Street, ☎ 01 836 50 03, Fax 01 855 03 10 – 15rm ⌂ ♪ TV CC Renovated Georgian house with quiet, comfortable rooms.

Celtic Lodge Guest House, 82 Talbot Street, ☎ 01 677 99 55 / 878 87 32, Fax 01 878 86 98, celticguesthouse@tinet.ie – 29rm ⌂ ♪ TV CC In a traffic-free shopping street, this small hotel has attractive rooms decorated in shades of blue and ochre. Better value than the establishments in Lower Gardiner Street.

• **Parnell Square area** (Plan I D2, Plan II D1)

Under €13
Mount Eccles Court, 42 North Great George Street, ☎ 01 878 00 71 / 872 63 01, Fax 01 874 64 72 – 124 beds. Georgian building next door to James Joyce Centre. Dormitories with 4-16 beds, most with own facilities, plus some double rooms.

Between €65-90
🏠 **Harvey's Guest House**, 11 Upper Gardiner Street, ☎ 01 874 83 84 / 874 51 40, Fax 01 874 55 10 – 14rm ⌂ ♪ TV CC Charming Georgian building near Mountjoy Square, in a quiet street shared with a number of other B&Bs. Most of the rooms, especially those on the ground and first floors, ooze elegance. All bathrooms have bathtubs. Excellent breakfast served in a lovely dining room.

Stella Maris Guest House, 13 Upper Gardiner Street, ☎ 01 874 08 35 / 874 08 39 – 8rm ⌂ ♪ TV Next door to the above and not quite up to the same standard in terms of comfort and décor. But the two first floor rooms have a certain charm, though most rooms lack their own facilities.

Parkway Guesthouse, 5 Gardiner Place, ☎ 01 874 04 69 – 14rm ⌂ This old-fashioned establishment will be appreciated by visitors who have an eye for faded charms. Variable level of comfort in the different rooms, though all clean and well kept. Some have facilities on the landing. A useful place to know when everywhere else is full.

Between €100-130

The Castle Hotel, Great Denmark Street, ☎ 01 874 69 49 / 874 35 31, Fax 01 872 76 74 – 45rm ⌂ ♬ TV CC This well-worn establishment – three Georgian houses run together – has a certain charm, and is only a short distance from the Gate Theatre and O'Connell Street. The public areas could do with a spot of attention, but the rooms are quiet, clean and attractive.

Walton's Hotel, 2-5 North Frederick Street, ☎ 01 878 31 31, Fax 01 878 30 90 – 50rm ⌂ ♬ TV ✕ CC Comfortable hotel in a recently renovated Georgian building. The pleasantly furnished rooms are quiet, spacious and bright. The restaurant is nothing out of the ordinary.

St George Hotel, 7 Parnell Square, ☎ 01 874 56 11, Fax 01 874 55 82 – 46rm ⌂ ♬ TV CC Opposite the Gate Theatre this mildly prestigious establishment has elegantly decorated rooms at reasonable rates for its category.

More than €130

Cassidy's Hotel, Cavendish Row, Upper O'Connell Street, ☎ 01 878 05 55, Fax 01 878 06 87 – 74rm ⌂ ♬ TV ✕ CC Next door to the above. Patrician establishment with splendid Victorian public rooms. Comfortable, quiet bedrooms with classical furnishings.

• **Smithfield Village** (Plan II B2)
More than €130

Chief O'Neill's Hotel, Smithfield Village, Dublin 7, ☎ 01 817 38 38, Fax 01 817 38 39, reservations@chiefoneills.com – 73rm ⌂ ♬ TV CC Built on the site of the old Jameson's Distillery (*see page 125*), this stylish modern hotel bears the name of the Irish adventurer who became Chicago's police

chief while at the same time assiduously collecting the tunes of old Irish ballads. Minimalist décor in the bedrooms. Bar and restaurant. Breakfast not included in room price.

• **Heuston Station area** (Plan I B2)
Under €13

⌂ **The Brewery Hostel**, 22-23 Thomas Street, Dublin 8, ☎ 01 453 86 00, Fax 01 453 86 16, breweryh@indigo.ie – 60 beds CC Next door to the Guinness brewery and a few steps from Heuston Station, this is a fine building which has been furnished with comfort in mind. As well as dormitories there are double and triple rooms. Very clean, good range of facilities, attractive rear courtyard for barbecues, guarded car park. One of the best establishments of its kind in Dublin.

Between €50-65

The Kingsbridge B&B, 14 Parkgate Street, Dublin 7, ☎ 01 671 05 41 / 677 32 63, Fax 01 821 24 18 – 7rm TV CC On the banks of the Liffey, this neat and well-kept small B&B is looked after by an elderly lady. Plain and not particularly quiet rooms, some with facilities on the landing. Own car park. Perfectly fine if nothing else is available.

Between €55-75

The Park Lodge Hotel, 7 North Circular Road, Dublin 7, ☎ 01 838 56 55 / 838 64 28, Fax 838 09 31 – 21rm ⌂ ♬ TV CC Right by the entrance to Phoenix Park, indubitably one of the least expensive establishments in its category. Nothing special to look at, but the rooms are well kept, quiet and spacious, and all have their own facilities including bathtub. Light meals available. Secure parking. Strict breakfast times: none served after 9.30am!

Between €75-100

Sadler's Inn, 15-16 Parkgate Street, Dublin 8, ☎ 01 671 07 77, Fax 01 671 08 12 – 13rm ⌂ TV CC With its green and yellow painted façade visible from afar, this inn is located in a busy part of town, on the banks of the Liffey opposite Heuston Station. Much favoured by celebrating football teams who seem to appreciate the strange Gothic décor of the pub on the ground floor. Despite all this, the rooms – same colours as the outside of the building – are reasonably quiet. Evening meal available until 10pm.

• **Phibsborough** (Plan I C1-2)
15min by bus from the airport and 20min walk from O'Connell Street, this is a lively part of the city, barely visited by tourists, and still living its own life.

Between €50-65
Mount Carmel B&B, 389 North Circular Road, ☎ 01 830 18 57 – 6rm [TV] Small and simple B&B, clean and good value for money. Hand-basin in the bedrooms, showers and WC on the landing. Mrs Cartland, the landlady, enjoys having guests and is a mine of information about the city. Good and copious breakfast.

St Peter's B&B, 312 North Circular Road, ☎ 01 830 07 23 – 5rm. Very well looked-after B&B which is excellent value because of its quiet situation, warm welcome and excellent breakfast. No private facilities. Guests may use the garden. Parking spaces in front of the house.

Between €75-115
Charleville Lodge, 268-272 North Circular Road, ☎ 01 838 66 33, Fax 01 838 58 54 – 30rm [📶] [�] [TV] [CC] Big red-brick Victorian mansion with attractive and comfortable accommodation. Good range of facilities, generous a-la-carte breakfast and large car park. Good value for Dublin.

• **Drumcondra** (Plan I D1)
This residential area in north Dublin has a range of B&B establishments, most on Drumcondra Road, which is noisy but convenient for the airport (buses 41, 41A, 41B and 41C) and the city centre (buses 3, 11, 13A, 16 and 16A).

Between €40-50
College House, 50 Upper Drumcondra Road, ☎ 01 836 70 70 – 3rm Small B&B with no particular charm apart from its price.

Errigal Guest Accommodation, 36 Upper Drumcondra Road, ☎ 01 837 66 15 / 836 74 95, Fax 01 837 66 15 – 11rm [📶] [TV] [CC]

Easily the best value in this area. All the rooms are comfortable and have their own facilities. Copious a-la-carte breakfast. Own car park.

Willow House, 130 Upper Drumcondra Road, ☎ 01 837 57 33 – 6rm [📶] [TV] [CC] Pleasant red-brick B&B with tasteful décor. Most rooms have their own facilities. Advance booking advisable.

Baldara House, 126 Upper Drumcondra Road, ☎ 01 836 86 68 – 5rm [📶] [TV] Very reasonable accommodation for the price. All bedrooms decorated in shades of green and blue. Private parking.

Breffni House, 45 Upper Drumcondra Road, ☎ 01 836 07 14 – 7rm [📶] [TV] Christine and Jim have rooms which are unpretentiously decorated but are quiet and have their own shower and WC. Pleasant Victorian-style dining room.

Between €75-130
The Doyle Skylon Hotel, 29 Upper Drumcondra Road, ☎ 01 837 91 21, Fax 01 837 27 78 – 88rm [📶] [✎] [TV] [✕] [CC] One of a chain of hotels of a fairly high standard. Room décor is Victorian in inspiration and quite attractive. All have private facilities with bathtub. Rates vary according to time of year and day of the week. Restaurant open until 10.30pm. Secure car park.

• **Clontarf** (Plan I F1)
Close to the sea and the mouth of the Liffey, this outer suburban residential area has little of interest for the visitor apart from its numerous B&B establishments. Clontarf Road with its heavy traffic is best avoided.

Between €50-65
Aishling House B&B, 19-20 St Lawrence Road, ☎ 01 833 90 97, Fax 01 833 84 00 – 10rm [📶] [✎] [TV] [CC] Just off Clontarf Road in a quiet area, a charming B&B in Victorian style, exceptionally well kept.

Tara B&B, 21 St Lawrence Road, ☎ 01 853 02 73, Fax 01 853 02 29 – 5rm [TV] [CC] Next door to the above but marginally less attractive.

Lawrence Lodge B&B, 26 St Lawrence Road, ☎ 01 833 25 25 – 5rm [📶] [✎] [TV] [CC] Brick-built residence of around 1900 with recently tastefully renovated interior.

Barry B&B, 98 Clontarf Road, ☎ 01 833 39 50 – 4rm [TV] [CC] Well looked after B&B with views over Dublin Bay, or to be precise, over warehouses and an oil refinery. Showers and WC on the landing, though one 4-bed room has its own facilities.

Ferryview House B&B, 96 Clontarf Road, ☎ 01 833 58 93, Fax 01 853 21 41 – 7rm [🍴] [TV] [CC] Next door to the above and with the same outlook. Family room on the ground floor.

More than €130

Clontarf Castle, Castle Avenue, ☎ 01 833 23 21, Fax 01 833 04 18 – 111rm [🍴] [♿] [TV] [✕] [CC] Recent hotel in striking style on the site of a 13C castle rebuilt around 1830. Flashy mock-medieval décor. Spacious, quiet, and extremely comfortable rooms. Choice of bars and restaurants with reasonable food at reasonable prices.

EATING OUT

See also "Eating out late".

Dublin has an abundance of restaurants, fast-food outlets, pubs and chip shops. All the museums have cafeterias where a decent meal costs between €6.50 and €10, but the best value at lunchtime are the various carveries (*See page 92*). Choice is more limited in the evening; few pubs serve an evening meal and it can be difficult to find a table in a restaurant without reserving beforehand.

• Temple Bar area (Plan II)

Under €13

The Bad Ass Café, Crown Alley (D3), ☎ 01 671 25 96. Open 9pm to the early hours, this old warehouse is a must-see Temple Bar institution. Usually bursting at the seams and amazingly noisy, it is a good place to get an idea of what today's Dublin is all about. The menu features pizza, pasta, grills, and Tex-Mex dishes. Orders wing their way to the kitchen by means of an ingenious system of wires and pulleys.

Irish Film Centre, 6 Eustace Street (D3), ☎ 01 677 87 88. Daily 10.30am-9.30pm. In the heart of Temple Bar, this is a pleasant place to eat, well away from the tourist hordes. It's a pub-restaurant, housed in the offices of the Irish documentary film centre. Varied cuisine and good value for money.

The Winding Stair Bookshop & Café, 40 Lower Ormond Quay (D2), ☎ 01 873 32 92. Monday-Saturday 10am-6pm; Sunday 1pm-6pm. An unusual establishment on the quayside opposite Temple Bar, a few steps from Ha'Penny Bridge. It's a secondhand bookshop with a pair of cafés, one on the first, the other on the second floor. Uncomplicated food served among the bookshelves with a view over the Liffey.

Mongolian Barbecue, 7 Anglesea Road (D3), ☎ 01 670 41 54. Weekdays 12pm-3pm / 5pm-10.30pm; weekends 6pm-11.30pm. In the middle of Temple Bar, this place gets its clientele to choose the ingredients for their meal themselves (vegetables, prawns, thinly cut slices of meat, sauces...) which are then cooked by the table on a hot-plate. The food is good, inexpensive (though dearer in the evening), and second helpings are allowed. Reservations absolutely necessary.

Gallagher's Boxty House, 20-21 Temple Bar (D3), ☎ 01 677 27 62, daily 12pm-11.30pm. This is easily the most exotic eating place in all of Temple Bar, serving as it does typically Irish food. It may even be the only establishment of its kind in the city as a whole. A victim of its own success, it is often packed out in the evening. Anyone not booking in advance is likely to have to queue before enjoying their Irish stew or their "boxty" – a meat or fish and potato pancake. Rustic décor and noisy atmosphere, though it's quieter at lunchtime.

Between €20-25

La Mezza Luna, 1 Temple Lane (D3), ☎ 01 671 28 40, daily 12pm-1pm. One of the first places to colonise Temple Bar and help it come up in the world, the Mezza Luna has acquired an enviable reputation for its "world cuisine" and its vegetarian food. Attractive setting, relaxed atmosphere, friendly service. Try tortellini with spinach or fillet of shark.

- **Grafton Street area** (Plan II)
Under €13
Bewley's Oriental Café, 78-79 Grafton Street (D3), ☎ 01 635 54 70. Daily at lunchtime and in the evening. This Art Deco café-restaurant is a real institution, originally founded in 1840 by Samuel Bewley, a Quaker tea merchant. The first Bewley's Café opened its doors in 1894 in South Great George Street, and the Grafton Street branch dates from 1927. Bob Geldof began his career here in 1977. In the 1990s the place lost some of its charm when part of it became a self-service cafeteria. But the atmosphere is still cosy, and there are tasty cakes and pastries and generous main dishes. Other branches, without the same charm, are at 40 Mary Street, ☎ 01 677 67 71 and 11-17 Westmoreland Street, ☎ 01 677 67 61.

Café Bell, Clarendon Street (D3), in the courtyard of St Theresa's Church. Monday-Saturday 9am-6pm. Staff from the church let themselves be tempted by the sin of gluttony in the quiet ambience of this establishment which has some of the attributes of a classical Viennese café, down to the miniature grand piano. No drinks licence, but excellent open sandwiches as well as cakes and inexpensive dishes of the day.

Café en Seine, 40 Dawson Street (E4), ☎ 01 677 43 69. Daily 8am-10pm, self-service at lunchtime; Thursday-Saturday 8am-2am (with DJ in attendance), Sunday brunch 12pm-4pm. Pleasant renovated gallery-like café with Art Nouveau décor. Sweet and savoury specialities, superb chandeliers, immensely long copper-topped bar.

Alpha Restaurant, 37 Wicklow Street (D3), ☎ 01 677 02 13. Monday-Saturday 9am-7pm. Snack bar on the first floor of a city centre building, quiet and very inexpensive. No drinks licence. Details of pop concerts plastered all over the stairway.

Café Rouge, 1 St Andrew Street (D3), ☎ 01 679 13 57. Daily 10am-11pm (10.30pm Sunday). This French bistro-style establishment is one of many franchised cafés of the same name.

Nevertheless, there's a friendly atmosphere and the "International-Irish" dishes served are perfectly acceptable.
Tosca, 29 Suffolk Street (D3), ☎ 01 679 67 44. Daily 12pm-3.30pm / 5.30pm-11pm. Recently-opened Italian restaurant.
More than €25
QV2, 14-15 St Andrew Street (D3), ☎ 01 677 33 63. Monday-Saturday 12pm-3pm / 6pm-12.30am. Highly recommended. A few steps away from the tourist office, this establishment is characterised by a cuisine as inventive as its décor, and is much appreciated by local yuppies. Everything is remarkably fresh, tasty and not at all expensive given the quality, from steamed mussels with citronella to Barbary duck in plum and ginger sauce and fillet of ostrich in mushroom sauce. Good wine list.

- **Around Merrion Square**
Between €20-25
Rubicon, 6 Merrion Row (Plan II E4), ☎ 01 676 59 55. Monday-Saturday 12pm-3pm / 5.30pm-10.30pm; Sunday 5pm-10pm. Almost next door to Merrion Square and O'Donoghue's famous musical pub, this restaurant offers a refined and ultimately unclassifiable cuisine, though there is a clear Italian-cum-Oriental influence. The whole world features on the wine list.
More than €25
Mangetout, 112 Lower Baggot Street (Plan I D3), ☎ 01 676 78 66. Tuesday-Saturday 12.30pm-2.15pm / 7pm-11pm, closed Saturday lunchtime, all day Sunday and Monday. In the short space of time since it opened, Mangetout has earned itself a solid reputation in the small world of Dublin gastronomes. French-inspired, but ever ready to take a liberty or two. Everything is fresh, delicious and the prices are reasonable.
L'écrivain, 109 Lower Baggot Street (Plan I D3), ☎ 01 661 19 19. Monday-Friday 12.30pm-2.30pm; Monday-Saturday: 6.30pm-11pm. Easily one of the best places to eat in Dublin. Inventive, fresh, and determinedly contemporary dishes served in a classical, comfortable setting. More

expensive later in the evening, but very reasonable prices at lunchtime and early in the evening.

Around O'Connell Street (Plan II)
Under €13

Judes, 151-152 Parnell Street (D1). One of the area's best pubs, relatively unspoiled and still with its local clientele of seasoned drinkers. Far from quiet, but worth it for the €6-8 plates of Irish stew served at lunch and until 9pm in the evening.

Frazers, at the corner of O'Connell Street and Parnell Street (D1), ☎ 01 878 75 05. Opposite the Parnell memorial, this modern restaurant offers mainstream dishes for lunch and dinner as well as generous beef or smoked salmon sandwiches with salad and chips.

Flanagans Restaurant and Pizzeria, 61 Upper O'Connell Street (D1), ☎ 01 873 13 88. Bang in the middle of O'Connell Street (almost opposite the tourist office), this restaurant is a favourite with family groups. Range of lunch and supper dishes including pizza, pasta, braised salmon, grilled plaice and steaks.

101 Talbot, 100-102 Talbot Street (E2), ☎ 01 874 50 11. Daily 5pm-11pm except Sunday and Monday. Frequented by a youngish and sometimes noisy crowd, this is a trendy establishment only open in the evening and serving Mediterranean-type food in a modern setting.

Messrs Maguire, 1-2 Burgh Quay (E2), ☎ 01 670 57 77. Daily 11am-9.30pm. Close to O'Connell Bridge, this pub pulls pints of its own beer in a décor which is a puzzling mixture of Gothic, Art Nouveau, Rococo and Oriental. There's a self-service restaurant and several dining rooms on two floors. Traditional music Sunday and Monday evenings.

Between €20-25

Restaurant Six, 6 Cavendish Row, Upper O'Connell Street (D1), ☎ 01 872 55 05. Monday-Saturday 12.30pm-2.30pm; Thursday-Saturday 6pm-10pm and Sunday-Wednesday 6pm-9.30pm. Chic establishment

favoured by the Gate Theatre crowd before and after performances. Try the mussels grilled in garlic butter or the chicken supreme with creamed leeks.

• Smithfield Village (Plan II)
Under €13

Old Jameson Distillery cafeteria, Bow Street, Smithfield Village (B2), ☎ 01 807 23 55. Daily 9.30am-5pm. Pleasant self-service cafeteria and café.

Chief O'Neill's Café & Bar, Smithfield Village (B2), ☎ 01 817 38 60. The bar-restaurant of the traditional music centre serves generous portions of traditional food in an old warehouse with modern décor. To get served, note your table number and order at the counter. Traditional music played live in the evenings and at Sunday lunchtime.

• Heuston Station area (Plan I)
Between €20-25

Nancy Hands Pub & Restaurant, 30-32 Parkgate Street (B2), ☎ 01 677 01 49. Opposite Heuston Station close to Ryan's Pub and Phoenix Park. 12pm-3pm (5pm weekends) / 6pm-10pm. Huge and cheerful pub, always busy, with a décor unable to make its mind up whether it's Irish Rustic, Victorian Drawing Room or Bavarian Beer Hall. Upper floor restaurant with a view over the Liffey. There are generously sized steaks and other classic and tasty dishes. The bar has the biggest range of whiskeys in Dublin.

WHERE TO EAT OUT LATE

Most local people like to eat before going out in the evening, and after 10pm it can be difficult to find a meal. But habits are changing, and a dozen or so places now stay open to a late hour.

• Around Trinity College (Plan II)
Under €13

Fast-food can be had all night long at the Westmoreland Street branch of **Abrakebabra** (D2) just up from the Liffey.

Kaffe Moka, 39-40 South William Street (D3). Daily 8am-4am. Very pleasant café-snack bar with modern décor and young clientele. Generous breakfasts, excellent open sandwiches, delicious cakes and pastries. No drinks licence, but thirty different kinds of coffee and chess sets laid out for customers' use. Backgammon and draughts too. Literary evenings on the second floor on Monday evenings.

Between €13-20

Good World Chinese Restaurant, 18 South Great George Street (D3), ☎ 01 677 53 73. Daily 12.30pm-3am. Decent, fairly inexpensive Chinese establishment serving copious portions.

● **Phibsborough** (Plan I)

Between €13-20

MacGowans, 16 Phibsborough Road (C1), ☎ 01 830 66 06. One of the very few places open continuously until 2am. Raucous Irish-American country-style pub with wooden tables and panelled walls. Immensely long ground floor bar and discotheque upstairs. Menu featuring cod steaks, burgers and variations on the theme of fry-up, including a massive "Potential Coronary" plateful.

HAVING A DRINK

No-one seems ever to have tried to count the number of pubs in Dublin. But then the object of love should never be the subject of rational calculation. What is certain is that it's rare to wander for more than 100 yards or so before coming across a welcome doorway leading to a friendly interior with its regulars lined up along the bar.

Even more than in the rest of the country, pubs are at the centre of social life for all classes and age groups. Many a pub has been a place of literary or artistic inspiration, and every year, the **James Joyce Pub Award** is given to establishments which have best kept up this tradition. While each pub has its regulars, patrons are becoming more and more varied. It is difficult, well-nigh impossible in fact, to stand at a bar for more than a few minutes without being engaged in conversation. Dubliners are both inquisitive and talkative, and delight in human contact. There's little hesitation in offering strangers a pint of what they fancy. One of the few unpleasant features of this appealing scene is the growing tendency, especially in the city centre, to employ bouncers, a practice which goes completely against the grain of the Irish idea of hospitality. Wedded to a kinder image of their country, some Dubliners have decided to boycott this kind of establishment.

Pub-crawling

Most visitors will have no difficulty in doing the rounds of the pubs without a guiding hand, but for those in a hurry or with a particular interest in mind there are such things as organised pub-crawls. **Jameson Literary Pub Crawl**, ☎ 01 670 56 02, Fax 01 670 56 03. Meeting-point at The Duke, a pub in Duke Street (Plan II D3), a few steps from the Powerscourt Townhouse Shopping Centre. Starting times: Easter-31 October: Monday-Saturday 7.30pm; 1 January-Easter (except 20 December-5 January): Thursday-Sunday 7.30pm. Additional tour Sunday 12pm all year. An entertaining 2hr30min walking tour with professional actors, stops at the principal pubs featuring in the city's literary heritage. €8.30, drinks extra.

Musical Pub Crawl, ☎ 01 478 01 93. Meeting point on the first floor of the Oliver St John Gogarthy pub, Temple Bar (Plan II D3). 1 May-30 October: daily 7.30pm. Musical walking tour of 2hr30min visiting five different pubs in the company of a pair of professional musicians in love with traditional music.

Traditional pubs

● **Around Trinity College**

Stag's Head, 1 Dame Court, ☎ 01 679 37 01. The passageway entrance to this famous pub from Dame Street is marked by a pavement mosaic depicting a stag's head. The pub has kept its Victorian interior with its splendid time-worn bar, above which another stag's head keeps watch. Eight draught beers, including Breo.

The Mercantile, 28 Dame Street, ☎ 01 679 05 22. Almost next door to the above establishment, this is a lively place, especially in the evening when a well-heeled youngish clientele comes here to listen to the music and hang around the late bar. It's quieter during the day, when visitors can enjoy a satisfying lunch and admire the splendid plasterwork of the ceiling.

Mulligan's, 8 Poolbeg Street, ☎ 01 677 55 82. Behind its yellow façade, this is one of the city's oldest and most famous pubs, much frequented by the gentlemen of the press. Future president John F Kennedy often used to drink here when he worked in Dublin as a journalist.

O'Neill's, Suffolk Street, ☎ 01 679 36 71. Very close to the tourist office. Huge traditional pub in a good location with patrons of all ages. Good self-service food at lunchtime.

The International Bar, 23 Wicklow Street, ☎ 01 697 92 50. Quiet little pub in the very centre of town popular with a young crowd. Above the bar is a fascinating array of sculpted busts. Actors from the Studio and International Theatre Group stage performances on the upper floor Monday-Saturday at 7pm, alternating with blues groups (tickets from the bar), and musicians get together for informal sessions Sunday lunchtime at around 12.30pm.

The Long Hall, 51 South Great George Street, ☎ 01 475 15 90. Splendid Victorian décor untouched since 1880, giving the impression that Phineas Fogg might walk in at any moment having completed his tour of the globe. Quiet and friendly atmosphere, ideal for a contemplative pint or two.

Dohenny & Nesbitt, 5 Lower Baggot Street, ☎ 01 676 29 45. Classic pub with a clientele of office workers, notably from the nearby Finance Ministry. Hence the witticism that there exists a Dohenny & Nesbitt School of Economics.

• Around the Custom House (Plan II E2)

The Madigan's, 25 North Earl Street, ☎ 01 874 54 49. Near O'Connell Street and the James Joyce Statue. Attractive Art Nouveau décor with new windows but the original glass and woodwork. A bust of Joyce keeps an eye on the proceedings.

Cleary's, 36 Amiens Street, ☎ 01 855 29 52. By the railway bridge near Connolly Station. Nothing could be more authentic than this reeking establishment with its nicotine-stained walls and ceiling and clientele to match, and nothing much seems to have changed since 1916, when Michael Collins held his meetings here.

• Phibsborough and Drumcondra (Plan I C-D1)

The Bohemian, on the corner of Phibsborough Road and the North Circular Road. The outside may not be much to look at, but inside is all Rococo plasterwork, Art Nouveau lamps and a clientele of similar vintage.

The Big Tree, North Circular Road, ☎ 01 855 78 05. With décor undecided whether it is Tudor cottage or Bavarian beer-hall, this is popular with local youth, who come here at the weekend to let off steam to the loud disco music. Open until 1am Friday evening.

The Cat and Cage, 74 / 76 Upper Drumcondra Road, ☎ 01 837 53 82. Appealing pub, a useful port of call for anyone staying in this suburban area who can't face the journey into town. Especially lively at the weekend when the clientele is mostly young. There is an upstairs restaurant serving reasonable traditional food.

• Heuston Station area (Plan I B2)

Ryan's, Parkgate Street, ☎ 01 677 60 97 / 671 93 52 (restaurant). Opposite the railway station, this splendid example of a Victorian pub with the whole panoply of glass, mirrors and woodwork is known for its carefully prepared food. Monday-Friday: lunch 12.30pm-2.30pm; dinner: Tuesday-Saturday 7pm-10.30pm.

Pubs with music

• Parnell Square area (Plan I D2, Plan II D1)

O'Hooley's, Gardiner Row, next to the Hotel Belvedere. Nothing out of the ordinary during the week, but on Saturday night the place is transformed when the clientele make their own entertainment, and everyone gets the chance to belt out their favourite ballad or country number. The quality of the performance isn't the point, it's the fun that counts for what is mostly a clientele no longer in the first flush of youth. A must for anyone wanting to extend their experience of Dublin life.

- **Christ Church Cathedral area** (Plan II C3)

Mother Redcaps, Backlane, High Street, ☎ 01 453 83 06. Friendly tavern next door to a sort of covered flea market. Pop and rock groups Friday and Saturday evenings 10pm-12.30am. Traditional music Sunday lunchtime 12.30pm-3pm.

Brazen Head, Bridge Street, ☎ 01 679 51 86. Music every evening from 9.30pm and Sunday from 12.30pm-2.30pm. Get here at least an hour beforehand for a seat or a place at the bar. One of Dublin's oldest pubs likes to present itself as something of a hang-out for brigands. A real city institution, it is popular with tourists, but this doesn't take away from the quality of the music or the friendly atmosphere.

- **Temple Bar** (Plan II D3)

The Quays, 12-13 Temple Bar, ☎ 01 671 39 22. This pub might look venerable enough, but in fact it only dates from the 1990s. Its main attraction is the traditional music played every evening. Ultra-crowded at the weekend.

The Auld Dubliner, Fleet Street, ☎ 01 677 05 27. Relatively recent pub which quickly acquired a solid reputation for its traditional music played every evening Thursday-Sunday.

Turks Head Chop House, Parliament Street, ☎ 01 679 26 06. Slightly weird décor possibly derived from Gaudí and late-19C Barcelona. Sociable atmosphere. Known for its 1970s sounds. Disco from 10.30pm.

- **Around St Stephen's Green** (Plan II D-E4)

Bruxelles, 7-8 Harry Street, ☎ 01 677 53 62. Young, trendy establishment close to Grafton Street. A place to have a drink or meal and listen to rock or blues, Sunday 6pm-8pm and Monday from 11pm-1am.

O'Donoghue's, 14-15 Merrion Row, ☎ 01 660 71 94 / 676 28 07. Fairly touristy, but superb authentic traditional music every evening and all day Sunday. This is where The Dubliners started out in 1962. Often crowded, especially at the weekend.

Grattan's, 47-48 Baggot Street. Very lively at the weekend. Live rock Thursday, Friday and Saturday evenings and nightclub until 3am.

The Mean Fiddler, 26 Wexford Street, ☎ 01 475 85 55. One of Dublin's liveliest night-spots, with every kind of music on the menu. The trendy bar in the basement stays open until the early hours.

Whelans, 25 Wexford Street, ☎ 01 478 07 66. Next door to the above establishment. Emphasis on Irish music, but always with a tinge of rock or blues. No under-21s admitted. And anyone over 25 is liable to get strange looks.

Other bars (Plan II)

The Globe, 11 South George Street, ☎ 01 671 12 20. Young, fashionable place, part of the celebrated Rí-Rá disco. Décor in Ancient Rome style. Good sandwiches.

The George, 89 South George Street, ☎ 01 478 29 83. Dublin's oldest and most celebrated gay bar. Disco attached.

Out on the Liffey, 27 Upper Ormond Quay, ☎ 01 872 24 80. Another rendezvous for Dublin's gay community.

Zanzibar, Lower Ormond Quay, ☎ 01 878 72 12. Huge bar attracting a young and fashion-conscious crowd with over-the-top oriental décor which makes a nice contrast to Dublin's grey skies. Disco upstairs.

Hot Press Irish Music Hall of Fame, 57 Middle Abbey Street, ☎ 01 874 90 66, Fax 01 874 90 67. A new and very popular place to go, on the right bank of the Liffey. There is also a restaurant, **The Jam**, a bar, a hi-tech exhibition on Irish rock music and a 600-seater auditorium for concerts featuring the latest groups.

The Porter House, 16 Parliament Street, ☎ 01 679 88 47. Next to the Clarence, the hotel owned by U2. "We might be a micro-brewery, but we certainly don't serve micro-beer" according to the owner, who brews a dozen or so beers here, each one more astonishing than the last. It's the only pub in Dublin not to serve Guinness.

NIGHTCLUBS

Discotheques – As the pubs turn out, around 11.30pm, discos take over, until 2am or 3am in the morning. Night buses are there to take revellers home, leaving from College Green (Plan II D3) (See "Getting around").

Buskers, Fleet Street (Plan II D3), ☎ 01 677 33 33. Young, lively atmosphere despite the somewhat intimidating presence of bouncers at the entrance. Live music in the bar every Friday night, and **The Boomerang** discotheque in the basement.

The P.O.D. (Place of Dance), Harcourt Street (Plan II D4), ☎ 01 478 02 25. Southwest of St Stephen's Green. Mostly "hard" sounds. Extremely popular, but getting in is almost impossible especially at the weekend and even more so if would-be clubbers fail to reach certain sartorial standards.

Rí-Rá, 37 Drury Street (Plan II D3), ☎ 01 677 04 85. Daily 11pm-2am. Dublin's most celebrated discotheque, on two levels. Very young, very noisy, very trendy, and not cheap either.

Break for the Border, Johnson's Place (Plan II D4) (200m from St Stephen's Green), ☎ 01 478 03 00. Vast establishment, but relaxed atmosphere. Drink at the bar or enjoy a meal in the restaurant.

The Kitchen, 6 / 8 Wellington Quay (Plan II C3), in the basement of U2's Clarence Hotel, ☎ 01 662 30 66. Famous for its very original décor and its mildly snobbish ambience, it's worth a visit (though getting in is far from guaranteed). Expensive.

Eamon Doran's, 3 Crown Alley (Plan II D3), ☎ 01 679 97 73. This place has a good reputation for the groups who perform here regularly. Certainly one of the best night-spots in the Temple Bar area. Meals available too.

OTHER THINGS TO DO

There's always something going on in this bubbling city. The tourist office publishes a **Calendar of Events** detailing nearly all cultural, musical, artistic and sporting events. Also available is **In Dublin**, a monthly with day-by-day details of all kinds of activities and performances, in particular concerts and shows.

Cinemas – Cinemas are not Dublin's strong point. They are relatively few and far between and the films shown tend to be limited to the latest American blockbusters. The **Irish Film Centre**, Eustace Street (Plan II D3), Temple Bar, ☎ 01 639 34 77, has a permanent programme of Irish films and classics and has seasons devoted to particular cinematic themes.

The main cinemas are on O'Connell Street, notably the **Savoy**, ☎ 01 874 60 00, and **Virgin**, ☎ 01 872 84 00.

Theatres – As in London, theatre here occupies an important place in cultural life, not least because the history of modern Irish drama is intimately linked to the history of the country itself.

This is particularly true of the **Abbey Theatre**, 26 Lower Abbey Street (Plan II E2), ☎ 01 878 72 22. Ticket office open Monday-Saturday 10.30am-7pm. The building may be less than impressive, but it is one of the great symbols of Irish culture. All the great Irish dramatists are staged here regularly, from Shaw and Synge to Yeats and O'Casey, as well as their less well-known colleagues. The **Peacock Theatre**, a sort of annexe to the Abbey, concentrates on more recent work.

Gate Theatre, 1 Cavendish Row (Plan II D1), ☎ 01 874 14 45. Ticket office open Monday-Saturday 10.30am-7pm. Another city institution, founded in the 1920s, the Gate also stages plays by foreign dramatists.

Olympia Theatre, 72 Dame Street (Plan II C3), ☎ 01 677 77 44. Ticket office open Monday-Saturday 10am-6.30pm. Dublin's solitary Victorian theatre to have survived fire and destruction has a varied programme including all kinds of concerts as well as musicals.

Sport and recreation – Ireland's national sport is of course **hurling** (the women's version is called "camogie"). Somewhat akin to hockey and also played on grass, it is extremely fast and sometimes violent. It is played all year round but the most important matches take place in July and August and are watched with passion in the pubs. The All-Ireland Final is played in September at Croke Park, Dublin 3 (in the north-east part of the city). Buses 3, 11, 11A, 16, 16A and 123 from O'Connell Street.

Gaelic football is popular too. The principal matches are also played at Croke Park in September. There is a good introduction to these sports at the **Gaelic Athletics Association (GAA) Museum** in Croke Park. May-September: daily 9.30am-5pm; rest of year: Tuesday-Saturday 10am-5pm; Sunday 2pm-5pm.

Greyhound racing – Events take place at **Shelbourne Park**, Dublin 4 (Plan I E3), ☎ 01 850 64 65 66 / 668 35 02. Monday, Wednesday, Thursday and Saturday 8pm-10pm. Also at **Harold's Cross**, Dublin 6, ☎ 01 497 10 81. Tuesday, Thursday and Friday 8pm-10pm.

SHOPPING

Music – Traditional instruments like flutes and tambourines are popular souvenirs, a bulky harp less so. Anyone really interested in developing their own traditional music talents might take home some printed music, perhaps with an accompanying cassette, all available from specialist shops.

Walton's Music, 2-5 North Frederick Street (Plan II D1), close to Parnell Square, ☎ 01 874 78 05. Monday-Saturday 9am-5.30pm. Good stock and staff can provide helpful advice. Another branch at 69-70 South Great George Street (Plan II D3) opposite Market Arcades, ☎ 01 475 06 61.

Celtic Note, Nassau Street (Plan II E3). Traditional music specialists, with a huge choice of CDs and cassettes.

Clothing – Tweeds, oilskins, and woollens from Aran are very popular with tourists from abroad, but are difficult to buy except from specialist shops.

Kevin & Howlin, 31 Nassau Street (Plan II E3), ☎ 01 677 02 57. This shop is a temple to tweed. Tweed is here in all its forms: suits, waistcoats, jackets, caps. It

might be expensive, but that's the price paid for a material which is never out of fashion and is virtually everlasting. Vast choice of material sold by the length to have made up later.

Clery's, 18-27 Lower O'Connell Street (Plan II D2). 9am-5.30pm (8pm Thursday); closed Sunday. Large and popular establishment with a basement full of tweed caps, pullovers, and reproduction traditional jewellery.

Market Arcades (Plan II D3), entrance through a red-brick porch off South Great George Street. Twenty or so stalls, some selling cut-price clothes. There are good bargains to be had, for example with tweed jackets. **Harlequin**, 13 Castle Market, on the right on leaving the market towards South William Street, has the best selection, ☎ 01 671 02 02. Monday-Saturday 10.30am-6pm.

Blarney Woollen Mills, Nassau Street (Plan II E3) has a good range of woollens, including classic Aran sweaters and other more imaginative items. Other clothing too plus a choice of souvenirs.

Arts and crafts – Sad to say, there is little in the way of traditional crafts for sale, most items offered under this heading being standardised and mass-produced. The best buys are Waterford crystal and fine copies of traditional jewellery.

House of Ireland, Nassau and Dawson Street (Plan II E3). Large establishment with the complete range of traditional Irish items. Mostly quite expensive.

Kilkeeny, Nassau Street (Plan II E3), near the above establishment with a very similar selection. Cafeteria.

Antiques and flea markets – **Francis Street** (Plan II B3-B4) has the most antique and junk shops. Buyers should be aware that Dublin prices are highly inflated, not least because of the strong demand from Irish-American buyers for mementoes of the old country. The demand is sometimes met by systematic buying in of stock from abroad.

Mother's Redcaps, next to the similarly named pub (see "Pubs with music"). Friday, Saturday and Sunday 10am-5.30pm. Bric-a-brac piled high, and who knows what might lurk amongst it? Old clothes, bargain records, Aran sweaters, pots and pans, odds and ends of every conceivable kind.

Smoked salmon – Vacuum-packed smoked salmon is sold in most supermarkets. Fishmongers and other specialists are few and far between, but the firms given below should be able to provide a good quality product

Kish Fish, 40-42 Bow Street (Plan II B2), ☎ 01 872 82 11. Wednesday, Thursday and Friday 9am-4.30pm. Tiny fishmongers 100m on the left from the Old Jameson Distillery. Whole smoked salmon as well as the sliced variety from a producer in Galway. About €7 per pound.

Hanlon, 20-21 Moore Street (Plan I D1), ☎ 01 873 30 11. One of the limited number of real fishmongers in Dublin

with their own smoked salmon. Wild salmon from €10.50 per pound.

Magill's, 14 Clarendon Street (Plan II D3), ☎ 01 671 38 20. Monday-Saturday 9.15am-5.45pm. Near Powerscourt Shopping Centre, a delicatessen with wild smoked salmon at a reasonable price.

Whiskey – Most off-licences stock the full range of Irish whiskeys, as does the shop at the **Old Jameson Distillery** (see page 125).

Mitchell & Son, 21 Kildare Street (Plan II E4), ☎ 01 676 07 66, is a venerable institution selling "Green Spot", a whiskey matured in sherry casks for 8 years and bottled by Jamesons. They also have an incredible range of wines from around the world.

Making the most of the Howth peninsula

COMING AND GOING

By train – Howth is the northern terminus of the **DART**.

By bus – Bus 31 runs from Lower Abbey Street in the city centre to Howth Harbour and bus 31B climbs to the summit of the peninsula.

WHERE TO STAY

Between €40-65

Inisradharc B&B, Balkill Road, ☎ 01 832 23 06 – 3rm 🍴 TV CC 1.5km from the harbour, up the road to the right from Howth Church. Modern, nicely decorated house with lovely sea views.

Highfield B&B, Thromanby Road, ☎ 01 832 39 36 – 3rm 🍴 TV CC Little house just out of the town embedded in greenery. Attractively furnished rooms.

Glenn Na Smól B&B, Nashville Road, ☎ 01 832 29 36 – 4rm 🍴 TV CC Comfortable well-furnished B&B just outside the town. Generous breakfast with home-baked rolls.

EATING OUT

There are plenty of Indian, Tex-Mex and Italian restaurants around the harbour, plus fish and chips and various fast food outlets. Less choice in the evening.

Under €13

De Gee's Coffee Shop, ☎ 01 989 26 41. Directly opposite the DART station, snack bar and café with generous helpings of fish and chips and burgers served all day. Good choice of cakes and pastries and decent coffee.

🦪 **Ye Old Abbey Tavern**, Abbey Street, near the ruins of St Mary's Abbey, ☎ 01 839 03 07. Daily 11am-2.30pm / 6pm-10pm. A welcoming inn, one of the two dozen or so claiming to be the "oldest pub in Ireland". The claim here is substantiated by some of the wall being part of the 15C abbey. Good platefuls of seafood and smoked salmon at lunchtime. In the evening, the **Abbot** restaurant upstairs serves a rather more refined cuisine at higher prices in a very chic setting. Reservations essential for dinner in summer.

Between €25-40

King Sitric, Harbour Road, East Pier, ☎ 01 832 52 35, Fax 01 839 24 42. Closed Sunday and two weeks in January. Only open for lunch in summer. Chic harbourside restaurant with maritime décor serving excellent seafood prepared in an international style. Good wine list.

HAVING A DRINK

Cock Tavern, opposite the Big Blue restaurant (above St Mary's Abbey). Traditional music every Thursday and Saturday evening, and Sunday morning. **Ye Old Abbey Tavern** (see "Eating Out"). Name bands play traditional music every evening at 9pm except Monday. It gets extremely crowded and those in the know take their places an hour beforehand. Admission charge. **Stream**, underneath the DART station. Traditional music and the occasional rock band Monday evening.

SHOPPING

Smoked salmon – Two shops in the harbour area (to the left on leaving the DART station) sell vacuum-packed smoked salmon and other kinds of seafood.

Wrights of Howth, daily until 6pm and to 9pm Wednesday and Thursday. Wild and farmed salmon, kippers and smoked trout. Their products can also be purchased at Dublin airport.

Beshoffs of Howth charge more, but the smoked salmon is their own.

Making the most of Dún Laoghaire

COMING AND GOING

By train – There are DART stations at Dún Laoghaire, Sandycove and Dalkey.

By bus – From Dublin, buses 7, 7A, 8 and 46A. Bus 8 goes to Burgh Quay, near O'Connell Bridge.

By boat – See "Making the most of Dublin".

ADDRESS BOOK

Tourist information – **Dublin Tourist Information Centre** in the ferry terminal. Monday-Friday 9am-5pm.

Banks / Currency exchange – The bureau de change in the ferry terminal opens to coincide with arrivals and departures. Cash machines in George Street in the town centre.

Post office / Telephone – George Street Upper (9am-6pm; Tuesday 9.30am-6pm; Saturday 9am-5.30pm).

WHERE TO STAY

Under €13

The Old Schoolhouse Hostel, Eblana Avenue, ☎ 01 280 87 70, Fax 01 284 22 66 – 170 beds and 18 rooms. From the DART station, go up Royal Marine Road and turn right. 4-6 bed dormitories with shared showers. A well-kept hostel in an old school building. Cooking facilities. Car park. Break-fast not included but available in adjacent cafeteria.

Between €40-50

Marleen B&B, 9 Royal Marine Road, ☎ 01 280 24 56 – 6rm TV Good location close to the harbour and DART station. Reasonable rooms for this price, some with own facilities.

Rathoe B&B, 12 Rosmeen Gardens, ☎ 01 280 80 70 – 3rm ⌅ TV One of the best B&Bs in the area, with bright and impeccably kept rooms of great charm. Friendly reception.

Sea View House B&B, 2 Granite Hall, Rosmeen Gardens, ☎ 01 280 91 05 – 3rm ⌅ TV Small, charming B&B in a quiet area.

Bayside B&B, Seafront, 5 Haddington Terrace, ☎ 01 280 46 60, Fax 01 230 15 54 – 14rm Bright and well-kept rooms, some with sea views, but no private facilities.

Hotel Pierre, 3 Victoria Terrace, ☎ 01 280 02 91, Fax 01 284 33 32 – 30rm ⌅ TV CC Pleasant hotel with old-fashioned charm, seafront location. Comfortable rooms with sea views and antique furniture.

Moytura House B&B, Saval Park Road, Dalkey, ☎ 01 285 23 71, Fax 01 235 06 33 – 3rm ⌅ TV Open 1 April-31 October. Charming late-19C residence set amid parks and gardens with sea views. Tastefully decorated rooms.

EATING OUT

For those in a hurry there are plenty of fast-food outlets on George Street in the town centre.

The Purty Kitchen, 2 / 3 Old Dunleary Road, Monkstown, ☎ 01 284 35 76. Daily 10am-11pm. Traditional pub with cosy dining room. Seafood includes mussels, salmon, lobster, and paella. Pleasant atmosphere; traditional music Wednesday evening and jazz in the upstairs club.

Brasserie Na Mara, Dún Laoghaire Harbour, ☎ 01 280 67 67. Monday-Friday 12.30pm-2.30pm / 6.30pm-10pm. Pleasant location opposite the harbour in the converted buffet of the railway station. Refined seafood dishes in a sober, modern setting.

The Queens, Castle Street, Dalkey, ☎ 01 285 45 69. One of the liveliest places in the area, with good pub food in the daytime (12pm-5pm) and classical restaurant menu in the evening (6pm-11.30pm) featuring fish dishes and grilles.

Upstairs, the **Vico** restaurant is only open in the evening, serving more elaborate dishes with a Mediterranean touch in an elegant setting with a piano bar. Considerably more expensive than downstairs.

HAVING A DRINK

Culturlann na hÉireann, Belgrave Square, Monkstown, ☎ 01 280 02 95. Music Monday-Thursday from 9pm, dancing Friday and Saturday. Admission charge. Not to be missed is this cultural centre which is also a pub and dance hall. Particularly lively atmosphere in the ballroom on Friday evening, notwithstanding the advanced age of some of the participants in the set dancing.

The Café en Seine, Dublin

G Bludzin/MICHELIN

BOYNE VALLEY★
Co Louth and Co Meath – 40km from Drogheda to Trim
Allow a day and a half to include a visit to Brú na Bóinne
See map page 154 and Michelin map 923 L-M / 6-7

Not to be missed
The prehistoric site at Newgrange.
The High Crosses at Monasterboice at sunset.
Traditional dance evening at Rathcairn.

And remember...
A car is essential for visiting the monastic sites.
Avoid the crowds by visiting Brú na Bóinne early in the day.

For 60km or so the winding course of the River Boyne between Drogheda and Trim is marked by an extraordinary array of ancient and historic sites. Around 5 000 years ago, at a time when the pyramids of Ancient Egypt were being built, another advanced civilisation chose this part of Ireland to build a series of monumental tombs whose exact significance remains a mystery. This Neolithic "Valley of the Kings" is also fixed forever in Ireland's collective memory as the place in 1690 of William of Orange's victory over the Catholic army of James II, an event of European as well as local significance (*see page 19*). Rich in remains of an often turbulent past, the area nowadays presents a peaceful image of traditional Irish countryside.

Drogheda
50km north of Dublin – Pop 25 000

Straddling the estuary of the Boyne a short distance from its mouth, this harbour town in County Louth has kept a few reminders of its Viking and Norman past. Nowadays a busy commercial and shopping centre, it was one of the most important towns of medieval Ireland. In 1649, after a siege lasting several days, Cromwell's army broke into the town, massacring 2 000 of the inhabitants. Many of the remainder were transported to the West Indies. Drogheda revived, and went on to prosper in the 18C and 19C. A stopping place on the route between Dublin and Belfast, it is a useful centre for exploring the Boyne Valley.

Bring me the head of Oliver Plunkett
Archbishop of Armagh, Roman Catholic Primate of Ireland, a reformer and pioneer of popular education, Oliver Plunkett was a member of an Anglo-Irish family from Co Meath. During the anti-Catholic hysteria at the time of the "Popish Plot" of 1679, he was arrested and falsely accused of treason. Tried and found guilty, despite the obvious unreliability of those who testified against him, he was hung, drawn and quartered in 1681. After extraordinary journeyings around Europe, his mummified head was eventually brought back to Drogheda in the 18C, where it is exhibited in St Peter's Church. Oliver Plunkett was canonised in 1975. More recently, speculation grew about whether the head was really his. A DNA test using one of his remote descendants proved that indeed it was.

A walk around the town
Allow 2hr
A town landmark and good point at which to begin a walk around Drogheda is the **Tholsel** at the corner of Shop Street and West Street. This 18C limestone building with its clock-tower was the meeting-place of the town council until the end of the 19C.
Nearby, in West Street is **St Peter's Church** (Roman Catholic), where the memory of Oliver Plunkett is honoured.
Just beyond the town centre, Drogheda's other **St Peter's Church** (Anglican) was built in the mid-18C on the site of a 13C place of worship. In 1649, at the

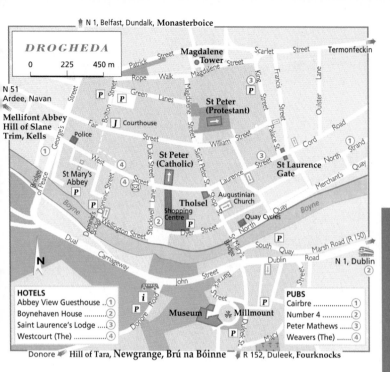

time of the siege, many of the town's inhabitants who had sought refuge inside the church were burnt to death when its wooden steeple was set alight. The building is normally closed except for services, but the graveyard is open, and along its inside wall (to the left of the entrance) are two fascinating **cadaver tombstones★** dating from 1561. The motifs on the shrouds bear an uncanny resemblance to the carving on some of the region's Neolithic monuments.

Not far from the church, on the site of the old fortifications, stands the battlemented **Magdelene Tower**, built as the bell-tower of a 14C priory.

Back at the Tholsel, it is a 500m walk to **St Laurence Gate★**, a three-storey barbican unique in Ireland, part of a fortified gateway erected in the 13C by the Normans using stone taken from the walls the Vikings had built.

Just outside the town on the right bank of the Boyne is **Millmount★**, a pre-Celtic tumulus which became in turn the site of a lookout tower, a Norman motte and then a castle. From its summit there is a panoramic view over the town. To the east, the railway viaduct was the longest of its kind in Europe at the time of its construction in 1855. The Martello tower here and the adjoining buildings house a restaurant, craft studios, and the **Millmount Museum** (*10am-5.30pm; Sunday 2.30pm-5.30pm. Admission charge*). This relatively small local museum has many fascinating exhibits, including guild banners, mementoes from the struggle for independence, and a reconstructed traditional kitchen. There is also an example of a coracle, a circular craft made from leather on a framework of branches. Coracles were used on lakes and rivers in this area from Neolithic times right up to the mid-20C.

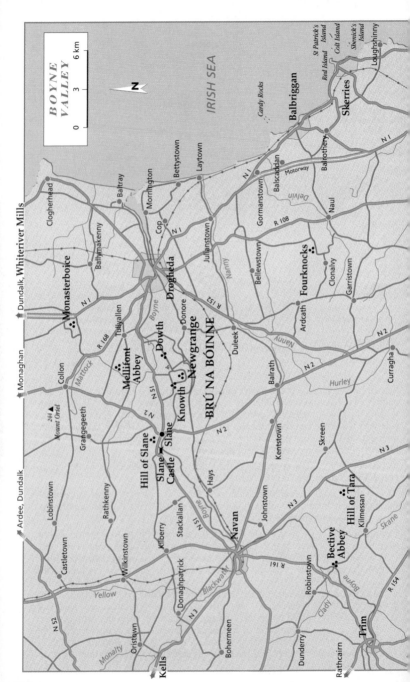

BOYE VALLEY

0 3 6 km

N

IRISH SEA

The prehistoric burial sites of Brú na Bóinne★★★

12km west of Drogheda towards Donore. The different sites can only be reached by shuttle bus from the Visitor Centre. Departures every 30min. March-April and October: 9.30am-5.30pm; May and mid-September to end September: 9am-6.30pm; June-mid-September: 9am-7pm; November-February: 9.30am-5pm. Bear in mind that there is no access to Dowth and that Knowth is closed 1 November-30 April. Admission charge. Compulsory guided tour. Allow half a day.

The term Brú na Bóinne ("Palace of the Boyne") covers that part of the Boyne valley between Drogheda and Slane. It was here, where the river winds in a series of meanders, that Neolithic people raised a number of spectacular **megalithic tombs** some 5 000 years ago. More than forty burial places have been counted, only three of which have been the subject of systematic excavation. The remainder are still buried beneath a thick layer of earth, forming a number of tumuli of variable size. The area is littered with other remains: stone circles, standing stones, medieval churches, all evidence of the cultures which have succeeded one another in Ireland over a period of almost 6 000 years.

The well-laid out **Visitor Centre** gives an overview of the Newgrange civilisation, which had much in common with people living at the same time in Brittany, southern Spain and around the mouth of the River Tagus in Portugal. The funeral rites of Neolithic times are explained and there is a reconstruction of a **thatched hut**, complete with background noises of birdsong and insects buzzing.

Newgrange★★

Western Europe's most spectacular **chambered tomb** was built around 5 000 years ago by people as yet ignorant of iron or the wheel. The tomb is a passage grave, covered by a **cairn** of stones about 100m in diameter, surrounded by a circle of **standing stones** and a facing of round granite boulders.

Excavated between 1962-75 and then restored, Newgrange has been adapted to give visitors access to the interior. The significance of the spiral motifs carved into the stone at the entrance remains unclear, but they may well represent some sort of "map" of the site. Above the opening, an ingenious system allowed the rays of the sun to illuminate the **burial chamber** on 21 December, the day of the winter solstice. The most gripping moment during a visit is the re-creation of this effect by means of an artificial ray of light which is shone 19m along the passageway into the main chamber. Here, the vault is 6m high, and above it are some 200 tonnes of earth, but there's no cause for alarm; the builders of Newgrange built to last, and their stonework hasn't moved from where it was set 5 000 years ago. The main chamber and its three recesses form a cross, an effect which did not go unnoticed by early Christian visitors to the site. In the recesses are stones carved in the form of basins; these contained offerings and the remains of cremated corpses, but little evidence has been found by archaeologists, the site probably having been pillaged on more than one occasion.

A work of titans

Like the Pyramids, the Newgrange tomb must have involved the deployment of huge resources of human labour over a considerable period of time. The material used was granite, blocks of which were partly faced with white quartz. As the nearest quartz outcrop is in the Wicklow Mountains, it is assumed that it was brought here by boat. Some of the blocks of granite weigh 4.5 tonnes and came from a quarry some 4km from the site. It has been estimated that it would have taken 80 labourers 45 days to shift a single block to its new location, using ropes and tree trunks.

Knowth★ and Dowth

To the west, the Knowth passage grave (interior not open to the public) is considerably larger than Newgrange, and is surrounded by

18 satellite tombs. From the Bronze Age to the beginning of the Christian era it was both a burial place and a residence. In Norman times a stone structure was built on top of the mound.

To the east of the Visitor Centre is **Dowth**, certainly the oldest of the Brú na Bóinne tombs, but the site is still being excavated and is not open to the public.

Further prehistoric sites

Hill of Tara

18km south of Navan via the N3. Audio-visual introduction to the site in the old church now used as a visitor centre. May-mid-June: 10am-5pm; mid-June-mid-September: 9.30am-6.30pm; mid-September-end October: 10am-5pm. Free admission. Heritage Site.

Apart from the panoramic **view**, over "the whispering and illimitable grasslands of Meath" (Benedict Kiely), the main feature of the hill seems to be the sheep grazing peacefully among the ancient earthworks. Until the 11C, the last of Ireland's High Kings ruled from this legendary height over a realm constantly expanding and contracting. The place took on an enhanced significance in the 19C as a growing Irish national identity began to be traced back to its Celtic roots. The famous Tara Brooch (*see page 116*), a triumph of Celtic craftsmanship, was discovered here.

Fourknocks

18km south of Drogheda via the R108. Turn right after 16km and ask for the key at the last house on the right before the stile.

Beneath its mound, this 3 000 to 4 000-year-old passage grave is accessible to the public and has a more intimate atmosphere than Newgrange. There are stones carved with interlacing patterns like those at Newgrange. Some sixty burials have been found in the main chamber and the lateral recesses.

Medieval sites

Monasterboice*

Signposted on the left, 13km north of Drogheda via the N1. Free admission. Where a 6C monastery once stood, a half-ruined round tower dominates a romantic old cemetery, a scene even more atmospheric when flocks of crows wheel cawing above it at twilight. Among the tombs stand three High Crosses, among the finest in the country. They are carved with scenes from both the Old and New Testament, possibly intended as a means of instruction for the monastery's novices. The carvings on the tallest of the crosses (7m) have been largely obliterated. The most richly decorated cross, to the right of the entrance, is 5.5m tall (*explanatory panel on the ground*).

Mellifont Abbey

8km northwest of Drogheda via the N51 and the R168 through Tullyallen. May-mid-June: 10am-5pm; mid-June-mid-September: 9.30am-6.30pm; mid-September-end October: 10am-5pm; closed October-May. Last admission 45min before closing time. Admission charge. Heritage Site.

The name Mellifont comes from the Latin *mellis fons* ("fountain of honey"), doubtless a reference to the beauty of the surrounding landscape. Tucked away in their valley setting, these poetic ruins are the remains of Ireland's first Cistercian abbey, founded in the 12C by Saint Malachie and monks from Clairvaux in France. The abbey and its church were burnt down and pillaged on several occasions, but the community survived until the 16C. The abbey buildings were used as headquarters by William of Orange during the Battle of the Boyne. Today all that remains are the bases of the nave columns, part of the octagonal building of the lavabo where the monks performed their ablutions, and a fragment of the colonnade from the cloisters.

Hill of Slane

14km west of Drogheda via the N51. Poorly signposted. In Slane, go for 500m towards Dundalk, then turn left in Abbey View. Free admission.

This hill has great symbolic importance for Irish Christianity since it is here that St Patrick is held to have lit a fire in order to defy the heathen king of Laoghaire. There is a fine **view** over the countryside from the summit with its cemetery and the ruins of a 16C church and monastery.

Trim*

37km northwest of Dublin via the N3 and the R154. This historic little township is a most attractive place, with a massive Norman castle and many other reminders of the past, plus an impressive number of pubs, which help guarantee a lively atmosphere at weekends.

The construction of **Trim Castle**** (*closed for restoration. The courtyard is visible from the observation platform*

Monasterboice High Cross

near the entrance, opposite the Garda station), the country's largest Norman castle, was begun in the 1170s on the orders of Hugh de Lacy. It was the headquarters of King John during his time in Ireland. Trim subsequently declined in importance, and by the 15C its physical fabric was in a poor state. It found a military role again during Cromwell's campaigns, but then gradually became the imposing ruin it is today, when it formed a backdrop to scenes in the film *Braveheart*.

Other reminders of Trim's glorious past can be seen in the course of a walk along the banks of the Boyne. They include **St John's Priory**, and the **Yellow Steeple**, all that is left of St Mary's Abbey, and so called because of the way it glows in the light of the setting sun.

Amid the ruins of the Cathedral, dedicated to **St Peter and St Paul**, are the tombs of the jealous man and woman. The recumbent effigies on this well-preserved tomb represent a man and a woman in Elizabethan dress, a

St Patrick's fire

On Easter eve in the year 433, St Patrick lit a great fire on the hilltop at Slane, knowing full well that the king of Laoghaire had forbidden any naked flame to be visible from the Hill of Tara. Warned by his druids of Patrick's magic powers, the king paid him a visit and finally decided to leave him in peace. It has to be said that the saint gave some cause for concern. In the course of the meeting, he killed one of the king's guards, let loose an earthquake, and explained the Trinity by means of a clover-leaf. Impressed by these achievements, Erc, a young servant of the king, converted to Christianity and became the first bishop of Slane. These events are still commemorated every Easter by the lighting of a fire on the hilltop.

Boyne Valley

The book of Kells

sword between them; the wife is supposed to have been guilty of an affair. The tomb is believed to cure warts; sufferers rub the offending blemish with a pin which is then left between the effigies. When the pin rusts, the wart will disappear.

Bective Abbey

Go 8km northeast of Trim via the R161 and turn right. Free admission. Bective was like a daughter establishment of Mellifont (*see above*), but by the 13C was more important than its parent. It was founded in 1146 by the king of Meath, Murcath O Maelshealchlainn. Its imposing ruins stand in the middle of a field among the inevitable sheep.

Kells

16km northwest of Navan via the N3. This little town, at its liveliest on market day, owes its fame to the **Book of Kells**, on show at Trinity College in Dublin *(see page 112)*. The world-famous book was begun on Iona, then brought here by monks fleeing from the Vikings. An important religious centre since the foundation here of a monastery in the 6C by St Columba, Kells was pillaged and burnt down by the Vikings on several occasions. Despite this, there remain a number of fascinating reminders of the place's past importance.

Parts of the monastery have survived in the graveyard around **St Columba's Church** *(only open to the public in summer)*. Close to the 11C **round tower** which has lost its conical cap, stands the 9C **South Cross**★, a fine example richly carved with Biblical scenes, among them Daniel in the lions' den and the sacrifice of Abraham. More crosses, unfinished, can also be seen.

It is thought that the Book of Kells was completed in the little drystone oratory which is known as **St Columba's House** (keys from the house with the vehicle entrance in Church Lane to the right of the church). Built in the 10C or 11C, this little edifice with its gloomy interior served as a dwelling at the beginning of the 20C. A steep ladder gives access to the "loft", which was probably a monk's cell.

A priceless head
On the death of the Norman knight Hugh de Lacy in 1195, his head was sent as a relic to St Thomas's Abbey in Dublin, while the rest of his body was buried at Bective. There followed a bitter quarrel between the two abbots, each of whom insisted that the whole of Hugh was their rightful property. The value of such important relics in promoting profitable pilgrimages may have had something to do with the matter. The dispute took on such proportions that the Pope felt obliged to intervene in person. A private meeting was held, but no solution was found. The quarrel only ended with the death of the two protagonists.

Boyne Valley

COMING AND GOING

By train – 7 express trains daily (4 Sunday) from Dublin's Connolly Station to Belfast calling at Drogheda (30min). Stopping trains from Pearse Station take twice as long. 9 trains daily (1 Sunday) in the reverse direction and 3 stopping trains.

By bus – There are Bus Éireann services 26 times a day (12 Sunday) from Dublin to Drogheda (75min). For Brú na Bóinne, there are 6 return services daily (3 Sunday) from Drogheda bus station to Dronore (10min). No services between Drogheda and Trim, but 6 buses daily (2 Sunday) from Dublin.

ADDRESS BOOK

Tourist information – *Drogheda Tourist Information*, in the bus station, ☎ 041 983 70 70. Monday-Saturday 9.30am-5.30pm; Sunday 11.45am-5pm. ***Trim Tourist Office***, Mill Street, ☎ 046 371 11. All year: 10am-12.30pm / 1.30pm-5pm; closed Sunday. Town walk brochure available. Craft shop. Next door is The Power and the Glory, a multi-media show about the town's history. Admission charge.

Banks / Currency exchange – Cash machines in West Street, Drogheda.

Post office / Telephone – West Street, Drogheda, Monday-Saturday 9am-5.30pm.

Bicycle hire – *Quay Cycles*, 11 North Quay, Drogheda, ☎ 041 345 26. Monday-Saturday 9am-1pm / 2pm-6pm.

WHERE TO STAY

• Drogheda
Between €40-50
St Laurence's Lodge, King Street, ☎ 041 983 34 10 / 983 78 41 – 12rm ⬛ TV The students' rooms in this old seminary building have been somewhat superficially smartened up but they are reasonably comfortable and the reception is friendly.
Abbey View Guesthouse, Mill Lane, Trinity Street, ☎ 041 983 14 70 – 10rm ⬛ TV CC Paula Johnson's rooms on the banks of the Boyne are plain but bright

and well-kept (4 have no facilities). Thoroughgoing modernisation planned.
Between €50-65
Boynehaven House, Dublin Road, ☎ 041 983 67 00 – 4rm ⬛ TV In a park 2km in the Dublin direction on the left. Spacious, comfortable and tastefully decorated rooms. Excellent breakfast.
Between €90-100
The Westcourt Hotel, West Street, ☎ 041 983 09 65, Fax 041 983 09 70 – 27rm ⬛ 🖊 TV ✕ CC The most famous guest here was former President Mary Robinson, and the hotel can rightly boast an exemplary level of comfort and service. Good food in ***The Courtyard***, the hotel restaurant.

• Monasterboice
Between €50-65
🐾 ***Tullyesker House***, ☎ 041 983 04 30, Fax 041 983 26 24 – 5rm ⬛ 🖊 TV Turn right beyond the main crossroads. Modern house with quiet rooms decorated with taste. The McDonnels cosset their guests and feed them a gargantuan breakfast, which includes porridge with whiskey, smoked salmon, freshly pressed fruit juice and home-made bread. Highly recommended. Closed 1 December-31 January.

• Slane
Between €40-55
O'Neill's B&B, Main Street, ☎ 041 982 40 90 – 3rm ⬛ ✕ CC This small B&B has plain but clean rooms. The ground floor restaurant serves unpretentious meals at a very reasonable price.
🐾 ***Glebe House***, ☎ 041 983 61 01 – 5rm ⬛ TV CC 10km from Drogheda via the N51 towards Slane. Follow signs before coming into Slane. Elizabeth Addison is a plant enthusiast and aromatherapist who has made this 18C house into a delight. Set in a splendid rose garden, it is only a few steps from Dowth prehistoric site. Rooms are furnished in country style. Dinner on request.

• Trim
Under €13
Bridge House Tourist Hostel, next to the Tourist Office, ☎ 046 318 46 –

21 beds. Small private hostel in a good location. Dormitories and rooms with basic comforts but well-kept. Attractive common room in a medieval hall with turf fire.

Between €40-50
Brogan's Guest House, High Street, ☎ 046 312 37, Fax 046 376 48 – 14rm 🛏 ♒ TV CC On the outskirts not far from the Yellow Steeple, this is an old inn which has been renovated. The rooms, in two separate buildings, are attractive, spacious and tastefully decorated.

● **Kells**
Under €13
Kells Hostel, ☎ 046 499 95, Fax 046 406 80 – 40 beds. The best hostel in the area, with sports and recreational facilities and a camp site. Double rooms and dormitories with 4-6 beds with own facilities, very well-kept. Laundry and cooking facilities.

EATING OUT

● **Drogheda**
Under €13
Raja Tandoori, 4 St Peter Street, ☎ 041 984 49 90. One of the very few places in the town centre where a reasonably priced meal can be found after 8.30pm. Generous portions of North Indian food served to the accompaniment of suitable music. Attentive service.
Moorland Café, West Street, ☎ 041 983 39 51. Monday-Saturday 9am-6pm. Right in the middle of town, a pleasant café serving lunches at very reasonable prices. No drinks licence.
The Black Bull Inn, Dublin Road, ☎ 041 983 71 19. One and a half kilometres out of town on the Dublin road. Meals served until 10pm. Huge country-style pub serving monster burgers and fish and chips. Inexpensive.

Between €15-25
🐌 **The Buttergate**, Millmount, ☎ and Fax 041 983 47 59. Daily 12.30pm-3pm / 6pm-10pm. Housed in the Martello tower, this is a rather smart establishment with a fine view over the town, serving refined dishes based on local fresh ingredients. Good wine list. Reservation advisable.

● **Drogheda**
No 4, Stockwell Lane, ☎ 041 984 5044. Drogheda's most "in" pub, with designer décor. Open until 2.30am weekends.
Cairbre, North Strand. The diametric opposite to the above establishment, with various odds and ends forming the basis of the décor. More or less traditional music Tuesday evening and Sunday lunchtime, and occasionally Wednesday evening.
Peter Matthews, 9 Laurence Street, ☎ 041 983 73 71. Easily the liveliest pub in town on weekend evenings. Rock music, jam-packed, young and noisy crowd. A bit quieter during the day.
The Weavers, 83 West Street, ☎ 041 983 28 16. Modernised classic pub, with good and inexpensive food. Blues or rock Wednesday evenings April-September.

● **Trim and around**
Emmet Tavern, Emmet Street, ☎ 046 313 78. Trim's liveliest pub has good smoked salmon or roast ham sandwiches at lunchtime. Rock and pop Thursday, Friday and Sunday evenings.
🐌 **The Bounty Bar**, close to the Tourist Office, ☎ 046 316 40. Decorative overload with old weaponry, domestic utensils, etc. Traditional music Sunday evening, and at unpredictable times during the week.
🐌 **Damsha na Bóinne**, Rathcairn. 15km northwest of Trim and 5km from Athboy, in a difficult-to-find hamlet, in the only area in this part of Ireland where Gaelic is spoken. This establishment is a centre of Gaelic teaching and its hall is used for concerts and dances. Traditional music and dance every Tuesday evening in summer. Not to be missed for festive atmosphere in an authentic setting.

Golf – There are three golf courses around Trim: Co Meath Golf Club, ☎ 046 314 63; Glebe Golf Course, ☎ 046 319 26, and South Meath Golf Club, ☎ 046 314 71.

Making the most of the Boyne Valley

DUNDALK AND COOLEY PENINSULA ★

Co Louth – Michelin map 923 M-N / 5-6

Not to be missed

An evening in McManus's pub in Dundalk.
A walk in the Cooley Mountains.
A plateful of Carlingford oysters.

On the border with Northern Ireland a granite promontory extends between Carlingford Lough and Dundalk Bay. This is the Cooley Peninsula, a granite upland of heather-covered hills, megaliths and conifer forests, teeming with legends like those gathered around the bold figure of **Cuchulain**, hero of the *Táin bo Cuainlge* ("The Cattle Raid of Cooley"), possibly the oldest vernacular epic in Western literature. The hills are threaded with tracks and footpaths, while the edge of Carlingford Lough is studded with fine sandy beaches.

Dundalk

85km north of Dublin – Allow 1hr on foot

Nestling on the shore of its bay, Dundalk is an industrial and harbour town, and with 25 800 inhabitants is the seventh largest urban area in the Republic. It was founded in the 12C, but was completely replanned in Georgian times by the Earl of Clanbrassil. There are few traces of the past left today, but although Dundalk has little to offer in the way of conventional tourist attractions, it's a lively place to spend an evening, and it makes a good base for exploring the surrounding area.

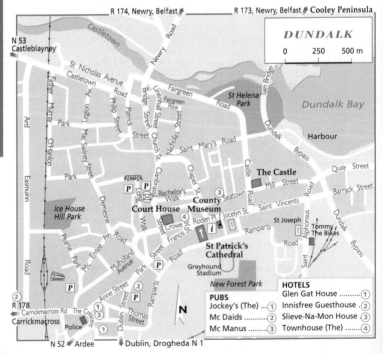

Dublin and around (side margin)

A short stroll around Dundalk

Dominating Roden Place, the huge neo-Gothic pile of **St Patrick's Church** was inspired by Cambridge's King's College Chapel and has an interior richly decorated with glass mosaic. On the far side of the square stands the massive neo-Classical building of the **Court House** with its imposing Doric portico. Occupying an old distillery next to the tourist office is the **County Museum** (*Tuesday-Saturday 10.30am-5.30pm; Sunday and public holidays 2pm-6pm. Admission charge*), with displays charting the history of Co Louth from Neolithic times to the present.

Cooley Peninsula drive★

73km tour starting at Dundalk.
Allow about 3hr including stops

The best way of exploring the Cooley Peninsula on foot is to walk the **Táin Way**. a well-signposted trail which can be followed at any time of the year. Starting from Carlingford, the circular walk (35km) takes most people a couple of days to complete, but shorter walks along sections of it can be enjoyed from either Carlingford or Omeath. Take sturdy footwear, rainproof clothing and carry a modicum of food and drink. Unofficial camping is frowned upon. Local tourist offices can provide copies of the detailed *Táin Way Map Guide*.

■ From Dundalk, set off towards Belfast on the N1, then turn right onto the R174 just beyond the Irish Secrets Coffee Shop in Dromad towards Ravensdale. On the left, **Ravensdale Forest Park** is a good place to stop for a picnic or a stroll in the forest.

Beyond Ravensdale continue for 3km and turn left towards Omeath.

■ The road climbs steeply to **Windy Gap★★**, one of the highest, and as the name implies, most exposed points in the peninsula. The hills are at their wild best in summer, when the violet of the heather alternates with the vivid yellow of the gorse and the dark green of the bracken. The road drops down again towards Omeath, giving splendid views over Carlingford Lough and the Mourne Mountains.

From Omeath opposite Warrenpoint on the far side of the lough, turn right towards Carlingford.

■ The charming little resort of **Carlingford★** faces the Mourne Mountains rising over the far shore of the lough in Northern Ireland. With plenty of pubs and restaurants, the township is at its busiest at the weekend, when it attracts crowds of visitors from the far side of the border. The place is famous for its **oysters**.

Carlingford has a number of reminders of the past in the shape of **King John's Castle**, a romantic little stronghold overlooking the sea, as well as **Taaffe's Castle**, a fortified merchant's residence dating from the 16C and set back a short distance from the quayside. Anyone wanting to find out more about the town's history should visit the **Holy Trinity Heritage Centre** (*in Churchyard Road, Sunday and public holidays 12pm-5pm. Admission charge*) in a deconsecrated medieval church which has been restored by volunteer labour.

■ 7km further on towards Dundalk an old mill, now restored, comes into view. Turn immediately left towards **Gyles Quay**, which includes among its amenities a beach, a camp site, and a pub.

■ Back again on the Dundalk road, pull into the car park of the luxury Ballymascanlon Hotel on the right. From here, a footpath leads to the **Proleek Dolmen★**, with a massive capstone weighing almost 50 tonnes.

From the next roundabout the N1 leads back to Dundalk.

COMING AND GOING

By train – Dundalk is on the Dublin-Belfast line and the trains serving Drogheda also stop here (see "Making the most of the Boyne Valley"). Allow an extra 20min travelling time.

By bus – Dublin-Dundalk (2hr) via Drogheda, 15 buses daily (7 Sunday), 14 in the reverse direction (7 Sunday). Dundalk-Carlingford (50-60min), 5 buses daily, Carlingford-Dundalk 6 buses daily, Monday-Saturday.

ADDRESS BOOK

Tourist information – *Tourist Information*, Jocelyn Street, Dundalk, ☎ 042 933 54 84. June-mid-September: Monday-Friday 9am-6pm; Saturday 9.30am-1pm / 2pm-5.30pm; closed Sunday; mid-September-May: Monday-Friday 9.30am-1pm / 2pm-5.30pm.

Teach Eolais Information Office, Old Quays Lane, Carlingford, ☎ 042 937 38 88. Normally 9.30am-5pm, but somewhat unpredictable.

Banks / Currency exchange – Cash machines in Clanbrassil Street, Dundalk.

Post office / Telephone – At the lower end of Clanbrassil Street, Dundalk, on the left coming out of the Courthouse. Monday-Saturday 9am(9.30am Tuesday)-5.30pm.

Bicycle hire – *Tommy the Bikes*, 11 Earl Street, Dundalk, ☎ 042 933 33 99.

WHERE TO STAY

• **Dundalk and around**
Under €40
Gyles Quay Camping, ☎ 042 937 62 72. ✗ 🛁 (🍴 CC Right turn off the R173 16km east of Dundalk. Extensive seaside site with pitches for tents, caravans and camper-vans, though most of it is given over to mobile homes. 1 May-30 September.

Between €40-50
The Townhouse, 5 Roden Place, Dundalk, ☎ 042 932 98 98 – 4rm 🍴 TV ✗ CC Well-located B&B opposite St Patrick's Church and next door to the town hall. Quiet, pleasant rooms facing away from the square.

Slieve-Na-Mon House, The Crescent, ☎ 042 933 13 95 – 5rm TV Classic B&B in a red brick house. Moderate level of comfort only.

Glen Gat House, 18-19 The Crescent, ☎ 042 933 79 38 – 16rm 🍴 TV CC Next door to the above establishment but marginally superior in terms of comfort. Attractive rooms and solid breakfast served in a dining-room with a panelled ceiling.

Innisfree Guesthouse, Carrick Road, ☎ 042 933 49 12 – 5rm 🍴 TV A short distance outside the town, well-kept rooms in a 1930s house. Parking available in front of the building.

🌸 **Gleneven Guest House**, Inniskeen, ☎ 042 782 94, Fax 042 785 60 – 5rm Turn right off the R171 by Conlon's pub 11km east of Dundalk. This charming house is looked after by an Irish-German couple. It stands on the banks of the River Fane, much appreciated for its trout. All the rooms are bright and spacious and have countryside views. Some have their own facilities, the others are due to get them. Inniskeen has a small museum dedicated to the writer Patrick Kavanagh.

• **Carlingford**
Under €25
Adventure Centre & Hostel, Tholsel Street, ☎ 042 937 36 51 – 62 beds. Small dormitories with 4-8 beds plus a number of double rooms, open to all but basically intended for patrons of the sports and recreation centre (See "Other things to do"). Open February-September.

Between €60-75
🌸 **Beaufort House**, ☎ 042 837 38 79, Fax 042 937 38 78 – 6rm 🍴 ✍ TV CC Turn right immediately on coming into Carlingford from the Dundalk direction, then continue for 400m parallel to the sea. Bright, attractive rooms with sea views in a recently built house painted a striking yellow colour. Excellent breakfast with smoked salmon for those that fancy it. Michael and Glinnis Caine can organise sailing trips and fishing expeditions.

Barnavave B&B, ☎ 042 937 37 42 – 5rm 🍴 TV CC Comfortable rooms with views of the Cooley Mountains in a white, recently built house, next door to Beaufort House.

Between €75-100

🐾 **Ghan House**, between the Heritage Centre and the harbour, ☎ 042 937 36 82 – 12rm 📶 TV ✗ CC Lovely restored Georgian house, tastefully decorated and furnished. The rooms are very comfortable with sea or mountain views. Evening meal available, served in a beautiful dining room with fine plasterwork.

EATING OUT

● **Dundalk**
Between €20-25
No.32, 32 Chapel Street, ☎ 042 933 11 13. Monday-Friday 12pm-3pm and Monday-Saturday 6.30pm-10.30pm. Small restaurant serving Italian / international dishes based on local seafood and other ingredients. Elegant, modern setting.

Windsor Inns, on the upper floor of The Windsor pub, Windsor Corner, Dublin Street, ☎ 042 933 81 46. Daily 6.30pm-10pm. Superior pub food and generous steaks in a Victorian setting.

Café Metz, Francis Street, ☎ 042 033 91 06, Fax 042 932 82 96. Monday-Saturday 12pm-3pm / 7pm-10.30pm, all day Sunday; closed Tuesday evening. Smart establishment serving international cuisine in a modern setting.

● **Carlingford**
Between €7.50-15
Carlingford Arms, Newry Street, ☎ 042 937 34 18. Monday-Saturday 12.30pm-10pm; Sunday 12.30pm-9.30pm. Pub with satisfying dishes such as poached salmon and leg of lamb. Traditional music Saturday evening.

Between €20-25
🐾 **The Oystercatcher**, Market Square, ☎ 042 937 39 22. Weekday 7pm-9.30pm; Sunday 12pm-3.30pm. Attractive little restaurant with nautical décor serving good traditional seafood plus some more adventurous dishes such as oysters in a blue cheese sauce. Accommodation available too, with double rooms from €65-75.

Jordan's Town House & Restaurant, entered from Newry Street or the quayside, ☎ 042 937 32 23. Monday-Saturday 6pm-9.30pm; Sunday 12.30pm-2.30pm; closed Tuesday and Sunday late

October-early March. Reservations advisable. Well-known establishment, famous for its refined cuisine featuring local meat and poultry. Small non-smoking section at the front, and a larger dining room facing the harbour. Rooms available all year round, but rather expensive.

HAVING A DRINK

● **Dundalk**
🐾 **McManus**, Seatown, ☎ 042 933 16 32. The best traditional pub in town, full of appealing bric-a-brac ranging from old sewing machines to soldiers' helmets and musical instruments. Folk music or traditional sounds Monday, Wednesday and Friday evening.

The Jockey's, opposite the Garda barracks near the station, ☎ 042 933 46 21. Another traditional pub which manages to be both reasonably quiet and very convivial. Good food at midday. Traditional music Friday evening.

McDaid's, Park Street, ☎ 042 932 98 90. THE place for Dundalk's young crowd, with live pop or rock at the weekend and disco every evening. Tex-Mex specialities.

● **Carlingford**
🐾 **O'Hare's**, Thosel Street, ☎ 042 937 31 06. Also known as PJ's, this is the best-known pub in Carlingford, a good place to gorge on oysters and enjoy traditional music Monday evening. The patron is no shrinking violet as far as publicity is concerned; a few years ago he succeeded in getting national TV to follow up his "discovery" of a pixie in the nearby hills.

Larkin's, Newry Street. Traditional pub with music (rock, pop or country) Tuesday evening and at the weekend.

OTHER THINGS TO DO

Watersports – Adventure Centre, Carlingford, offers a range of activities from windsurfing to sailing and rafting. The owner of **Beaufort House** also organises trips aboard his sailing boat (See "Where to stay").

Sea fishing – Apply to **Peadar Elmore**, North Commons, Carlingford, ☎ 042 937 32 39. Normally for groups only.

WEST OF DUBLIN
Co Kildare, Co Laois and Co Wicklow
Michelin map 923 K-L-M / 8 – Allow a day and a half

Not to be missed
The National Stud and Japanese Gardens at Kildare
Peatland World at Lullymore
The painting collection at Russborough House
And remember...
The best time to visit the National Stud is in the spring when the foals
are coming into the world.

Bounded to the north by the Liffey and to the east by the Wicklow Mountains, Co Kildare forms a sort of transition zone between the intensively built-up area around Dublin and the empty centre of the country, long crossed by important communication routes like the Grand Canal and the main road to Cork. There are few spectacular landscapes, but the springy turf of the Curragh has a world reputation for the breeding and racing of fine bloodstock.

Kildare and around
Allow at least half a day to include the National Stud.
50km southwest of Dublin – Pop 4 300

Despite its battering by heavy traffic, this busy little town on the main Dublin-Cork road has a number of fascinating historic features as well as friendly pubs. The county town of Co Kildare derives its name from the Celtic *Cill Dara* ("Church of the oak"), and the story goes that **St Brigid** founded a church here close to an oak tree around the year 480. The event is recalled every year with the placing of St Brigid's Crosses (made of plaited reeds) over doorways. But what is really celebrated in Kildare is the cult of the horse.

Kildare town
In the middle of town stands **St Brigid's Cathedral*** (*May-October: Monday-Saturday 10am-1pm / 2pm-5pm, Sunday 2pm-5pm. Free admission*). The original 13C church was almost completely rebuilt in the 19C. It has a number of fascinating Renaissance tombs as well as a fine timber roof built like the hull of a ship.
To the rear of the building stands a **round tower** (*Admission charge*) with an external stairway, the only one of its kind in Ireland. From the top there is a fine view over the town and the Curragh.

The kingdom of the horse
1.5km southeast of Kildare (signposted off the Dublin road), the Tully estate comprises the National Stud, the Japanese Gardens and St Fiachra's Garden. 12 February-12 November: daily 9.30am-6pm, last admission 5pm. Guided tour available. Admission charge.
The Tully estate belonged to William Hall-Walker, later Lord Wavertree, an immensely wealthy brewer of Scottish origin, who began breeding horses here in 1900. In 1915 he bequeathed the property to the Crown, when it became the British National Stud. Several years after independence it passed into the ownership of the Irish state.
Beyond the entrance are the **Japanese Gardens****, easily one of the finest of their kind in Europe, designed in 1906 on the initiative of Lord Wavertree by two Japanese landscape gardeners, Tassa Eida and his son Minoru. They represent the different stages in the life of Man, from his arrival in the world to death, beginning with the **Cave of Birth** and ending with the **Gateway to Eternity** via a series of symbolic

The Irish Derby

landscapes incorporating rockeries, bridges and waterfalls as well as native and exotic plants. The exit is marked by a Japanese-style pavilion housing a café, a useful spot to take a break.

On the left just beyond the entrance to the **National Stud**★★ is the **Sun Chariot Yard** with the stables which house pregnant mares and, from February to July, their yearlings as well. Beyond the yard is the foaling unit where the mares give birth. To the left are the ruins of **Black Abbey**, an 11C commandery of the Knights of St John, while to the right is the small **Horse Museum**. Its most striking exhibit is the skeleton of Arkle, the outstanding Irish racehorse whose run of successes was brought to a sad end when he fell at Kempton Park in 1966.

Beyond the exit of the museum are the stables for the stallions. At the right at the end of the avenue of oak trees is the approach to **St Fiachra's Gardens**. Created in 1998, the gardens are named after St Fiacre, an Irish holy man who spent much of his life in France where he became the patron saint of gardeners. Avenues lined with beeches, willows and birch trees lead to a number of **monks' cells**, which have been turned into a kind of underground garden, where Waterford crystal is on show, its beauty enhanced by special lighting effects.

The vast expanse of the **Curragh** is on the way out of Kildare on the N7 towards Newbridge. The area has been associated with horse racing since time immemorial, and ever since 1864 it has been the scene of the **Irish Derby**, which takes place on the first Sunday of July (*see "Making the most of Kildare"*). The Curragh was also used as a

Horses in Ireland

The first horses arrived in Ireland at the end of the last Ice Age, around 10 000 years ago. Over the following millennia, their relations with humans were mostly of a culinary nature, as is shown by the carvings depicting mealtimes which have been found at a number of Neolithic sites. Around the 4C BC, along with the use of iron, the Celts introduced domesticated horses, though they were used exclusively as draught animals. The first representation of a man on horseback dates only from around 700 AD, and the systematic breeding of horses for work and warfare had to await the arrival of the Normans.

military base. In March 1914, the near-mutiny later called the Curragh Incident took place, when British officers stationed here made known their unwillingness to put down the uprising planned by Ulster Protestants against Irish Home Rule.

Lullymore

25km north of Kildare via the R401 as far as Rathangan, then turn right on to the R414 just beyond the Grand Canal. Allow half a day.

Peatland World* *(9.30am-5pm; weekends 2pm-6pm. Admission charge)* tells its visitors everything they could possibly want to know about **peat**, what it is, how it was formed, and how it is used. The well-designed displays bring home the extent to which Irish life has revolved around peat, from its use in warming the home to its role in flavouring whiskey and in manufacturing cosmetics.

There is more on peat 800m away in the **Lullymore Heritage and Discovery Park** *(Easter-late October: Monday-Friday 9.30am-6pm; weekends 12pm-6pm. Admission charge)*. This fascinating open-air museum has reconstructions of prehistoric and later dwellings convincingly evoking the way in which traditional life was lived in the Irish countryside until quite recently.

Russborough House***

Co Wicklow. 27km east of Kildare via the N7 and the R413 and 20km southeast of Naas via the R410 and the N81. April and October: Sunday and public holidays: 10.30am-5.30pm; May and September: Monday-Saturday 10.30am-2.30pm; Sunday and public holidays 10.30am-5.30pm. Interior by guided tour only. Admission charge. Extra charge for upstairs rooms of limited interest. Allow 1hr30min.

On the banks of the vast **Poulaphouca Reservoir** whose waters mirror the surrounding mountains, this elegant Palladian mansion in Wicklow granite was begun in 1741 by Joseph Leeson, the future Earl of Milltown. A stucco caricature of the Earl appears above the door from the staircase hall to the entrance hall. Mahogany is used extensively in the interior, which has also kept its rich plasterwork and some of the original furniture. The estate was bought in 1952 by the South African millionaire Sir Alfred Beit, a descendant of another Alfred Beit who together with Cecil

Russborough House

Rhodes founded the De Beers diamond mining concern. In 1978 Sir Alfred left his priceless **picture collection**★★ to the Republic of Ireland *(some paintings are in the National Gallery in Dublin, see page 114)*, but on show at Russborough are works by some of the great European masters like Murillo, Ruysdael, Rubens, Reynolds, Poussin, Boucher and Franz Hals. The ceiling **stuccowork** in the Saloon, the Tapestry Room, Music Room and Library is of extraordinary richness.

Emo Court★★
Poorly signposted 23km west of Kildare via the N7. Interior by guided tour only. Mid-June-mid-September: 10.30am-4.15pm; closed Monday. Admission charge. Heritage Site. Gardens open all year dawn-dusk. Free admission. Guided tour of gardens 3pm Sunday July-August.

Standing among its **lovely gardens**, this elegant neo-Classical edifice was built in 1792 to the designs of James Gandon for Lord Portarlington, the former banker John Dawson. His descendants lived here until 1920, when the house was taken over by the Jesuits. The interior was restored in the 1970s. Particularly striking are the entrance **rotunda**, the splendid stuccowork in the **dining room** and in the **library**, which has a splendid Carrara marble chimneypiece.

Around Athy
Co Kildare – 23km south of Kildare

With a population of just over 5 000 people and no bigger than a large village, Athy is nevertheless a busy urban centre serving an extensive rural region. The Grand Canal and the River Barrow meet near here, and people come to the area for walking, boating and fishing holidays. There are few historical points of interest, but the town prides itself on its great religious diversity. As well as Catholic, Anglican and Presbyterian churches, there is a Kingdom Hall of the Jehovah's Witnesses, an Orthodox church, and even a number of Quaker families living in nearby Ballitore. But the Protestant Church of the Kellyites, founded a century ago here in Athy, has left no trace. In the middle of town, the old 18C town hall is now the seat of the tourist office as well as the **Athy Heritage Centre** *(March-October: Monday-Saturday 10am-6pm; Sunday and public holidays 2pm-6pm. Admission charge)*. The Centre has displays on local history and on local heroes like the famous Antarctic explorer Ernest Shackleton, as well as on the celebrated Gordon Bennett motor race.

Steam Museum★
In Stradbally, 15km northwest of Athy via the R428. Monday-Friday 11am-1pm / 2pm-4pm (liable to alteration). Otherwise key may be available from Ken Graham opposite. Admission charge. The narrow gauge railway at the far end of the village is in operation on some Sundays and public holidays, ☎ 0502 251 14 / 251 54.

Steam enthusiasts have been collecting the objects of their passion here for more than 20 years, and the results are on view in the form of old steam rollers, threshing machines, traction engines and the like. The village undergoes an annual invasion in the first weekend in August, when hundreds of such monsters clank, hiss and rumble their way here for a great **rally**.

Rock of Dunamase★
20km northwest of Athy via the R428 and the N80. Free admission. The striking silhouette of this ruined Norman castle rises abruptly on its hilltop site, dominating the surrounding rather flat countryside. Dating from 1170, the castle was destroyed by Cromwell's men in the mid-17C. A rough track leads to what is left of the keep, from where there is a fine **view**.

COMING AND GOING

By train – The station is in the northern part of the town along Milltown Road. 16 trains daily (9 Sunday) to and from Dublin Heuston Station (35min).

By bus – Hourly services daily between Dublin and Kildare (60min) by the Limerick bus. Buses also stop at the National Stud.

ADDRESS BOOK

Tourist information – **Tourist Information**, on the main square, ☎ 045 522 696. June-end September: 10am-1pm / 2pm-6pm, except Sunday.

Bank / Currency exchange – Cash machines in the town centre. Bureau de change at the **National Stud**.

Bicycle hire – **Kieran's Bike Shop**, Claregate Street, ☎ 045 522 254.

WHERE TO STAY

Between €45-50

Fremont B&B, Tully Road, very near the National Stud, ☎ 045 521 604 – 3rm Bright and quiet rooms (one with own facilities) in a modern house the main interest of which is its proximity to the Stud. Closed 1 November-mid-March.

Castleview B&B, ☎ 045 521 816 – 3rm Four kilometres west of Kildare via the N7. Go 2km along the main road, then turn right and follow signs for another 2km. Modern farmhouse in the middle of the countryside, opposite an old church and the ruins of a castle. Well-kept but basic comforts only. The cattle-raising owners are very welcoming and can supply visitors with all sorts of useful information about the area.

Cloncarlin House B&B, Monasterevan, ☎ 045 525 722 – 6rm Turn left off the N7 10.5km west of Kildare on the way into Monasterevan, then left again. Lovely 18C farmhouse, well away from the noise of the main road. Fairly basic comforts, but well-kept accommodation and friendly reception. Closed January.

EATING OUT

Under €13

The Gregory Tavern, Main Street, ☎ 045 520 099. Monday-Saturday 12pm-9pm. Good pub food served on rough-hewn tables. Seating outside on fine days.

The Silken Thomas, opposite the above establishment, ☎ 045 522 232. Daily 12.30pm-3pm / 6pm-10pm. Huge pub with classic Victorian décor and a wide choice of hearty dishes including steaks. Dinner served in the comfortable dining room is more refined and more expensive.

Giorgio's, The Square, near St Brigid's Church, ☎ 045 521 864. Tuesday-Sunday 5pm-11pm. Kildare's Italian outpost, serving generous portions of pizza and pasta.

HAVING A DRINK

All Kildare's pubs are in the main square.
The Gregory, traditional music Thursday and Sunday evening.

Silken Thomas, live music six nights a week.

Flanagan's, next door, as above but five nights only.

The Vatican, worth looking into for its connection with a local eccentric.

The Cush Inn, ☎ 045 523 467. Turn left off the N7 at Monasterevan 12km west of Kildare towards Athy. Dead as could be for most of the week, this pub fills up to bursting on weekend evenings. There's a variety of sounds, a nightclub for dancing, and a traditional music group performs at the bar on Sunday evening. Fortifying Irish stew available at all times.

OTHER THINGS TO DO

Racing – There are three racecourses in the area. A calendar is available at the tourist office. **The Curragh**, ☎ 045 441 205, Fax 045 441 442. **Naas**, 25km northeast of Kildare towards Dublin, ☎ 045 897 391, Fax 045 879 486. **Punchestown**, 10km south of Naas via the R411, ☎ 045 897 704, Fax 045 897 319.

Traditional clothing – *Aran Crafts*, Monasterevan, 10.5km west of Kildare via the N7, ☎ 045 525 319. Factory shop with range of pullovers, jackets and other woollens at very reasonable prices. 10am-5pm, closed Sunday.

Making the most of Athy and around

By train – The station is on the way out of town on the Dublin road. 6 trains daily to Dublin (3 Sunday) via Kildare (45-60min)

By bus – Buses from Dublin to Limerick and Clonmel stop at Athy (8 buses daily). No direct service Athy-Kildare.

ADDRESS BOOK

Tourist information – *Athy Heritage Centre*, in the old town hall in the centre of town, ☎ 0507 330 75. Monday-Saturday 10am-6pm; Sunday and public holidays March-October 2pm-6pm. Wide range of information about the area.

Banks / Currency exchange – There are several banks with cash machines in the main street.

WHERE TO STAY

Under €40
***Forest Farm & Caravan Park*,** Dublin Road, ☎ 0507 312 31 / 330 70. Newly laid-out caravan site sheltered by trees.

Between €40-45
***Moate Lodge*,** Dublin Road, ☎ 0507 261 37 – 4rm Turn left off the N78 just before Ardscull 6km east of Athy. This old house in the countryside close to the Norman motte at Ardscull has plain but decent accommodation.

***Balindrum Farm*,** Balindrum, ☎ 0507 262 94 – 5rm ⚲ TV CC Turn right off the N78 at a signpost about 4.5km east of Athy, then right again for about 1km. Modern farmhouse in the middle of the countryside. Immaculately kept rooms with standard décor. Evening meal can be arranged. Open 1 April-31 October.

⚲ ***Vicarstown Inn*,** Vicarstown, ☎ 0502 251 89 – 10rm ⚲ CC About 15km north of Athy via the minor road running parallel to the Grand Canal. Charming atmosphere of yesteryear in this little inn which is a favourite with fishermen and people sailing on the canal. A real haven of peace and quiet with an appealingly authentic feeling. Dinner available on request. Open March-November.

Between €65-75
***Coursetown Country House*,** ☎ 0507 311 01, Fax 0507 327 40 – 4rm ⚲ TV CC 2.5km from Athy on the R428 Stradbally road. Lavish breakfast served in a room opening out on to the garden.

EATING OUT

Between €13-20
***Smugglers*,** Duke Street, ☎ 0507 311 81. Daily 12pm-4pm / 6pm-9.30pm. Easily the best pub-restaurant in town, and certainly the liveliest. Spicy crab claws, smoked salmon and tandoori chicken among stone walls and exposed beams.

HAVING A DRINK

Smugglers (see "Eating Out"), has traditional or rock music Friday-Sunday, and there is a club next door.

⚲ ***The Anchor Inn*,** by the canal in Vicarstown. People come from all around for the famous Monday evening traditional music sessions.

Vicarstown Inn (see "Where to stay") has music Saturday and Sunday evenings.

CO WICKLOW★★★
FROM BRAY TO AVOCA VIA GLENDALOUGH
About 110km – Allow 2 days
Michelin map M-N / 8-9 and map page 173

Not to be missed
The wonderful gardens at Mount Usher.
A walk in the Wicklow Mountains.
Exploring the valley at Glendalough.
Tea-dance at The Meetings pub.

And remember...
When visiting Glendalough it's better to stay overnight
at Roundwood rather than Laragh.

Lying between the urbanised areas around Dublin and Wexford and bounded to the east by the Irish Sea, County Wicklow is a lovely land of forests, waterfalls, lakes and great country houses. Its name is derived from the little port which is the county town and from the mountain chain which runs north-south through the middle of the area. Far from the centre of power in Dublin, this remote region remained a bastion of Celtic Christianity for centuries, as evidenced by the romantic ruins of the monastery at Glendalough. Much later, the Anglo-Irish Ascendancy found in Wicklow's charming countryside ideal sites for their country houses and landscape parks.

■ Bray
20km south of Dublin – Allow 3hr

At the southern terminus of the DART railway line, Bray is a popular seaside resort and dormitory town for Dublin. With its faded Victorian charm, it is not very different from a hundred similar places along the coasts of Britain, depending nowadays more on day trippers from the city than on the prosperous folk who once took their summer holidays here.

The seafront
Behind the sand and shingle beach there are amusement arcades and fast-food outlets, but Bray's main individual attraction nowadays is probably the **National Sea-Life Centre** (*April-September: 11am-5.30pm; weekend 11am-6pm. Admission charge*), one of a chain of such establishments, with an array of aquariums and all kinds of interactive exhibits.

The area around Bray is a delight for garden-lovers. About 1.5km on the way out of town on the R761 are **Killruddery House Gardens★** (*April-September: 1pm-5pm. House open May, June and September only. Admission charge*). These superb formal gardens with their lakes and canals were laid out in the 17C by the Earls of Meath. Altered repeatedly to conform to changing fashions in landscape design, they have nevertheless kept much of the original layout with its hedges of box and beech. Almost completely remodelled in the 19C, the **house** has an extraordinary clock operated by water power.

Near Kilmacanoge 5km southwest of Bray via the N11, **Glencormac Gardens** (*daily 10am-5.30pm. Free admission*) give visitors an unusual opportunity to combine the enjoyment of natural beauty with a bit of shopping. The gardens were created in the 19C by James Jameson, a member of the famous family of distillers, and feature such rarities as a Himalayan weeping cypress. There is also a pleasant cafeteria (*see "Making the most of Wicklow"*) as well as **Avoca Handweavers**, the factory outlet for a range of traditional clothing.

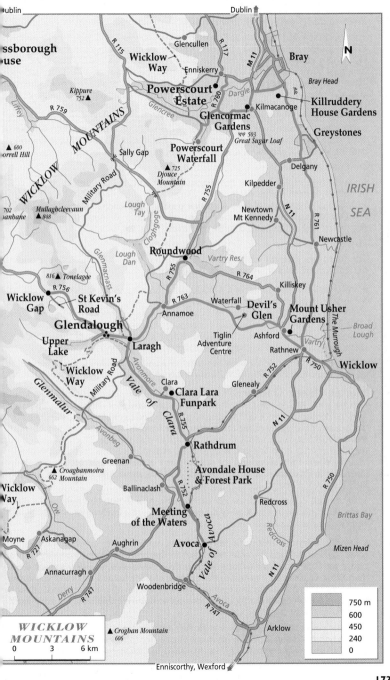

Dublin

Dublin

Glencullen

R 115

R 117

M 11

Bray

Wicklow Way

Enniskerry

Bray Head

ssborough use

Kippure
752 ▲

R 759

R 260

Dargle

Powerscourt Estate

Kilmacanoge

Killruddery House Gardens

Glencree

Glencormac Gardens

WICKLOW

MOUNTAINS

▲ 600
orrell Hill

Sally Gap

Powerscourt Waterfall

503
Great Sugar Loaf

Greystones

Military Road

R 755

Delgany

Djouce Mountain

Kilpedder

N 11

R 761

IRISH

702
oanbane

Mullaghcleevaun
▲ 848

Lough Tay

Newtown Mt Kennedy

Newcastle

SEA

Cloghoge

816 ▲ Tonelagee

Lough Dan

Glenmacnass

Roundwood

Vartry Res.

Wicklow Gap

R 756

St Kevin's Road

R 755

R 764

Killiskey

R 763

Waterfall

Devil's Glen

Mount Usher Gardens

Glendalough

Annamoe

The Murrough

Broad Lough

Upper Lake

Laragh

Tiglin Adventure Centre

Ashford

Vartry

Wicklow Way

Military Road

Rathnew

R 752

R 750

Wicklow

Glenmalur

Vale of Clara

Clara

Clara Lara Funpark

Gleneahy

Avonmore

R 755

Avonbeg

Rathdrum

Greenan

Avondale House & Forest Park

▲ Croaghanmoira
662 Mountain

Ballinaclash

R 752

Redcross

Brittas Bay

Wicklow Way

Ow

Meeting of the Waters

Vale of Avoca

N 11

Redcross

Mizen Head

Moyne

R 727

Askanagap

Aughrin

Avoca

Annacurragh

Derry

R 741

Woodenbridge

Avoca

R 747

Arklow

WICKLOW
MOUNTAINS

0   3   6 km

▲ Croghan Mountain
606

	750 m
	600
	450
	240
	0

Enniscorthy, Wexford

173

Return to the N1 and go north, following signs for Powerscourt Estate, 5km west of Bray.

The once splendid 18C house at **Powerscourt★★★** (*Gardens 9.30am-5.30pm. Waterfall: 9.30am-7.30pm; 10.30am-dusk in winter. Separate admission charges. Allow 90min*) fell victim to a great fire in 1974 and has been only partly restored. Some of the outbuildings house craft shops and there is a terrace cafeteria overlooking the gardens. The splendid formal **gardens** remain a great attraction. Dominated by a **monumental stairway★** they slope down gently to the **Lake** mirroring the distinctive outline of the nearby Sugar Loaf Mountain (503m). From the lake a Triton spews a 30m jet of water high into the air. The gardens were begun in 1840 and took 100 workmen 12 years to complete. Further downhill to the left of the stairway is the **Japanese Garden★** with its bridges and miniature pagodas. Other features include the **Pets' Cemetery** and the **Walled Gardens★★**, a summer delight of spectacular exotic blooms.

Turn right out of the car park, and drive 5km.

An attractive footpath leads to **Powerscourt Waterfall★**. These are the highest falls in Ireland, formed by the waters of the Dargle River plunging 130m down a jagged rock face in a horseshoe of hills. A **nature trail** (*leaflet available at the entrance*) leads for 2km through the leafy surroundings, where there are sequoias and monkey puzzles as well as the more familiar pine trees.

Return to Bray, then go south along the coast on the R761.

The road goes through the pretty little resort and harbour town of **Greystones★** nestling among cliffs and with a vast shingle beach.

■ **Wicklow★** – The capital of Co Wicklow is also a harbour town and a good base for exploring the mountains, with plenty of B&Bs, pubs and restaurants. The main visitor attraction is the formidable prison, now named **Wicklow Historic Gaol** (*March and October: 10am-5pm; April-September: 10am-6pm; last admission 1hr before closing; guided tour every 10min. Admission charge*). Convincing historical tableaux and costumed guides evoke the grim conditions endured by prisoners in the 18C and 19C.

If there is still time, continue down the coast road towards Arklow past extensive pebble beaches. If not, take the R750 and N11 to the village of Ashford 6.5km northwest of Wicklow.

Mount Usher Gardens★★ – *Signposted to the right off the road into Ashford from the south. Mid-March-31 October: 10.30am-6pm. Admission charge.* These luxuriant gardens contain almost 4 000 species of plants including many exotics. Seduced by the beauty of the valley of the River Vartry, the Dublin linen manufacturer **Edward Walpole** set out in the 1860s to create a horticultural paradise. Much influenced by the ideas of Irish-born William Robinson, he exploited the area's mild microclimate to grow plants from all around the world, many of which would not flourish easily elsewhere in this part of Ireland. The river itself was attractively landscaped, and the little suspension bridges are popular features.

From Ashford, take the R763 towards Glendalough. After 3.5km, turn right onto a stony track which winds round the flank of the mountain through a lovely forest of fir, birch and beech before reaching Devil's Glen.

■ **Devil's Glen★** – This particularly wild part of the country served as a refuge for some of the insurgents who had taken part in the 1798 Rebellion. Nowadays it is a refuge for those who love walking in unspoiled countryside, with few sounds other than those of birdsong, waterfalls, the buzzing of the bees and the wind sighing in the trees. Such attractions have tempted artists here from all over the world, and the woodland has become a setting for an open-air **sculpture exhibition**, featuring work made from timber harvested locally.

The main road continues to climb through the forest before reaching a right turn leading to the youth hostel and the Tiglin Adventure Centre (see "Making the most of Wicklow"). The R763 eventually meets the R755 at the hamlet of Annamoe on the banks of the river of the same name.

4km southwest of Annamoe on the R755 is the village, or rather hamlet of **Laragh**, nestling in a leafy valley not far from Glendalough. Laragh could be said to welcome visitors; there's hardly a building that isn't a B&B, restaurant or souvenir shop. This, together with the noise of tour buses and cars, has unfortunately had the effect of robbing the place of all its charm, and the sensitive tourist is advised to hurry on to Roundwood.

■ **Roundwood** – 4km northeast of Annamoe, this is the highest village in Ireland (238m), located close to a vast lake, the banks of which are unfortunately off-limits to the public *(in private ownership)*. With its cheerful pubs, camp site, hotels and restaurants, Roundwood is frequented by hikers doing the Wicklow Way, and is far more attractive than Laragh, as well as much quieter.

Go back to Laragh and take the R756 towards Glenalough, and in 3.5km turn left into a large car park.

■ Glendalough★★★

The best place to leave your vehicle is in the car park by the Visitor Centre, close to most of the site's attractions. The other car park is 1km further along on the left between the two lakes.
Mid-October-mid-March: 9.30am-5pm; mid-March-late May and September-mid-October: 9.30am-6pm; June-August: 9am-6.30pm. Last admission 45min before closing. Admission charge for the Visitor Centre (with a not particularly enthralling exhibition on Glendalough and Irish monasticism); guided tour available; free admission to the site. Heritage Site. Allow 2hr30min.

The round tower at Glendalough

J Brun/EXPLORER

A saint of ice and fire

Cóemhghein, anglicised to Kevin, means "well-born" in Gaelic, and the future saint was a member of a princely family from Leinster. It is said that his beauty had an almost supernatural quality, but to women his heart seemed made of ice. His rejection of the advances made by a princess was so forceful that the poor girl fell into the lake at Glendalough and drowned. Eaten by remorse, Kevin spent the rest of his life in meditation, far removed from the world. On the rare occasions when he opened his mouth, the words issued forth in letters of fire. He would spend days on end in the forest, lost in prayer, leaning against an oak with his arms outstretched, so motionless that the birds would use him as a perch. Not surprisingly, tradition has made Saint Kevin the protector of all birds.

In the year 570, accompanied by a group of monks, **Saint Kevin** chose this remote spot among the mountains to found a monastery. After his death in 617, Glendalough became a place of pilgrimage, a kind of monastic town, with churches, dwellings, workshops, a hospital and farm buildings. Despite numerous Viking raids, the site kept up its religious activity for almost 900 years, before entering a period of definitive decline.

The monastic site

Mostly located between the road and the Glendasan River, the ruins of Glendalough can only give a partial idea of the religious life of past centuries. They are reached through a monumental **gateway** made from a pair of granite arches, once the main entrance to the monastic enclosure which was subsequently used as a graveyard.

To the right is a **round tower★** dating from the 10C, which served at one and the same time as a look-out post, a belfry, a grain-store, and a place of refuge. Topped by a conical cap which was restored in 1876, the tower is 30m high, with a doorway 3.6m above ground level.

Little remains of the **cathedral**, which was once Glendalough's most imposing building. Several times rebuilt, but dating mostly from the 12C, it had a nave which at the time of its construction was one of the largest in the country. To the south of the cathedral stands St **Kevin's Cross**, an undecorated high cross. The cross marked the boundary of the graveyard, where the little **priests' house** still stands.

Down the slope towards the river is **St Kevin's Church★** with its dry-stone roof. The church is also known as St Kevin's Kitchen because of the chimney-like shape of its belfry. Close by are the bare ruins of **St Kieran's Church**, a little edifice which once stood outside the present monastic enclosure.

Go across the river and turn right on to the track which leads to the Lower Lake through an oak woodland.

The pathway leads past the Lower Lake. On the right just before the Upper Lake is the office of the Wicklow Mountains National Park (*see "Making the most of Wicklow"*), with a small **museum** with displays evoking the mining past of the Glendalough area, which was once important for the extraction of lead and silver.

The **Upper Lake★★** at Glendalough is a real jewel, its deep blue waters gloriously set in a semi-circle of hills carved out by glaciers and now clad with sombre conifer forests. A short

The all-purpose oak

One of the reasons for the choice of Glendalough as the site of a monastic settlement was its wealth of oak trees. The oak was regarded at the time as one of the great gifts of Nature, fulfilling a whole range of purposes. The trunk and larger branches were used as building timber while smaller branches were chopped up into firewood. The tannin contained in the bark was turned into medicines or used for tanning leather. The oak apples formed by a parasitic growth were ground down to form a base for the black ink employed by the monks in their manuscripts. As for the acorns, they made fine pig food, and could even be eaten by humans in times of famine, once the starch had been extracted. Even the leaves could be stuffed into straw mattresses or fed to animals in winter.

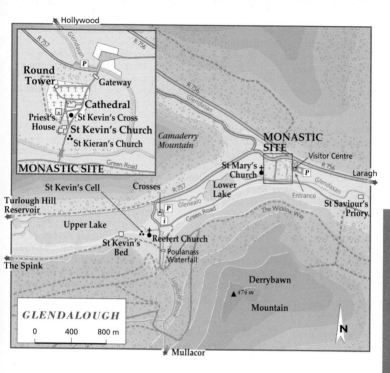

distance from the shore are a number of **crosses** placed to mark the boundary of the monastic enclosure. On the lower slopes amid the woodland stands **Reefert Church**★, traditionally the burial place of Celtic kings, and higher up, a ring of foundation stones marks the site of **St Kevin's Cell**. The cell in which the saint would spend his retreats from the world was probably built of corbelled stone on the same pattern as the beehive dwellings on Skellig Michael. From this spot a number of footpaths radiate out to link up eventually with the Wicklow Way.

Walks around Glendalough

Anyone with a little time to spare should take the opportunity while at Glendalough to explore the surrounding mountains along the network of well-signposted footpaths.

Glenealo River, Turlough Hill and Camaderry – *Circular walk of 14.5km. Allow 5-6hr.* From the car park at Glendalough, go to the north bank of the Upper Lake and continue westwards for just over 1km. Just before the point where the Glenealo River flows into the lake, a

The Wicklow Way

Inaugurated in 1984, the first official long distance footpath in Ireland runs for 136km from the southern suburbs of Dublin to the little village of Clonegal near Carlow. Divided into 19 sections, the path is clearly signposted and can be enjoyed at any time of the year given the right equipment, by riders and mountain bikers as well as by walkers. The route crosses the vast spaces of these granite uplands where dark conifer forests alternate with grassy open swathes grazed by sheep, then skirts lakes and passes just above the valley of Glendalough. It reaches its highest point (630m) at White Hill, and the longest section between places to stay is between Knockree and Roundwood, a distance of 22km.

narrow path turns off towards the scanty remains of the old lead mines. With the river to the left, the path climbs in a series of bends up the northern side of the hill. Carry on for about 3.5km to where a loop leads towards Turlough Hill Reservoir, a lovely lake which you skirt round to the south before beginning the climb up Camaderry (698m). This is the steepest part of the route, eventually reaching the flat summit, where a well-earned rest can be enjoyed close to the little **stone circles** of Neolithic date. The fairly straightforward descent passes beneath a rocky spur, after which it is only 4km back to the starting point.

The Spink, Mullacor and Derrybawn Ridge – *Circular walk of 12km. Allow 4-5hr.* Starting from the headquarters of the Wicklow Mountains National Park *(see above)*, turn right, cross over the little bridge and climb up to the lovely **Poulanass Waterfall**. Keep on along the forest track and at the first junction turn right. The route leads up the flank of the Spink, passing a sheer drop high above the lake *(keep well away from the edge)*. The effort of the climb is soon rewarded by a splendid **view*** of the lake and the Glendalough valley far below. Once you have got your breath back, carry on, leaving the forest on the left and then tackling the climb up Mullacor (657m). From the summit there are fine views over the whole region. The path descends along the forest edge and crosses a peat bog before reaching the foot of the rounded mass of Derrybawn (450m). A rocky climb leads to this summit, where you turn left to begin the descent towards the forest, which you must go through before reaching the **Wicklow Way** where you turn right. There now follows a series of zig-zag bends which lead downwards to the Poulanass waterfall and the start of the walk.

Return to Laragh and go towards Rathdrum. The R755 follows the winding course of the River Avonmore in its deep valley.

■ **Vale of Clara** – This valley used to have something of an industrial character, with a number of mills along its length, but nowadays tourism is more important here than industry. In summer, the **Clara-Lara Funpark** *(on the left 4km south of Laragh)* is an extremely popular open-air family attraction. It is only a short distance from the attractive little village of Rathdrum, which boasts the **Cartoon Inn**, a real shrine for fans of cartoon characters. A good place to relax is Rathdrum's vast green, just below the church.

Leave Rathdrum towards Avoca and follow signs for 1.5km to Avondale House.

■ **Avondale House & Forest Park**** – *May-September: 10am-6pm; October-April: 11am-5pm, closed public holidays, last admission 1hr before closing. Admission charge.*

Avondale House**, once the home of **Charles Stewart Parnell** (1846-91), is a slate-roofed Georgian residence of austere appearance somewhat relieved by its elegant porch. A portrait of Parnell greets visitors in the entrance hall, above it a fossilised moose head recovered from a bog. The first floor rooms are furnished in Victorian style and contain numerous mementoes of the personal and public life of this great leader of Irish nationalism.

The attractive **Avondale Forest Park*** stretches out around Parnell's house, threaded by numerous well-signposted woodland walks and trails. Since the 18C the park has been planted with a wide variety of **exotic trees**, particularly eucalyptus species. There are also majestic oaks and beeches, some of which are more than 250 years old, demonstrated by the exposed rings on the stump of a beech tree.

Return to the R752 and drive 4km towards Avoca.

The River Avonbeg joins the Avonmore at a spot called **Meeting of the Waters**, a place of inspiration for the poet Thomas Moore (1779-1852). The pub here, **The Meetings**, is known for its music, not only in the evenings but also on Sunday afternoons in summer, when the beer flows freely and a crooner in white shirt and tie charms couples of all ages on to the dance floor with his syrupy songs.

Return to the R752 and drive 5km towards Avoca.

■ **Avoca** – This pretty little village and its pub, **Fitzgerald's**, achieved immortality as **Ballykissangel** in the BBC TV soap opera of that name. A good proportion of the millions of viewers seem to have visited Avoca / Ballykissangel since the series was first screened in the 1990s, and there is a brisk trade in Ballykissangel merchandise. However, Avoca has another asset in the shape of **Avoca Handweavers** *(summer: 9am-5pm; November-April: 9.30am-5pm. Shop closes at 6pm all year,* ☎ 0402 351 05). Powered by its waterwheel, the 18C hand-weaving mill can be visited, and good quality woollens and knitwear are on sale in the factory shop.

Parnell's rise and fall

Charles Stewart Parnell was a Protestant landowner, deeply committed to the struggle for the Home Rule which would restore to the country the autonomy it had enjoyed before the Act of Union of 1800. He was instrumental in creating a disciplined Irish parliamentary party which returned 85 Nationalist MPs to Westminster in 1885. Convinced of Parnell's influence and of the importance of his cause, Liberal leader Gladstone was ready to support Home Rule. But, just as this great patriot's ambitions seemed likely to be realised, he was destroyed by a scandal. His relationship with Kitty O'Shea, a married woman, became public, and the British press seized on the scandal to blacken his name. Forced to resign, and with his health undermined by stress, Parnell died a few months later. Despite the disapproval of Church and State, the people of Dublin turned out in their tens of thousands for his funeral.

Making the most of Co Wicklow

COMING AND GOING

By train – Trains leave Dublin Connolly Street for Rosslare via Bray, Greystones, Wicklow, Rathdrum and Arklow. 3 trains daily in each direction. Bray is also the southern terminus of the suburban DART line (45min).

By bus – Several buses daily between Dublin, Bray, Wicklow and Ashford. There is no direct link to Powerscourt; get off at Enniskerry or take the DART to Bray then bus 185. In both cases the 2km between Enniskerry and Powerscourt will have to be covered on foot. Inexpensive excursions from Dublin to Glendalough via Roundwood are run by St Kevin's Bus Co, ☎ 01 281 81 19. One bus in each direction morning and afternoon.

ADDRESS BOOK

Tourist information – *Bray Tourism*, Main Street, in the old law courts, Bray, ☎ 01 286 4000, Fax 01 282 84 80. June-September:

9am-5pm; rest of year 10am-4pm. Small local history museum plus information on Bray and the Wicklow Mountains.
Tourist Information, Fitzwilliam Square, Wicklow, ☎ 0404 691 17, Fax 0404 691 18. June-September: 9am-6pm, closed Sunday; October-May: 9.30am-1pm / 2pm-5.30pm, except weekends. Useful information and maps for the Wicklow Mountains.
Wicklow Mountains National Park, 100m from the main car park and Upper Lake, Glendalough, ☎ 0404 454 25 / 453 38 (winter), Fax 0404 453 06. May-August: 10am-6pm; April-September: 10am-6pm weekends only. Free admission. Excellent walking maps and brochures, including the particularly useful "Exploring Glendalough".

Banks / Currency exchange – Cash machines in Main Street in Bray and in Wicklow.

Bicycle hire – *Bray Sports Centre*, 8 Main Street, Bray, ☎ 01 286 30 46 / 282 83 94. ***ER Harris & Sons***, 87c

Green Park Road, Bray, ☎ 01 286 33 57.
Dave's Diner, in Bray DART station.
Wicklow Hire, Abbey Street, Wicklow,
☎ 0404 681 49. Daily 8.30am-5.30pm,
except Sunday.

WHERE TO STAY

• **Bray**
Under €45
Bayswell House, Strand Road,
☎ 01 286 39 84 – 6rm Open 31 May-
30 September. Facing the sea, inexpensive but basic level of comfort.

Between €45-50
Sea Breeze House, 1 Marine Terrace,
☎ 01 286 83 37 – 7rm ⌂ TV CC
Closed 15 December-31 January. Some
of Ms Grace's classically furnished rooms
have sea views.
Ulysses Guest House, Strand Road,
Wavecrest Terrace, ☎ 01 286 38 60 –
10rm ⌂ TV CC Closed in June. Some
of the rooms have sea views. Rather garish decor but decent accommodation.

• **Enniskerry**
Under €13
Lacken House, Knockree,
☎ 01 286 40 36 – 58 beds, 6km south
of Enniskerry. Turn left at the
newsagents in the village and follow
signs to Glencree. From Bray, take the
No 85 bus, get off at Barnmire and walk
the last 500m. This old farmstead among
the mountains and close to the Wicklow
Way has been turned into a hostel. It is
a firm favourite with people walking the
Way, and offers a very basic but acceptable level of comfort, given the price.

Between €50-65
Ferndale B&B, in the centre of the
village. ☎ and Fax 01 286 35 18 – 4rm
⌂ TV CC Closed December-February.
This attractive little house in its garden
has comfortable rooms furnished in Victorian style. Excellent breakfast with
choice of fresh fruit juices, scrambled
eggs with smoked salmon etc

• **Newtown Mt Kennedy**
13.5km south of Bray via the N11.

Between €45-55
Springmount House, 500m from
the church towards Wicklow,
☎ 01 281 91 95 –2rm ⌂ TV Open
April-November. The rooms in this

lovely Georgian farmhouse are quiet,
comfortable and furnished with taste.
Warm welcome from the owners, who
have a 150-acre farm. Evening meal
using farm produce can be provided if
ordered in advance.

• **Wicklow**
Between €25-30
Wicklow Bay Hostel, to the north of
the town, also called **Marine House**,
☎ and Fax 0404 692 13 – 60 beds and
2rm Open all year. Pleasant hostel in a
restored 18C building facing the sea.
The 4-8 bed dormitories are bright and
clean. Pleasant atmosphere and numerous facilities.

Between €45-50
MacReamon Town House, Summer-
hill, ☎ 0404 611 13 – 4rm ⌂ Well located just a few steps from the main
pubs and restaurants, this pretty town
house with its yellow painted façade has
bright, quiet rooms which are attractively decorated.

• **Ashford**
Between €13-20
Tiglin Hostel, 6km west of Ashford
via the R783, ☎ and Fax 0404 490 49
– 50 beds. Open all year, reception open
before 10am and after 5pm. Together
with the Adventure Centre, this hostel is
in old farm buildings on the fringe of the
forest at Devil's Glen. This is deep
countryside, and visitors should not be
surprised if a deer peers through their
window. Basic comfort in the 4-12 bed
dormitories, but there's a friendly atmosphere (NB No smoking or drinking).
Cooking facilities and mountain bikes
for hire. Lots of useful information about
walking in the area.

Between €45-50
Carrig Lodge, Ballylusk,
☎ 0404 402 78 – 4rm ⌂ CC Turn right
just beyond the petrol station on the way
out of Ashford towards Glenealy. In the
middle of the countryside, this modern
house has bright, well-kept rooms all
decorated in different pastel colours.
Ballyknocken House,
☎ 0404 446 27, Fax 0404 446 96 – 7rm
⌂ TV ✗ CC 4km south of Ashford towards Glenealy. The sheep-raising Byrne
family turned their farmhouse into a

180

B&B 20 years ago. The simply-furnished rooms are comfortable. Visitors will appreciate the lounge with its turf fire, especially on those all-too-common days when the drizzle seems never-ending. Tasty evening meal available if ordered in advance.

Between €75-90
🐾 *Bel Air Hotel*, ☎ 0404 4012 09, Fax 0404 401 88 – 12rm ⌂ 🏷 📺 ✗ 🐎 cc Signposted on the right on the way out of Ashford towards Glenealy. This tiny castle in the middle of the countryside has a proud bearing and plenty of charm, though a face-lift wouldn't do any harm. The décor has hardly been tampered with for a century or so, but the rooms nevertheless have every modern comfort. Evening meal can be provided if ordered in advance. Visitors are welcome at the riding school run by the owners.

● **Roundwood**
Under €13
Roundwood Caravan & Camping Park, ☎ 01 281 81 63 ✗ ✗ cc Open 1 April-26 September. Vast caravan and camp site by a lake. Numerous facilities include a shop, restaurant and play areas.

Between €45-50
The Coach House, in the centre of the village, ☎ 01 281 81 57, Fax 01 281 84 49 – 14rm ⌂ 📺 ✗ cc Pleasant inn with bar and restaurant, popular with walkers doing the Wicklow Way. Plain but tastefully furnished and comfortable rooms in the main building or an annexe.

● **Around Glendalough**
Under €13
The Wicklow Way Hostel, Laragh, ☎ 0404 453 98 – 32 beds. Open all year. Small private hostel with average-only welcome, comfort and cleanliness. Dormitories with 6-14 beds. Breakfast not included in the price.
The Lodge Hostel, near the monastic site, ☎ 0404 453 42, Fax 0404 456 90 – 120 beds ✗ cc Open all year and reception open all day. Huge, recently restored building, a favourite with walkers. Breakfast and evening meal available. Advance booking advisable in summer.

Between €45-50
Carmel's B&B, ☎ 0404 452 97 – 4rm ⌂ 📺 4.5km northwest of Glendalough, between Laragh and Annamoe. Attractive, quiet rooms all on the same floor of a modern house set back from the road. Friendly reception and good breakfast.

Between €75-90
🐾 **Derrybawn House**, ☎ 0404 451 34 – 6rm ⌂ Turn right off the R755 into a tree-lined avenue 1km south of Laragh. This lovely 18C residence smothered in Virginia creeper stands among the ancient oaks of its parkland. Visitors can lead a life of luxury in rooms tastefully furnished in country style. Wide choice at breakfast-time. Billiard room available for the use of guests.

● **Rathdrum**
Under €13
Avonmore Riverside Caravan and Camping, ☎ 0404 460 80, on the banks of the Avonmore, this small camp site is only open in summer.

Between €20-30
The Old Presbytery, The Fairgreen, ☎ 0404 469 30, Fax 0404 466 04 – 48 beds and 8rm cc As its name implies, this hostel is located in what used to be the home of the parish priest. Cooking facilities. Bicycle hire. Camping allowed.

EATING OUT
● **Bray**
Between €8-13
Molloy's, 14 Quinsboro Road, 7am-6pm; Sunday 10am-6pm. Huge cafeteria serving good cakes and pastries and generous helpings of the dish of the day at very reasonable prices.
The Porter House, on the seafront. Daily 12.30pm-2.30pm / 4.30pm-9pm. The busiest seafront pub has a choice of more than 100 beers including several brewed here. The strongest (7%) is An Brain Blasta. Tex-Mex and sausage and chips on the menu, but it can take a while to get served.
Avoca Handweavers, Kilmacanoge, ☎ 01 286 74 66. Open Monday-Saturday 9.30am-5pm; Sunday 10am-5pm. 5km south of Bray via the N11. Big cafeteria with good and generously

proportioned salads, among other dishes. Outside eating in the summer in the attractive gardens.

• Enniskerry
Under €13

Poppies, in the middle of the village, ☎ 01 282 88 69. Open Monday-Friday 9am-5pm; weekend 9am-8pm. Small restaurant with chocolate-box décor serving dishes like beef in Guinness followed by a hearty pudding.

• Wicklow
Under €13

The Coffee Shop, Fitzwilliam Square, ☎ 0404 680 06. Inexpensive snack bar with lunchtime salads, sandwiches, good cakes and pastries and a limited number of dishes of the day. No drinks licence.

Between €20-25

The Quays Bistro, South Quay, ☎ 0404 619 00. Tuesday-Sunday 6pm-10pm. Fashionable establishment with Spanish-flavoured international cuisine. Sunday "Tapas evenings" with musical accompaniment.

• Ashford
Between €13-25

Ashford House, on the way into the village from the Dublin direction, ☎ 0404 404 81, Fax 0404 409 90. Daily 12pm-3.30pm / 5.30pm-9.30pm. This recently restored house manages to combine tradition and modernity. People come from far and wide to enjoy Conor Spacey's imaginative cooking, in which only fresh fish and local organic produce are used. Relatively inexpensive at midday, dearer in the evening. Jazz evening every Thursday at 9pm.

• Roundwood
Under €13

The Coach House, (see "Where to stay"). Open 12pm-10pm. Rustic pub serving solid food.

Between €13-20

The Roundwood Inn, in the middle of the village, ☎ 01 281 81 07. Daily 1pm-3pm and Wednesday-Saturday 7.30pm-10pm. Village inn with good pub food for less than €13 at midday and more elaborate cuisine in the evening. Game specialities when in season.

• Laragh
Under €13

The Wicklow Heather, in the hamlet, ☎ 0404 451 57, Fax 0404 456 69. Daily 12.30pm-10pm. Friendly inn with excellent ham or smoked salmon sandwiches available at any time. More sophisticated food in the evening.

• Rathdrum
Under €13

The Meetings, 4km south of Rathdrum towards Avoca, ☎ 0402 352 26, Fax 0402 355 58. Daily 12pm-10pm. The liveliest and friendliest pub for miles around serves straightforward pub food all day. In the evening, and on Sunday, things become somewhat more refined, with dishes like rainbow trout, Wicklow lamb and duck à l'orange. The place is famous for its summer Sunday afternoon dances (April-October).

HAVING A DRINK

• Bray
There's traditional music virtually every evening in the numerous pubs in town or on the seafront. Monday evening, **Cois Farraige**, Strand Road; Tuesday, Thursday and Sunday evenings, **Clancy's**, Quinsboro Road; Tuesday, Thursday and Saturday evenings, **Mayfair**, Florence Terrace; Friday and Sunday, **Lenihan's**, Main Street; Friday, **Jim Doyle's**, Strand Road, and Sunday evening, **Harbour Bar**, Seafront.

• Wicklow
Various musical evenings at the **Bridge Tavern**, Bridge Street, Thursday-Sunday evenings in summer and Sunday only in winter. Traditional music at **Mulvihill's**, Market Street, Thursday-Monday evenings. **Paddy O'Connor's** in the town centre has a good reputation for its traditional music evenings (variable timings). **The Beehive Inn**, Coolbeg Cross, on the N11, and the **Leitrim Lounge**, facing the sea, also have music on weekend evenings.

• Ashford
The Woodpecker, in the village, ☎ 0404 401 62, has groups Friday and Saturday evenings and at midday Sunday.

• Roundwood

Vartry House, above the village, ☎ 01 281 81 05, is well-known for its traditional music and its lively atmosphere at the weekend. *The Coach House* (see "Where to stay"), also has music sessions at the weekend.

• Laragh

Lynham's, in the centre of the village next to the hostel, ☎ 0404 453 45, is the liveliest pub in the village. If it's full inside, drinkers spill out into the square. Good pub grub for the hungry and traditional music most evenings in summer.

• Rathdrum

The Parnell, in the village, ☎ 0404 466 54. Enjoyable music some evenings in this Victorian pub devoted to the memory of the 19C political leader.

Phelan's, Ballynaclash, 5.5km south of Rathdrum, ☎ 0404 463 68. Slightly strange establishment which sells groceries as well as drinks. Good traditional music sessions at the weekend and in the week as well in summer.

The Meetings (see "Eating out")

OTHER THINGS TO DO

Fishing – The *Dargle River*, which runs into the Glencree above Bray, has an exceptional reputation for trout between April and September, and for salmon in April and May. Angling permit compulsory, valid for the whole season, available for €25 from *Bray Sports Centre*, 8 Main Street, Bray, ☎ 01 286 30 46.

Sea fishing – All kinds of fishing goes on in Bray, from the beach or from Bray Head to the south of the town. Information from A Downes, 15 King Edward Park, ☎ 01 286 23 73.

The whole coastline from Greystones to Wicklow is known for its onshore fishing. Bass, plaice and cod can all be

caught. Contact J Byrne, 24 Seafield Road, Wicklow Town, ☎ 0404 677 16.

Golf – The area has a good thirty golf courses of all kinds, most with fairly steep fees. The least expensive are *Bray Golf Club* (9 holes), Ravenswell Road, Bray, ☎ 01 286 24 84, open to non-members Tuesday-Friday, €22 per day; *Greystones Golf Club* (two 9-hole courses), Whitshed Road, Greystones, ☎ 01 287 41 36, pitch and putt, Monday, Tuesday and Friday; *Wicklow Golf Club* (18 holes), Dunbur Road, Greystones, ☎ 0404 673 79, sited on the clifftop overlooking the Irish Sea, non-members welcome Tuesday-Friday, daily fee €25; *Roundwood Golf Club*, Roundwood, ☎ 01 281 84 88, Monday-Friday, €25.

Riding – The Wicklow area is ideal for riding, and there are several equestrian centres where horses can be hired for a day or longer. It's best to book in advance. *Bel Air Hotel* (see "Where to stay"), Ashford; *Clarabeg Country House*, Roundwood, ☎ 0404 464 61, day rides; *Laragh Trekking Centre*, Glenmacnass Road, Laragh, ☎ 0402 452 82. This trekking specialist takes riders along the trails around Glendalough, but bookings need to be made at least a week in advance.

SHOPPING

Traditional clothing and souvenirs – *Glendalough Woollen Mills*, on the right on the way out of Laragh towards Avoca, ☎ 0404 451 56. Good range of pullovers and other woollens, tweed jackets and reproductions of traditional jewellery. 9.30am-5pm.

Old Avoca Mill, Avoca, ☎ 0402 351 05. This weaving mill has traditional sweaters and tweed. There is another shop at Kilmacanogue, south of Bray, under the name of *Avoca Handweavers* (see "Eating out"), summer: 9am-6pm; November-April: 9.30am-6pm.

Jerpoint Abbey

THE SOUTHEAST

The southeastern coast and its hinterland are among Ireland's most attractive regions. There's no wild and spectacular scenery as in the west of the country, but the area's river valleys and broad estuaries, rich and rolling farmlands, fishing ports and neat houses combine to create an atmosphere of well-being, further enhanced by the kindly climate and a deep sense of history.

This is indeed the driest and sunniest part of Ireland, a fact which no doubt played a role in attracting foreigners to the area. The Vikings came at first to raid and plunder, but in the 9C began to settle, making use of the sheltered anchorages of the river estuaries and founding the towns of Wexford and Waterford. More or less identical with the ancient province of Leinster, the area not only enjoyed a pleasant climate and natural harbours, but also benefited from the presence of a trio of rivers giving easy access inland. The Barrow, Nore and Slaney encouraged trade between the interior, and the coast, even to foreign shores, and the links thus forged were bound to have an effect on customs and attitudes. The Vikings were soon converted to Christianity and the Anglo-Normans were quickly absorbed into the Celtic population, intermarriage between people of different cultures apparently causing few if any problems. This spirit of tolerance may partly explain how it was here that, inspired by the ideals of the French Revolution, Catholics and Protestants came together to fight as United Irishmen for their country's freedom. All over the southeast, a sometimes benevolent, sometimes tragic past makes its presence felt, in town, village and countryside alike.

CO WEXFORD★

Michelin map 923 L-M / 10-11 and map page 189

Not to be missed
An evening at the Centenary Stores in Wexford.
A seafood meal at the Silver Fox in Kilmore Quay.
A clifftop walk at Hook Head.
The enchanting gardens at Kilmokea.

And remember...
Pick up a copy of the "South East Holidays" brochure from one of the tourist offices
for a wealth of information about the area.

In the extreme southeastern corner of the island, the area around Wexford has the
country's best sunshine record as well as charming landscapes and friendly harbour
towns. This is an Ireland with just a touch of the Mediterranean about it, a place
with a smile on its face, where the living is easy.

Enniscorthy
109km south of Dublin – 21km north of Wexford

In the heart of Co Wexford, Enniscorthy (Pop 3 800) stretches out along the banks
of the Slaney surrounded by farming countryside famous for its **strawberry** crop.
Every year, the girls of the area compete for the coveted title of "Strawberry Queen".
Founded by the Normans in the 13C, the town developed in Tudor times thanks to
its ironworks. Later prosperity was due to distilling and brewing and to ceramics.
But Enniscorthy's most historic moment came in 1798, when the United Irishmen
made their last stand against the British army at the **Battle of Vinegar Hill**.

The town
Allow 2hr. Dominated by its Norman castle and its cathedral, Enniscorthy seems an
austere sort of place at first glance. But a walk around the town soon reveals cheerful
streets of shops and friendly pubs. Topped by a slender spire, **St Aidan's Cathedral**
was designed by Pugin and begun in 1846 but only completed a century later. The
interior has fine polychrome **frescoes**.
Go down Main Street into bustling Market Square lined with shops and restaurants.
A statue of **John Murphy**, one of the leaders of the 1798 Rebellion, stands here.

A not very Catholic priest
Despite his Catholic faith, Father John Murphy
took the part of the Protestant dominated
United Irishmen, and emerged as a leader of the
rebellious masses encamped on Vinegar Hill.
With the help of a Protestant, he managed to escape from the scene of battle, but was betrayed
the following day by a Catholic and executed. Exe-
crated by his bishop as a drunkard and de-
bauchee, Father Murphy was eventually taken
back into the fold at the time of the Vinegar Hill
centenary in 1898. The battle was now seen as
part of a seamless web of patriotic, Catholic
struggle, and the good Father was considered to
have fought for "Faith and Fatherland". Portraits
of him wearing the rebels' red kerchief were doc-
tored to show him with his priest's white collar.

At the top of Castle Hill rises the
sombre outline of **Enniscorthy
Castle**★ *(June-September: 10am-
6pm; Sunday 2pm-5.30pm; October,
November, February and May:
daily 2pm-5.30pm; December-January: 2pm-5pm Sunday only. Admission charge)*. This formidable
fortress with its four corner
towers was built by the Normans
in 1205 to command the River
Slaney. After several centuries in
the hands of the Normans' allies,
the native MacMurrough family,
the castle became Crown property in 1550. Elizabeth I thought
of giving it to her favourite, the
poet Edmund Spenser, who only

The Southeast

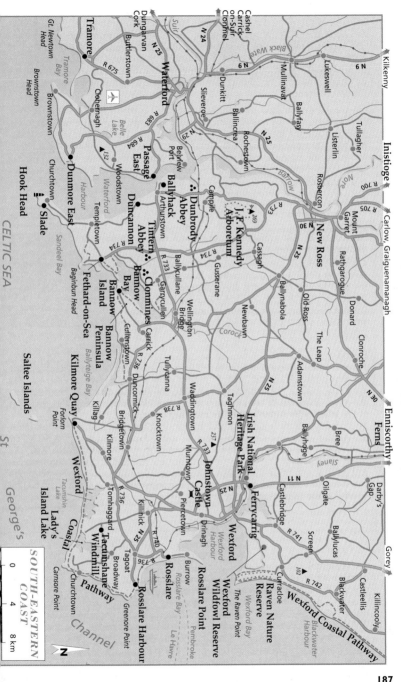

SOUTH-EASTERN COAST

0   4   8 km

N

187

held out in its icy interior for three days before departing. After the 1798 Rebellion the castle served as a prison, and the picture of an armed man scratched on a wall by a captured rebel can still be seen in one of the dungeons. The **Wexford County Museum**⋆ is housed in the castle. The displays on the first floor include many mementoes of the Rebellion and the Battle of Vinegar Hill, while an upper floor has an astonishing array of oddments, ranging from old agricultural implements to a mammoth's tooth.

On the New Ross road outside the town, the **National 1798 Visitor Centre**⋆ (*9.30am-6pm; Sunday 11am-6pm, last admission 5pm. Admission charge*) was opened in 1998 to mark the bicentenary of the 1798 Rebellion. The excellent interactive displays help in understanding the far from simple issues leading up to the insurrection, and stress the international dimensions of the affair, with its links to the American Declaration of Independence and the French Revolutionary creed of Liberty, Equality and Fraternity.

Enniscorthy Pottery Trail
The Enniscorthy area is proud of its long pottery-manufacturing tradition. Potteries flourished here right up to the 1960s, when decline set in. Nowadays the skills are maintained by just a few craftspeople, who enjoy meeting visitors who take the trouble to follow this trail.

Carley's Bridge Pottery (*8.30am-5.45pm; 10am-4pm Saturday in summer; closed Sunday, ☎ 054 351 07*) is on the New Ross road 2km to the west of Enniscorthy just beyond the dog track. It is the oldest pottery in Ireland. Here too is **Hillview Potteries** (*9am-9pm, ☎ 054 354 43*), created about twenty years ago.

Pots for all occasions can be found at the **Kiltrea Bridge Pottery** (*Monday-Saturday 10am-5.30pm, ☎ 054 351 07*) which is 5km from Enniscorthy on the R702 towards Kilteady (*follow signs*).

Ferns⋆
13km northeast of Enniscorthy via the N11. In the early Middle Ages, Ferns was the religious capital of Leinster, with **St Mary's Abbey** (*on the way out of the village to the north*), built at the beginning of the 12C by King Dermot MacMurrough. The abbey was burnt down in 1154, then rebuilt, but little remains of it other than part of the walls by **St Aidan's Church**, plus the **tower**, on its own in a field.

In the middle of the village, behind the modern church, rises the **castle**⋆ (*June-late August: 10am-1pm / 2pm-5pm, except Saturday. Free admission. Key at the tourist information office at the castle entrance*). Erected by the Normans in the 13C, the castle has kept its walls, its moat, and its keep, the last complete with murder holes and battlements. From the top of the keep there is a panoramic **view**⋆ over Ferns and its surroundings. Also visible are the openings through which hot tar, boiling oil and other unpleasant substances could be poured on to the heads of any attackers.

Wexford⋆
130km south of Dublin – Pop 10 000

A commercial and fishing port close to the mouth of the River Slaney, this lively county town owes its foundation and its name to the Vikings, who called it *Waesfjord* ("mud-flats harbour") when they settled here in the 10C.

Cromwell passed this way in 1649, massacring a good number of citizens in the market place. In 1798 the town was one of the main centres of the rebellion of the United Irishmen. Then, in the course of the 19C, it prospered as a port, as it does today, thanks to the country's economic boom. Visitors should spend a little time here walking the main street with its shops and pubs and savouring the charm of a town whose vitality is expressed each autumn with its famous **Opera Festival**.

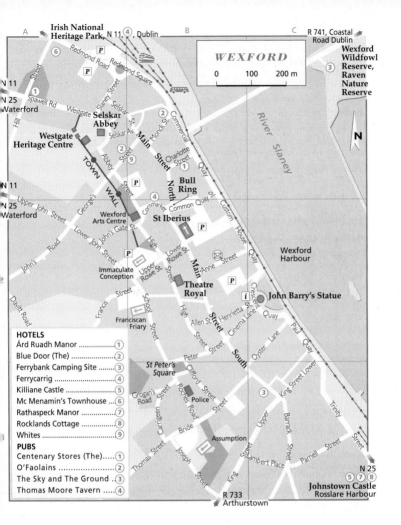

A short walk in Wexford

Allow half a day. Wexford stretches out from north to south for almost a kilometre along its **Main Street*** (B1-B2), its bustling commercial axis.

On the right at the beginning of North Main Street, Selskar Avenue leads in 100m to the ruins of **Selskar Abbey** (A1) *(Free admission)*. All that is left are a few fragments of walls and windows of the original abbey built by the Normans in the 12C. Close by is **Westgate** (A1), one of the medieval town's five gates, now housing the **Westgate Heritage Centre** *(9.30am-4pm summer only. Admission charge)*, with an audio-visual presentation of the town's often turbulent history.

Go back to North Main Street and turn south. The small square is still called the **Bull Ring** (B2), where the Normans once indulged in the unpleasant sport of bull-baiting. The statue here represents a **pikeman**, one of the armed peasants who took part in the events of 1798. Back from the square is the **covered market** of 1775.

A short distance further down North Main Street on the left is the Venetian-style façade of the Anglican **St Iberius' Church**★ (B2) *(April-October: 10am-5pm; November-March: 10am-3pm; closed Sunday all year. Free admission but donation welcomed).* Dedicated to the saint who brought Christianity to the area, the church dates mainly from the 18C. The Georgian interior has an unusual gallery and splendid Corinthian columns screening the choir.

Go along Rowe Street opposite the church and turn immediately left into the High Street.

This narrow lane gives access to the **Theatre Royal** (B2), a modest structure dating from 1832. In October each year it is the principal venue for Wexford's internationally renowned **Opera Festival**.

Continue along the High Street and turn left into the even narrower Peter Street. Cross Main Street South into Cinema Lane which leads to the quayside.

The main railway line running along the quayside somewhat spoils the view. The statue of **John Berry** (C2) on Crescent Quay pays tribute to this Co Wexford man born in 1745 who became the founder of the US Navy.

Places to visit around Wexford

A number of places of interest are within easy reach of Wexford, but they are in different directions and to see them all it will be necessary to come back through the town more than once.

The **Irish National Heritage Park**★★ *(1 March-31 October: 9.30am-6.30pm, last admission 5pm. Admission charge. Allow 2hr30min)* is close to the mouth of the Slaney at Ferrycarrig about 4km northwest of Wexford via the N11. A visitors' trail links

Crannóg at the Irish National Heritage Park

together the 17 sites in which 9 000 years of Irish history have been recreated, from the primitive dwelling of a prehistoric family to the round tower of medieval times. The individual sites are brought to life by the presence of costumed interpreters.

Eight kilometres southwest of Wexford via the N25 *(then follow signs to the right)* is **Johnstown Castle***, an elegant neo-Gothic edifice which is now an agricultural research centre. This is not open to the public, but its outbuildings house the **Irish Agricultural Museum*** *(June-August: 9am-5pm; weekends and public holidays 2pm-5pm; April-May and September-2 November: 9am-12.30pm / 1.30pm-5pm; weekends and public holidays 2pm-5pm; 3 November-31 March: 9am-12.30pm / 1.30pm-5pm; closed weekends and public holidays. Admission charge).* This well-presented museum explains the country's rural life and agricultural heritage in a series of buildings devoted to particular themes. Among the array of tools, old machinery and other items, there is a fine example of the type of **caravan** used by travellers *(see page 48)*. A special hall is devoted to the **Great Famine** and the role of the potato in nutrition. Upstairs rooms contain implements of all kinds as well as traditional country furniture.

It is worthwhile taking a walk in the **ornamental grounds*** *(May-October only: 9am-5.30pm. Admission charge)*. The lovely 20-hectare park contains more than 200 varieties of trees and shrubs, walled gardens, lakes and hot-houses.

To the north of Wexford *(beyond the bridge continue along the R741 for just under 3km towards Gorey, then turn right along the sea-wall)* the estuary of the Slaney is flanked by the mud-flats known as **slobs**, reclaimed from the sea in the 19C. They form the **Wexford Wildfowl Reserve** *(16 April-30 September: 9am-6pm; 1 October-15 April: 10am-5pm. Free admission. Allow 60min)*. There are few birds here in summer, but between October and April, the abundant fauna of insects and worms sustains migrating birds who gather here in huge numbers, among them most of the world's population of Greenland white-fronted geese. *The Interpretative Centre,* ☎ *053 231 29 has an audio-visual presentation and can arrange guided tours.*

Return to the R741 and go towards Gorey, then turn right in 500m towards Curracloe. Turn right opposite the post office in the village and after 900m take the first track on the right for another 1.8km.

The sandy spit forming the northern side of the great bay of Wexford Harbour is designated as the **Raven Point Nature Reserve*** *(Free admission. Allow 1hr30min to 2hr)*. Pathways wind through the dunes and pine trees of the 589-hectare reserve, the sandy beaches offer good bathing, and there is even the chance of seeing grey seals at the southern extremity of the point *(1hr50min boat trips from Wexford,* ☎ *053 212 08)*.

The coast from Rosslare Strand to Ballyhack
85km round tour – Allow 2 days.

One of the main ports of entry to Ireland, **Rosslare Harbour** is not a place to linger long in. But it's a good starting point for visiting the little places along the coast like Kilmore Quay and the Saltee Islands or the marshy landscapes around Tacumshane. And for visitors with some time to spare, further along the coast is the Hook Head Peninsula with its wonderful walks.

■ **Rosslare Strand and around** – *18km south of Wexford via the N25 and R470, and 8km north of Rosslare Harbour.* This little seaside resort has an unusual feature, an avenue of yew trees bordering its sandy beach.

To the north, on the way to **Rosslare Point**, a section of the **Wexford Coastal Pathway** parallels the southern shoreline of Wexford Harbour. Numerous seabirds can be seen foraging for food in the muddy strand.

From Rosslare Strand follow the R736 for 4km, go through Tagoat and continue for a further 1.5km, then turn left and continue for a further 4km.

The Wexford Coastal Pathway

This long-distance footpath runs between Courtown in the north and Wexford in the south through a landscape of dunes, sandbanks, pebbly beaches and cliffs. Beyond Wexford it continues to Waterford for a distance of almost 200km. The path can be picked up at any point along its length. There are no difficult stretches though a tide table is useful for some sections (Maps 76 and 77 in the Discovery series give more detailed information).

Lady's Island Lake* was an important religious site in Neolithic times. Surrounded by marshland, the lagoon then became a pilgrimage centre associated with the Virgin Mary. Next to the ruins of an Augustinian friary on a peninsula protruding into the lake, a little chapel is the site of pilgrimages on 15 August and 8 September.

From Lady's Island, go 1km towards Rosslare Strand then take the first turning on the left and continue for about 500m before turning left again. Carry on for 3.5km to Tacumshane.

Tacumshane Windmill* *(Apply to the general store-cum-pub next to the windmill. Admission charge)* is one of only three surviving windmills in Ireland. Restored, it's in good shape, with a thatched cap, sails, and a "tailpole" for turning the sails into the wind. Inside, the millstones and gear-wheels can be seen.

On leaving the mill, turn left and then right after 1km. Turn left onto the R736 and continue for 15km to Kilmore Quay.

■ **Kilmore Quay*** **and Saltee Islands*** – This fishing village has a lot going for it, including houses with thatched roofs, fine sandy beaches, a maritime museum, inviting pubs, and last but not least, one of Ireland's finest seafood restaurants. Kilmore is rarely crowded except during the annual **Seafood Festival** *(second week in July)*, and is altogether a tempting place to take a break.

The **Guillemot Maritime Museum*** *(June-September: 12pm-6pm. Admission charge. Guided tour)* is housed in an old lightship now embedded in concrete on the quayside. Inside it has all sorts of exhibits recovered from wrecks and elsewhere evoking the tough life led by seafaring folk. Kilmore Quay itself had a tough time of it too in 1989, when waves 15m high swept in causing much damage.

Keen walkers can exercise their legs by exploring the **Ballyteige Burrow Nature Trail** *(from opposite Walsh's grocery shop go along the road leading towards the shore, then cross the footbridge over the canal and carry on into the dunes)*. The 9km trail follows the line of sand-dunes enclosing the **Cull** lagoon to the northwest of Kilmore Quay. The area is at its most lovely between May and mid-July, when larks hover overhead and the grass is speckled with wildflowers.

Four kilometres offshore, the **Saltee Islands*** are well worth a trip *(30min crossing aboard the Saltees Princess. Departures every morning at 10.30am from Kilmore Quay, weather permitting; return between 3pm-4pm; €15. Take a picnic. Apply to Declan Bates, ☎ 053 296 84 or mobile 087 529 536, Fax 053 297 90)*. Within sight of Kilmore Quay, these two little islands are one of the country's most important bird sanctuaries, harbouring some 375 species, including gannets, guillemots and puffins. There are also grey seals. All these creatures are considered to be his "subjects", by the self-styled "Prince of the Saltees", one Michael Neale.

Nowadays the islands are uninhabited for most of the time, but in Neolithic times, when Little Saltee was still linked to the mainland by a land bridge, people lived and worshipped here.

Go north on the R738 for 3km then turn left towards Duncormick.

As the road runs along the Cull a number of castle ruins come into view, their jagged outlines an unexpected sight in this flat landscape. The R736 is reached at **Duncormick**, a little village founded in Norman times. Three kilometres beyond the village is **Coolhull Castle**, a 16C structure which could do with some attention. A further 2km along the road is the pretty village of **Carrick** or *Carig*, where the church has a medieval **font** with fine interlaced carving.

Carrick marks the beginning of the little **Bannow Peninsula***, an area of lovely undulating countryside between Bannow Bay and Ballyteige Bay.

The road comes to an end at **Bannow Island** at the tip of the peninsula. Now attached to the mainland, the island was the point where the Normans made their first landing in Ireland in 1169.

The R736 continues towards Wellington Bridge on top of an embankment parallel to the shore of **Bannow Bay***. It is worth stopping to take in the landscape and the many seabirds which inhabit this important bird sanctuary.
Visible on the far bank are the ruins of the old monastic settlement of **Clonmines***, founded in the 12C. The abbey here prospered on the income of the lead and silver mines in the area right up to the mid-19C. On the right-hand side of the road going towards Wellington Bridge, the old brick chimney of the last of the mines is covered in a dense growth of ivy.

Beyond Wellington Bridge follow the R733 for 7km, then turn left towards Tintern Abbey.

Hook Head Peninsula**
The peninsula extends into the sea between Waterford Harbour to the west and the open sea of St George's Channel to the east. This lovely area with its sandy beaches and steep cliffs is ideal for walkers, riders and cyclists.

■ **Tintern Abbey*** *(June-late October: 9.30am-6.30pm. Admission charge)* a daughter house of the Cistercian abbey of the same name in Wales, stands at the extreme northeastern end of the peninsula. Nestling in its valley location, it was founded in 1200 by the Norman William de Clare, who had sworn to build an abbey if he survived a violent storm at sea during his first crossing to Ireland. The monks lived here until the Dissolution, when the abbey became the property of the Colclough family who made it their home for 400 years. The well-preserved ruins of the abbey, which include a massive crenellated tower, make a fine picture when viewed from the fortified bridge. There are good **walks** in the surrounding countryside, described in detail in a leaflet obtainable from local tourist offices.

A minor road leads to the tiny village of Saltmills. Continue past the village and join the R734 which brings you to Fethard.

■ **Fethard-on-Sea*** is a pleasant little resort with a lovely sandy beach along which runs a section of the **Wexford Coastal Pathway**. At the far northern end of the beach, **Big Burrow** is an important nesting site for seabirds. In the village itself, the entire **façade** of a garage is covered in seashells, while a short distance away the old **castle** of the Bishops of Ferns has a dungeon in the base of its battlemented tower.

Take the main road south towards Hook Head for 8km, then turn left towards Slade.

The ruins of a medieval **castle** overlook the delightful little port of **Slade*** with its fishermen's cottages. It is a 30 minute walk to the tip of the peninsula and the Hook Head lighthouse; the clifftop beyond the village is exposed to wind and spray, and an anorak is likely to come in handy.

The lighthouse can also be reached by car – 2km drive.

■ **Hook Head Lighthouse****, 25m high, stands on the site where a light has been maintained continuously ever since the 5C. Below the lighthouse, the black rocks undergo a constant battering from wind and waves. *A visitor centre is planned,* ☎ 051 389 46 54.

Return to the main road and drive 12km north to Duncannon.

■ Nestling at the foot of its fort, the village of **Duncannon*** livens up once a year in the first fortnight of July for its **Cockle Festival**.
Duncannon Fort* *(June-mid-September: 10am-5.30pm. Admission charge)* was built in 1584 in anticipation of an attack from the Spanish Armada, strengthened in the early 19C for fear of Napoleon, and reinforced again during the Second World War. None of these attacks materialised, so the fort's impregnability was never called into question.

From the ramparts there is a superb **view**** over the Rivers Suir and Barrow, from Waterford in the west to New Ross in the north.

Carry on northwards along the main road for 3.5km to Arthurstown, then for a further 2.5km to Ballyhack.

■ The most important thing about the little harbour village of **Ballyhack*** is its **ferry** *(October-March: 7am-8pm; April-September: 8am-10pm; first crossing 9.30am Sunday all year. Crossing time: 5min. Fare: €6 for car and passengers)* which crosses the estuary of the Suir to the village of **Passage East** with its prettily painted houses *(see page 209)*. Ballyhack has an austere beauty about it, an impression reinforced by **Ballyhack Castle*** *(mid-June-late September: 10am-1pm / 2pm-6pm; Saturday and Sunday: 10am-6pm. Admission charge)*. A visit to this massive six-storey tower house built in the 15C-16C by the Knights Templar gives a good idea of the construction techniques used at the time.

New Ross
34km west of Wexford via the N25 – 27km northeast of Waterford

This old port town well inland on the River Barrow is now a quiet place of some 5 000 inhabitants. Its main attraction is its row of pubs lining the quayside, but it is a useful base for tourists wanting to visit some of the sights in the countryside around the town such as the Kennedy Arboretum or the charming village of Inistioge.

The town
Allow 1hr30min. On the quayside by the bridge, the **JF Kennedy Trust*** *(July-August: 10am-7pm; October-March: 12pm-5pm, last admission 4.30pm. Admission charge)* is devoted to the US President whose family originally came from this area. The foundation is an important genealogical centre for Irish-Americans wanting to trace their

Johnston Castle

F. Baume/MICHELIN

origins. There is a museum of emigration but the star turn is the three-masted **Dunbrody**★, a replica of a famine ship which crossed the Atlantic with its cargo of people escaping the tribulations of their homeland (www.dunbrody.com).

Go along Quay Street at right angles to the river, opposite the bridge, to the **Tholsel** on the corner of South Street. Dating from 1749 and now the home of the municipal offices, this building was used as a barracks by the British garrison during the 1798 Rebellion. On the far side of the street, the statue of the **Croppy Boy** raises his fist in memory of the close-cropped insurgents of the time.

Go along Mary Street, the continuation of Quay Street, then turn left into Church Lane.

St Mary's Church★, an early 19C Anglican establishment (if closed, ask for the key at No 6 Church Lane). This church was built on the site of what was one of the largest medieval abbey churches in Ireland, of which only ruins remain surrounded by a graveyard. The adjoining Catholic church dates from the 19C.

South of New Ross

12km south of New Ross via the R733 and the R734, then follow signs on the right. The **John Fitzgerald Kennedy Arboretum**★★ *(May-August: 10am-8pm; April and September: 10am-6.30pm; October-March: 10am-5pm. Admission charge)* is a popular place for family walks. Opened in 1968 and dedicated to the memory of the US President assassinated in 1963, the beautifully maintained park extends over an area of 252 hectares and has more than 6 000 plant species including 500 varieties of rhododendron.

Back on the R733, drive for 3km towards New Ross then follow signs on the left indicating the Kennedy Homestead.

Not easy to find, the whitewashed cottage of the **Kennedy Homestead** *(May-September: 10am-5.30pm. Admission charge)* was the birthplace in 1820 of JF Kennedy's great-grandfather, and Kennedys still live in this remote part of Ireland. One room has Kennedy memorabilia, including mementoes of JFK's visit here a mere two months before his death.

Return to the R733 by the JFK Arboretum and go towards Ballyhack for about 1.5km before turning right at signs indicating Great Island and Kilmokea Gardens and continuing for a further 2.5km.

What is perhaps the most beautiful garden in the southeast has been laid out next to a Georgian glebe house which is now a B&B *(see "Making the most of New Ross")*. **Kilmokea Gardens**★★ *(April-November: 9am-5pm; December-March: 1pm-4pm. Admission charge including tea)* consists of a walled garden with ornamental plants and a jungle-like but carefully controlled wild area laid out along the narrow valley of a tiny stream.

Return to the R733 and turn right towards Ballyhack. Dunbrody Abbey is 3km further on.

Towards the end of the 12C the Norman knight Hervey de Montmorency founded **Dunbrody Abbey**★ *(May, June and September: 10am-6pm; July-August: 10am-7pm. Admission charge).* For many years the abbey led a prosperous existence, but fell victim to Henry VIII at the Dissolution. Its substantial and attractive ruins stand on the banks of a tributary of the River Barrow.

On the other side of the road, the ruinous **castle** *(same opening times. Admission charge)* was built in the 17C by the Etchingham family into whose hands the abbey had passed. The adjacent **visitor centre** is worth a visit even if only for the newly-created yew maze.

A side-trip into Co Kilkenny

13.5km north of New Ross via the N30 and the R700. Delightfully set among wooded hills overlooking the River Nore, the charming village of **Inistioge**★ has an attractive square lined with lime trees and London planes. There's not a lot to do here, but it is very pleasant strolling along the riverside and there are a number of ruins to investigate.

The **Woodstock Forest Park**, 1.5km to the south of the village, has footpaths giving lovely **views*** over the valley.

To avoid going back the way you have come, take the minor road between Inistioge and Graiguenamanagh, a distance of 11km.

The riverside township of **Graiguenamanagh*** is a popular stopping point for people taking a house-boat holiday on the Barrow. It is not just a haven for boats, but with 13 pubs for a population of only 1 500, for thirsty drinkers too.

The place is dominated by the restored **Duiske Abbey***, a Cistercian foundation dating from the 12C and still much visited by believers. The abbey has a wonderful **effigy*** of a 14C knight in chain mail brandishing his sword, and there is a small **museum** in the monks' quarters with items relating to the abbey.

The tranquil Nore at Inistioge

B Kaufmann/MICHELIN

COMING AND GOING

By train – The railway station is on the left bank of the River Slaney, reached by turning right beyond the bridge. Three trains daily to Dublin (2hr10min) and to Rosslare (70min) via Wexford (25min).

By bus – Buses leaves from Templeshannon Quay, opposite the castle on the left bank of the Slaney. The n° 2 bus runs 8 times daily (5 on Sunday) to Dublin (2hr20min) and to Rosslare (50min) via Wexford (25min), and bus n° 5 runs 3 times daily to Waterford (1hr).

ADDRESS BOOK

Tourist information – In the castle, ☎ 054 345 99, same opening times as the castle (*see page 186*).

Banks / Currency exchange – Several cash machines around Market Street.

Post office – Abbey Quay.

Bicycle hire – *Kenny's Bike*, Slaney Street, on the quayside to the left of the Antique Tavern, ☎ 054 332 55. Paul Nolan is a good source of tips for touring the area by bike.

WHERE TO STAY

• **Enniscorthy and around**
Between €40-50
Old Bridge B&B, Slaney Place, ☎ 054 342 22 – 4rm ↑ TV CC Good location on the quayside close to the castle, slightly garish décor but reasonable rates.

Between €50-55
Salville House, ☎ 054 352 52 – 3rm ↑ ⟋ TV ✗ CC Follow signs on the Wexford road. Lovely 19C country residence on a rise overlooking the river. The simply furnished rooms are bright and spacious. The place is known for its fine cuisine (€23 per head), for which advance booking is essential.

• **Ferns**
Between €65-90
Clone House, ☎ 054 661 13, Fax 054 662 25 – 5rm ↑ TV CC Three kilometres along a minor road on the left when driving north out of the village.

One of the best places to stay in this area, Betty Breens' farmhouse is a real little paradise. The rooms are exceptionally comfortable, furnished with exquisite taste, and the delicious breakfast consists of home-produced ingredients.

EATING OUT

• **Enniscorthy**
Under €13
The Antique Tavern, on the quayside, ☎ 054 334 28. Furnished and decorated in the manner of a pirates' hideout, this old tavern deserves its name. Good pub food which in summer can be enjoyed on a little open-air terrace.

The Mill House, next to the **Riverside Park Hotel** in the southern part of the town. 12.20pm-10pm. This very pleasant pub and self-service restaurant is in the storehouse of an old mill. Country décor and cosy atmosphere.

HAVING A DRINK

Doreen's, opposite the Antique Tavern, has music Saturday and Sunday evenings, with the clientele singing along to the accordion player.

OTHER THINGS TO DO

Greyhound racing – On the way out of town in the New Ross direction, ☎ 054 331 72, Monday and Thursday evening at 8pm.

Golf – *Enniscorthy Golf Club*, Knockmarshall, 2km on the New Ross road, ☎ 054 331 91. Dawn to dusk. Fee: €19 weekdays, €23 at weekends.

Fishing – Details on fishing in the estuary of the River Slaney from Myles Keogh's Bar, Castle Hill, ☎ 054 335 88.

Riding – *Boro Hill Equestrian Centre*, Clonroche, ☎ 054 44 117, 12km southwest of Enniscorthy via the N30, has horses for hire all year round.

Bicycle hire – *South East Cycle Tours*, 1 Mary Street, ☎ 054 332 55, will help set up a week or fortnight cycling round the area on minor roads, with a guide and hotel and restaurant reservations.

COMING AND GOING

By train – The railway station is in Redmond Square (B1) close to the centre of town. Trains from Wexford run to Dublin Connolly Station (2hr40min) and in the other direction to Rosslare Harbour (28min) 3 times daily.

By bus – Service n° 2 runs 10 times daily between Wexford and Dublin (3hr10min) and to Rosslare (25min), and bus n° 55 runs 9 times daily to Waterford (1hr). Buses 370 and 371 also run to Waterford (2hr30min), but via New Ross.

ADDRESS BOOK

Tourist information – *Tourist Information*, Crescent Quay (B2-C2), ☎ 053 231 11, Fax 053 417 43. January-March and November-December: 9.30am-1pm / 2pm-5.30pm except weekends; April-October: 9am-6pm except Sunday (July-August 11am-5pm Sunday). Their "Southeast Holiday Guidebook" has a town plan and much useful information on the area.

Bank / Currency exchange – Numerous cash machines in Main Street.

Post office – *Main Post Office* in Anne Street (B2). Another post office in Mulcahy's newsagents, North Main Street (B1).

Bicycle hire – *Hayes Cycles*, 108 South Main Street (C3), ☎ 053 224 62.

WHERE TO STAY

Under €25
Ferrybank Camping Site, ☎ 053 443 78/432 74 ⏚ ✗ CC From Wexford, cross the bridge and turn immediately right. Well-managed camping and caravan site with swimming pool, in parkland close to the river.

Between €50-55
The Blue Door, 18 Lower George Street, ☎ 053 210 47 – 4rm ⓝ TV A good place to stay in the middle of town. Hanging baskets and window boxes full of flowers, plus well-kept and pleasantly decorated rooms. The landlady has lots of useful tips about the area.

Killian Castle, Drinagh, ☎ and Fax 053 588 85 / 588 98 – 9rm ⓝ TV CC Turn left off the Rosslare road just beyond the Farmer's Kitchen restaurant 3km from Wexford. Enjoy the aristocratic life in a building next door to an old manor house in the middle of the countryside. Level of comfort varies between the rooms, but very acceptable for the most part.

Rathaspeck Manor, ☎ 053 426 61 / 451 48 – 6rm ⓝ TV CC Turn right off the Rosslare road 5km from Wexford and follow signs. Vast historical residence with bedrooms with an odd array of furniture and good value for the price.

Between €50-55
Árd Ruadh Manor, ☎ 053 231 94 – 8rm ⓝ TV CC Big brick building resembling a manor house with rooms furnished in Art Nouveau style.

McMenamin's Townhouse, 3 Auburn Terrace, ☎ and Fax 053 464 42 – 6rm ⓝ TV CC Victorian house in the station area, quiet and tastefully furnished. Gargantuan breakfast including herrings and smoked salmon and porridge. Private car park.

Rocklands Cottage, ☎ 053 435 89, Fax 053 436 01 – 2rm ⓝ TV On the Rosslare raod 2km from Wexford. Vast Victorian residence in parkland, with bright, quiet rooms and very ordinary furnishings. But overall a high degree of charm.

Between €90-115
White's Hotel, George Street, ☎ 053 223 11, Fax 053 450 00 – 82rm ⓝ 🄿 TV ✗ CC Huge traditional town centre hotel with spacious and carefully furnished rooms. Private facilities include bathtubs, and a jacuzzi is also available.

More than €130
Ferrycarrig Hotel, Ferrycarrig, ☎ 053 209 99, Fax 053 419 82 – 90rm ⓝ 🄿 TV ✗ CC On the N11 4.5km north of the town. De luxe establishment, refurbished in 1997, on the banks of the Slaney and only a few steps from the Irish National Heritage Park. There is a swimming pool, a fitness centre, an aerobics studio as well as several restaurants decorated in maritime style.

Under €13

Into the Blue, 80 South Main Street (B3), ☎ 053 220 11. Snack bar: 8am-5pm; restaurant: Wednesday-Saturday 6.30pm-9.30pm. A good place to come for lunch with generously filled sandwiches. In the evening there are more refined dishes such as haddock coated in mustard seeds or salmon with sweet potato and coriander.

The Star, next door to the above (B3). 9am-5.30pm; closed Sunday. This bakery-cum-café has delicious traditional cakes and excellent meat and fish pies to eat in or take away.

The Harpers, North Main Street (B1) adjacent to White's Hotel, ☎ 053 223 11. Daily 12pm-10pm. Huge hall in a style halfway between Gothic cathedral and Bavarian beer-hall. Moderately priced lunch, with cold meat dishes, fried pollock, etc. In the evening, prices rise for dishes such as smoked salmon with horseradish or confit of duck with honey and ginger.

Dragon Heen, Redmond Square (A1), ☎ 053 213 32. Daily 12.30pm-2.30pm/5.30pm-11.30pm. On the first floor of a building near the station, this Chinese restaurant serves a very acceptable version of Szechwan cuisine. Prices are lower at lunchtime, while in the evening it makes sense to order the €40 menu for two which includes six different dishes.

Asple's, Crescent Quay (C2), ☎ 053 241 97. Open 11am-9.30pm. Attractive country-style décor with grills and salads at midday. In the evening, the adjacent restaurant serves all kinds of seafood specialities at a higher price.

Between €13-20

🍴 **Tim's Tavern**, 51 South Main Street (B2), ☎ 053 238 61. Daily 12pm-10pm, dinner from 6pm. Huge and lively tavern with tasty pub food at midday. More refined dishes in the evening, including a very acceptable duck à l'orange.

Between €20-25

Heavens Above Restaurant, 112 South Main Street (C3), ☎ 053 212 73, Fax 053 218 32. Monday-Saturday 6.30pm-10pm; closed Sunday. The décor of this restaurant is calculated to make diners feel they are aboard ship. Seafood is the predictable speciality, including paupiettes of pollock with crab, fillets of sole or seafood selection. The more straightforward dishes are, however, the better bet.

HAVING A DRINK

🍴 **The Centenary Stores**, Charlotte Street, ☎ 053 244 24. This huge pub consists of several rooms fitted out like old chandlers' stores. Evenings tend to be lively, with traditional music on Monday and Wednesday, as well as Sunday lunchtime. On Tuesday there is folk or blues, and there is a nightclub to 2am Thursday to Sunday.

The Thomas Moore Tavern, Cornmarket Street, by contrast, is an intimate little pub in the building where the mother of the poet Thomas Moore used to live.

The Sky and the Ground, 112 South Main Street, ☎ 053 212 73. Classic pub on the upper floor of the Heavens Above restaurant. Traditional music all week except Friday and Saturday.

🍴 **O'Faoláins**, Monck Street, ☎ 053 238 77. Traditional tunes Monday evening and Sunday lunchtime, ballads Tuesday and Friday evening, mixed styles Thursday evening and DJs at the back of the building Friday, Saturday and Sunday evening to 2am.

OTHER THINGS TO DO

Fishing – The Rivers Slaney and Sow are famous for salmon and trout, and there is sea fishing north and south of the mouth of the Slaney.

Further details from **Murphy's Tackle Shop**, 92 North Main Street, ☎ 053 247 17. For sea fishing aboard the Patsy J II, contact Peter Jackson, ☎ 053 212 08 or 08 72 86 90 87 (mobile).

Riding – For hire of horses for riding in the countryside or along the beach, contact: **Shelmalier Riding Stables**, Trinity, Fourth Mountain, Taghmon, ☎ 053 392 51. Turn left off the R25 on to the R738 10km west of Wexford.

Making the most of Wexford

Golf – Wexford Country Club, Mulgannon, 1km south of town, ☎ 053 422 38, Fax 053 422 42. 18 holes. Fee: €23 weekdays, €25 weekends.

Festival – The **Wexford Opera Festival** takes place in the last two weeks of October. Most performances are in the Theatre Royal, ☎ 053 221 44 / 224 00, others in St Iberius' Church. Tickets are much sought after and should be booked at least three months in advance.

Making the most of Rosslare

COMING AND GOING

By train – Trains meet ferry passengers at Rosslare's Europort. Three trains daily between Rosslare Europort and Dublin (3hr05min), calling at Wexford (25min) and Rosslare Strand (6min).

By bus – Bus station in the port. Service n° 2 runs 29 times daily between Rosslare Europort and Dublin (3hr10min) via Wexford (20min). Bus 40 runs 3 times daily (twice Sunday) between Rosslare Europort and Cork (4hr15min) via Waterford (1hr50min). No 55 runs between Rosslare Europort and Waterford (1hr20min) via Wexford 7 times daily.

By ferry – Stena Line, ☎ 053 331 15, runs 6 times daily between Rosslare and Fishguard in Wales, using a conventional ferry (3hr30min) or a faster catamaran (1hr40min). Irish Ferries, ☎ 053 331 58, run twice daily between Rosslare and Pembroke Dock in Wales (4hr30min). There is also a service to and from Cherbourg or Roscoff in France 3-5 times weekly between late March and late September. Around 20hr.

ADDRESS BOOK

Tourist information – A small tourist information office opens in the Europort terminal to coincide with ferry arrivals, ☎ 053 332 32.

Rosslare Kilrane Tourist Office, ☎ 053 336 22, Fax 053 334 21. On the left of the main road, 1.5km from the harbour. May-September: daily 11am-8pm; October-April: Tuesday-Sunday 2pm-8pm. Plentiful information about the whole of Ireland as well as the southeast.

Banks / Currency exchange – No cash machine in the Europort but a bureau de change opens to coincide with ferry arrivals. Cash machine at the Bank of Ireland next to the modern church in the village. Bureau de change at the post office in Rosslare Strand.

Post office – On the road out from Rosslare Harbour in the Super Valu shop. Near the station in Rosslare Strand.

Car hire – In the Europort terminal: Hertz, ☎ 053 332 38, Europcar, ☎ 053 336 34.

WHERE TO STAY

• **Rosslare Strand**
Between €65-115
Churchtown House, ☎ and Fax 053 325 55 – 14rm ⌂ ♪ 🖃 ✗ 🆑 Three kilometres from Rosslare Strand on the road to Tagoat. Lovely Georgian house in parkland. The rooms are very comfortable even though the furnishings are on the flashy side. Evening meal available if ordered in advance.

• **Rosslare Harbour**
Under €13
Rosslare Harbour Youth Hostel, Goulding Street, ☎ 053 333 99, Fax 053 336 24 – 82 beds. Guests are accommodated even if catching a night boat, but there is also a midnight curfew. Dormitories are a bit basic.

Between €45-50
Ailsa Lodge, ☎ 053 332 30, Fax 053 335 81 – 10rm ⌂ ♪ 🖃 🆑 Only 5min from the ferry terminal. The spacious rooms in this attractive white

house have fine sea views, which to some extent makes up for the choice of furniture.

• Near Rosslare Harbour
Under €25
St Margaret's Beach Caravan & Camping Park, ☎ 053 311 69. ⚘ Turn left off the N25 at Tagoat 9km from Rosslare Harbour and follow signs for 5km. Private camp site with family atmosphere and basic facilities, close to the beach. Open Easter-31 October.

Between €45-50
Furziestown House, ☎ 053 313 76 – 2rm ⚑ Deep in the countryside, this farmhouse will delight anyone looking for peace and quiet... always provided that they can find it. Turn left off the N25 towards Kilmore Quay in Tagoat 10.5km from Rosslare Harbour, continue for 1.9km and turn right at the crossroads, then immediately left. Continue for 2.2km, turn left towards Furziestown and continue in the same direction until a sign appears on the left. From the moment of your arrival, Yvonne Pim will be at pains to make you feel at home. Breakfast features fresh fruit juice, home-made jams and eggs from her hens. Additional accommodation to rent for 4 people @ €320 per week.

EATING OUT
• Rosslare Strand
Between €25-30
Oyster Restaurant, in the village, ☎ 053 324 39. Easter to late November: 12pm-3pm / 5.30pm-9pm, closed Tuesday and Wednesday. Despite its name, there are no oysters on offer here, though various other kinds of seafood are on the menu. Inexpensive "Ferry Menu" at midday, dearer dishes in the evening.

• Carne
Between €13-20
The Lobster Pot, ☎ 053 311 10, Fax 053 314 01. Daily 12pm-10pm, reservation advisable. People come from far and wide to enjoy the fish dishes served in this little inn with its décor of hundreds and thousands of bits and pieces. A €13 lunch can consist of a satisfying assortment of fish, smoked and unsmoked. In the evening, the slightly more expensive house speciality is "Lobster Pot Pourri", a kind of fish stew.

HAVING A DRINK
Crosbie Cedars Hotel, to the north of Rosslare Strand. Modern hotel with a pleasant pub, as well as a discotheque Friday, Saturday and Sunday evening from 11pm-2am.

Making the most of Kilmore Quay

ADDRESS BOOK
Tourist information – Stella Maris Community Centre, ☎ 053 299 22. Three hundred metres on the left on the way up from the harbour. Supposedly open 9am-2pm. This is Kilmore Quay's social centre, and if there is anyone there they can supply a good range of information on Kilmore Quay and Saltee Islands.

Bicycle hire – Kilmore Quay Bike Hire, Island View House, ☎ 053 297 81. Quay House (see "Where to stay") also has bikes for hire.

WHERE TO STAY
Under €13
Kilturk Hostel, ☎ 053 298 83. In the Kilmore Quay, but 2km from the harbour. This is a small independent hostel with basic facilities, but OK if you are really pushed.

Between €50-65
The Ridge Cottage, ☎ 053 299 82 – 3rm ⚑ On the left on the way into Kilmore Quay, 1.5km from the harbour. Absolutely delightful thatched cottage, perfectly restored and furnished with impeccable taste, whether

in terms of rustic chairs and tables, curtains and fabrics, or the elegant bathroom belonging to the upstairs room. Excellent value for money.

EATING OUT

Between €20-25

Silver Fox, near the harbour, ☎ 053 298 88. Open 12.30pm-9.30pm (9pm Sunday); closed last week in January and first week in February. Essential to book in advance. This is easily the best fish restaurant in the southeast. Especially good are the brill Saint-Jacques and the grilled plaice in cream sauce. If there's any room left for dessert, the profiteroles are well worth a try. Everything is as fresh as could be, the prices are not excessive and there is a good wine list.

HAVING A DRINK

Kehoes, in Kilmore Quay, ☎ 053 298 30. A notice asks you to leave your diving suit at the door, and this lively pub is a real little maritime museum, with all kinds of objects recovered from various wrecks. Traditional music at the weekend.

OTHER THINGS TO DO

Sea fishing – Dick Hayes, ☎ 053 297 04, and **Joe Walsh**, ☎ 053 354 19 can take visitors aboard their craft in search of blue shark and other prey.

Diving – Some of the finest diving in Ireland can be had here, and the Saltee Islands in particular have a wealth of wrecked vessels of all kinds. **Kilmore Quay Diving Centre**, ☎ 053 299 88, has qualified instructors and can hire all the necessary equipment for fascinating underwater expeditions.

Making the most of the Hook Head Peninsula

ADDRESS BOOK

Tourist information – The **ticket office** at Duncannon Fort has some useful information about the area.
Tourist office at Ballyhack Castle, summer only 10am-1pm / 2pm-6pm.
Tourist Information, Fethard-on-Sea, next to the castle, ☎ 051 397 502/ 397 378. Summer: 9am-5.30pm, 11am-3pm Saturday and Sunday; rest of year: 9am-5.30pm; closed weekends. Information on the area plus bicycle hire.

Banks / Currency exchange – Small bureau de change at the King's Bay Inn in Arthurstown.

Bicycle hire – Apply to the youth hostel in Arthurstown (see "Where to stay").

WHERE TO STAY

• **Fethard-on-Sea**
Between €45-50
Hotel Naomh Seosamh, in the village, ☎ 051 307 129, Fax 051 397 560 – 15rm 🛏 🅿 TV ✕ CC Charming small hotel with rooms that are not particularly spacious but good value. Substantial breakfasts, including kipper pancakes. The hotel has a fine restaurant too (see "Eating out").

• **Arthurstown**
Under €13
Arthurstown Youth Hostel, ☎ 051 389 411 – 32 beds. On the right on the road out of Arthurstown towards Ballyhack. This small private hostel is in an old coastguards' house on a headland overlooking the sea. There are double rooms as well as dormitories. Cooking facilities and bike hire. Open June-September.

Between €50-55
Glendine Country House, ☎ 051 389 258, Fax 051 389 677 – 4rm 🛏 TV ✕ CC On the right on the way into the village from the R733. The house dates from 1830, most of the furniture is hardly more recent. All the rooms are

tastefully furnished and decorated, especially the dining room. Breakfast includes delicious home-made jams and bread.

EATING OUT

• Duncannon
Under €13
Strand Tavern, ☎ 051 389 09. Monday-Saturday 12.30pm-3pm / 6pm-9.30pm, Sunday 12.30pm-9.30pm. Family pub popular with local people. Generous sandwiches at lunchtime as well as fine fish dishes.
Templars Inn, Templetown, ☎ 051 397 162. Daily 12pm-9pm. 7km south of Duncannon on the road to Hook Head. Seaside inn at the foot of a cliff and opposite a ruined church, known for its seafood, grills, and very reasonable prices.

• Fethard-on-Sea
Between €20-25
Naomh Seosamh (see "Where to stay"), Bar food: 10am-9pm, restaurant: 6.30pm-9pm. Good fish restaurant with attractive décor. Crab claws in garlic butter and coquilles St-Jacques in white wine sauce cannot fail to leave happy memories.

• Arthurstown
Between €25-45
👜 **Dunbrody Restaurant**, on the way into the village, ☎ 051 389 600, Fax 051 389 601. Daily 1pm-2.30pm / 6.30pm-9.30pm. This restaurant belongs to a luxury hotel in a lovely Georgian building standing in parkland. Sophisticated cuisine with a local flavour enhanced by Mediterranean touches. Few diners could remain indifferent to the grilled terrine of vegetables with shavings of Parmesan or the leg of Wexford lamb in orange, whiskey and basil sauce. The products of many countries feature on the excellent wine list.

• Ballyhack
More than €25
Neptune, by the harbour, ☎ 051 389 254, Fax 051 389 356. April-late September: 6.30pm-9pm, open Sunday lunchtime but not evening; October-late March: open only Saturday evening and Sunday lunchtime. Reservations essential. The food here outshines the décor. The cooking is refined without being pretentious. Particularly good are the coquilles Saint-Jacques Mornay, the wonderful guinea fowl in Bailey's Cream, and the excellent desserts.

OTHER THINGS TO DO

Riding – Seaview Trekking Centre, Saltmills (near Tintern Abbey), ☎ 051 562 239, organises treks around the Hook Head Peninsula.

Walking – One way of exploring the historical riches of the Hook area is to go on a guided walk with Phil Conway, Saltmills, ☎ 051 562 142.

Making the most of New Ross

COMING AND GOING

By bus – New Ross has no rail service, but there are reasonable connections by bus. Service n° 5 between Dublin (3hr) and Waterford (20min) calls at the bus station and the quayside 7 times daily. The n° 55 runs 7 times daily to and from Rosslare Harbour (1hr) and Wexford (40min). No 40 links New Ross and Cork (2hr40min) 5 times daily except Sunday.

ADDRESS BOOK

Tourist information – Tourist Information, 22 The Quay, ☎ 051 421 857. June-September: 10am-6pm, except Sunday.

Banks / Currency exchange – Banks with cash machines in South Street and one on the quayside.

Post office – In Charles Street, near the quayside, 9am-5.30pm; 10am-12pm Saturday; closed Sunday.

WHERE TO STAY

• New Ross
Under €13
MacMurrough Farm Hostel, ☎ 051 421 383. Signposted off the N30 about 4km to the north of town. Difficult to find, but guests can be picked up if they telephone. Brian and Jenny Nutall have turned their farm into a hostel with dormitories of 7-8 beds and one double room, and make their guests feel very welcome.

Between €45-50
Rivesdale House, Lower William Street, ☎ 051 422 515, Fax 051 422 800 – 4rm ⁴⌐ Open March-September. Attractive house in the upper part of town with its own car park. Quiet, functional rooms with all comforts.

Between €115-140
Kilmokea Country Manor (see "Kilmokea Gardens" page *195*), ☎ 051 388 109, Fax 051 388 776 – 4rm ⁴⌐ TV CC Mark and Emma Hewlett have lovingly restored this old glebe house of 1794 in its fabulous gardens. The house is entirely furnished in Victorian style, and the rooms with their canopied beds look out over the gardens. Dinner available if booked in advance for around €25.

• Inistioge
Between €45-50
Grove Farmhouse, ☎ 056 584 67 – 4rm ⁴⌐ CC Take the R700 towards Thomastown for about 4km, then follow signs on the left just after the bridge. 19C farmhouse on a hilltop overlooking attractive countryside. Quiet, bright rooms with floral décor. Generous breakfast in a dining room overlooking the garden. Open April-October.

EATING OUT

• New Ross
The town does not set out to attract gourmets, and it can be difficult to find a decent meal after about 8pm.

Under €13
John V's, The Quay, ☎ 051 425 188. Fairly standard, unpretentious pub with acceptable food.

Mannion's, Mount Elliott, ☎ 051 421 412. 1.5km south on the N25. Friendly atmosphere and generous helpings of classic cooking.

Between €13-30
The best but most expensive way of eating here is to book a river cruise aboard the Galley, ☎ 051 421 723. Lunch: 12.30pm May-October, €16; afternoon tea: 3pm in June, July and August, €10; dinner: 7pm May-September, €25-30. The cruise on the Barrow takes between two and three hours and the meal and views are enjoyed from a panoramic saloon.

• Inistioge
Under €13
The Old School House Café Delightful café serving well-filled sandwiches and home-made cakes. No drinks licence.

Between €25-30
The Motte, Plas Newydd Lodge, ☎ 056 586 55. On the left on the way out of the village towards Thomastown. Dinner only, Tuesday-Saturday 7pm-9.15pm, closed one week in autumn, one week in Spring, and one week at Christmas. This little house in its flowery garden might not look like a restaurant, but it is and it serves some of the best food in the area. The atmosphere may seem a little stiff to begin with, but the mood quickly lightens when the food arrives, made from local, fresh ingredients and prepared in a determinedly innovative way. Well worth trying are the cheese profiteroles and the farmyard chicken with apricot couscous. A gourmet's treat, well off the beaten track.

HAVING A DRINK
Corcoran's, New Ross. In the old part of the town, this is a comfortable and cheerful stone-built pub with traditional music and other sounds, plus dancing at the weekend.

OTHER THINGS TO DO
Golf – Tinnerany Golf Club, 2km from the centre of New Ross, ☎ 051 421 433, Fax 051 420 098. 18-

hole course open to visitors Monday-Saturday. Fee: €17-20.

Fishing – *O'Leary & Sons*, Graiguenamanagh, in the main street, can provide a fishing licence as well as all kinds of fishing gear.

River cruises – *The Ultimate Boat Hire*, Graiguenamanagh, ☎ 0503 249 45, Fax 0503 248 89, has 4-6 berth houseboats for hire by the week for cruising on the Barrow downstream as far as Waterford. Bicycles can be hired and taken on board too. Book at least a week in advance. Deposit of 25% of hire charge. Reckon on €580-€1 300 per week depending on the time of year and size of boat.

SHOPPING

Traditional clothing – *Butler Island Craft Centre*, New Ross, on the N25 towards Wexford, ☎ 051 422 612. Open 8am-8pm; 8am-9pm in summer. Sweaters, tweeds, waxed jackets and other traditional wear. Souvenir shop and cafeteria open all day.

WATERFORD AND AROUND ★

Co Waterford
140km south of Dublin – Pop 43 000
Michelin map n° 923 K-L / 11 – See map page 187

Not to be missed
A tour of the Waterford Crystal factory.
An evening at Doolan's pub.
Delicious seafood at McAlpin's in Cheekpoint.

And remember...
Waterford is best explored on foot – cars can be parked on the quayside
or in the shopping centre car park.

Rising over the quayside, Reginald's Tower is a potent reminder of the long history of this thousand-year-old town, which, far from dwelling on past glories, has its face turned resolutely to the future. Pride of place may still be occupied by its world-famous glass factory, but the town has understood the value of diversification, and,

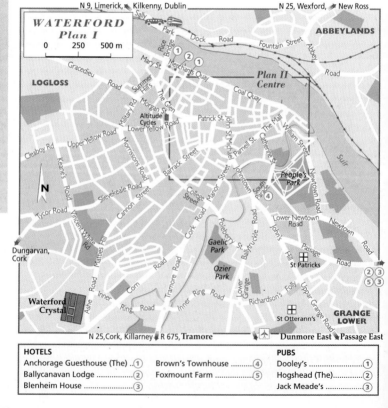

HOTELS		PUBS
Anchorage Guesthouse (The) ..①	Brown's Townhouse ....④	Dooley's ....①
Ballycanavan Lodge ....②	Foxmount Farm ....⑤	Hogshead (The).............②
Blenheim House ....③		Jack Meade's ....③

thanks to various economic inducements, has been able to persuade a good number of firms from abroad to set up here. For the visitor, it's an enjoyable place for a stroll, with bustling traffic-free streets and a long quayside facing the River Suir.

Historic river port

Founded by the Vikings in the 9C, *Vadrafjord* was sited to control shipping entering both the Suir and the Barrow. Three centuries later, its strategic location made it the target of one of the first Anglo-Norman expeditions commanded by Henry II. As in the other towns in the southeast, the mixing of peoples and cultures proceeded without too much friction. While remaining profoundly Irish and Catholic, Waterford was loyal to the Crown, and put up a determined and successful defence against Cromwell's army in 1649.

The town
Allow half a day

Waterford Crystal** (Plan I)

2km from the town centre towards Cork. Guided tours start at the Visitor Centre. April-October: daily 8.30am-4pm; November-March: Monday-Friday 9am-3.15pm. Admission charge. The Visitor Centre, which includes a tourist office, closes one hour later. Showroom and sales: daily 8.30am-6pm, except weekends January-February. Allow 2hr.

The fascinating factory tour gives a comprehensive idea of **crystal manufacture**, starting with the molten glass and ending with the delicate work of cutting. As a prelude to the tour there is a documentary film on the history of glass-making in Ireland in general and Waterford in particular. Visitors are then taken through a series of specially designed workshops. The people involved in production are highly skilled and take real pleasure in displaying their talents. The creation of an individual

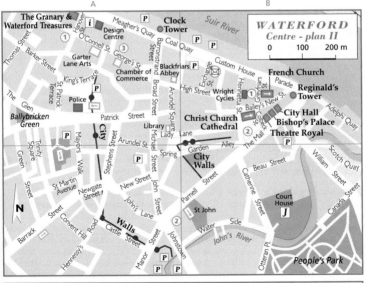

HOTELS CENTRE		PUBS		
Barnacle's Viking	①	Roxy (The)	①	T & H Doolans ....③
Mary Ryan B&B	②	Rubys	②	

B Pérousse/MICHELIN

Waterford at night

piece of glass by blowing, then by shaping it in a mould may seem almost childishly simple, but is of course the result of many years of patient practice. As for the sculptors and engravers who produce unique works to order, their mastery of drills and buffing wheels is a wonder to behold. A fine selection of the factory's products can be admired or purchased in the showroom at the Visitor Centre.

Crystal's glittering history
The earliest traces of glassworking in Ireland date from 1585. The first glassworks were in the countryside, close to the timber which the furnaces consumed in huge quantities, one of the main causes of the deforestation of the Irish landscape. From the 17C coal began to be used, and the works could now be located in towns. The brothers George and William Penrose set up the Waterford factory in 1783, using silica, potassium and litharge, a lead oxide which gave the glass great brilliance and hardness. The industry flourished at Waterford until the Second World War, after which it went into decline. It was revived in the 1960s thanks to the arrival here of Czech craftsmen and the initiative of a new set of owners.

Around Reginald's Tower (Plan II B1)
Originally built by the Vikings in 1013, **Reginald's Tower and Museum** (*June-August: Monday-Friday 8.30am-8.30pm; Saturday 8.30am-5pm; September: daily 10am-1pm / 2pm-5pm; October: Monday-Friday 10am-1pm / 2pm-5pm. Admission charge to the museum. Heritage Site*) is a good place to begin an exploration of the town centre. The three-storey tower was rebuilt by the Normans, and served successively as an observation post, a look-out tower, a fortress, a mint and a prison. The displays in the rooms on the various floors are devoted to the history of fortresses and are hardly worth the trouble.

From the tower, turn right into The Mall which leads to **City Hall** (*Monday-Friday 9am-4pm. Free admission*). This formidable 18C building once housed the city exchange, and now contains a fine collection of **crystal** as well as a **portrait gallery**.

City Hall is also the setting for the **Waterford Show**, a kind of musical about the city's history *(details and tickets from the tourist office or at the Waterford Crystal Visitor Centre)*. Next door is the **Theatre Royal**, its interior a fine example of Victorian theatre design, but only open for performances.

Turn right turn into Colbeck Street then left into Spring Garden Alley, which leads to a section of the **City Walls**, well preserved fragments of the Viking fortifications including the remains of a **look-out tower**.

Go back the way you came towards the Anglican **Christ Church Cathedral**★ (also known as the **Cathedral of the Blessed Trinity**). The original church here was built around 1096, the time when the Vikings were converted to Christianity. The present building in English neo-Classical style dates mostly from the late 18C, with neo-Gothic alterations following a fire in 1815. From the medieval church there survives the tomb and ghoulish **effigy**★ of the 15C Mayor James Rice, who ordered that his body should be shown as it would be a year after his burial, in an advanced state of decomposition. A Latin inscription admonishes the reader to reflect on our earthly destiny.

On leaving the cathedral, turn right and cross the square, then turn left into Greyfriars Street to the **French Church** *(keys from No 5 Greyfriars Street)*. The church was once part of a Franciscan priory dating from 1240. In 1539 it was converted into a hospital. The chapel was given to the French Huguenots who came here in the late 17C, and Protestant services were held in it from 1693 to 1815.

Along the quayside (Plan II)
This part of the quayside is not particularly enthralling; a little further upstream, the 19C **Clock Tower** (A1) seems to be keeping an eye on the cars lined up on the huge quayside car park.

Beyond the tourist office is the **Granary** (A1) on the corner of Merchants' Quay and Hanover Street. This massive stone structure has been restored at great expense to house the **Waterford Treasures** *(June-August: daily 9.30am-9pm; September-May: 10am-5pm. Admission charge)*. Many archaeological finds from the area have been collected here and are displayed with the aid of all the latest interactive hi-tech gadgetry. Particularly fascinating are items of Viking origin from ancient *Vadrafjord*. Many visitors are tempted into creating a souvenir of their visit by having their picture taken in the seat once used by the Mayor of Waterford at meetings of the city council.

Around Waterford
Allow half a day

Passage East
13km east via the R683 and the L157. The ferry from Ballyhack docks in this tiny little place with its brightly painted houses nestling at the foot of a cliff on the western shore of Waterford Harbour *(see page 194)*. There is a brace of friendly pubs, but Pas-

sage East really comes alive during the second weekend of September, the time of the **Mussel Festival**, when the shellfish are consumed in the open air accompanied by every kind of sauce imaginable. Details of this and other local activities can be found at **Carvey's**, the general store-cum-post office.

Three kilometres from Passage East, the road towards Dunmore East passes (*on the right*) the impressive ruins of **New Geneva**, a planned settlement created at the end of the 18C to accommodate Swiss Protestant immigrants. The project never came to fruition, and the buildings were converted into barracks which became notorious for the ill-treatment meted out to prisoners who had participated in the 1798 Rebellion.

Dunmore East★
19km southeast via the R683 and the R684. With its B&Bs and restaurants, this is an exceptionally chic fishing village, with thatched cottages and neat villas among pines and yews. Nearby are several attractive little coves, and the village is a good starting point for several lovely walks along the clifftops. The most popular walk is known as the **Woodwalks**, and begins at the *Ship* restaurant by the church. It is also possible to go down the track opposite the church which leads to **Lady's Cove**, a sandy bay which is a great favourite with local people and visitors.

Tramore
14km south via the R675.
Tramore is a very different kettle of fish from Dunmore East. One of Ireland's main holiday resorts, it attracts the crowds with a big amusement park as well as an extensive beach of fine sand. There are plenty of pubs too. If these delights pall, a clifftop walk leads south along the Doneraile cliffs, and Great Newtown Head to the west has a group of 19C navigational pillars, one of which is topped by the Tramore Metal Man, a 4m-high cast-iron figure in blue jacket and white trousers.

COMING AND GOING

By plane – Waterford has an **Airport** (off Plan I), ☎ 051 875 589, about 10km to the south of the city, served by a number of British and Irish operators. Flights to a number of UK destinations (http://homepage.eircom.net/~wra/timetab.htm).

By train – **Plunkett Station** is on the north bank of the River Suir (Plan I). Four trains daily (3 Sunday) between Waterford and Dublin (2hr30min); 4 trains daily to Kilkenny (40min); 3 trains daily to Rosslare Harbour (1hr), and 2 trains daily to Limerick (2hr15min).

By bus – **Bus Éireann** at the railway station (Plan I), ☎ 051 879 000. Twelve buses daily between Waterford and Dublin (2hr15min to 3hr30min), n° 4 via Kilkenny and n° 5 via New Ross and Enniscorthy.

Bus n° 40 runs 3 times daily (twice Sunday) between Waterford, Wexford (65min) and Rosslare Harbour (1hr20min) and between Waterford and Cork (2hr15min).

ADDRESS BOOK

Tourist information – **Tourist Information**, 41 Merchants Quay (Plan II A1), ☎ 051 875 823 or 852 444, Fax 051 877 388. January-March and November-December: 9am-5pm; closed weekends; April-September: Monday-Saturday 9am-6pm, Sunday 11am-5pm; July-August and October: Monday-Saturday 9am-5pm. A city plan and a South East Holiday Guide are available at no charge, and a wide range of other useful publications is for sale.

Waterford Crystal Visitor Centre (Plan I), ☎ 051 358 397. January-March: 9.30am-5.30pm; closed weekends; April-October: daily 9.30am-6pm; November-December: daily 9.30am-5.30pm. Same facilities and services as the tourist information centre plus bureau de change and hotel reservations.

Banks / Currency exchange – Several cash machines in the city centre and on the quayside, particularly near the post office. Bureau de change at the **Waterford Crystal Visitor Centre**.

Post office – Main post office on the quayside at the corner of Keyser Street (Plan II B1). Monday-Friday 9am-5.30pm; Saturday 9am-1pm.

Medical service – **Ardkeen Hospital**, near the quayside in the eastern part of the city, ☎ 051 873 321.

Bicycle hire – **Wright Cycle Depot**, Henrietta Street (Plan II B1), ☎ 051 874 411. May-September: Monday-Saturday 9.30am-1pm / 2pm-6pm. **Altitude Cycle** (Plan I), 22 Ballybricken, ☎ 051 870 356, Fax 051 858 433.

WHERE TO STAY

• **Waterford**

Under €13

Barnacles Viking House, Coffee House Lane, ☎ 051 853 827, Fax 051 871 730 – 109 beds. Independent hostel in a good location just back from the quayside near Reginald's Tower. Numerous facilities and several double rooms, but not a particularly welcoming reception.

Between €40-50

Mary Ryan B&B, 7 Cathedral Square, ☎ 051 876 677 – 3rm The rooms in this B&B close to Christ Church Cathedral are small but quiet and well kept. Shared facilities.

Blenheim House, Blenheim Heights, ☎ 051 874 115 – 6rm ⌘ TV CC 5.5km east of the city on the Passage East road. The parkland surrounding this lovely Georgian house is inhabited by deer who have no inhibitions about making guests welcome. The rooms are not large but comfortable and furnished with care.

Ballycanavan Lodge, Faithlegg, Halfway House, ☎ 051 873 928 – 3rm TV 5km east via the R683 towards Cheekpoint. The rooms in this prominently sited modern house are bright and quiet. The general style is nothing to write home about but the breakfast certainly is. Open mid-March to late October.

Between €65-70

The Anchorage Guest House, 9 The Quay, ☎ 051 854 302 or 086 810 2222 (mobile) – 14rm 📶 🔌 TV CC Small, recently renovated establishment offering the same level of comfort as a hotel but at a cheaper price. The rooms at the back of the building are quieter than those at the front.

Between €70-75

📶 **Brown's Townhouse**, 29 South Parade, ☎ 051 870 594, Fax 051 871 923 – 6rm 📶 🔌 TV CC In a residential street in the city centre, this Victorian house may not look like much but it offers all the comforts of a good hotel.

📶 **Foxmount Farm**, Passage East Road, ☎ 051 743 08, Fax 051 549 06 – 5rm 📶 6km east of the city on the R683 towards Cheekpoint. In the middle of the countryside, this is a lovely old house with attractively decorated rooms with rustic furnishings. Generous à la carte breakfast. Open 1 March to early November.

• **Dunmore East**

Between €45-50

Church Villa, near the church, ☎ 051 583 390, Fax 051 383 023 – 6rm TV Very pleasant B&B in the upper part of the village. Some of the rooms have shared facilities but all are attractively decorated.

Creaden View, in the village, ☎ 051 383 339 – 5rm 📶 TV Open March to late October. Three of the rooms in this pretty little house have superb sea and cliff views.

• **Tramore**

Between €45-50

The Cliff, Church Road, ☎ 051 381 363, Fax 051 390 363 – 20rm Basic rooms with or without facilities in the local YMCA. The best thing about the establishment is its matchless view of beach and sea.

Cliff House, Cliff Road, ☎ 051 381 497 – 6rm 📶 TV Open 1 February to late November. This modern house is in a hilltop residential area with sea views. Comfortable rooms. Breakfast is served in a conservatory facing the garden and the sea.

EATING OUT

• **Waterford**

Under €13

The Reginald, behind Reginald's Tower (Plan II B1) with an entrance to the rear of the French Church. Daily 11.30am-3pm / 6pm-9.30pm. Huge pub-restaurant with mock-medieval décor serving decent and inexpensive food at midday.

Design Centre Cafeteria, 44 Merchants Quay (Plan II A1), by the tourist office, ☎ 051 876 677. Open 9am-5pm. The Design Centre has a pleasant cafeteria with exposed beams, a view of the quayside, and satisfying lunches. No drinks licence.

📶 **Haricots**, 11 O'Connell Street (Plan II A1), ☎ 051 841 299. Monday-Friday 9am-8pm; Saturday 9.30am-6pm. No colorants or additives in the food here (nor in the clientele, for that matter); this is an eco-friendly establishment of a distinctly green hue. Excellent smoked haddock and baked apple or well-filled sandwiches. No drinks licence, but BYO.

📶 **T & H Doolans**, George's Street (Plan II A1), ☎ 051 841 504. Daily 11am-10pm. Atmospheric tavern in a timber-framed house right in the middle of town, famous for its music. As well as the inevitable Irish stew, there are mussels, oysters, smoked salmon...

The Brasserie, Arundel Square (Plan II A1), ☎ 051 857 774. Friendly establishment close to the main shopping centre. Popular with late risers, with a monster breakfast served until midday. Otherwise Tex-Mex, pizzas and open sandwiches.

Between €20-25

📶 **Dwyers**, Mary Street (Plan I) (near the harbour), ☎ 051 877 478. Dinner only: 6pm-10pm; closed Sunday. A good place for a fine meal in a friendly setting. The chef has set out to produce a sophisticated version of traditional cuisine, something which happens sufficiently rarely to be worth pointing out and is definitely worth the detour.

📶 **McAlpin's Suir Inn**, Cheekpoint, ☎ 051 382 182. Dinner only: 5.30pm-10pm; closed Sunday all year and Monday and Tuesday in winter. 12km east of Waterford via the R683. The view of the huge power station on the far side of the estuary is not exactly enthralling, but it's the food visitors come to admire, justifiably so. From the seafood gratin to the crab claws with garlic butter via the generous smoked salmon salad, everything is fresh and delicious in the convivial and welcoming little pub. Advance booking strongly recommended.

● **Dunmore East**
Between €25-30
🏠 **The Ship**, close to the church, ☎ 051 383 141, Fax 051 383 144. June-September: 12.30pm-2pm / 6pm-10pm; September-May: dinner only. Highly regarded seafood restaurant with maritime décor. Recommended dishes include grilled turbot or coquilles St-Jacques with tomato risotto and spinach. Less expensive at lunchtime with mussels in white wine or haddock and potatoes.

HAVING A DRINK

● **Waterford**
🏠 **Jack Meade's**, ☎ 051 873 187. 6.5km east of town, under the viaduct on the Cheekpoint road. This out-of-the-way pub prides itself on its reputation as a robbers' den and a place where freebooters plied their public with illegal booze a hundred years ago. People come here for a pint and a bite to eat but especially for the Wednesday evening music. Jolly barbecues on summer Sundays.
T & H Doolans (see "Eating out") is a good place for listening to traditional music with a different group every evening.
Dooley's Hotel, The Quay, ☎ 051 873 531. This grand hotel on the quayside has a very lively pub with traditional music on Wednesday evening and country style sounds on Friday and Saturday evenings.
The Hogshead, 15 The Quay, ☎ 051 852 006, is one of the most popular pubs in town for its live music in the evening. Blues, rock, country and jazz from Thursday to Sunday.
The Roxy, O'Connell Street, ☎ 051 854 325. Cavernous establishment filled with ear-splitting sounds most evenings and patronised by a particularly young and equally raucous crowd.
Ruby's, Parnell Street, ☎ 051 858 128. Chinese pagoda outside, more Scottish castle inside, this is one of the trendiest spots in town, with a pub on the ground floor, a saloon with a view on the first

floor and a discotheque from Tuesday to Sunday 11.30pm-2am.

● **Passage East**
The New Geneva, in the village. Traditional pub with music Wednesday and weekend evenings.

● **Tramore**
O'Brien's Bar, Strand Street, ☎ 051 301 090. Traditional music sessions every evening in summer and Monday, Wednesday and Friday evenings until late October.
The "Vic", Queen Street, ☎ 051 390 338. The best place in town for rock music, with big-name bands lined up all year. Possible admission charge.

SHOPPING

Crafts – Waterford Design Centre, 44 Merchants Quay (Plan II A1), by the tourist office, ☎ 051 856 666. Open 9am-6pm; closed Sunday and public holidays January-April. Comprehensive selection on two floors of Irish craft products, from crystal and ceramics to woollens and ironwork. Craftspeople sometimes give demonstrations of their skills on the second floor.

OTHER THINGS TO DO

Greyhound racing – Kilcohan Park, 2km west of Waterford on the Cork road, ☎ 051 874 531. Racing Thursday and Saturday evenings at 8pm.

Golf – The Island, 4km east of Waterford on the Dunmore East road. 18-hole course on a little island in the Suir estuary. Fee: €30-€34.
Tramore Golf Club, Newton Hill, Tramore, ☎ 051 386 170, Fax 051 390 961. Vast 18-hole course open to visitors all week. Fee: €31 weekdays and €38 at weekends.

Sea fishing – Dunmore Sea Angling, Dunmore East, ☎ 051 383 397 or 088 682 794 (mobile) organise fishing trips including hire of equipment.

Water-based activities – Dunmore East Adventure Centre, Stoney Cove, near Dunmore East harbour, ☎ 051 383 783, Fax 051 381 423. The centre runs a whole range of activities including archery and climbing as well as water-based sports like windsurfing, sailing and canoeing.

KILKENNY AND AROUND★★

Co Kilkenny – Pop 8 600
124km southwest of Dublin – Michelin map 923 K / 9-10

Not to be missed
Doing the rounds of Kilkenny's pubs.
Climbing the tower of St Canice's Cathedral.
Jerpoint Abbey.

And remember...
Kilkenny Castle attracts the crowds; buy your ticket an hour or two in
advance and use the time to explore the town.

Dominated by its great castle, capital of its county and important cultural centre, Kilkenny is one of Ireland's most attractive towns, its medieval core largely intact. It's a busy place, with bustling streets and an active student life.

Canny Kilkenny

Kilkenny's location on the River Nore at the meeting point of a number of major routeways gave it a strategic importance early in its history.

The Butlers of Ormonde – Capital of the Celtic kingdom of Ossory at the start of the Christian era, Kilkenny owes its name to the 6C Bishop St Canice. In the Middle Ages, the town flourished under the domination of the Anglo-Norman Butler family. The Butlers got on well with their Irish neighbours and adopted many of their customs as well as their language, but this cultural osmosis was not to the liking of their English sovereigns. In 1366 they promulgated the **Statutes of Kilkenny** which forbade the Anglo-Normans to use the Gaelic tongue, wear native clothing or practice Celtic customs (see page 17). But the process of intermingling had gone too far to be reversed, the law was widely ignored, and the area remained a cultural anomaly.

A taste for independence – In the 17C, the "Old English" Catholics and the Irish came together to found the **Confederation of Kilkenny** which functioned for several years as an independent parliament. This era came to an end when Cromwell's men laid siege to the town in 1650; on this occasion there were no reprisals and no massacre, and the Irish army was permitted to march out of the city. In the course of the following centuries Kilkenny continued to prosper in the shadow of its castle and today it is still proud of its identity and its vibrant spirit of independence.

The town

Allow half a day including the castle, but stay longer if possible.

Kilkenny Castle★★ (C2)

Guided tour only (50min), every 20min. April-May: daily 10.30am-5pm; June-September: daily 10am-7pm; October-March: Tuesday-Saturday 10.30am-12.45pm / 2pm-5pm, Sunday opening time 11am. Gardens: daily 10am-8.30pm, guided tour at 3pm in July-August. Admission charge. Heritage Site.

The illustrious **Strongbow**, Earl of Clare, erected a timber fortress here in 1172. Twenty years later, his son-in-law built the first stone structure to stand on the site, a castle with four corner towers, of which three have been incorporated into today's castle. In the late 14C it passed into the hands of the Anglo-Norman Butler d'Ormonde family, whose wealth was partly based on the import of wine from France. For 550 years this family dominated the southeast of Ireland from their Kilkenny stronghold, and the state of the castle at various times reflected the state of their fortunes, for good or ill. In the 19C they transformed their ancient residence into a splendid palace, but their prosperity was coming to an end. In 1935, the last

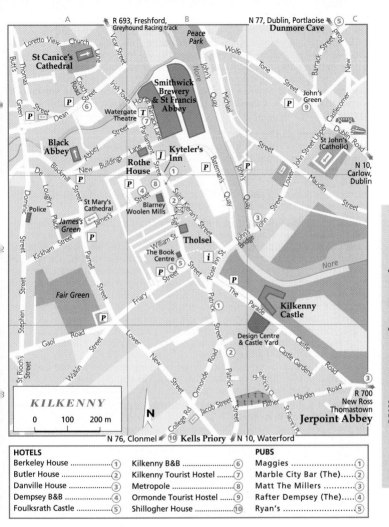

HOTELS

Berkeley House ....①	Kilkenny B&B ....⑥
Butler House ....②	Kilkenny Tourist Hostel ....⑦
Danville House ....③	Metropole ....⑧
Dempsey B&B ....④	Ormonde Tourist Hostel ......⑨
Foulksrath Castle ....⑤	Shillogher House ....⑩

PUBS

Maggies ....①
Marble City Bar (The).....②
Matt The Millers ....③
Rafter Dempsey (The).....④
Ryan's ....⑤

Marquess of Ormond instructed Sothebys to auction the furniture, and in 1967 the castle itself, now in a ruinous state, was bought by the Irish state for the sum of £60. Restoration has been under way for some time, with uneven and not always happy results, like the fluorescent green carpet in the Library. But the film shown at the beginning of a tour of the castle gives a good idea of the lifestyle of the Anglo-Irish aristocracy over the centuries.

Among the finest features in the castle interior are lovely examples of **wallpaper*** hand-painted in Chinese style, and the impressive **portrait collection** in the **Long Gallery**** with its hammerbeam roof decorated in pre-Raphaelite style. The **Butler Gallery** in the basement houses temporary exhibitions of contemporary work by Irish artists.

215

The attractive parkland around the castle is laid out in formal style, and makes for a pleasant stroll before visiting the **Design Centre** (*1 April-late September: Monday-Saturday 9am-6pm; Sunday 10am-6pm*) housed in the monumental stable buildings (*on the opposite side of the street facing the castle entrance*). The Centre was previously used as craft studios, but is now a kind of souvenir supermarket offering a range of more or less tasteful wares to the international crowds. A number of **workshops** survive on the far side of the stable courtyard, but the craftspeople's products are far from being bargains.

A stroll through the town

At the beginning of Rose Inn Street, on the left, the **Shee Alms House★** (B2), a 16C hospice, makes an attractive home for the **Tourist Information Office**.

In the busy High Street, the colonnaded building on the right is the **Tholsel** (B2) (*Monday-Friday 9am-1pm / 2pm-5pm*). Dating from 1761, this is where the town's financial affairs were conducted; it now contains among other items, **guild charters** the oldest of which – that of the butchers – was issued in 1200.

A hundred metres further on, in Parliament Street, the continuation of the High Street, is the lovely Tudor façade of **Rothe House★** (B1). This 16C merchant's dwelling bears the name of one of its owners, Peter Rothe, who took part in the Confederation of Kilkenny. Badly damaged at the beginning of the 19C, the building served as a meeting place for members of the nationalistic Gaelic League (*see page 23*). In 1962, the Kilkenny Archaeological Association purchased what had become little more than a heap of ruins, restored it and converted the upper floor into the fascinating museum of local history (*April-October: 10.30am-5pm; Sunday 3pm-5pm; November-March: 1pm-5pm; Sunday 3pm-5pm. Admission charge*). There are all kinds of everyday implements, nationalist memorabilia, and a fine collection of lace and old fashions. On display on the first floor are examples of pledges of abstinence made under the influence of **Father Mathew**.

On the right, further along Parliament Street is the entrance to what was a cinema. Refurbished in 1994, this is now the **Watergate Theatre** (B1), the venue for most of Kilkenny's drama and other performances.

To the right just before the bridge over a little tributary of the Nore is the entrance to the **Smithwick Brewery** (B1) (*tickets from the tourist office; guided tour only – 1hr30min: June-August: Monday-Friday 3pm. Free admission including a tasting*). Part of the Guinness group, the brewery produces Smithwick and Kilkenny ales and American Budweiser under licence. The tour includes a video explaining the mysteries of the brewing process and a tasting – one pint only, unlike the old days when visitors could "taste" as much as they liked... In the brewery courtyard, incongruously, are the remains of **St Francis' Abbey**, a Franciscan foundation.

150m beyond the bridge are steps leading up to the Anglican **St Canice's Cathedral★★** (A1) (*Easter-September: 9am-1pm / 2pm-6pm; rest of year: 10am-1pm / 2pm-4pm; Sunday 2pm-6pm; closed 25 December-1 January. No admission during services. Donation appreciated*). St Canice may well have built a church on this hilltop site

The apostle of temperance
Born in Co Tipperary in 1790, Theobald Mathew studied in Kilkenny and returned here a few years later. Dismayed by the ravages of alcoholism among the poor, this Capuchin friar – now aged 49 – undertook a crusade against the demon drink. At the end of his stirring sermons, the faithful would flock to sign pledges of abstinence, while innkeepers swore for their part to dispense neither beer nor whiskey on Sundays. Theobald Mathew's persuasive powers were such that he was invited to preach in the United States. During the Great Famine he was noted for his activities in relieving the distress of those most affected. Worshipped by both Catholics and Protestants, after his death he was given a statue on Dublin's O'Connell Street, and one of the capital's bridges was named after him.

in the 6C, but the present building, in Early English style and restored several times over, dates mainly from the 13C. The **nave**, one of the longest in Ireland, is of great majesty. There are numerous tombs, including one with the remarkable 16C **effigy★** in black Kilkenny marble of Piers Butler, Earl of Ormond and Ossory, together with his wife Margaret Fitzgerald, the pair of them in Tudor costume. The stone, in reality a hard limestone rather than marble, has a shiny appearance thanks to having been touched by virtually every visitor to the cathedral. In front of the altar, the floor tiles are made from the country's four types of marble, black Kilkenny, green Connemara, red Cork and grey Tyrone.

The Kilkenny witch

In 1324, Dame Alice Kyteler was accused by the Bishop of Kilkenny of witchcraft and heresy. Suspicion had been aroused by her nightly sorties in the company of her sister and her servant Petronella, and she had been seen sweeping the street in front of her son's door while muttering a spell intended to deprive the neighbours of their possessions. She was also accused of meeting an evil spirit at a crossroads and of having sacrificed nine cockerels to him. She was found guilty of diabolical practices, but she recanted and was pardoned, for a while at least. When she and her "accomplices" were brought to trial again, they were all condemned to death. Dame Alice and her sister succeeded in making their escape, leaving the unfortunate Petronella to be burnt at the stake before an appreciative public.

Outside, the 30m-high **round tower** (*9am-12.30pm / 2pm-5.30pm; Sunday 2pm-5.30pm; closed 25 December-1 January. Admission charge*), is all that is left of a church of the 8C. In clear weather, it is well worth scaling the staircase to enjoy the **view★** over Kilkenny and the surrounding area.

Back again by the brewery, turn right into narrow Abbey Street which leads to **Black Abbey** (A1) (*7.30am-7pm. No entry during services. Free admission*). Founded by the Dominicans in the 13C, Black Abbey is the oldest medieval church in Ireland in which services are still held. Inside there are fine examples of both old and modern stained glass, and in a glass case near the altar there is a fine 15C carving of the **Holy Trinity★**.

In St Kieran's Street, a narrow lane between the Nore and the High Streeet, **Kyteler's Inn** (B1) (*see "Making the most of Kilkenny and around"*) occupies an old timber-framed building. This was the home of Alice Kyteler, a local women condemned as a witch in 1324.

Matt the Millers pub at Kilkenny

W Buss/HOA QUI

Around Kilkenny
Allow half a day

Dunmore Cave★★

9.5km north via the N77. Buggys Coaches run 4 buses daily from Kilkenny bus station to Castlecomer. 15 March-15 June: daily 10am-5pm; 15 June-15 September: daily 10am-7pm; 15 September-31 October: daily 10am-5pm; rest of year: 10am-5pm weekends and public holidays only. Last admission 45min before closing. Admission charge. Heritage Site. Allow 1hr.
Hollowed out of the limestone of the Castlecomer plateau, this **cave** is one of the most famous in Ireland, less for its size than for its beauty and its archaeological interest, and has fascinated archaeologists and speleologists for a long time. Its series of "rooms", linked by a narrow corridor, have been given more or less imaginative names – the Cathedral, the Town Hall, the Hall – inspired by the shape of the stalactites and stalagmites whose characteristics are enhanced by a sophisticated lighting system.

The cave appears in Celtic legends around the 9C as the lair of a gigantic cat, the "Lord of the Mice". A 10C tale associates the site with a raid and massacre of the type commonly perpetrated by the Vikings. And human remains have indeed been recovered here – parts of 19 adults and 25 children, 13 of them less than 6 years old. The veracity of the legend was given extra credence when Viking coins were discovered as well.

Kells Priory★★

14km south of Kilkenny via the R697. When coming from Kilkenny, take the minor road running along the river just before the bridge. Free admission. Little visited by tourists, the beautiful and important ruins of this fortified **Augustinian priory** are among the finest in the whole country. The remains extend along the Kings River among sheep-grazed meadows. The first buildings here were erected in 1193 and burnt down a century later before being reconstructed. The setting can be appreciated from the picnic area to the south, on the right bank of the river. By the bridge there is a large **water mill**, recently restored and converted into a visitor centre.

Thomastown

18km south of Kilkenny via the R700. Built on both banks of the Nore, this is a charming little market town prettily located among green hills and placid rivers. A walk upstream leads to three of the **mills** which were once the town's main activity. In the town itself there are remains of the 14C **walls** and of **St Mary's Church**.

Ladywell Street leads to the **Camphill Community Water Garden**★ (*Tuesday-Friday 10am-5pm; Sunday 12pm-5.30pm. Admission charge*). Managed by an association of the disabled, this luxuriant garden laid out along a little stream has a wealth of exotic plants flourishing in the mild microclimate. There is a cafeteria and a shop with plants and seeds for sale.

Jerpoint Abbey★★★

2km south of Thomastown. March-May and mid-September-mid-November: 10am-5pm; closed Monday; June-mid-September: daily 9.30am-6.30pm; mid-November-late November: 10am-4pm. Admission charge. Heritage Site. Allow 1hr.
In a central position in the network of abbeys between Kilkenny and Waterford, Ireland's finest Cistercian foundation dates from 1180, when monks came here from Baltinglass in Co Wicklow and established themselves on the spot first occupied by a Benedictine monastery. The plan of the abbey is classically Cistercian, with a church in the shape of a Latin cross. The central tower was added to the crossing in the 15C. Jerpoint is famous above all for the carvings on the tombs in the chapels in the north transept; the **group of mourners**★★ is particularly fine, even if the subjects do appear to be smiling. In the south transept chapel, a **carved tombstone**★ shows "the brothers", two 13C knights in chain mail.

The **cloisters**★ have kept part of their arcades, restored in 1953. The columns have fascinating carvings of people in medieval costume. Especially notable are the **knight and his lady**★ and a **bishop** in the western colonnade.

Kilfane Glen and waterfall★

Follow signs off the N9 3km north of Thomastown. April-September: Sunday 2pm-6pm; July-August: daily 11am-6pm. Admission charge. A fine example of Romantic garden-making in a lovely wooded setting, this is a little paradise, apparently natural but in fact totally artificial, which has remained unchanged for 200 years. There is a water-fall and a remarkable *cottage orné*, and a foundation has been established which encourages contemporary artists to install their works in the gardens and along the woodland walks. The most striking contribution is James Turrell's barn-like struc-ture, open to the sky and inviting visitors to take a new look at the ever-changing heavens.

Making the most of Kilkenny and around

COMING AND GOING

By train – The railway station is in Dublin Road in the northeastern part of town (C1). 4 trains daily to and from Dublin Heuston station (2hr) and Waterford (45min).

By bus – The bus station is by the rail-way station. Service n° 7 links Kilkenny and Dublin (2hr) 5 times daily via Athy, and the n° 130 Dublin-Waterford bus calls at Kilkenny 5 times daily.

ADDRESS BOOK

Tourist information – *Tourist Infor-mation*, Shee Alms House, Rose Inn Street (B2), ☎ 056 515 00, Fax 056 639 55. October-March: Mon-day-Saturday 9am-5pm; April and September: Monday-Saturday 9am-6pm; July-August: Monday-Saturday 9am-8pm; open Sunday 11am-5pm May-September. Charge for most infor-mation.

Banks/Currency exchange – Several cash machines in the High Street (B2) and bureau de change at the Tourist In-formation office.

Post office – High Street (B2). Mon-day-Saturday 9am-5.30pm.

Bicycle hire – *JJ Wall*, Maudlin Street (C2), ☎ 056 212 36. Monday-Saturday 9am-5.30pm. Bikes for hire by the day or (more economically) for longer periods.

Bookshop – *The Book Centre*, 10 High Street (B2) has a good selection of maps and guides.

WHERE TO STAY

• **Kilkenny**
Under €13
Kilkenny Tourist Hostel, 35 Parlia-ment Street, ☎ 056 635 41 – 60 beds. Well- located hostel right in the middle of town, very practical for backpackers. 4-6 bed dormitories. Cheerful atmos-phere. No smoking. Cooking facilities. Plenty of information available on the area.

Ormonde Tourist Hostel, John's Green, near the station, ☎ 056 527 33 – 40 beds. Less intimate than the above establishment, with everything neat and tidy in almost military fashion. A few double rooms, much in demand in sum-mer. Cooking and laundry facilities.

🏚 ***Foulksrath Castle***, Jenkinstown, ☎ and Fax 056 671 44 – 52 beds. 15km to the north via the N77. Take the Bug-gys Coaches bus which leaves from in front of Kilkenny Castle at 11.30am and 5.30pm and get off at Canahy Cross, which is 300m from the hostel. Highly recommended for budget travellers, close to a lovely well-wooded park. Guests can live like lords in this 15C Norman castle with its dining hall complete with ancient fireplace. Cooking facilities, or meals can be provided.

Between €45-50
Dempsey B&B, 26 James's Street, ☎ 056 219 54 – 6rm Quiet little B&B, nothing special but good town centre location. Friendly reception.

Danville House, New Ross Road, indicated on the left beyond the first roundabout, ☎ 056 215 12 – 5rm 📶 TV Open 15 March-1 November. Lovely Georgian house in a countryside setting, full of rare objects including Cromwellian armour. The rooms are quiet and decorated with taste. Guests eat breakfast at a shared table.

Kilkenny B&B, Dean Street, ☎ 056 640 40 – 5rm 📶 TV Close to St Canice's Cathedral, this B&B is recognisable by its pretty flower garden. The rooms are not large and the decoration fairly ordinary, but there's a warm welcome.

Shilloger House, Callan Road, ☎ 056 632 49, Fax 056 648 65 – 8rm 📶 🖋 TV CC 1km from the town centre via the N76. Michael and Gorette Hennessy have made their house as attractive as possible for their guests. The perfectly kept rooms wouldn't disgrace a first-rate hotel.

Between €57-75
Metropole Hotel, High Street, ☎ 056 637 78, Fax 056 702 32 – 12rm 📶 🖋 TV CC Small hotel without special charm but good location in the centre of the old town.

Berkeley House, 5 Lower Patrick Street, ☎ 056 648 48, Fax 056 648 29 – 10rm 📶 TV CC Closed Christmas week. Town house near the castle, standard accommodation.

More than €130
Butler House Guest House, 16 Patrick Street, ☎ 056 657 07, Fax 056 656 26 – 13rm 📶 🖋 TV CC Closed Christmas week. Lovely private establishment in an 18C building with tasteful rooms overlooking a formal garden.

• **Thomastown**
Between €50-75
Abbey House, opposite the entrance to Jerpoint Abbey, ☎ 056 241 66, Fax 056 241 92 – 7rm 📶 🖋 TV CC Flower-print curtains and Victorian furniture in a lovely old building surrounded by its garden. Excellent à la carte breakfast with fresh fruit juice and home-made scones.

Ballyduff House, ☎ 056 584 88 – 4rm 📶 CC Not easy to find. From Thomastown, go towards Jerpoint Abbey, then opposite Redgwood's shop on the way out of town turn left towards Grove Farmhouse, and continue along the lane for about 2.5km. On the banks of the Nore, this little manor house run by the exuberant Breda Thomas is a real paradise, where guests are treated like members of the family. All the rooms are stylishly furnished and decorated, and breakfast is taken overlooking the river beneath the gaze of the family portraits which are scattered throughout the house. Open January to October.

EATING OUT

• **Kilkenny**
Under €13
Paris Texas, 92 High Street (B2), ☎ 056 618 22. Daily 12pm-10pm. Huge and lively pub with décor as varied as the menu which includes Tex-Mex, Thai, and a blend of Franco-American-Irish cuisine.

Pump House, corner of Parliament Street and Abbey Street (B1), ☎ 056 639 24. French-style menu including such delicacies as ragout de poulet aux champignons en croûte. Traditional music several evenings a week.

Kyteler's Inn, St Kieran's Street (B1), ☎ 056 210 64. Daily 11.30am-11.30pm. Pub-restaurant in a medieval building devoted to the memory of Dame Alice, the Kilkenny witch. Very acceptable and inexpensive lunches and for dinner, served in the vaulted cellar, a hotch-potch of dishes in various styles (generous helpings).

Between €13-20
Lautrec's Bistro, on the right at the beginning of St Kieran's Street (B2) coming from Rose Inn Street, ☎ 056 627 20. Weekdays: 12pm-2pm / 6pm-10.30pm, later closing at the weekend. French-owned (another establishment at Thomastown), this bistro serves inventive, Italian-inspired and Asian-influenced dishes. Cosy and inexpensive, with attentive service, good wine list and reasonable prices.

The Basement Restaurant, Butler House (see "Where to stay"), ☎ 056

612 43. Tuesday-Saturday 8am-4pm / 6pm-10pm. Bright red and yellow décor in the basement of a fine Georgian building. Standard dishes at lunchtime, more sophisticated dishes in the evening such as baked turbot with leeks and tomatoes in balsamic sauce.

Ristorante Rinuccini, The Parade (B2), ☎ 056 615 75. Daily 12.30pm-3pm / 6pm-10pm. Basement Italian restaurant with an intimate and relaxing atmosphere serving good pasta and other more elaborate dishes with more than a touch of the Mediterranean about them.

• **Thomastown**
Between €20-40
🍴 **The Silk**, Marshes Street, ☎ 056 544 00. Tuesday-Sunday 12.30pm-3.30pm / 6.30pm-9.30pm; closed Tuesday, Wednesday, and Thursday at lunchtime. The owner hails from St-Tropez and has worked in London, but Ireland has become his great love. The restaurant is in an old school building with sparkling new décor. The food is innovative Mediterranean, with memorable dishes such as chicken breast à la citronelle on a sweet potato galette or leg of lamb in a herb crust with garlic sauce.

HAVING A DRINK

• **Kilkenny**
The Marble City Bar, 66 High Street, on the right beyond the post office, ☎ 056 620 91. Traditional music 5pm-7pm Sunday and ballads Monday evening.

Maggie's, St Kieran's Street, ☎ 056 622 73. Lively pub with youngish clientele has traditional music Tuesday, Wednesday and Thursday evenings.

Ryan's, Friary Street. Low-ceilinged but colourful pub, packed out on Sunday and Thursday evenings when traditional and folk groups provide the entertainment.

The "Rafter" Dempsey, next door to the above establishment, ☎ 056 229 70. More or less "alternative" rock groups turn up the volume here on Sunday evenings, no doubt much appreciated by the residents of the B&B in the upstairs rooms.

Matt the Millers, by the bridge. Jam-packed, especially at the weekend, when the crowds squash up against the immensely long bar to listen to rock and occasional country groups. Admission charge.

• **Thomastown**
Carrols, Logan Street, ☎ 056 242 73. Genuine pub with a beer garden in summer. Well-known traditional bands Wednesday evenings.

OTHER THINGS TO DO

Festival – The **Kilkenny Arts Festival**, ☎ 056 521 75, goes on for about ten days during the second half of August. There are classical, jazz and pop concerts, plays and entertainments of all kinds in Kilkenny and the villages around.

Theatre – Watergate Theatre, Parliament Street (B1), ☎ 056 616 74. Advance booking and sales: Monday-Friday 10am-7pm; Saturday 2pm-6pm. The local repertory company puts on quality plays all year round.

Music – Jazz and other music at the **Newpark Hotel**, Castlecomer Road in the northeast part of town, ☎ 056 221 22. Every Thursday evening July-August.

Golf – Kilkenny Golf Club, Glendine on the way out of town to the north, ☎ 056 654 00. 18-hole course with a fierce reputation. Fee: €25 weekdays, €28 weekends.

Greyhound racing – St James's Park, Freshford Road (off A1 on plan), ☎ 056 212 14. Races all year Wednesday and Friday at 8.15pm.

SHOPPING

Traditional clothing – Blarney Woollen Mills, High Street (B2), Kilkenny, ☎ 056 527 88. Good range of sweaters, wax jackets and other traditional garments as well as Waterford crystal and ceramics.

Redgwood, Grennan Watermill, on the right on the way out of Thomastown towards Jerpoint Abbey, ☎ 056 247 88. Factory outlet with traditional waxed outerwear and other good quality clothing.

CLONMEL AND AROUND★

Co Tipperary – Pop 15 500
47km northwest of Waterford
Michelin map 923 I-J / 10-11

Not to be missed
A walk in the Comeragh Mountains.
The Tooreen Drive megaliths.
Ormond Castle at Carrick-on-Suir.

The many megaliths in the area around Clonmel prove that the region was inhabited in prehistoric times, but the town itself dates from the 10C, when it was founded on the north bank of the Suir by the Vikings who had sailed upstream from Waterford. Its name derives from the Irish for "meadow of honey", a reference to the fertile soil of the valley. The most important town in Co Tipperary, busy Clonmel is a handsome place with plenty of B&Bs for visitors passing through or using the town as a base for exploring the surrounding area. To the southeast, in Co Waterford, are the high hills and narrow valleys of the Comeragh Mountains, a lovely landscape of peat bogs and sombre forests of firs. There are many opportunities for walking and riding, while anyone with even a slight interest in archaeology will find much to fascinate them.

The town
Allow 2hr

The town centre is largely defined by O'Connell Street and Parnell Street, traffic-free and running parallel to quayside and river.

The 19C **Town Hall** stands on a site once occupied by a 17C merchant's house. The statue opposite is of a participant in the 1798 Rebellion. On the far side of the street, **Hearn's Hotel** is an old coaching inn dating from 1792. It was from here that Charles Bianconi ran his famous coaching business.

To the left of the entrance to the Town Hall, narrow Dowd's Lane is lined by the buildings of Bulmer's cider works, though production using apples from the area is carried on nowadays in a modern plant just outside the town.

Parnell Street leads to the **County Museum** (*Tuesday-Saturday 10am-1pm / 2pm-5pm; move planned to town library*). As well as civil and military memorabilia relating to Co Tipperary, the museum has a fascinating collection of prehistoric items and a number of Roman coins, brought here no doubt from England.

An Irishman from Italy

Born in Lombardy, Charles Bianconi (1786-1875) was sent to Ireland at the age of 16 because of a scandalous love affair. In 1815 he cannily bought up some of the horses which were going at bargain prices following the ending of the Napoleonic wars, and started a carriage service between Clonmel and Cahir. A shrewd businessman and uncompromising boss, he went on to create the punctual and reliable communication system which had been totally lacking in Ireland beforehand. By 1847 his vehicles were serving 22 counties and covering a distance of almost 7 000km a day. A friend of Daniel O'Connell, Bianconi helped finance the nationalist cause and was twice elected Mayor of Clonmel. Between 1826 and 1834 he resided in what is now Hearn's Hotel.

In the western part of town, close to the remains of the walls, is the Anglican **Old St Mary's Church**. The original building dating from the 13C was modified in the 15C and 16C and its imposing **tower** was restored in the 19C.

At the western end of O'Connell Street, the 19C **West Gate** stands on the site of an older gateway which separated the Anglo-Norman town from Irishtown, the suburb in which the native Irish were supposed to reside.

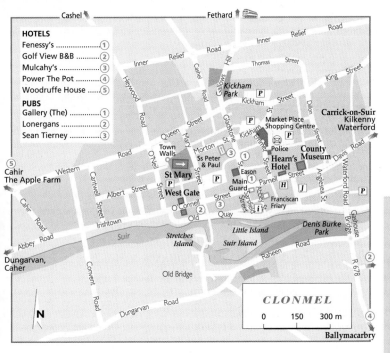

Around Clonmel

Keen walkers will want to investigate the **East Munster Way**, a well-signposted long-distance footpath running from Ormond Castle in Carrick-on-Suir via Clonmel to Clogheen. The route crosses the Comeragh Mountains and the **Knockmealdown Mountains** and presents no special difficulties (*the "East Munster Way Map Guide" includes a 1:50 000 map as well as detailed practical and other information and is available from local tourist offices*).

Among the Comeragh Mountains

These green uplands with their forests and peat bogs are crossed by the River Nier. There are several megalithic sites and plenty of fine views, some of which can be enjoyed from the **Nier Valley Scenic Route**★ winding through the area (*64km tour leaving Clonmel on the R678 and continuing to Ballymacarbry, then returning via the R671. Allow half a day*).

Another route, shorter but equally pleasant, leads to Ballymacarbry by crossing the Comeragh Mountains via Harney Cross (*leave Clonmel on the R678 and go as far as the golf course, then turn off towards Harney Cross*). A good place to stop and have a picnic or a meal is the **Power the Pot** inn and camp site (*see "Making the most of Clonmel and around"*). Details of walks in the area can be obtained here, and there is a spectacular **view**★ of the hills all around. The narrow road continues right across the heath and bog of the mountains. To the right of the road is **Moanyarha Bog**, where the peat is being worked for commercial purposes and which can be viewed from along a track.

Continue in the same direction for 5km. After a series of bends, a small bridge is crossed. Continue for a further 2.5km, then turn left along a narrow road towards Tooreen, then left again at a junction. Continue for 2.5km as far as the ruins of an old lime kiln on the right, then park the car 50m further on by a house. The route is not signposted.

The **Tooreen Drive**★ gives access to a series of megalithic sites (*the gate along the way may be closed but is easily opened*). About 10m away on the left beyond the verge, a signpost in the bracken indicates the way to a fascinating **stone circle**★ of Bronze Age date. The 12 standing stones are thought to form part of a calendar since they indicate the seasons with great accuracy at the time of the solstices and equinoxes. On the other side of the road, an arrow points to a line of four stones 50cm high close to a little **funeral mound**★ hidden in the heather. A stone marks the entrance. Return to the road and continue for about another 100m. To the left, bounded by the forest is an open area with an Iron Age **stone circle**. Scattered in the forest are many other megalithic remains of less importance and interest.

Return to the main road and turn left. It is 3.5km to Ballymacarbry.

Ballymacarbry★, a tiny valley-hamlet on the banks of the Nier, is a starting point for walks and treks in the area (*see "Making the most of Clonmel and around"*).

Carrick-on-Suir

24km east of Clonmel via the N24. Allow 2hr including a tour of the castle. This quiet little town is inordinately proud of one of its sons, the champion cyclist Sean Kelly who distinguished himself more than once in the Tour de France.

Apart from the lovely 15C arched **bridge** over the Suir, the main attraction, just outside the town (*follow signs*) is **Ormond Castle**★★ (*1 June-late September: daily 9.30am-5.30pm, last tour 4.45pm; closed rest of year. Guided tour. Admission charge. Heritage Site*). The first castle was built here in the 15C by Piers Butler, whose tomb can be seen in St Canice's Cathedral in Kilkenny (*see page 216*). Two centuries later, parts of what remained of his stronghold were incorporated into a splendid Tudor mansion built by Thomas Butler, the 10th Earl of Ormond, known as Black Tom. In the **Long Gallery**★ occupying the whole of the first floor of the east wing is a plaster frieze depicting personages from the courts of Henry VIII and Elizabeth I. The servants' quarters beneath the impressively carpentered roof are well worth a visit. Back on the ground floor, visitors can marvel at a fine array of **charters**★★ conferring titles and privileges on members of the Ormond family. One of them has a striking **medallion** showing William of Orange and, her bosom bared, Queen Mary.

Making the most of Clonmel and around

COMING AND GOING

By train – Railway station in Prior Park Road 1.5km from the centre in the northern part of town. Two trains daily to Limerick (1hr15min) and two to Waterford (50min).

By bus – By the railway station. Service n° 5 calls here three times daily on the Cork (1hr45min) to Dublin (3hr15min) route. Bus n° 55 runs 4 times daily between Waterford (50min) and Limerick (1hr30min).

ADDRESS BOOK

Tourist information – *Tourist Information*, Sarsfield Street, ☎ 052 229 60. Monday-Friday 9.30am-5.30pm and Saturday 10.30am-4pm. Useful town plan and the "South East Holiday Guidebook" available free, and other guides and maps for sale including a very comprehensive town guide and details of walks.
Details of walks, treks, bike routes, accommodation, fishing and virtually anything else from the genial Patrick Melody at *Melody's* in Ballymacarbry, a sort of pub-cum-general store-cum-equestrian centre-cum tourist information office. For detailed information about megaliths, contact *Andrew Ryan*, ☎ 052 361 41, a teacher who knows all there is to know about the area. For guided walks and walking tours, contact *Michael Desmond*, ☎ 052 362 28.

Banks / Currency exchange – Several banks and cash machines in O'Connell Street.

Post office – Main post office in Emmet Street. Monday-Friday 9am-5.30pm (9.30am Tuesday, but 9am first Tuesday of the month); Saturday 9am-1pm.

Bookshop – *Eason*, 19 / 20 Gladstone Street has a good range of maps and guides.

Bicycle hire – *Clonmel Classic Cycle*, 8 Mary Street, ☎ 052 278 27.

WHERE TO STAY

• **Clonmel area**
Under €13
🐾*Power the Pot*, Harney's Cross, ☎ 052 230 85 – 12 beds ✗ About 9km

south via the R678. Small private hostel, with plain but well-kept dormitories plus one double room. Fine location, 345m up in the hills, and a good starting point for various walks. Owners can give any help necessary in planning excursions. Camp site and restaurant. Open 1 May-15 October.

Between €45-50
Woodruffe House, Cahir Road, ☎ 052 352 43 – 4rm 🍴 Three kilometres east via the N24. Even though their farmhouse is only 20 years old, the O'Donnells have succeeded in giving it the charm of much older places. The rooms are spacious and comfortable. Two of them share a bathroom. Mrs O'Donnell can provide light meals if booked in advance. Open 1 April-1 November.

Between €50-65
🐾*Fenessy's Hotel*, Gladstone Street, ☎ 052 236 80 – 14rm 🍴 🚿 TV CC Charming old hotel, newly renovated, in what was once the mayor's residence. Quiet, attractive rooms, each with different décor. Good value for this type of establishment.

Mulcahy's, 47 Gladstone Street, ☎ 052 250 54, Fax 052 245 44 – 10rm 🍴 TV CC Bright, quiet and cosy rooms in the building which is also Clonmel's oldest pub (see "Having a drink").

Golf View B&B, Lyreanear Avenue, ☎ 052 231 59 – 2rm Two kilometres outside town towards the golf club. Very acceptable rooms in a modern house with lovely country views. Open May-September.

• **Ballymacarbry**
Between €45-50
🐾*Cnoc-Na-Ri*, ☎ 052 362 39 – 4rm 🍴 TV CC At the metal bridge 5km to the east of the hamlet take the left turn, a cul-de-sac. Walkers or anyone looking for peace and quiet will appreciate this restored old house in the middle of the countryside. An ideal place to recover in after a hard day's hiking. Evening meal provided if booked in advance.

EATING OUT
Under €13
Sean Tierney, 13 O'Connell Street, ☎ 052 244 67. Monday-Saturday 10.30am-9pm, Sunday 12.30pm-9pm.

One of Clonmels most celebrated pubs with a décor midway between Wild West and mock medieval. Generously filled open sandwiches at midday. Dinner in the upstairs restaurant has a strong emphasis on hearty meat dishes, such as the Gaelic steak in whiskey sauce.

Angela's Restaurant, Abbey Street, ☎ 052 268 99. Monday-Saturday 9am-5.45pm. Generous breakfast, plus Italian-inspired dishes in this little cafeteria with a green and yellow façade.

Hearn's Hotel, Parnell Street, ☎ 052 216 11. Daily 12.15pm-3pm / 6pm-9.30pm. Clonmel's most famous hotel is a good place to dine in comfort at a very reasonable price.

Mr Bumbles, Kickham Street, ☎ 052 291 88. Daily 12pm-3pm / 6pm-10pm. Bistro-like establishment, bright and welcoming décor, with excellent grills at midday, and more sophisticated and expensive dishes in the evening.

HAVING A DRINK

Mulcahy's (see "Where to stay"). The biggest pub in town, with several rooms decorated in country style. Traditional music Wednesday evening, blues or rock Friday-Sunday. The **Dannos** nightclub (entrance on Market Street) is part of the same establishment and functions from Thursday to Sunday 11pm-2.30am.

Sean Tierney, one of the best pubs in town (see "Eating out").

The pub in **Fenessy's Hotel** (see "Where to stay") has occasional traditional or folk evenings at weekends.

The Gallery, Gladstone Street. Varied sounds at the weekend. Ditto **Lonergans**, near Westgate.

Ballymacarbry

Melody's, the unmissable institution hereabouts, has traditional music on Tuesday and Wednesday evening.

OTHER THINGS TO DO

Riding – Davern Equestrian Centre, Tannersrath Lower, ☎ 052 273 27, Fax 052 298 00. Mark and Mary Davern organise riding parties all year.

Melody's Nire Valley Equestrian, Ballymacarbry, ☎ 052 361 47. Can provide mounts for a few hours or for a trek lasting several days if you really want to get to know the hills. Pat Melody, the daughter of Patrick (see "Tourist information") has horses and ponies for experienced riders or beginners and will act as companion and guide.

Fishing – Kavanagh's Sports Shop, Upper O'Connell Street, ☎ 052 212 79. The local fishing association has its headquarters here and can provide whatever information visiting fishermen need.

Golf – Clonmel Golf Club, Lyreanaerla, 4km south via the R678, ☎ 052 240 50. 18-hole course, hillside location in lovely surroundings. Fee: €23 Monday-Friday, €25 weekends.

COMING AND GOING

By train – The station is on the north side of town in the Kilkenny direction. One train weekdays only to Cork or to Rosslare Harbour via Waterford.

By bus – Buses call at Greenside, a park by the R24. Service n° 7 runs 4 times daily to Dublin (3hr) via Kilkenny, and to Cork (2hr) 3 times daily. Service n° 55 links Carrick with Clonmel (20min) 4 times daily and continues to Waterford (1hr35min), Wexford (1hr30min) and Rosslare Harbour (1hr50min).

ADDRESS BOOK

Tourist information – Heritage Centre, Main Street, just off the street by the Bell and Salmon Hotel, ☎ 051 640 200. October-May: Monday-Friday 10am-5pm; June-September: daily 10am-5pm. Limited range of information on the area and opening and closing times are erratic.

Banks – Cash machines in Main Street.

Post office – In Main Street. Monday-Friday 9am-5.30pm, Saturday 9am-12pm.

Bicycle hire – OK Sports, New Street, ☎ 051 640 626.

WHERE TO STAY

Under €13
Carrick-on-Suir Caravan & Camping Park, Kilkenny Road, ☎ 051 640 461. Near the town centre, small, simple campsite, friendly welcome.

Between €30-40
The Gables, Main Street, ☎ 051 641 400 – 5rm ⁂] This B&B's rooms are in what used to be a girls' boarding school. Attractive dining room, but otherwise limited comfort only.

The Bell & Salmon Arms, Main Street, ☎ 051 645 555, Fax 051 641 293 – 13rm ⁂] ♪ TV ✕ CC Traditional hotel

of somewhat faded charms with completely refurbished bedrooms done out in pastel colours.

EATING OUT

Between €13-25
Very acceptable lunches in the restaurant of the **Bell & Salmon Arms** and at the **Carraig Hotel** in Main Street. Both establishments have more gastronomic offerings in the evening at around €20.

HAVING A DRINK

The bar of the **Bell & Salmon Arms** has different groups on Wednesday, Thursday, Saturday and Sunday evenings, and there is a nightclub at weekends.

N Cooneys, opposite the Carraig Hotel. A good place for a pint while sitting at a table made from an old sewing machine. **Tír Na nÓg**, just next door, ☎ 051 640 656. "The land of eternal youth" earns its name by attracting a young crowd with traditional music Monday-Wednesday and disco Thursday-Sunday.

OTHER THINGS TO DO

Fishing – Foley's Tackleshop, 34 Bridge Street, ☎ 051 640 318, sells permits as well as the right equipment for catching trout and salmon in the Suir.

SHOPPING

Glassware – Tipperary Crystal, Ballynoran, 5km west via the N24, ☎ 051 641 188. Monday-Friday 9am-5.30pm; Saturday 9am-5pm; Sunday 11am-5pm; 6pm closing time in summer. Free guided tour mid-March-late September: Monday-Thursday 9am-4.30pm; Friday 9am-3.30pm. This glass factory is more intimate than its equivalent at Waterford and has a pleasant restaurant and a shop in a pair of thatched cottages.

CASHEL ★★★

Co Tipperary – 158km southwest of Dublin
Michelin map 923 I / 10

Not to be missed
The Rock of Cashel by moonlight.

And remember...
The town is on a lorry route; bear this in mind when choosing overnight
accommodation.

On their lonely limestone outcrop, Cashel's round tower and romantically ruined
cathedral exude an air of mystery which intensifies at nightfall. This is – literally as
well as metaphorically – one of the high places of Ireland, where the Celtic kings of
Munster ruled and where one of them was baptised by St Patrick himself. Few places
convey so intensely the spirit of early Celtic Christianity, and even today the Rock
of Cashel continues to occupy an important place in the collective Irish imagination.

Town and Rock
Allow half a day

The Rock is the great attraction at Cashel, but the little township too has a number
of sights of interest, despite the constant procession of heavy lorries on the main road.

Rock of Cashel★★★

*Mid-September-mid-March: daily 9am-4.30pm; mid-March-mid-June: daily 9am-5.30pm;
mid-June-mid-September: daily 9am-7.30pm. Guided tour every hour, last tour 45min
before closing time. Admission charge. Heritage Site. Allow 1hr30min.*

Most visitors to the Rock begin
their tour at the museum, housed
in the undercroft of the Hall of the
Vicars Choral, a restored 15C
building. Among the various rep-
licas of religious objects is the 12C
cross of St Patrick★ mounted on
a 4C votive stone used by the kings
of Munster in their coronation ceremony.

Cashel's oldest religious building is
Cormac's Chapel★★, a well-preserved and richly decorated 12C
structure built by monks from Germany. Its ornamental carvings in-

Smitten by a saintly staff
In the year of grace 450 St Patrick came to
Cashel to baptise Aenghus, king of the Éo-
ganacht. In the course of the ceremony the
saint wished to emphasise his words by striking the ground with his staff, but its pointed tip
pierced the king's foot. Thinking that this was
part of his initiation, the stoic ruler remained
silent and did not flinch. His conversion failed
to save him from later misfortune; having
emerged the loser from more than 40 battles,
Aenghus decided that paganism was the better
bet after all and renounced his Christian faith.

clude motifs unique in Ireland, like the helmeted **centaur** aiming an arrow at a lion
(*tympanum of the north doorway*). There are also traditional Celtic motifs like human
heads and figures of animals (*chapel vault*). By contrast, the superb interlace carving
on the remains of a **prince's sarcophagus** is of Viking inspiration.

The **Cathedral★**, impressively proportioned, was set on fire and pillaged in 1647 by
one of Cromwell's allies. Built in the 13C on a cruciform plan, it has a central tower
erected a century later. In the choir, a niche (*south side*) contains the remains of
Bishop Miller McGrath, twice married and father of nine offspring, deceased in 1621
having served both Protestant and Catholic faiths.

Outside, by the north transept, the 12C **round tower** rises to a height of 28m. It
has five storeys connected by ladders and its entrance is 3.5m above ground level.

Near the car park at the foot of the Rock, the **Brú Ború Cultural Centre** (*Monday-Friday 9am-5pm. Free admission*) is a place to get a meal or browse through souvenirs. In the evening there are folklore performances (*see "Making the most of Cashel"*).

At the foot of the Rock

From the Rock, arrows indicate Bishop's Walk to the right. The pathway winds across fields to the gardens at the rear of **Cashel Palace***, the Palladian mansion built in 1730 for Archbishop Theophilus Bolton and now a luxury hotel.

On the far side of Main Street, John Street leads to the Anglican **St John's Cathedral** built in the 18C to replace the derelict cathedral on the Rock.

Next to the cathedral is the **Bolton Library*** (*June-August: Tuesday-Sunday 10am-6pm; rest of year: Monday-Friday 9.30am-5.30pm. Admission charge*), with 12 000 volumes from the libraries of various bishops. They include many rarities, such as an almanac and mathematical treatise of 1168, a Bible which may be the smallest in the world, and a note signed by Jonathan Swift.

Back on Main Street, turn right then left into Dominic Street. The **Folk Village** (*March-October: daily 10am-6pm; rest of year: Monday-Saturday 9.30am-4.30pm*) is a small private museum in a house with a thatched roof. In it are objects evoking rural life as it used to be lived as well as memorabilia from the 1916 Uprising.

A little further along the street on the right are the ruins of a 13C **Dominican Friary** (*keys from Ms McDonnell at n° 19*), consisting of the tower and part of the walls.

Just under 1km outside the town (*along the Dundrum road*) are the ruins of **Hore Abbey**, begun in 1272 and the last Cistercian establishment to be founded in Ireland. From the field in which it stands there is a fine view of the Rock of Cashel.

Cahir**

18km south of Cashel – allow half a day.

In the 11C Cahir (or Caher, both pronounced "care") was a residence of **Brian Ború**, one of the High Kings of Ireland. Dominated by its Anglo-Norman castle, the historic township is a busy little place, a starting point for walks along the banks of the lovely River Suir.

The **castle**** (*mid-March-mid-June and mid-September-mid-October: daily 9.30am-5.30pm; mid-June-mid-September: daily 9am-7.30pm; mid-October-mid-March: 9.30am-4.30pm. Admission charge. Heritage Site*) stands on a small island in the Suir. The formidable 13C stronghold soon passed into the ownership of the Anglo-Norman **Butler** family who reigned over much of the southeast. In the **Banqueting Hall** a giant moose's head recovered from a peat bog surveys the scene, mostly the result of 19C restoration. The rest of the castle seems to consist of a succession of corridors, spiral staircases, secret hiding places and sentry walks, a perfect background for the shooting of scenes from films such as *Excalibur* or *Barry Lyndon*.

From the castle, a riverside walk along the Suir leads to the Swiss Cottage. By car, 2km south on the R670.

The exuberantly thatched **Swiss Cottage**** (*mid-March-late April and October-November: 10am-1pm / 2pm-4.30pm; closes 5pm in April; closed Monday except public holidays; May-September: daily 10am-6pm. Guided tour only. Admission charge. Heritage Site*), despite its name, has as much of the South Pacific as the Alps about it. It dates from the early years of the 19C and was built by Lord Caher as a hunting and fishing lodge, probably to a design by John Nash. Recently restored with great care and attention to detail, it has in one of the ground floor rooms a wonderful example of French **hand-painted wallpaper** showing an Oriental landscape. Other rooms are charmingly furnished with original 19C furniture.

COMING AND GOING

By bus – Buses stop in Main Street near Biancon's Bistro. Service n° 9 between Dublin (2hr50min) and Cork (1hr35min) via Cahir (15min) calls here three times daily in the week and twice on Sunday.

ADDRESS BOOK

**Tourist information – *Tourist Information*, Town Hall, Main Street, ☎ 062 514 57. May-September: Monday-Friday 9.30am-5.30pm; July-August: daily 9.30am-5.30pm. Useful information on the town and its surroundings, plus tickets for a ride aboard a "train" around the town. The Heritage Centre here has a multi-media exhibition about the area.

Banks/Currency exchange – Cash machine in Main Street and bureau de change at Tourist Information.

Post office – Main Street. Monday-Friday 9am-1pm / 2pm-5.30pm; Tuesday 9.30am-1pm / 2pm-5.30pm; Saturday 9am-1pm; closed Sunday.

WHERE TO STAY

Under €16

Cashel Holiday Hostel, John Street, ☎ 062 623 30, Fax 062 624 45 – 50 beds. Pleasant youth hostel in a restored Georgian building. Small 4-6 person dormitories with facilities and three double rooms with facilities on the landing.

Between €50-55

Ashmore House, John Street, ☎ 062 612 86, Fax 062 627 89 – 5rm ⌇ TV CC A Georgian building with very ordinary but quiet rooms. Friendly welcome.

Rahard Lodge, Dualla Road, ☎ 062 612 65 – 3rm ⌇ Six kilometres east of Cashel via the R691. Recent, yellow-painted house with a fine view of the Rock of Cashel rising from the surrounding pastureland. Plain but acceptable rooms. Open 1 April-30 November.

Ballyhoven House, Dualla, ☎ 062 612 65 – 3rm ⌇ Turn right 6km east of

Cashel via the N8 and follow signs. Standing in parkland, this fine 18C manor house has somewhat rustic comforts with furniture to match. But it's all very charming, and it's fun to take a walk in the surrounding countryside with your host's labrador as guide. Open May-September.

Ardmayle House, near Goold's Cross, ☎ 0504 423 99, Fax 0504 424 20 – 6rm ⌇ CC Annette Hunt does everything in her power to make guests feel at home in her pretty farmhouse in the middle of the countryside. The rooms are attractively decorated in country style and breakfast is a memorable occasion. Evening meal if ordered in advance. Open 1 April-1 October.

EATING OUT

Under €13

Granny's Kitchen, at the foot of the Rock, close to the car park, ☎ 062 618 61. March-September: 9.30am-7.30pm; September-October 9.30am-6pm. Delightful little pink-painted café embedded in flowers. No drinks licence.

Alexander Knox & Co, Main Street, ☎ 062 614 41. Daily 12pm-3pm and 5.30pm-10pm. Traditional pub, very comfortable, with good honest food.

Between €13-20

Bailey's of Cashel, Main Street, ☎ 062 619 37 / 618 46. Rustic inn open every evening 6pm-10pm, with good local dishes such as chicken in Cashel blue cheese sauce and lamb stew with Guinness. Rooms available, but they are not cheap and rather noisy.

More than €20

Chez Hans, Moor Lane, at the foot of the Rock, ☎ 062 611 77, Tuesday-Saturday 6pm-10pm. Slightly incongruous setting of an old Wesleyan chapel for the sophisticated international dishes offered by the German proprietor.

HAVING A DRINK

There are plenty of pubs with music in Main Street. Traditional sounds at **Feehan's** on Wednesday evening and at

Darvan's on Monday and Wednesday. The **Moor Lane Tavern** has different kinds of bands Thursday-Sunday. Rock music Friday and Saturday evening at **Alexander Knox & Co**.

The **Brú Ború Cultural Centre** at the foot of the Rock, ☎ 062 611 22, combines a meal with a folklore performance every evening June-September. There's also a bar.

Making the most of Cahir

COMING AND GOING

By train – The railway station is located near St Paul's Church at the end of Church Street. One train a day to Limerick and in the other direction to Waterford and Rosslare.

By bus – The bus station is near the castle and the tourist office. Service n° 8 links Cahir with Dublin (3hr) three times daily and with Cork (1hr20min). Service n° 55 runs 3 times daily to Galway (2hr35min) and to Waterford (55min). Service n° 56 links Cahir with Cashel (15min) 4 times daily Monday-Saturday and three times Sunday.

ADDRESS BOOK

Tourist information – Tourist Information, by the castle, ☎ 052 414 53. April-June and September: Monday-Saturday 10am-1pm / 2pm-5.30pm; July-August: daily 9.30am-6pm. Very professional service and lots of useful information about the area.

Bank – Cash machine in Castle Street and another in the main square.

Post office – Church Street. Monday-Friday 9.30am-1pm / 2pm-5.30pm; Saturday 9.30am-1pm.

WHERE TO STAY
Under €13
Lisakyle Hostel and Camping, Ardfinnan Road, ☎ 052 419 63 – 17 beds. Two kilometres outside Cahir. Somewhat spartan dormitories plus small camp site. Maurice and Bridget Condon will come and pick you up from the bus or railway station if necessary. Bicycles for hire.

Between €40-45
The Rectory, ☎ 052 414 06 – 5rm On the way out of town towards Cashel, this is a restored 18C rectory with plain but tastefully furnished rooms. Pleasant atmosphere and friendly welcome.

EATING OUT
Under €13
The Castel Arms, Castle Street, ☎ 052 425 06. Good unpretentious pub food.
Galtee Inn, The Square, ☎ 052 412 47. Daily 12pm-3pm / 5pm-10.30pm. Traditional inn with straightforward country cooking at midday, more expensive in the evening, with excellent and generously proportioned steaks.

HAVING A DRINK
Join the local black-clad bikers for weekend rock sessions at **Black Tom's**, Limerick Road.

OTHER THINGS TO DO

Fishing – The Suir is famous for its trout. For equipment and permits, contact **Conba Fishing Tackle**, Old Church Street, ☎ 052 423 48.

Riding – **Cahir Equestrian Centre**, Ardfinnan Road, ☎ 052 414 26. Day rides and longer treks all year under the guidance of Fiona Hyland.

Golf – **Cahir Park Golf Club**, ☎ 052 414 74, Fax 052 427 17. 18-hole course on the banks of the Suir, not far from the Swiss Cottage. Fee €18 all week.

DUNGARVAN AND AROUND
Co Waterford and Co Cork
Michelin map 923 H-I-J / 11-12

Not to be missed
Helvick Head at sundown.
An evening with music at the An Seanachaí pub near Dungarvan.
And remember...
Make sure you have a good road map; road signs are only in Gaelic in the An Rinn
Gaeltacht.

The little harbour town of Dungarvan (pop 7 000) has a fine site astride the River
Colligan where it flows into the broad bay known as Dungarvan Harbour. There may
not be all that much to see here, but the town is a good starting point for exploring
the cliffs of Helvick Head and the Gaelic-speaking area of An Rinn, as well as the
country inland, rich in reminders of the past of which the most splendid is the great
castle at Lismore.

Dungarvan and around*
Co Waterford – 46km west of Waterford

The town
Allow 2hr. On the west bank of the Colligan near the quayside are the ruins of **King
John's Castle**, built by this monarch in 1185 and a reminder that the town owes
its origin to the Anglo-Normans. In a lane behind the castle, the local museum *(may
move)* is housed in the **Old Market House** dating from the 17C.
On the east bank is the suburb of **Abbeyside**, which derives its name from the 12C
Augustinian abbey of which there remains a tower and most of the nave. From the
abbey there is a fine **view*** over Dungarvan Harbour and **Cunnigar Point**, the sandy
spit rich in bird life which protects the harbour from storms.

Around Dungarvan Harbour
*Leave the town on the N25 towards Cork and drive for about 3km, then turn left onto the
R674 towards Helvick Head.*
All the signs along the road to Helvick Head are in Gaelic because this is the **An
Rinn Gealtacht**, the only Irish-speaking area left along the south coast. Here, some
800 people have succeeded in preserving their traditional culture and use Gaelic in
their everyday life as a matter of course.

The road runs parallel to the shore along the hillside for almost 10km before
reaching **Helvick Head****. From here there is an extraordinary **panorama**** over
Dungarvan Harbour and the coast as far as Tramore. The scene is all the more
striking at sunset, when the last rays bring out the purple tints of the cliffs in spectacular fashion.

Ardmore*
20km southwest of Dungarvan via the N25 and the R673. A seaside resort famous for its
beach of fine sand backed by high cliffs, Ardmore prides itself on being one of the
country's most venerable Christian sites, founded by St Declan in 416.
The 29m-high **round tower*** and the neighbouring **church*** enjoy a very fine
view** over the cliffs and the sea, which in sunny weather takes on an intense
turquoise colour. This is the starting point of the long distance footpath of
St Declan's Way, which runs for almost 100km as far as Cashel. A somewhat
shorter walk, which nevertheless offers superb views, is from the Cliff House Hotel
to **Ram Head**

Lismore and around★★
17km northwest of Dungarvan

This quiet little place is well worth seeing for its majestic castle and gardens and its cathedral. To find out more about the area and its history, call at the Heritage Centre which has an exhibition and an excellent documentary film (*see "Making the most of Lismore and around"*).

The village

The best views of the **castle**★★ (*private property*) are from the riverside or the cathedral graveyard. The original medieval fortress was owned for a while by Sir Walter Raleigh. The present building, a splendid 19C re-creation of a Tudor stronghold, was built around the remains of the old castle to plans by Joseph Paxton, the Irishman who also designed London's Crystal Palace. It is not open to the public, but the **gardens**★ are (*11 April-27 September: daily 1.45pm-4.45pm. Admission charge*). The lower garden has a magnificent hedge of ancient yews, while the upper garden, dating in its present form from the reign of James I, is a harmonious mixture of fruit trees, roses, vegetables, bulbs and greenhouses with vines.

The main street leads to **St Carthage's Cathedral**, the romanised name of St Carthach, founder of the first monastery at Lismore. The present building dates from the 17C; inside there are several fascinating tombs and effigies as well as a fine timber pulpit sculpted in the 18C.

Ireland's only vineyard

About 7km along the road from Lismore to Dungarvan at **Cappoquin** is **The Vineyard** (*signposted in the village*), the creation around 1990 of David and Patricia McGrath. Their grapes are Schönburger, a German variety. Thanks in part to the advice of a grower from the Beaujolais area, they produce a dry and slightly astringent white wine which can be tasted.

Youghal and around★
On the N25 29km west of Dungarvan and 46km east of Cork.

Once an important naval and commercial port, Youghal (pronounced "yawl") in Co Cork is a lively place with 5 700 inhabitants, attractively located on the west bank of the Blackwater estuary. Like most of the towns along the south coast, Youghal was founded by the Vikings, then developed under the Anglo-Normans. **Sir Walter Raleigh** served as mayor here, and it was due to him that both tobacco and the potato made their first appearance in Ireland.

The old town

Full of character, Youghal made a convincing background for many of the scenes in the film of *Moby Dick*, shot here in 1954. **Market Square** was at the centre of much of the action, and the **Moby Dick pub** has memorabilia from the filming and the time spent in the town by Captain Ahab (played by Gregory Peck). In Fox's Lane leading towards Main Street is the **Fox's Lane Folk Museum** (*April-October: Tuesday-Saturday 10am-1pm / 2pm-6pm. Admission charge*) with a fascinating collection of everyday objects from the past.

The Clock Gate★ marks the junction with Main Street. Dating from the 18C, it is a four-storey structure which was used for many years as a prison. Anyone condemned to death here would be hanged from the windows in order to impress the populace. From Main Street, Church Street leads to **St Mary's Collegiate Church**★, flanked by a stretch of the **town walls**. The church stands on what is one of the oldest places of worship in Ireland, St Declan having founded an oratory on this spot at the beginning of the 5C. The present building mostly dates from the 18C and 19C; inside is the huge **monument**★ to Richard Boyle, 1st Earl of Cork, the richest man in Ireland in the 18C.

B Pérousse/MICHELIN

Youghal harbour

Ballycotton*

Co Cork. 37km west of Youghal via the N25 and R632. With its pretty houses and gardens, this delightful little resort makes the most of its setting among the cliffs of this coastline. It is particularly popular with deep-sea fishermen and scuba divers, and there are plenty of places to stay and good restaurants to eat in.

The best of the cliff walks starts from the car park at the western end of the village. After 200m, the path drops steeply to a stairway cut into the cliff which leads down to a sort of natural swimming pool called **The Paradise***, where bathers frolic in a spectacular setting of rocks and cliffs.

COMING AND GOING

By bus – Buses stop on Davitt's Quay. There are four n° 4 buses daily linking Dungarvan with Waterford (1hr) and Dublin (2hr45min). Service n° 40 runs 9 times daily (6 Sunday) to Cork (1hr15min), and in the other direction to New Ross, Wexford and Rosslare Harbour. Service n° 362 runs 3 times daily (not Sunday) between Dungarvan and Ardmore.

ADDRESS BOOK

Tourist information – *Tourist Information*, The Square, ☎ 058 417 41. May-September: Monday-Friday 9am-6pm; July-August: Monday-Friday 9am-9pm; Saturday 9am-6pm; Sunday 11am-6pm.

Banks – Cash machines in The Square and in Meagher Street.

Post office – Bridge Street. Monday-Friday 9am-5.30pm; Saturday 9am-1pm.

Bicycle hire – *Murphy's Cycles*, 68 Main Street, ☎ 058 413 76. Monday-Saturday 9am-6pm.

WHERE TO STAY

Under €13
Dungarvan Holiday Hostel – Youghal Road, on the way out of town towards Cork, ☎ 058 443 40, Fax 058 362 94 – 52 beds. Small, clean and well-kept hostel with four double rooms as well as dormitories. Good range of facilities and warm welcome.

Between €45-50
Ballyguiry Farm, ☎ 058 411 94 – 6rm Three kilometres out of town on the N25 Cork road, turn right opposite the road to Helvick Head and follow signs. Large Victorian house on a hillside with lovely countryside views. The rooms furnished in country style do not all have their own facilities, but the general level of comfort is more than satisfactory. Open 1 April-late October.

Between €50-65
Gortnadiha House, Ring, ☎ 058 461 42, Fax 058 465 38 – 3rm Follow signs 3km out of town on

the N25 Cork road. Pleasant farmhouse in a lovely park with sea views. Very comfortable rooms, and tasty home-made cheeses at breakfast-time.

● **Ardmore**
Under €13
Ardmore Beach Hostel, Main Street, ☎ 024 945 01 – 27 beds. Open Easter-October and rest of year by booking in advance. Small private hostel with two 5- and 6-bed family rooms.

Newtown View Farmhouse, Grange, ☎ 024 927 03 – 4rm Signposted on the N25 14km before Youghal coming from the Dungarvan direction. Modern house with quiet, spacious and tastefully furnished rooms. Good choice of dishes at breakfast-time.

EATING OUT

● **Dungarvan**
Under €13
The Shamrock, O'Connell Street, ☎ 058 422 42. Daily 12.15pm-9pm, except Sunday evening. Small cafeteria with good salads, pies and home-made puddings.

An Seanchaí, 8km from Dungarvan on the N25 towards Cork. This traditional-style pub with its thatched roof is close to a mass tomb holding victims of the Great Famine, but no-one is likely to leave these premises famished, particularly if they partake of the excellent Irish stew. Add to this a friendly atmosphere and evening music sessions which attract people from far and wide Thursday-Sunday.

Between €13-25
The Tannery, 10 Quay Street, ☎ 058 454 20. Tuesday-Saturday 12.30pm-2.30pm / 6.30pm-10pm. Paul Flynn has gained a solid reputation for his inventive and freshly prepared "world food" served in an attractive contemporary setting. Very reasonably priced at lunchtime, more expensive in the evening.

● **Ardmore**
Under €13
Beachcombers, Seafront, ☎ 024 943 21. April-late September: daily 10.30am-9pm; rest of year: weekends

only. Pleasant little restaurant with chocolate box décor and satisfying and inexpensive dishes like lamb stew or smoked salmon.

HAVING A DRINK

Dungarvan has plenty of pubs with music, most of them in Main Street or on the quayside. Traditional music every evening at the **Marine Bar**, likewise on Tuesday and Friday at the **Lady Belle**, Thursday and Saturday at **Kiely's Cross**, Thursday-Sunday at **Bridi Dees**, Grattan Friday-Sunday at **Bridgie Terrie's** and Thursday, Saturday and Sunday at **Bean A Leanna**.

Mooney's, on the road to Helvick Head. Everyone here speaks Gaelic, there's a really great atmosphere, and there's traditional music every weekend. Not to be missed.

OTHER THINGS TO DO

Sea fishing – Seve Baumann, ☎ 058 413 95, takes visitors out in his boat every morning at 10am. Equipment provided. For comprehensive information on fishing in the area, contact the **Dungarvan Sea Angling Club**, ☎ 058 449 62 or 088 633 242 (mobile).

Riding – John and Louise Moloney have mounts for hire all year round at their **Colligan Equestrian Centre**, ☎ 058 682 61.

Golf – West Waterford Golf & Country Club, around 5km west of Dungarvan, indicated on the left on the way out of town, ☎ 058 432 16, Fax 058 443 43. 18-hole course in a setting of green hills. Fee: €25 weekdays, €30 weekends.

Making the most of Lismore and around

COMING AND GOING

By bus – One n° 4 bus a day to Dublin (4hr) via Dungarvan, Waterford and Kilkenny.

ADDRESS BOOK

Tourist information – Tourist Information and Heritage Centre, Grattan Square, ☎ 058 549 75. April-May and September-October: 9.30am-5.30pm; Sunday 12pm-5.30pm; June-August: 9.30am-6pm; Sunday 12pm-5.30pm. Good range of information on the area, plus small exhibition and documentary film about the history of Lismore (admission charge).

Post office – In the upper part of Main Street.

WHERE TO STAY

Under €13

Kilmorna Farm Hostel, ☎ 058 543 15 – 5rm and 9 beds. 1.5km outside Lismore (follow signs). Small private hostel in an old coaching inn. Reasonably comfortable double rooms (bathroom on the landing) and dormitory. Relaxed atmosphere. Cooking and laundry facilities.

EATING OUT

Under €13

The Madden's, in the upper part of Main Street opposite the post office. ☎ 058 541 48. Monday-Friday 12.30pm-2.30pm. Patronised by Fred Astaire on his sojurns in Lismore. Good pub lunch at midday, open sandwiches and excellent home-made cakes at other times. Traditional music some evenings.

COMING AND GOING

By bus – Service n° 40 links Youghal with Waterford and Cork 9 times daily Monday-Saturday and 7 times daily Sunday.

Service n° 240 runs between Cork and Ballycotton via Middleton 3 times daily Monday-Friday and once on Saturday in summer.

ADDRESS BOOK

Tourist information – *Tourist Information & Heritage Centre*, Market Square, ☎ 024 924 47. October-late April: 9.30am-5.30pm, except weekends; May, June and September: 10am-6pm, except weekends; July-August: 9am-7pm; weekends 10am-6pm. Good range of information on Youghal, plus historical exhibition (admission charge).

Bank – Cash machine in North Main Street by the post office.

Post office – In North Main Street.

WHERE TO STAY

• Youghal

Between €13-20

Stella Maris Holiday Hostel, 3 Strand Street, ☎ 024 918 20 – 86 beds. Close to the beach, this is a standard kind of hostel with several 3-bed rooms with their own facilities.

Between €45-50

Carn na Radharc, ☎ 024 927 03 – 3rm 🍴 Turn right just before the bridge 2km before Youghal when coming from Dungarvan on the N25. Modern house with acceptable rooms and a dining room with lovely views.

🍴 **Castle Farm**, 3 Strand Street, Ballycrenane, ☎ 024 981 65 – 6rm 🍴 Near Ballymacoda 11km southwest of Youghal on the R633. Restored old farmhouse with rooms furnished in country style with fine coastal views. Visitors who happen to be here at the beginning of July may find themselves invited to the Matchmaking Fair organised by the owners. Open 1 April-31 October.

• Ballycotton

Between €40-45

Congress House, ☎ 0214 646 728 – 4rm ✖ At the far western end of the village, perched on the very edge of the clifftop. Lots of charm but general level of comfort leaves something to be desired.

EATING OUT

• Youghal

Under €13

Several fast-food outlets and cafés in Main Street.

Between €13-40

Aherne's, 163 North Main Street, ☎ 024 924 24. Daily 12.30pm-2pm / 6.30pm-9.30pm and bar open all day. Luxury hotel-restaurant with reasonably priced seafood dishes at the bar and more sophisticated restaurant offerings in the evening at a much higher price.

Tides, Upper Strand, ☎ 024 931 27. Daily 12pm-10pm. On the left on the way out of town towards Cork. Good "Franco-Irish" cuisine and generous helpings of seafood in a relaxed atmosphere. Rooms available too.

• Ballycotton

More than €25

🍴 **Spanish Point Seafood Restaurant**, in the village, ☎ 0214 646 177. Closed January and until mid-February and open at weekends summer only. Excellent fish restaurant with fine seaviews which alone justify the trip out to Ballycotton.

HAVING A DRINK

• Youghal

The Nook, 20 North Main Street. The most characterful and liveliest pub in town, with traditional music Monday and Wednesday evening. Groups also play at the **Central Star** and the **Clock Tavern** also in North Main Street.

OTHER THINGS TO DO

Sea fishing – Ballycotton is a good place for fishermen. For full information on fishing trips contact **Dietmar Scharf**, ☎ 0214 646 056, or **Peter Manning**, ☎ 0214 646 773.

Some of Skellig Michael's 2 300 steps

X Zimbardo/HOA QUI

THE SOUTHWEST

To the west of the city of Cork, the southern gateway to the Republic, lies a succession of inlets running deep inland. Bathed by the Gulf Stream, this is a coast whose mild climate supports a plant life of almost Mediterranean luxuriance, with yuccas and an abundance of flowers. Gentle hills, wooded river valleys and brightly painted villages give this part of Ireland an even friendlier face than usual. Beyond Skibbereen, the landscape changes. The rocky fingers of five peninsulas reach westward into the Atlantic, the hilltops are ridged with crags, the shorelines fringed by wild cliffs and battered by the ocean swell. Little seems to thrive here among the scattered cottages apart from the black-faced sheep. This is the austere Ireland of legend, a place of violent storms and lonely monasteries, of holy men and smugglers, the cradle of a rebellious nation, where moonshine once enlivened the harshness of daily life. Further inland, though, the countryside resembles a vast garden, with mountains rising over lovely lakes with wooded shores. In Killarney, where the roads are lined with rhododendrons, nature seems tamer still.

Everywhere there is the sense of a long history littered with battles, with fighting among the clans, resistance to pirates, Vikings and English, all for a piece of barren, but much-loved land.

CORK ★

County town of Co Cork
The Republic's second city – Pop 140 000
256km southwest of Dublin

Not to be missed
A stroll through the English Market.
The Crawford Gallery and the area around Paul Street.
An afternoon trip to Cobh.

And remember...
A good plan is to explore Cork in the morning, have a pub lunch, then visit Cobh in the afternoon to make the most of the light.
When shopping, don't forget that most places close at 5pm or 5.30pm.

The best way of coming to Cork is aboard one of the ferries from Wales or France. The boat moves up the long estuary of the Lee, the breeze a stimulating blend of salty air and the promise of the land. White cottages stand in the fields, then come the brightly painted buildings of the little port of Cobh and finally Cork itself, the island city between two arms of the Lee, backed by hills. In the past, the waters flowed throughout the town, linking the arms of the Lee by a network of canals, long since filled in. To the north, the slope rises abruptly, with streets as steep as stairways climbing up to a summit topped by a pair of churches. With endearing exaggeration, locals love to compare their city with Venice (for its canals) and Paris (for church-crowned Montmartre).

Cork is a place of paradox, an industrial centre which is an outlet for the agricultural produce of the prosperous interior. A university city, it has a young population as well as new enterprises based on electronics and information technology. There's an intense atmosphere of activity of all kinds, accompanied by the music of violinists, flautists and *bodhrán* players (*see page 62*), all adding to the fun of a stroll through the streets or an evening spent in a friendly pub.

From colonisation to rebellion

Built on the marshlands bordering the Lee, Cork in Gaelic is *Corcaigh*, meaning marshy place or swamp. In the year 650, a monk by the name of **Fin Barre** founded a monastery on the hill which soon became a place of refuge from Viking raids. Eventually the Norsemen came to stay, settling on an island in the river and intermixing with the native population. In the 12C it was the turn of the Anglo-Normans, who succeeded in attaching the area to the English kingdom. They fortified Cork and laid out the system of canals which allowed ships to sail right up to the city gates. Cork prospered, and its commercial strength helped support its aspirations of independence, winning it a reputation as "Rebel Cork". In 1492, the mayor supported Perkin Warbeck, pretender to the English throne, an ill-judged move for which he was hanged. In 1649 Cromwell marched in, causing much havoc, followed a few decades later in 1690 when King William's army destroyed the walls and other fortifications. In the 19C and early 20C the city was in the forefront of the nationalist struggle, giving the movement some of its fiercest fighters and figureheads, including two of its Lord Mayors, Terence McSwiney, who died on hunger strike in Brixton prison, and Tomás McCurtain, shot in his own home. In 1920, in reprisal for an ambush in which they had lost several men, the Black and Tans set fire to part of the city centre and prevented firemen from putting out the blaze. Then in the Civil War that followed British withdrawal, Cork was a stronghold of opposition to the government, and had to be brought to heel by Free State troops.

Land and water meet at Cork

240

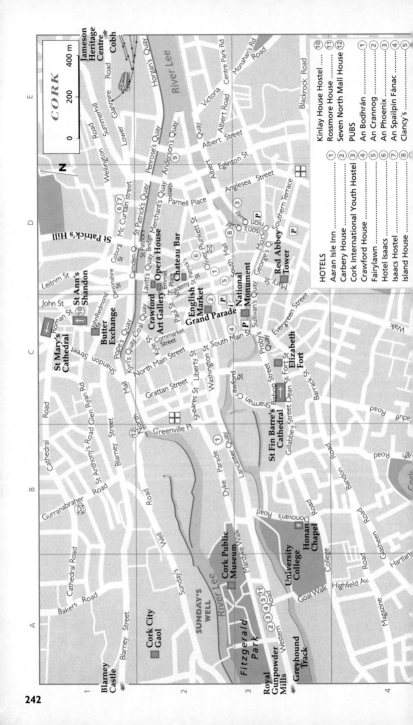

CORK

0 — 200 — 400 m

N

HOTELS

Aaran Isle Inn	①
Carbery House	②
Cork International Youth Hostel	③
Crawford House	④
Fairylawn	⑤
Hotel Isaacs	⑥
Isaacs Hostel	⑦
Island House	⑧
Kinlay House Hostel	⑩
Rossmore House	⑪
Seven North Mall House	⑫

PUBS

An Bodhrán	①
An Crannóg	②
An Phoenix	③
An Spailpín Fánac	④
Clancy's	⑤

Jameson Heritage Centre
Cobh

River Lee

St Patrick's Hill

St Ann's Shandon
Butter Exchange
St Mary's Cathedral

Opera House
Chateau Bar
Crawford Art Gallery
English Market
National Monument
Grand Parade
Red Abbey Tower

St Fin Barre's Cathedral
Elizabeth Fort

Cork City Gaol

Cork Public Museum
University College
Honan Chapel

Royal Gunpowder Mills
Greyhound Track

Fitzgerald Park
SUNDAY'S WELL

242

The city centre

Allow 2hr. The centre is compact; the two car parks in Grand Parade are close to the tourist information centre which is a good starting point for a tour on foot

Embraced by the two arms of the Lee, the city centre has two main arteries, the broad semi-circular avenue of St Patrick's Street and ruler-straight **Grand Parade** (C2). The southern end of Grand Parade by the river is marked by the **National Monument** (C3) commemorating those who fell in the struggle for independence. Several splendid **18C houses** have survived, some with bow fronts and some still with the steps which led down to the water when Grand Parade was an open channel linking the branches of the Lee. Running eastwards is Oliver Plunkett Street, once the quarter of furriers and jewellers.

On Grand Parade is one of the entrances to the **English Market★** (C2), the covered market which was established here in 1610. At the time the market's main avenue was still a waterway, only filled in at the beginning of the 19C, enabling merchandise to be brought in by boat. The market is full of the banter of stallholders promoting their wares; the butchers' stalls are particularly fascinating, with their displays of *drisheen* (black pudding) and *crúibín* (pigs' trotters). The avenues lead to an atrium overlooked by the Farm Gate Café, much prized for its excellent lunches *(see "Making the most of Cork")*.

A bent for business

The fine buildings lining the quaysides of Cork are proof that the city's merchant class knew how to turn a pretty penny despite the place's often turbulent history. By the 18C international trade was well developed, and fortunes were being made from shipping emigrants across the Atlantic as well as from dealing in beef and butter. The lucrative export trade in butter was centralised in the Butter Exchange, which set prices and exercised quality control. By the 20C other industries had begun to develop, in part funded by the Irish who had made good in North America. Shipyards were established and Henry Ford (whose family came from near Clonakility in Co Cork) set up his first overseas car plant here.

At the corner of Grand Parade and St Patrick's Street, a narrow road leads to **Cornmarket Street** (C2), lined with gaudy shop-fronts aggressively proclaiming the bargains within. The street is the venue for the morning **Coal Quay Market**, a kind of flea market even more raucous than the English Market.

St Patrick's Street (D2) is the city's main shopping thoroughfare, lined with tall residences in pastel colours as well as department stores and speciality shops. The **Chateau Bar★** occupies an 18C building, a fine example of a merchant's house dating from 1793. It can be recognised by the stairs leading to its raised ground floor and by the doorway beneath, used for unloading goods from boats when St Patrick's Street was still a waterway.

St Patrick'Fs Street is busy enough, but the lanes running off it are teeming with life. French Church Street leads to **Paul Street** (C2-D2), the chic part of town, with lots of boutiques, trendy furniture shops, bars and cafés.

Go east along Paul Street to Emmet Place.

An elegant red-brick building houses the **Crawford Art Gallery★** (D2) *(9am-5pm; closed Saturday afternoon and Sunday. Free admission)*, founded by the wealthy William Crawford to accommodate artists' studios and picture and sculpture galleries. Among the works is a fine collection of Irish 19C and 20C painting including canvases by Jack Yeats.

The French come to Cork

The Huguenot or French Quarter between St Patrick Street and Paul Street owes its name to the Protestants who fled here in the 18C from religious persecution in their native France. The Cork area was very anglicised, and welcomed these newcomers, who devoted their energies to trade and commerce, notably in wine and textiles. Their presence here gave a boost to business with France.

Not far from the gallery, on the quayside along the northern branch of the Lee, stands the **Opera House** (D2). A massive and not particularly beautiful building, it is the venue for a whole range of concerts and performances, including a famous October jazz festival (*see "Making the most of Cork"*).

Continue east along the quayside, then cross Patrick's Bridge towards the northern hillside.

North Cork
Don't try and explore this part of Cork by car; the streets are steep and narrow and the one-way system is confusing – allow 1hr, or 3hr if going to Cork City Gaol on foot

Once over the bridge, cross McCurtain Street with its array of bars and clubs of every kind, to the foot of **St Patrick's Hill** (D1). The pavement leads steeply upwards, lined with houses painted in cheerful colours, to a fine **viewpoint** over the city and its harbour.

Go back down the hill to the junction with McCurtain Street and turn right into Coburg Street. Go along Devonshire Street and turn half-right into John Redmond Street which takes you to a point just below the church of St Anne's Shandon.

St Anne's Shandon (C1) (*10am-5pm; closed Sunday. Admission charge*) is one of Cork's symbols, easily identified by its distinctive outline and its **tower** topped by a **weathercock**, a splendid 3m long salmon. Dating from 1722, the Anglican church

The tower of St Ann's Shandon and the rooftops of Cork

F Baume/MICHELIN

is unusual in that two of its sides are built in red sandstone and two in grey limestone. Inside there is a fine collection of **17C books**. Anyone not bothered by heights should climb the tower and try their hand at playing a tune on the church's famous **bells** (*fee*); there are eight of them, each producing a different note, and sheet music is provided.

Near the church is the **Butter Exchange** (C1) built in 1770 to handle the flourishing trade in the salty butter produced in the countryside around and exported to Britain, the continent of Europe and as far as the West Indies. This trade sustained the economy of the city throughout the 19C. Nowadays the building houses the **Shandon Craft Centre** (*9am-5.30pm; closed Sunday*) where craftspeople can be seen at work fashioning all kinds of objects, from pottery and textiles to glassware and sculpture. In the narrow street facing the entrance to the craft centre stands an old shop, established in this part of town for many years. Its ancient sign proclaims it to be the **Exchange Toffee Works**, and it must be the oldest hand-made sweet-shop in this part of Ireland. Four generations of the same family have been turning out marshmallows and other sweet things to the delight of local children, and you don't have to be in the first flush of youth to put your head round the door and enjoy the aroma of hot sugar and fruity syrups.

Go back past the entrance to St Anne's and along Chapel Street.

St Mary's Cathedral (C1) is the area's Catholic place of worship, identifiable by its colonnaded porch. It is a not particularly interesting example of 19C church architecture, but its **registers** of births and deaths go back to 1748 and are a valuable resource for people trying to trace their ancestry.

Go down Shandon Street to the quayside and walk west for 15-20min to the City Gaol.

Cork City Gaol★ (A2) (*9.30am-5pm in summer; 10am-4pm in winter. Admission charge*) has been completely restored. The cells now contain life-like tableaux of prisoners and evoke in a very realistic way the harsh treatment once meted out to those who had fallen foul of the law. The small café is a good place for a pause before the longish walk back into town.

Return to the starting point of the walk near the tourist office, then cross the footbridge over the southern branch of the Lee at the end of Grand Parade and turn left.

South Cork
Allow an hour

The buildings along the quayside here are particularly picturesque, interspersed with any number of pubs and the occasional real oddity like the junk shop adorned with ancient bric-a-brac of all kinds.

To the right between Sullivan's Quay and George's Quay, Mary Street leads to **Red Abbey Tower** (D3). The only structure remaining from the medieval town, the square tower was part of an Augustinian monastery founded in the 13C. King William's artillerymen used it as a gun emplacement during their bombardment of the city in 1690.

Go back along the quayside towards the cathedral, and at the sign indicating the **Elizabeth Fort** (C3) turn left up Keyser's Hill, a narrow lane running between walls painted a bright yellow. Steps lead up to the **star-shaped fort** of 1603. After being severely damaged in the 1690 siege, it became a prison, then a barracks. It is now a Garda station, but there is nothing to stop visitors from stepping inside to admire the fine **view** over the city. Almost directly below are the big steel vats of **Beamish's brewery**, and further away, the towers of St Anne's Shandon and St Mary's.

Continue west along Proby's Quay then along Bishop Street.

St Fin Barre's Cathedral★ (C3) *(10am-5pm)*, an Anglican establishment, stands on the site of the city's founding monastery. The present building, designed by William Burges, only dates from 1878 and is in a highly decorated version of 13C French Gothic style. Built from a pale limestone, it is crowned by a 73m-high **spire**. Particularly striking are the three lavishly sculpted western **doorways**, and, inside, the **stained glass** and the richly carved **coffer ceiling** depicting the life of Christ.

West city

A car is useful for this part of town. Drive down Western Road in the Killarney / Tralee direction and park on the road opposite the university or in the road running parallel to the Lee.

This residential area is also the site of **University College**, founded by Queen Victoria in 1849 (she is commemorated at the entrance to a park on the left of Western Road). The university buildings are in a mixture of mostly traditional styles, scattered over an attractive campus. In the grounds is the college's **Honan Chapel★**. Built in 1915 in Irish Romanesque style, its rich interior decoration makes it an outstanding example of the Celtic Revival style, with stained glass and other ornamentation by leading artists and craftspeople of the time.

Cross over Western Road to Mardyke Walk and the luxuriant riverside Fitzgerald Park.

Built by a wealthy brewer, the Georgian mansion in the park now houses the **Cork Public Museum★** (A2) *(11am-1pm / 2.15pm-5pm except Saturday, Sunday morning and public holidays. Free admission)*. The museum retraces local history since prehistoric times with models, old documents, prints and many other items. The commercial, cultural, political and social development of the city is evoked by means of such objects as lovely old lacework, a finely crafted golden bird, rare silverware, and paintings.

Three times a week, Western Road is the scene of intense activity as the crowds stream towards the **Greyhound Track★** (A3). The dogs themselves may be the main attraction, but the spectators' faces too repay study, especially in the frantic seconds before the completion of the final lap.

Around Cork★★

The Royal Gunpowder Mills and Blarney Castle (15km) are to the west of Cork. Fota Island, Cobh and Midleton make up a separate trip (about 60km in total). Crosshaven can be combined with a boat trip to make a whole day excursion. In each case it is more pleasant to stay somewhere close by rather than in Cork itself. Allow 2 days if making all these excursions.

Royal Gunpowder Mills★
Leave Cork on Western Road towards Killarney and continue on the N22 to Ballincollig, 7km from Cork, and follow signs. April-September: 10am-6pm. Admission charge.

These gunpowder mills were founded by a banker in 1794, and flourished throughout the 19C thanks to the heavy demand from European armies as well as Britain. The largest of their kind in Ireland, and the second largest in the United Kingdom as a whole, they were a major factor in the local economy until gunpowder was made redundant by the invention of dynamite and nitroglycerine. They closed in 1903. Spread over an extensive site, many of the buildings have been restored, and there is a museum helping to explain the importance of what is the largest remaining example of such a complex in Europe.

Go back towards Cork and turn left on the R618 towards Macroom. Turn right in 1km on to the R579 and continue for 4km before turning right again onto the R617 towards Tower and Blarney.

Blarney Castle★

July-August: 9am-7pm (the rest of the year until dusk). Admission charge to the castle only, or combined ticket including Blarney House and gardens.

The village of Blarney itself is nothing special, but the huge woollens shop and the castle attract visitors in their thousands, mostly Irish and Americans.

The castle ruins include several halls and a series of dungeons, but the most prominent feature is the great **keep** dating from 1446. This is really a tower house, battlemented and very typical of its period. The famous **Blarney Stone** is set inside the parapet at the top of the tower; as everyone knows, kissing it is supposed to endow the kisser with the gift of eloquent speech. This is quite a procedure, usually involving waiting in a queue, lying down and being dangled over the battlements with your legs held by a guide. Definitely only for those with a head for heights.

Blarney House *(late June-mid-September: 12pm-6pm; closed Sunday)* is a large 19C edifice built in Scottish Baronial style in the castle gardens.

Rock Close★ is a rock garden laid out in the 19C around a **druidic site** close to the river. There is what is supposed to be a sacrificial stone, a wishing staircase which should be negotiated downwards with one's eyes closed, a rock shaped like a witch's face, some caves, and a pair of **dolmens**.

In the middle of Blarney village are the **Blarney Woollen Mills**. Woollens were the basis of the place's economy in the days before tourism, and still do a roaring trade with visitors. At the end of the 18C a model community was founded, with workers housed in small individual homes. At the peak of activity there were 13 mills operating in the area, producing tweeds mainly for military use.

Cobh★★

23km east of Cork via the N8, N25 and R624. Cobh (pronounced "cove" is a good place to stay for visitors with a car).

No-one staying in the Cork area should miss out on this side trip to Cobh, Ireland's premier transatlantic port. Once a simple fishing village, Cobh became an important base for the Royal Navy in the American War of Independence and during the Napoleonic wars. When Queen Victoria disembarked here on her first visit to Ireland the place was renamed Queenstown in her honour. In the heyday of luxury transatlantic travel in the first half of the 20C many of the great liners would call at Cobh, but the port is famous above all as the place where hundreds of thousands of emigrants bade their last farewell to their native land before setting off to America. It was also the last port of call for the ill-fated Titanic.

The blarney

A number of tales surround the origin of the Blarney Stone. Was it brought back from the Crusades? Or was it given to the King of Munster by a witch in gratitude for saving her life? Wherever the stone came from, there's no doubt about what is meant when someone is said to have the gift of the blarney. Queen Elizabeth I was so exasperated by the way in which the castle's owner used his charm and eloquence to frustrate all her attempts to take the castle from him, that she declared "This is all Blarney, he never means to do what he says!" The expression passed into the English language.

The Cobh Heritage Centre★★ *(early March-late December: 10am-6pm. Admission charge)* evokes this sombre history

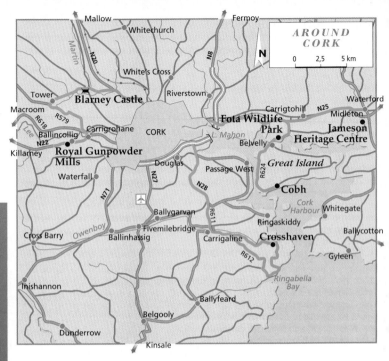

in a very moving way. Under the title **The Queenstown Story**, the exhibition recalls the conditions aboard ship, the epic story of emigration, the tragedies of the Titanic and the Lusitania, the evolution of the port and its strategic role in wartime.

A stroll along the quayside reveals a wealth of fine residences evocative of past splendours. The use of bright colours enlivens the scene, particularly in the case of the delightful red and green Town Hall with its splendid clock.

Atop the hill is the imposing Gothic Revival Roman Catholic **St Colman's Cathedral**, with a slender spire and a famous **carillon** of 48 bells. There is a fine view from here of the town and harbour. An unusual feature is the tap, which, when turned, produces holy water.

Six kilometres north of Cobh on the R624 is **Fota Island***. Here is the **Fota Wildlife Park** *(April-October: 10am-5pm. Admission charge. Heritage Site)* and **Arboretum**. Exotic tree and shrub species from all five continents flourish in the mild climate, as do animals from all over the world in an environment where many of them can wander freely.

Jameson Heritage Centre*
20km east of cork via the N25 towards Midleton. 10am-6pm. Closed weekends November-February. Admission charge.

Midleton has been associated with the distilling of whiskey since the early years of the 19C. All the big names have their headquarter offices here, among them Paddy, Jameson and Powers. There is a guided tour of the old distillery where the mysteries of whiskey production are explained. The largest still in the world is here, with a capacity of 130 000 litres. The tour ends with a tasting.

Crosshaven

23km southeast of Cork via the N28 and R611 to Carrigaline, then via the R612. The final stretch of road runs along the River Owenboy. Crosshaven is a popular excursion for people from Cork and traffic is heavy at weekends.

It was inevitable that this attractive fishing village should become a resort and sailing centre for well-off people from Cork. The place began to develop in the 19C when a paddle-steamer service to and from Cork was inaugurated, and the arrival of the railway in 1904 accelerated the process. The British military base of Camden Fort commanded the seaward approach. Crosshaven is the headquarters of the Royal Cork Yacht Club, the successor to the world's oldest yachting fraternity, the Water Club, founded at Cobh in 1720.

Pleasure craft abound here, and **sea fishing** is very popular. There are good **bathing beaches** too, at Church Bay, Myrtleville, Ringabella Bay, Rocky Cove and elsewhere. Attractive walks lead to **Camden Fort** with its view over the harbour where dolphins can sometimes be seen, to Church Bay (beyond Cronin's pub), or along the **cliffs** between Rocky Cove and Robert's Cove. Oysterhaven, much further south towards Kinsale, is very popular with **windsurfers**.

Emigrant agony

The failure of the potato crop in 1845 and in subsequent years left countless thousands faced with a choice between starvation and emigration. Rather than slowly die of hunger, many chose to leave their homes for the New World, and a high proportion of those that left passed through Cobh. Arriving at the port on foot or by train, the would-be emigrants might have to wait days on end for a place on a boat. Many were relieved of their last pennies by unscrupulous operators and packed aboard vessels which came to be known as "coffin ships". Over a period of 100 years more than a million and half people left Ireland for America.

COMING AND GOING

By plane – **Cork Airport** (off D4), ☎ 0214 313 131, is 8km south of the city on the Kinsale road. An airport bus goes to Parnell bus station in town. There are flights to and from Dublin and major cities in the UK.

By train – **Kent Station**, Lower Glanmire Road (E1), ☎ 0214 506 766, is on the north bank of the Lee, 15min on foot from the city centre. 6 to 9 trains daily to Dublin (3hr), 4 to 8 trains daily to Limerick (1hr30min), 3 to 5 daily to Tralee (2hr30min) and Killarney (2hr). 12 trains daily weekdays and 5 Sundays to Cobh (25min) via Fota.

By bus – **Parnell Central Bus Station**, Parnell Place (D2), ☎ 0214 508 188, is just behind St Patrick's Street, near the quayside. 5 or 6 services daily to Waterford (2hr15min), 3 or 4 to Dublin (4hr30min), 5 to 7 to Killarney (2hr), 4 or 5 to Galway (4hr), 5 or 6 to Sligo (7hr) and one to Donegal (9hr). There are regular services to the south coast (see under "Making the most of..." for each destination), as well as to Crosshaven and Blarney.

By boat – Ferries from the UK and France dock at the Ringaskiddy terminal 14km south of the city, ☎ 0214 378 111. From here there is a bus service to Parnell Bus Station (30min).

GETTING AROUND

Cork is best explored on foot as parking space is scarce. Anyone staying in the western suburbs will find it easier to leave the car there and walk into town along Western Road (A3-B3). A disc parking scheme is in operation. A road tunnel under the Lee between Douglas in the south and the N8 and N25 in the north was opened in 1999, making it easier to get through the centre towards Cobh and the northeast.

By bus – Buses run frequently on several routes. Service n° 8 (from St Patrick's Street) runs along Western Road and serves the University and the greyhound track. Service n° 11 links Parnell bus station and Cork City Gaol, and n° 2, also from the bus station, goes to St Mary's Cathedral.

By taxi – Taxis can be found throughout the city centre. The main taxi stands are in St Patrick's Street (C2-D2) and South Mall (D2) and in front of the major hotels.

Car hire – **Budget**, Tourist Office, Grand Parade (C2-C3), ☎ 0214 274 755. **Great Island Car Rentals**, 47 McCurtain Street (D1), ☎ 0214 503 536. The major international rental firms have desks at the airport. Most firms require drivers to be at least 21, possibly 23 years old.

ADDRESS BOOK

Tourist information – **Tourist House**, Grand Parade (C2-C3), ☎ 0214 273 251. Summer: 9am-7pm except Sunday afternoon; rest of year 9am-12.45pm / 2.15pm-5.30pm; closed Sunday. Wide range of books, maps and plans for sale plus some free publications (including basic city plan). Bureau de change. Hotel reservations and car hire. Tickets for open-top bus tour of Cork and for boat trips around the harbour and to Cobh.

Banks / Currency exchange – There are branches of the principal banks in South Mall (D2) and St Patrick's Street (C2-D2). They close at the weekend, but most have a cash machine. Travellers' cheques can be cashed at major hotels and at the tourist office, as well as at some shops and other outlets used to dealing with tourists (but check the rate of exchange offered).

Post office – The main post office is in Oliver Plunkett Street (D2). 9am-5.30pm; closed Sunday.

Telephone – There are still plenty of coin-operated telephone boxes, but phone cards are more practical for making international calls. In Cork, as in other large towns, there is a distinction between the blue and white telephone boxes of Eircom and a private service with green call boxes. The latter are cheaper, but rarer.

Internet – Get connected at **Favourite**, 122 St Patrick's Street (D2) close to Patrick's Bridge, daily 9am-10.30pm, ☎ 0214 272 646. Bring along some €1 coins.

Medical service – *Cork Regional Hospital*, ☎ 0214 546 400.

Apart from the big hotels in the city centre, most of Cork's accommodation is in B&Bs on the western side of town. Anyone with a car should consider staying in Blarney or Cobh where accommodation is better value.

• Cork
Under €13
Youth hostels are the only places in Cork which offer accommodation at this price and they are often full.
Cork International Youth Hostel, Western Road, ☎ 0214 543 289 – 100 beds in dormitories and double rooms CC Opposite the University and on the n° 8 bus route. In a lovely garden, this large building has bright and clean rooms. The double rooms are more expensive. Essential to book in advance and have proof of YHA membership. Breakfast extra. Laundry facilities.
Isaacs Hostel, 48 McCurtain Street, ☎ 0214 508 388 – 64 beds in dormitories and family rooms. ✕ Private hostel in ideal location between the railway station and city centre. Well-equipped communal kitchen. Characterful warehouse conversion. Additional charge for breakfast.
Kinlay House, Shandon, ☎ 0214 508 966 – 140 beds in dormitories and smaller rooms CC Large new building in a quiet street by St Anne's Shandon. Inexpensive. Linen supplied and continental breakfast included. Cooking and laundry facilities. Safe available.

Between €40-50
Aaran Isle Inn, 14 Dyke Parade, ☎ 0214 278 158 – 16rm ⬜ ℘ TV CC Good location on the western edge of the city centre, big yellow-painted and tastefully renovated building.
Rossmore House, Western Road, ☎ 0214 274 908 – 5rm ⬜ TV CC Closed at Christmas. Opposite the entrance to the University and only a 10-minute walk from the city centre, this pretty dark blue house is kept spotless by the friendly and energetic Patricia Downing. The rooms without facilities

are less expensive. Private parking. Tea-making facilities in the room.
Carbery House, Western Road, ☎ 0214 272 217 – 6rm ⬜ CC Slightly more expensive than the above establishment, but very comfortable, this attractive house is kept by a charming couple. Rooms without their own facilities are less expensive. Secure parking at the back of the building.
Island House, Morrison's Quay, ☎ 0214 271 716 – 51rm ⬜ ℘ TV ✕ CC Modern and comfortable, Island House is located on one of the canals, very close to the city centre but in a quiet situation. The rooms are modern and the kitchen can be used by guests. Favourable rates for family rooms and 3-bed rooms. Parking available.

Between €65-90
Jurys Cork Inn, Anderson's Quay, ☎ 0214 276 444 – 133rm ⬜ ℘ ✕ CC Right by the bus station on the banks of the Lee, this huge and impersonal international hotel is good value and very comfortable. Rates (€70) are by room and not per person (3 adults or 2 adults and 2 children).
Crawford House, Western Road, ☎ 0214 279 000 – 12rm ⬜ ℘ TV CC The somewhat severe exterior belies a refined minimalist interior with pale wood floors, designer furniture, huge beds and whirlpool baths. Reduced low season rates. Private parking.
Fairylawn, Western Road, ☎ 0214 543 444 – 14rm ⬜ ℘ TV CC Completely renovated, this huge building has the atmosphere of a small private hotel. Very near the University and Cork Museum, it offers attractive surroundings and a high degree of comfort. It may be possible to negotiate a favourable rate out of season or when staying for longer periods. Large private car park.
Hotel Isaacs, 48 McCurtain Street, ☎ 0214 500 011 – 36rm ⬜ ℘ TV ✕ CC Next to the hostel of the same name, close to the bus and railway stations and the city centre, at the end of a covered passageway with a fountain, this is a good place to stay, albeit on the expensive side. Comfortable 2-3 room apartments are available too, by the

night or week, at relatively favourable rates (€70-80 per night depending on the number of rooms and the season).

🐌 **Seven North Mall House**, 7 North Mall, ☎ 0214 397 191 – 7rm 🛏️ 🖋️ TV CC Stately 18C town house of unique charm by the northern branch of the Lee. There's no signboard; Angela Hegarty prefers privacy and discretion. There are architects in the family, and the hand of the designer can be seen in the décor and the labyrinthine staircases. Each room is different, with huge bathrooms and bathtubs fit for giants. The footbridge to the city centre and its restaurants is close by. Private car park.

• **Blarney**
Between €40-50
Traveller's Joy, Tower, ☎ 0214 385 541 – 3rm CC The village of Tower is clearly signposted on the R617 4km from Blarney. The landlady, the lovely Gertie O'Shea is a mine of information on the area, and the garden of her little bungalow will delight all plant-lovers.

Ashlee Lodge, Tower, ☎ 0214 385 346 – 6rm 🛏️ 🖋️ TV CC A good place to stay, this attractive bungalow has prettily decorated rooms with tea-making facilities and a wide choice of alternatives at breakfast-time. Guests may use the delightful living-room with its library full of useful information about the area and its attractions.

Between €50-75
🐌 **Maranatha House**, Tower, ☎ 0214 385 102 – 6rm 🛏️ CC At the end of a lovely tree-lined avenue, this Victorian manor house is almost submerged in flowers. Antique furniture, canopied beds, tasteful draperies, breakfast on the veranda, plus charming hosts, perfection indeed.

• **Cobh**
Between €45-50
Ardeen B&B, 3 Harbour Hill, ☎ 0214 811 803 – 5rm 🛏️ TV Close to the cathedral in a street running parallel to the quayside, this is a pretty and well-kept B&B. It is worth getting a room facing the sea. Reduced rates between November and May.

Harley's B&B, 24 Harbour Row, ☎ 0214 814 290 – 6rm 🛏️ 🖋️ TV CC Overlooking the harbour in the continuation of the street beneath the cathedral. Bright rooms with views of the river, their décor a mixture of wood, white paint, lace and pretty bedspreads. Room 3 is at the back of the building, but its décor and whirlpool bath more than make up for the lack of view. An additional advantage is that the landlady owns the laundrette next door.

• **Crosshaven**
Between €55-70
🐌 **Whispering Pines Hotel**, ☎ 0214 831 843 – 15rm 🛏️ 🖋️ TV ✕ CC All the spacious rooms have a view of the river. Public rooms are comfortable, and the bar and gardens are pleasant enough though not particularly characterful. Barry Twomey is an expert fisherman and can arrange fishing trips, as well as tours in the hotel's own bus. Bikes can be hired too. Restaurant specialising in ultra-fresh seafood.

EATING OUT

• **Cork**
It is possible to eat for less than €6.50 in the majority of pubs. Soups are an especially good idea, served with bread and butter or with toasted sandwiches.
Between €6.50-13
🐌 **Café Paradiso**, 16 Lancaster Quay (B2), ☎ 0214 277 939. In a street running west off Grand Parade, this is a vegetarian restaurant with a choice of light dishes, including soups and salads with home-made bread and olive oil. At dinner-time, there are more sophisticated dishes at higher prices. Wine is expensive, but is available by the glass. Closed Sunday.

Reardens, Washington Street (C2). Big western-style pub close to Grand Parade. Loud music and much in favour amongst the young. Traditional snacks or more substantial offerings like cajun chicken, lasagne and curries.

The Mongolian Barbecue, 97 South Main Street (C2), ☎ 0214 279 880. Near Cornmarket Street, pick and mix buffet guaranteed to satisfy the heartiest appetite. Meat grilled before your eyes and enlivened by a variety of sauces. Lunch costs as little as €6.50.

Bodega, 46 Cornmarket Street (C2), ☎ 0214 272 878. An old warehouse with contemporary paintings on the walls, this is one of the places where "le tout Cork" comes to see and be seen. Sunday jazz, DJ on Thursday and Saturday. Satisfying bar meals for less than €13 including a variety of soups, salads, pastas, grills and fish dishes. The restaurant is more expensive, reckon on between €20-25.

McGuire's Warehouse Bar, Paul Street (C2). This old warehouse has been given a new lease of life with a clever facelift using brick, stone and bright colours. Traditional lunches including soups, salads and sandwiches. Popular with the fashionable crowd, best at lunchtime.

Kethner's, Paul Street (C2), ☎ 0214 272 868. Open all day. Straightforward establishment serving good quality fast food including burgers, pizzas and home-made pasta. Lunch for less than €6.50, more expensive in the evening, but bigger portions.

Gingerbread House, Paul Street (C2), ☎ 0214 276 411. Big bakery-cum-café, eat in or take away. Delicious scones, muffins and other cakes and pastries for elevenses and various types of quiche for lunch.

Café Mexicana, Carey's Lane (C2), ☎ 0214 276 433. Intimate little place in the Paul Street area with south of the border décor and dishes to match at a reasonable price. Wine available by the glass.

Food, Etc Café, French Church Street and Academy Street (D2). Open 8.30am-6pm, this is a friendly café with restful décor linked to a shop specialising in interior design. Popular with "ladies who shop". Excellent coffee and light lunches, including omelettes, quiches, warm salads and a choice of pastries.

Crawford Gallery Café, Emmet Place (D2), ☎ 0214 274 415. The gallery's café-restaurant occupies a large, bright room with pictures, sculptures and flowers on the tables. Salads, sandwiches and cakes, and a limited range of full meals. Good lunchtime choice.

Farm Gate Café, English Market (C2). 8.30am-5.30pm; closed weekends. Meals are served around the mezzanine overlooking the vegetable market and a pretty fountain. Savoury flans, hot or cold, spiced chicken, salads and cakes. A good place for lunch.

The Oyster, 4 Market Lane (C2), ☎ 0214 272 716. Closed Sunday. In a cul-de-sac off St Patrick's Street by the English Market. With strikingly renovated décor of false marble and wrought iron, this restaurant founded in 1792 is one of the city's oldest. Traditional pub dishes including Irish stew and chicken and ham, plus soups and sandwiches, all for less than €7.50. More expensive in the evening but still very affordable.

Valparaiso, 115 Oliver Plunkett Street (D2), ☎ 0214 275 488. Open 12.30pm-3pm / 5pm-11pm. Tapas and other dishes of Spanish or Mediterranean inspiration served in a big bright interior. Reckon on around €7.50 at lunchtime, a bit more in the evening.

Clancey's, Prince's Street and Marlborough Street (D2), ☎ 0214 276 097. With entrances on both streets, this is one of those typical long bars, with plenty of nooks and crannies, low ceilings and a good atmosphere. Full meals or sandwiches at lunchtime. In the evening restaurant meals work out at around €15-20.

Quay Co-op, 24 Sullivan's Quay (C3), ☎ 0214 317 660. Monday-Saturday, 9am-9pm; closed Sunday. Take-away available. Opposite the footbridge at the end of Grand Parade, this restaurant is above a health-food shop, and is much favoured by vegetarians, with healthy snacks, salads and soups.

Proby's Bistro, Proby's Quay (C3), ☎ 0214 316 531. In the street leading to St Fin Barre's Cathedral, this restaurant has dishes for under €6.50 at midday and from €7.50 upwards in the evening. International cuisine ranging from Greek to Malaysian.

No 5 Fenn's Quay, 5 Sheares Street (C2), ☎ 0214 279 527. From 10am in the morning; closed Sunday and on Monday evening. In the street parallel to Washington Street to the rear of the courthouse, this popular restaurant serves well-prepared food made from fresh ingredients at very reasonable prices.

Isaac's Restaurant, 48 McCurtain Street (D1), ☎ 0214 503 805. Range of tasty and copious dishes served in a series of spacious rooms with walls of exposed brick. Popular and very busy establishment. Cosmopolitan cuisine.

More than €18

🍴 **Arbutus Lodge**, Middle Glanmire Road, Montenotte (off E1), ☎ 0214 501 237. One of Ireland's best restaurants, in a lovely building. Luxurious setting and exquisite food, plus a superb wine list. Expensive, but well worth it. Ownership may change.

• **Blarney**

Around €13

Blair's Inn, Cloghroe, ☎ 0214 381 470. Five kilometres from Blarney via the R617 to Tower, then via the R579 (well signposted). Traditional country pub with good fresh food served in an informal setting. Dishes include generous helpings of Irish stew, pork in cider with apple sauce, and seafood and salmon gratin.

• **Cobh**

More than €6.50

🍴 **The Bistro**, East Beach, ☎ 0214 811 237. Open 10am-10pm; closed Sunday evening. Violet-coloured building on the quayside by the town hall. The French chef specialises in dishes which successfully marry a variety of cuisines. There is ultra-fresh fish and seafood, and perfectly cooked meats. Try mussels in cream sauce, crab claws in garlic butter, or baked salmon in spinach sauce. Dinner will cost at least €16. Morning coffee and scones are equally classy.

HAVING A DRINK

Cork is a city of bars and of two great beers, or rather stouts, Murphy's and Beamish. Each has its adherents, though Beamish is cheaper. Murphy's drinkers claim their brew is smoother and less bitter than Guinness, and while this may be true, the regional rivalry between Cork and the capital quite possibly has something to do with it too.

🍴 **Hi-B Bar**, 108 Oliver Plunkett Street (opposite the post office, on the upper floor). Brian O'Donnell's pub is a Cork institution, its décor unaffected by the passage of time, a perfect setting for a quiet conversation over a pint of whatever takes your fancy. The proprietor is a classical music fan, and there's an incredible CD collection stacked up behind the bar. But there's room for blues and traditional sounds too.

An Bodhrán, 42 Oliver Plunkett Street. Traditional groups every evening. Good atmosphere and snacks available at lunchtime.

An Crannóg, 74 Oliver Plunkett Street. Bar much in favour with a young crowd, with rock music and a DJ in the evening Thursday-Saturday. Good value light lunches.

An Phoenix, 3 Union Quay. On two floors, with a décor based on old beer barrels, this pub has excellent blues or traditional sounds every evening.

🍴 **An Spailpín Fánach**, 28 South Main Street. Right opposite the Beamish brewery, this establishment is much in favour with fans of traditional Irish music and blues. The programme is full of variety and there is music most evenings. Irish stew on offer at lunchtime for less than €6.50.

🍴 **Clancy's**, Princes' Street and Marlborough Street. See "Where to eat".

OTHER THINGS TO DO

Festivals – Guinness International Jazz Festival, ☎ 0214 270 463 / 270 022, annually in late October. The nerve centre of the festival is the Opera House, but there are sessions in pubs and hotels all over town. This is a prestigious event with a terrific atmosphere; there is great pressure on accommodation, so book well in advance.

Greyhound racing – Cork Greyhound Track, Western Road (A3), ☎ 0214 543 095. Open 8pm Monday, Wednesday and Saturday. Admission €4. It's worth coming early to watch the dogs arrive with their owners.

Golf – Lee Valley Golf Club, Clashanure, Ovens, to the west of the city, ☎ 0214 331 721, par 72, 18-hole course. **Blarney Golf Course**, Stoneview, Blarney, ☎ 0214 382 455, par 70, 18 holes. **Fota Island Golf Club**, ☎ 0214 883 710, par 72, 18 holes.

Cobh

C Legrand/MICHELIN

THE SOUTH COAST★
FROM KINSALE TO BALTIMORE
Co Cork
140km via the coast road – allow 2 or 3 days
Michelin map 923 D-E-F-G / 12-13

Not to be missed
The walk to Charles Fort and Old Head of Kinsale.
De Barra's pub at Clonakilty.
Baltimore at the time of the Fiddle Fair.

And remember...
The road signs are more than usually unreliable in this area
and a good road map is a necessity.
There aren't many bargains to be had in the shops at Kinsale.

Beyond the fishing village of Kinsale, the coast is cut into by a series of inlets and estuaries. The westward-running road is never very far from the shore and every now and then it gives sea views. Inland is a landscape of rolling green hills and roads enclosed by hedgerows. The drive from Cork to Bantry via Macroom is a fine alternative to the coastal route, winding as it does along the valley of the Lee through an ancient upland now covered in coniferous forests.

Kinsale

■ Kinsale★

In summer and at the weekend traffic is heavy and parking is problematic. It's best to get here in the morning, giving time to explore the town and walk out to Charles Fort. Allow half a day.

Sometimes thought of as Ireland's St Tropez, Kinsale is prettily located at the mouth of the Bandon River and is one of the most popular places in the southwest. Its spruce houses, restaurants and October gourmet festival attract hordes of visitors, mostly Americans. As well as its fishing harbour, the town is divided into three distinct districts, the centre, Scilly and Charles Fort.

A port of some importance
Kinsale developed as a fishing and commercial port soon after the Anglo-Norman invasions. The siege of the town in 1601-02 was of great significance in the course of Irish history. A Spanish force, come to help the rebellion led by O'Neill, occupied the town despite the fact that the rebels were fighting in the far north. The Spaniards were besieged by the English, who were in turn besieged by

O'Neill's men. Unaided by the Spanish, who stayed within the town, the Irish were routed, a defeat which led in the space of a few years to "the flight of the Earls" and the end of the old Gaelic order. In 1641 the town prudently declared for Cromwell and was spared the usual slaughter and devastation. King James II landed here in 1689 on his way to defeat at the Battle of the Boyne, and it was from Kinsale that he departed into permanent exile.

In the 17C and 18C Kinsale was heavily fortified and became an important shipyard for the Royal Navy. But ships grew too large for the harbour, and the industry declined. The town has only really revived with the growth of tourism.

Town centre

After strolling through the pretty little lanes around the main square, climb up to the top of the town via Main Street, Guardwell and Church Street.

The square Norman tower of the late 12C Anglican **St Multose's Church** rises over the overgrown graveyard with its higgledy-piggledy tombstones. There is eroded Norman zig-zag decoration over the **north door**. In the south aisle are a number of ancient tombstones laid against the wall or forming part of the floor.

Go back down Church Street to Market Square.

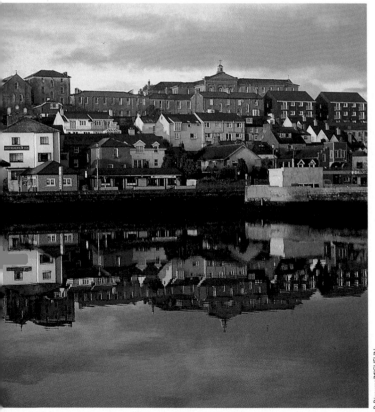

B Pérousse/MICHELIN

The Lusitania disaster

The great liner was torpedoed off Kinsale by a German submarine on 7 May 1915 and her wreck lies on the seabed 19km offshore. 1 500 died in the disaster, which helped change the climate of opinion in America and contributed to her entry into the war two years later. For months after the sinking, bodies and wreckage continued to be washed ashore all along this coast.

Kinsale Regional Museum (*2pm-5.30pm, but may vary because staffed by volunteers. Admission charge*) is housed in the courthouse of 1600. The Dutch-gabled façade was added in 1706. Inside is a wonderful array of bits and pieces evoking the history of the town and its surroundings. There is also some memorabilia connected with the sinking of the *Lusitania*, the inquiry into which was held here.

Go along Market Street and Cork Street.

Desmond Castle (*June-September: 10am-1pm / 2pm-6pm. Admission charge. Heritage Site. Check times as the castle is also staffed by volunteers*) is a three-storey tower house rather than a castle, built at the end of the 15C. Initially a residence of the Earls of Desmond, it was used as an arsenal by the Spanish during the siege of 1601-02, then by the English as a prison for foreign captives, mostly Frenchmen, hence its other name of "French Prison". In 1747, 54 of the inmates died in a terrible fire. Two floors of the building now house a **museum of wine**, a reminder of the trade which enriched the town. There are also displays on some of the great Irish families who went into exile. Some disappeared into obscurity, while others made their fortune, among them the Hennessy dynasty of brandy distillers.

Walks around Kinsale

The coast around the town offers good walking as well as the chance of a swim. Anyone with a little time to spare should take the long way round via the Bandon River rather than the direct route to Courtmacsherry Bay.

Leave Kinsale on the R600 towards Cork. On the way out of town turn right to Charles Fort. The fort can also be reached on foot via the attractive Scilly Walk and Summer Cove.

Charles Fort★★ (*March-October: 10am-6pm; rest of year weekends only. Admission charge. Heritage Site. Keep children well under control*) was built in the 17C as part of a system of defences which included the less well-preserved James Fort on the far side of the bay. Its star-shaped plan is that of the typical Baroque fortress. The fort consists of two huge **bastions** facing the sea and encloses what is virtually a complete town. The British occupied it right up until 1922, when the town was abandoned to the Irish. Although ruinous, the buildings are still redolent of the atmosphere when the garrison stood ready to repel any attack, and there are fine **views★** of Kinsale and the estuary from the ramparts.

Beyond the fort there is a pleasant **coastal walk★** to the tip of the headland.

Go back to Kinsale and take the R604 south. On the way out of town just beyond the bridge, turn left towards Castle Park Marina.

James Fort, high up on the clifftop, makes a good destination for a walk starting from the pub by the youth hostel. There is even a little bathing beach.

Return to the R600, then take the R604 towards the Old Head of Kinsale, 12km from Kinsale.

Seeing off the Spanish

At the end of the 16C and the beginning of the 17C, the whole of Europe was affected by the Wars of Religion and the power struggles associated with them. In Ireland as elsewhere, the Spaniards acted as a rapid reaction force charged with protecting Roman Catholicism and all it represented. In 1588 many of the ships of the Spanish Armada were wrecked off the Irish coast. In 1602, the Spanish forces of Don Juan de Aguila which had occupied Kinsale watched on while their Irish allies were defeated. The battle over, de Aguila surrendered ignominiously.

C Boisvieux/HOA QUI

Charles Fort

The **Old Head of Kinsale**★ offers attractive walks along its cliffs and the beach to the west. The ruins which can be seen beyond the car park are those of one of the many castles built by the powerful De Courcy family. It was within sight of this desolate headland that the Lusitania was sunk.

Return to Kinsale and take the R606 then the R605 for 13km to Inishannon. In Inishannon, cross the bridge and take the minor road along the right bank of the river. After about 4km, turn left towards Kilmacsimon.

The hamlet of **Kilmacsimon**★ stretches out along the **Bandon River**, whose well-wooded banks have something of a Scandinavian look about them, at least when the tide is in. But the scattered little houses, together with a tiny shipyard, a waterside pub, broad pasturelands and circling crows, all combine to make visitors feel that this is the real Ireland. The best way to experience the area (apart from dropping in at the pub) is to take a walk along the river beyond the shipbuilders.

Courtmacsherry Bay★

Beyond Kinsale, the R600 winds through a landscape of green hills before passing through **Ballinspittle**, famous ever since thousands of witnesses testified to having seen a statue of the Virgin Mary move in 1985. The road then runs along the shore of Courtmacsherry Bay to Timoleague.

■ **Timoleague** – *25.5km from Kinsale*. With the ruins of its ancient abbey dominating the estuary of the Argideen, the village looks like something out of an old print. The **Franciscan abbey**★ *(free admission)*, founded in the 13C, grew rich on the wine trade with Spain, but was sacked by Cromwell's men in 1642. An exploration of the ruins reveals the Gothic choir, the cloisters, the monks' dormitory, the refectory with its superb windows, the wine cellars, and a leper hospital.

On the far side of the village, beyond the big Catholic church perched on the headland, are the **Timoleague Castle Gardens** *(mid-May-mid-September: 11am-5.30pm. Admission charge)* with a wealth of flowering shrubs. By the entrance is a little **Anglican chapel**, its interior completely covered in mosaic and multicoloured friezes. The building and its elaborate decoration was paid for by the Maharajah of Gwalior in recognition of the devoted service of his doctor, a native of Timoleague.

259

Continue on the R601 to Courtmacsherry. Birds flock in large numbers to this inlet which runs far inland, attracted by the rich feeding grounds of the mudbanks exposed at low tide.

■ **Courtmacsherry –** This little place with its colourful array of houses is an ideal base for walking and deep-sea fishing. A number of **footpaths** lead to the headland (3.5km) through woods and past little bays.

Anyone with time to spare should drive to Clonakilty via Butlerstown. The **coast road** winds past cliffs and beaches across the **Seven Heads Peninsula**. A good place to stop is **Dunworley Bay**, its sandy beach framed by sheer cliffs.

■ Clonakilty
Allow 1hr for a quick tour

Clonakilty prospered in the past thanks to linen manufacture, but nowadays it is famous as a centre for Gaelic traditions, particularly music. Nationalist leader **Michael Collins** *(see page 24)* was born here, or to be exact, at Sam's Cross 5km to the west. It's a busy little place, with attractive shop signs and plenty of bars and pubs, including the famous De Barra's

A short stroll
At the centre of town is **Emmet Square**, a fine example of an English-style Georgian square, with tall town houses with elegant and colourful **doorways** surmounted by pretty fanlights.

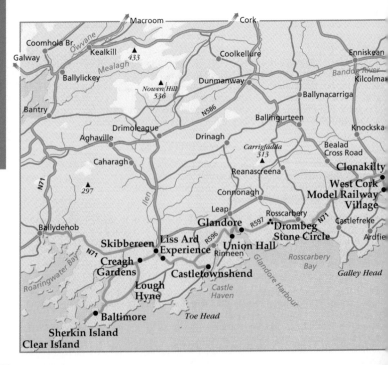

Towards the end of the main street in the Skibbereen direction is the **West Cork Regional Museum** (*May-October: 10.30am-5.30pm, Sunday 3pm-5pm; rest of year: daily 3pm-5pm. Admission charge*). The fascinating items evoking the history of the area include documents and photographs, and there is an abundance of material on the War of Independence and the career of Michael Collins.

Around Clonakilty

On the Inchydoney road to the south of the town is the **West Cork Model Railway Village★** (*March-October: 11am-5pm. Admission charge*) with wonderfully detailed miniature reconstructions of villages as they were in the 1940s, all linked together by a model railway.

An ideal spot for a swim or a picnic is at **Inchydoney beach★**, 2.4km south of Kinsale and backed by sand dunes.

Resist the temptation to go directly to Skibbereen which would mean missing delightful but out-of-the-way sights like the little harbours at Union Hall and Castletownshend.

The estuaries route★★

From Clonakilty follow the N71 for 13km to Rosscarbery, then take the picturesque and hilly R597 towards Glandore. Look out for the sign to Drombeg Stone Circle, 5km beyond Rosscarbery.

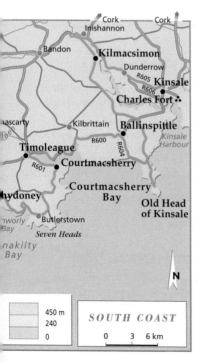

■ **Drombeg Stone Circle★** – *Well-signposted off the main road. 300m walk from the car park.* Consisting of 17 individual monoliths, the **stone circle** is 9m in diameter and dates from the 2C BC. The entrance to the circle is marked by two taller stones facing an altar which catches the rays of the setting sun at the time of the winter solstice. The nearby hole was a cooking pit, where heated stones would be placed to boil water.

■ **Glandore★** – This well-sheltered little haven still has a number of fishing boats. Its Gaelic name Cuan Dor means "harbour of the oaks", a reference to the dense woodlands that once covered the area. The two tiny islands beyond the harbour are called Adam and Eve; sailors feeling their way into port used to be instructed to "avoid Adam and hug Eve".

Just under 1km after leaving Glandore towards Leap, cross the estuary on the narrow bridge.

■ **Union Hall★** – This little place with its harbour, church, brightly painted pubs and trawlers, seems to come straight out of the pages of a children's picture book. It owes its name to the Act of Union of 1800.

About 2km off the Castletownshend road is a real little curiosity, the cottage housing the **Céim Hill Museum** *(10am-7pm. Admission charge)*. This "witches cave" is cram full of bric-a-brac of all kinds supposedly illustrating the evolution of mankind from prehistoric times to the present day. Don't miss the dinosaur jaw.

Continue on minor roads to Rinneen, then Castletownshend (R596).

■ **Castletownshend**★ – The village's substantial stone houses and their gardens are in striking contrast to the buildings found elsewhere in this area. Castletownshend was founded by Cromwellian soldiers who had done well out of the wars and who settled here, becoming traders and merchants.

The steep main street runs down to the quayside. Anglican **St Barrahane's Church** is perched charmingly atop a rise among yuccas and hortensias, and is reached up a series of flights of steps. In the porch is a souvenir from the wreck of the *Lusitania*, an oar from one of her lifeboats. At the back of the church are the graves of **Edith Somerville** and **Violet Martin**, cousins who together wrote stories about their minor gentry milieu, the most famous being *Some Experiences of an Irish R M* (1899).

Continue on the R596 to Skibbereen.

■ Skibbereen and around★

A good place to stay when there's no more room on the coast or if you are travelling by bus – otherwise it is worth just a brief stop

Skibbereen's origins are unusual; in 1631, when nearby Baltimore was raided by pirates, the survivors fled here and founded a new settlement. Skibbereen suffered particularly acutely during the Great Famine. Later in the 19C the little town made its debut on the international stage when the local paper, the Skibbereen Eagle, announced during a European political crisis, that it "was keeping its eye on the Czar of Russia". The weighty warning was taken up by the world's press, and became the most famous line ever printed in an Irish newspaper, though the Russian ruler's reaction remains unrecorded.

With only 2 000 inhabitants, Skibbereen is a lively place, especially on Wednesday, cattle market day, and Friday, when the market for country produce is held.

Liss Ard Experience

1km out of town on the Castletownshend road. May-September: 9am-6pm; closed Saturday and Sunday morning. Admission charge.

This large estate has been transformed into a kind of **conceptual park**. It is an ambitious project, still in its early stages and thus difficult to evaluate. Visitors are invited to experience Nature through a series of themed "rooms", a woodland walk, a wild flower meadow, a lake... The American artist James Turrell is responsible for the Crater, part of a planned Sky Garden. This is a place whose meaning and message will become clearer as it matures and develops.

Creagh Gardens★

6km southwest of Skibbereen via the R595 towards Baltimore. March-October: 10am-6pm. Admission charge.

This is a most attractive garden, laid out along traditional lines with a wealth of exotic shrubs, an artistically designed vegetable garden, pools, sweet-scented magnolias, and grassy slopes descending to the banks of the **River Ilen**. The elegant Georgian mansion is not open to the public.

B. Pérousse/MICHELIN

Quiet days in Baltimore

Lough Hyne★★

Indicated on the left 4km along the road to Baltimore. This saltwater lagoon linked by a narrow channel to the sea is a **marine nature reserve** with many rare and unusual species. Bathing in the particularly warm and unpolluted waters is possible, but paddlers and swimmers need to beware of sea urchins. The western and southern shores are threaded by attractive **footpaths**.

■ Baltimore

13km from Skibbereen

This remote fishing village lies at the end of a winding road which gives good views of the many islands in the bay. For many years the place was dominated by the powerful and piratical O'Driscoll clan and even today this is the most common family name in the area. A total of no fewer than nine ruined fortresses are evidence of a stormy past. In 1631 Baltimore was raided by pirates from Algeria, who sacked the town and killed many of the inhabitants or carried them off to be sold as slaves. The remainder fled to Skibbereen. The great city of Baltimore on Chesapeake Bay takes its name from this tiny place.

Every year in May Baltimore is the scene of the annual traditional music festival known as the **Fiddle Fair★★**. There are impromtu sessions in the street, musical evenings in the pubs, and a great atmosphere generally. The other big event in Baltimore's calendar is the July / August regatta, held every other year. Some of the sailing takes place in the dangerous waters off Cape Clear Island, guarded by the famous **Fastnet lighthouse** (*see panel page 270*). A good idea of the wild land- and sea-scape hereabouts can be had by walking the windswept cliffs to **Baltimore Beacon★★**, a white-painted medieval marker on the headland, shaped like the proverbial pillar of salt and known as "Lot's Wife".

Islands off Baltimore

Reached by ferries from Baltimore. See "Making the most of the south coast".

Sherkin Island★ (*day visit possible*) is proud of its three lovely beaches, the ruins of an O'Driscoll stronghold, and the remains of a 15C Franciscan monastery.

Clear Island★★ is further offshore, and wilder. It is one of the most important seabird sanctuaries in Ireland, and as well as birds, ornithologists gather here in considerable numbers, many of them staying in basic accommodation at the observatory. Clear Island is part of the Gaeltacht and people come here to take advanced courses in the Irish language. It is a stiff climb up from the landing-stage, but the view is well worth the effort. **Lough Erroll**, close to the O'Driscoll fort, is inhabited by a micro-organism capable of cleaning clothes immersed in its waters. A walk around the island passes the ruins of the 12C **St Kieran's Church** as well as some fascinating **megaliths**.

COMING AND GOING

By car – From Cork take the N71 southwest towards Kinsale. If returning to Cork, it's a good idea to come back via the inland route which leads through attractive hilly scenery (N71 to Bantry and Ballylickey, then the R584 to Macroom and finally the R618).

By bus – There is a regular service between Cork (Parnell bus station) and Kinsale (45min, 6 buses daily, 10 in summer, about half these numbers on Sunday). Most of the towns have a service to Cork; the main route is via Bandon, Clonakilty, Rosscarbery and Skibbereen (3 buses daily from Cork and 2 in the reverse direction, Cork-Skibbereen 2hr45min). From Skibbereen there is a bus to Baltimore and another north to Bantry, Glengarriff and Killarney.

By boat – Regular ferries (3 daily all year, 8 in summer) between Baltimore and Sherkin Island: 15min, €5 return. One to three boats daily to Clear Island: 45min, €10 return. Information: Sherkin Island, ☎ 028 201 25 / 202 18; Clear Island, ☎ 028 391 19. In summer there is also a ferry to Schull (3 trips daily) which also carries bikes and is a short cut to Mizen Head.

ADDRESS BOOK

Tourist information – *Tourist Office*, Pier Road, Kinsale, ☎ 0214 772 234, open March-November, helpful advice including free plans and accommodation lists. The tourist office at Skibbereen is open all year, the office at Clonakilty only in July and August.

Banks / Currency exchange – There are banks at Kinsale, Clonakilty and Skibbereen, and cash machines at Kinsale and Skibbereen.

Medical service – *Kinsale Hospital*, ☎ 0214 772 202. ***Skibbereen Hospital*,** ☎ 028 216 77.

WHERE TO STAY

Prices are higher (and probably rising) at Kinsale, and it makes sense to stay at more unspoiled places like Clonakilty and Skibbereen which are equally good bases for further exploration.

• Kinsale and around

Under €13

Dempsey's Hostel, Eastern Road, ☎ 0214 772 124 – 32 beds in dormitories and family rooms (slightly more expensive). In the centre of Kinsale near Dempsey's Garage and on the main bus route (the bus will stop if requested).

Castlepark Marina Centre, Castlepark, ☎ 0214 774 959 – 50 beds in dormitories and double rooms 🜄 CC On the far side of the bay from Kinsale, beyond the fishing harbour, the hostel is a 45min walk from the town centre but in summer there is a daytime ferry. The dormitories and the double rooms (more expensive but still good value) are in modern stone buildings laid out around a courtyard. Disabled access. Own restaurant in summer and barbecue for use of guests. The centre also organises water-based activities (see "Other things to do") and there is a pub next door.

Between €45-50

Tierney's Guest House, 70 Main Street, ☎ 0214 772 205 – 9rm ⌂ Good central location and a charming and warm-hearted landlady who charges a fair price.

Ashling, Bandon Road, ☎ 0214 774 127 – 5rm ⌂ Five minutes on foot from the centre, this is a modern house in a quiet location (even at the height of the season).

Kilcaw House, Kilcaw, ☎ 0214 774 155 – 4rm ⌂ ♪ TV CC On the way into Kinsale on the Cork road (R600), a rather more expensive establishment than those listed above, but more comfortable and attractively decorated.

Harbour Hill Farm, Knockduff, ☎ 0214 774 479 – 4rm ⌂ ✕ Just over 3km outside Kinsale, clearly signposted off the R600 towards Cork. Beautifully kept and very peaceful, this is a sheep and dairy farm, and breakfast consists largely of home-produced ingredients (evening meal too on request). There is a superb view of the bay and a lovely walk down to the shore and Charles Fort.

Between €55-75

Glebe Country House, Ballinadee, Bandon, ☎ 0214 778 294 – 4rm ⌂ 🛁 ✕ [CC] Leave Kinsale towards Clonakilty and turn left at signs indicating Ballinadee and Bandon (10km). This charming and cosy Georgian vicarage has antique furniture, huge fireplaces, and a garden full of scented plants. The landlady is an expert on organic food; if requested she will prepare delicious evening meals, and her breakfasts are full of tasty surprises. There are three 5-person apartments to rent too in one of the other old buildings on the property.

Between €75-130

Desmond House, 42 Cork Street, ☎ 0214 773 575 – 4rm ⌂ 🛁 [TV] [CC] Directly opposite Desmond Castle, this town house has been renovated with a sure and tasteful hand. Bright, spacious rooms. Luxurious and characterful interior with lots of antiques and souvenirs of travels.

Scilly House Inn, Scilly, ☎ 0214 772 413 – 7rm ⌂ 🛁 [TV] ✕ [CC] In the Scilly part of town opposite The Spaniard inn. Karen Young is a painter and maker of fabulous patchwork quilts. Her works enhance the house and give it a very special atmosphere. There is antique furniture, all kinds of interesting objects dotted here and there, watercolours and cut flowers, and even the garden has a charm all of its own.

● **Timoleague**
More than €55

Lettercollum House, ☎ 023 462 51 – 9rm ⌂ 🛁 ✕ [CC] One kilometre outside the village on the Clonakilty road. Imposing 19C manor house in an extensive park. Huge rooms (some family size) and elegant minimalist decor make this an exceptionally attractive place to stay.

● **Courtmacsherry**
Between €45-50

Travera Lodge, ☎ 023 464 93 – 6rm ⌂ [CC] On the R601 4km from Timoleague. Looking out over Courtmacsherry Bay, this is an attractive, well-kept house which has been recently renovated.

● **Butlerstown**
More than €90

Butlerstown House, ☎ 023 401 37 – 4rm ⌂ [CC] Built in 1805, this Regency residence is set in parkland just outside the village. The elegant interior has a spectacular staircase and antique furniture beautifully restored by the owner himself. Warm but not over-effusive reception, varied and generous breakfast, and rates which reduce according to the length of time spent here. A fine place to stay.

● **Clonakilty**
Under €13

Old Brewery Hostel, Emmet Square, ☎ 023 335 25 – 45 beds. Choice of 4, 6 and 8-bed dormitories, as well as double and family rooms. The jolly owner knows the area like the back of his hand, has bikes for hire, and will arrange guided tours of the town and surroundings.

Wytchwood, Emmet Square, ☎ 023 335 25 – 6rm ⌂ [CC] Just opposite the hostel run by her husband, Clare Hayes welcomes her guests with great good humour. Peace and quiet and comfort are assured in this large yellow-painted house close to the centre of town.

Nordav, Fernhill Road, ☎ 023 336 55 – 5rm ⌂ [TV] About 300m from the centre in a street running into Western Road, the McMahon family offer the best in Irish hospitality. Attractive garden and impeccable interior.

● **Union Hall**
Between €13-45

Maria's Schoolhouse, ☎ 028 330 02 – 10 beds in a dormitory and 8 rooms ✕ Outside the village just beyond the new school. Alternative atmosphere in this old schoolhouse with its colourful décor. The hosts join their guests for meals and musical evenings. Breakfast is extra, but the kitchen is available for guests' use. Laundry facilities and bicycle hire. Baby-sitting. Disabled access.

Seascape B&B, ☎ 028 339 20 – 4rm ⌂ The rooms (two of which have a shared bathroom) have been very tastefully decorated by Julie O'Donovan.

There is a garden terrace with a view down to the harbour. Generous breakfast and warm welcome.

Between €45-50
Ardagh House, ☎ 028 335 71 – 5rm ◌ TV CC The good-humoured Ann O'Connell can tell her guests about everything that's going on in the area and gives good advice on fishing and diving. Her home is extremely well-kept and has a fine situation facing the bay.

• **Skibbereen**
Between €60-75
Eldon Hotel, Bridge Street, ☎ 028 220 00 – 19rm ◌ ℘ TV ✕ CC Michael Collins ate his last meal at this hotel just before his assassination. The panelled bar is a cosy setting for an evening pint. Single travellers should ask for the business rate. Secure parking.

• **Baltimore**
Under €13
Rolf's Hostel, ☎ 028 202 89 – 40 beds. Very pleasant youth hostel in an old building in an elevated location well away from the road on the way into Baltimore. As well as the 10-bed dormitories there are double rooms at a slightly higher rate. Bicycle hire. Camping possible.

Between €45-50
Fastnet House B&B, ☎ 028 205 15 – 6rm ◌ Plain but comfortable accommodation, almost at the bottom of the road leading to the harbour, and handy for the pubs.
◌ **Slipway**, The Cove, ☎ 028 201 34 – 5rm ◌ Looking out over a quiet inlet on the way to Baltimore Beacon, this is a charming place to stay. Wilmie Owen is a weaver and she has decorated her house with taste, mixing wood, stone and her own work. As well as a great traveller, her husband David is an oyster-farmer, and in theory oysters can be served at breakfast.

Between €50-60
Baltimore Bay Guest House, ☎ 028 206 00 – 9rm ◌ TV CC Spacious and charming rooms just above the harbour in this little hotel which is run by a Frenchman from Brittany who also has two restaurants in town, La Jolie Brise and Chez Youen.

• **Sharkin and Cape Clear Islands**
Under €45
Island House, Sherkin, ☎ 028 203 14 – 5rm Plain accommodation in this farmhouse about 1km along the road from the landing stage. Splendid views.
Cuina House, Sherkin, ☎ 028 203 14 – 5rm CC This house is closer to the landing stage (behind the Jolly Roger). Unpretentious but comfortable rooms. Evening meal if ordered in advance.
Cape Clear Island Adventure Centre and Hostel, ☎ 028 391 44 – 40 beds ◌ A few minutes on foot from the landing stage, this stone-built youth hostel has fairly basic dormitories. The activities on offer include fishing, canoeing, and diving.
Cluain Mara, Clear Island, ☎ 028 391 53 – 4rm ◌ CC Right next door to the pub, this B&B is kept by a very pleasant family who can take their guests on boat trips. Evening meal can be provided. Accommodation should be booked well in advance.

EATING OUT

• **Kinsale**
Under €13
Crackpots, 3 Cork Street, ☎ 0214 772 847. Daily 12.30pm-2pm / 7pm-10pm. Right by Desmond Castle, international cuisine made from fresh ingredients and served in generous portions. The menu might feature fish of the day, chicken à la libanaise or mussels Thai style. Meals are served on plates made in the upstairs pottery, which can be inspected.
The Spaniard, Scilly, ☎ 0214 772 436. Popular pub in the Scilly part of town on the far side of the harbour. Inexpensive, straightforward and delicious food served at the bar at lunchtime and up to 7pm in the evening.

Between €13-25
The Blue Haven, 3 Pearse Street, ☎ 0214 772 209. This highly-rated restaurant has a reputation for excellent fish and seafood. Midday prices for bar food are reasonable; choose from seafood soup, quiches or delicious sandwiches. The evening meal – set menu or à la carte – will cost €25 or more, especially with wine. No orders taken after 9.30pm.

Jim Edwards, Market Quay, ☎ 0214 772 541. Another of the area's star establishments, open all day to 10.30pm. Choose fish and seafood or bar meals. Quite expensive, but good value nevertheless.

Casino House, Coolmain Bay, Kilbrittain, ☎ 023 499 44. 15km from Kinsale on the R600 towards Timoleague. Enchanting surroundings, original décor plus inventive and refined cuisine. Ultra-fresh seafood and good wine list. Lunch and dinner every day in July and August, evening only rest of year and closed Wednesday. Only open at weekends in winter. There is also a charming little cottage to rent at the entrance to the park (for 2 or 3 people).

More than €25
The Vintage, Main Street, ☎ 0214 772 502. With one of the best reputations in the south, this establishment only opens for dinner. The food is good, albeit expensive, and served in a romantic setting. Specialities include pavé of smoked salmon and oysters in white wine.

● **Timoleague**
Under €13
Grainne's, ☎ 023 463 48. Lunch served until 2.30pm, dinner until 9pm. In the main street of the village, this pub with its big fireplace has soups, quiches, toasted sandwiches, fish, chicken and generous portions of stew, all at very reasonable prices.

Between €13-25
Lettercollum House, ☎ 023 462 51. Dinner only, reserve before midday. About 1km from the village on the Clonakilty road. Good wine list and a healthy and refined cuisine based on seafood and vegetarian dishes made from homegrown ingredients. Full menu only in theory, but you may order a single dish if you wish.

● **Clonakilty**
Under €13
An Sugan, Strand Road, ☎ 023 334 98. On the way into town, this pub serves generous portions of bar food at midday in a pleasantly cosy atmosphere enhanced by a turf fire when the weather

shows the slightest sign of turning cool. Dinner is more expensive, but the seafood dishes are a real treat.

● **Union Hall**
Between €6-13
Dinty's Bar. All in pink, this bar is known for its grills, highly rated by local people. Usual pub snacks available as well.

Casey's Bar. Recognisable far away by its bright green front. Typical pub food, plain but satisfying, and very inexpensive. Lunch and dinner too.

● **Castletownshend**
Under €13
Mary Ann's, ☎ 028 361 46. No orders taken after 9pm. Halfway down the main street, this pub has low ceilings with massive beams and a warm and welcoming atmosphere. Beer garden at the rear. The usual seafood, grills, salads and soups are excellent.

● **Skibbereen**
Between €6-13
Bernard's, Main Street, ☎ 028 217 72. Right in the middle of town, varied and inexpensive food. Lasagne, salads, seafood and well-filled sandwiches.

● **Baltimore**
Under €13
La Jolie Brise, ☎ 028 206 00. By the harbour, a straightforward and inexpensive place to eat, with mussels and chips, snacks, cakes and pastries. Slightly dearer fish dishes. The outside terrace is particularly attractive.

Between €13-25
Customs House, ☎ 028 202 00. In the street running down to the harbour, one of the very best restaurants in the area. Choice of two menus, each equally tempting. Fresh and carefully prepared ingredients, an elegant and sober setting in a series of small rooms. Dinner only, best booked in advance. Open Thursday-Saturday only except at the height of the season. Closed November-March.

HAVING A DRINK
Every place has its pubs, many with a reputation for good music.

• Kinsale

The Spaniard, Scilly. Great atmosphere in this pub, known all over Ireland and more or less unchanged for decades (it's 300 years old). Traditional music Wednesday evening.

The Shanakee, Market Street. Full of character, divided up into snugs. Blues and traditional music every evening in summer.

• Clonakilty

De Barra, Pearse Street. Wonderfully cluttered interior and a rendezvous for the best interpreters of the traditional Irish repertoire (the gaeltacht isn't far away), as well as blues and rock. There's something on nearly every evening.

• Baltimore

McCarthy's, by the harbour. Declan McCarthy's bar is a tasteful shade of violet. He is a traditional music fan and has made his place into a Mecca for the like-minded. Two or three evening sessions during the week. Good atmosphere guaranteed; all visiting musicians welcome. Bar meals.

OTHER THINGS TO DO

Festivals – The Fiddle Fair is a 10-day festival of traditional music, held annually in Baltimore in May. Incredible crowds and terrific atmosphere, especially at McCarthy's pub. Some might be put off by the crowds, and in any case accommodation should be booked well in advance.

Golf – Most of the places along the south coast have at least one golf course. Among the most attractive are: **Old Head of Kinsale Golf Links**, ☎ 0214 778 444, 18 holes, especially pleasant course by the sea 10km from Kinsale; **Bandon Golf Club**, ☎ 023 411 11, 18 holes. Founded in 1906, probably the best in the area; **Lisselan Golf Club**, Lisselan Estate, Clonakilty, ☎ 023 332 49, impeccably maintained 9-hole course 3km from the town.

Water-based activities – The **Castle Park Marina Centre** in Kinsale, ☎ 0214 774 959 (by the youth hostel) offers a wide range of activities including boat hire, canoeing, and deep-sea fishing. **Atlantic Sea Kayaking** in Union Hall, ☎ 028 330 02 has canoes for hire and offers lessons for all age groups and abilities as well as day excursions or longer trips. The **Baltimore Watersports Centre**, ☎ 028 203 00, is a recognised diving instruction centre, and will help scuba divers explore the numerous wrecks in the area and even meet up with dolphins.

MIZEN HEAD AND BANTRY BAY★★
FROM BALLYDEHOB TO GLENGARIFF

Co Cork
Around 140km – Allow 2 to 3 days
Michelin map 923 C-D / 12-13

Not to be missed
The landscapes of Mizen Head.
Sheep's Head and the Goat's Path.
A walk in Glengariff Woods.
A dip in the sea at Barley Cove.

And remember...
The Goat's Path should not be attempted by camper vans or cars towing caravans.
Fill up before beginning the drive around the peninsulas.

Mizen Head★★
About 60km – Allow a day

Guarded by the villages of Ballydehob, Schull and Durrus, the peninsula consists of a succession of superb landscapes, ideal for walking.

■ **Balleydehob** – This little place with its brightly-painted houses stretches out along a road running down to **Roaring Water Bay** and its many islands. Like much of the rest of the area, it has attracted writers and artists in search of peace and quiet, many of them from Britain and the continent of Europe. The **old railway bridge** with its twelve stonework arches has not seen a train since the Skull and Skibbereen Tramway closed in 1947. It is now a walkway.

On the way into Ballydehob take the R592 for 7km.

■ **Schull★** – This old fishing village nestling in its bay owes its name to the Gaelic scoil Mhuire (school of Mary), a reference to a Christian community. The ruins of the 16C **St Mary's Chapel** can be seen in the graveyard, but old documents refer to a church on this site as early as the 12C.

Schull is known for its regattas (in particular Calves Week at the beginning of August) and the place also attracts astronomers who come to Ireland's only **planetarium** *(April-May: 3pm-5pm Sunday only; June: 3pm-5pm Tuesday, Thursday and Saturday; July-August: 2pm-5pm, 7pm-9pm Monday; closed Sunday. Admission charge. ☎ 028 285 52).*

A legendary light
The Fastnet rock has given its name to a weather zone which features in every shipping forecast. The use of the rock as a base for a lighthouse to guide vessels through the often turbulent waters off the southwestern coast goes back to 1853, when a cast-iron tower was erected. In 1896 it was decided to build something taller and more substantial. More than two thousand blocks of Cornish granite weighing 4 633 tonnes were brought here and lifted into place. The work took four years, based on a construction yard at Crookhaven on the tip of the peninsula. The Fastnet light was automated in 1989. Prior to this, it was looked after day and night by four lighthouse keepers who lived on the rock for a month before spending a fortnight's leave ashore.

The village is the starting-point for walks *(brochure available)*. The best is the **Colla Pier walk★**, which takes in a number of superb viewpoints over the bay and islands (*go along the coast opposite Long Island, then turn right before the Hotel Colla and return to Schull along the inland path and through Gubbeen, known for its cheeses*). The **Fastnet lighthouse** is visible to the south. A close-up view of the famous light can be had in the course of a boat trip from Schull.

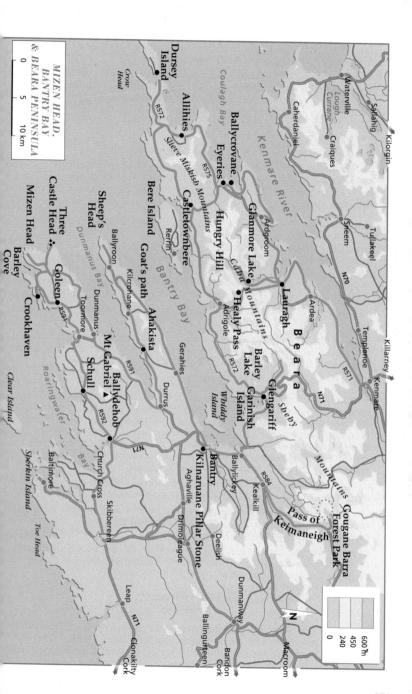

MIZEN HEAD,
BANTRY BAY
& BEARA PENINSULA

0   5   10 km

600 m
450
240
0

N

Dursey
Island

Crow
Head

Allihies

R572

Ballycrovane
Eyeries

R575

Slieve Miskish Mountains

Coulagh Bay

Kenmare River

Glanmore Lake

Ardgroom

Caherdaniel

Lough
Currane

Waterville

Sallahig

Kilorgin

Craigues

Tullakeel

Sneem

N70

Templenoe

Killarney

Kenmare

R571

Ardea

Lauragh

Beara

Sheehy

Cougane Barra
Forest Park

Pass of
Keimaneigh

R584

Kealkil

Deelish

Mountains

N71

Castletownbere

Hungry
Hill

Caha Mountains

Healy Pass

Barley
Lake

Glengariff

Garinish
Island

Whiddy
Island

Bantry

Ballylickey

Bere Island

Goat's path

Rerrin

Kilcrohane

Adrigole

Gerahies

R572

Aghaville

Drimoleague

Dunmanway

Ballingurteen

Macroom

Bandon
Cork

Sheep's
Head

Dunmanus Bay

Ballyroon

Ahakista

Durrus

Kilnaruane Pillar Stone

Church
Cross

Skibbereen

Three
Castle Head

Goleen

Toormore

R591

Dunmanus

R591

Mt Cabriel ▲
Schull

Ballydehob

Roaringwater

Bay

Baltimore

Leap

N71

Clonakilty
Cork

Mizen Head

Barley
Cove

Crookhaven

R591

Clear Island

Sherkin Island

Toe Head

271

Every other year the participants in the Fastnet Yacht Race set off westward from the Isle of Wight, using the lighthouse as their outermost marker. In the 1979 race, fierce storms struck, claiming a total of 15 victims.

To the north, the country inland is dominated by the imposing outline of **Mount Gabriel***, which can be reached from Schull along **Gap Road** (Walkers note: this is a demanding and tiring route and there are dangerous shafts from old copper mines along the way). From the 407m summit there is a fine panorama over the bay. In the Second World War a German aircraft crashed into the hill; nowadays there is an aircraft tracking station at the summit, marked by the pair of white domes.

Leave Schull on the R592 as far as Toormore, then take the R591.

The road passes through a rocky landscape of moorland and little inlets to reach **Goleen** above its tiny fishing harbour. Look for the sign to Crookhaven and follow the coast road between sea and cliffs. On the right are the remains of old **copper mines** which in the late 19C were one of the area's main sources of employment.

■ **Crookhaven*** – It is difficult to imagine that this far-off village at the end of the peninsula was a place of some importance in the 18C and 19C, when it was a busy fishing harbour as well as a safe anchorage and a stopping-point for ships sailing to and from the West Indies. The church on the edge of the village was especially built for sailors.

In 1902 at nearby Brow Head, Marconi set up the first **transatlantic telegraph station**, of which a few remains are left.

On the way out of Crookhaven, take the road to the left which runs along the edge of the caravan park and follow the coast to Mizen Head.

The road runs alongside the **magnificent beach*** at Barleycove, framed by cliffs and very popular with surfers. The scene changes with the tide; when it is out it reveals extensive sandbanks much frequented by seabirds.

Beyond the beach, the road on the left leads in 5.6km to Mizen Head.

■ **Mizen Head*** – From near the car park, a footpath climbs up the hillside revealing fine views. The remote-controlled **lighthouse** on its island can be reached via a footbridge 45m above the waves. Crossing it is quite an experience, especially in stormy weather, but it is expensive (mid-March-late October: 10.30am-5pm; November-mid-March: 11am-4pm weekends only. Admission charge). On the far side, the not particularly interesting little **museum** traces the history of the lighthouse and signal station and the building of the Fastnet lighthouse.

Go back towards Barleycove and turn left after the Barleycove Hotel. At the T-junction turn right. The road winds among hills then comes to an end by the sea.

The gate on the right (ask for permission at the farm above the road) gives access to a **spectacular footpath**** to **Three Castle Head*** where there are the ruins of a 12C **castle** which belonged to the O'Mahony clan.

Return the way you came. Go past the Barleycove Hotel and turn left at Kilmoe Church. Drive along Dunmanus Bay on the north shore of the peninsula, then take the R591 to Durrus. Follow signs to Sheep's Head.

Sheep's Head**
Tour of 48km

From Durrus the road runs by the shore through the charming little port of **Ahakista** and the village of Kilcrohane. One bay succeeds another, then the landscape becomes more rugged and wind-blasted as the road nears Sheep's Head. Huge blocks of rock mark the approach to the headland which is at its most spectacular in stormy weather (footpaths can be very exposed and dangerously slippery).

Back in Kilcrohane take care not to miss the junction and the left turn before you get to the church *(the road partly turns back on itself)*. This is the start of the **Goat's Path★** to Bantry. It is a superb route, though poorly surfaced in places. On the far shore of Bantry Bay is the Beara Peninsula, dominated by the heights of the Caha Mountains.

The road meets the N71 about 2km short of Bantry.

Around Bantry Bay★
Tour of 64km

Before going on into Bantry it is worth stopping at the **Kilnaruane Pillar Stone★★** *(signposted on the way into the town from the Cork direction, near the West Lodge Hotel. After 800m, park the car by the sign and walk across the field to the right)*. On its hilltop, the 7C stone no doubt formed part of a high cross. The carving on one face shows a boat with oarsmen and rams. On the other side a praying figure can be made out *(a replica is on show at the Skellig Heritage Centre on Valentia Island in Kerry, see page 288)*.

■ **Bantry★** – Bantry was once the home of an important fishing fleet. In 1968 a large oil refinery was built on Whiddy Island in the bay, but the explosion of the tanker *Betelgeuse* in 1979 caused 50 deaths and the complex was closed.

On the way into Bantry from Cork stands the White family's country mansion, **Bantry House★** *(9am-5pm. Admission charge. Combined ticket for house and gardens, or gardens only)*. The main part of the house, which the Whites acquired in 1750, dates from 1720, but the façade overlooking the bay was added in the mid-19C by the second Earl of Bantry. He was also responsible for the fine furniture and works of art on display, as well as the Italian-style **terraced gardens**: a great stairway with 106 steps rises up behind the house to give superb views over the bay.

Inside the house are pictures, documents and personal memorabilia tracing the history of the White family. The spectacular dining room with its royal blue walls has portraits of King George III and Queen Charlotte dating from the time of Richard

The Dining Room at Bantry House

C Legrand/MICHELIN

The French Armada

Bantry Bay was the scene of a dramatic episode in British and Irish history, when in 1796 a formidable French fleet sailed in to aid the United Irishmen in their rebellion. The force was commanded by the brilliant young General Hoche, accompanied by Wolfe Tone who was also wearing French uniform. As with the Spanish Armada in 1588, it was the weather that saw off England's enemies rather than any great effort on her part. First the French ran into thick fog, then a storm blew up; only 16 of the 43 ships made it into the bay. The storm continued to rage, and eventually even these ships had to cut anchor, return to the open sea and abandon all thoughts of invasion. Had the ships landed the thousands of soldiers aboard, the course of history could have been very different. Against them was ranged a feeble force: the men of the Bantry militia and a few members of the yeomanry led by local landowner Richard White, whom George III subsequently created Lord Bantry for his pains.

White's ennoblement. The furniture, from all over the world, includes a number of rare items, among them a Russian reliquary with 15C and 16C icons, Aubusson tapestries once owned by Marie-Antoinette and staircase panels in Spanish leather.

The stables house the **1796 French Armada Exhibition Centre**, which explains the debacle by means of models, documents and a number of finds.

In Ballylickey, 5km beyond Bantry in the Glengariff direction, turn right on to the R584 towards Gougane Barra (22.5km further on).

The road climbs inland through a wild landscape, crossing the **Pass of Keimaneigh*** between vertical walls of rock.

■ **Gougane Barra Forest Park**** — The park includes a lake surrounded by mountains which is the source of the River Lee. An island in the lake was the site of the **hermitage** of St Fin Barre, the saintly founder of the city of Cork. The present chapel is the site of **pilgrimages** which take place on the Sunday following 12 September (St Fin Barre's saint's day). The forest park and mountain slopes are threaded with **attractive walks*** and nature trails.

■ **Glengariff** — The beauty of its surroundings, the mildness of its climate and the lushness of its vegetation made Glengariff a destination for 19C tourists, among them Queen Victoria and George Bernard Shaw, who wrote part of his St Joan here and on Garinish Island. Nowadays the town is highly commercialised and not really of great interest in itself.

Out in the bay, **Garinish Island**** (*Ilnacullin* in Gaelic) is the site of an extraordinary Italian-style garden designed by the early 20C landscape architect Harold Peto, lavishly planted with exotic shrubs and dotted with little Classical buildings (*March-October: 10am-5.30pm. Admission charge. Heritage Site. NB the price of the boat trip does not include entry to the gardens*).

Equally ravishing but costing nothing, **Glengariff Woods**** have lovely walks along signposted footpaths (*car parks 1.5km along the road towards Kenmare or 2km along the road towards Castletownbere*).

A free brochure sets out a dozen or so attractive routes, among them one leading to **Barley Lake***. The path passes through a hilly landscape with rivers rich in fish, lined with rhododendrons and huge moss-covered rocks.

COMING AND GOING

By car – To drive around the peninsula, take the N71 beyond Skibbereen, the R592 to Toormore, and the R591. Minor roads lead around Sheep's Head, then the N71 continues towards Bantry and Glengariff. Parking in Main Street in Schull is strictly regulated in summer and fines are common.

By bus – 3 buses daily between Schull and Cork and one bus daily to Killarney. The stop is in Main Street opposite Griffith's pub. During school terms there is a service between Schull and Bantry. Bantry is linked to Cork (3 buses daily), to Killarney (2 buses daily between June and September), and to Glengariff and Skibbereen. The stop is in Wolfe Tone Square, opposite Lynch's pub. Further details from the nearby tourist office.

By boat – Between June and September boats ply between Schull and Cape Clear Island, Sherkin Island and Baltimore. Details are posted on the quayside, or contact Kieran Molloy, ☎ 028 281 38 or Ciarán O'Driscoll, ☎ 028 391 53. Bicycles carried free of charge.

ADDRESS BOOK

Tourist information – *Tourist Office*, Wolfe Tone Square, Bantry, ☎ 027 502 29.

Banks / Currency exchange – Banks are rare in this thinly populated area and not all B&Bs accept credit cards. The only two cash machines are the one in the upper part of the main street in Schull, and the other in Wolfe Tone Square in Bantry.

Medical service – There are chemist's shops and doctors in Schull and Bantry. *Bantry Hospital*, ☎ 027 501 33.

WHERE TO STAY

Other than in Schull and Bantry, accommodation is scattered around this wild and spectacular landscape.

• **Schull**

Under €13

Backpackers' Lodge Hostel, Colla Road, ☎ 028 286 81 – 35 beds in dormitories or private rooms. CC 5mins on foot from the top of Main Street towards Colla Point. This big wooden building beneath the trees has a friendly atmosphere and a pleasant garden where tents can be pitched. Good level of facilities including kitchen and laundrette. Bicycle hire.

Between €45-50

White House, ☎ 028 283 06 – 3rm TV In the street running off Main Street by the bank. New, spotless house with quiet and comfortable rooms with tea-making facilities. Private parking.

Old Bank House, Colla Road, ☎ 028 283 06 – 4rm TV CC Mrs Donovan has converted the old bank premises into an attractive B&B. The garden is a haven of greenery. Open April-September.

Stanley House, Colla Road, ☎ 028 284 25 – 4rm CC About 1km from the village, this house overlooks the bay; the view is particularly good from the lounge and the veranda. Well-kept establishment, generous breakfast. Open March-October. The owners also have comfortable 2-6 person cottages to let.

Harbour Command, South Schull, ☎ 028 282 35 – 2rm 3km from the village along the Colla road, clearly signposted down a track to the right. This bungalow commands a splendid panorama over the whole of the bay. The owner is a keen amateur mason, and the garden is an extraordinary mixture of walls and ramparts, terraces and turrets, set off with magnificent shrubs. Peace and quiet are guaranteed. Less expensive than elsewhere.

Between €50-65

Fortview House, Gurtyowen, Toormore, ☎ 028 353 24 – 5rm Nine kilometres from Schull and 2km from Toormore on the R591 towards Durrus and Bantry. The good-humoured Violet Connell has turned her home into one of the most attractive places to stay in the area. There's antique furniture, charming rooms, knick-knacks everywhere, stencilled décor, plush sofas... and if that wasn't enough, the breakfast is superlative, with fish, home-made bread and cakes, fresh fruit, fresh vegetable juice.

The only drawback – no credit cards, but potential guests should not allow this to put them off. There is also a cottage to rent.

🐾 **Rock Cottage**, Barnatonicane, Toormore, ☎ 028 355 38 – 3rm 🍴✕ CC On the R591 very close to the establishment described above, this is another really delightful place to stay, a small Georgian hunting lodge and farm on the edge of sheep-grazed pastures. Restful lodgings. Elegant décor, dinner if ordered in advance, and a 3-person designer-decorated cottage to let in the farmyard.

More than €75

Grove House, Colla Road, ☎ 028 280 67 – 5rm 🍴 TV ✕ CC On the way out of Schull, this fine Georgian residence welcomes its guests into rooms which have housed the likes of Jack B Yeats, George Bernard Shaw and Edith Somerville. Recently restored. Dinner if ordered in advance. A bit on the expensive side nevertheless.

• **Goleen**

More than €45

Heron's Cove, ☎ 028 352 25 – 5rm 🍴 🐾 TV ✕ CC Right on the edge of a rocky inlet, this house has the air of a small hotel about it. Most of the rooms have sea views, and the outside terrace overlooks the water. Warm-hearted Sue Hill does everything she can for her guests. Generous helpings at mealtimes. Open March-November.

🐾 **The Ewe**, ☎ 028 354 92 🍴 CC Clearly signposted high up on the way into the village. This arts and crafts centre offers accommodation by the week including courses in ceramics, pottery and sculpture. There are three small 2-4 person tastefully decorated apartments, and the terraced Japanese garden facing the sea is a fine place to retreat to. A place apart of great serenity.

• **Crookhaven**

More than €45

Galleycove House, ☎ 028 351 37 – 5rm 🍴 TV CC 1km short of this little fishing port. In an isolated position facing the ocean, this bungalow is ideal for people seeking solitude by the sea. The beach is nearby, pubs and other facilities in the village.

• **Sheep's Head**

Between €40-50

Grove House, Ahakista Bar, ☎ 027 670 60 – 5rm 🍴✕ A short distance beyond Ahakista Bar on the same side of the road, this white farmhouse is close to the sea, with a pebble beach at the bottom of its lovely garden. Rooms are well-kept and comfortable, the less expensive ones sharing a bathroom. Dinner can be ordered, generous breakfast served on a pretty veranda.

Hillcrest House, ☎ 027 670 45 – 4rm 🍴 ✕ Clearly signposted 1km out of Ahakista on the way to the headland, this big stone farmhouse overlooking the bay is 5mins on foot from the beach. Meals can be provided, prepared with produce from the farm. Baby-sitting can be arranged. Reduced rates for longer stays. Deposit required when booking. Open April-October.

Reenmore Farmhouse, Ahakista, ☎ 027 670 51 – 6rm 🍴 ✕ Two kilometres west of Ahakista towards Kilcrohane, right by the sea. This isolated place, ideal for walking, is kept by a charming and welcoming lady. Meals by arrangement, based on farm produce. Two of the rooms have sea views. Open mid-March to mid-November.

Sea Mount, Glenlough West, Goat's Path, ☎ 027 612 26 – 6rm 🍴 ✕ Just beyond Sheep's Head on Bantry Bay, 12km from Bantry. Typical traditional farmhouse, with a pretty garden on the bay. A long walk in the hills around will work up a good appetite for the landlady's delicious home-made cakes. Plain, comfortable rooms. Meals by arrangement. Open April-October.

Fuchsia Cottage, Gerahies, Goat's Path, ☎ 027 614 11 – 2rm 🍴 Not far from the establishment described above, this pretty house in its landscaped garden is 11km from Bantry in the Sheep's Head direction. Friendly reception. Open all year.

• **Bantry**

Between €40-50

🐾 **The Mill**, Newtown, ☎ 027 502 78 – 6rm 🍴 TV CC On the way out of Bantry on the Glengariff road. Tosca Kramer is a charming Dutch lady who runs her establishment with great style. Good breakfasts and a veranda to relax on. Her partner has bikes for hire and spends his spare time painting. Laundry facilities can be arranged. Open April-November.

Atlantic Shore, Newtown, ☎ 027 513 10 – 6rm ⚑ TV CC Clearly signposted on a minor road going off to the right on the way out of Bantry towards Glengariff. Big modern bungalow, well-kept, with a superb view over the bay. One room with disabled facilities. Open April-September.

Ard Na Greine, Newtown, ☎ 027 511 69 – 4rm ⚑ CC Clearly indicated on the way out of Bantry on the same road as the establishment above. Quiet and comfortable house without a lot of character but with a lovely garden with country views. Courteous reception. Open April-October.

More than €170

Bantry House, ☎ 027 500 47 – 9rm ⚑ ✐ ✗ CC Live like a lord in one of the splendid rooms of this historic house. The owner is a music lover and organises frequent concerts in the library. Meals by arrangement. Billiard room and access to those parts of the house open to the public. Open March-October.

• **Ballylickey**

Around €13

🏠 **Hazel Wood Lodge**, ☎ 027 524 44 – 55 beds in dormitories and private rooms. ⚑ CC A big yellow-painted building off the N71 5km from Bantry. This is an excellent place to stay for backpackers who pay less than €13 for a dormitory bed as well as for couples and families who are accommodated in very comfortable rooms for not much more. Some of the rooms are more like small suites. There is a well-equipped kitchen on each floor. Laundry facilities, games rooms, baby-sitting and bike garage.

Margaret Sullivan, Seacrest, ☎ 027 506 40 – ⚑ TV CC Margaret restores old cottages with great care and lets them for between €150-450 per week according to the season (up to 6 people). Very comfortable and very central for exploring this area.

• **Glengariff**

Between €45-50

🏠 **Ardnagashel Lodge**, ☎ 027 516 87 – 3rm ⚑ TV CC On the N71 between Ballylickey and Glengariff 9km from Bantry. A peaceful and relaxing atmosphere in this lovely house, run by a most amiable couple who can talk entertainingly on any subject. Reduced rate for light breakfast.

🏠 **Cois Coille**, ☎ 027 632 02 – 6rm ⚑ On a minor road off a bend in the N71 on the way out of Glengariff in the Bantry direction, close to the Eccles Hotel. Built on a slope with a lovely terraced garden, between sea and mountain. Very quiet, attractive rooms, generous and varied breakfast. Open April-October.

WHERE TO EAT

With a few exceptions, most of the restaurants in this very popular area are expensive for what they offer. A better bet are the pubs and cafés, where the food is not only cheaper but often very good.

• **Schull**

Between €6-13

Adele's Café, Main Street, ☎ 028 284 59. This bakery offers a choice of flans and cooked meals to take away. The upstairs café has straightforward but well-prepared dishes including quiches, sandwiches, local cheeses, pasta, fish and cakes. Wine by the glass. Reckon on €6 for lunch and double that for dinner.

The Courtyard, Main Street, ☎ 028 283 90. This is a grocery with all the usual stock plus some local products, including Gubbeen cheeses. The café at the back of the shop has inexpensive light snacks and cakes, ideal for elevenses.

The Bunratty Inn, Main Street, ☎ 028 283 41. Traditional pub grub served all day, local specialities, soups and sandwiches, in a cheerful atmosphere with occasional live music.

An Tigín, Main Street, ☎ 028 288 30. Great atmosphere in this friendly pub with live music at the weekend.

• **Goleen**

Between €13-20

Heron's Cove Restaurant, ☎ 028 352 25. Ultra-fresh seafood is the speciality here, some of it coming from the proprietors' own lobster pots, plus excellent grills. As soon as it turns at all cold, Sue Hill lights the fire in the big fireplace. Friendly atmosphere in a seaside setting.

• **Durrus**

Under €13

Ivo's, ☎ 027 611 09. In the middle of the village, this friendly pub is a favourite with the cosmopolitan crowd. Inexpensive dishes of the day and live music at the weekend.

More than €30

Blair's Cove, ☎ 027 611 27. Two kilometres from Durrus on the R591 Toormore road. This restaurant in its elegant Georgian building is in French ownership. Starters and desserts from the buffet, excellent fish dishes and grills prepared on an open fire. Romantic atmosphere, bare stone walls, chandeliers etc. Advance booking essential. Open March-October, except Sunday and Monday out of season, or Sunday in summer. Suites and apartments available, but expensive.

• **Ahakista**

More than €50

🍴 **Shiro**, ☎ 027 670 30. This establishment comes as a complete surprise to those not in the know; beyond the doorway of the grand Georgian house is a subtle and refined interior, the creation of Kei Pilz, the Japanese lady of the house. The food offered reflects the best in her country's cuisine, with exquisite choice of ingredients and meticulous preparation and presentation. Dinner only. Closed Christmas to late February. Reservation essential; this is recognised as one of the finest places to eat in Ireland.

• **Bantry**

Between €6-13

The Snug, The Quay, ☎ 027 500 57. This pub serves a good choice of generous platefuls all day (no evening meal after 8pm). Seating is on benches or around the bar in a convivial atmosphere.

HAVING A DRINK

• **Ahakista**

Ahakista Bar, on the left of the road on the way to Sheep's Head. With its wobbly metal roof this bar is unmissable. Cheerful atmosphere, frequent live music.

• **Bantry**

The Anchor, New Street and William Street. In the road leading off Wolfe Tone Square to the right of the tourist office. The décor is a reminder that the landlord is an old sea dog, retired in principle but still taking off on the occasional voyage, trusting his faithful clientele to hold the fort. They do.

OTHER THINGS TO DO

Festivals – Bantry has a number of festivals. In mid-May, **Murphy's International Mussel Festival** is very popular, a good excuse for freely-flowing liquor and lots of live music in pub and street. Anyone wanting to stay here during this period will need to book their accommodation well in advance.

The **West Cork Chamber Music Festival** takes place at the end of June / early July in Bantry House, ☎ 027 611 05. Chamber concerts of very high quality.

The **Bantry Bay Regatta** lasts for a fortnight in August, with all kinds of associated events taking place over the whole area between Bantry Bay and Schull. Details available locally.

Golf – Bantry Park Golf Club, Donemark, ☎ 027 505 79 is an 18-hole course in a superb setting overlooking Bantry Bay. **Glengariff Golf Course**, ☎ 027 631 16 is a 9-hole course, ideal for novices.

Fishing – Fishing is very popular along this coast. Bars are often the best source of local information.

Deep-sea fishing trips are run by **Schull Deep Angling Centre**, ☎ 028 376 60. Equipment supplied. Another firm: **Schull Watersports Centre**, ☎ 028 285 54.

There is fishing for trout and salmon in the Glengariff. The necessary permit can be obtained from the **Glengariff Anglers Association**, ☎ 027 630 21. Full details locally.

(vertical left margin) **The Southwest**

Watersports – *Schull Watersports Centre*, The Pier, ☎ 028 28554. Diving, boat and dinghy hire. Instruction available.

Crafts and clothes – *Naturally*, Main Street, Schull, ☎ 028 281 65. Browsing is a pleasure in this well-above-average shop with its classical Irish woollens, luxurious items in silk and linen, refined ceramics and original engravings.

Timberland Factory Shop, William Street, Bantry. In a side street not far from the tourist office. Timberland items at reduced prices from the firm's Irish factory. A few bargains, especially walking shoes / boots, but mostly quite expensive.

Garinish Island from the air

E Quémére/DIAF

Mizen Head and Bantry Bay

BEARA PENINSULA★★

Co Cork and Co Kerry
Tour of about 160km
Michelin map 923 B-C / 12-13 and map page 271

Not to be missed
The road along the north shore of the peninsula.
Glanmore Lake and Healy Pass.

And remember...
The Beara Peninsula has some of Ireland's finest walking, but always remember that
the weather is very changeable and you need to be properly equipped.

Less spoiled by tourism than the peninsulas in neighbouring Kerry, this rocky finger
of land has some of the southwest's wildest and most spectacular scenery. Studded
with lakes, the **Caha Mountains** are the backbone of the peninsula and, though
never any higher than 700m, have some of the characteristics of Alpine landscapes.
The much indented coastline is backed by pastoral countryside.

South shore★

*Leave Glengariff on the R572 (signposted Beara Ring) and continue for around 19km.
The conical outline of Sugar Loaf Mountain (574m) appears on the right. Continue
through Adrigole (leaving Healy Pass for later – it's better driven north-south), and in
around 7km look out for the sign to Rossmackowne and turn right to Hungry Hill. Leave
the car by the gate, and walk up the hill to the right of the lake.*

■ **Hungry Hill**★ – *Minimum of 5hr walking. Good walking shoes or boots essential.
Take water and check weather conditions. The path can be slippery in fog.*
The 684m-high hill owes its fame to the Daphne du Maurier saga of the same name.
It's a good three hours to the summit, where there is a stone circle, a lovely **water-
fall** *(north side)* and a magnificent view.

Continue on the R572 for 7.5km to Castletownbere.

The road runs alongside **Bere Haven**. This sheltered anchorage in the lee of Bere
Island was a Royal Navy base until 1938, when it was returned to the Republic by
Britain despite fierce opposition from Winston Churchill. **Bere Island** itself is inhabited by a few families and has a sailing school. It is linked to the mainland by
ferries *(every 2hr from 9.30am. Return fare €6)* which leave from the quayside on the
way into Castletownbere.

O'Sullivan v Puxley
The immensely rich Puxley family owed
their unpopularity less to their Welsh origin than to the help they gave to the authorities in their efforts to stamp out the
smuggling which was the principal economic activity of the area. This earned
them the undying enmity of the O'Sullivans, who controlled the contraband
trade in league with the French and Spanish. Years of conflict came to a climax
when the most prominent Puxley met his
end on the way to church, assassinated by
one of the O'Sullivans, never short of an
excuse to raise the standard of rebellion.

■ **Castletownbere** – This is an important fishing port, with a working
harbour full of massive trawlers, a re-
freshing change from similar places
which have sold their soul to tourism.
Russian factory ships moor in Bere
Haven and Slavonic sounds can sometimes be heard in the streets. In the hills
around the town there are a number of
stone circles like the clearly signposted
example at **Derrintaggart**.

Just under 3km along the R572 to the
west of Castletownbere is the unmistakable tower marking the entrance to
Dunboy Castle★ *(Admission charge)*.

The park contains two sets of ruins. **Puxley's Castle** was the huge 19C manor house of the Welsh family who owned the local copper mines and whose fortunes inspired Daphne du Maurier's *Hungry Hill*. The house was burnt down by the IRA in 1921 during the War of Independence. A little further on, **Dunboy Castle** was the stronghold of the O'Sullivan clan, a star-shaped fortress of which very little remains. It was the last place to hold out against the English in 1602, when a small Spanish / Irish force put up a stout resistance against their far more numerous besiegers, and were massacred for their pains.

Carry on along the R572 coast road for 13km. At the junction, turn left and continue to Dursey Island. Alternatively, if not visiting the island (additional 15km), carry straight on for 4km along the R575 to Allihies.

■ Dursey Island★

To avoid being stranded on the island, check the cable-car return times very carefully and don't rely on the official timetable

Dursey Island is linked to the mainland by Ireland's only **cable railway**, which was built in 1970 and designed to carry six people or one man and a cow across the 220m straits *(every 15min between 9am-11am, 2.30pm-5pm, then at 7pm and 8pm; Sunday between 9am-10.15am, at 12pm, 1pm, 7pm and 8pm. €3 return)*.

Close to the island station of the cable-car is a deep cleft in the cliff, the scene of a particularly unedifying episode in Anglo-Irish relations. In 1602, moving on from their assault on Dunboy Castle, the English attacked Dursey Island and killed its defenders, together with some of the civilian population, by hurling them into the sea here. Those survivors who had sought sanctuary in the church were burnt alive. A short distance away on the left, surrounded by tombstones, are the ruins of a **monastery** founded in the 16C, and later plundered by pirates. Nearby, on the islet of Oilean Beg are more remains, in this case those of a **castle**, with well-preserved steps leading to the drawbridge. Further on are more ruins still. **St Michael's Chapel** is linked to the hermitage of the same name on Skellig Island and was the scene of the terrible events of 1602.

Off Dursey Island to the west, three great chunks of rock are called the **Bull**, **Cow**, and **Calf**. Legend has it that the Bull marks the entrance to the Great Beyond...

North shore★★

Leaving behind the peace and quiet and high cliffs of Dursey Island, return to the **coast road★★** and head towards Allihies. The landscape is one of rust-coloured moorland and lush pastureland enclosed by stone walls and great stone boulders.

■ **Allihies★** – With its pubs and garishly coloured shop-fronts, this picture-postcard village has become something of a Mecca for New-Agers on the quest for Celtic culture. On the way into the village, the beach at **Ballydonegan** has been formed from waste sand from the old mines scattered over the countryside. The village's past prosperity came from **copper**. At their height, the mines owned by the Puxleys employed some 1 200 people, 400 of them actual miners, mostly from Wales. Local people resented this invasion, and showed their disapproval by refusing to sell the newcomers food and other supplies. Everything had to be brought in from Wales. The mines closed in the 1930s and despite sporadic attempts to revive them, remain closed. Fine **walks** on the slopes of the orange-tinted hills lead to the old workings, with their tall chimneys and disused tunnels *(on the way out of the village to the north, go as far as the junction of several roads and turn right. The old mine shafts can be dangerous and care is necessary)*.

The R575 carries on through this mining landscape for about 15.5km to **Eyeries★**, another brightly painted village which served as a backdrop for some of the scenes in the film *The Mauve Taxi*.

Continue along the coast road beyond Eyeries and turn off to the pretty little port of **Ballycrovane***, famous for the tallest pillar stone in Ireland (5.18m) with its Oghom inscription *(see Art and Architecture page 29)*.

Carry on to Ardgroom along the **coast road****. This long stretch has fine views over the great inlet known as the **Kenmare River** and of the highly indented coastline with its cliffs and rocks of black stone. The strings of little buoys are an indication of the shellfish farming which is a speciality of the area.

At Ardgroom, turn left on the R571 towards Lauragh.

■ **Around Lauragh** – On the way into Lauragh are **Derreen Gardens*** *(April-September: 11am-6pm. Admission charge)*, laid out in 1870 by the 5th Lord Lansdowne and famous for their tree ferns, rhododendrons and azaleas.

Not far from the gardens there is a sign to **Glanmore Lake***. The dark surface of the lake reflects the surrounding steep slopes. The seemingly mountainous landscape offers good walking.

Return to Lauragh and take the R574 to the right in order to climb up to **Healy Pass****. The road ascends among open country littered with great boulders, and gives a spectacular **panorama**** of the lake far below, particularly impressive at sunset. At the pass itself there are superb views of both shores of the Beara Peninsula.

Making the most of the Beara Peninsula

COMING AND GOING

By bus – In summer there are two services daily between Castletownbere and Kenmare, Killarney and Glengariff, and one bus on Thursday to Cork.

On foot – The 196km Beara Way is a long-distance trail starting at Glengariff or Kenmare.

ADDRESS BOOK

Banks / Currency exchange – There is a bank and cash machine at Castletownbere and another at Kenmare. Bureaux de change at the Eccles Hotel, in the souvenir shops and supermarket at Glengariff and the general store at Allihies.

Medical service – Chemists at Bantry, Castletownbere and Kenmare.

WHERE TO STAY

• **South shore**
Under €13
⌂ **Garanes Hostel**, ☎ 027 731 47 – 22 beds CC On the Allihies road 9km west of Castletownbere, indicated by a sign on the left. Fantastic views and friendly common room. The girls'

dormitory is nicer than the men's. The nearby Buddhist retreat helps create a contemplative atmosphere. Apartments to rent by the week.

Between €30-50

Island's End, Rossmackowen, ☎ 027 600 40 – 5rm ✕ On the R572 2km beyond Adrigole. Kept by a friendly German lady, this inexpensive B&B is open all year. The rooms share a bathroom and shower. Evening meal if ordered in advance (generous portions).

Sea Point, Castletownbere, ☎ 027 702 92 – 3rm ⁜ ✕ cc Two kilometres short of Castletownbere. Ann Black knows the area like the back of her hand and can give all sorts of useful tips about how to spend one's time. Pretty view from the garden. Meals provided to order, including vegetarian food. Laundry facilities.

Rodeen Country House, Castletownbere, ☎ 027 701 58 – 6rm ⁜ ✕ cc Clearly signposted on the right 2km short of the village. Sub-tropical garden, superb view, small but cosy rooms and a warm welcome from cordon bleu cook Ellen Gowan, make this a good choice of place to stay. Delicious breakfast and main meals to order based on organic produce or from her own garden.

More than €50

The Old Presbytery, Castletownbere, ☎ 027 704 20 – 5rm ⁜ ℘ ✕ cc With its vast lawn, facing the fishing harbour, this 18C glebe house is clearly signposted on the way into Castletownbere when coming from Glengariff. Very comfortable and characterful rooms, more expensive if with a view. Breakfast served in the pleasant conservatory.

- **Opposite Dursey Island**

Between €30-50

Windy Point House, Dursey Sound, ☎ 027 730 17 – 4rm ⁜ ✕ cc Just before the cable-car for Dursey Island, this house has superb views. Open April-October, restaurant in summer.

- **North shore**

Under €13

Allihies Village Hostel, Allihies, ☎ 027 731 07 – 20 beds and 4 rooms. Traditional cottage painted blue and white, pleasant and clean, handy for the pubs. Laundry facilities.

Between €30-50

Sea View House, Allihies, ☎ 027 732 11 – 10rm ⁜ ℘ ✕ cc This small hotel in the middle of the village is painted yellow and violet. Well-kept and comfortable, with tea-making facilities in the bedrooms.

Crowley's Glor na Mara, Kilcatherine, Eyeries, ☎ 027 740 12 – 3rm ⁜ ✕ cc On Coast Road 4.5km north of Eyeries, this establishment has a magnificent location on the rocky coast. Well-kept and inexpensive rooms. Fresh seafood, including lobster, to order.

Sea Villa, Ardgroom, ☎ 027 743 69 – 3rm ⁜ ✕ cc On Coast Road between Eyeries and Ardgroom, this house offers peace and quiet and comfort among the hills plus a wonderful view.

Mountain View, Healy Pass Road, Lauragh, ☎ 064 831 43 – 3rm ⁜ ✕ On the Kenmare side of the turn leading to the Healy Pass, this is an isolated farmhouse with a pleasant view over its surroundings. Meals to order, specialising in seafood.

Josie's Lakeside House & Restaurant, Glanmore Lake, ☎ 064 831 55 – 3rm ⁜ ✕ cc Comfortable rooms and a charming restaurant in a serene location on the banks of the lake. Lunch available for €6.50, and evening meal from €13.

WHERE TO EAT

Under €13

The Village Inn, Ardgroom, ☎ 027 740 67. All the usual kinds of pub food to suit every pocket, in the centre of the village. More sophisticated dishes in the evening. Convivial atmosphere.

Between €13-30

Lawrence Cove House, Bere Island, ☎ 027 750 63. Authentic cuisine of high quality making the most of freshly caught fish and shellfish. Own boat fetches guests from the pontoon 4km east of Castletownbere (€3.80). Book food and ferry at the same time.

IVERAGH PENINSULA★★
(RING OF KERRY)

Co Kerry
172km drive around the Ring of Kerry (with no side trips) – Allow 2 days
Michelin map 923 A-B-C-D / 11-12 and map page 285

Not to be missed
Derrymane and Lamb's Head.
A dip in the sea at Derrymane.
The Skelligs and the Skellig Heritage Centre.

And remember...
Coach parties are taken in an anti-clockwise direction around the Ring of Kerry,
so it's better to drive round in the opposite direction,
ie Kenmare-Waterville-Cahersiveen.
Sneem, Waterville and Cahersiveen are often over-run by tour groups.
The best trout and salmon fishing is in Lough Currane and Lough Caragh.

Concentrated in this peninsula are Ireland's finest landscapes, a superb synthesis of rocky bays, superb sandy beaches, mountains, lakes and woodland. Most visitors experience the area by driving round the **Ring of Kerry★★**, the name given to the coast road and sometimes to the peninsula itself. Not surprisingly, this is the most popular part of Ireland for visitors from abroad, many of them from America, and it can get very crowded. But there are still some parts of it which have been spared the full force of the tourist assault.

■ Kenmare★
34km south of Killarney – Allow 1hr.

Backed by a semicircle of mountains, this lively market town is located at the point where three rivers, the Roughty, Finihy and Sheen run into the long inlet of the sea known as the Kenmare River. The road into Kenmare from the Beara Peninsula *(see page 280)* runs through shoreline woodlands, a lovely leafy setting just outside the town for the **Sheen Falls★**.

The English imprint
Kenmare was a planned town, laid out in the form of a cross by its founder, a certain **William Petty**, who had served as physician-general in Cromwell's army. Like many of his fellow-soldiers, he was rewarded for his services with grants of land. By astute purchase, Petty maximised his holding, and soon owned a quarter of Co Kerry. He strove to make Kenmare a model centre of commerce and industry, encouraging Protestant settlers from Wales, Cornwall and the rest of England to come here, thereby reinforcing the area's British character. In the 19C the town was a thriving place, proud of its butter market, its banks, and its Turkish bath. But by now the native Irish birth rate meant that Catholics were in the majority, and the town eventually became a bastion of *Sinn Féin* and the Gaelic League.

Petty's projects
William (later Sir William) Petty (1623-87) was something of a polymath, a cosmopolitan scholar and medical man who studied in France, Holland and in Oxford, and was a devotee of the teachings of Francis Bacon. His move to Ireland led him to abandon medicine in favour of cartography and applied geography. He carried out a survey of County Down, and as well as developing Kenmare and its surroundings, he mapped much of Ireland and in 1685 published the country's first atlas, the *"Hiberniae delineatio"*. Later came *"The Political Anatomy of Ireland"*, a scientific description of the country's people and resources. Despite having been one of Cromwell's men, he continued to be favoured at the Restoration, and was knighted by Charles II.

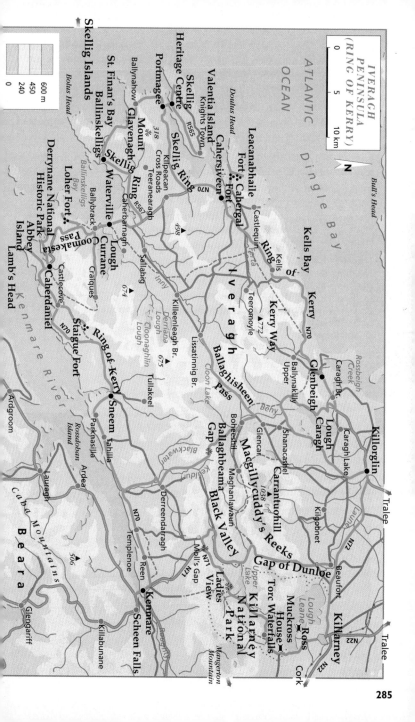

The town

Kenmare is laid out around a little triangle-shaped park and its two main streets are lined with shops, restaurants and trendy boutiques. Close to the park, at the rear of the tourist office, the **Kenmare Heritage Centre** *(Easter-September: 10am-5.30pm; closed Sunday; July-August: daily 10am-7pm. Admission charge)* has displays on local megaliths, the history of the town since its foundation, and the sufferings of the population during the Famine. The fascinating section on Kenmare lace shows how local girls were taught lace-making techniques by nuns while their brothers learnt more masculine trades like carpentry.

On the upper floor, the **Lace and Design Centre** *(same opening hours)* has examples of wonderfully delicate Kenmare lace, made with techniques first developed in Italy and incorporating lovely Celtic Revival motifs.

In Market Street in the southwestern part of town is the **Druids' Circle**, a Bronze Age stone circle of 15 monoliths surrounding a central stone.

Anyone with a little time to spare should take a boat trip down the **Kenmare River★**, where there is a large colony of seals *(Seafari River Cruises on the quayside near the bridge)*.

Into the hills

Follow the Ring of Kerry signs on the road out of Kenmare to the west (N70). The main road runs alongside the Kenmare River. In 12km there is a fascinating side-trip to be made into the wild mountains rising to the north. Turn right towards **Ballaghbeama Gap★**, Boheeshil, and **Ballaghisheen Pass★** *(allow 50min there and back)*. The mountains rise to over 700m, threaded by rivers and studded with lakes, all teeming with fish.

Late afternoon light Skellig Ring

G Biudzin/MICHELIN

Ring of Kerry – southern section
36km – allow half a day (whole day including side-trips)

■ **Sneem** – This is a another village of brightly painted houses, prettily laid out around a square by a river. Perhaps inevitably, it is a popular stop for coach parties, and has several craft shops and cafés. One famous visitor was General de Gaulle, who came here to recuperate after his fall from power in 1969.

Continue west on the N70. In Castlecove, 17.5km further on, turn right towards Staigue Fort.

■ **Staigue fort★** – *Narrow access road. The Visitor Centre is expensive and not really worth it.* This is one of the finest prehistoric forts in Ireland. Dating from about the 5C BC, it is a drystone structure on a prominent site commanding the surrounding area and probably housed a small community. The walls are 4m high and 5m thick, with steps on the inside face to provide access to the parapet.

Go back to the N70 and continue to Caherdaniel.

■ **Caherdaniel★★** – The village itself is nothing out of the ordinary, but there are some fascinating sights nearby.
The first trip to make is to **Lamb's Head★★** *(Turn left on the bend on the way into the village. About 6km there and back on foot or by car).* The way leads past a lagoon with a large bird population before reaching the rocky coastline. Beyond a strange boat-shaped house overlooking Derrynane Bay there is a tiny harbour.

Return to Caherdaniel and follow the signs to the **Derrynane National Historic Park★** *(May-September: 9am-6pm; 11am-7pm Sunday; April and October: closed Monday; November-March:1pm-5pm weekends only. Admission charge, free entry to park. Heritage Site).* In the middle of a lovely park planted with rare species stands the house where Daniel O'Connell spent his childhood before being sent away to school first at Cobh, then in France. The 19C **house** contains fascinating mementoes of the great nationalist leader including personal items, documents, furniture, and family portraits, including one of the great man depicted as Hercules breaking his chains!
Now drive to **Derrynane Harbour★**, a Mecca for windsurfers. Go down to the **beach★★** *(to the left of the car park)* and walk along it to **Abbey Island★** which can be reached on foot at low tide. In the middle of an overgrown **sailors' graveyard** are the ruins of an ancient abbey, possibly founded by St Finan, and overlooking what is one of Ireland's most beautiful beaches.

Return to the N70 and continue to Waterville.

■ **Waterville** – This little resort on the isthmus between the lough and the sea is sometimes almost overwhelmed by the numbers of tourist coaches, but it is nevertheless a good base for exploring the wild and unspoiled landscapes all around.
Lough Currane★*(turn inland at the road junction 1.5km from Waterville towards Caherdaniel)* is known for its **salmon** and **sea trout**. There is a fine **walk★** (or drive) along the rocky shoreline and among the hills *(16km there and back).*

Leave Waterville to the north on the N70 towards Cahersiveen. Turn left after 3km and follow signs to Skellig Ring (R567).

Skellig Ring★★
40km round trip leaving out Valentia Island

The village of **Ballinskelligs** marks the beginning of part of the *Gaeltacht*. The **beach★** of fine sand is a good place to stop for a swim.
The road now turns away from the coast temporarily towards **St Finan's Bay★★**, from where the characteristic outline of the Skellig Islands *(see below)* can be made out. A series of hairpin bends follows, leading up the side of **Mount Glavenagh**

(318m) to a pass, from where there is a marvellous **panorama****. Then comes a steep descent to **Portmagee**, a lively little fishing village with brightly painted house-fronts. On the far side of Portmagee Channel is Valentia Island, which has given its name to one of the sea areas featuring in the BBC's shipping forecasts.

■ **Valentia Island** – *Access via the bridge at the end of the quayside in Portmagee.* Immediately on the left after the bridge is the **Skellig Heritage Centre**** (*Easter-September: 10am-6.30pm. Admission charge. The Centre runs boat trips around the islands*), which brings to vivid life the history of the Skellig Islands through films, models, reconstructions and photographs. Valentia is often bypassed by visitors in a hurry, but anyone with a little time to spare should do the lovely **walk*** to Bray Head, opposite the cliffs of Skellig Ring (*Turn left beyond the Heritage Centre and at the beginning of the footpath leading to the tip of the island and the lookout tower*). At the eastern end of the island the peaceful little port of **Knight's Town** (*with a ferry service to Cahersiveen*) has as its symbol an unusual weather-boarded orange **clock tower** on the quayside.

H Choimet/MICHELIN

Puffin

■ **Skellig Islands***** – *Enquire on the quayside or at the Heritage Centre about crossing to the islands by fishing boat – only in calm conditions. Reckon on €25.*

No landing is allowed on **Little Skellig**, but it can be sailed around to observe the seabirds, among which is an important colony of gannets, as well as petrels, guillemots, and puffins.

Skellig Michael*** (or Great Skellig), rising to 218m, is the larger of the two islands, the site of one of the most important Early Christian monasteries, and recently declared a World Heritage Site. It is a place of austere beauty, evoking perhaps more than anywhere else both the austerities and contemplative joys of the monastic life. Not that the monks were wholly without material comforts. They may have rowed themselves in their cumbersome craft to this westernmost point of Europe, but they were by no means cut off from the world, importing wine from the Middle East and cloth from North Africa. Despite the Viking raids, they clung to their rock until the 12C, when they abandoned the island and moved the monastery to Ballinskellig. The history of the **monastery** goes back to its foundation in the 6C by St Finian. It consists of a group of well-preserved drystone structures perched on a high and narrow platform on the cliff edge. There are remains of the **church**, of two **oratories**, and of six beehive-shaped **cells**. Stones protruding from the main structure were no doubt there to hold an insulating layer of earth in place. The monks collected rainwater in a cistern, and basic heating was provided by a small fire of peat or wood brought from the mainland.

The island has a total of 2 300 steps cut into the rock; images of the monks toiling up to the monastery in a storm come vividly to mind (*anyone without a good head for heights needs to take special care*).

Ring of Kerry north
66km – Allow half a day

■ **Cahersiveen** – Neither the town nor the **Barracks Heritage Centre** are particularly remarkable, and Cahersiveen's greatest claim to fame is that it was the birthplace of Daniel O'Connell. However, at Kinnego West on the far side of the estuary are two of the finest prehistoric forts in Kerry.

Little Skeillig

Cross the bridge over the estuary at the foot of the Barracks, turn left at the T-junction and drive to where the outline of the forts comes into view. Leave the car here and walk along the rough track.

The great mass of **Cahergal Fort**★ is visible from a point close to the road. It is the larger and better preserved of the two drystone forts, with two superimposed internal terraces.

Even though less prominent and partly smothered in grass *(follow the road to the right and go up the access path on foot)* **Leacanabuaile Fort**★★ has a lot of charm. Inside the ramparts are the remains of the foundations of six houses and a passageway leading to a chamber. The romantic ruins visible below belong to **Ballycarbery Castle**, a 15C stronghold built by the McCarthy clan, and subsequently owned by the O'Connells *(can be seen from the road but not open to the public).*

Return to Cahersiveen and continue east along the Ring of Kerry.

In 16km a minor road turns off to the left towards **Kells Bay**, with a pretty beach backed by trees but unfortunately spoiled by the presence of caravans. Back on the Ring of Kerry, the road runs parallel to the coast on a corniche with views northward to the Dingle Peninsula. **Glenbeigh** is a resort just inland where many Irish people spend their holidays. The sand-dunes of **Rossbeigh Strand** protrude 5km into Dingle Bay.

Turn right 4km beyond Glenbeigh towards Caragh Lake, then immediately right again towards Glencar.

The wooded landscape around **Lough Caragh**★★ is in total contrast to the coast. Beautifully built in stone above a mass of tumbled rocks in the Caragh River, Blackstones Bridge is the starting point for a pleasant **forest walk**. The **Kerry Way**★★ long distance footpath crosses the country, giving superb views over Lough Caragh from the section between Glencar and Glenbeigh.

■ **Killorglin** – This little town is the scene every year in the second week of August of the **Puck Fair★★**, one of the biggest fairs in Ireland. Its origins go back to harvest festivals and worship of the god Lug. A billy-goat is enthroned with great ceremony as king of the fair, and revelry continues for three days and three nights.

Making the most of the Iveragh Peninsula

COMING AND GOING

By car – Kenmare is 94km from Cork. Take the N22 via Macroom and Cloonken, then the R569.

By train – Five to seven trains daily between Cork and Killarney (2hr), and 4 trains daily between Dublin and Killarney (3hr50min) via Tralee.

By bus – Two to three buses daily between Kenmare and Tralee all year; June-September two buses daily between Kenmare and Cork; June-September two buses daily from Killarney (bus station opposite the Great Southern Hotel) to the Ring of Kerry.

ADDRESS BOOK

Tourist information – *Tourist Office*, The Square, Kenmare, ☎ 064 412 33. Open 9am-6pm; closed Sunday except July-August.

Banks / Currency exchange – Banks and cash machines in Kenmare, Cahersiveen and Killorglin.

WHERE TO STAY

• **Kenmare**

Between €40-50

Ard na Mara, Pier Road, ☎ 064 413 99 – 4rm On the way out of town towards Glengariff, in the road just before the bridge. Quiet, spacious rooms with a superb view of the Kenmare River. Tea-making facilities.

Druid's Cottage, Sneem Road, ☎ 064 418 03 – 3rm Cute little stone-built house on the Ring of Kerry with small but pretty rooms, run by a friendly landlady.

The Nook, Muxnaw, ☎ 064 411 96 – 4rm TV ✗ On the Glengariff road 1.5km from the centre of town opposite the Riversdale Hotel. With flower-covered pergolas, walls yellowed by the sun and a view of the Caha Mountains, this is a wonderful place to stay. There's a warm welcome, and evening meals can be provided if wished. Nothing could be more relaxing than nodding off in the garden here...

Ceann Mara, Killowen, ☎ 064 412 20 – 4rm ✗ One kilometre from Kenmare on the Cork road (R569). The great thing about this house is its garden. There's access to the river and a tennis lawn. Dinner by arrangement, vegetarian if wished. Open May-September.

Finnihy Lodge, Killarney Road, ☎ 064 411 98 – 5rm On the way out of Kenmare towards Killarney, this is a large house set back from the road. Courteous reception, well-kept rooms, some sharing a bathroom and more expensive. Baby-sitting can be arranged.

Tara Farm, Tubrid, ☎ 064 412 72 – 6rm TV ✗ CC Look for the sign on the left on the way out of town towards Sneem (N70). Well away from the hustle and bustle of town, an impeccably kept bungalow overlooking the Kenmare River. Rooms with a view of the sea are slightly more expensive; the other rooms overlook the countryside. Fish supper by arrangement.

Between €50-70

Mylestone House, Killowen Road, ☎ 064 417 53 – 5rm CC On the way out of Kenmare towards Cork. Five minutes on foot from the middle of town, this modern house has a friendly land-

Lough Caragh, an angler's paradise

lady and is attractively decorated and very well-kept. The least expensive B&B in this category.

@ **Muxnaw Lodge**, Castletownbere Road, ☎ 064 412 52 – 5rm ⌂ TV ✗ ⚘ One kilometre southwest of Kenmare on the R571. This elegant residence of 1801 is built on rising ground and is set in a lovely garden with a tennis court. Cosy interior with family furniture, musical instruments and old prints. Very good value.

The Rose Garden, Sneem Road, ☎ 064 422 88 – 8rm ⌂ ℘ TV ✗ CC This brand-new building is almost like a hotel. Reduced rates for longer stays. À la carte restaurant. Very professional welcome.

More than €100

Sallyport House, ☎ 064 420 66 – 5rm ⌂ ℘ TV CC On the left off the Glengariff road just before the bridge. Antique furniture and sophisticated comforts. Impeccable service, spacious and attractively decorated rooms, sumptuous breakfast. But it is expensive.

@ **Dromquinna Manor**, Blackwater Bridge, ☎ 064 416 57 – 46rm ⌂ ℘ TV ✗ 🛁 🏊 ⚘ CC This establishment maintains the best traditions of the luxury hotel, with refined décor, four-poster beds and every comfort. The rooms in the main building are more expensive but have a view of the Kenmare River and are worth it. There's fishing in the hotel's private park.

• **Sneem**

Under €13

Harbour View Hostel, ☎ 064 452 76 – 40 beds and 12rm ✗ CC On the N70 on the way in from Kenmare. A motel which has been refurbished as inexpensive accommodation and includes a camp site. Reduction for use of own sleeping bag. More expensive 2-3 bed rooms. Huge kitchen, laundry facilities. Lively bar.

Between €40-50

@ **Old Convent House**, Pier Road, ☎ 064 451 81 – 6rm ⌂ ✗ Just below the main street in Sneem, this is an old stone building set in its tranquil garden and enjoying lovely views. Charming, characterful décor. Access to the Kenmare River. Meals by arrangement.

The Bank House, North Square, ☎ 064 452 26 – 6rm ⌂ TV CC The bright green front of this house on the road out to Caherdaniel is unmistakable. Very pleasant reception.

• **Caherdaniel**

Under €13

Traveller's Rest Hostel, ☎ 066 947 5175 – 12 beds. In a prominent position opposite the petrol station, this cottage is a welcoming place with a cosmopolitan clientele. Double rooms available too.

Caherdaniel Village Hostel, ☎ 066 947 5277 – 12 beds. Extension planned. Well-kept 2-bed rooms with shower and toilet on the landing. Cooking facilities. Handy for the Blind Piper pub next door.

Between €45-50

Derrynane Bay House, ☎ 066 9475 436 – 6rm ⌂ ℘ TV CC On the way out of the village towards Waterville. Big modern bungalow, well-kept and comfortable. Generous breakfast. Tea-making facilities.

Harbour View Farmhouse, Farraniaragh, ☎ 066 9475 292 – 3rm ⌂ ✗ Turn left off the Waterville road past the viewpoint overlooking Derrynane just below the big restaurant, and follow signs. Superb views over this indented coastline. Meals by arrangement.

@ **Moran's Farmhouse**, Bunavalla, ☎ 066 9475 208 – 4rm ⌂ ✗ Follow signs beyond Harbour View Farmhouse. An isolated farmhouse by the sea, a tiny garden overlooking Derrynane Bay, seafood straight from the water on to the table, this is ideal for people looking for peace and quiet and unspoiled surroundings.

• **Ballinskelligs**

Under €13

Ballinskelligs Youth Hostel, ☎ 066 947 9229 – 22 beds and 1 family room. Rudimentary accommodation, but close to the beach and on the Kerry Way. Member of An Oige.

Between €45-50

The Old School House B&B, Cloon, ☎ 066 9479 340 – 5rm ⌂ ✗ CC Next to Rascals Restaurant on the R566, well-signposted off the R567 Waterville-

Ballinskelligs road. Pretty little rooms in a quiet location in a converted schoolroom, less than 2km from the beach.

🐌 **Tig Báigh Fionán**, St Finan's Bay, ☎ 066 9479 301 – 4rm 🍴 TV CC On one of the loveliest bays in the area, this little house has been tastefully redecorated by a friendly young couple. Two of the rooms are cheaper and share a bathroom. Breathtaking views at breakfasttime. Open April-September. Book well in advance.

• **Waterville**

Between €45-50

Seaview, Toor, ☎ 066 9474 297 – 3rm 🍴 Near Loher Fort 4km from Waterville.

Turn off the N70 between Caherdaniel and Waterville by the church towards Hog's Head. Superb view of Ballinskelligs Bay. Very quiet location.

Atlantic View, Toor, ☎ 066 9474 335 – 5rm 🍴 Next to the above establishment, this B&B has the same unspoiled surroundings. Wonderful walks nearby.

Between €50-65

Lakelands Guesthouse, Lake Road, ☎ 066 9474 303 – 12rm 🍴 🛁 TV ✗ CC 3km from Waterville on Lough Currane. Well-signposted on the N70 2km before Waterville when coming from Caherdaniel. This comfortable modern house by the waterside is virtually a hotel. The landlord hunts (November-January) and fishes (January-September), and will arrange for guests to do likewise. Boat and other equipment available. Sumptuous meals prepared by the landlady. Less expensive out of season. Superb walking all around.

• **Cahersiveen**

Between €40-50

Sea Breeze, Reenard Road, ☎ 066 9472 609 – 6rm 🍴 CC On the way into Cahersiveen from the west going towards Reenard Point. The rooms are small but well-kept. The ones with shared bathroom are less expensive. Pleasant conservatory for watching the sun go down.

Ocean View, Reenard Road, ☎ 066 9472 261 – 6rm 🍴 ✗ A little further along the same road as the above

establishment. Lovely view of the bay, attractive décor. Evening meal by arrangement.

Reenard House, Reenard Road, ☎ 066 9473 307 – 6rm 🍴 🛁 TV ✗ CC On the corner of the road leading to Reenard Point, this big pink-painted house is brand-new. Very comfortable with warm welcome. Tea-making facilities in the rooms. Baby-sitting by arrangement.

Harbour Hill, Knockeens, ☎ 066 9472 844 – 4rm 🍴 CC Three kilometres from Cahersiveen. Look for the sign on the left on the road out towards Waterville. Alone on its hill, this plain and simple house has an impressive panorama over the bay and Valentia Island.

Iveragh Heights, Carhan Road, ☎ 066 9472 545 – 5rm 🍴 TV ✗ On the side of the hill to the right on the way out of Cahersiveen towards Killorglin (N70). Watch out for vehicles coming in the other direction when entering. Lovely views over hills and river. Meals by arrangement. Good advice on walks in the area.

• **Glenbeigh**

Between €40-50

🐌 **Ross na Rí House**, Station Road, ☎ 066 9768 472 – 3rm 🍴 In a road by the sea on the way out of Glenbeigh towards Killorglin. Charming little place inside and out with a delightful landlady and very reasonable rates.

• **Killorglin and Lough Caragh**

Under €13

Laune Valley Farm Hostel, Banshagh, Killorglin, ☎ 066 9761 488 – 30 beds and 4 family rooms. Clearly signposted on the right 1.5km from the bridge on the Tralee road. Big farmhouse in the middle of the countryside facing the mountains. Laundry facilities, camp site and meals made with produce from the farm.

Between €45-50

🐌 **Blackstones House**, Glencar, ☎ 066 9760 164 – 6rm 🍴 ✗ CC Clearly signposted by Blackstones Bridge on the Kerry Way (if coming from Lough Caragh or from Killorglin, follow signs to Blackstones). 18km from

Killorglin, on the banks of a river full of fish, among forests and mountains. Ideal for huntin', fishin' and walkin', and not expensive either.

River's Edge, Killorglin, ☎ 066 9761 750 – 6rm ⚲ At the bottom of the main street before the bridge. This fine modern house is an excellent base for anyone preferring a bit of town life. Well-kept and nicely decorated.

More than €150

⊛**Ard na Sidhe Hotel**, Caragh Lake, Killorglin, ☎ 066 9769 105 – 19rm ⚲ 𝒫 ✗ CC Total luxury in a grand Victorian manor house where every detail has been attended to. Wonderful gardens going down to the lakeside. Boats available. Free admission to the facilities in the other hotels in Killarney belonging to this chain (swimming pool, tennis courts, sauna, riding...). Expensive, but utterly charming. The best rooms are in the main building.

WHERE TO EAT

Ireland's most popular tourist area has a good number of restaurants and cafés serving fairly standard fare. Lunch is not usually a problem, but eating out in the evenings can soon empty your pocket.

• **Kenmare**
Between €6-13
The New Delight, Henry Street, 10am-10pm in summer, 10am-4pm rest of year. Vegetarian restaurant with relaxed atmosphere. Satisfying and not expensive. Between €5-7.50 at midday, rather more in the evening.

More than €13

⊛**Lime Tree**, Shelbourne Street, ☎ 064 412 25. In the enchanting setting of an old school smothered in greenery, refined and ultra-fresh food. Local fish and lamb specialities. Evening only, dinner à la carte.

D'Arcy's, Main Street, ☎ 064 415 89. A more traditional type of restaurant with good food prepared with a French touch using local ingredients. Try the pan-fried monkfish in tomato sauce or heather-flavoured ice cream. But quite pricey.

• **Caherdaniel**
Between €6-13
The Blind Piper, in the middle of Cahersiveen in the road leading to Derrynane. Cheerful pub with traditional bar food from €5 upwards.

The Stepping Stone, ☎ 066 9475 444. Plain décor and food based on traditional ingredients. No smoking.

• **Cahersiveen**
Between €6-13
The Shebeen Bar, Main Street, on the way out towards Tralee. Another pub serving a variety of inexpensive dishes. Live music Thursday evening.

O'Neill's Point Bar, Reenard Point, ☎ 066 9472 165. Facing the landing stage for Valentia Island, this is a friendly pub with excellent seafood dishes. Generous portions from €10 upwards. Very popular with local people.

OTHER THINGS TO DO

Walking – The Kerry Way long distance footpath runs for 214km. Although it winds its way through the highest mountain range in Ireland, the path does not climb higher than 385m. The summits of the mountains are for experienced walkers only (see "Making the most of Killarney"). Buy the "Kerry Way Map Guide" or nos 70, 78, 83, 84 and 85 of the Ordnance Survey Discovery Series maps.

Golf – The 18-hole 71 par **Kenmare Golf Club**, ☎ 064 412 91, is very popular with American and British visitors, fee €22. **Waterville Golf Links**, ☎ 066 9474 102, par 72, 18-hole course, fee €76, overlooks the ocean and is one of the world's top golf courses. **Dooks Golf Club**, Glenbeigh, ☎ 066 9768 205, par 70, 18-hole, fee €32, is among the sand-dunes of Dingle Bay. **Killorglin Golf Club**, ☎ 066 9761 979, par 72, 18-hole, fee €20.

Watersports – **Skelligs Aquatics**, Caherdaniel, ☎ 066 9475 277, offers diving among shipwrecks, submarine caves and ocean life. Sailing instruction, deep-sea fishing, survival techniques. All ages welcome, by the day, weekend or week.

Derrynane Watersports Centre, Derrynane Harbour, ☎ 066 9474 266. The centre benefits from its location on a bay very suitable for windsurfing and canoeing. Hire of equipment, sailing instruction, water-skiing, etc. **Des Lavelle's**, Knightstown, Valentia Island, ☎ 066 9476 124, runs diving courses as well as mini-cruises to the Skellig Islands.

Riding – The **Dromquinna Stables**, Kenmare, ☎ 064 410 43. Lovely rides along the Kenmare River by horse or pony. **Eagle Rock Equestrian Centre**, Caherdaniel, ☎ 066 9475 145, accompanies visitors through the dunes and along beaches around Derrynane.

Fishing – Trout and salmon fishing in all the rivers in the peninsula. The best stretches are in Lough Currane (free) and Lough Caragh (details from the Glencar Hotel, ☎ 066 9760 102). For the rivers around Kenmare, contact **O'Hare's Fishing Tackle Shop**, 21 Main Street.

For sea fishing, the best areas are the Kenmare River off Sneem (pollock, conger eel, trout), Derrynane (sea perch and bass), Hog's Head, Waterville beach (sea perch and bass), St Finan's Bay (bass), Valentia Harbour and Glenbeigh.

Deep sea fishing trips can be arranged at Derrynane, contact **Skelligs Aquatics**, ☎ 066 9475 277, or at Portmagee, contact **Michael O'Sullivan**, ☎ 066 9474 255.

SHOPPING

Tweeds and woollens – **Quill's Woollen Market**, Kenmare and Sneem. Family business with branches all over the Southwest (eg in Cork and Killarney), but the shop in Kenmare seems to be the least expensive, particularly for machine-knitted pullovers ("hand-loomed"). Wide range of types and stitches. A few good tweed jackets and of course caps.

Crafts – Between Waterville and Ballinskelligs, the big circular thatched building of **Cill Rialaigh** is a showcase for the work of contemporary artists and craftspeople. There are pots, sculpture, watercolours, oil paintings, and all sorts of decorative objects, plus a few chairs drawn up in front of the fire where you can enjoy a cup of tea with delicious scones.

KILLARNEY AND AROUND ★★★

Co Kerry – Pop 7 300
At the foot of Macgillycuddy's Reeks
300km from Dublin and 87km from Cork
Michelin map 923 D / 11-12 and map page 285

Not to be missed
Muckross House and the Traditional Farms.
A walk or bike ride around the lakes.
A boat trip to Dunloe and Black Valley.

And remember...
Woollens and tweeds are expensive here, but don't be afraid to bargain.
Don't let yourself be hassled by constant calls to take a trip
in a pony trap or jaunting car.
The ascent of Carrantuohill is a strenuous climb, certainly not to be thought
of as a straightforward afternoon stroll.

The town spreads out at the foot of Macgillycuddy's Reeks, the highest mountain range in Ireland, dominated by Carrantuohill. The town as such is far less interesting than this magnificent natural setting, certainly in terms of its architecture. Like other places in the west, it has lots of brightly-painted buildings, plus a cathedral, a castle and a country house, and an array of souvenir shops. There is music everywhere, almost always worth listening to even though most of it is staged for the crowds of visitors who come to what is one of the country's foremost tourist towns.

Monks, clansmen and a Queen
The area around Killarney has plenty of evidence showing that it was occupied from the Bronze Age onwards. In the 7C AD a monastery was founded on the little island of Innisfallen, and it was here that one of Ireland's earliest historical chronicles, the **Annals of Innisfallen** were written, of which the sole example, in Latin and Gaelic, is in Oxford's Bodleian Library. The little monastic community attracted both scholars and the powerful, very much like a university.

There followed a period in the course of which a number of clans divided up the area among themselves. The O'Donoghues built Ross Castle on the eastern shore of the lake, while the McCarthys appropriated Muckross and the O'Sullivans lorded it over Dunloe. Cromwell's wars put an end to this happy state of affairs. Under the sway of the English, the town developed thanks to linen and woollen manufacturing. In the 19C tourism was born, coming of age when Queen Victoria paid a visit.

When coming in on the road from Killorglin, look out for the sign to Aghadoe Heights on the left about 3km short of Killarney; from here, the magnificent panorama is the best possible introduction to the town in its setting of lakes and mountains.

The town

Allow 1hr (half a day including the walk to Ross Castle). The town is very crowded in summer. The most practical car parks are around the cathedral and to the rear of the post office in New Street. Go northeast along New Street to get to the High Street and Main Street

Around the Market Cross
New Street runs into the town's principal thoroughfare, called High Street (*to the left*) and Main Street (*to the right*). The junction still bears the name of Market Cross, a reminder of the markets of yesteryear, when peasants would pour in from the surrounding countryside to sell whatever they could to pay the rent: eggs, milk,

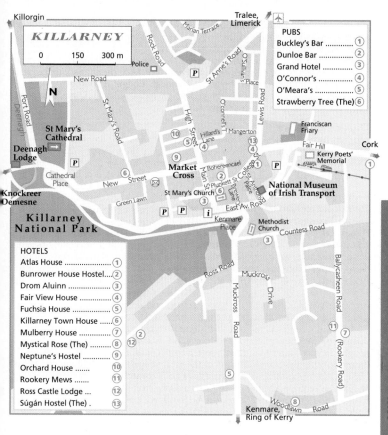

butter, peat and cloth. Nowadays the Market Cross is the commercial heart of the town, whose charm comes from the bustle around the restored shop fronts and the atmosphere inside the pubs.

Go south along Main Street. Beyond St Mary's Church, at the bend in the road, is where the jaunting cars stand ready to take visitors to the edge of town (between €4.50-10 per person). To avoid the barrage of offers, keep to the pavement on the same side as the church, continue into East Avenue Road and look out for the signboard of the National Museum of Irish Transport.

In the gardens of Scott's Hotel stands the astonishing **National Museum of Irish Transport*** *(April-October: 10am-6pm. Admission charge)*, with its array of vehicles and motoring memorabilia: there are bicycles from every era, motor-cars (including a unique Rolls-Royce Silver Stream), fire engines, a 1910 Wolseley once driven by Countess Markievicz and William Butler Yeats, countless old advertisements, posters and magazines.

Go back the way you came to the end of New Street.

The architect of the Gothic Revival Roman Catholic **St Mary's Cathedral** (1842-55) was Pugin, who gave it a tall spire, untypical of Ireland. The building is not of great interest; construction stopped between 1848 and 1853, when it was used as a shelter for the victims of the Famine. Many of those who died of starvation or disease were buried in a common grave here.

On the far side of the street, railings protect the **Knockreer Demesne**★, the estate which forms part of the Killarney National Park *(see below)*. The entrance to the estate is guarded by a little thatched building, **Deenagh Lodge**. A **footpath**★★ leads to Knockreer House and runs across the park to the banks of Lough Leane, then south along the shore to Ross Castle *(20min on foot)*.

Outside the town

Access by car to the southwest of town along Muckross Road and Ross Road.

A very simple structure like many 15C strongholds, **Ross Castle**★ *(Easter-October: 10am-5pm; closed Monday in October. Admission charge. Heritage Site. Guided tour only)* is a well-restored fortified tower. The interior gives a good idea of life as led at the time, with everyone piling promiscuously into the same bedroom; a bench with holes serving as a communal latrine, etc. There is contemporary furniture, and interesting insights into methods of construction, like the ingenious system of interwoven willow rods forming the shuttering for vaults.

Beating the tax-man
The lack of a roof on many an Irish castle was deliberate. Taxes were calculated not on land but on houses, defined by the existence of a roof. The rich tended not to live on their estates, simply drawing their revenues from them, and were quite happy to have a roof built when they were in occupation, then have it removed when they left.

Attractive footpaths lead into the woods around and along the lakeside to the peninsula of **Ross Island**★, where copper was once mined.

To follow in the steps of the pious who counted among their number the High King Brian Ború, make the pilgrimage to **Innisfallen Island**★, one of the many islands in Lough Leane or Lower Lake *(boat from the landing stage at Ross Castle, reckon on €5)*. From the water there are fine views of the great ramparts of Macgillycuddy's Reeks, while on the island there are the remains of a 12C **oratory** and a **carved doorway**, and, in the centre of the monastery, a sacred yew tree.

Innisfallen was thought by Macaulay to be "not a reflex of heaven, but a bit of heaven itself".

Macgillycuddy's Reeks★★★
Walking is the only way to escape the crowds – Allow 2 days

The unspoiled nature of this majestic landscape has long been under siege from mass tourism. Nevertheless, it is possible to get off the beaten track and discover places where nature is intact, where native woodland still flourishes, where dark waters fill the lakes, and rugged crags hang high overhead.

The mildness of the climate means that exotic vegetation flourishes, and the area is famous for its evergreen arbutus (or strawberry trees). The richness of the flora led in 1981 to the park's being designated a UNESCO Biosphere Reserve.

Killarney National Park★★★
Vehicle access to the park is on the right, 6km south of the town on the N71, about 1km past Muckross Park Hotel. Pedestrians have two additional access points closer to town off the same road.

Covering an area of 101sqkm, the National Park includes three lakes – Lower, Middle and Upper Lake – which are linked by a river, and set in a highly varied landscape offering all sorts of walking possibilities. Some are content to stroll around the gardens, others head for the hills or go right round Middle Lake, perhaps by bike, passing the **Meeting of the Waters**, the point at which the waters of the Upper and Middle Lake mingle.

Most people begin their acquaintance with the National Park with a visit to **Muckross House, Gardens and Farms**** *(house and gardens open all year, farms open May-October and the weekend of 21 March-late April: 9am-6pm, July-August 9am-7pm. Free admission to gardens, admission charge for house and gardens, combined ticket available. Heritage Site).* The superbly landscaped lakeside **gardens**** are the estate's pride and joy, with an astonishing variety of shrubs and other plants seen against the background of rocky islands, wooded slopes and rugged crags. When the rhododendrons and azaleas flower in May the spectacle is even more striking. Dating from 1843, **Muckross House*** is a splendid mansion in neo-Tudor style, presented to the state in 1932 by its Californian owners, Mr and Mrs William Bowers Bourn. The interior is furnished in early-20C style. In the basement there are working displays of traditional trades like weaving, pottery, cobbling and bookbinding.

The **Traditional Farms**** consist of half a dozen buildings, ranging from a farmstead to a labourer's cabin, forming an open-air museum devoted to the recreation of rural life in the early 20C. Farm animals wander around, tools and implements are on display, and costumed guides recreate the activities of yesteryear such as butter-making, blacksmithing, and carpentry *(allow 1hr)*.

The ruins of the 15C Franciscan **Muckross Friary*** can be seen in the park. The well-preserved cloisters, the great square tower of the church, and a number of domestic buildings evoke the monastic life as led towards the end of the Middle Ages.

About 1km further along the N71 *(car park on the left)* are the **Torc Waterfalls***, a relatively modest cascade 18m high but in an enchanting wooded setting *(easy 150m walk from the car park).* To the left of the falls, a stairway up the side of the hill with 173 steps climbs to a viewpoint with a fine **prospect*** over the lakes *(allow at least 2hr for falls and viewpoint).*

Continue along the N71 towards Kenmare. The road runs along **Muckross Lake** (Middle Lake) and winds among walls of naturalised rhododendron which flower purple in May. At the **Upper Lake** the landscape changes, there is bare rock, and woodland gives way to peat bogs. **Ladies View**** *(16km from Killarney)* owes its name to the visit paid by Queen Victoria and her ladies-in-waiting who stopped here to wonder at the superb panorama. It's a popular spot, and deservedly so.

Eight kilometres further on, turn off the N71 at **Moll's Gap** and follow signs to **Black Valley*****. A minor road to the right descends into a wild and unspoiled valley still inhabited by a few hardy countryfolk. From here the Gap of Dunloe is accessible on foot or by bike.

Muckross House

B Pérousse/MICHELIN

Gap of Dunloe★★★

Southern approach – *The best approach is from Black Valley to the south. The landscapes are wilder and just as lovely, and it's one way of avoiding being pestered to take a carriage ride. A shorter and in some ways even more attractive alternative is to take a boat from Ross Castle to the foot of the Gap (€9 one way, bikes carried, leaves at 11am). It is 2.5km uphill to the Gap, followed by a descent of 12km.*

Northern approach – *Leave Killarney to the west towards Killorglin (N72). In 9km turn left towards Beaufort and Gap of Dunloe. The surfaced road ends at Kate Kearney's Cottage, an old coaching inn, and from here on becomes a track. Only take a ride in a pony and trap if you are tired or in a hurry (it is a short, expensive trip); on foot or by mountain bike is much better as long as you are fit. Some sections of the 12km route are steep, but the going is easy. Once beyond the first 2km or so, the crowds thin out noticeably.*

Circular tour – *It is a 60km circuit by bike from Killarney, returning via Black Valley, Moll's Gap and the N71. It can be reduced to 30km by following the Kerry Way along Upper Lake, though this involves a lot of getting off and pushing.*

The **Gap** is a narrow, rock-strewn gorge, a U-shaped breach in the mountains carved out by glaciers. The track winds up in a series of hairpin bends, accompanied by a tumbling stream. All around are sheer walls of rock rising more than 400m. The route leads past several little lakes, peat bogs, and abandoned buildings, among them the old Royal Irish Constabulary barracks by Auger Lake. From the top of the gorge there is a stupendous **view**★★ of Black Valley and the Upper Lake.

Carrantuohill★★

Go towards Beaufort as for the Gap of Dunloe, then follow signs. Car park (parking charge in summer). Allow 6hr hard walking there and back. Not to be attempted after heavy rain or in fog, and proper walking footwear is essential.

At 1 038m this is the country's highest summit. Rock outcrops, waterlogged ground and some steep sections make it a demanding climb, but the effort is well rewarded when you reach the roof of Ireland and take in the splendid and far-reaching views.

Making the most of Killarney

COMING AND GOING

By plane – *Kerry Airport*, ☎ 066 976 4644, is at Farranfore 15km north of Killarney. Flights from London, Manchester and Dublin.

By car – Cork-Killarney via the N22; Dublin-Killarney via the N7 to Limerick, the N21 to Castleisland, then the N22.

By train – The railway station is by the Great Southern Hotel in East Avenue Road, ☎ 064 310 67. Five trains daily (3 Sunday) to Cork (2hr), and 4 services daily to Dublin (4hr).

By bus – The bus station, ☎ 064 347 77, is by the railway station. There are services to Cork (6 buses daily), Dublin (3 buses daily), Tralee (at least 3 buses daily), Limerick and Galway.

GETTING AROUND

Bicycle hire – There are several bike rental firms in town, at Market Cross, in Plunkett Street and College Street. Reckon on €8 per day.

Boat hire – Muckross House Boathouse, at Muckross and Ross Castle Pier. With or without crew, about €5 per hour per person.

ADDRESS BOOK

Tourist information – Tourist Office, Beech Road (near the car park between New Street and Main Street), ☎ 064 316 33. Open 9am-5.30pm except Sunday; June-September: open later and on Sunday. Efficient staff and a good source of information, including maps and books on the area as well as the "Where Killarney" brochure which describes walking routes and has excellent maps.

Banks / Currency exchange – All the main banks have branches with cash machines in Main Street. Many shops accept travellers' cheques and the tourist office acts as a bureau de change.

Internet – Café Internet, New Street, opposite the cathedral.

WHERE TO STAY

Killarney gets very full in season and on public holidays. Book in advance and at busy times make use of the tourist office which can almost always find somewhere to stay (charge).

• In town
Under €13
The Súgán Hostel, Lewis Road, ☎ 064 331 04 – 18 beds. Good location close to the bus and rail stations and the town centre. The hostel attracts hippy types from all over the world. Fairly basic accommodation, but good atmosphere. Bicycle hire. Lots of useful tips.
Neptune's Hostel, New Street, ☎ 064 352 55 – 100 beds in dormitories and smaller rooms ⒸⒸ Central location, well-kept and with good range of facilities including large kitchen, launderette, left luggage, safes and bicycle hire. Continental breakfast €2. Single rooms around €18.
Atlas House, Park Road, ☎ 064 361 44 – 136 beds in dormitories or smaller rooms ⒸⒸ Ultramodern building without much character but very practical, with laundry facilities and bi-

cycle hire. Continental breakfast included in the price. Double rooms cost around €30.
Bunrower House Hotel, Ross Road, ☎ 064 339 14 – 28 beds. Twenty minutes on foot from the bus and rail stations (or free pick-up). Close to town despite being in a countryside setting by the lake and the National Park. Camping possible. Bicycle hire.
Between €40-50
Orchard House, Fleming's Lane, ☎064 318 79 – 4rm ⌂ In a side-street in the middle of town, clearly signposted from the High Street, this little house is kept by an energetic couple. Warm welcome, quiet surroundings, handy for the pubs. The least expensive in this category.
Drom Aluinn, Countess Road, ☎ 064 350 39 – 4rm ⌂ Ⓣ Ⓥ Only 5min on foot from the centre in a quiet position, this is a large, well-kept and comfortable house. Tea-making facilities in the rooms. Car park. Good value.
The Mystical Road, Woodlawn Road, ☎ 064 314 53 – 6rm ⌂ Ⓣ Ⓥ Noreen Mahoney's home can hardly be seen for flowers. This landlady is full of high spirits and very friendly. Parking available.
Ross Castle Lodge, Ross Road, ☎ 064 369 42 – 4rm ⌂ Ⓣ Ⓥ On the road to Ross Castle, surrounded by trees, this lovely cottage and its garden are looked after by an extremely pleasant couple. Lots of good walks all around and right next to a golf course.
Rookery Mews, Rookery Road, ☎ 064 335 70 – 16 apartments for 3-5 people. Quite close to the centre of town in a quiet location. Can be rented for 2-3 nights or by the week. From €115 per weekend (2 nights for 5 people off-season) to €450 per week (7 nights for 5 people in July-August).
Between €50-65
Mulberry House, Rookery Road, ☎ 064 341 12 – 5rm ⌂ Ⓣ Ⓥ ⒸⒸ Quiet, well away from traffic, but only 10min on foot from the town centre. Brand-new house, all comforts and sophisticated décor. Excellent value.
Killarney Town House, 31 New Street, ☎ 064 352 59 – 11rm ⌂ ⌀ Ⓣ Ⓥ ⒸⒸ Small and urbane hotel in the very

Making the most of Killarney and around

centre of town, near the post office. All comforts. Rather more expensive than equivalent B&Bs.

Fair View House, College Street, ☎ 064 341 64 – 11rm 🖥 𝓟 TV CC Good central location, this large town house is virtually a hotel. Some of the rooms are reasonably inexpensive, but prices really go up in high season. Don't be shy of bargaining and make sure exactly what has been agreed on. Apart from this one cavil, the place is highly recommended.

More than €80

😊**Fuchsia House**, Muckross Road, ☎ 064 365 88 – 10rm 🖥 𝓟 TV CC This charming Victorian-style residence has refined décor and an enchanting conservatory overlooking a walled garden. Delicious breakfast with a huge choice, including vegetarian.

- **Outside the town**

Under €13

😊**Aghadoe House Hostel**, Aghadoe, ☎ 064 312 40 – 200 beds. Five kilometres from Killarney, off the Killorglin road (free pick-up from the station). Superb manor house in parkland with some of the finest views in the area. Laundry facilities and bicycle hire. Often fully booked in summer. Member of the Irish YHA.

😊**Black Valley Youth Hostel**, Black Valley, Beaufort, ☎ 064 347 12 – 50 beds. This is about as isolated as it gets, among the mountains at the beginning of the southern approach to the Gap of Dunloe. Superb landscapes all around. Small general store. Plain food.

Between €45-50

Tara House, Fossa, ☎ 064 443 55 – 5rm 🖥 CC Signposted on the Killorglin road 4km from Killarney just beyond the Hotel Europe. Long low house in a pretty garden. The owners are very attentive and will help you plan your walking trips.

Inverary House, Beaufort, ☎ 064 442 24 – 9rm 🖥 𝓟 ✗ CC Off the Killorglin road 9km from Killarney. Go past the Gap of Dunloe junction and turn left opposite the petrol station and general store, then left again a short distance beyond the Beaufort Bar. Big rooms, with fine mountain views. Generous meals by

arrangement, seafood specialities. Attractive garden with fishing rights.

😊**Carriglea House**, Muckross Road, ☎ 064 311 16 – 8rm 🖥 TV CC On the left of the Muckross road on the way out of town, opposite the Lake Hotel. Set back from the road in an elevated position, this is a grand Georgian building with a superb view of lake and mountain. Very reasonable rates considering the quality of the accommodation.

Crabtree Cottage, Mangerton Road, ☎ 064 331 69 – 4rm 🖥 ✗ Look out on the N71 on the far side of Muckross for the Muckross Park Hotel and turn left (clearly signposted). Little cottage in a charming and luxuriantly planted garden. Lovely conservatory. Fine walking country all around. The room without its own facilities is less expensive. Evening meal by arrangement.

😊**Friars Glen**, Mangerton Road, ☎ 064 375 00 – 10rm 🖥 𝓟 TV CC Beautiful house in the middle of the countryside with woodland at the bottom of the garden. Big fireplaces in the lounges, and breakfast (excellent) in the conservatory, large but cosy rooms and a drying room for wet walking gear. One of the best places to stay in the area.

EATING OUT

The Killarney Manor Banquet pulls in the coach party crowds with its cabaret-style folklore performances but it's expensive and hardly the most authentic of experiences.

Under €13

Mike's Take Away, Plunkett Street. Probably the best take-away in town, with generous servings of non-greasy fish and chips.

Grunt's, New Street. Opposite the post office, a place to eat copious salads, quiches or other straightforward dishes. Breakfast and lunch.

The Green Onion, Fleming's Lane (off the High Street). Good sandwiches, salads, soups and cakes. 11am-6pm; closed Sunday.

Between €6-13

😊**Greenes Vegetarian Restaurant**, Bridewell Lane (in New Street, opposite Dunnes Stores), ☎ 064 330 83. Open 10.30am-3pm / 6pm-9.30pm.

Cosmopolitan dishes, generous portions of satisfying food. No frills and very friendly.

Teo's, New Street, ☎ 064 363 44. Mediterranean atmosphere and flavours, including pasta, salads, and various grilled dishes.

Between €13-20

Sceilig Restaurant, High Street, ☎ 064 330 62. A traditional kind of place, with dishes of the day or à la carte. Special offers Sunday lunchtimes.

The Celtic Cauldron, 27 Plunkett Street, ☎ 064 368 21. Irish cuisine served in a pleasantly rustic setting. Good atmosphere.

More than €20

The Strawberry Tree, 24 Plunkett Street, ☎ 064 326 88. Convivial pub atmosphere and highly inventive and constantly changing menu, using local produce. Best to book in advance in summer.

Gaby's, High Street, ☎ 064 325 19. Specialising in seafood. Expensive, but this has not put off the customers who have been coming here for over 20 years. Various kinds of smoked fish, crab claws and lobsters. Reservation advisable in summer and at the weekend.

HAVING A DRINK

It's a good idea to stroll around town checking what is on in the various pubs. When there's music, the entrance fee is usually only charged after 9.30pm, so can be avoided by getting there earlier.

O'Meara's, 12 High Street. A good place for traditional music. Music every evening in season.

O'Connor's, 7 High Street. Another place where locals go for their pint. Good music, Monday, Thursday and at the weekend.

Buckley's Bar and **Failte Bar**, College Street. Traditional music every evening in one or other of these bars.

Dunloe Bar, Plunkett Street. Regular traditional music evenings.

The Strawberry Tree, Plunkett Street. The restaurant might be on the expensive side, but the bar is a good place for a pint or two. Friendly atmosphere.

Grand Hotel, Main Street. The hotel bar is a favourite with local people. The music (and occasional dancing) is good and there are fewer tourists than elsewhere. Get here early if you don't want to pay the €5 charge.

OTHER THINGS TO DO

Golf – Killarney Golf & Fishing Club, Killorglin Road, ☎ 064 310 34, is recognised as one of the most beautiful in the world, with two 18-hole lakeside courses; Fee: €40. **Ross Golf Club**, Ross Road, ☎ 064 311 25, close to the centre of town, 9-hole course, attractive setting, fee €15.

Riding – Black Valley Equestrian, Black Valley, ☎ 064 371 33, easy riding or longer treks in a unique setting.

Fishing – O'Neill's Fishing Tackle Shop, 6 Plunkett Street, ☎ 064 319 70, is the place for local information and permits. Hire of equipment, fishing parties arranged.

SHOPPING

Music – The Irish Music Centre, College Street, sells CDs and cassettes of all the Irish groups and singers, plus a few instruments.

Crafts – Don't rush into the first "factory outlet" you see along the tourist trail. Most are simply shops selling the usual souvenirs at inflated prices. If something takes your fancy, don't be afraid to bargain.

Quills Woollen Market, High Street, belongs to the same firm as the one in Kenmare, but is more expensive. Good selection of woollens and tweeds. Blarney Woollen Mills, is a branch of the main shop in Blarney near Cork. It's more expensive, but also has better quality articles. **Crystals & Linen at Quills**, High Street, specialises in lace and linen and in Irish crystal. On the northern approach to the Gap of Dunloe, **Moriarty's** has a particularly good stock of tweed jackets, caps, skirts and rolls of cloth, as well as mohair travelling rugs and pullovers and the inevitable souvenirs.

DINGLE PENINSULA★★★

Co Kerry
197km tour – Allow 2 to 3 days
Michelin map 923 A-B-C / 11 and map page 307

Not to be missed
Kerry Museum and the Geraldine Tralee Show.
Brandon Bay and Brandon Mountain.
The road to Slea Head and the beehive huts.

And remember...
Make time to walk at least part of the Dingle Way.
Shopping is less expensive in Tralee than in Dingle.
Book accommodation well in advance for a stay in Dingle.

The contrast between the area around Killarney and the northernmost of the peninsulas of the Southwest is a striking one; no more exotic blooms and lush parklands, but a spectacular landscape of dramatic views and sheer cliffs. The violence of the coast in its turn is juxtaposed with the inland patchwork of tiny fields bounded by drystone walls. On the very edge of Europe, this is mythical Ireland, a heartland of the *gaeltacht*, a place where the living has been as hard as the harsh beauty of the landscape.

■ Tralee★

The town is a good base for exploring the area – allow half a day

At the head of its bay and backed by mountains, Kerry's county town is no picture postcard, but carries on with its own life without taking too much notice of the tourists passing through. On market day, the place fills up with cattle trucks and the pubs fill up with farmers grumbling about the terrible prices they've been getting. But as well as being a long-established market town, Tralee has attracted new activities, and the farmers might well find themselves sharing the bar with fresh-faced whizz-kids from some hi-tech enterprise set up only yesterday.

Native chieftains and foreign lords
Up to the end of the 12C and the Norman invasions, society in this part of the world was dominated by petty chieftains and organised in scattered rural communities. The powerful Anglo-Norman **Fitzgerald** family seized the northern part of Kerry and in 1216 founded the town of Tralee. The town was given a castle and protective walls and above all a harbour, through which passed commodities such as timber, fleeces, linen, wine, salt fish and meat. The place even had a travel agent who arranged pilgrimages to the shrine of St James in Santiago de Compostela. By the 16C the Fitzgeralds had become the Earls of Desmond, and, like many of the "Old English" in Ireland, had gone native. With Spanish and Papal help, the 15th Earl rebelled against Elizabeth I, but was defeated, executed and his head put on a spike in the Tower of London. The Desmond lands, including Tralee and its castle, were given to Sir Henry Denny, who had played a leading role in the massacre at Smerwick Bay in 1590. Three centuries of Denny rule here helped make Tralee a stronghold of Irish nationalism.

The town
Park the car near the tourist office and begin a walk around the town at the Ashe Memorial Hall at the end of Denny Street.
Tralee was largely destroyed in the 17C and there is not very much in the way of fine architecture, but the town and its park are nevertheless full of character. The place is particularly lively during **Panceltic Week** in early April, a time of Celtic

celebrations and events of various kinds, as well as during the **Rose of Tralee International Festival** in August. The latter event attracts participants and visitors from all over the world; all girls of Irish descent are eligible to win the title of "Rose of Tralee" provided she is

> *"...lovely and fair*
> *As the rose of the summer"*

The festival lasts several days, and as well as a beauty contest is the occasion for much merriment.

Kerry County Museum** or **Kerry, the Kingdom** (*March-December: 10am-6pm. Admission charge. Allow 1hr15min*) is one of Ireland's most fascinating museums. It consists of two distinct parts. The first has life-size tableaux evoking Irish history from the Stone Age onwards, with special attention paid to rebellion, Celtic culture, and great national events. Also called the **Geraldine Tralee Show****, the second part is a multi-media "medieval experience", in which visitors are carried through the streets of the Tralee of the Fitzgeralds, complete down to the authentic odours of the time.

Turn right on leaving the museum to the **Town Park**, appropriately ablaze with roses between June and September. On the far side of the park is **St John's Church**, with a tap dispensing holy water. Beyond the church is Castle Street, a left turn into which leads back to the centre of town.

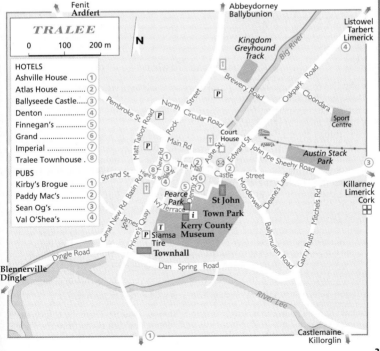

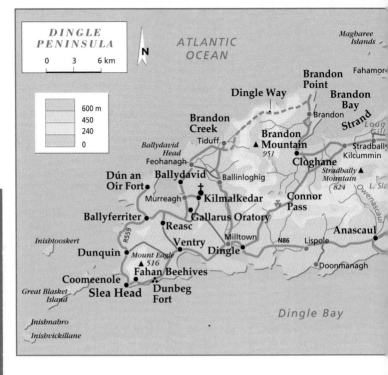

Around Tralee★

■ **Ardfert★** – *9km northwest of Tralee towards Ballyheige via the R551.*
This quiet little township once belonged to the bishops of Kerry and, with churches, cathedral and Franciscan friary, was far more important than Tralee. But the lack of a harbour meant eventual eclipse by its rival.

The ruins of the **cathedral** and **churches★** *(May-September: 9.30am-6pm. Admission charge. Heritage Site)* are very evocative of the spirit of medieval faith. A number of **tombs** remain from the time of the first monastery here, founded by St Brendan the Navigator in the 6C. The cathedral itself (13C) may have walls open to the sky but the elegance of its high lancet windows is still impressive. The statue in a niche in the northwest corner of the building is said to be of St Brendan. The Irish-Romanesque western doorway and decorated arch belong to an earlier 12C church.

Further along the same road is a car park giving access *(200m on foot. Free admission)* to the remains of **Ardfert Friary★**. In the middle of the fields, this Franciscan establishment was founded in the 13C and rebuilt in the 15C. The well-preserved cloister has a lot of charm, its tall windows echoing the graceful shapes of those in the cathedral. The stone tiles of the roof are a marvel of constructional ingenuity.

Leave Ardfert to the southwest towards Fenit and follow signs to Barrow.

Beyond the golf course in its lovely setting is **Barrow Beach★**. From the clifftop there is a view of the Slieve Mish Mountains and Mount Brandon rising from the Dingle Peninsula on the far side of Tralee Bay. To the right, the vast sandy beach stretches

Roots

The local enthusiasts investigating the fate of people who had emigrated from Tralee soon found that they had started more than they had bargained for. Attempting to trace the descendants of the passengers aboard "Jeanie Johnston", they burrowed in the archives, placed advertisements, and surfed the web... Their compilations grew into a kind of worldwide census of all the Irish who had ever emigrated from Ireland, England or Scotland. Tracing family roots has always been a favourite Irish sport, and all sorts of extraordinary stories and incidents have emerged: babies born on board, even the descendants of people who smuggled themselves on to the "Jeanie Johnston", have all been identified.

out for 8km to **Banna Strand★**, where some of the scenes in *Ryan's Daughter* were filmed in 1968. It was here too that Sir Roger Casement landed from a German submarine on Good Friday 1916 hoping to persuade the leaders of the Easter Rising of its hopelessness. Ill and exhausted, he was almost immediately recognised by a local farmer, denounced and arrested.

Return to Tralee via the little port of Fenit and along the north shore of Tralee Bay with superb views to the south. Go through Tralee and follow signs towards Dingle. The village of Blennerville is 2km from Tralee.

■ **Blennerville** – At the head of the bay, this village attracts crowds of visitors with its narrow-gauge steam railway, its marina, and its huge **windmill★** built in 1780. In 1830, Blennerville became one of the country's emigrant ports, and flourished to the extent that in 1846 it became worthwhile building a canal allowing ships to come upstream as far as Tralee. The **Blennerville Visitor Centre★** *(April-October: 10am-6pm. Admission charge)* evokes the story of emigration and gives all kinds of fascinating and often poignant details about life aboard an emigrant ship, through letters and other documents. One such boat, the *Jeanie Johnston*, which like her sister ships took human cargoes westward to Quebec and returned with Canadian timber, is being restored. The museum staff can provide many an anecdote about the fate of particular individuals in the epic of emigration. The mill is linked to the visitor centre. It has been superbly restored to working order, and from its upper storeys there is a fine **view** over the bay.

From Tralee to Dingle via Connor Pass★★
76km including the side-trip to Brandon Bay – take a picnic and sturdy footwear.

The N86 leaves Tralee and runs along the southern shore of Tralee Bay at the foot of the **Slieve Mish Mountains** which rise to more than 800m. At Camp *(15km from Tralee)*, follow signs to Dingle via Connor Pass. Beyond the turn to Castlegregory,

Dingle Peninsula

307

the road rises bit by bit to dominate **Stradbally Strand** and **Fermoyle Beach**, a seemingly endless stretch of sand backed by pastureland. The imposing outline of Brandon Mountain (951m) looms up in the distance over Brandon Bay.

Look out for the sign to Cloghane and Brandon, and turn right to a part of the peninsula little frequented by tourists.

■ **Brandon Bay**★★ – The first village along the way is **Cloghane**, a tiny place sited at the head of a sandy bay, with a beach that changes its appearance dramatically with the ebb and flow of the tides. Turn right about 3km beyond the village to **Cappagh beach**★, an unspoiled spot with good salmon fishing.

On the far side of Brandon village, the road winds along **Brandon Point**★★ at the foot of Brandon Mountain. The landscape is one of little stone-walled fields grazed by sheep. The car can be left at the end of the road, from where a footpath leads to the left along the top of impressive cliffs. There are good walks in the area, including the climb up **Brandon Mountain**★★ *(starting from Cloghane)*, the section of the **Dingle Way**★★ to the west between Brandon and Brandon Point, and around **Loch an Dúin**★★ to the south, among desolate and rock-strewn mountains *(full details at Cloghane)*.

Return the way you came and carry on towards Connor Pass.

■ **Connor Pass**★★ – The road climbs higher and higher above a deep and peaty valley. There are lakes, rivers, braided streams and waterfalls carving their way through the grey rock. Hugging the flank of the mountain, the road then reaches the pass, at 456m the highest in Ireland. From the car park there is a wonderful **panorama**★★ over both sides of the peninsula, grey and austere to the north, greener and gentler to the south. Then it's downhill all the way to Dingle *(8km away)*.

■ Dingle
Allow half a day

Dingle has a well-sheltered harbour at the head of a deep inlet. Its Gaelic name, *An Daingean*, means fortress, and refers to the role the town played in various rebellions. After the arrival of the Normans the town devoted itself to fishing and to trade, principally with Spain. A number of Spaniards settled here, but they were regarded with suspicion and were obliged to live outside the walls. Their presence is recalled by plaques above some of the doorways in Green Street. It is said that the dark hair and eyes of some of Dingle's present-day inhabitants can be traced back to these immigrants from the south.

The town

Dingle's interest is limited to its brightly-painted house fronts and the **quayside**, quite a spectacle when the fishing fleet comes in. Pubs are plentiful; in the past the place is supposed to have had more drinking premises than inhabitants, but nowadays there's a mere 50 or so for the population of about 1 500. Another spot to linger awhile is the **Café Liteartha**, a kind of café-cum-bookshop, a good place to read the papers and enjoy some conversation.

But Dingle's most celebrated attraction is **Fungie**. The famous dolphin has lived in the bay since 1983 when he was in the first flush of youth. He's not quite as frisky as he used to be, and possibly a little tired of people and their carryings-on. Rather than make his acquaintance in the course of a boat trip with a crowd of other tourists (*costing a rather steep €8*), it's better to swim out on your own (*leave Dingle towards Anascaul early in the morning or in the evening. Turn right at the Skellig Hotel towards the beach marked by a stone tower. Swim out making plenty of noise*).

Leave Dingle to the west on the R559 towards Ventry and Slea Head.

From Dingle to Brandon Creek via the coast★★★
Allow a day including stops

The sea is reached again at **Ventry Bay**, its beauty not enhanced by the presence of caravans near the beach.

Continue towards Slea Head and stop on the left at the **Celtic and Prehistoric Museum** (*April-October: 10am-6pm. Admission charge. 30min guided tour*) with fascinating collections including fossils, Bronze Age tools and implements and Celtic jewellery. The museum café is a good place to stop for a break.

The road dips inland, comes out on the coast again on the southern flank of Mount Eagle (516m), then passes Dunbeg Fort and Fahan.

■ **Fahan**★★ — *Admission charge.* The landscape here is stunningly beautiful, with black cliffs topped by bright green pastures and a patchwork of fields running up the mountainside. Here too is one of the most unusual archaeological sites in Ireland.

Dingle harbour

Dingle Peninsula

Fahan is the overall name for the clusters of more than 400 **drystone huts**, circular forts including **Dunbeg Fort**, and underground passageways. The beehive-shaped huts are called *clocháns* in Gaelic; their origins are mysterious but probably go back to the end of the pre-Christian period or to the very early days of Christianity. Given their diminutive size, it might be supposed that the people of that time were of small stature. They were certainly good organisers, as is proved by the existence here of dwellings with several rooms, well protected by cliffs and mountains, and within easy reach of all the resources of the sea. The whole complex of structures may well have been a kind of proto-town, or at the very least, an extensive community.

Further clusters of *clocháns* can be seen by the roadside all the way to the headland. They are all on private property, but to have a closer look at them, leave the car in one of the rudimentary lay-bys, and note where local landowners have put up signs indicating payment. One of the most interesting is **Caher Conor** (*admission charge*) a group consisting of five dwellings surrounded by a circular wall. Several more remains are visible from here, a short distance further on (*free admission, but ask for permission and be careful to close all gates*).

Before the road reaches Slea Head, there is a big bend and a ford across a stream coming down from a cleft in the mountain.

■ **Slea Head★★★** – Marked by a cross, like many other prominent points in the Irish landscape, the headland commands a grandiose **panorama**. The sheer cliffs are immensely impressive. Visible to the south in clear conditions are the heights of Valentia Island. To the west is the outline of the Blasket Islands, and to the north is the ravishing curve of **Coomeenole beach**, another Ryan's Daughter location. On the slopes there are more stone huts, some covered with earth and grass. On the left on the way to the beach are a number of abandoned houses; their gardens are still in use, the soil fertilised by a mixture of sand and seaweed, cultivated entirely by hand. Because of the steepness of the slope, the plough only made a belated appearance in this part of the world.

Beyond Coomeenole on the way to Dunquin (about 5km), the cliffs are lower and the landscape lusher. Keep well away from the edge of the road; the cliffs are unstable, and 20 years ago part of the carriageway fell into the sea.

Beehive huts at Fahan

C Legrand/MICHELIN

■ **Dunquin** – The one feature of the village that stands out is its **quay**, a narrow block of stone attached to the cliff, lapped by the deep green sea. It is from here that boats leave for the **Blasket Islands** *(April-September: boats to Great Blasket every 30min from 10am in fine weather; €13 return trip, €6.50 children. To go right round the islands on a 2-3hr trip, ☎ 066 91565 33, £16).*

This group of seven islands was formed by volcanic action and their summits are in effect the continuation of the mainland mountain range. Uninhabited since 1953, they have ruins and remains which testify to the harshness of the daily life of their former population. The final exodus of the inhabitants took place as a result of the death of a young man who could not be given medical attention in time to save his life. Nowadays the islands are a paradise for birds and rabbits. There are a few sheep too as well as occasional seals, and Great Blasket's beach is reckoned to be one of the finest in the west.

Appreciation of the islands can be enhanced by a visit to the **Blasket Islands Visitor Centre*** *(Easter-October: 10am-6pm. Admission charge. Heritage Site)*, despite the building's incongruous design. The museum has well-thought out displays on the islanders' everyday life, their emigration to America, and their extraordinary literary heritage, which includes *Twenty Years A'Growing* by Maurice O'Sullivan, *The Islandman*, by Tomás ÓCriomhthain, *Peig* by Peig Sayers (translated from the Gaelic), and *Western Island* by Robin Flower. These and other works are on sale in the small bookshop, as are cassettes and other material on and in Gaelic – Dunquin is a stronghold of the language.

Continue towards Ballyferriter past the strange outline of the hills known as the Three Sisters.

■ **Ballyferriter** – *Around the village are some of the most fascinating sights (clearly signposted) of the Dingle Peninsula.*

The small **Corca Dhuibhne Regional Museum** *(May-September: 10am-5.30pm; April and October: 10am-12pm / 2pm-4pm except weekends. Admission charge)* has displays on many aspects of the area, including its flora, geology, its customs and heritage.

About 5.5km north of the village, the promontory fortress of **Dún an Óir** makes a good destination for a walk along Smerwick Bay. In 1580, at the time of the Desmond Rebellion, it was the scene of a ferocious battle between the English and a mixed force of Irish and their Spanish and Italian allies. The foreign officers were spared by the English victors, but some 600 common soldiers were butchered, together with a few civilians for good measure.

Back in the village, follow the R559 eastwards, then in 2km turn right and follow signs to **Riasc monastery*** *(free admission)*. This 6C monastery is surrounded by a circular **wall**, and includes the remains of an **oratory** and of several **huts** which served as cells for the monks. A number of **crosses** have been discovered here, beautifully engraved with **Celtic motifs** of pre-Christian inspiration.

By the road between Ballyferriter and Ballydavid stands **Gallarus Oratory**** *(free admission)*, an extraordinary example of early Christian architecture. In the shape of an inverted boat, it is built of carefully corbelled stonework of considerable sophistication and strength, and has resisted the depredations of the weather for 1 200 years without the benefit of a single dab of mortar. There is a little **Visitor Centre** *(admission charge)* where a film is shown *(irregular times)* explaining the techniques of this kind of construction and describing some of the other sites in the area.

The sailor's cabbage

Sea-kale or crambe grows widely on Great Blasket. Since Roman times it has been preserved in salt or vinegar. Rich in Vitamin C, it helps protect against scurvy, something known to sailors long before medical men were able to trace the source of the disease. A supply was usually kept aboard ship. Great Blasket folk would collect the kale, dry it, then sell it to ships' captains on the mainland.

A holy traveller

Miracles started to happen almost as soon as Brendan was born. On taking up the monastic life, he founded the monastery at Ardfert, then built the oratory on the summit of Brandon Mountain. Then, perhaps tiring of these earth-bound exploits, he succumbed to the lure of the ocean, embarking with 14 other monks on a voyage to lands unknown. The legend has it that he reached America and returned safe and sound. Enthusiasts who attempted to repeat his journey in 1976 took 13 months to reach Newfoundland.

Continue along the R559 towards Ballydavid and look out for the sign on the right to **Kilmakedar Church**★, a Romanesque edifice of the 12C. It has a **doorway** with geometric carvings and depictions of heads, including the keystone which represents the monastery's founding saint. There is also a **sundial**, a stone engraved with the Latin alphabet, and an **Ogham stone**.

Tranquil little **Ballydavid** seems like a place at the end of the world, with its tiny quay, seaweed smells, soft sandy beach, and a matchless view over the water to the Three Sisters.

Follow signs to Brandon Creek.

■ **Brandon Creek** – Brendan the Navigator is said to have departed from this spot on the first ever transatlantic voyage, in the 6C. Given the austere surroundings of high cliffs and the dark and stormy waters, one can only marvel at his courage. A short distance away is the hamlet of Ballingloghig, the start of a path climbing up **Brandon Mountain**. The summit is crowned by the remains of an oratory, which on the nearest Sunday to St Brendan's saint's day (16 May) is the scene of a **pilgrimage**, as well as a mass on the last Sunday in June.

Return to Dingle by the direct route (signposted).

From Dingle to Tralee via Inch★
56km round trip

From Dingle take the N86 Tralee road along the south of the peninsula towards Anascaul. Before getting to Anascaul, turn right on to the R561 towards Inch and Castlemain.

An absolute must of a short detour before getting to Inch is **Anascaul**, with famous Dan Foley's, a pink and blue pub which features on every other postcard of the area.

■ **Inch**★ – The road continues through a short defile before emerging onto the coast opposite the Iveragh Peninsula. From here there is a view of a long and narrow **promontory**, a sandbar protruding at right angles into Dingle Bay and almost closing it off from Castlemaine Harbour. The Atlantic breakers constantly hurl themselves at it, much to the delight of surfers. Cars are allowed on to the beach, and in fact driving on to the hard sand is the only way to get round the picnickers clustered around the start of the beach. Driving to the far end of the promontory leaves any crowds far behind, and the sand dunes which seemed so insignificant from the road now appear enormous. Behind them is a vast marshy area teeming with birds.

From the beach get back on to the R561 towards Castlemaine, reaching the village of Aughils in 8km. Look out for a minor road to the left signposted "Scenic route to Camp".

■ **Scenic route to Camp**★★ – This 8km route is steep and narrow and caravans and camper-vans are not allowed.

The road penetrates into the heart of the **Slieve Mish Mountains**, with wonderful views back to the coast. Desolate slopes rise from the deep valley, populated solely by a few sheep. The road terminates at the village of Camp, at a bend near the bridge over the Finglass River.

Return to Tralee on the N86.

The indented coastline of the Dingle Peninsula

The Southwest

COMING AND GOING

By train – **_Tralee station_** is at the corner of John Joe Sheehy Road and Edward Street, ☎ 066 7123 522. Five trains daily to Cork (2hr30min), 3 Sunday; 4 trains daily to Dublin (4hr), 3 Sunday; 1 train daily except Sunday to Rosslare (5hr30min); 5 trains daily to Killarney (40min), 4 Sunday, and 3 daily to Galway.

By bus – Same location as station, ☎ 066 7123 566. Regular services to most towns. 5 buses daily (4 Sunday) to Dublin (6hr); 6 buses daily (4 Sunday) to Cork (2hr30min); 5 buses daily (4 Sunday) to Limerick (2hr15min); 5 buses daily (14 in summer, 6 Sunday) to Killarney; 5 buses daily (4 Sunday) to Galway; 4 buses daily (9 in summer), 2 Sunday (6 in summer) stop on the Ring Road at Dingle (1hr15min).

ADDRESS BOOK

Tourist information – **_Tourist Office_**, Ashe Hall (at the end of Denny Street), Tralee, ☎ 066 7121 288. Open daily; closed Sunday out of season. The staff here really put themselves out for visitors. There are maps, books and other material for sale, absolutely necessary for anyone who wants to do some serious walking. They are normally able to find accommodation even in the busiest periods (nominal charge). There is another tourist office in Strand Street, Dingle (on the quayside), ☎ 066 9151 188, open March-October.

Banks / Currency exchange – In Tralee there are banks and cash machines in Denny Street and Castle Street. In Dingle the two banks with cash machines are in Main Street.

Post office – Main Street in Tralee, and Main Street in Dingle.

Medical service – **_Tralee County General Hospital_** for emergencies, ☎ 066 7126 222, on the way out of town towards Killarney.

Internet – **_Cyberpost_**, Upper Castle Street, Tralee, ☎ 066 7122 541. **_Dingleweb_**, Main Street, Dingle, ☎ 066 9152 477.

Bicycle hire – In Tralee: **_Tralee Gas Supplies_**, High Street; **_O'Halloran_**, Boherbee: **_Jim Caball Himself Ltd_**, Staughtons Row.
In Dingle: **_The Mountain Man_**, Strand Street; **_Paddy's Rent-a-Bike_**, Dykegate Street.

WHERE TO STAY

The area gets very busy at weekends and in the summer and it makes sense to book accommodation in advance. At festival time and on race days (late August) all the B&Bs in Tralee are fully booked. When staying somewhere out of town on the coast or in the countryside it is cheaper to shop for picnic provisions in Tralee or Dingle rather than locally. Long distance walkers should bear in mind that there is little accommodation along the Dingle Way and that they should make their arrangements well in advance.

• Tralee
Under €13

🐌 **_Atlas House_**, corner of Castle Street and McCowen's Lane, ☎ 066 7120 722 – 180 beds in dormitories and smaller rooms. ᴄᴄ New, well-kept establishment right in the centre of town and only 5min from the bus and rail station. Price includes continental breakfast. Double rooms more expensive. Laundry facilities.

Finnegan's Hostel, 17 Denny Street, ☎ 066 7127 610 – 60 beds in dormitories and smaller rooms. Close to the park, this converted town house also has private rooms with their own facilities. Laundry facilities and bike hire.

Between €45-50

Denton, Oakpark Road, ☎ 066 7127 637 – 5rm ⁄ TV ᴄᴄ On the way out of town towards Listowel, this is a big modern house painted pink and white. Reduced rates for stays lasting more than one night. Generous and varied breakfast.

Ashville House, Ballyard, ☎ 066 7123 717 – 6rm ⁄ TV ᴄᴄ Leave the town centre along Prince's Quay and cross over the Dingle road. The Ballyard part of town is on higher ground beyond the bridge. As the road rises, the sign for Ashville House is on the left. Friendly reception. Open fire as soon as the weather starts to cool down. Special arrangements and rates for New Year.

Tralee Townhouse, High Street, ☎ 066 7181 111 – 20rm ⚐ ℘ TV CC The little hotel has a lift and is very well placed for going out in the evening. Excellent service, and the owner will do everything in his power to help his visitors plan their time.

Between €65-75
Imperial Hotel, Denny Street, ☎ 066 7127 755 – 30rm ⚐ ℘ TV ✕ CC Reasonably priced hotel, with friendly bar and comfortable rooms. Bang in the middle of town and a bit noisy in the mornings. Ask for a room with own facilities – it's no more expensive.

The Grand Hotel, Denny Street, ☎ 066 7121 499 – 40rm ⚐ ℘ TV ✕ CC A bit more expensive than the above establishment, but refurbished and very well-kept rooms. Bathrooms have a bathtub. Attractive bar.

More than €140
Ballyseeded Castle Hotel, on the Killarney road, ☎ 066 7125 799 – 12rm ⚐ ℘ TV ✕ CC A real Fitzgerald castle standing in its own extensive park. Imposing hallway, superb dining room, attractive lounges, dark panelled bar, rooms with varied décor. A place to live like a lord, or at least like one of the gentry.

• **Cloghane**
Under €13
Mount Brandon Hostel, ☎ 066 7138 299 – 16 beds and 1 room. On the Dingle Way, next to the village pub. Laundry facilities. Bicycle hire.

Between €40-45
Abhainn Mhór, ☎ 066 7138 211 – 4rm ⚐ On the road into the village, a comfortable bungalow close to the beaches and footpaths.

Benagh B&B, ☎ 066 7138 142 – 4 rooms ⚐ Between Cloghane and Brandon with a superb view of the bay. A source too of useful information on where to walk and on little-known

things to see in the area. Wonderful for nature lovers and people looking for peace and quiet.

• **Dingle**
Under €13
The Sleeping Giant, Green Street, ☎ 066 9152 666 – 8 beds in dormitories and 5 smaller rooms. Very central, halfway between the youth hostel and the B&Bs. The rooms are hardly any dearer than the dormitories. Friendly reception.

The Grapevine Hostel, Dykegate Lane, ☎ 066 9151 434 – 32 beds. Good location in a quiet street in the middle of town. Cheerful common room with an open fire.

Ballintaggart House, 2km out on the way towards Anascaul, ☎ 066 9152 207 – 130 beds in dormitories and 12 smaller rooms CC Camping possible. A huge hostel big enough to lose yourself in, but everything is well organised. Shuttle service to Dingle, laundry facilities, bike hire, big paved courtyards for eating out in. Friendly place to stay with a cosmopolitan atmosphere, a bit crowded in summer.

Between €30-45
Dillon's, Connor Pass Road, ☎ 066 9151 724 – 3rm ⚐ On the way out of town towards Connor Pass, the least expensive in this category, provided you choose the continental breakfast. Plain but well-kept.

O'Shea's, Connor Pass Road, ☎ 066 9151 368 – 3rm ⚐ On the same road as the above establishment but a bit closer to town. A good place to stay, very well-kept, with lovely views of the mountains.

Montbretia, Greenmount, ☎ 066 91523 276 – 4rm ⚐ CC On rising ground to the south of the town. Cheerful rooms with pale wood décor. Some of the rooms overlook the town and the bay. Very peaceful.

Quayside, The Tracks, ☎ 066 9152 276 – 4rm ⚐ TV By the fishing harbour, this stone-built house has several attractive rooms on the first floor overlooking the water. Reduced rates in low season.

Between €45-50

Devane's, Goat Street (above Main Street), ☎ 066 9151 193 – 6rm ⁿ⃞ TV⃞ Comfortable big pink house in the upper part of town.

Boland's, Goat Street, ☎ 066 9151 426 – 7rm ⁿ⃞ TV⃞ Next door to the above establishment, another well-kept B&B. Tea-making facilities in the rooms

😊 **The Lighthouse**, High Road, ☎ 066 9151 829 – 6rm ⁿ⃞ Main Street leads west past the hospital to this modern house overlooking the bay. Brightly decorated interior with lots of cheerful fabrics and attractive wooded furniture. Ask for one of the rooms with a view. Model hosts.

Between €65-100

😊 **Captain's House**, The Mall, ☎ 066 9151 079 – 8rm ⁿ⃞ 🖉 TV⃞ CC⃞ A classically elegant interior, a conservatory for tea-time, and an enchanting garden reached across a little bridge, everything to make guests feel content, plus amiable and efficient service.

😊 **Doyle's Townhouse**, John Street, ☎ 066 9151 174 – 8rm ⁿ⃞ 🖉 TV⃞ CC⃞ This house is unmistakable; the restaurant is red and white and the B&B next door sports the same colours. Spacious and pleasantly decorated rooms all with own facilities including bathtub. But a bit expensive nevertheless.

• **Around Dingle**

Under €13

Dunquin Youth Hostel, Dunquin, Ballyferriter, ☎ 066 9156 121 – 52 beds and family rooms. Close to the Blasket Islands Visitor Centre. Member of the Irish YHA.

Tigh an Phóist, Ballydavid, ☎ 066 9155 109 – 27 beds and 4rm Near the sea by Carraig church, this is an attractive and friendly establishment. Laundrette, bike hire, store.

Fuchsia Lodge, Anascaul, ☎ 066 9157 150 – 20 beds and 8rm CC⃞ 16km from Dingle and 1km beyond Anascaul on the Tralee road. Camping possible. Bicycle hire, laundrette, good kitchen, small store. Lifts to and from Tralee or Dingle can be arranged. A good place to stay in the middle of the countryside.

Between €35-40

😊 **Clare Nagle's B&B**, Dunquin, ☎ 066 9156 412 – 2rm Just short of the Blasket Islands Visitor Centre, behind the youth hostel. This plain but charming stone cottage is kept by a friendly weaver lady. The pair of tiny but utterly delightful and inexpensive rooms share a bathroom. Clare Nagle also lets out the 3-room house next door for between £125-400 per week according to the season.

😊 **Cois Farraige**, Feohnagh, Ballydavid, ☎ 066 9155 460 – 5rm ✗ Between Ballydavid and Brandon Creek, this is an archetypal Irish location with the sea just behind the house and desolate but totally unspoiled landscapes all around, plus a pub just 100m away. There are several shared bathrooms. Meals provided on request. Excellent breakfast. The landlady is a person of taste who fashions delightful objects, pictures and cards.

😊 **Red Cliff House**, Inch, Anascaul, ☎ 066 9157 136 – 5rm ⁿ⃞ ✗ CC⃞ A place straight out of a Daphne du Maurier novel: a lovely house built in red stone in the middle of a superb park high above the sea. Antique décor and furnishings. Excellent breakfast. Other meals by arrangement, vegetarian specialities. Baby-sitting can be arranged. Very good value.

Between €45-50

Ceann Trá Heights, Ventry, ☎ 066 9159 866 – 5rm ⁿ⃞ TV⃞ CC⃞ Follow signs beyond the post office in the village. Modern, well-kept and pleasant house with rooms overlooking Ventry Bay. Generous and varied breakfast.

Ard an Chaisleáin, Ventry, ☎ 066 9159 846 – 5rm ⁿ⃞ ✗ CC⃞ On a minor road leading off the R559 at the head of Ventry Bay. Large farmhouse overlooking the bay at the foot of a ruined Fitzgerald castle. Spacious rooms. Lavish meals provided on request, using farm ingredients.

Cois Corraigh, Emila, Ballyferriter, ☎ 066 9156 282 – 5rm ⁿ⃞ Just short of Ballyferriter, a traditional house without very much character, but well-kept.

😊 **Suanas**, Ballydavid, ☎ 066 9155 268 – 5rm ⁿ⃞ On the Ballydavid road beyond Murreagh, this house overlooks

Smerwick Bay in splendid isolation. Impeccable interior. Beach close at hand.

Ard na Carraige, Carrig, Ballydavid, ☎ 066 9155 295 – 4rm ⚓] Between Murreagh and Feohanagh some distance inland. If all else fails.

Begley's B&B, Brandon Creek, ☎ 066 9155 399 – 4rm ⚓] ✗ This little stone-built house is on the Dingle Way in wild and desolate surroundings at the foot of Brandon Mountain. Wonderful walks all around. Meals by arrangement. Reduced rates for longer stays.

An Bóthar Pub, Cuas (Brandon Creek), ☎ 066 9155 342 – 6rm ⚓] ✗ ⓒⓒ On its own out in the country, this pub has bathtubs in the bathrooms. Traditional music many evenings. Open fire in the bar. Magnificent walks nearby.

Between €60-75

Smerwick Harbour Hotel, Gallarus Cross, ☎ 066 9156 470 – 16rm ⚓] ⓟ ⓣⓥ ✗ ⓒⓒ Near Gallarus Oratory, this brand-new hotel is very comfortable. Bar with open fire. Traditional music every evening in summer.

EATING OUT

• **Tralee**

Under €13

Sean O'G's, Bridge Street. Straightforward pub with soups, salads, sandwiches and other snacks at lunchtime.

The Snackery, The Mall. Inexpensive traditional breakfasts and lunches, much in favour with local people.

ⓐ **The Greyhound Bar**, Pembroke Street. Traditional local pub, with rooms running deep into the interior plus cosy little corners. The usual pub food, including Irish stew, roast lamb, bacon and cabbage... Untouched by tourism.

The Grand Hotel, Denny Street. The bar of this traditional hotel has pastries for elevenses and inexpensive snacks at lunchtime.

Between €13-25

ⓐ **Finnegan's Cellar Restaurant**, Denny Street, ☎ 066 7181 400. This stone-walled cellar comes as a pleasant surprise. Straightforward, cheerful, décor, subtle lighting, an open fire and

check tablecloths all help create a bistro-like atmosphere. Good selection of international dishes.

Val O'Shea's, Lower Bridge Street, ☎ 066 7121 559. Another convivial pub. Excellent bar food at midday and a good restaurant upstairs for traditional and well-prepared dishes.

The Oyster Tavern, The Spa (7km towards Fenit), ☎ 066 7136 102. Has been serving its fishy specialities to great public acclaim for more than 20 years. Popular with local people and great atmosphere.

ⓐ **James Ashe's Pub** and **Cardy's**, Camp (16km from Tralee on the Dingle road), ☎ 066 7130 133. In the middle of the village, a really charming pub. Midday bar meal for less than £10. More sophisticated and expensive food in the evening. Good for a pint even if you're not eating.

• **Dingle**

Under €6

ⓐ **An Café Liteartha**, Dykegate Street. A Dingle institution. Morning and afternoon tea or coffee with scones. Generously filled sandwiches and good salads at lunchtime. The café is in the back room of a bookshop specialising in all things Gaelic. Newspapers to read and good conversation. A place to remember for those rainy days.

Around €13

Fenton Restaurant, Green Street, ☎ 066 9151 588. In an elegant and refined setting, this is one of the best places to eat in Dingle. Concentrate on the seafood dishes based on what has just been landed from the fishing fleet. Between €6.50-13 at lunchtime, €13-25 in the evening.

More than €20

Doyle's Seafood Bar, John Street, ☎ 066 9151 174. Model ships, panelling and maritime décor create a promising atmosphere, amply fulfilled by the subtle and refined seafood dishes. Superb ingredients, original presentation.

• **Around Dingle**

Under €6.50

Dunquin Pottery and Café, Dunquin. To the right of the road between Coomeenole Strand and Dunquin, this pottery with the upturned curragh outside is unmistakable. The shop's café has delicious creations such as Porter Cake made with Guinness, plus soups and sandwiches, all served on big wooden tables with magnificent views. Not to be missed, especially when the weather turns funny.

🍺 **Tigh an tSaorsaigh**, Ballyferriter, ☎ 066 9156 344. Easily one of the best pubs in the area (B&B as well). At midday or in the evening there are snacks and sandwiches or traditional meals to suit all budgets. A good place to drop anchor.

Between €6-13
Gorman's, Glaise Bheag, Ballydavid, ☎ 066 9155 162. Between Ballydavid and Feohanagh, a restaurant and B&B with fine views as well as good food. Snacks at all prices at lunchtime, more expensive after 6pm. Seafood especially good.

HAVING A DRINK

● **Tralee**
Kirby's Brogue, Rock Street. A Tralee institution. Music every evening in summer in a big room with stone walls and slate floor. Out of season, people sometimes bring their own instruments along for impromptu sessions. Great atmosphere.

Val O'Shea's, Lower Bridge Street. Cheerful atmosphere, and less touristy that the above establishment.

Paddy Mac's, The Mall. Inspired décor made from all sorts of odds and ends. Young, lively atmosphere.

Sean Óg's, Bridge Street. Convivial atmosphere around the enormous open fire. Music almost every evening.

● **Dingle**
Dick Mack's, Green Street. Opposite the church, this is another pub which features on postcards, not least because of its red and blue front. Successfully combining the professions of cobbler and barman, the landlord creates a cheerful atmosphere. Good music. Crowded in summer.

O'Flaherty's (or rather, since the pub sign is in Gaelic, **Ua Flaithbheartaigh**), Bridge Street. Rustic décor, all exposed

stonework and unfinished wood. Used to be the local of one of the country's best bodhrán champions. Excellent traditional music every evening in summer.

Droichead Beag, Main Street, on the corner with the road to Connor Pass. Very popular with local people, this pub reckons it has more live music than anywhere else. Certainly there's music and a good atmosphere every evening.

OTHER THINGS TO DO

Festivals – The **Panceltic Week** which takes place in Tralee in early April involves musicians from all parts of the Celtic world, Cornwall, Brittany, Scotland, Wales as well as Ireland. There are concerts, dance competitions, songs and so on. During the **Rose of Tralee International Festival**, in late August, the town organises many concerts, street events, family games in the park, and, of course, the election of lovely Rose herself.

Performances – **Siamsa Tíre**, National Folk Theatre, Ivy Terrace (near Ashe Hall), Tralee, ☎ 066 7123 055. Gaelic culture presented through songs, dance and mime in performances of high quality, perfectly accessible to non-Gaelic speakers. Daily at 8.30pm.

Water park – **Aquadrome**, on the Ballyard road (at the end of Prince's Street), Tralee. Pool with waves, slides, rapids, saunas, Turkish bath. Adults €7.50, children €5.

Greyhound racing – **Kingdom Greyhound Stadium**, Oakview, Tralee: racing Tuesday, Friday and Saturday, from 8pm. Admission €3.80.

Gaelic football – Kerry is one of the bastions of the sport, and the county has carried off the championship 31 times. Tralee has 4 teams, and there's an electric atmosphere on match evenings. Every Sunday at **Austin Stack Park**, John Joe Sheehy Road.

Walking – **Walk Information Centre**, 40 Ashe Street, Tralee, ☎ 066 7128 733. The best place for detailed information about all kinds of walking including guided treks.

Riding – El Rancho Riding Stables, Ballyard, Tralee, ☎ 066 7121 840. Horses by the hour or half day for rides in the mountains, or for several days on longer treks.

Kennedy Equine Centre, Carirwisheen, Tralee, ☎ 066 7126 453. At the foot of the mountains, same provision as the above establishment. **Dingle Horse Riding**, Ballinaboula, Dingle. ☎ 066 9152 018. These stables are on the mountain-side above Dingle. Apartments to rent as well.

Golf – Ballybunion Golf Club, ☎ 068 271 46. One of the world's ten most beautiful golf courses, 2 x 18 holes overlooking the sea. Fee: €38-70. **Tralee Golf Club**, West Barrow, ☎ 066 7136 379. Designed by Arnold Palmer, this 18-hole course is also among the world's finest, in a really superb setting. Fee: €55. **Dingle Golf Club**, Ballyferriter, ☎ 066 9156 255, 18-hole. Fee: €25.

Watersports – Dingle Sailing Club, The Marina, ☎ 066 9151 984. **Dingle Marina Diving Centre**, The Marina, ☎ 066 9152 422, underwater instruction for beginners and sea diving.

Fishing – Fishing from the beach goes on all along the shores of the peninsula. Between Tralee and Dingle there are good spots at Blennerville, Derrymore and Camp, and further away at Stradbally and Fermoyle. Cloghane has bass and sea trout. At the end of the peninsula, Smerwick Harbour and Ballyferriter have bass and various kinds of flat fish, as does Inch.

For deep-sea fishing, contact **John Young** at Brandon, ☎ 066 9138 264, or **Nicholas O'Connor**, Angler's Rest, Ventry, ☎ 066 9159 947.

The walls of Aran

THE WEST COAST

The dynamic and cosmopolitan gateway to the west, Limerick bestrides the Shannon, the longest, and most languorous of Ireland's rivers. Torn for centuries between English rule and Irish roots, the town paid a high price for its strategic location on the country's most important communication route. Today's Shannon may have lost its function as a great trading axis, but has revived thanks to water-borne tourism. It's a peaceful and relaxing experience to cruise its slowly-moving waters rich in bird life, past pretty villages, ruined monasteries, and hopeful figures waiting for that elusive catch.

Nearer the coast, the contrast is total. Here is a wild, rocky landscape, battered by winds coming straight off the ocean. The tall black cliffs of Moher form a proud rampart vainly attacked by the breakers at their feet, while the silent limestone terraces of the seemingly desolate Burren are a botanist's delight, their crevices teeming with gentian, wild geranium, burnet rose and an array of orchids. Offshore float what seem to be detached fragments of the mainland; these are the Arans and other islands, held together by a dense mesh of drystone walls, bulwarks built to foil wind and tide.

Remote, and largely unspoiled, the West is far from being serene or bucolic. It's a place where people sing and dance to spite the elements, where tales are told by smoky fires, where winds bend walkers double, where dwellings turn their backs to the sea, where men work a mean and stony soil.

LIMERICK★

County town of Co Limerick
Third city of the Republic – Pop 79 000

Not to be missed
King John's Castle.
The Hunt Museum.
Bunratty Folk Park.

And remember...
A good way of dividing up the day is to go to Bunratty in the morning,
eat at Durty Nelly's, explore Limerick city in the afternoon,
then finish off with an evening at Nancy Blake's.

A difficult history combined with economic stagnation left Limerick with an unattractive and crime-ridden image. But better times have now arrived, with new sources of employment and a thriving university. The city has enjoyed something of a cultural renaissance, with a music and drama scene of great vitality. The main part of the city is laid out on a grid, giving it something of the feeling of an American town, minus the skyscrapers. In architectural terms there is little that is outstanding, though there are plenty of red-brick terraces and Georgian doorways. But overall there is a good urban atmosphere, and Limerick has certainly not been swamped by tourist coaches like other places in this part of the world.

Angela's Ashes
Frank McCourt became a local celebrity when this novel of his was awarded the Pulitzer Prize in 1997. The book tells the story of the author's wretched childhood in the Limerick of the 1930s and 40s. The city's response to an influx of visitors anxious to see the places which feature in the novel has been to set up a trail, with accompanying interpretive material. McCourt's fans don't seem to be put off by all the changes that have taken place since the period in which he set his narrative.

A succession of sieges

The first to come here were the Vikings, who built a stronghold and used it as a base from which to plunder the surrounding countryside. They were eventually driven out by the Irish, but then came the Normans, who built no fewer than 400 castles in the area. Loyal to the English crown throughout the Middle Ages, Limerick was divided into distinct English and Irish towns, whose populations rarely mixed. But in the end the Irish revolted and took over the whole of the city. The Cromwellian force which later laid siege to the city took six months to overcome its defences. Forty years later another siege began, this time by King William III's army. The city's brave and resourceful commander, **Patrick Sarsfield**, resisted the assault and the royal force withdrew. But reinforcements arrived, and after more fighting, Sarsfield surrendered the city on terms that guaranteed the rights of the Catholic population and allowed the rebels to go unhindered into exile. But the English Parliament repudiated the agreement and anti-Catholic activity intensified. The consequence was extreme dissatisfaction with English rule, and in the 19C and 20C Limerick became a stronghold of nationalism and republicanism. In 1919 a general strike took place against British military rule, and for a while the town even had its own soviet, or workers' council.

The city
Allow half a day

Limerick is built on both banks of the Abbey River and the Shannon. The medieval **English Town** (or King's Island) was laid out around the castle and was defended by walls, while the **Irish Town** extended over the land to the south of the Abbey River.

From the Hunt Museum to King's Island** (B1)

Start this walk by enjoying the view along the Shannon to the castle from the little park behind the tourist office. Then follow signs to the castle and the Hunt Musuem, in Rutland Street.

The Georgian Custom House makes an elegant home for the **Hunt Museum**** (*10am-5pm; 2pm-5pm Sunday; closed Monday. Admission charge*), the finest museum in the Republic after the National Museum in Dublin. The collections were amassed by John Hunt, an historian specialising in Celtic culture. Among the multitude of objects from the Stone Age to the 20C are treasures such as a coin said to be one of Judas's thirty pieces of silver, the 9C bronze and enamel Antrim Cross, rare jewellery, and a superlative array of medieval crucifixes.

Go north along the Shannon and cross Mathew Bridge over the Abbey River to King's Island.

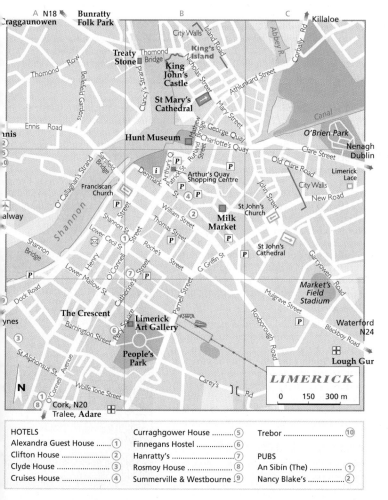

HOTELS	Curraghgower House .... ⑤	Trebor .... ⑩
Alexandra Guest House .... ①	Finnegans Hostel .... ⑥	
Clifton House .... ②	Hanratty's .... ⑦	PUBS
Clyde House .... ③	Rosmoy House .... ⑧	An Sibín (The) .... ①
Cruises House .... ④	Summerville & Westbourne .⑨	Nancy Blake's .... ②

King John

The royal John after whom Limerick's castle is named never visited the town as King, though he did come here when still uncrowned in 1197, at a time when Limerick had only just been taken by the Anglo-Normans. Prince John seems to have made little attempt to placate the Irish chieftains with whom he needed to keep on good terms in these early days of tentative colonisation. Greeted by a group of dignitaries on landing at Waterford, the prince's retinue amused themselves by tweaking their hosts' beards. Not surprisingly, the local lords continued to cause trouble for their far-off ruler once he became king, and John had to return more than once to try and put his Irish house in order. When the barons back home in England asserted their independence by forcing him to sign Magna Carta, the inept John found it even more difficult to restrain his Irish "vassals".

On the north bank of the river is the city's oldest quayside, together with the remains of the **Potato Market**.

Opposite rises the distinctive battlemented tower of **St Mary's Cathedral***, the city's oldest building, founded in 1168 after the Vikings had been driven away. From this period are the lovely **Romanesque doorway**, the nave, and part of the transepts. The remainder of the building (tower, choir, chapels and windows) dates from the 15C. The **choirstalls*** in black oak have remarkable carvings of grotesque people and fantastical animals depicting the struggle between good and evil.

Walk along the river towards the castle. By the pub, take the lane running along the walls and turn left.

King John's Castle** (*April-October: 9am-5.30pm. Admission charge*) is a formidable Norman stronghold, built from 1200 onwards on the site of the Viking settlement. The massive gateway with its two flanking towers has been spoiled by the construction of a modern entrance, but a tour of the great fortress is well worthwhile. Open to view are archaeological excavations which have revealed a number of 12C dwellings with their plank walls and stone doorways.

In the courtyard, reproductions of arms and implements give an idea of living conditions in the Middle Ages. Timber and osier (willow) scaffolding helps in an understanding of medieval construction methods, and there are explanations of the techniques of siege warfare; the most effective way of overcoming defensive walls was to burrow beneath them, fill the excavation with straw and set it alight, thereby causing them to collapse. A film is shown which traces the city's violent and unsettled history through the centuries.

On leaving the castle, turn left back towards the Shannon.

A little Gothic Revival tollhouse guards the approach to Thomond Bridge from King's Island. On the far side of the river is the **Treaty Stone** where the terms of surrender were agreed after the siege of 1691.

Go south along the riverbank for a superb **view** of the castle. Powerful currents disturb the surface of the tidal Shannon. At low tide this stretch of the river is much frequented by fishermen.

Cross the river by going over Sarsfield Bridge, carry on along Sarsfield Street, then turn right into Limerick's principal thoroughfare, O'Connell Street.

City centre

O'Connell Street (A2-B2) is lined with tall brick-built **Georgian houses**, which, finely detailed and well-proportioned, make an attractive townscape. At the **Crescent★** (A3), the road widens, a dignified setting for the **statue of Daniel O'Connell**.

A left turn into Barrington Street leads to the pleasant **People's Park** (B3), bounded on the west by Pery Square. Here, in the heart of the Georgian town, is the **Limerick City Art Gallery** (*10am-1pm / 2pm-6pm; closed weekends. Free admission*), with a collection of modern Irish paintings as well as frequent visiting exhibitions.

Return to the city centre along Mallow Street at the north corner of the park. Turn right into O'Connell Street towards the main shopping area.

On the left of O'Connell Street, **Arthur's Quay Shopping Centre** incorporates a number of craft shops. Running off to the left of the street are narrow little lanes making up an extensive and attractive traffic-free area between Cruises Street and Denmark Street. Denmark Street runs behind the church to the **Milk Market**, a picturesque scene on Fridays and Saturdays when the traders come to town.

South of Limerick★
74km round trip.

Adare

17km from Limerick. Leave the city on the N20 towards Tralee and Killarney, then turn off on the N21 to Adare. The Limerick-Tralee bus calls at Adare, which is a popular stop on coach tours.

Adare is the stuff of which picture postcards are made, largely because of its incongruous **thatched houses**. These were built in the mid-19C for his tenants by the local landowner, Lord Adare, seemingly with the idea of making the place look as rustically English as possible. Visible from the road on the way into the village are the lovely ruins of a 15C **Franciscan friary**. They stand in the park of the castle, now a golf course and hotel.

Limerick

King's Island

W Buss/HOA QUI

325

The village has more monastery remains, including those of a 13C **Trinitarian Abbey**, the church of which is still in use. It stands in Main Street, as do the ruins of a 14C **Augustinian priory**.

Go back 2km along the Limerick road and turn right to Croom, where a road running off to the left leads towards Monaster, Holycross and Lough Gur.

Lough Gur

Local people love to walk around this little **lake** tucked away in the hills. All around are archaeological remains including dolmens and stone circles. The **Interpretive Centre** *(mid-May-September. Admission charge. Video film)* explains the history of the area since Neolithic times.

Northwest of Limerick into County Clare⋆
47km to Ennis

This alternative to the main Limerick-Ennis road *(N18 – 37km)* takes in a range of sights from prehistoric times onwards.

■ **Bunratty** – *13km northwest of Limerick via the N18.* One of the most popular visitor attractions in the area, **Bunratty Castle & Folk Park**⋆⋆ *(September and June: 9.30am-5.30pm; July-August: 9am-6.30pm. Admission charge)* can get very busy, and the only way to avoid the crowds is to be here at opening time. The well-preserved 15C **castle** has furniture, fittings and tapestries of the time. "Medieval" banquets are held twice nightly, much to the delight of the tour groups being waited on by prettily costumed serving wenches.

The Folk Park is another matter altogether, a conscientious reconstruction of a **village** as it would have been at the start of the 20C. As well as a school and post office, there are **traditional shops** like an ironmonger's, complete with authentic-looking window displays and enamel advertisements. Further on there are a number of **vernacular dwellings**, a farm, a fisherman's cottage and a forge.

A walk around the village can be satisfactorily rounded off by dropping into the pub bearing the endearing name of **Durty Nelly's**.

Get back on to the N18, turn right on the R471 towards Sixmilebridge, then on to the R469 towards Quin. There are interesting sights on both sides of the road. Look out between Sixmilebridge and Quin for signs to Craggaunowen.

■ **Craggaunowen**⋆ – *Mid-March-October: 10am-6pm. Admission charge.* This is the site of a project involving the reconstruction of various types of building from Ireland's prehistoric past. There is one of the little artificial islands known as a **crannóg**, a **ringfort**, and a **tower house**. Perhaps the most fascinating object here is the replica of a boat of the type which St Brendan might have used in his pioneering crossing of the Atlantic, and which itself made the voyage in 1976.

A little further along the R469, follow the sign to **Knappogue Castle**, another Norman fortress *(free admission)*, which is also a venue for mock-medieval banquets.

■ **Quin** – This village has the ruins of a **Franciscan abbey** *(free admission)*, which has kept its **tower** as well as its lovely 15C **cloisters**. Some of the **tombs** are more than 400 years old.

■ **Ennis** – An important place for shopping, the little capital of County Clare hums with activity. Irish music enthusiasts make for Custy's Music Shop. The town is at its busiest on Saturday, market day.

Ennis's best known sight is its **Friary**⋆*(April-September: 9am-6.30pm. Admission charge. Heritage Site)*, right in the middle of town. Founded in the 13C, it has a superb **east window** as well as some fascinating **sculpture**; there is a figure of Christ with the instruments of the Passion (corner of nave and south transept), a Virgin and Child, a St Francis (between nave and choir), and the 15C **McMahon tomb**, carved with scenes from the Passion. The friary was one of the largest of its kind, with 350 monks and 600 pupils.

Making the most of Limerick

COMING AND GOING

By plane – **Shannon Airport** (off A2 on plan), ☎ 061 471 444, is 24km northwest of the town on the Galway road. Regular airport bus service from the bus and rail stations. €4.50. Daily flights to and from Dublin, London and major British cities, the USA and a number of European destinations.

By train – **Colbert Station**, Parnell Street (B3), ☎ 061 315 555, is five minutes' walk east of the city centre near People's Park. 8 to 10 trains daily to Dublin (2hr), 4 to 8 daily to Cork (90min), 2 daily to Rosslare, Tralee and Killarney.

By bus – **Colbert Station**, Parnell Street (B3). This is one of Ireland's most important coach stations, with several buses daily to Ennis, 7 to Galway and Tralee, 6 to Killarney and Sligo, 6 to Cork, and 8 to Rosslare.

GETTING AROUND

The city centre is compact and best explored on foot. Leave the car in one of the multi-storey car parks on the riverside or by the tourist office. On-street disc parking.

By car – Limerick's central location in the west means that it can get very congested, and allowance needs to be made for this when en route to airport or ferry. A minor compensation is that the grid layout of the streets means that it is easy to get your bearings again if you take a wrong turn somewhere.

By taxi – **Top Cabs**, ☎ 061 417 417.

Car hire – **Sixt Car Rentals**, Ennis Road (A1), ☎ 061 453 049.

ADDRESS BOOK

Tourist information – **Tourist Office**, Arthur's Quay Park (B2), ☎ 061 317 522. On the riverside at the end of O'Connell Street, this branch has a good range of useful material, especially for walkers.

Banks / Currency exchange – The main banks, all with cash machines, are in O'Connell Street. The **Anglo-Irish Bank (AIB)** has a bureau de change which opens on Sunday. The major hotels and gift shops mostly have exchange facilities.

Post office – The main post office is in Lower Cecil Street (A2). 9am-9pm, except Sunday.

Internet – Daily surfing at **Webster's Internet Café**, Thomas Street (B2): €1.90 per 15min 9am-9pm, 1pm-9pm Sunday.

Medical service – **Limerick Hospital** (off A3 on plan), ☎ 061 301 111.

WHERE TO STAY

• **Limerick**

Under €20

Summerville and Westbourne, Dock Road, ☎ 061 302 500 – 16 beds in dormitories and 139 smaller rooms. 🍴 CC Small, well-kept modern complex of several buildings with 113 single rooms and 26 doubles. Separate charge for breakfast, laundry and cooking facilities. Reduced weekly rates.

Finnegan's Hostel, 6 Pery Square, ☎ 061 310 308 – 50 beds in dormitories and 2 smaller rooms. Five minutes from the railway station, this big Georgian building overlooks People's Park. Inside it's showing its age, and the dormitories are rather lacking in facilities. The smaller rooms (same price) have better facilities.

Between €45-50

Clyde House, St Alphonsus Street, ☎ 061 314 727 – 40rm 🍴 TV CC 10 minutes on foot from the city centre, these spacious studios have a kitchen and bathroom, and a laundrette is available. Car park. Continental breakfast included. Reduced rates if staying longer than 3 days.

Curraghgower House, Ennis Road, ☎ 061 454 716 – 4rm ⌂ TV Two of the rooms share a bathroom and are less expensive. Traditional house and friendly reception.

Between €55-65
☺ **Rosmay House**, O'Connell Street, ☎ 061 314 556 – 4rm ⌂ TV CC At the end of a charming garden, a red door leads to attractively decorated rooms. Friendly welcome in this pretty red-brick house designed to make guests feel at home straightaway.

Cruises House, Denmark Street, ☎ 061 315 320 – 29rm ⌂ ℰ TV CC Right in the city centre, this is a comfortable small hotel. The best rooms are those on the same side as the church (larger and more comfortable than the ones on the same side as the pub). Supervised car park nearby. Ideal for anyone spending the evening in the Nancy Blake pub, only a step away.

Alexandra Guest House, O'Connell Street, ☎ 061 318 472 – 12rm ⌂ ℰ TV CC 10 minutes walk from the centre. The rooms sharing a bathroom are less expensive.

Clifton House, Ennis Road, ☎ 061 451 166 – 16rm ⌂ ℰ TV CC Set back from the road on rising ground on the way out of Limerick towards Ennis. This large and rather impersonal but very comfortable establishment is more like a hotel than a B&B. Car park.

More than €65
Hanratty's Hotel, 5 Glentworth Street, ☎ 061 410 999 – 22rm ⌂ ℰ TV CC Right in the centre not far from the station, this is a big yellow-painted building on 4 storeys (no lift). Comfortable, with spacious and well-kept rooms. Cars can be parked free overnight in the adjacent public car park.

• Bunratty
Between €45-50
Cecilia Lodge, Low Road (between the castle and Durty Nelly's), ☎ 061 369 766 – 8rm ⌂ TV CC An unusual establishment admirably run by nuns. Warm welcome, peace and quiet, efficient service.

• Ennis
Between €13-45
Clare Lodge Hostel, The Cornmarket, ☎ 065 293 70 – 50 beds in dormitories and 14 smaller rooms. restaurant CC Brand-new building on the main street in the town centre. Comfortable and well-kept. The double rooms are good value, but the dormitories are on the expensive side for what is offered. No cooking facilities, though there is a restaurant.

Between €45-50
☺ **Druimín**, Golf Links Road, ☎ 065 241 83 – 5rm ⌂ TV CC On the north side of town 2km from the centre on the way out towards Milton Malbay. Delightful garden, attractive rooms, and a warm family welcome. The owner is a golfer and can arrange accommodation and golfing packages. A great place to stay.

Banner House, Limerick Road, ☎ 065 227 51 – 9rm ⌂ ℰ TV CC In a road off to the right on the way into town, this is virtually a miniature hotel. Well-kept, modern and comfortable.

EATING OUT

• Limerick
Between €3.50-9
☺ **Chimes Restaurant**, The Belltable Arts Centre, O'Connell Street (A3), ☎ 061 319 866. In an artistically decorated basement opposite the County Council offices, good selection of snacks, quiches, lasagne, chicken, baked potatoes, etc. Daily papers provided. Good espresso.

☺ **Hunt Museum Restaurant**, Custom House, Rutland Street (B1), ☎ 061 312 662. On the ground floor of the museum, open 10am-5pm (2pm-5pm Sunday). Good range of salads and hot dishes.

Between €6-13
☺ **The Green Onion**, Old Town Hall, Rutland Street (B2), ☎ 061 400 710. Daring décor in red and blue. Variety of delicious dishes to suit all budgets. Wine is expensive, but is available by the glass. Closed Sunday.

Nestor's Café & Restaurant, 28 O'Connell Street (B2), ☎ 061 317 333. Pub on the ground floor with restaurant above. Attractive stone interior. Delicious bar food.

Texas Steak Out, 116 O'Connell Street (B2), ☎ 061 410 350. Décor to match the name and a wide choice of Tex-Mex, grills, and vegetarian.

Castle Lane Tavern, 4 Market Lane (B1), ☎ 061 360 788. In a lane running alongside the castle, pleasant pub with good carvery at lunchtime. The evening meal-cum-cabaret upstairs is very touristy.

More than €13

The Locke Bar & Restaurant, 3 George Quay (B1), ☎ 061 413 733. Big pub on the ground floor, restaurant above overlooking the Abbey River by St Mary's Church. Attractive outside seating beneath the trees in summer. Easy to park.

● **Bunratty**

Between €6-13

Durty Nelly's, In a prominent location at the foot of the castle, this might seem like the tourist-trap par excellence, but it has somehow kept its original décor and genuine atmosphere, with a succession of snug little low-ceilinged bars stretching away to the back of the building. The usual pub food at lunchtime, more expensive evening meals in the upper floor restaurant.

HAVING A DRINK

Nancy Blake's, Denmark Street. Old-fashioned pub opening out on to the street, easily the best place to have a drink in Limerick. Traditional music at least four nights a week. The back bar is called **The Outback** and is popular with the young in-crowd. In summer the courtyard is filled with tables and there's a great atmosphere.

The An Sibín, O'Connell Street. The basement bar of the Royal George Hotel is fitted out like a traditional country pub. Good atmosphere and music every evening, though touristy in summer.

OTHER THINGS TO DO

Greyhound racing – Market's Field Stadium, Mulgrave Street (C3), Monday and Thursday at 8pm, Saturday at 7.30pm.

SHOPPING

Woollens and tweed – Arthur's Quay Shopping Centre (B2) has several shops selling hand- or machine-made woollens as well as Irish designer-wear in linen, tweed or cotton.

Crafts – Mary Gleeson Pottery, Denmark Street (B2), has pretty pots as well as candles in every possible shade of blue. Hand-made greeting cards and pictures as well.

Bookshop – Celtic Book Shop, Rutland Street (B1) (near the Hunt Museum). Extensive range of Celtic books, cards and posters.

Music – Definitely not to be missed in Ennis is **Custy's Traditional Music Shop**, possibly the best place in the west for traditional music. Apart from superb individually made musical instruments, there is an original and varied selection of recordings of independent musicians not to be found anywhere else, perhaps not surprising, given that Co Clare is one of the great strongholds of traditional music.

THE SHANNON VALLEY
FROM LIMERICK TO ROSCOMMON
Co Clare, Co Tipperary, Co Offaly, Co Roscommon & Co Leitrim
Circular tour of around 260km – 2 days

Not to be missed
Clonfert Cathedral.
Clonmacnoise Monastery.
And remember...
If you are simply using this route as an alternative to the direct road
between Limerick and the north of the country, it may be enough
just to stop at Clonfert and Clonmacnoise.

Linked by the Grand Canal and Royal Canal to the east of the country and to the north by the Shannon-Erne Waterway, the Shannon was once a communication route of the first importance. Its flat and marshy banks are lined with reed-beds teeming with bird-life. Every now and then the river broadens out, forming numerous little lakes. Upstream from Limerick it flows through a pastoral landscape whose monotony is only broken by the ruins of monasteries sacked by Vikings and Normans.

Leave Limerick (see page 322) to the east on the N7 Dublin road, take the left fork 8km from the city centre and follow signs showing Castleconnell, O'Briensbridge and Lough Derg Drive.

The Shannon is reached at the well-manicured village of **Castleconnell**, set in leafy countryside and a real delight, with trees, flowers, trim houses and old-fashioned shops. The shady lane leading to the riverside makes an attractive short walk.

The route continues towards O'Briensbridge, where the Shannon is crossed, and carries on via the R463 towards Killaloe.

Lough Derg★
60km from Killaloe to Portumna –
The Lough Derg Drive runs right round the lake, a distance of 160km

Many places around Lough Derg are starting-points for boat trips or longer cruises on what is the largest *(40km long, 15km across)* of the Shannon lakes, its southern shores bordered by well-wooded hills.

■ **Killaloe** — *26km from Limerick.* This pretty village with its steeply sloping streets marks the start of Lough Derg. There is a marina here, but Killaloe is especially worth stopping in because of the 12C-13C **St Flannan's Cathedral**★, one of the finest in the area. Its **Romanesque doorway** has elaborately carved motifs which mix flowers and zigzag ornament. In addition, there is one of the great 12C **Kilfenora crosses** and, near the doorway, a **cross shaft** with ogham and Scandinavian runic inscriptions. Nearby stands a delightful **Romanesque oratory** dating from the early 12C; it has a steeply-sloping stone-tiled roof as well as carved capitals depicting animals. If there is time to spare, cross the lovely **stone bridge** to **Ballina** on the left bank of the lough. Killaloe and Ballina are more or less a single town, but the former is in Co Clare while the latter is in Co Tipperary. The **Lough Derg Drive** leads from Ballina to a viewpoint over the water.

On the way back, look out for the sign to **Leinstermen's Graves**, and park the car at the foot of a hill. The "graves of the men of Leinster" consist of a group of pre-historic stones on the 461m summit, from where there is a superb **panorama**★ over the lough and its hilly setting.

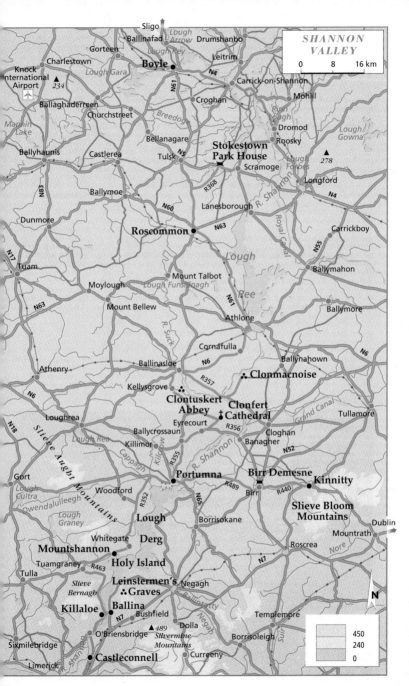

SHANNON VALLEY

0   8   16 km

Sligo
Ballinafad
Drumshanbo
Gorteen
Leitrim
Charlestown
Boyle
Lough Arrow
Lough Key
Carrick-on-Shannon
Knock International Airport
▲ 234
Croghan
Mohill
Lough Gara
N61
N4
Ballaghaderreen
Churchstreet
Breedog
Rinn Lough
Dromod
Roosky
Lough Gowna
Ballyhaunis
Castlerea
Bellanagare
Tulsk
N5
Stokestown Park House
Scramoge
Lough Forbes
▲ 278
Mannin Lake
Longford
N83
Ballymoe
R368
N60
Lanesborough
N4
Dunmore
Roscommon
N63
Carrickboy
N7
Tuam
Mount Talbot
Lough
N55
Ballymahon
Moylough
Lough Funshinagh
Ree
Mount Bellew
Athlone
Ballymore
N63
R. Suck
Cornafulla
Ballynahown
N6
Athenry
Ballinasloe
N6
R357
Clonmacnoise
N6
Kellysgrove
Clontuskert Abbey
Clonfert † Cathedral
Grand Canal
Tullamore
Loughrea
Eyrecourt
R356
Cloghan
N18
Ballycrossaun
R. Shannon
Banagher
N52
Slieve Aught Mountains
Lough Rea
Killimor
R355
Kilcorn
Gort
Cappagh
Portumna
Birr Demesne
Kinnitty
Lough Cultra
Woodford
R352
R489
Birr
R440
Owendalulleegh
Lough Graney
Lough
Derg
Borrisokane
Slieve Bloom Mountains
Dublin
Mountrath
Whitegate
N65
Roscrea
Nore
Mountshannon
Holy Island
Tuamgraney
R463
N7
Tulla
Slieve Bernagh
Leinstermen's Graves
Negagh
Ballyfinnaty
Killaloe
Ballina
Templemore
Bushfield
Negagh
Suir
Sixmilebridge
O'Briensbridge
Dolla
▲ 489
Silvermine Mountains
Borrisoleigh
N7
Castleconnell
Curreeny
Limerick
Shannon

N

450
240
0

331

The R463 runs north from Killaloe, giving fine views over the lake and the undulating countryside. The village of Tuamgraney is reached in 15km, and Mountshannon is 10km further on.

■ **Mountshannon** – With a southward prospect over the water, this village is a good place from which to savour the discreet charm of Lough Derg. The marina here, its cruisers and sailing boats moored among overhanging trees, is one of the most attractive on the lough. Mountshannon is also a popular angling centre.

■ **Holy Island**★ – *June-September. Admission charge. Access by boat from either Mountshannon or Tuamgraney.* Holy Island (*Inis Cealtra* "Burial Island" in Gaelic) is one of those many islands to which hermits retreated in order to live the contemplative life. The place still has something of the atmosphere of Early Christianity, of the time in the 7C when the monastery founded a century earlier had evolved into a famous centre of learning, attracting the erudite from all over Ireland. After being sacked by the Vikings, the monastery was re-founded by the great **Brian Ború**, a native of Killaloe, and the island became the focus of a pilgrimage. This well-attended and festive event was suppressed in the 19C by the church authorities because of its pagan overtones.

The extensive ruins include the remains of five **churches**, a monk's cell, a round tower, inscribed tombs, a holy fountain, and strange stones with hollow channels, possibly intended for pagan rites and then reused as receptacles for holy water.

Follow the R352 and then the R353 to Portumna, 29.5km further on.

■ **Portumna** – Located at the point where the Shannon flows into the northern end of Lough Derg, Portumna in Co Galway is an important staging-post for migratory birds and an excellent point from which to observe them.

Portumna Castle *(May-September: 10am-5pm; closed Mondays in May. Admission charge)* is a fine example of a 17C fortified manor house, with formal gardens and an imposing doorway. It was partly destroyed by fire in 1826, and since only the hall is open to the public, the interior is not of great interest.

Pleasure craft on the Shannon

C. Legrand/MICHELIN

To the south, by the remains of a **Cistercian priory**, several signposted **footpaths** make pleasant walks through the lakeside woodlands.

Leave Portumna to the east on the N65, then turn left on to the R489 towards Birr (25.5km).

Slieve Bloom Mountains
120km round trip

The Georgian town of **Birr** is the first place in Co Offaly after leaving Co Tipperary. It is a pleasant little place with fine houses lining its shady avenues. The main attraction of what was originally a British garrison town is the **Birr Demesne★** *(May-September: 9am-6pm; 9am-1pm / 2pm-5pm rest of year. Admission charge, less expensive out of season).* With its two rivers and an artificial lake, this vast estate is planted with more than 1 000 species of exotic trees and shrubs, the flora of China and the Himalayas being particularly well represented. There are formal gardens too, with the tallest box hedges (12m) in the world. The gardens were largely the creation of the 6th Earl of Rosse, whose descendants still live in the castle. This remarkable family has many achievements and inventions to its credit, including a suspension bridge and a pioneering giant telescope which is on display in the grounds. *Apart from a gallery celebrating their activities, the castle is not open to the public.*

To the east of Birr via the R440, the green summits of the Slieve Bloom Mountains rise to just over 500m. Carry on beyond the charming village of **Kinnitty** *(13km from Birr)* on the R440, and walk all or part of the long-distance footpath called **Slieve Bloom Way** which threads its way along the boggy slopes and conifer woods.

Go back to Portumna and follow the R335 northwards towards Ballinasloe. After 7km, turn right towards Ballycrossaun and Eyrecourt. At Eyrecourt take the R356 and fork almost immediately left towards Clonfert.

The monastery trail
Around 70km

The monasteries along this route include some of the area's most fascinating sights.

■ **Clonfert Cathedral★** — *Free admission.* Lost in the countryside in the middle of its overgrown graveyard, this 12C cathedral is a real jewel of medieval architecture and one of the most magical places in all Ireland. Its best-known feature is its wonderful **Romanesque doorway★★** topped by a triangular gable. Carved in sandstone, it represents "the apogee of the Irish Romanesque mason's love of ornamentation" (Peter Harbison), combining geometric designs with depictions of human faces and animals *(best seen in afternoon light).* Inside the building, on the arcade leading to the choir, are later, 15C **carvings** of angels and a siren.

Go back to the major junction and turn right towards Ballinasloe. At the next crossroads turn right again and continue for 5km.

In a field to the right of the road, opposite a pink-painted cottage, are the ruins of the 13C **Clontuskert Abbey**. Of a rebuilding carried out in the 15C, there remains a good part of the **cloisters**, a rose window, and a fascinating **western doorway** with carvings of four saints (St Michael, St John, St Catherine and St Augustine).

In Ballinasloe (very lively at the beginning of October at the time of the horse fair), follow signs towards Athlone, then turn right towards Clonmacnoise on the R357.

■ **Clonmacnoise★★** — *10am-6pm; 9am-7pm in summer. Admission charge. Heritage Site.* The kings of Connaught and Tara were buried at Clonmacnoise, the country's largest and richest monastic foundation, on an elevated site overlooking the winding Shannon. The monks chose this site because of its strategic location at the point where the river met the high road linking Dublin, Tara and the west of the country.

The first monastery was founded by **St Kieran**, a fine scholar who made it a centre of learning whose influence was widespread in spite of repeated raids by Irish, Vikings and Anglo-Normans. Most of the visible remains go back to the period between the 10C and 12C. The overall pattern of the monastic settlement can be discerned, with its eight **churches**, a **cathedral**, two **round towers** (the larger of which served as a refuge from raiders), a number of **tombs** and three **high crosses** (*the originals of the crosses and the finest tombs are on display in the Visitor Centre*). The early 10C **Cross of the Scriptures★★** is a kind of Biblical strip cartoon in high relief; the **South Cross** to the right is decorated with spirals and interlacing related to the ornamentation of similar crosses at Kells and on Iona, while the **North Cross**, the oldest of the three, dating from the 9C, consists only of a decorated shaft (the cross-legged figure on the side facing the river may represent the Celtic god Cernunnos).

After leaving Clonmacnoise, continue on the same road across an almost lunar landscape stretching away into the far distance. This is **Blackwater Bog**, part of the world's highest raised bog, being chewed away by giant machinery to fuel the electricity generating station at Shannonbridge.

At the next junction, take the turning towards Athlone, a small town with no major sights, and continue to Roscommon, 29km northwest.

Roscommon and around
Allow 1hr

Little Roscommon is the capital of the county of the same name, the centre of rich cattle and sheep country. The imposing ruins of its Norman **castle**, just outside the town, testify to the place's former importance. Its massive towers and high walls held off many an attacker before it was taken by Cromwell, who ordered it to be destroyed.

More evidence of past glories can be seen in the remains of the 13C **Dominican Friary**, which houses the tomb of its founder, the ruler Felim O'Connor.

The last hangwoman in Ireland
In the centre of Roscommon, the old county gaol harbours the memory of the sinister figure known as "Lady Betty". Sentenced to death for murder, Betty took advantage of the failure of the hangman to turn up by suggesting she be spared if she took over his duties. Once in post, she amused herself by drawing a portrait of each condemned person on the wall of the prison before stringing them up.

Leave Roscommon to the north towards Boyle. In about 9km, turn right on to the R368 towards Strokestown.

Strokestown Park House★
June-September: 12pm-5pm; closed Monday. Admission charge. This elegant 18C Palladian mansion was designed in the 1730s for the Mahon family, descendants of one of Cromwell's lieutenants. The interior has fine original **furniture**. Among the most fascinating rooms are the nursery, the schoolroom, and the great **kitchen**, incorporating a gallery allowing the housekeeper to supervise operations.

The stables have been adapted to house a **Famine Museum** of compelling interest. The well-documented and detailed displays trace the history of the house and estate and place the Great Famine in the context of its time, throwing into sharp relief the callous indifference of the British government to the disaster.

Follow signs to Carrick-on-Shannon. The capital of Co Leitrim is not particularly interesting in itself, but makes a good base for trips on the Shannon as well as for fishing holidays. Motorists heading north should follow signs to Boyle and Sligo.

COMING AND GOING

By car – The area is thinly populated, with only a few small towns, and there are no roads consistently following the course of the Shannon. But the river can be reached at a number of places, notably by driving east from Limerick towards Lough Derg. An alternative is to tour the lakes to the south of Sligo (*see page 394*).

By bus – It is almost impossible to explore the area by bus; nearly all the interesting sights are well away from main roads and bus routes. One way of getting to Clonmacnoise and Clonfert would be by bus to Ballinasloe and hiring a bicycle from there; 2 buses daily to Ballinasloe from Galway (1hr), 12 daily from Dublin.

By boat – The Shannon's 200km of navigable waterway can be explored aboard a cabin cruiser, but most of the river's course is unexciting and the riverbank villages with their identical landing stages are not enthralling either. Most visitors begin a river cruise at Killaloe or Carrick-on-Shannon at either end of the main navigation, and there are several marinas along the course of the river where facilities are available. Boats can be hired for the weekend or by the week. Reckon on €500 for a small 4-berth boat in low season, and €2550 for a 10-berth vessel in high season. **Emerald Star**, Carrick-on-Shannon, ☎ 078 202 34 or **Ireland Line Cruisers**, Killaloe, ☎ 061 376 364. The larger villages along the river all have boats for hire too.

On foot – Sections of the riverbank can be walked along signposted footpaths. The **Lough Derg Way** can be reached along the towpath from Limerick. Further upstream, the banks are marshy and less accessible, but there are some footpaths giving views over the various loughs – enquire at local tourist offices.

ADDRESS BOOK

Tourist information – *Killaloe Tourist Office*, ☎ 061 376 866. *Ireland West Tourism Office*, Galway, ☎ 091 630 81. *Shannon Development Tourism Group*, Shannon, ☎ 061 361 555.

Banks / Currency exchange – Banks and cash machines at Killaloe, Ballinasloe, Roscommon and Carrick-on-Shannon.

WHERE TO STAY

Between €45-50

Rivergrove, World's End, Castleconnell, Co Limerick, ☎ 061 377 107 – 4rm ⬛ TV CC This is an ideal place for fishermen or anyone looking for peace and quiet, with the trees and reedbeds of the Shannon at the bottom of the garden and attractive rooms with river views. It's handy for pubs and places to eat as well.

Radharc na Sionna, Logan's Bridge, Mountshannon, Co Clare, ☎ 061 927 406 – 2rm ⬛ TV CC Pretty stone cottage opposite the service station with a friendly landlady. Baby-sitting by arrangement.

The Sails Guesthouse, Mountshannon, Co Clare, ☎ 061 927 496 – 6rm ⬛ TV CC Opposite the above establishment, this lovely yellow-painted newly-built house has bright and cheerful big rooms.

Willmount House, Willmount, Portumna, Co Galway, ☎ 0509 411 14 – 4rm ⬛ CC One kilometre outside Portumna on the Ballinasloe road. Fine Georgian house of 1748 with spacious and completely refurbished rooms overlooking sheep-grazed fields. Excellent value.

The Rose Cottage, Creagh, Ballinasloe, Co Galway, ☎ 0905 453 02 – 3rm On the Dublin road out of Ballinasloe in the direction of Clonmacnoise, this two-hundred-year-old cottage looks like something out of Hansel and Gretel. Plain but well-kept rooms, open fires and warm welcome.

More than €50

Kincora Guesthouse, Church Street, Killaloe, Co Clare, ☎ 061 376 149 – 4rm ⬛ CC In the main street, this old house painted a buttercup-yellow is full of nooks and crannies and twisting staircases. Small but comfortable rooms. Own car park.

Glencarne House, Ardcane, Carrick-on-Shannon, Co Leitrim, ☎ 079 670 13 – 5rm 🍴 On the N4 between Carrick-on-Shannon and Boyle, this is a country gentleman's residence at the end of a long avenue. Very comfortable rooms (one smaller than the others). Dinner by arrangement, with generous portions, and prepared using exclusively organic produce.

EATING OUT

Between €6-13

Crotty's Pub, Killaloe, ☎ 061 376 965. Up the lane opposite the bridge, this traditional pub has a courtyard decorated with old enamel advertisements. Good atmosphere and satisfying food, served in generous helpings. Various international dishes plus the usual bar food. 12pm-3pm July-August; 5pm-10pm all year. Good evening music sessions in the pub opposite.

An Cupán Caife, Mountshannon, ☎ 061 927 275. Daily 10am-9pm. Easy to spot because of its thatched porch, this little restaurant has varied and straightforward dishes for all wallets, including soups, sandwiches and salads.

OTHER THINGS TO DO

Fishing – Lough Derg is a paradise for fishermen, with trout, perch and pike. Boats can be hired by the day or week all along the river. Reckon on €13 per hour, €38 per day and €165 per week. **Whelan's**, Killaloe, ☎ 061 376 159. **Gerald Madden**, Mountshannon, ☎ 061 921 615. **D & H Clarke Ltd**, Portumna, ☎ 0509 410 49.

SHOPPING

Weavers – Eugene and Anke Mc Kernan Handweavers, Tuamgraney, Co Clare, ☎ 061 921 527. Between Killaloe and Mountshannon, this weaving workshop has scarves, shawls and cardigans in soft and subtle colours.

THE BURREN ★★★
AND WEST CLARE
Co Clare – Michelin map 923 D-E / 8-9
Short trip (109km) along the coast starting from Ennis
Longer tour (220km) to include all main sights – allow 1 to 2 days

Not to be missed
The cliffs at Moher.
The Black Head Coast Road.
The Burren Way.
An evening set dancing at Kilfenora.

And remember...
Look out for the "Green Road" signposts; they indicate an ancient roadway
which is almost always worth exploring.
Look for somewhere to stay on the coast or in the countryside rather than in town.
Shops are few and far between; stock up on film and other necessities
and make sure you have enough cash for everyday purchases.

"The very bones of Ireland's landscape break through its skin on the Burren" (William Trevor), and this ancient limestone plateau is indeed a slightly sinister, but at the same time strangely compelling place. The centuries have denuded it of all vegetation, save for the flowers which flourish in the fissures known as grykes, which break up the otherwise implacable surface. In these indentations running parallel to one

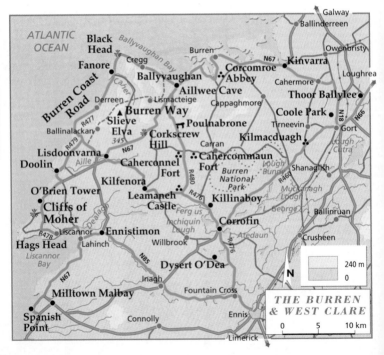

The west coast

338

another, there is an astonishing variety of plants, with Mediterranean and arctic-alpine species growing side by side, a botanist's delight and a source of wonder to anyone, especially in late Spring when many are in flower. Rain quickly percolates through the porous limestone, eroding the underground into caverns and secret rivers. The surface hollows or sinkholes sometimes fill with water and become temporary lakes called turloughs, a phenomenon unique to the Burren.

The living was never easy here, but there are many traces of early settlement, with an abundance of dolmens and ring forts as well as Early Christian monuments. Much later, Oliver Cromwell is supposed to have commented that the area had "not wood enough to hang a man, nor water enough to drown him, nor earth to bury him", an evidently suitable dumping ground for the native Irish driven off the lusher land east of the Shannon. For today's visitors, the Burren is one of the most fascinating parts of Ireland, for its austere geology, its glorious floral diversity, and its sense of a mythical and legendary past.

On foot in the Burren

The best local guide is the Ordnance Survey's 1:50 000 map n° 51 in the Discovery Series (also covers the Aran Islands). Walking is the best way to explore the Burren. The **Burren Way***** is a superb footpath running for 45km between Ballyvaughan in the northeast and Liscannor to the south of the Cliffs of Moher. It can easily be broken up into a series of one-day walks.

Something of the famous **Cliffs of Moher***** can be experienced by taking the path from Doolin to Hag's Head, but the most spectacular section is between **Ballyvaughan** and **Ballinalackan***** *(a little under 20km)*. The path starts from the coast road 1km from Ballyvaughan towards Black Head.

This section of the path can be reduced by a third *(making it a feasible day walk)* by taking the N67 from Ballyvaughan towards Lisdoonvarna, then turning right in 3km towards Lismacteige and continuing for as far as possible (this road is part of the Burren Way). Park the car and continue on foot among the stony hills. After the crossing of the **Caher Valley** comes a climb up the flank of **Slieve Elva** *(with a series of breathtaking views)*. The path goes round this mountain and continues southward to meet the coast road at Ballinalackan.

West Clare coast*

21km from Ennistimon to Doolin (not including the side-trip via Spanish Point)

The N85 runs northwest from Ennis *(see Limerick page 322)*, and 26km from the county town of Co Clare passes through **Ennistimon**, a peaceful little place well endowed with pubs which springs into picturesque life at the time of its horse fair.

Leave the town to the west towards the Cliffs of Moher. The popular but fairly ordinary resort of Lahinch is reached in 4km. From here there is an easy excursion southward to Milltown Malbay and Spanish Point.

■ **Spanish Point** — *30km there and back.* The coast here is flat, and its sandy beaches have not been enhanced by the building development which has taken place. Spanish Point is popular with surfers and golfers, but otherwise the only real attraction is for devotees of traditional music. The **Willie Clancy Summer School**, named after a famous piper from the area, and held in the little resort of **Milltown Malbay** takes place during the first week in July, with informal "classes" in the pubs tending to go on well into the night.

■ **The Cliffs of Moher***** — *Parking charge. The best effect of the light is in the afternoon. The cliff edge is extremely dangerous in rain or high winds.*
These black cliffs of alternating bands of mossy sandstone and schist, inhabited by countless seabirds, are one of Ireland's most spectacular natural sights. Eight kilometres in length, they rise to the giddy height of 200m above the surging sea. Not surprisingly, the cliffs draw crowds of sightseers, but humanity, however numerous,

is dwarfed by the grandeur of Nature. The well-designed car park is the starting point for a number of **footpaths★★★**, which lead away from the crowds to wild places, thronged with guillemots, puffins, fulmars, storm petrels and cormorants.

To the west, the clifftop path leading to **Hag's Head★★** has a stunning overall **view★★★** of the line of cliffs whose awesome scale makes their visitors look like swarms of ants.

To the north, the path runs past **O'Brien's Tower** (*Admission charge to the viewing platform, but the view is really no better than from the ground*) and continues for what is one of the most spectacular sections of the **Burren Way★★★**.

Go left out of the car park towards Lisdoonvarna on the R478. After about 5km turn left towards Doolin.

■ **Doolin★** – West Clare is of course famous as the heartland of **traditional Irish music**, and this little place on the Atlantic shore is perhaps where its pulse beats most strongly. Things began in the 1960s with the Russell brothers performing in O'Connor's pub, and nowadays a steady stream of musical pilgrims flows this way from far and wide, filling the handful of pubs and all available accommodation, especially in summer.

Other than its music, there's not a lot to be said about Doolin. The village is divided into two parts, and at the far end there is a **landing stage** for boats to the Aran Islands (*see page 350*). A **long-distance footpath** takes off southward along the coast from Fisherstreet at the lower end of the village (*near Castleview Guesthouse*). It eventually leads to the Cliffs of Moher after having passed **Doonagore Castle**, built in the 15C by the O'Briens (*whole day walk there and back, walking shoes or boots essential, path slippery in rain*).

On the way out of Doolin, turn left off the Lisdoonvarna road at the junction (R479). After about 6km, turn left on to the R477.

The Burren coast★★★
62km from Doolin to Kinvarra (including side-trips)

For anyone not intending to stay in the area, this route gives some idea of the spectacular **geology** responsible for the landscape of the Burren. By the coast, it consists of a succession of smooth, flat limestone terraces, scored with lengthy crevasses and interrupted by the occasional pebbly cove. Inland, the sparse grasslands among the limestone are grazed by sheep, cattle and donkeys. Rising over the road, **Slieve Elva** (345m) is entirely made up of heaped masses of rock. The limestone has taken on strange forms; there are chimneys, canyons, and pavements, divided by valleys and punctuated by great **boulders** like the playthings of a race of giants. In spring

The woman who fell to Earth
Legend has it that the Burren owes its origin to a lunar quarrel. One night, the giant and giantess who lived on the Moon got drunk, quarrelled, and began hurling stones at each other. The woman was frightened, and hid behind a mass of rocks. Her furious husband scooped her up, rocks and all, and hurled the lot earthwards. It was a hard landing, which she did not survive. The villagers of Fanore came out and buried her beneath an enormous heap of sand, the dunes one still sees today. As for the rocks which came with her, they formed the Burren.

and summer, wherever there is a scarce patch of soil, the area becomes a great rock garden, with **Mediterranean** and **arctic-alpine plants** flowering in glorious profusion side by side; there are blue gentians, burnet roses, wild geranium and orchids. Progress on foot through this stony and ankle-twisting landscape may not be easy, with endless detours and deviations, but it is well worth it for the feeling of penetrating an alien, mineralised landscape which could be the surface of some other planet.

The Cliffs of Moher

■ **Fanore** – The village with its dunes and **beach** of pale sand comes as something of a surprise in the middle of the stony landscape of the Burren. Unfortunately it has been overwhelmed by caravan parks and bungalows, and gets crowded and noisy in summer.

Just before crossing the river, turn right towards the **Caher Valley★★**. The road winds among the rocky terraces and penetrates some distance into the typical landscape of the Burren.

Go back the way you came and continue on the coast road to Black Head.

■ **Black Head★** – The rocky headland with its limestone cliffs is a viewpoint from which dolphins and seals can sometimes be spotted. Far below, a little **lighthouse** marks the southern limit of Galway Bay.

The more energetic will want to climb the hillside up to **Cathair Dhún Iorrais**, an Iron Age hillfort from which there is an exceptionally fine **panorama★★**.

Further away by the shore is **Gleninagh Castle** *(not open to the public)*, a tall stone tower dating from the 16C.

From the hamlet of Cregg, a **footpath** takes off into the hills between Mount Gleninagh and Mount Cappanawalla, reaching a splendid **viewpoint★★** overlooking the sea and Burren before linking up, to the south, with the Burren Way.

Continue along the coast road. To the right of the road is a strange little building known as the **Pinnacle Well**. It once served the community as a source of water, and the story has it that anyone who walked round it three times would be granted three wishes.

The landscape now becomes more leafy and the road is lined with trees on the approach to Ballyvaughan.

■ **Ballyvaughan** – Nestling at the head of its bay, this old harbour village is a welcome sight after so much bare rock, even though it is now largely given over to tourism. To the east, the edge of Galway Bay is dotted with pretty cottages and marked by deep inlets, while the country inland is a patchwork of little stone-walled fields.

Continue towards Galway, and turn right in 6.5km towards Corcomroe Abbey.

■ **Corcomroe Abbey★** – *Free admission.* **Carvings** of enigmatic heads, effigies and floral motifs are the most interesting feature of this ruined 12C Cistercian foundation. Among the latter are several identifiable medicinal species which were doubtless grown by the monks – the Cistercians had a good reputation as gardeners. The dedication of the abbey to St Mary of the Fertile Rock may be some sort of reference to this, or possibly to the contrast between the arid wastes of the Burren and its floristic richness.

Return to the main road and continue towards Galway for 13km as far as Kinvarra.

■ **Kinvarra★** – Tucked away at the head of Galway Bay, this charming little port stages a popular traditional music event called the Cuckoo Fleadh *(first weekend in May)*, while later in the year *(early August)* the old fishing boats known as **Galway Hookers** assemble in the harbour. When the tide goes out, the mud and seaweed of the harbour floor attract swarms of seabirds.

On the far side of the harbour rises the austere outline of **Dunguaire Castle★** *(May-September: 9.30am-5pm. Admission charge)*, a four-storey tower house built in 1520 by a descendant of the kings of Connaught. Some of the rooms have ceilings made of wickerwork. From the top of the building there is a superb **view★**. The castle is a venue for medieval banquets *(5.30pm and 8.45pm, around €40)*, where guests are served and entertained by costumed attendants, appropriate music is played in the background, and much quaffing, feasting and general revelry is the order of the evening.

The main road continues to Galway *(28km)*. However, for those who have time, there is much more of the strange world of the Burren to be explored. From Kinvarra, follow signs towards Gort through a vast and stony landscape.

Inland Burren★

37km from Kinvarra to Corrofin

■ **Thoor Ballylee**★ — *On the N66 between Gort (4km) and Loughrea (20km). April-September: 10am-6pm. Admission charge.* The 16C **tower house** contains many mementoes of WB Yeats, whose work was strongly influenced by the landscape all around:

> *"An acre of stony ground,*
> *Where the symbolic rose can break in flower..."*

> (from *My House, Meditations In Time Of Civil War*, 1923)

One reason for choosing this place in 1917 as his summer residence was its proximity to Coole Park, the country house of Lady Gregory with whom he had founded Dublin's Abbey Theatre.

From Gort, take the N18 north for 3km.

■ **Coole Park** — *April-September: 10am-5pm; closed Monday; summer: daily 9.30am-6.30pm. Admission charge to Visitor Centre. Free admission to park all year.* Lady Gregory's house is no more, but the park has pleasant walks and in the walled garden is the famous **autograph tree**, a great copper beech into which many of the country's literary greats carved their names, among them WB Yeats, George Bernard Shaw, JM Synge and Sean O'Casey.

Go back to Gort and take the R460 towards Corrofin. On the right in 6km are the ruins of Kilmacduagh.

■ **Kilmacduagh Monastery**★ — *Free admission.* Founded in the 7C, then sacked by the Vikings in the 9C and 10C, this monastic complex spreads over a surprisingly extensive area. It is recognisable far away by the slightly leaning 11C or 12C **round tower** with its conical cap. Other buildings, all in ruins, include a 13C **cathedral**, several 11C and 12C **churches**, and the **Glebe House**, a 15C two-storied structure which may have been the abbot's lodging.

The road continues towards Corrofin (17km), running past a little lake and across more limestone pavements.

The secret Burren★

About 60km – allow at least half a day.

■ **Corrofin** — This is an unpretentious little place frequented by fishermen making the most of the opportunities along the delightful **River Fergus** and the numerous loughs.

The old church in Corrofin also houses the **Clare Heritage Centre & Museum** *(10am-6pm; closed weekends November-Easter. Admission charge).* As well as evoking 19C daily life with displays of implements and other items to do with weaving, butter-making and other farming activities, the centre deals with the miseries experienced in the region at the time of the Famine, when more than 100 000 of its inhabitants took the path of emigration.

On the other side of the road, the **Genealogical Research Centre** (☎ 065 379 55) has extensive records used to help the descendants of these and other emigrants to trace their roots.

■ **Dysert O'Dea**★ — *Follow signs to the right 2km south of Corrofin on the R476 towards Ennis.* The site of an ancient hermitage, this was also the scene in 1318 of a great Irish victory over the Anglo-Normans, which delayed English control of the area for almost two hundred years.

A 15C **tower house** is now an **Archaeological Centre** *(May-September: 10am-6pm. Admission charge)* with a film on local history. *A visit to the tower is not essential – it is not very different from many others in the area, but the ruins should be explored. Leave the* car park by the dirt track, go through the gate on the right and along the edge of the field. Right in the middle of the field rises the superb **White Cross of Tola***, a 12C high cross which is a perfect example of Celtic art with **geometrical carving** showing Scandinavian influence. The lower part has **Biblical scenes** (Adam and Eve, Daniel in the Lions' Den, etc), while gracing the shaft are figures of **Christ** and a **bishop**. Towards the far side of the field, at the foot of an 11C **round tower** demolished by Cromwell's men, are the serene remains of an 11C **Romanesque church**. It has a magnificent **doorway**** with carvings of strange heads and columns with intricate interlace ornamentation.

Go back through Corrofin and take the R476 towards Kilfenora. The hamlet of Killinaboy is reached in 3km.

■ **Killinaboy** – The village's 11C or 12C ruined **church** once formed part of a nunnery. The gable over the main doorway has a **cross of Lorraine**, usually an indication of the presence of a fragment of the True Cross brought back from the Crusades. Above the south door is a flagrant example of a **sheela na gig**; such figures of a woman flaunting her sexuality are not uncommon in Ireland and may be of pagan origin, possibly as an evocation of fertility or as a warning against sexual desire.

About 5km further along the road to Kilfenora are the sparse remains of **Leamaneh Castle**, once a stronghold of the O'Briens, which was re-fortified in the 17C.

■ **Kilfenora*** – *10.5km from Killinaboy.* This village has its own ceilidh band and twice a week there are evening sessions of **set dancing**** *(see page 62).* There are other attractions too.

The **Burren Display Centre*** *(March-October: 10am-5pm, 6pm in summer. Admission charge)* explains the geology and natural history of the Burren by means of a film and models and there are displays on the history of the area's monuments.

The village has a **cathedral*** dating from the 12C. Partly ruined, it has kept a number of features such as a **bishop's head** above the doorway, a delicately carved **window**, and superb **captials** with figurative carvings. On each side of the nave is a 14C **tombstone** with the effigy of a bishop in high relief. A third tombstone with the incised figure of a bishop dates from the same period. But the most interesting objects here are the three high crosses outside, among them the famous **Doorty's Cross****, which unfortunately is very eroded. On the eastern, best preserved face, the figure of a bishop can be made out above two other personages, while on the west face, almost indistinguishable, is a representation of Christ. A second, very plain cross without a circle, stands in the northern part of the enclosure. The third cross can be found by following the path leading from the cathedral into a field. On its eastern face it has figures of Christ and an animal, as well as interlacing.

Take the N476 northwest out of Kilfenora to Lisdoonvarna (8km).

■ **Lisdoonvarna** – This small town is a spa which owes its fame to its **sulphur springs** and to its celebrated matchmaking festival. The springs attract health-seekers, the festival brings in hordes of spruced-up farmer's boys (often quite elderly boys) in search of a spouse.

Lisdoonvarna's evil-tasting waters are supposed to help in the treatment of rheumatism and thyroid problems. They can be tried by the glass or by taking a dip *(Spa Wells Centre, ☎ 065 740 23, June-October. Charge).*

The September **Matchmaking Festival** is a more complicated affair. It has a serious history; farmers living deep in the countryside had little opportunity to meet suitable sweethearts, and professional matchmakers were employed to rectify the deficiency and bring potential partners together. Nowadays the festival is less concerned with prolonging the family line and more of an excuse for a prolonged booze-up, probably best avoided by sensitive souls and those who recoil from crowds.

Take the N67 northwest out of Lisdoonvarna towards Ballyvaughan (16km).

In about 8km, the road begins the descent of **Corkscrew Hill****, from where there is a magnificent panorama of the terraced hills.

Just short of Ballyvaughan, take an almost 180° turn to the right on to the R480, continue for 1.5km and park the car on the left.

■ **Aillwee Cave*** – *March-October: 10am-5.30pm except weekends; July-August: daily 10am-6.30pm. Admission charge.* The only cave in the Burren open to the public forms part of a complex underground system extending beneath the whole of the area. The bones of a brown bear were found in this 1km-deep cavern, and much is made of this discovery.

The Swiss cheese effect

The calcareous rock of the Burren lends itself to erosion and the formation of ravines. Rivers follow a capricious course, appearing and disappearing in an apparently arbitrary manner. Beneath the surface they have worn out a vast network of caves and underground chambers. On the surface, water gathers in depressions called sinkholes, and normally drains away swiftly. But in certain conditions it remains awhile, forming temporary lakes or "turloughs", which disappear in their turn. The underground world of the Burren remains largely secret; the caves are closed to the public because of the risks involved when underground water levels change without warning.

Continue south along the R480. To either side are ring forts and burial mounds. Look out on the left in about 6km for the sign to Poulnabrone.

■ **Poulnabrone**** – *Light effects and general atmosphere are best in the early morning or late evening.* Amid a splendid stark and rocky landscape, this grand **dolmen** is a fine example of a Megalithic tomb, with a capacity of more than twenty corpses and their accompanying burial offerings of pottery and jewellery.

The stony wastes of the Burren

The Burren

One kilometre further on, to the rear of a house on the right, is **Caherconnell Fort**

Turn left about 1.5km beyond the dolmen towards Carran (5.5km)

To the east of the village of Carran is the **Burren Perfumery** (*9am-7pm. Free admission*) where perfumes are distilled based on the richly varied local flora.

Go south out of Carran and at the junction fork left on the minor road towards Killinaboy. Look out in about 2km for the sign to Cahercommaun.

■ **Cahercommaun Fort**★★ (Cathair Chomáin) – Perched on the edge of a cliff, this fort with its three lines of defences is one of the finest in Ireland. It seems to have been built during the Iron Age and occupied right up to the 9C. Roman items have been found here, indicating interesting trading links between its cattle-raising inhabitants and the wider world (*20min on foot, but check that the farmer permits access*).

Making the most of the Burren

COMING AND GOING

By bus – The Burren is not well served by buses, but there are some services from Limerick, Ennis and Galway. From Ennis bus station, Station Road, ☎ 065 241 77, **West Clare Line** has daily services to Ennistimon, Lahinch, Milltown Malbay, Lisdoonvarna and Doolin. Two buses daily (except Sunday) leave Ennis post office to Doolin and there is a single bus daily (except Sunday) to Corrofin. From Galway, ☎ 091 562 000, there are daily services to Kinvarra, Ballyvaughan, Lisdoonvarna and Doolin. The **West Clare Shuttle**, ☎ 091 767 801 links Galway and Doolin via Fanore or Lisdoonvarna (telephone in advance).
There is a daily service from both Cork and Dublin to Doolin.

GETTING AROUND

Bicycle hire – **Burke's Garage** at Lisdoonvarna. **Doolin Bike Store**, at Doolin. Reckon on €7.60 per day.

ADDRESS BOOK

Tourist information – The best places for local information are the **Tourist Office** at the Cliffs of Moher and the **Burren Display Centre** at Kilfenora.

Banks / Currency exchange – There is a bank and cash machine in Parliament Street at Ennistimon. Money can be changed at the Cliffs of Moher Tourist Office, the post office at Doolin and the Burren Display Centre at Kilfenora.

• By the sea

Under €13

The Bridge Hostel, Fanore, ☎ 065 707 6134 – 16 beds and 4 rm ✕ Right at the beginning of the Caher Valley, this very pleasant hostel is run by a friendly couple and is ideal for walkers. Washing machine, additional charge for breakfast, evening meal by arrangement.

The Doolin Hostel, Doolin, ☎ 065 707 4006 – 130 beds ✖ CC In the lower part of the village before the bridge, this is a well-managed hostel with laundrette, bicycle hire, safe, bureau de change and even a little shop. Some private rooms.

The Aille River Hostel, Doolin, ☎ 065 707 4260 – 34 beds in dormitories and double rooms. On the riverbank halfway between the two parts of the village, this cheerful establishment has inexpensive double rooms. Linen supplied free, payment for drying clothes.

Flanagan's Village Hostel, Doolin, ☎ 065 707 4564 – 24 beds and 4 rooms. In the upper part of the village just before the church, this is a modern bungalow with inexpensive double rooms. Laundry facilities, general shop nearby.

Between €30-45

Atlantic View, Liscannor (Cliffs of Moher), ☎ 065 708 1214 – 4rm Four kilometres beyond Liscannor and 1.5km before the Cliffs of Moher, this pretty and well-kept house is set back from the road. The two rooms which share a bathroom are less expensive.

Puffin Cottage, Boherboy, Doolin, ☎ 065 707 4912 – 4rm About 2km from Doolin on the R479 towards Lisdoonvarna. Delightful little house with cheerful decoration kept by a young couple keen on DIY. Two of the rooms share a bathroom. Superb sea views.

McGanns Cottage, Boherboy, Doolin, ☎ 065 707 4790 – 3rm Almost opposite the above establishment, this is a nicely decorated modern cottage.

The Blue Dolphin, Doolin, ☎ 065 707 4692 – 4rm In a road running at right angles off the main road by the Doolin Bike Store. The landlord is one of the most skilled makers of "bodhráns" in Ireland, and can tell his guests anything they want to know about traditional music. Friendly welcome and not expensive. The room with bathroom on the landing is marginally less expensive.

Doolin Cottage, Doolin, ☎ 065 707 4762 – 4rm Next door to the previous establishment and same rates, making it a good alternative when the Blue Dolphin is full.

Monica's B&B, Fanore, ☎ 065 707 6141 – 4rm By Fanore beach at the foot of the hill, this grey and white house is very well-kept.

Ard na Hona, Munnia, Burren, ☎ 065 707 8220 – 5rm Halfway between Ballyvaughan and Kinvarra, this large house stands on the hillside overlooking Galway Bay. Superb views, charming reception and attractive decor.

Between €45-50

Moher Lodge, Liscannor, ☎ 065 708 1269 – 5rm Three kilometres beyond Liscannor towards the Cliffs of Moher, this large farmhouse stands in a commanding position overlooking the road. Comfortable rooms.

Doonagore Farmhouse, Doonagore, Doolin, ☎ 065 707 4170 – 5rm About 4km beyond Moher towards Doolin. Friendly reception in this big farmhouse very close to the sea.

Trildoon House, Doolin, ☎ 065 707 4870 – 7rm On the road between Moher and Doolin with lovely views over the sea and the village. Comfortable, quiet house and friendly landlady.

Castle View Farmhouse, Doolin, ☎ 065 707 4289 – 3rm CC A location to dream about, in the middle of the countryside right by Doonagore Castle. Ideal for walkers wanting to do the clifftop path.

Riverfield House, Doolin, ☎ 065 707 4113 – 5rm CC At the top end of the village, 5min walk from the pubs, well-kept and comfortable and with a pretty garden. Less expensive out of season.

Burren Way Cottage, Doolin, ☎ 065 707 4516 – 3rm At the top end of the village between the pubs and the

Making the most of the Burren

church, pretty little red and white house with lots of flowers, tastefully decorated and run by a charming landlady full of ideas about how her guests could spend their time. She's happy to let you sit by the peat fire and browse her books to the sound of classical recordings.

Between €50-65

Cullinan's Guesthouse, Doolin, ☎ 065 707 4183 – 6rm ⓜ ℘ ✗ cc In the middle of the village. Cheerful and comfortable. The welcome couldn't be friendlier and as a bonus it is the best place to eat in Doolin (see "Where to eat").

Ballyvaughan Lodge, Ballyvaughan, ☎ 065 707 7292 – 8rm ⓜ ℘ TV cc In the middle of Ballyvaughan, this is a lovely house with every comfort. Pine and patchwork is the theme of the décor. Generous and varied breakfast. Efficient service. Reduced rates out of season.

Between €100-130

Aran View House, Doolin, ☎ 065 707 4420 – 19rm ⓜ ℘ TV ✗ cc Beyond the church on the way out of Doolin, this substantial residence of 1738 has been converted into a comfortable hotel. Views of the sea and the Aran Islands. Special rates for stays of 2, 3 or 7 days.

Hyland's Hotel, Ballyvaughan, ☎ 065 707 7037 – 30rm ⓜ ℘ TV ✗ cc Comfortable, cheerful hotel in the village. Lounge and bar with open fire.

• **Inland**

Under €13

Corrofin Hostel, Corrofin, ☎ 065 683 7683 – 30 beds and 3rm Pleasant place to stay in the middle of the village. Laundry facilities and camping possible. *Clare's Rock*, Carran, ☎ 065 708 9129 – 40 beds. Recently built hostel in wild countryside, ideal for walkers and cyclists. Comfortable, good facilities including bike hire, laundry, meals by arrangement. Children welcome. Rooms can be booked in advance.

Between €45-50

Burren House, Killinaboy, Corrofin, ☎ 065 683 7143 – 3rm ⓜ ✗ Bright, well-kept accommodation by the side of the road between Corrofin and Kilfenora. Evening meal by arrangement.

Lakefield Lodge, Corrofin, ☎ 065 683 7675 – 4rm ⓜ ✗ On the way out of Corrofin towards Ennis, much frequented by fishermen (the landlord is a keen one himself). Evening meal by arrangement.

Burren Farmhouse, Ballybreen West, Kilfenora, ☎ 065 707 1363 – 3rm ✗ Two kilometres outside the village on the Ennistimon road. Traditional, very plain farmhouse. Mary Doorty is a village character and a set dancing enthusiast. If you're lucky she might even take you dancing. Wonderful home-made bread and copious meals (by arrangement).

Kilcarragh B&B, Kilcarragh, Kilfenora, ☎ 065 708 8042 – 4rm ⓜ Well-kept establishment on the Ennistimon road. Fine if there's nowhere else.

Grovemount House, Lahinch Road, Ennistimon, ☎ 065 707 1431 – 6rm ⓜ ℘ TV cc One kilometre outside the village on the N67 towards the Cliffs of Moher. The most expensive establishment in this category, but very high level of comfort and efficient and friendly service. Much lower rates out of season.

Hillbrook Farm, Lahinch Road, Ennistimon, ☎ 065 707 1164 – 4rm ⓜ cc About 1.5km from the village, a bit further out than the previous establishment. Very well-kept, every comfort, set back from the main road.

Greenlawn Lodge, Galway Road, Lisdoonvarna, ☎ 065 707 4861 – 4rm ⓜ TV cc Large and attractive house in a quiet setting on the way out of Lisdoonvarna.

Ballinsheen House, Galway Road, Lisdoonvarna, ☎ 065 707 4806 – 5rm ⓜ TV cc This lovely yellow house is on rising ground almost opposite the previous establishment. Friendly reception, pleasant décor, good value.

Benrue Farmhouse, Lisdoonvarna, ☎ 065 707 4059 – 6rm ⓜ ✗ Turn right 4km north of Lisdoonvarna on the N67 and follow signs to this isolated farmhouse 2km further on. Huge breakfast, evening meal by arrangement, tea and scones on arrival.

Lismacteige, Ballyvaughan, ☎ 065 707 7040 – 4rm ⓜ From Ballyvaughan head towards Lisdoonvarna, and turn right after 1.5km on the Green Road (clearly signposted). Modern cottage to the rear of a thatched house lost among the hills along the Burren Way. Both houses are run by an elderly lady who adores receiving guests. Very quiet.

Merryjig Farmhouse, Lismacteige, ☎ 065 707 7120 – 4rm 🛏 ✖ Next door to the previous establishment, this house has less character, but has wonderful views over the hills and guests are made to feel very welcome. Delicious evening meal by arrangement. Ideal starting point for the most interesting part of the Burren Way.

WHERE TO EAT

Between €6-13
McDermott's Pub, Doolin. Traditional bar food, all the usual Irish fare plus some more exotic dishes and vegetarian meals. Food served until 9.30pm.
McGann's Pub, Doolin. Opposite the previous establishment, same opening times, classic cuisine.
Roadside Tavern, Lisdoonvarna. ☎ 065 707 4432. Everything is great about this pub with its highly varied décor: the atmosphere, the landlord who plays the bodhrán, the home-smoked salmon... Sandwiches, salads and desserts for under €13.
Vaughan's Bar, Kilfenora. Pub serving generous portions of high-quality food. Traditional dishes for around €6.50.
Monk's Bar, Ballyvaughan, ☎ 065 707 7059. On the quayside, this place is much sought after for its fresh and well-prepared seafood. Between €6.50-13, more in the evening.
The Tea Rooms, Ballyvaughan, quayside cottage with a garden. Salads, soups, sandwiches and delicious cakes. Open 11am-6pm.
Between €13-25
Bayview Restaurant, Church Street, Lahinch, ☎ 065 708 1040. Near the church, good range of straightforward and inexpensive dishes. Lunch around €7.50, dinner between €13.50-18.
Barrtra, Lahinch, ☎ 065 708 1280. Seafood specialities in the evening. Less expensive between 5pm-7pm.
Cullinan's, Doolin, ☎ 065 707 4183. Small, pleasant establishment, simple but tasty cooking for €20 and upwards. Evening meal only.

OTHER THINGS TO DO

Music and dance – Co Clare has more pubs with music than anywhere else in the country, and visitors can tour around for days on end and not spend a single evening without some sort of musical entertainment. Every village has a ceilidh several evenings a week, and there is set dancing on Thursday and Friday evenings at **Vaughan's Pub** in Kilfenora (details of other set dancing establishments from here or from Burren Farmhouse). The majority of pubs have traditional music every evening in summer; among the best are the **Roadside Tavern** at Lisdoonvarna, and **McDermott's**, **McGann's** and **O'Connor's** in Doolin.

Cards – "45" is an extremely popular card game played by two teams of four, and even if you don't acquire a perfect grasp of the rules, a game can be a sight worth seeing. In the winter, pubs like **McDermott's** (Wednesday evening) and **O'Connor's** (Thursday evening) fill up with passionate players.

Fishing – The River Fergus and its tributaries to the east of Corrofin have a fine reputation for trout, perch and pike. To the west of Corrofin, Inchiquin Lough is teeming with trout (no permit necessary for trout). **Shannon Regional Fisheries Board**, ☎ 065 682 7675.

Surfing – Surfboards can be hired near the beach at Lahinch. The whole of the coastline to the south of Lahinch has good surfing.

Golf – **Lahinch Golf Club**, ☎ 065 708 1592, has a world reputation; two 18-hole courses, fee €57.

SHOPPING

Music – **Traditional Music Shop**, at the lower end of Doolin. Good selection of less well-known groups and individual musicians, plus hand-made instruments.

Perfume – **The Burren Perfumery**, Carran. Perfumes made from the wild flowers of the Burren.

Fish – **The Burren Smokehouse**, Lisdoonvarna. Salmon smoked over oak chippings.

Making the most of the Burren

THE ARAN ISLANDS★★
Co Galway
Inishmore, Inishmaan and Insiheer – Pop 1 500
Michelin map 923 C-D / 8

Not to be missed
Dún Aengus and the Gort na gCapall road on Inishmore.
Dún Chonchuir and a walk along the lanes on Inishmaan.

And remember...
Dún Aengus is best early or late in the day when there are no crowds.
The best time to watch seals is when they haul out at low tide.
Aran sweaters are more expensive here than elsewhere!
There are cars on the islands, and they tend to drive in the middle of the road –
cyclists beware!

Guarding the seaward approach to Galway Bay, these great slabs of limestone with
their bays and black cliffs have the same geological structure as the Burren on the mainland. Here are the same lunar landscapes, the same grid of tiny stone-walled fields
stretching out endlessly, the same close-cropped grass speckled with more than

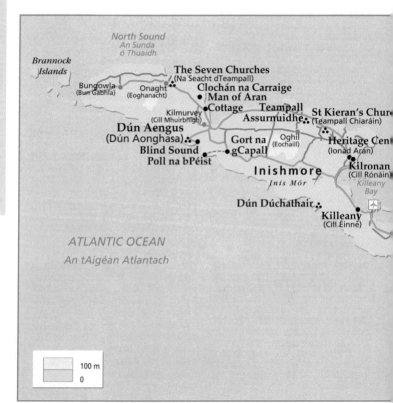

400 species of flowers. This austere terrain is at its most poignant on drizzly days, when sea, sky and surface fuse together in the infinitely subtle tones of a Chinese water-colour. The strung-out cottages of the island settlements are still a bastion of the Gaelic language, but anyone coming here with the idea of experiencing the traditional life described so movingly in JM Synge's *The Aran Islands (see page 66)* will be disappointed, because here, as everywhere, life has moved on. It is better to enjoy these unique islands and their severe beauty free from any romantic preconceptions.

Three men in a boat
The symbol of the Aran Islands is the curragh, the Celtic version of a dug-out, powered by three men using oars without blades. The black shapes of upturned curraghs can still be seen on the beaches here. Traditionally, they were made from the hide of a cow covered in pitch and stretched over a light wooden framework. Later, the cowhide was replaced by tar-cloth. Nowadays a curragh will be made out of fibre-glass and pushed along by an outboard motor, but the shape is still as it always was. Every year there is a fiercely contested curragh rowing competition which recalls the ancestral struggle of Man against the Ocean.

Inishmore** (Inis Mór)

12.8km long by 3.3km wide. While it is possible to get round the island in a day by bike or taxi, its spirit and its altogether different sense of time can only be appreciated by spending at least one night here.

Legend has it that the islands were originally populated by the Fir Bolg tribe, expelled from the mainland by Celtic invaders. What is certain is that they have been inhabited for a long time, as indicated by the presence here of numerous Iron Age ring forts dating from around 500 BC. A thousand years later, Christianity arrived, brought by St Enda, who founded a monastery. Monastic leaders from the mainland followed him here, to learn from his teachings and to absorb the contemplative atmosphere of this remote place. In medieval times and later, the overlordship of the islands became a matter of dispute between the O'Briens, rulers of Clare, and the pro-English O'Flahertys. They finally fell under English rule, and suffered the usual scourge of absentee landlordism. The Famine and growing poverty drove many of the islanders to emigrate, to Britain or America.

Kilronan (Cill Rónáin)
Boats from the mainland tie up at Kilronan's long **pier**. It can get very busy here, what with tractor-borne farmers supervising the loading of large flocks of unwilling sheep while other supplies like building materials and consumer goods of all kinds are brought ashore.

Waiting for tourists at the exit from the harbour is an array of horse-drawn vehicles or mini-buses, which take their clients on the classic route around the island. The alternative is to walk or cycle. The road to follow leads off to the right, climbing past the post office and the **Heritage Centre** (*April-October: 10am-7pm. Admission charge*), with displays on the natural heritage and traditions of the island.

Aran cottage

Westward on Inishmore

Around 13.5km to the western tip of the island. Turn right 600m from the harbour into Lower Road opposite Joe Watty's pub. Going round in this direction is easier for cyclists. The narrow road runs parallel to the sea between stone walls. It is worth while taking time to look carefully at how the walls are constructed and at the grey stone itself, fissured as if it had been subject to some forgotten cataclysm. One bay follows another, each one with a beach of smooth round pebbles (some contain fossils) which scrunch beneath the action of the waves. To the left, signs indicate the ruins of **St Kieran's Church** (Teampall Chiaráin), dating from the 9C and 12C, as well as the remains of **Teampall Assurnuidhe**, from where there is a pleasant **view**.

The road then runs directly above the sea to the ruins of an old seaweed fertiliser plant. A careful look out to sea may reveal a strange sight – dozens of black triangles on the surface of the water, which turn out to be the noses of a **colony of seals**.

About 6km from Kilronan is **Kilmurvey beach** (Cill Mhuirbhigh) and beyond it the **Man of Aran Cottage***, built in 1932 by Robert Flaherty while making his film *Man of Aran* (regular showings at the Heritage Centre). The cottage is now a B&B and restaurant.

Go back halfway along the beach and continue for 500m along the road leading to **Dún Aengus***** (*free admission*) – Aengus was a Fir Bolg chieftain. Bicycles must be left at the foot of the hill (*10min on foot to the summit*). The imposing outline of the fort stands out on the top of a cliff more than 80m high (*take great care – the enclosure reaches right to the cliff edge*). One of the finest prehistoric monuments in Europe, Dún Aengus consists of three concentric earthen ramparts more than 5m thick. The area between the outer and middle rampart is sown with pointed blocks of stone – chevaux de frise – intended as an additional barrier to slow down any attacker. To the right of the fort there is a fine view of successive lines of cliff stretching out westward.

Leave the fort to the west, and carry on along the clifftop, climbing a series of walls. There is a view down into **Blind Sound****, an indentation in the cliffs which here are highly laminated and hollowed out at the bottom, providing perches for thousands of seabirds.

Come down from the fort to a group of shops and take the road to the left. The road soon makes a sharp turn, and in about 1km joins the main road leading to the western tip of the island (which can be left out if time is short).

At the junction with the main road, a footpath opposite leads in 200m to a well-preserved **clochán** or beehive hut, an evocative reminder of the simple and solitary life of the first monks.

The main road continues to the **Seven Churches** (Na Seacht dTeampall), a somewhat grandiose term for what is a rather modest group of ruins, the remains of a monastic community which boasted not seven, but merely two churches. The road comes to an end at the western tip of Inishmore, from where the Brannock Islands can be seen.

The best way back to Kilronan is along the Gort na gCapall road. Go back to Kilmurvey beach, and turn right at the head of the bay towards the hamlet of Gort na gCapall (the main road to Kilronan is more direct but not as interesting and is lined with B&B establishments).

The Gort na gCapall road★★

About 5.5km. Allow 90min to get to Killeany Bay just to the south of Kilronan. The last section of this route is very stony and inexperienced mountain bikers may find it easier to get off and push.

Once past the hamlet of Gort na gCapall, the road passes through a landscape of **stony terraces** overlooking sea and cliffs. It is worthwhile making a short side-trip to the shore to the southeast of the hamlet to see **Poll na bPéist★**, a rectangular hole at the foot of the cliff. It makes an impressive sight when being filled by the incoming tide.

Continue along the road *(not without difficulty, it's very steep)* to the highest part of the island, a totally unspoiled landscape. The road degenerates into a footpath invaded by grass and bordered by wild flowers including wild strawberries. The eye is led to the sea across the countless stone walls attempting vainly to break the force of the wind. Solitude and silence is total.

Around Killeany Bay

About 2km south of Kilronan, the tiny settlement of **Killeany** (Cill Éinne) marks the beginning of the southernmost part of Inishmore, the flattest area in the island, with its biggest sandy beach. Just after a first little beach *(on the way out of Kilronan)* and before Killeany, there is a sign indicating **Dún Dúchathair★★** (Black Fort) to the right. Built on the cliff edge like Dún Aengus but not quite on the same scale, it is nevertheless full of charm and atmosphere.

In the footsteps of JM Synge on Inishmaan★★★ (Inis Meán)
Inishmaan is 5km long by 2km wide and can be visited in a day.

Inishmaan, and in particular its western cliffs, was the inspiration for the book *The Aran Islands* by **JM Synge**. Bleaker and more desolate than its bigger neighbour, the island remains a stronghold of Gaelic culture.

The signposted footpath called the **Inishmaan Way★★★** *(8km, 2hr)* begins to the left of the pier and penetrates the island's interior. Beyond a first fort, **Dún Fearbhaí★** with its view of the mainland, is a little settlement with the island's only pub, a long thatched cabin.

A little further on the left, beyond **Synge's Cottage**, and among the remains of a number of **clocháns** is the huge mass of **Dún Chonchúir★★** *(see page 28)*. The prehistoric fort owes its name to Chonchúir (or Connor), the brother of Aengus, the leader of the Fir Bolg. From the top there is a stunning **panorama★★** of the mainland and of the island's innumerable stone walls.

Further west is the shoreline facing Inishmore. The footpath, marked by splashes of white paint on the stone, leads to **Synge's Chair****, a rocky sheltered spot where the great man would spend long hours meditating or writing. The way back through the little stone-walled fields passes by a **knitwear workshop**, making modern versions of one of the traditional island crafts.

Inisheer** (Inis Oírr)
The island is 4km long and 2.5km across – Day trip from Doolin

The smallest of the Aran Islands is also the flattest and the nearest *(8km)* to the coast of Co Clare. Most of its dwellings are on the northern coast, and the remainder of the island, though certainly quite wild, has gentler landscapes than those of its neighbours, best explored along the signposted **Inisheer Way**** *(10.5km, reckon on 2hr30min to 3hr)*. With its dunes, its rocky coast, and its little fields with their inevitable drystone walls, the island undergoes a metamorphosis in springtime, when it is covered with **daffodils**, one of its main exports.

There are a number of individual sights, among them **St Cavan's Church** (Teampall Chaomháin), an extraordinary 10C chapel half buried in the sand, which houses the tomb of St Cavan (Chaomháin), brother of Kevin, the founder of the great monastery at Glendalough.

The island also has an **O'Brien castle**, erected in the Middle Ages in the centre of the prehistoric fort of **Dún Formna****.

Making the most of Inishmore

By boat – Island Ferries, Victoria Place, Galway. ☎ 091 572 050 / 568 903, is the only firm operating all year round. There is a bus service from Galway to the port of Rossaveel 38km to the west via the R336. Three boats daily (more in July and August) between Rossaveel and Inishmore (35min), €19 return, and one boat daily to and from Inishmaan and Inisheer. Details of services between the islands by telephone. Between April and September **Doolin Ferries**, Doolin (in the Burren), ☎ 065 707 4455, serve Inisheer (30min), €19 return, and Inishmore (1hr), €25 return. Tickets at the quayside. Check times of sailings by telephone, as they vary according to tides and weather conditions.

O'Brien Shipping, Galway, ☎ 091 567 283, operates daily services to all three islands between June and September (90min) for €23, and three times weekly out of season. Fare includes transport of bicycles. Daily service Inishmore and Inishmaan between June and September, €13 return.

By plane – Hourly flights (4 daily out of season) operated by **Aer Árann**, ☎ 091 593 034, between Connemara Regional Airport at Galway and the three islands (10min). Reckon on €44 return or €37 one way and return by boat (or vice-versa).

GETTING AROUND

By bus – The island bus leaves daily from the supermarket at 10.30am (except Thursday), 1pm, 2.30pm, 5pm (except Monday and Thursday) and 7.20pm. Reckon on €2 to Dún Aengus and €2.50 for the whole journey (one-way).

By carriage or minibus – Island excursions starting at the harbour. Around €6 for the standard route.

Bicycle hire – On the pier. Allow €6 for a day's hire and €26 per week.

On foot – There is a little map of the Inishmore Way. Alternatively use the Ordnance Survey Discovery Series sheet n° 51 covering all three islands and most of the Burren.

ADDRESS BOOK

Tourist information – *Tourist Information*, on the pier, daily 10am-4pm, closed one day a week out of season. Camera film (including slide film) for sale at same prices as mainland, though there is less choice. Left luggage.

Banks / Currency exchange – The bank at Kilronan opens on Wednesday and on Thursday as well between June and September. No cash machine. Bureau de change at the tourist office and post office (9am-5pm; closed Saturday pm and Sunday).

WHERE TO STAY

Under €13

Kilronan Hostel, Kilronan, ☎ 099 612 55 – 44 beds cc By the harbour next to the Ti Joe Mac pub. Pleasant, practical accommodation in dormitories.

Between €40-50

Seacrest House, Kilronan, ☎ 099 612 92 – 6rm Very close to the harbour, straightforward well-kept accommodation, very friendly reception. Evening meal (€13) available in winter.

Man of Aran Cottage, Kilmurvey, ☎ 099 613 01 – 3rm ✕ cc Lovely little rooms in a thatched cottage full of charm. The one room with its own facilities is more expensive. Maura's cooking is delicious (see "Where to eat").

Ard Éinne, Killeany, ☎ 099 611 26 – 15rm ✕ cc Right by the landing strip, this is a well-run large establishment. The less expensive rooms have shared facilities. Dinner by arrangement (€15). Transfer to and from the pier if required.

Between €50-65

Kilmurvey House, Kilmurvey, ☎ 099 612 18 – 12rm ✕ cc At the foot of Dún Aengus, this substantial residence is admirably run by a mother-daughter partnership. Warm welcome, varied cuisine and delicious cakes.

Pier House, Kilronan, ☎ 099 614 17 – 12rm TV cc Facing the pier, large and very comfortable modern building.

Tigh Fitz, Killeany, ☎ 099 612 13 – 12rm TV ✕ cc 1.5km from the harbour (transfer by minibus if required), comfortable rooms above a pub, with snacks available until 6pm. Dinner by arrangement (€18). Excellent value.

EATING OUT

Establishments are not categorised by price because charges vary widely according to the type of meal and time of day.

The Old Pier, Kilronan, take-away or eat in. Classic fast food including salads, fish, or tasty grilled chicken.

The Aran Fisherman, Kilronan, ☎ 099 611 04. High quality cuisine based on seafood. Quite expensive salads, vegetarian dishes, plus light meals at midday, between €7.50-10. Reckon on €15-23 in the evening.

Joe Watty's Bar, Kilronan, on the rise just beyond the post office. Good traditional bar food.

Man of Aran Cottage, Kilmurvey. Inventive cuisine prepared by the landlady of the B&B of the same name, using organic produce from her husband's garden, including some interestingly unfamiliar vegetables. Sittings for dinner at 7.30pm and 8.30pm, between €19-23. Reservation essential. Snacks, soups and cakes served during the day.

B Kaufmann/MICHELIN

Achill Island

CONNEMARA
AND MAYO

One of Ireland's most vibrant cities, Galway leads an intense artistic and cultural life, with busy streets with art galleries and bookshops at every corner and pubs and cafés where music is king. Pride in its Gaelic heritage has not held up modernity and renewal, and with its numerous students much of the city wears a youthful face. A place to revel in, it is also the gateway to the wild and westernmost part of the country.

Connemara is one of Ireland's most celebrated landscapes, and one of its bleakest. Its desolate mountain ranges and great stretches of bog drenched by the incessant rain seem almost bereft of inhabitants other than a few wild ponies. But it has a stunning beauty all its own, and its abundant rivers and lakes teem with trout and salmon waiting to be taken. Bays and inlets break up the coastline, and offshore lie a host of islands.

Further north, Mayo remains largely neglected, though the holy mountain of Croagh Patrick attracts thousands of pilgrims. For walkers, this is a challenging landscape, with more vast tracts of peatland and heather-clad hills. The lonely sandy beaches are a dream, at least when the sun deigns to shine on them. Elsewhere, only straggling power lines and wind turbines break the monotony. Along much of the coast, great cliffs like those at Downpatrick Head and on Achill Island rear up against the Atlantic storms.

GALWAY★

County town of Co Galway – Pop 58 000
Fourth largest town in the Republic (after Dublin, Cork and Limerick)

Not to be missed
A stroll through the traffic-free streets.
Music in the pubs.

And remember...
The city on its own can easily be seen in the course of a half-day visit,
but spend at least one evening in the pubs.
Accommodation needs to be booked well in advance in summer,
and it is a good idea to offer a deposit.

If any one place summed up all Ireland's charm, it would be Galway. There may be nothing special about its architectural heritage, but nowhere else has quite the allure of its lively streets, its little restaurants and countless pubs. The university, with its many students from abroad, helps create a cosmopolitan atmosphere, and the harbour and up-to-date industries add their bit to the bustle and the go-ahead ambience. When the sun shines, and the streets are thronged with people and the cafés spread out onto the pavement, Galway could almost be a port city on the Mediterranean, though the omnipresent musical background remains resolutely Irish. The city is the gateway to Connemara and the Aran Islands, which together make up one of the most significant parts of the Gaeltacht, and despite its international feel, remains a stronghold of Gaelic culture. Literature, theatre, and dance and music are its lifeblood.

Legend has it that the first settlement here was a Celtic encampment, founded at the point where a chieftain had lost his daughter by drowning. Later, on the right bank of the river came **Claddagh**, a fishing village consisting of thatched dwellings straggling along the shoreline.

In the 13C, slowly taking possession of Ireland, the Normans saw the advantages of the sheltered anchorage here, half-way along the country's western coast. They erected a castle, then built what amounted to a fortified town surrounded by walls. English and Welsh settlers were encouraged to come here and populate the place. Power was eventually split among fourteen prominent families, whose wealth was derived from trade with Spain and Portugal, and who were known as "The Tribes". And for many years Galway was called **"The city of the Tribes"**. A bastion of English power in the middle of a hostile region, the city imposed strict rules intended to keep Irish influence at bay; the Irish were forbidden to enter the city and those of them that had resided here were expelled. As elsewhere, a separate Irish town grew up outside the walls, in this case to the west of the city on the edge of the bay. Despite the animosity of the Gaelic clansmen in neighbouring Connemara, Galway did not really suffer from its isolation, thanks to its imports of wine and brandy and its exports of fish, wool and meat. But in the 17C, with the religious wars tearing the country apart, decline set in. The city suffered two sieges, one by Cromwell in 1652, a second in 1691 by William of Orange, and maritime trade diminished. Renewal began with the revival of Gaelic culture in the late 19C, which brought artists, writers and other visitors to the region.

The ubiquitous potato

The city
Allow 2-3hr on foot

Built at the head of the bay which bears its name, Galway stretches out along the Corrib River. On the right bank of the river is the site of the original fishermen's village of Claddagh with its many pubs, while on the left bank are the remains of the medieval town, old streets and quaysides. To the northeast, Eyre Square is the focal point of the Georgian town.

Medieval Galway*

A good starting point for a walk around the medieval town is the riverside near Wolfe Tone Bridge. On the right are the remains of the 13C medieval quayside, including the **Spanish Arch** (C3), a fragment of the city gateway which owes its name to Galway's trading links with Spain. The arches (originally there were four) supported a fort watching over the activities of the quayside. To the south of the gateway is a 20m section of the **city walls**.

Close by, the **Galway City Museum** (C3) *(10am-1pm / 2.15pm-5.15pm. Admission charge)* has many items relating to everyday life across the centuries. Particularly noteworthy are photographs of the old settlement of Claddagh before it was torn down. From the museum terrace there is a fine **view** of the estuary.

Go along Quay Street and its continuation, the High Street. There are many picturesque stone houses, bars and brightly painted shop fronts. One place that should not be missed is **Kenny's Bookshop** *(see "Making the most of Galway")*, a city institution and a favourite haunt of local literati.

At the end of the High Street, turn left towards **St Nicholas' Church** (C2) *(9.30am-4.30pm. Free admission. Optional guided tour)*. Dedicated to the patron saint of seafarers, the church was founded in 1320 and added to in the 15C and 16C. Christopher Columbus is supposed to have prayed here when on business in Galway in 1477. Inside there is a medieval **stoup**, as well as numerous **tombstones**, including one of a Crusader (12C-13C).

Every Saturday morning in Market Street near the church there is a lively **market**, with lots of local crafts and produce.

An early tourist trap

In 1493, Walter Lynch, a member of one of Galway's "Tribes", murdered his best friend in a fit of jealousy. His own father, acting as judge, condemned him to death. No executioner was willing to hang the young man, so the father resolved to perform the task himself. A plaque in Market Street, by the northeastern corner of the church, supposedly marks the spot where the execution took place. In fact it was placed there in 1854 by a local priest with the idea of encouraging visitors, and has remained to this day, as has the tale itself.

Not far from St Nicholas' Church, in Bowling Green, is **Nora Barnacle's House** (C2) *(May-September: 10am-1pm / 2pm-5pm; closed Sunday. Admission charge)*, the residence of James Joyce's wife-to-be and now a small museum. Joyce himself stayed at his mother-in-law's home on two occasions, and those days are recalled by letters, photographs, and other memorabilia.

Go round the church and into Shop Street.

At the corner of Shop Street and Upper Abbeygate Street rises the imposing façade of **Lynch's Castle*** (C2), a superb 15C town mansion which now houses the Allied Irish Bank. There are **gargoyles** and elaborately worked lintels above the **windows**, as well as a rectangular panel with Henry VII's coat of arms. The "castle" was confiscated in the 17C when Cromwell took the town, the Lynches having unwisely supported the Royalist cause. Inside the porch is an account of Judge Lynch's execution of his own son.

Go along Shop Street and Williamsgate to Eyre Square.

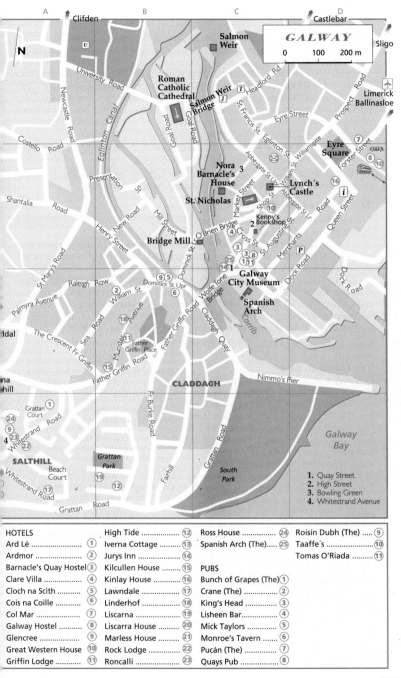

GALWAY

0   100   200 m

1. Quay Street
2. High Street
3. Bowling Green
4. Whitestrand Avenue

Eyre Square (D1-D2)

Galway's principal square focuses on gardens dedicated to the memory of US President John F Kennedy who received a hero's welcome when he visited the city in 1963.

The gardens are not particularly interesting in themselves, but act as a meeting-place for folk with nothing else to do. There are several statues, including one of the Gaelic writer **Patrick O'Connor**, and another of **Liam Mellows**, a participant in the Easter Uprising who was subsequently shot without trial by the Free State government during the Civil War. The **Browne doorway** is all that remains of the one of the square's finest residences, a late medieval mansion now demolished.

A section of the **town walls** together with the remains of two towers have been integrated with the new Eyre Square shopping centre.

Go back along Williamsgate and turn right into Eglinton Square and its continuation Francis Street. Turn left towards the riverbank and Salmon Weir Bridge.

The banks of the Corrib

Salmon Weir Bridge (C1) was built in 1819 to link the law courts and the prison, located on the far bank on the site of the present cathedral.

At this point the river is narrow and the current very strong. The **salmon weir** itself is a little way upstream, a fine sight in springtime when hundreds of returning salmon pass through on their way to the lakes to the north.

On the right bank of the river, built on one of several islands, stands the huge **Roman Catholic Cathedral** (B1), dedicated to Our Lady of Assumption and St Nicholas and completed in 1965. It is a structure of unrelieved pretentiousness and an incredible mixture of styles, and not surprisingly has been the object of much negative comment. But it is difficult not to be impressed by the sheer scale of the interior.

Go back southwards to O'Brien Bridge, the third of the trio of city-centre bridges.

The Claddagh Ring

This ring is on sale all over Ireland. It features a heart clasped by two hands surmounted by a crown. It was first created in the 17C by a young Galway man who had been kidnapped by pirates and sold to an Arab jeweller, who taught him his skills. Eventually the young man returned home, and designed the ring as a pledge of fidelity. In Claddagh, where it was often the only item of jewellery in the family, it was handed down from mother to daughter. During the period of betrothal, the ring is worn with the heart pointing to the fingertip, while after the wedding it is worn the other way round.

Overlooking the river by the bridge is **Bridge Mill** (C2), dating from the 18C and converted into an attractive commercial gallery. It has an outside café in summer, a good place to take a break from sightseeing.

Go south along Dominick Street with its many bars to the starting point of the walk, Wolfe Tone Bridge. To the south of the bridge is the old district of Claddagh.

Claddagh (B3-C3), the old fishermen's settlement, was where the poorer Irish lived beyond the walls of the English town. Consisting in modern times of unsanitary cabins, it was completely demolished in the 1930s and rebuilt as an extremely ordinary housing estate. But its lively traditions meant that it lived on in popular memory. It used to elect its own "king", the last of whom died in 1934 at the age of 90.

The riverbank leads westward to the **Salthill** (A4) area, a residential suburb with a beach lined with video arcades, leisure centres and discotheques.

COMING AND GOING

By plane – *Galway Airport* (off D1 on plan), ☎ 091 is at Carnmore, 15km east of the city. Three flights daily to Dublin. Airport bus €3.20, taxi around €15.

By train – *Ceannt Station* (D2), near Eyre Square and very close to the city centre behind the Great Southern Hotel, ☎ 091 561 444. Three to five trains daily to Dublin (3hr), changing at Athlone for other destinations.

By bus – The ***Central Bus Station*** is next to the railway station (D2), ☎ 091 562 000. ***Bus Eireann*** has daily links to all major towns, but numerous private firms offer superior services (less expensive and faster) to certain destinations (eg Dublin, Donegal and the North). Check before purchasing your ticket. ***Nestor Travel*** (Dublin), ☎ 091 797 144, ***O'Donnell Travel*** (Sligo, Donegal), ☎ 091 761 656, ***Citylink*** (Dublin), ☎ 091 564 163, ***Michael Nee*** (Clifden), ☎ 095 510 82.

GETTING AROUND

The city centre is partly pedestrianised and cars should be left at the car park on the Salthill side of town (A4) (free parking, 10min on foot from the centre). On-street parking by disk. There are multistorey car parks by the river and docks.

By bus – Most services leave from Eyre Square (D2), among them the bus to and from Salthill. Every 10min in summer up to 11.30pm.

By taxi – *Galway Taxis*, ☎ 091 561 111, ***Big O Taxis*,** ☎ 091 585 858.

Car hire – *Budget*, Eyre Square (D2), ☎ 091 566 376, ***Hertz*,** airport desk, ☎ 091 752 502.

Bicycle hire – At the youth hostels.

ADDRESS BOOK

Tourist information – *Tourist Information*, Victoria Place (D2) near Eyre Square, ☎ 091 563 081. Open 9am-5.45pm; closed weekends. Open Saturday morning in May, daily July-August.

Banks / Currency exchange – The main banks and cash machines are in Eyre Square (D2) and Shop Street (C2).

Post office – The main post office is in Eglinton Street (C2), 9am-6pm except Sunday.

Internet – *Hotlines* and *Jamie Starlights*, Upper Dominick Street (B3), 9am-midnight weekdays, 12pm-midnight Sunday.

Medical service – *University College Hospital*, Newcastle Road (A1), ☎ 095 524 222.

WHERE TO STAY

Galway's success as a visitor destination seems to have gone to the heads of some B&B owners, who see nothing wrong in gross overcharging in summer and transform their establishments into tourist processing plants. Bord Failte approved places and those registered with Town & Country have more or less stable prices. The best area to stay is on the west side of town, which is quiet and close to the centre. Galway has an impressive number of hostels, but most are fairly basic, and some get very scruffy in summer. Listed below are some of the more recent establishments. The places where guests are received with courtesy are unfortunately getting harder and harder to find. Advance booking is advisable all year round, and essential in July-August and at festival time. It may be possible to get reductions between October and April.

• **Left bank**
Between €13-25
☞ ***Kinlay House*,** Merchants Road, ☎ 091 565 244 – 150 beds, 12rm **CC** Right in the middle of town, large and well-built building. Bright, spacious dormitories and smaller rooms. Friendly reception. Laundrette, lockers, left luggage, continental breakfast included in price.

☞ ***Barnacle's Quay Hostel*,** 10 Quay Street, ☎ 091 568 644 – 110 beds, 5rm **CC** In the middle of the pedestrian area, this hostel is cheerful and very well-kept. Breakfast included, laundrette, lockers and left luggage.

Making the most of Galway

Galway Hostel, Eyre Square, ☎ 091 566 959 – 78 beds. The dormitories and rooms are pretty minimal, but this is a good location just opposite the station.

Great Western House, Eyre Square, ☎ 091 561 150 – 191 beds, 22rm CC Very comfortable, laundrette, free left luggage, sauna, the Rolls-Royce of the hostels, but the reception leaves something to be desired.

More than €90

Jury's Inn, Quay Street, ☎ 091 566 444 – 128rm ⚓ 🅿 TV ✕ CC Classic international hotel, vast and impersonal, but with excellent facilities. Rooms overlook the bay. Top rates in season, significant reductions and special offers out of season.

More than €115

The Spanish Arch Hotel, Quay Street, ☎ 091 569 600 – 20rm ⚓ 🅿 TV ✕ CC Elegant and welcoming, tastefully decorated and comfortable rooms, but a bit expensive given their small size.

• Right bank

Between €45-50

⬡ **Linderhof**, 25 Munster Avenue, ☎ 091 588 518 – 4rm ⚓ TV Wonderful place to stay, well-run, quiet, 5min on foot from the city centre and close to the best pubs. Added to all that, a really friendly landlady who makes her guests feel like old friends and who is a mine of useful information.

⬡ **Griffin Lodge**, 3 Father Griffin Place, ☎ 091 589 440 – 6rm ⚓ TV CC Close to the previous establishment with the same advantages. Slightly more expensive, but well-run, attractive and comfortable.

Kilcullen House, 38 Father Griffin Road, ☎ 091 586 736 – 8rm ⚓ TV A less than ideal location on a through road, this big building nevertheless has a number of quieter rooms facing the rear. Convenient for the centre, less than 10min away on foot.

• Salthill

Between €45-50

Ard Lé, 25 Grattan Court, ☎ 091 586 513 – 5rm ⚓ ✕ CC In a quiet position 15min walk west of the centre. Large and welcoming house with a warm-hearted and energetic landlady.

Rock Lodge, Whitestrand Road, ☎ 091 583 789 – 6rm ⚓ TV CC 15min on foot from the centre. Bright, attractive rooms. Very pleasant landlady.

Glencree, 20 Whitestrand Avenue, ☎ 091 581 061 – 4rm Immaculately-kept, in a street close to the previous establishment at the same distance from the centre.

Roncalli, 24 Whitestrand Avenue, ☎ 091 584 159 – 6rm ⚓ TV CC Comfortable house, with charming landlord and lady whose great claim to fame is that they once had Chelsea Clinton as their guest. Well-run.

Ross House, 14 Whitestrand Avenue, ☎ 091 587 431 – 4rm ⚓ TV CC Cheerful and elegant décor, quiet house with a lovely back patio. Very close to the previous establishments.

High Tide, 9 Grattan Park, ☎ 091 584 324 – 5rm ⚓ TV CC Slightly set back from the seafront road, but facing the bay. Friendly reception and a wide range of breakfast dishes, including fish.

Liscarna, 22 Grattan Park, ☎ 091 585 086 – 6rm ⚓ TV In a quiet road close to the sea. Generous breakfast.

Lawndale, 5 Beach Court, ☎ 091 586 676 – 5rm ⚓ TV This attractive red-brick house faces the sea. Comfortable, but not especially friendly reception.

Clare Villa, 38 Threadneedle Road, ☎ 091 522 520 – 6rm ⚓ About 3km from the centre, on the Salthill bus route (stop opposite). To get here by car, go along the seafront from the centre over the big Salthill roundabout and turn second right after the Galway Bay Hotel. Large, bright residence, spacious rooms decorated in pastel colours.

Liscarra House, 6 Threadneedle Road, ☎ 091 521 290 – 5rm ⚓ TV CC On the same bus route as the previous establishment (the driver will stop directly in front of the house on request). Really comfortable, run by an extremely pleasant landlady who greets her guests with tea and scones. Impressive breakfast. Slightly more expensive than the others, but well worth it.

Marless House, Threadneedle Road, ☎ 091 523 931 – 6rm ⌂ TV CC Next door to the above establishment, same rates. Immaculately-run, attractive décor, sumptuous breakfast, well worth the extra expense. A good place to stay.

• **Spiddal**
17km west of Galway, on the coast road towards Connemara.

Between €45-50
Cloch na Scíth, Kellough, ☎ 091 553 364 – 3rm ⌂ 2km before Spiddal on the same side as the sea, this is a white-painted thatched-roof dwelling, with guest rooms in a modern extension at the back. Ask for the room with a sea view. Attractive cottage-style décor.

Cois na Coille, Shanavooneen, ☎ 091 553 352 – 4rm ⌂ On the way out of Spiddal towards Connemara, turn right and continue for 2km to this pretty farmhouse in the middle of the countryside. The two rooms with shared bathroom cost less.

Ardmor, Greenhill, ☎ 091 553 145 – 7rm ⌂ TV CC Less than 1km out of Spiddal on the Connemara road. Attractive bungalow in a pretty garden by the roadside. Every comfort, efficient service. There are sea views from the back garden.

🏠 **Iveran Cottage**, Salahoona, ☎ 091 553 762 – 4rm ⌂ Delightful stone-built cottage, 1.5km beyond Spiddal on the Connemara road. Cheerful, original décor in a house full of character with lots of books and antiques. Copious breakfast with ultra-fresh ingredients.

🏠 **Col Mar**, Salahoona, ☎ 091 553 247 – 5rm ⌂ CC Large house in a quiet position, clearly signposted on the right from the R336, a short distance further on from the previous establishment. Very friendly reception from charming landlord and lady. Attractive garden.

EATING OUT
Galway's abundance of small restaurants and its cosmopolitan atmosphere make it a good place to have a change from pub food and the like (good as it is). Try any one of the numerous places frequented by the city's many students, and eat a modest – and probably very tasty and inexpensive – meal by candlelight.

Under £6
La Boulangerie Francaise, Cross Street (C2). The real thing, run by a Frenchman, with authentic French cakes, good coffee, and three croissants for £1.

Café de Paris. Inexpensive snacks in a passageway (C2) next to the previous establishment.

Couch Potatoes, 40 Upper Abbeygate Street (C2). An original establishment much liked by locals. Baked potatoes of every imaginable sort. Inexpensive, friendly atmosphere.

Food for Thoughts, 5 Lower Abbeygate Street (C2). Ideal for a quick and inexpensive lunch, eaten from high stools. Good quiches, lasagne, vegetarian dishes, salads and a range of herbal teas. Much in favour with local people.

🏠 **McSwiggans**, Eyre Street (C1). Traditional pub with cheerful décor serving the usual pub grub including generous heaped-up salads.

Café du Journal, Quay Street (C2) is a good place to enjoy a sandwich or a soup. Friendly atmosphere and excellent coffee.

Fat Freddy, right next to the above, good pizzas.

🏠 **McDonagh**, Quay Street (C2) is the best place for fresh, delicious fish, to take away or eat in, at a very reasonable price.

The Bridge Mill, O'Brien Bridge (C2). Restaurant open 12pm-5pm serving straightforward dishes, salads, sandwiches and soups in the old mill building which also houses several shops. The outside section overlooking the river is great in summer.

Pasta Paradiso, 51 Lower Dominick Street (B2). A spacious, attractive and quiet establishment with good pub-type food and pasta with all kinds of sauces. Newspapers to read, relaxed atmosphere.

Between €6.50-13
🏠 **The River God**, 2 Quay Street (C2), ☎ 091 565 811. Intimate little upper-floor restaurant serving exotic dishes and vegetarian food, generous portions

and inexpensive. Desserts have psychedelic names. "River God Platters" at €6.50 are delicious and satisfying.

Sev'nth Heav'n, Courthouse Lane (C2), a little lane running off Quay Street. Open until midnight. Traditional Irish dishes, but mostly succulent vegetarian food.

KC Blakes, Quay Street (C2), next door to Jury's Inn. Good range and quality including exotic dishes, pizzas, grills. A bit more elegant and dearer than the previous establishments.

🍴 **Nimmo's**, Spanish Arch (C3), ☎ 091 561 114. Reached via the Spanish Arch, this is a charming restaurant with intimate little tables and exposed stonework. The ground floor wine bar has dishes for between €7.50 at midday and in the evening. The upper-floor restaurant has a classic meat and fish menu at rather higher rates. Sunday jazz at 5.30pm.

HAVING A DRINK

It's difficult to choose among the myriad pubs, each one as friendly as the next. Music tends to start up in the town centre pubs as early as 3pm or 5pm, while the Dominick Street area is probably better for evening sessions, when the music might not begin until 10pm or even later. The Salthill area is full of late-night establishments and the atmosphere here can get pretty hectic as the evening wears on.

● **Left bank**

Taafe's, Shop Street. This is a good place for daytime drinking with live music between 3pm and 9pm. Lively atmosphere and varied clientele.

Quays Pub, Quay Street, much in favour with the young crowd and always packed. Varied music, not always traditional. Charge made for the music upstairs, but it can still be heard downstairs.

King's Head, Quay Street, also attracts the young. Mock-medieval décor. Good music including traditional, blues, rock and soul. Sunday brunch with jazz.

The Bunch of Grapes, Quay Street, is the ideal place for the early evening, more of a bar for a drink and a chat in a pleasant atmosphere.

🍴 **Tomás ÓRiada**, Quay Street, is full of little hidey-holes on various levels. Music between 5pm-9pm, fine for early evening drinking. Convivial atmosphere and inexpensive food.

Lisheen Bar, Bridge Street. Good traditional music every evening and Sunday morning. Pretty touristy in summer.

The Púcán, Forster Street, is a pub with an incredible atmosphere some nights of the week. Traditional music, singing, and even dancing. Spectators are expected to join the fray. Great atmosphere.

● **Right bank**

🍴 **Monroe's Tavern**, Fairhill Road and Dominick Street, is a huge pub which is almost always packed out because of the high quality of the traditional music played here. Convivial atmosphere and the beer flows freely. You will find it difficult to tear yourself away if you arrive after 10pm.

The Róisín Dubh, Dominick Street, is where the celebrities come to play. There's an entrance charge when there's a concert on, but the music can be heard from the pub even if the musicians remain invisible, and the atmosphere more than makes up for this.

Mick Taylors, Dominick Street, good local pub not frequented by tourists, where the beer is served correctly and the music is fine. Courtyard in summer.

🍴 **The Crane**, Sea Road, southwest from Dominick Street. Smoky pub for beer and conversation on the ground floor. On the upper floor (staircase to the side), music by as yet unknown performers in an intimate setting (no amplification, no charge), and a really friendly atmosphere. Frequently one of the best places to spend an evening.

● **Festivals**

Galway Poetry & Literature Festival (April) brings writers and readers together for talks and readings at various locales around town.

Early Music Festival (mid-May), numerous concerts over a three-day period.

Arts Festival (late July) includes music, drama, and a whole range of events and performances. Great atmosphere, but the town gets very crowded.

Galway Races (3rd or 4th week in July). Again, the place is full, but the pub scene has to be experienced to be believed.

Oyster Festival (late September) celebrates a great local speciality which gets eaten everywhere, including on the streets. Normally washed down with beer. Musical accompaniments of various kinds, and a prize for the champion oyster-opener. Crowds again, and terrific atmosphere over a period of four days.

SHOPPING

Tweeds and woollens – Shop Street, the High Street and Quay Street are full of tourist shops selling woollens at similar and far from inexpensive prices. But it is well worthwhile comparing. **ÓMáille**, in the High Street, claims to have had John Wayne and Maureen O'Hara as customers, and to have provided the costumes for the film "The Quiet Man".

Crystal and porcelain – **Galway Irish Crystal**, on the Dublin road on the way out of town, is devoted to one of the town's specialities, and is cheaper than the shops in town. Craftspeople can be seen at work. Daily 9am-6pm. **Royal Tara China**, also on the Dublin road is a factory producing this famous porcelain, which can be visited, and there is a factory shop. Daily 9am-6pm, factory visits Monday-Friday, video screening Saturday and Sunday.

Crafts – The **Design Concourse Ireland**, Kirwan's Lane (C2) (near Barnacle's Quay Hostel) is a showcase for a fine selection of Irish crafts, traditional and resolutely contemporary side by side.

Jewellery – The Claddagh Ring is available at all the jewellery shops. Try **Faller's** in Williamsgate Street (D2).

Bookshops – **Kenny's Bookshop** (C2) should not be missed. First of all there are the books on three levels, then there is an art gallery with old engravings side by side with often really fascinating contemporary work. There is a huge choice of books, with many rarities and titles unobtainable elsewhere. Take the time to have a good look at the photographs of the famous authors who have been here, including a number of Nobel Prize-winners. **The Gallery Bookshop**, Bridgewater Court (B3) (on the far side of the river, near Monroe's Tavern) is a bookshop-cum-café in a completely different style. There may not be such a vast choice, but it is easier to find your way around, it's very friendly, snacks are available, and the book of your choice can be studied while reclining in a comfortable sofa.

Traditional music – **Mulligan Records**, Middle Street (C2), is the best place, with a very complete range. Advice readily given by friendly staff. Many of the best musicians come from Galway, like De Danaan and Dolores Keane. For instruments, **Musical Instruments**, 38 Dominick Street (B3) has the likes of U2 and Van Morrison among its customers.

CONNEMARA ★★

Co Galway – Michelin map 923 C-D-E-F / 7-8
270km two-day basic tour – allow an extra day for side-trips

Not to be missed
Inchagoill Island and Cong Abbey.
Kylemore Abbey and the Inagh Valley.
The Bog Road from Roundstone.

And remember...
In southern Connemara check place-names on the map
since most road signs are in Gaelic only.
It is absolutely essential to have waterproof footwear for walking.
Buy camera film before setting out.

After the bustle of Galway, Connemara is a different world altogether, a place of peat bogs, gleaming lakes, swirling mists and austere, rain-drenched mountains. To travel the few roads penetrating this empty land is to experience Nature in wild and desolate guise. This is a place of rocky wastes, clad in rust-coloured grasses and pitted with ponds and little lakes, with a coastline punctuated by deep bays clogged with fronds of orange seaweed.

Trials and tribulations of the Gaelic clans
Connemara was once the preserve of the powerful O'Flaherty clan, whom the Normans failed to dislodge. But the Gaelic hold on the land was eventually broken by Cromwell's men, who instituted a reign of terror from their base on Inishbofin; the monks were imprisoned or deported, and the population forbidden to live within 5km of the coast. This condemned them to misery and destitution by depriving them of access to the seaweed needed to fertilise the poor soil of their little fields. Two centuries later, the effects of the Famine were particularly severe in this area, and most of the survivors emigrated or were only kept alive by employment on public works projects.

The decline of this Gaelic stronghold was to some extent checked by the revival of Gaelic culture at the end of the 19C, and today southern Connemara forms the largest *Gaeltacht* in Ireland.

The coast road from Galway to Clifden ★
126km – Allow half a day

From Galway (see page 358) take the R336 towards Spiddal (an Spidéal), 17.5km away. There are fine views of the Burren on the far side of the bay. At the junction 18.5km further on, the road to the left leads to Rossaveel (Ros á Mhíl), while the road to the right runs through a wild and unspoiled landscape to Oughterard (Uachtar Ard) and Lough Corrib. The coast road continues to Costelloe (Casla), where a left turn leads to Carraroe.

■ **Carraroe** (An Cheathrú Rua) is a little peninsula with attractive beaches. The principal man-made attraction is **Beyond the Pale**, an open-air sculpture exhibition featuring the work in metal of the contemporary artist Edward Delaney, who lives here and whose sculptures grace many an urban scene around the country.

Go back to Costelloe and continue on the R336 for 13km to Screeb Cross, turning right on the R340 to Gortmore (An Gort Mór) 4km further on. Look out for signs to Rosmuc and Pearse's Cottage.

A land of mist and mountains

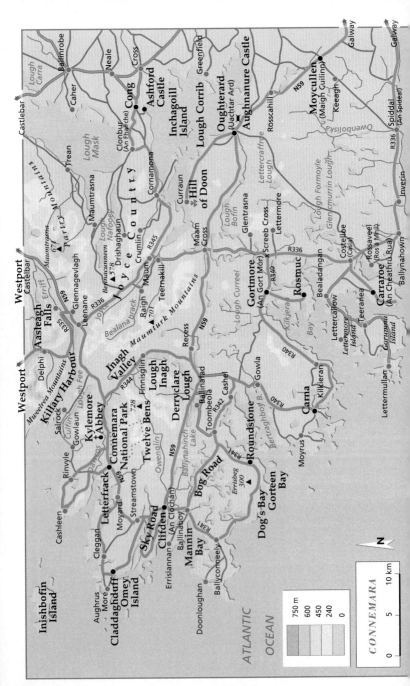

CONNEMARA

■ In Rosmuc, **Pearse's Cottage** *(mid-June-mid-September: 9.30am-6.30pm. Admission charge. Heritage Site)* was the holiday retreat of the poet and educationalist Patrick Pearse. One of the architects of the Gaelic renaissance, he came to believe that there was no alternative to Ireland's freeing herself from British rule except by force. During the Easter Uprising, he assumed the office of President of the Provisional Government, and was one of the first to be executed once the revolt was crushed.

Go back to the R340.

■ 20km further on, the fishing village of **Carna** lies hidden among an incredible mass of grey rock. The ruddy terrain reflects the colour of the masses of seaweed in the bays.

■ The road now threads its way between the steep slopes to landward and the low-lying, highly indented shore. **Roundstone** *(30km from Carna on the R340 and R342)*, is a delightful little port famous for its traditional musical instrument **workshop** *(see "Making the most of Connemara")*. The village was founded in the 19C by the Scottish engineer Alexander Nimmo, who built most of Galway's harbours and roads, and encouraged Scottish settlers to come to the area.

About 4km from Roundstone towards Ballyconneely is **Gorteen Bay**, one of Connemara's finest beaches. **Dog's Bay** follows soon after.

Return to Roundstone and continue towards Galway for 6km, then turn left towards Clifden.

The narrow, bumpy **Bog Road**★★ runs through a magical landscape of **bogland** studded with countless little lakes filled with waters of the blackest black.

This route ends in Ballinaboy at the head of **Mannin Bay** with its string of lovely beaches. To the right, the R341 leads north to Clifden.

From Galway to Clifden via Lough Corrib★
79km excluding side-trips
Allow 2hr (or a whole day including the boat trip)

This is the direct, and very beautiful route to Clifden, but anyone with a day to spare should think seriously about taking a boat trip on Lough Corrib.

Beyond **Moycullen** (Maigh Cuilinn) and its **Connemara marble** factory the N59 runs along the lough.

■ **Aughnanure Castle**★ – *25km from Galway. Mid-June-mid-September: 9.30am-6.30pm. Admission charge. Heritage Site.* Built on a rocky promontory eaten away by the waters of Lough Corrib, this is an imposing six-storeyed **tower house** dating from the time of the 13C Norman incursions. It soon fell into the hands of the O'Flahertys, then Cromwell's men took it over to guard the approaches to Galway. The interior layout is the conventional one, with the main hall on the top floor and a rooftop terrace with a superb **view** over the lough.

■ **Oughterard** (Uachtar Ard) – *3.5km beyond the castle.* This lakeside village is much favoured by fishermen. There are fine walks in the area, such as the one along **Glann Road** *(to the north)* leading to the **Hill of Doon**★, from where there is a splendid **panorama**★ over the lough and its islands. The continuation of Glann Road is called **Western Way**, a footpath running along the lakeside and terminating at Maum.

■ **Inchagoill Island**★ – *Access by boat from Oughterard. The boat leaves around 11am and returns around 4.30pm. €16. Stops are made at the island of Inchagoill (30min), Cong (2hr) on the far side of the lough (see page 374), and there is another stop at the island on the way back. Detailed information from the tourist office.*
In the middle of Lough Corrib, this island was settled by monks as early as the 5C. Of the two ruined churches here, the more interesting is the 12C **Church of the Saints** with a magnificent Romanesque doorway with carvings of heads.

From Oughterard continue on the N59 towards Clifden.

Connemara

Maam Cross (15km from Oughterard), a crossroads in the middle of the countryside, marks the beginning of the typical Connemara landscape of desolate hills and countless lakes.

Beyond Recess, the N59 runs along the banks of **Derryclare Lough**, one of Connemara's iconic images. *If there is time it is well worthwhile making a short side trip into the Inagh Valley along the R344 (see page 374).*

The road now winds round the base of the myth-laden mountains known as the **Twelve Bens**. The more energetic will want to climb to the top of **Ben Lettery** (580m), starting at the youth hostel of the same name *(turn right 3km beyond the junction for Roundstone)*, and be rewarded with a stunning **view**★★ from the summit.

North Connemara★
Around 65km – allow a day (not including walks)

■ **Clifden** (An Clochán) – *Allow half a day.* Clifden is the only settlement in Connemara which is anything like a town. It attracts lots of tourists, from America as well as from other European countries, and from springtime onwards there's nothing much Irish about it at all.

Alcock and Brown
Clifden makes much of these pioneer aviators who were the first to cross the Atlantic; their names appear again and again around the town, and there is a monument to them too. Taking off from Newfoundland, they crash-landed in a bog 5km from here on 15 June 1919 after a flight lasting 15 hours and 57 minutes, winning the prize of £10 000 offered by the Daily Mail. The telegram announcing their arrival was despatched from Clifden's post office.

However, once outside the centre, unspoilt country and deserted bays are no distance away. One excursion not to be missed is the **Sky Road**★★ *(the Lower Sky Road is better for walkers, while drivers should take the Upper Sky Road as far as the N59 towards Westport).* To begin with there are fine views down across Clifden Bay and its islands, then the road runs along Streamstown Bay, a narrow 6km inlet between the hills.

Leave Clifden on the N59 towards Westport. After 3.5km, turn left towards Claddaghduff (11km).

■ **Omey Island** – From the tiny village of **Claddaghduff** it is possible to walk at low tide to this little island with its handful of houses and lovely sandy beaches. In summer there are pony races on the sands.

Continue to Cleggan, a lively little fishing village 6km further on.

■ **Inishbofin Island**★★ – *2 or 3 boats daily from Cleggan. Crossing of 30-45min. €15 return trip, bicycles carried free. Guided walks can be arranged with an archaeologist from the Connemara Walking Centre at Clifden (See "Making the most of Connemara").*

The island, a lovely combination of pastureland, sandy beaches and dramatic cliffs, was first the home of monks, then of the notorious female pirate Grace O'Malley *(see panel, page 381).* Cromwell took over the island in order to make it into a stronghold and an internment centre for likely future rebels. Low tide reveals a rock at the foot of the **fort** he built; the condemned were bound to the rock so that their fellow-prisoners could watch them expire as the water rose. At the tip of the island, near the ruins of the abbey, are some 7C **tombstones**.

From Cleggan, return to the N59 at Moyard (8km), then continue to Letterfrack 7km further on.

■ **Letterfrack** – This neat village was laid out in the 19C by a Quaker couple, and was one of a number of such mission settlements founded along the Connemara coast. The local bishop ran an orphanage here, followed by a school, which was noted for the severity of its regime. In the graveyard of the church there is a **tombstone** erected in memory of the more than 60 pupils who perished here in the course of their education!

On the way out of the village, the **Connemara National Park Visitor Centre**⋆ *(Easter-October: 10am-5.30pm; July-August: 9.30am-6.30pm. Admission charge. Heritage Site)* has displays on the flora and fauna of the area. In the park itself, a number of easy footpaths have been laid out, and information is available on the more ambitious walks in the area, including the Twelve Bens. *(From here it is feasible to walk in a day to the youth hostel at Ben Lettery, but only for experienced walkers with the right equipment).*

■ **Kylemore Abbey** – *6km to the east of Letterfrack. Mid-March-October: 9am-6pm; November-mid-March: 10am-4pm. Free access to car park and shop, admission charge to park, building and Victorian Garden.*

At the foot of lush woodlands and overlooking a lake, this imposing Gothic Revival mansion is now an **abbey** and private college. It was originally built by the wealthy English businessman Mitchell Henry for his Irish wife, and for many years was the scene of lavish high society living. In the First World War it was taken over by the Roman Catholic Church to house a Belgian community of Benedictine nuns who had to flee their homeland. The nuns are still here, with sufficient business acumen to run a **pottery** and souvenir shop for their visitors.

There are lovely walks in the **park**, particularly along the path leading up to a statue, from where there is a fine **panorama**⋆ over mansion and lake.

To the west of the abbey is the **Victorian Garden**, a fine example of a walled garden.

On leaving the abbey, take the N59 eastwards to a junction. From here there are the alternatives of continuing along the shore of Killary Harbour or taking the R344 along the Inagh Valley.

Kylemore Abbey

B Pérousse/MICHELIN

The **Inagh Valley**✶✶ is one of the prettiest in Connemara, framed to the north by the Maumturk Mountains whose summit rises to 700m, and to the south by the Twelve Bens. Beyond **Lough Inagh** the road runs alongside **Derryclare Lough** in a landscape of bleak bogland.

On reaching the N59, turn towards Galway. At Maam Cross, turn towards Maum, then take the R345 to Cong along the north shore of Lough Corrib.

Cong and the Joyce Country
Allow half a day

■ **Cong** – *Access by boat (see above) or by road.* Built on a narrow sliver of land between Lough Corrib and Lough Mask, the village of Cong (Co Mayo) featured in the making of John Ford's 1952 film *The Quiet Man*, starring John Wayne in what many consider to have been his best performance. Some of the scenes were shot at **Ashford Castle**, an impressive edifice built between lough and river, and at one time in the ownership of the Guinness family. Now one of the world's most prestigious hotels, the castle has numbered President Reagan among its distinguished guests. The building is for residents only, but the park *(Admission charge)* is open to the public.

In the village, the **Quiet Man Heritage Cottage** *(Admission charge)*, a replica of one used in the film , is really only of interest to committed *Quiet Man* fans.

By contrast, the ruins of the **abbey**✶ *(access via the main road or the graveyard. Free admission)* are well worth a visit. The abbey was built in the 12C on the site of a monastic foundation of the 6C or 7C by Turlough O'Connor, King of Connaught and High King of Ireland. His son Roderick, the last native king of Ireland, died here in 1198. There is a fine Romanesque doorway, and the wonderfully serene **cloisters** have a number of capitals from the same era. On an island in the river is the **monks' fishing house**; it had an ingenious contraption which rang a bell when a fish was netted, freeing a monk for other duties!

A footpath off to the left beyond the fishing house leads to some **natural caves** carved out by the river, and to **Giant's Grave**, a prehistoric burial chamber.

On the way out of Cong towards Clonbur, the first turn on the right leads to the so-called **Dry Canal**.

Go back to the R345 at Clonbur and continue to Leenane.

The road passes through the area which has come to be called the **Joyce Country**✶ – not because of any associations with the writer, but because of the River Joyce, which runs down a green valley among steep-sided hills whose summits are often lost in mist.

At Leenane, a tiny settlement without much character, the R336 reaches **Killary Harbour**✶✶, a narrow fjord bounded by mountains, fed by the River Erriff *(3km east of Leenane)*. Here are the **Aasleagh Falls**, which can be reached in the course of an attractive walk.

A canal without water
The 7km-long channel was intended to link Lough Mask and Lough Corrib. Men employed on Famine relief work laboured for a miserable wage for six years, but when the attempt was made in 1854 to fill the canal with water, it disappeared almost at once through the porous rock beneath. The problem was left unsolved, as the viability of such a waterway was already being threatened by railway building.

COMING AND GOING

By bus – The private **Michael Nee** bus company, ☎ 095 510 82, runs 3 services daily between Clifden and Galway. **Bus Éireann** have one bus daily out of season (4 to 6 in season) from Galway to Oughterard and Clifden, 1 to 2 buses daily to Cong, 1 to 2 daily between Clifden and Westport via Letterfrack and Leenane.

ADDRESS BOOK

Tourist information – Tourist Office, Market Street, Clifden, ☎ 095 211 63. Abbey Street, Cong, ☎ 092 465 42.

Banks / Currency exchange – Banks and cash machines at Clifden and Oughterard.

Internet – Two Dog Café, Church Hill, Clifden.

Medical service – Chemists at Clifden and Oughterard. Photographers might well stock up in advance with their favourite film.

Bicycle hire – Mannion's, Bridge Street, Clifden. Reckon on €7.50 per day.

WHERE TO STAY

• Roundstone
Between €45-50
Wits End, ☎ 095 359 51 – 3rm ⌁ In the middle of the village, this pink-painted house is next to the post office and looks out to sea. Small rooms, charming landlady.

Heather Glen, ☎ 095 358 37 – 4rm ⌁ On the way out of Roundstone towards Recess, this bungalow overlooks the bay, and has superb views from the lounge and bedrooms (no 7 is the most attractive).

Ivy Rock, ☎ 095 358 72 – 6rm ⌁ cc Not far away from the previous establishment and with the same sea views. The rooms are all comfortable, but the better ones are upstairs.

• Oughterard
Between €13-20
Canrawer House, Station Road, ☎ 091 823 88 – 46 beds, 6rm Brand-

new large hostel, in a road to the right on the way out of the village towards Clifden. Bright, spacious dormitories, laundrette, bicycle hire, camping allowed. Inexpensive family rooms (€55 for five-bed room).

Between €45-50
Fough East, ☎ 091 552 957 – 5rm ⌁ Turn into Glann Road right in the middle of the village. Modern, attractive house, very well run by a German lady. Fresh, pleasant decor. The least expensive in this category.

Waterfall Lodge, ☎ 091 552 168 – 6rm ⌁ tv On the road out towards Clifden, this is a lovely Georgian building in parkland bordering on a rushing stream. Elegant interior, exceptionally spacious rooms (including some overlooking the stream) and a good range of choices at breakfast-time.

Corrib Wave House, Portacarron, ☎ 091 552 147 – 11rm ⌁ tv ✗ cc Clearly signposted off the Galway road 1.5km from the centre. On the banks of Lough Corrib, this establishment is run by a keen fisherman and has its regulars who keep on coming back to benefit from his advice. Boat and fishing gear can be hired. Evening meal by arrangement.

Lakeland, Portcarron, ☎ 091 552 121 – 9rm ⌁ ✗ cc Close to the previous establishment, in a pleasant garden by the waterside. Comfortable contemporary building with attractive lounges. The rooms overlooking the lake are the best. The fisherman owner hires out boats. Evening meal by arrangement.

Waterfront House, Ardnasilla, ☎ 091 552 797 – 6rm ⌁ 🖉 tv cc Take the road towards the golf course on the way out of the village towards Galway. Large new and impeccably run house set among lovely lawns on the edge of the lough. Nice bright rooms.

Lake Side Country House, Ardnasilla, ☎ 091 552 846 – 4rm ⌁ cc Very near the previous establishment, this ordinary-looking house by the lough is run by a very friendly couple. Very attractive garden with tables and chairs overlooking the lough, tea and scones served on arrival, and maybe a boat-trip with the landlord.

Camillaun, Eighterard, ☎ 091 552 678 – 4rm ⌂ CC Attractive house set among trees by a little river and with views of the lough. The owner can arrange fishing parties and has several boats.

● **Clifden**

Under €13

Clifden Town Hostel, Market Street, ☎ 095 210 76 – 20 beds, 2rm Right in the middle of town, this well-known youth hostel is often full; be sure to book in advance. Well-run and friendly, ideal location.

Between €13-25

Dún Gibbons Inn, Westport Road, ☎ 095 213 79 – 39rm ⌂ ℰ TV CC Just on the way out of town towards Westport, this large new stone building has an excellent range of facilities (kitchen, laundrette, restaurant, bike store...). It is a kind of de luxe hostel (€13 per person in a six-bed room, without breakfast) which also caters for families or anyone wanting to cook for themselves, catch up with the laundry, etc.

Between €45-50

Harbour Lodge, Beach Road, ☎ 095 216 65 – 9rm ⌂ Close to the quayside, but set back from the road in a quiet position high up. Large and rather impersonal establishment but well-run. All the rooms are identical, but the ones to go for are nos 6 and 9 on the upper floor.

Bay View, Westport Road, ☎ 095 212 86 – 5rm ⌂ TV CC On the Westport road about 3km from Clifden, this bungalow overlooks the sea. Very well-kept. Room n° 1 has a superb view.

Dun Aengus Country Home, Sky Road, ☎ 095 210 69 – 6rm ⌂ In a convenient location only 800m from the centre, a rather characterless house but quiet and comfortable.

Hillside Lodge, Sky Road, ☎ 095 214 63 – 6rm ⌂ CC Pretty pale-pink house, 1.5km along Sky Road, well-run and very comfortable. Some of the rooms have good views. Cheerful lounge with open fire for when it starts getting cool.

Lighthouse View, Sky Road, ☎ 095 221 13 – 4rm ⌂ CC Small but very pleasant rooms. Lower rates out of season.

Letterdean Farmhouse, Westport Road, ☎ 095 211 73 – 3rm ⌂ TV On the hillside 3km in the Westport direction, this little farmhouse is run by a cheerful landlord with a great sense of humour. The best room is the large one with the corner window.

White Heather House, The Square, ☎ 095 216 55 – 6rm CC In a quiet location 2km from Clifden on the Ballyconneely road. The rooms with shared facilities are less expensive.

Faul House Farmhouse, Ballyconneely Road, ☎ 095 212 39 – 6rm ⌂ Quite close to the previous establishment, a cheerful farmhouse in a quiet location. The very pleasant landlady does everything to make her guests feel at home. Generous and varied breakfast.

Between €50-65

⌂ ***Mallmore House***, Ballyconneely Road, ☎ 095 214 60 – 6rm ⌂ On the Ballyconneely road about 2km outside Clifden, this is like a little manor house with a rather grand entrance portico. Refined decor, large and cosy lounge, open fires, delightful garden, very varied breakfast. Excellent value.

Seaview House, ☎ 095 214 41 – 6rm ⌂ CC On the road leading to the harbour in Clifden, a fine stone-built house, attractively decorated and very comfortable with bright and spacious rooms.

More than €115

⌂ ***The Quay House***, Beach Road, ☎ 095 213 69 – 14rm ⌂ ℰ TV CC Right by the quayside, this is a large building full of character, expensive but with great charm. Elegant, unusual and refined decor, huge rooms furnished with antiques (some rooms have a kitchenette, all have a bath-tub). Breakfast is taken in a delightful conservatory full of flowers. Rates for the few rooms without a view might be negotiable.

● **North Connemara**

Under €13

⌂ ***Old Monastery Hostel***, Letterfrack, ☎ 095 411 32 – 50 beds, 4rm CC Cat's whiskers of a hostel in what used to be a convent. Breakfast included in the price, leafy setting, friendly landlord, comfortable, camping permitted, laundry facilities and bicycle hire.

Between €13-25

Renvyle Thatched Cottages, Renvyle, ☎ 095 434 64. A dozen pretty little thatched houses in the middle of Renvyle. The inside of each comfortable cottage is a bit dark, but the peat fires cheer things up. Accommodation for between 4 and 7 people. Reckon on €490-600 per week in July-August, much less out of season.

Between €45-50

Waterfront Rest, Derreen, ☎ 095 217 16 – 9rm ⁴⃝ TV CC On a side road to the left off the Westport road 3km outside Clifden. Rather impersonal, a bit like a small hotel, but well-kept and comfortable, in a completely unspoiled and wild setting. All the rooms have views.

Cnoc Breac, Cleggan, ☎ 095 446 88 – 4rm ⁴⃝ CC Well-kept quiet accommodation 800m from the village. Two of the rooms have sea views.

Ben Breen House, Toreen, Moyard, ☎ 095 411 71 – 6rm ⁴⃝ TV CC Clearly signposted from the N59 7km from Clifden towards Letterfrack. The helpful landlady is full of good advice on how to set about exploring the area. Her house is very comfortable, beautifully kept and quiet.

Corner Stones, Crocnaraw, Moyard, ☎ 095 413 64 – 3rm ⁴⃝ Clearly signposted from the main road 1km out of Moyard towards Clifden. Rather characterless house but very pleasant all the same and one of the least expensive in this category.

Rockfield Lodge, Moyard, ☎ 095 413 66 – 8rm ⁴⃝ TV 🍽 CC On the N59 just short of Moyard when coming from Clifden. Modern, comfortable house. The better rooms are upstairs. Breakfast is taken in the conservatory, which has fine views.

⊛ Old Castle House, Curragh, Renvyle, ☎ 095 434 61 – 5rm ⁴⃝ ✗ Poorly signposted, but keep a look-out for the castle 4km beyond Renvyle on the bay road. In a remote and wild setting by the sea and in the shadow of a ruined castle, this place is for those wanting to stay

amidst unspoiled Nature. Pretty rooms with lots of pine and snug duvets. Splendid walking. Evening meal by arrangement.

Between €50-65

⊛ Ker Mor, Claddaghduff, ☎ 095 449 54 – 5rm ⁴⃝ CC Turn left towards Claddaghduff off the Westport road 3.5km outside Clifden and continue for 5km. Deep in the countryside, this pleasant cottage is kept by a lady oyster farmer from Brittany. Her oysters can be sampled. Meals by arrangement in her lovely kitchen. Lots of tips on what to do in the area which she has fallen in love with.

The Diamond Lodge, Kylemore Road, Letterfrack, ☎ 095 413 80 – 3rm ⁴⃝ CC Elegant house painted a pale pink and set in parkland on the way out of the village towards Leenane. Refined and very comfortable.

Doneen Lodge, Barnaderg Bay, Letterfrack, ☎ 095 410 60 – 6rm ⁴⃝ 🖉 TV CC On the Clifden road 2km outside Letterfrack. Lovely wooded surroundings. Relaxing lounge and conservatory. Generous breakfast, choice of traditional or fresh fish and smoked salmon.

Between €65-90

⊛ Garraunbaun House, Moyard, ☎ 065 416 49 – 3rm ⁴⃝ CC Look out for a not very prominent sign on the way out of Moyard towards Clifden and continue for another 1.5km. This Georgian house in its park overlooks the bay. Its rooms are bright and tastefully furnished, there are books everywhere and an appreciation of fine things. The multilingual landlady serves delicious tit-bits in her great big kitchen in the heart of the house. Most guests find it difficult to leave. Less expensive out of season (€65 for two).

• Cong and around

Between €13-25

Cong Travel Inn, ☎ 092 463 10 – 15rm ⁴⃝ In the middle of the village, brand-new accommodation, comfortable and not expensive, but a bit on the dark side.

The Quiet Man Hostel, ☎ 092 460 89 – 30 beds, 6rm Near the previous establishment, this is a traditional and very welcoming hostel. Big kitchen, laundrette, bicycle hire. Also available are 4-bed cottages, let by the day out of season (€32), and by the week in season (€315).

Forest View Apartments, Culleen, ☎ 092 465 32. ⌂ In the middle of the countryside, two apartments to rent by the night or week. The ground-floor apartment is quite small but sleeps 4 (€25-50 per night according to the season). The larger apartment on the upper floor has facilities like a washing machine and dishwasher as well as country views (€430 per week or €75 per night for 6-8 people).

Inisfree House, Ashford, ☎ 092 460 82 – 4rm ⌂ On its own deep in the country, 1.5km west of Cong, large traditional farmhouse, plain and comfortable.

Nymphsfield House, Gortroe, ☎ 092 463 20 – 4rm ⌂ CC New and well-run house on the road running off opposite the main doorway of Ashford castle. Quieter location than in the village.

River Lodge, ☎ 092 460 57 – 5rm ⌂ TV CC On the riverbank in the middle of the village, with comfortable bedrooms but impersonal public rooms.

Robin's Roost, Drumshiel, ☎ 092 460 51 – 4rm ⌂ ✕ Go west out of the village and turn right by the bridge and the Esso petrol station (it's clearly signposted). A house on several levels, full of nooks and crannies and set in a delightful garden. The landlady is an expert fish cook (evening meal by arrangement).

Hazel Grove B&B, Drumshiel, ☎ 092 460 60 – 5rm ⌂ CC Very close to the previous establishment, well-kept by a very friendly landlady.

⌂ **Ballykine House**, Clonbur, ☎ 092 461 50 – 5rm ⌂ Clearly signposted to the right off the Clonbur road 3.5km from Cong, this is an imposing residence in parkland overlooking Lough Mask. Lovely walks in the neighbourhood. Very pleasant landlady full of useful information about the area. A bit more expensive than the other establishments in this category, but well worth it.

• **Leenane**
Between €40-50
Ben Gorm Farm, Bundorragha, ☎ 095 422 05 – 5rm ⌂ On the R335

towards Louisborough 10km from Leenane, this farmhouse overlooks Killary Harbour in a splendid setting. Friendly reception, peat fires and good tips for walkers.

Killary House, Leenane, ☎ 095 422 54 – 7rm Big house overlooking Killary Harbour on the road towards Letterfrack. The rooms which share a bathroom are less expensive.

Between €50-70
Portfinn Lodge, Leenane, ☎ 095 422 65 – 8rm ⌂ ✎ ✕ CC Excellent location on the way out of the village towards Letterfrack, a comfortable and tastefully decorated establishment. Room n° 2 is tiny for the price, but the rooms overlooking the bay are much better. Nevertheless rather expensive in season. A good place to eat (see "Eating out").

EATING OUT

Restaurants and other establishments are not categorised by price, as the cost of a meal will vary greatly according to the type of dish chosen and the time of day.

• **Oughterard**
O'Fathartha's, Main Street, ☎ 091 552 692. Good reputation for its fish specialities, including hot smoked trout and eel stuffed with smoked salmon. Lunch €6.50-7.50, dinner more expensive.

The Golf Club Restaurant, ☎ 091 552 131. Three kilometres outside the village towards Galway. Straightforward cooking, generous portions. Open all day to 9.30pm. Lunch €5-8, and dinner €10-15.

Clifden and around
Two Dog Café, Church Hill. Stripped-down designer establishment, good for elevenses or a soup and roll, but otherwise very expensive. Daily newspapers to read.

Mitchell's, Market Street, ☎ 095 218 67. Cheerful setting and well-prepared traditional food. Light lunches available. In the evening dishes vary between €13-18.

Destry's, Main Street, ☎ 095 217 22. Unusual and delicious dishes based on local produce given an innovative treatment. Between €20-25.

Eldon's Hotel, Roundstone, ☎ 095 359 33. Fish and seafood specialities. Cooking of a high standard with ultra-fresh ingredients. Reckon on between €20-25.

High Moors, Doneen, ☎ 095 213 42. On the Ballyconneely road 1km out of Clifden, this restaurant in a private house is run by people passionate about healthy, natural eating. Super local ingredients prepared with considerable talent. Main dishes between €13-18. Dinner only; closed Monday and Tuesday; reservation advisable.

Erriseask House Restaurant, Ballyconneely, ☎ 095 235 53. Delicious and elegant cuisine in an attractive setting. Dinner only. Booking advisable. Reckon on at least €25.

North Connemara

Olivers, Cleggan, ☎ 095 446 40. Bar and restaurant, reasonably priced and tasty seafood meals. Lunchtime snacks are generous and not at all expensive.

Pangur Bán, Letterfrack, ☎ 095 412 43. Pretty thatched house in the village, an intimate setting for straightforward but delicious cooking. Irish stew, salads, sandwiches for lunch for between €2.50-7.50, and more elaborate traditional or more exotic dishes in the evening for between €13-19.

Portfinn Lodge, Leenane, ☎ 095 422 65. Good choice of food made from local ingredients, particularly seafood. Pleasant dining room. Reckon on €19-plus.

HAVING A DRINK

• **Clifden**

Mannion's Bar, Market Street. The friendliest and least touristy of Clifden's pubs. Excellent traditional music. Pub grub at lunchtime and early evening.

• **Letterfrack**

Veldon's, cheerful pub, lots of atmosphere, traditional music at the weekend.
Molly's, local people's favourite bar. Music at the weekend.

OTHER THINGS TO DO

Fishing – Connemara is one of the world's great places for freshwater fishing. Permits can be obtained from

Western Regional Fisheries, Weir Lodge, Galway (near the Cathedral), or in one of the numerous fishing equipment shops around the area. Trout and salmon may be caught between February and late September. The best fishing centre is Oughterard. **Tuck's Fishing Tackle Shop** or **Lakeland Angling Centre**, ☎ 091 821 21.

Walking – Peat bogs are very treacherous and signposted footpaths virtually non-existent. It is essential to get advice from local experts before setting off. Information, maps, and guides are all available at the **Connemara Walking Centre**, Market Street, Clifden, ☎ 095 213 79. **Connemara Safari**, Sky Road, Clifden, ☎ 095 210 71, organises 5-day walking tours.

Riding – **Cleggan Trekking Centre**, Cleggan, ☎ 095 447 46. **Glen Valley Stables**, Glencroff, Leenane, ☎ 095 422 69.

Festivals

Bog Week, at Letterfrack last week in May. Traditional festival, with concerts and dance.

Connemara Pony Show, at Clifden in August. Buyers come from all over the world to this very atmospheric horse fair starring the area's famous ponies.

Clifden Arts Week, last week in September. Free concerts, theatre performances, poetry readings, and most of all, a great atmosphere in the pubs.

SHOPPING

Marble – **Connemara Marble Factory**, on the N59, Moycullen, ☎ 091 555 102, has all kinds of jewellery and many other items made from the green marble of Connemara, at prices to suit all pockets.

Music – **Roundstone Musical Instruments**, Roundstone, ☎ 095 358 75, is a place no music enthusiast should miss. All kinds of traditional instruments, including harps, Irish flutes and bodhráns.

Smoked salmon – **Salmon Factory**, Salt Lake Manor, Clifden (2km along the Ballyconneely road), ☎ 095 212 78. Expertly smoked wild salmon. Postal delivery can be arranged.

Making the most of Connemara

SOUTH MAYO★
WESTPORT
Co Mayo
Michelin map 923 C-D / 6-7

Not to be missed
A picnic on Silver Strand.
The climb up Croagh Patrick.

And remember...
Countryside lovers should spend the daytime walking and save
Westport for late afternoon / early evening.
Stout footwear is needed for climbing Croagh Patrick.

With its lonely mountains and vast sandy beaches, Mayo is even wilder and more unspoiled than neighbouring Connemara. It is also a sacred land; the pilgrims come in their thousands to Croagh Patrick to pay homage to the country's patron saint, and ever since the Virgin Mary appeared to the people of Knock in 1879, this village has become the Irish equivalent of Lourdes, with an ultra-modern airport and a huge basilica.

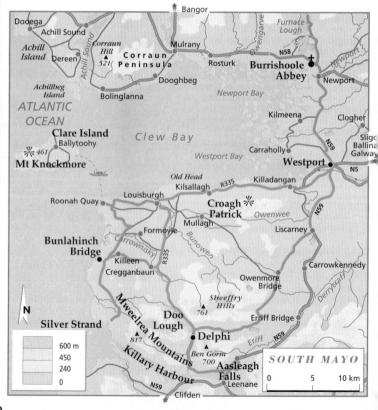

From Killary Harbour to Westport★★

*Around 75km including a side-trip to Silver Strand –
36km via the Scenic Road*

Thirty metres deep at its mouth, **Killary Harbour** (*see page 374*) is an arm of the sea running 14km inland between rugged cliffs. Imposing uplands border it to the north, the highest summit being that of Mweelrea (817m).

The R335 runs through the mountains, Ben Gorm to the right, Mweelrea to the left, before coming to the oddly-named **Delphi**, called thus because the shrine in Greece took the fancy of the Earl of Sligo on his travels.

Just beyond Delphi, a bumpy road takes off to the right, forming the direct route to Westport. This is the **Scenic Road★★**, which winds for 20km through a wild and partly afforested mountain landscape before joining the N59 at Liscarney.

To take the longer coastal route to Westport, continue on the R335.

After the junction with the Scenic Road, the R335 runs along the shore of **Doo Lough**, a romantic mountain lough between Mweelrea and the Sheeffry Hills.
A path from the northern end of the lough gives experienced walkers the chance to climb **Ben Bury** (795m) and even **Mweelrea★★** itself (*16km, reckon on 8hr of difficult walking to the summit, and take a map*), from where the **views★★** over the region are simply breathtaking.

To get to the coast, turn left about 6km beyond the lough and follow Scenic Road signs to Silver Strand. At the village of Killeen turn towards the sea by the graveyard.

A sign points towards **Bunlahinch Bridge★**, an extraordinary clapper bridge over the river made by laying flat slabs on stone piles.

Go back the way you came and continue south to Silver Strand.

Silver Strand★★ is a vast beach of pale sand, backed by dunes and mountains, which together make up one of the classic images of this part of Ireland.

Go back the way you came and continue towards Louisburgh (16km). Before getting there, turn left to Roonagh Quay, the port for Clare Island.

■ **Clare Island★★** – *Clare Island Ferries, Roonagh Pier, ☎ 098 282 88, has at least three crossings daily between May-September, and 8 in July-August; €13, bicycles carried free. Buses leave from Westport Harbour daily at 10am. Enquire by phone out of season.*
Guarding the entrance to Clew Bay, this island with a population of 140 owes its fame to the pirates who made it their lair. The 16C lady pirate **Grace O'Malley** is supposed to be buried in the ruins of the island's Cistercian **abbey** close to the beach. Unusually for Ireland, the abbey has traces of **frescoes** on its ceiling.

With fewer visitors than the Aran Islands, but just as beautiful, Clare Island has very impressive 90m-high **cliffs**, dominated by **Mount Knockmore** (461m); the difficult climb to the summit is rewarded by a splendid **view★★**. But the cliffs and heights as seen from down below are spectacular too, and the best way to enjoy them is by taking a walk to the **lighthouse**.

Go back to Louisburgh and continue towards Westport. After about 13km turn into the car park at Croagh Patrick.

Queen of the West

Widow of an O'Flaherty killed in the course of a raid on the English at Galway, Grace O'Malley or Granuaile was a sailor of matchless abilities. Her life as a pirate preying on ships travelling along the west coast was a dramatic one. She once gave birth in the middle of an engagement with a Turkish vessel, but tore herself away from her newborn child in order to take up the fight. When her second husband made a pact with the English, she threw him out. Captured by her old opponents, she made her escape with the help of her son. Nicknamed the Queen of the West, she made a trip to the English court and pleaded successfully for the release of her brother and son.

■ **Croagh Patrick**★★ – *Allow 3hr there and back.* The climb up the sacred mountain presents no special difficulties though the stony surface can make the going tedious. Thousands of the faithful of all ages make the ascent, some of them barefoot, to take part in the famous **pilgrimage** (*see "Making the most of South Mayo"*). The panel giving would-be pilgrims useful advice is well worth a look. The climb gives ever more impressive views of **Clew Bay** and its countless islands, and from the summit there is the reward of a **panorama**★★ over the whole of Mayo.

■ Westport

Co Mayo – Pop 3 800
Allow half a day to explore the town and its surroundings

In striking contrast to its setting in a landscape of great austerity, Westport is an elegant and lively place strung out along the Carrowbeg River. The town's Georgian architecture recalls the days of British domination; it is an interesting example of an 18C planned urban settlement, carried out by James Wyatt for the local great landowners, the Brownes, who were later ennobled as the Marquesses of Sligo.

Westport Quay

The old port with its fine stone warehouses is on the western outskirts of the town. This is the location too of **Westport House**★★ (*June-September: 2pm-6pm; July-August: 10.30am-6pm. Admission charge*), the former residence of the Browne family, a fine Classical mansion begun in 1730 by Richard Castle with later additions by Thomas

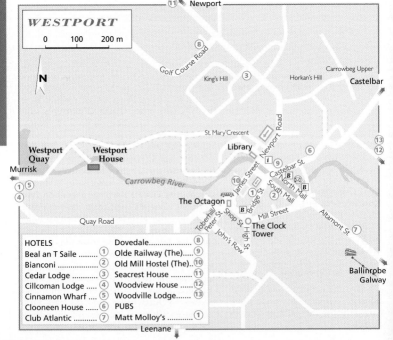

WESTPORT

0   100   200 m

N

Newport

Golf Course Road

King's Hill

Horkan's Hill

Carrowbeg Upper

Castelbar

St Mary'Crescent

Library

Newport Road

Castelbar St.

North Mall

South Mall

Murrisk

Westport Quay

Westport House

Carrowbeg River

The Octagon

James Street

Bridge St.

Toberthill

Peter St.

Shop St.

Mill Street

The Clock Tower

Quay Road

John's Row

High St.

Altamont St.

Ballinrobe
Galway

HOTELS		
Beal an T Saile	①	Dovedale ⑧
Bianconi	②	Olde Railway (The) ⑨
Cedar Lodge	③	Old Mill Hostel (The) ⑩
Cillcoman Lodge	④	Seacrest House ⑪
Cinnamon Wharf	⑤	Woodview House ⑫
Clooneen House	⑥	Woodville Lodge ⑬
Club Atlantic	⑦	**PUBS**
		Matt Molloy's ①

Leenane

Westport Horse Fair

Ivory and by Wyatt. The fascinating interior has fine **furniture**, a grand library, **family portraits**, china and porcelain, and many other items reflecting the life-style of the Anglo-Irish Ascendancy.

The **park** has a small zoo and is ideal for family walks.

North of Westport

Leave the town on the N59, then turn left in 2.4km after passing through Newport. Built on an arm of the sea, **Burrishoole Abbey**, a 15C Dominican foundation, is a place of great serenity.

Anyone heading for Ballina or Sligo should take advantage of the excellent scenic short cut called the **Nephin Drive**★★ *(look out for signs on the N59 to the north of Newport)*. This route winds through rhododendron-clad hill country and past a pretty lake. After Furnace Lough and Lough Feeagh, the road degenerates somewhat and crosses a densely forested area at the foot of the mountains. Then comes a col, from where there is a superb **panorama** over the whole of north Mayo. Standing out from the ocean of dark bogland are the slender white forms of wind turbines and the outline of a power station.

COMING AND GOING

By bus – Buses start and terminate at the Octagon in Westport. 3 services daily to Galway, 1 or 2 daily to Clifden and 2 daily to Sligo.

By train – Westport's station is in Altamont Street. 3 trains daily to Dublin (3hr30min).

ADDRESS BOOK

Tourist information – *Tourist Office*, The Mall, Westport, ☎ 098 257 11.

Banks / Currency exchange – Banks and cash machines at Westport.

Internet – *Dunning's Cyber Pub*, The Octagon.

WHERE TO STAY

• **Around Killary Harbour**
Between €40-45
Delphi Adventure Centre, Leenane, ☎ 095 423 07 – 90 beds, 20rm TV 🏄 CC Among the mountains between Leenane and Louisburgh, an architecturally ambitious building with a mixture of accommodation and facilities. Part is a comfortable hostel on the conventional pattern, part a hotel (considerably more expensive) with access to saunas, jacuzzi, gym, etc. The two parts share the open-air sports and recreational facilities (rock-climbing, canoeing...).
Between €75-150
🏠***Delphi Lodge***, Leenane, ☎ 095 422 11 – 12rm 🏄 ✗ CC Elegant Georgian mansion up against the mountain with a private fishing lake reserved for guest use. Cheerful and refined setting, good food, extra-ordinary landscapes. Cottages to rent.

• **Silver Strand**
Between €40-45
Bayside Farmhouse, Killadoon, Louisburgh, ☎ 098 686 13 – 5rm 🏄 On the way to Silver Strand, this is a plain but welcoming little farmhouse close to the beach. Wild countryside all around, good for walking.

• **Clare Island**
Under €13
Bay View Hostel, ☎ 098 263 07 – 16 beds. Basic accommodation attached to

the pub. OK for one night's stay on the island. Also has some hotel-standard rooms.
Between €100-115
🏠***The Lighthouse***, ☎ 098 451 20 – 5rm 🏄 CC The old lighthouse has been adapted to house guests while retaining all of its essential character. The views are breathtaking and the solitude is absolute. Transport from the landing stage if needed. Dinner €25.

• **Westport and around**
Between €13-25
🏠***Traenlaur Lodge***, Lough Feeagh, Newport, ☎ 098 413 58 – 32 beds. Dream location for walkers and other nature lovers, embedded among rhododendrons and by a stream rushing down to the lough. In an isolated position 8km from Newport on the Nephin Drive, this big old house is very welcoming. There is a little shop, laundrette and kitchen. Meals available. Superb walking country all around.
The Old Mill Hostel, James Street, Westport, ☎ 098 270 45 – 46 beds, 2rm CC An old but completely renovated building in a very central location, well-kept and comfortable. Reservations only possible with credit card.
Club Atlantic, Altamont Street, Westport, ☎ 098 266 44 – 120 beds, 12rm Opposite the station on the Galway road, 5min on foot from the centre. Large modern building with very good facilities (billiards, ping-pong, laundrette, large kitchen, small shop...)
Between €40-45
Cedar Lodge, Kings Hill, ☎ 098 254 17 – 4rm 🏄 TV CC In a residential area very close to the centre on the Newport side of town. Friendly reception, family atmosphere and generous breakfast.
Dovedale, Golfcourse Road, ☎ 098 251 54 – 4rm 🏄 CC On the way out of town towards Newport. Spacious and very quiet rooms. Lovely garden.
Woodview House, Buckwaria, ☎ 098 278 79 – 6rm 🏄 TV CC Leave Westport on the N5 in the Dublin direction and turn right just before the Knockranny Hotel. Large, very quiet house, 1.5km from the centre. Warm, spontaneous welcome.

Woodville Lodge, Knockranny, ☎ 098 278 22 – 4rm ⌖] [TV] Attractive, new house in the same road as the previous establishment, next to the hotel.

Seacrest House, Claggan, Kilmeena, ☎ 098 416 31 – 6rm ⌖] ✕ [CC] Turn left off the Newport road 6km from town and continue for a further 3km. In the middle of the countryside overlooking Clew Bay, very well-kept by an amiable landlady who is also a good cook (evening meal by arrangement). The blue room is the best, both in terms of view and price (shared bathroom).

Cillcoman Lodge, Rossbeg, ☎ 098 263 79 – 6rm ⌖] [TV] [CC] Signposted to the right on leaving Westport Quay towards Louisburgh. Quiet and very comfortable.

⌂**Beal an tSáile**, Murrisk, ☎ 098 640 12 – 3rm ⌖] [TV] On the coast road towards Louisburgh 9km from Westport. Delightful garden giving directly onto the sea, exuberant and refined décor, lux-urious rooms, superb views, friendly reception, and all this at a price barely more than the average.

Between €55-65

Cloneen House, Castlebar Street, ☎ 098 253 61 – 16rm ⌖] 🖉 [TV] Very near the centre of town on the Dublin road, this large house is almost like a hotel. Comfortable but impersonal. The rooms at the rear are quieter.

Apartments to rent

Bianconi Apartments, South Mall, ☎ 098 278 00. Right in the middle of town, two-room apartments with all comforts. June-September only, between €380-500 per week for 4.

Cinnamon Wharf Apartments, The Quay, ☎ 098 276 81. Next door to Westport House, these apartments are in a converted stone-built warehouse. All comforts. The best rooms are upstairs. To rent by the day or week. Reckon on €235 per week for 4 people out of season, rising to €600 between mid-July-mid-August.

Eating out

• Westport

Kinara Café, Market Lane, ☎ 098 260 29. Delicious exotic and unusual dishes, quiches, at all price levels. Lunch menu valid to 6.30pm, when prices rise.

The Lemon Peel, The Octagon. Traditional dishes or classic cuisine à la carte. "Early Bird" meals with generous helpings served between 5pm-7pm for €15.

The Quay Cottage, Westport Quay, specialises in fish and seafood. Reckon on €15-20 for a main course.

Having a drink

⌂**Matt Molloy's**, Bridge Street, is Westport's most celebrated pub, not least because the landlord is one of the Chieftains. Music every evening during the season.

Festivals

Croagh Patrick Pilgrimage, last Sunday in July. An opportunity to experience the full extent of Irish piety. Not for anyone who doesn't like crowds, and Westport itself is full of visitors.

Arts Festival, late September, involves readings, drama, and music in all the town's pubs. The standard is high and the atmosphere great.

Horse & Pony Show, late September. The streets become a huge market where the horse is king. Incredible atmosphere helped along by lashings of beer.

Making the most of South Mayo

NORTH MAYO ★
ACHILL ISLAND
Co Mayo
Michelin map 923 C-C-E-F / 5-6

Not to be missed
Atlantic Drive on Achill Island.

And remember...
Avoid driving into the sun by doing the Atlantic Drive in the morning.

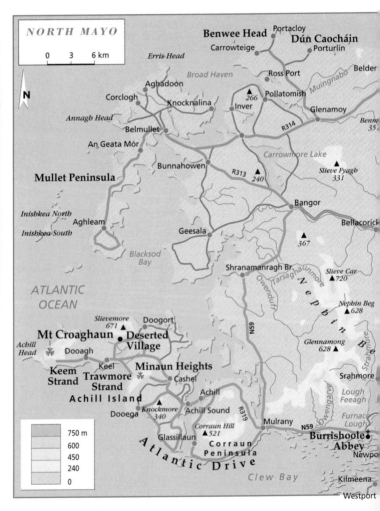

NORTH MAYO

0   3   6 km

N

Benwee Head
Portacloy
Dún Caocháin
Carrowteige
Porturlin
Erris Head
Belder
Broad Haven
Ross Port
Muingnabo
Aghadoon
Pollatomish
266
Glenamoy
Corclogh
Knocknalina
Inver
R314
Benm 35
Annagh Head
Belmullet
Carrowmore Lake
An Geata Mór
Bunnahowen
R313
240
Slieve Fyagh 331
Mullet Peninsula
Bangor
Inishkea North
Bellacorick
Aghleam
Geesala
Inishkea South
367
ATLANTIC OCEAN
Blacksod Bay
Shranamanragh Br.
Tarsaghaunmore
Slieve Car 720
Owenduff
Nephin Beg
Slievemore 671
Doogort
Nephin Beg 628
Mt Croaghaun
Deserted Village
Achill Head
Dooagh
N59
Glennamong 628
Keem Strand
Keel
Minaun Heights
Trawmore Strand
Cashel
Srahmore
Achill Island
Achill
Lough Feeagh
Dooega
Knockmore 340
Achill Sound
R319
Corraun Hill 521
Mulrany
N59
Furnace Lough
Glassillaun
Corraun Peninsula
Burrishoole Abbey
Owengarve
Srahmore
Newpo
A t l a n t i c   D r i v e
Clew Bay
Kilmeena
Westport

750 m
600
450
240
0

Connemara and Mayo

North Mayo is unknown Ireland, most of it a great damp desert of blanket bog. While the austere panoramas of Achill Island attract numerous visitors, the rest of the county is completely unspoiled, its roads free of traffic, its empty immensity devoid of people.

Visitors coming into the area from Westport (*see page 382*) should follow the **Atlantic Drive★★★** signs. From the village of Mulrany, this route winds round the peninsula giving lovely **views★** towards Achill Island on the far side of the isthmus.

Achill Island★★
24km by 19km
Round trip of about 100km – allow a day

Linked to the mainland by a bridge, Achill Island is a splendid mixture of sheer cliffs, sand or pebble beaches, and mountains like Slievemore (670m) and Croaghaun (666m).

The village of Achill Sound stands at the end of the isthmus; from here, Atlantic Drive hugs the south coast of the island in a great bend, passing one of Grace O'Malley's **tower houses**. Once past the point, it is a succession of bleak cliffs and deserted bays all the way to Dooega. Just short of Cashel, a left turn leads towards **Minaun Heights★★** (464m), a summit giving a unique panorama over the whole of the island. Return to Atlantic Drive, and after the road has skirted round the north of Minaun Heights, turn left at a sign indicating the **Fr Sweeney Monument**. This road leads to **Trawmore Strand★**, a beach at the foot of high cliffs, where the peace and quiet is only broken by the sound of the waves on the shingle and by the sight of an occasional dolphin. Return to the main road and continue to Keel, the island's miniature capital, then on through Dooagh to **Keem Strand★★**, a beach of fine sand nestling at the foot of the island's highest mountain. The more energetic may want to climb **Mount Croaghaun★★★**, the spectacular western flank of which drops almost vertically into the sea.

Return to Mulrany and continue north on the N59 to Bangor.

North Mayo coast
Around 150km – allow half a day including stops

In north Mayo, the landscape becomes even wilder, a peaty Sahara undulating to the horizon with not a single tree or trace of habitation.

■ Beyond Bangor, take the R313 towards Belmullet *(19km)* at the base of the **Mullet Peninsula**. The flat countryside of the peninsula may lack dramatic scenery, but, untouched by tourism, it is a paradise for sea anglers and cyclists.

Go back through Belmullet and turn onto the R314 in about 5km. 22.5km beyond Belmullet, turn left towards Portacloy.

■ This detour to **Benwee Head**★★ passes through a remote area which is fine walking country *(starting out from Portacloy head west, or even better east)*. One of the best routes is the one leading to the **Dún Caocháin cliffs**★★.

From Portacloy, go southeast for 13.5km and turn left on to the R314 towards Céide Fields, 17km further on.

■ Standing in an elevated position, the archaeological site of **Céide Fields**★★ *(June-September: 9.30am-6.30pm; rest of year: 10am-5pm. Admission charge. Heritage Site)* has revealed much valuable detail about how the landscape of Mayo has evolved since prehistoric times. While the excavations themselves are of no great interest to the untrained eye, the visitor centre engages the imagination with its displays on the 5 000-year old settlement pattern they have revealed, together with a fascinating explanation of the evolution of its 4m-deep covering of blanket bog. There is also a superb film evoking the natural wonders of the area. Near the car park there is a fine **viewpoint**★ overlooking the sombre cliffs and the sea.

Carry on along the R314 to Ballycastle and turn left (18.5km detour).

■ **Downpatrick Head**★ comes into view along the coast road. It is a striking illustration of the geological structure of this part of the coast, with its eroded cliff and its detached rock stack.

Continue along this road to the R314. From here it is 5.5km to Killala.

Cutting peat

C. Legrand/MICHELIN

■ The quiet little port of **Killala** is also an old-fashioned seaside resort. It is the place where the French general Humbert landed in the hope of playing an active part in the 1798 Rebellion. Despite initial successes against a nominally superior British force, he was eventually defeated, though one of his chief difficulties in the meantime was coping with his undisciplined Irish allies, many of whom only spoke Gaelic. Killala has a little cathedral and a 12C **round tower**, 25m high, which served as a refuge in times of peril.

Ballina and around
12km south of Killala
Allow 3hr to include a visit to Foxford Woollen Mills

The largest town in north Mayo may be lacking in distinctive character, but it makes a good base and it is much frequented by anglers because of the fine fishing on the River Moy. Every summer in July Ballina hosts a **Salmon Festival**, a lively affair which is part town fair and part fishing competition.

Fifteen kilometres to the south of the town on the N26 are the **Foxford Woollen Mills**★ *(10am-6pm except Sunday; 45min factory tour Monday-Friday. Admission charge)*, producing tweeds and plaids. The factory was founded in the late 19C by a nun determined to relieve the extreme poverty of the local population. As well as the factory she also set up a free school with the aim of encouraging weaving families to settle nearby.

Making the most of North Mayo

COMING AND GOING
By bus – Ballina has 3 buses a day to Dublin, 9 to Galway, 3 to Westport and 4 to Sligo.

By train – Three trains daily between Ballina and Dublin.

ADDRESS BOOK
Banks / Currency exchange – Banks and cash machines at Ballina and Belmullet. Bureau de change at the post office in Achill.

Medical service – Chemists at Belmullet and Ballina (1hr film processing).

WHERE TO STAY
Bear in mind that outside the few villages the area is virtually uninhabited, B&Bs are very thin on the ground, and you should plan your tour accordingly.

● **Achill Island**
Between €9-20
Wild Haven Hostel, Achill Sound, ☎ 098 453 92 – 26 beds. This large establishment is a bit off the through road but near the village and offers a very friendly reception.

Between €40-45
Hy Breasal, Achill Sound, ☎ 098 451 14 – 4rm ⚹ TV CC This new and pretty house is clearly signposted on arriving on Achill Island. It is in a quiet location but near the village.

Woodview House, Springvale, Achill Sound, ☎ 098 452 61 – 4rm ⚹ Clearly signposted on the way out of Achill Sound towards Dooagh. Small but well-kept rooms and sea views.

West End House, Dooagh, ☎ 098 432 04 – 4rm ⚹ TV CC Very close to the sea, this house has a charming landlady. Breakfast is taken in an attractive conservatory.

Between €45-50
⊕ **Stella Maris**, Keel, ☎ 098 432 97 – 8rm ⚹ TV CC Traditional house in the village with somewhat over-the-top decor. Lavish facilities include bidets in every bedroom and there are wonderful

views. The rooms with four-poster beds are more expensive. The most attractive room is n° 6.

More than €65
Bervie, Keel, ☎ 098 431 14 – 15 rooms, 🛏 TV CC This establishment consists of a pleasantly laid out series of long, low buildings by the beach. The more expensive rooms have sea views (no 28 is a little jewel, with unforgettable views, just the thing for a romantic holiday).

😋 **Joyce's Marian Villa**, Keel, ☎ 098 431 34 – 20rm 🛏 TV This older house has been tastefully renovated. Attractive, refined décor, hearty welcome and efficient service. Tea and scones served on arrival. A good place to stay despite the rather high rates.

• Belmullet
Between €9-20
😋 **Kilcommon Lodge**, Pollatomish, Ballina, ☎ 097 846 21 – 20 beds, 4rm Turn left off the R314 between Belmullet and Portacloy. Delightful cottage in a flowery garden at the foot of the hill. Well-kept and comfortable, ideal for walkers. Laundrette.

Between €40-45
Conan House, Attycunnane, Ballina Road, Belmullet, ☎ 097 812 94 – 3rm 🛏 Plain, inexpensive accommodation, family atmosphere and friendly welcome.

Kemar House, Carne, Bellmullet, ☎ 097 813 81 – 7rm 🛏 🖉 TV Clearly signposted off the road leading to the golf course and the Mullet Peninsula. Big building on rising ground, very comfortable and with a superb view.

• Killala
Between €40-45
Avondale B&B, ☎ 096 322 29 – 4rm 🛏 Plain, well-kept little house by the quayside.

Beach View House, Ross, ☎ 096 320 23 – 4rm 🛏 Turn right towards the beach 3km out of Killala in the Ballycastle direction. Almost completely on its own, this is a pleasant bungalow close to the beach.

• Ballina
Under €45
Quay House, The Quay, ☎ 096 212 08 – 3rm 🛏 On the riverside road on the

way into Ballina from the Sligo direction. Nothing special about the accommodation but very friendly reception. Car park to the rear.

Between €45-50
Suncroft B&B, 3 Cathedral Close, ☎ 096 215 73 – 5rm 🛏 CC Very close to the centre of Ballina behind the cathedral. Small but comfortable rooms. Those with shared facilities are less expensive.

😋 **Red River Lodge**, Iceford, Quay Road, ☎ 096 228 41 – 4rm 🛏 CC Beyond The Quay 6km from Ballina along the river, this is a very large house, impeccably run by its charming owner. Fine views, delicious breakfast, no charge for receiving email.

Woodlands B&B, Sligo Road, ☎ 096 229 56 – 6rm 🛏 On the main road. Small but well-kept rooms. A bit noisy, but fine if there's nothing else.

😋 **Cnoc Brendain**, Quay Road, ☎ 096 221 45 – 4rm 🛏 ✗ CC 2km along the river beyond The Quay. Lovely garden. Friendly welcome. Open May-mid-September.

Michael Swartz Apartments, Ballina Angling Centre, Dillon Terrace, ☎ 096 218 50 – 2rm 🛏 TV CC 4 to 6-bed apartments in the middle of Ballina. All facilities. €63 per night, €380 per week.

More than €75
Bartra House Hotel, Pearse Street, ☎ 096 222 00 – 21rm 🛏 🖉 TV ✗ CC Small and comfortable hotel in the centre of Ballina, a little expensive. Single travellers should take advantage of the commercial rate out of season.

EATING OUT
• Achill Island
The Beehive, Keel, is ideal for lunch and for snacks at other times.

The Chalet, Keel, has dinners of quality at higher prices – dishes upwards of €13.

• Belmullet
The Golf Club Restaurant, is the best bet for generous meals at reasonable prices.

Western Strands Hotel, in Belmullet, is much prized by local people. Traditional meals at traditional rates (€13-15 per dish).

• **Ballina**

Gaughan's Pub, O'Rahilly's Street. Behind the delightful front with its display of old books, this establishment offers traditional pub grub.

Murphy's, Sligo Road, is the best place to go to eat at any time. Bar food prices at lunchtime, more expensive upstairs in the evening. Dishes from €13-20.

Tulios, Pearce Street, makes a change from the pub, with pizza and pasta specialities costing at least €9.

OTHER THINGS TO DO

Seaweed baths, about 13km from Ballina in the Sligo direction, ***Kilcullen's Seaweed Baths***, Enniscrone, ☎ 096 362 38, practice the ancient Irish tradition of a seaweed bath taken in warm seawater. €10 fee to feel completely revived.

Keem Strand on Achill Island

The vastness of Donegal

THE NORTHWEST

Well away from the main tourist trail, northwestern Ireland has the country's most dramatic and unspoiled landscapes as well as an incomparable sense of space and freedom. The rhythm of life slows down here, in keeping with the glow of peat fires, the short winter days, the frugal light and the long rain-streaked roads. Legends live on in these parts, and the spirits of dead queens, solitary hermits and romantic poets still haunt the present. Mountain-top tombs are crowned by strange mounds, and battlemented castles and crouching cabins together defy the constant winds.

In Sligo, the shade of Yeats seems to hover around the shores of Lake Gill and at the foot of strangely shaped Benbulben. Further away, Queen Maeve, legendary ruler of Connaught, keeps watch over her sacred mountain.

In Donegal, where the roads are sometimes so narrow that you can touch the walls on either side, sea and mountain are as wild and savage as one another. The few houses strewn around the hills like carelessly discarded toys seem lost in the immensity of the landscape. The mountains of Slieve League have the highest cliffs in all Europe, while the near-perfect cone of Errigal Mountain is sometimes capped with snow like a modest Mount Fuji. Were it not for the ever-present chill in the air, Donegal's beaches would be an earthly paradise. People do not come here for the sun, however, but for the exhilaration of spray and spindrift, of gales blowing in from the Atlantic, of another Ireland at the very edge of the world.

SLIGO AND AROUND★★
Co Sligo, Co Leitrim and Co Roscommon
Allow 2 days, using either Sligo or Boyle as a base
Michelin map 923 G-H-I / 4-5-6 and map page 396

Not to be missed
Knocknarea and Queen Maeve's grave.
The view from Carrowkeel in clear weather.
The climb up Benbulben.

And remember...
Don't rush through Co Sligo; the county has some of Ireland's best walks and cycle rides.
Read some of Yeats' poetry.
Wear an anorak for the climb up Benbulben, and don't attempt it in rainy weather.

Sligo owes much of its fame to WB Yeats, winner of the Nobel Prize for literature in 1923. Together with his brother, Jack Yeats, he used to spend his summers in the area, which inspired some of his finest poems. The town still has a special feeling for literature and the arts. It's a busy place, and a good starting point for a whole range of superb walks.

A long history
The first traces of human activity in the Sligo area go back to Neolithic times, when hunter-gatherers (with a particular liking for shellfish) erected an astonishing number of dolmens, stone circles and burial mounds. Later came numerous ring-forts, some of which remained in use right down to medieval times. At the time of the coming

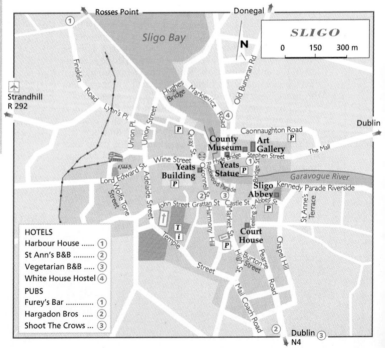

of the Normans, the area was the subject of dispute among several Gaelic clans, specifically the Fitzgerald family. The clans managed to retain part of the area and keep their culture and way of life intact up to the 17C, when the English began a systematic process of colonisation. In the 18C Sligo prospered, thanks to a lively trade in beer, spirits, linen, rope and leather, and it was also one of the main ports through which emigrants passed on their way to North America.

The town

Follow signs to the Town Centre when coming in on the N4 from the south. Go along Teeling Street past the Gothic Revival law courts and turn right towards Sligo Abbey. There is unrestricted parking along the N4 just short of the town centre, as well as a pay car park near the Abbey. Allow 2hr for a look around the town.

Sligo Abbey★ *(June-September: 9.30am-6.30pm. Admission charge. Heritage Site)*, dates from the 13C and is the town's oldest building. In the 15C it suffered badly in a fire, though the fine triple-arched rood screen and the choir were mostly unharmed. Most of the rest of the present ruined structure dates from the subsequent rebuilding; the **cloisters**★ are particularly fine, but the outstanding feature is the **carved altar**★ of nine panels, the only one of its kind in Ireland.

Go back the way you came, turn right into Bridge Street and cross the bridge to Stephen Street.

Housed in the old presbytery, the **County Museum** *(June-September: 10.30am-12.30pm / 2.30pm-4.30pm, closed Sunday; April, May and October: 10.30am-12.30pm, except Sunday; March and November: 10.30am-12.30pm Tuesday, Thursday and Saturday. Free admission)* has an array of items relating to the Yeats brothers and their links with the town (including the Nobel Prize) as well as archaeological finds from the area.

The town's **Art Gallery** *(same opening times as the museum; free admission)* in the adjacent building has a good selection of works by Jack Yeats and other modern Irish painters such as Paul Henry and Sean Keating.

Continue along Stephen Street to Hyde Bridge.

In front of the neo-Renaissance Ulster Bank building is a fine statue of WB Yeats, its base carved with extracts from his poems.

The brick-built edifice on the far side of the bridge is the **Yeats Building & Art Gallery**, housing a library and visiting exhibitions of contemporary art. **The Winding Stairs Bookshop** opposite stocks new and secondhand copies of most of the great man's works, and also has a pleasant upstairs café.

A right turn leads to the quayside with its poignant **Famine Memorial**, a statue of a distressed family ready to emigrate.

The main shopping streets can be reached by going back the way you came, walking along O'Connell Street, then turning left into Grattan Street and back to the Abbey.

West of Sligo★
Allow half a day

■ **Strandhill** — *8km from Sligo via the R292.* This popular seaside resort has been spoiled by over-development, but it does have a splendid **beach** backed by dunes. The huge breakers rolling in from the Atlantic are great for surfers and bodyboarders, but bathing is dangerous for inexperienced swimmers.

The R292 runs round the peninsula, giving fine **views** over Ballysadare Bay. Turn left off it onto a minor road marked "Scenic Drive" and park the car at the **View Point**★. Walk back to the well on the mountain side of the road, and climb up the embankment for the start of a particularly attractive **walk**★ *(2km there and back, not difficult but muddy in wet weather)* through a luxuriantly verdant gorge.

Continue to the sign on the left pointing to Knocknarea.

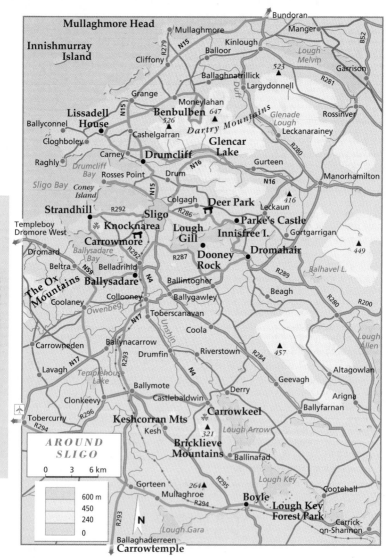

■ **Knocknarea**★★ – *Allow 1hr there and back. The climb is not difficult and the path is clearly signposted.* This austere hill overlooking Sligo Bay can be distinguished from far and wide because of the round burial mound on its summit. From the top there is a magnificent **view**★★; to the north are Slieve League and Donegal, to the east Lough Gill, to the south, Mayo and Croagh Patrick, and all around the deeply indented coastline and shining sands. Close up, the mound is truly massive, 10m high and 55m across; it is supposed to contain the grave of **Queen Maeve**, legendary ruler of Connaught. What is beyond dispute is that it was constructed 5 000 years ago. To the northwest, 400m away, the circular foundations of stone huts can be made out.

Continue along the road to the sign indicating Carrowmore.

■ **Carrowmore**★ – This prehistoric site comprises an extraordinary number of dolmens and stone circles scattered over an area several hundred metres across. The **Visitor Centre** *(May-September: 9.30am-6.30pm. Admission charge. Heritage Site)* has interpretive displays on what is one of Europe's most important Megalithic necropolises.

A splendid individual **dolmen** can be seen in a field to the left a short distance from the car park on the way back to Sligo.

Turn south on the N4, then continue on to the N59 to **Ballysadare**, where the river tumbles seawards down a series of **waterfalls**.

Continue on the N59 for about 5km and turn left towards Glen Wood and Coolaney, then onto Carrowneden. Turn right at a signpost indicating Scenic Drive and Ladies' Brae.
The road runs through the heart of the **Ox Mountains**, a landscape of forests and wild hills, before arriving at a lovely **viewpoint**★ overlooking the coast and Knocknarea.

Carry straight on and turn left onto the N59. Go through Templeboy and turn left in Dromore West towards Tobercurry. The road runs along Lough Easky at the foot of the Ox Mountains. In Tobercurry, an important centre for traditional music, take the R294 towards Boyle. In 15km, turn right on the R293 towards Ballaghaderreen, and look out for signs to Carrowtemple Burial Grounds.

Dolmen number 7 at Carrowmore

W Buss/HOA QUI

South of Sligo★
Allow half a day

■ **Carrowtemple** – This Early Christian monastic enclosure has a wealth of lovely but much eroded 8C-10C **engraved stones★** with interlace carving.

Go back the way you came and head for Boyle on the R294.

■ **Boyle and around** – This little town in Co Roscommon has an **abbey★** *(April-October: 9.30am-6.30pm. Admission charge. Heritage Site)* which is one of the loveliest in Ireland. Founded by Cistercians from Mellifont in 1161, it has a square tower, a rarity for this order, in a style combining English, Celtic, and Burgundian influences. The **capitals★** are particularly fine, with carvings of animals and people.

Built in the 18C for the King family who originally came to the area with orders to subjugate the native Irish, **King House** *(May-mid-October: 10am-6pm; April and late October: weekends only. Admission charge)* was later used as a base for the Connaught Rangers. There is an exhibition on successive rulers of Connaught, from Irish chieftains to the Anglo-Irish of the Ascendancy.

There are pleasant picnic spots at the vast **Lough Key Forest Park★** just over 3km along the Carrick-on-Shannon road. Attractive footpaths lead through the forest and boat trips can be taken on the lough.

Leave Boyle and head towards Sligo on the N4.

In 3km turn right onto the **Arigna Scenic Drive**, which gives fine **views** over Lough Key.

Turn left and follow the road along the banks of Lough Arrow. In Castlebaldwin, cross over the N4 towards Carrowkeel.

■ **Carrowkeel★★** – The road up to the Megalithic site of Carrowkeel *(6.5km from Castlebaldwin)* runs among the cliffs of the **Bricklieve Mountains** (321m) and passes through a gate *(please close it behind you)* to a car park. From here there is a magnificent **walk★★** through abandoned peat workings *(1hr there and back)*. At the

Boyle Abbey

Y Travert/DIAF

summit there is a group of burial mounds covering passage graves dating from the 4th millenium BC. The **panorama**** is splendid, taking in Co Sligo and its lakes as far as Benbulben. Down the slope to the east it is possible to make out the remains of about 80 **round huts**, which were no doubt the dwellings of the builders of the graves. To the west, **Keshcorran Mountain** is also topped by a substantial burial mound.

Go back to the road and turn left, away from Castlebaldwin. In about 5km, turn onto the R295 towards Ballymote and continue to the village of Kesh.

■ **Keshcorran Mountain*** – *At the post office in Kesh, go down towards Boyle and turn off the R295 towards St Kevin's Church. Turn left at the T-junction and go along the narrow lane on foot. The caves are on the right. Go along the cliff and come back into Kesh along the R295 towards Ballymote. You will need to take care on the approach to the caves because the ground is unstable.*

Keshcorran Mountain is easily recognisable because of its huge burial mound. A **walk*** *(1hr30min there and back)* leads to **Keshcorran caves** which were lived in by prehistoric people, and were the setting for the pagan cult of Lughnasa as well as being the source of numerous legends.

The R295 goes through Ballymote and joins the N4 south of Sligo. Before coming into town, turn right towards Lough Gill.

Around Lough Gill*
Allow half a day by car –
28km tour with few gradients, easily done by bicycle

On reaching the lough, turn left towards **Tobernalt Holy Well**. Legend has it that St Patrick touched the stone in front of the well; visitors placing their hand in the imprint of his will be cured of all their ills. Water from the well is in fact supposed to be good for headaches and eye problems. The well itself has been venerated since pagan times, and the pilgrimage here on the last Sunday in July corresponds to the beginning of the Celtic harvest festival. Tokens are still left on a tree by the steps.

Follow the road through the forest by the lakeside and turn left onto the R287.

A short distance further on leave the car in the car park and climb **Dooney Rock*** overlooking the lough.

Further on a 3km detour leads to Innisfree and its jetty, from where there is a view of **Innisfree Island** *(crossing on demand, ☎ 071 640 79, €5)*, immortalised by Yeats, who imagined longingly how it would be to *"...live alone in the bee-loud glade"* (from *The Lake Isle of Innisfree*).

Go back on the R287 to **Dromahair** in Co Leitrim and the 16C Franciscan **Creevelea Abbey**.

Continue to Parke's Castle.

Parke's Castle* *(April-May and October: 10am-5pm; closed Monday; June-September: 9.30am-6.30pm. Admission charge. Heritage Site)* is a fortified mansion built in the early 17C by the planter Captain Robert Parke. Its solid walls rise directly from the waters of the lough, opposite Innisfree. There is a fascinating 45min **audio-visual presentation** on the history of the area, and there are boat trips on the lough *(from 12.30pm onwards, for 1hr (€6.50) or 2hr (€8), irregular timetable)*.

Carry on along the lough on the R286 towards Sligo. Turn right in 3km towards Calry, then turn left at the T-junction to a car park and the sign indicating Deer Park and Giant's Grave.

An attractive **walk*** through the woods leads *(follow signs, 40min there and back)* to a hilltop with **Deer Park***, a fine example of a **Neolithic grave** consisting of two vast ovals bounded by **dolmens**.

The distinctive silhouette of Benbulben

North of Sligo★★
Allow half a day

■ **Drumcliff** – *9km north of Sligo via the N15 towards Donegal.* The distinctive outline of Belbulben rises over the village of Drumcliff where Yeats wished to be buried. His **gravestone** in the churchyard is inscribed with the epitaph he wrote himself. Drumcliff also has a **round tower** and an early 11C **high cross★** carved with Biblical scenes, a reminder of the first monastery founded by St Columba in the 6C.

■ **Lissadell House** – *Turn left just beyond Drumcliff towards Carney. June-September: 10.30am-12.15pm / 2pm-4.15pm; closed Sunday. Admission charge. Free admission to park.*
This austere neo-Classical country house is still the home of the Gore-Booth family, whose most famous member was Constance, later **Countess Markievicz**, one of the leading figures in the Easter Uprising of 1916 and subsequently the first woman to be elected to the Dáil. The interior evokes a rather faded grandeur, with family portraits and an oval gallery used as a music room.

Go back towards Sligo and follow signs to Enniskillen and the N16.

■ **Glencar Lake** – A short distance beyond the town the road runs above Glencar Lake, whose dark waters are dominated by Truskmore and Benbulben, massive blocks of limestone which rise to dramatic cliffs pitted with deep vertical fissures and streaked with waterfalls.
Follow the road round the lake towards Glencar village and stop at **Glencar waterfall**, a lovely cascade immortalised by Yeats.

Continue along the shady north shore of the lake and turn right at the fork along the foot of Benbulben.

The Northwest

■ **Benbulben**★★ – *3hr there and back, not difficult.* To make the **climb**★★ up to the summit (526m) of Benbulben, take the path to the left of Glenvale Farmhouse B&B. At a wall, bear left in a northwesterly direction to **King's Gully**. Once on the flat top of the mountain it is possible to make a circular walk along the clifftop.

To see more of Benbulben by road, go back to the N15 between Sligo and Donegal. Beyond Drumcliff look out on the right for a little church with a tower. Turn right just beyond it towards Ballintrillick, then take the first turning on the right. Take the road signposted North Sligo Watersupply, and go through the green gates. Park the car at the junction and continue on foot.

The easy footpath runs along a rushing stream on the **north flank**★★ of Benbulben among desolate bogland. A backward look takes in the whole of the north of Co Sligo and the Slieve League part of Donegal.

Go back to the N15 and drive north. At Cliffony, take the R279 towards Mullaghmore.

■ **The Mullaghmore Peninsula**★ – The peninsula protrudes northward into Donegal Bay with views of the summits of Slieve League. The romantic silhouette perched on a grassy cliff is that of **Classiebawn Castle**, once the residence of Lord Mountbatten. In 1979 the retired naval commander and statesman was killed by the IRA when they blew up his sailing boat in the bay.

The surrounding area has wonderful **walks**★ along the cliffs of **Mullaghmore Head**★ facing Innishmurray Island.

■ **Inishmurray Island**★ – Boat from Mullaghmore harbour *(minimum 6 people,* ☏ 071 661 24). The island has a remarkable monastic **enclosure** laid out in the middle of a **ring fort** like those in Kerry or on the Aran Islands. There is a church, an oratory, a stone hut, altars, tombstones...

Making the most of Sligo and around

COMING AND GOING

By bus – *Sligo Airport*, Strandhill, ☏ 071 682 80. One flight daily to Dublin.

By train – *Railway station*, Lord Edward Street, ☏ 071 698 88. 3 trains daily to Dublin.

By bus – Same location as the railway station in Lord Edward Street, ☏ 071 600 66. Three to four buses daily to Dublin, 4 daily to Galway, Donegal, Londonderry, and Belfast. Enquire locally for details of services to Boyle, Glencar, and Strandhill.

ADDRESS BOOK

Tourist information – *Tourist Information Office*, Temple Street, Sligo, ☏ 071 612 01. October-May: 9am-5pm except Sunday; June and September: 9am-6pm except Sunday; July-August: 9am-8pm daily.

Banks / Currency exchange – Banks and cash machines in Boyle and Sligo.

Internet – *Galaxy Cyber Café*, Milbrook, Riverside. In the basement of a general store and video rental shop, 10am-midnight. Snacks available.

The Northwest

• **Sligo**

Between €13-25

Harbour House, Finiskin Road, ☎ 071 692 56 – 48 beds in dormitories and private rooms. `CC` By the quayside, 15min on foot from the station and town centre, this hostel is in a well-run stone building. Comfortable beds, friendly landlord.

The White House Hostel, Markievicz Road, ☎ 071 451 60 – 31 beds. Close to the centre on the N15 in the Donegal direction. Classic and rather spacious hostel accommodation with river views.

Between €45-50

Vegetarian B&B, Tonaphubble Lane, ☎ 071 705 18 – 3rm `TV` `CC` Clearly signposted off the N4 Pearse Road 20min on foot from the centre, this is a serenely attractive house, tastefully decorated. The landlady serves delicious meals using organic and vegetarian ingredients.

St Ann's B&B, Pearse Road, ☎ 071 431 88 – 4rm `TV` `CC` On the N4 on the way into the town (5min on foot from the centre), this house has a small swimming pool in its little garden. The rooms at the rear are better.

• **Around Sligo**

Between €45-50

Ard Cuilinn Lodge, on the R284, Drumiskabole, ☎ 071 629 25 – 5rm `CC` Take the R284 at the roundabout on the Dublin road. 5km from Sligo. Superb mountain views, big garden, friendly hosts, good advice on what to do in the area. Guests are made to feel at home straightaway. The two rooms with shared facilities are less expensive. The landlord is a keen genealogist with a good record for tracing the local origins of visitors of Irish descent.

Stanford's Inn, Dromahaire, ☎ 071 641 40 – 6rm `TV` `CC` In a riverside setting in the middle of a pretty village at the end of Lough Gill, this is a pleasant place to stay with a friendly pub nearby (see "Eating out"). Comfortable, recently redecorated rooms.

Benbulben Farm, Drumcliff, ☎ 071 632 11 – 6rm `^` Two kilometres from Drumcliff at the foot of Ben-

bulben, with splendid views of the coast. Pretty garden. Slightly faded decor, but very comfortable.

Mountain View Farmhouse, Carney, Drumcliff, ☎ 071 632 90 – 5rm `TV` Nine kilometres from Sligo. Turn left just beyond the Yeats Tavern at Drumcliff and continue for 2.5km. Fine views of Benbulben. Very well-kept house, friendly reception.

Dunfore Farmhouse, Ballinfull, ☎ 071 631 37 – 4rm `TV` `CC` Carry on for 9km past the previous establishment, go past Lissadell House and follow signs. Friendly farmhouse, full of animals and run by a poetess of a landlady (cassette available of her poems). Good breakfast.

More than €65

Glebe House, Coolaney Road, Coolaney, ☎ 071 677 87 – 6rm `X` `CC` Clearly signposted on the left off the old Sligo road on the way out of Coolaney. Completely refurbished and very comfortable large Georgian residence. Fine country living, including excellent food.

• **Boyle and around**

Between €45-50

Abbey House, Boyle, ☎ 079 623 85 – 6rm `TV` Just to the rear of Boyle Abbey, this is an imposing house with a garden going down to the river. Spacious, comfortable rooms, attractive lounge with turf fire lit as soon as it becomes chilly. Small apartments also available.

Rosdarrig House, Dublin Road, Boyle, ☎ 079 620 40 – 4rm `TV` `CC` On the way out towards Dublin. Comfortable, bright rooms in a new house. Attractive garden.

More than €50

Riversdale Farmhouse, Knockvicar, Boyle, Co Roscommon, ☎ 079 670 12 – 5rm `^` On the banks of Lough Key 12km from Boyle, signposted off the road between Boyle and Carrick. This is another Georgian house, sited in extensive parkland. The decor has seen better days but the welcome is friendly and service efficient. The landlord, a keen fisherman, owns several lakes and boats (for the use of guests) and can give all sorts of useful fishing tips.

More than €100
Temple House, Ballymote, ☎ 071 833 29 – 5rm 🔔 ✗ ⓒⓒ Leave Sligo on the N17 towards Tobercurry and turn left beyond Ballynacarrow; a park wall soon comes into view. Furnished with antiques and expertly run, this big Georgian mansion would be just the place for a special treat. Wonderful for walking, the estate covers 500 hectares and includes the ruins of a medieval castle. Dinner by arrangement (€23), with ingredients from the estate, sumptuous breakfast in the dining hall. The only drawback is that the hostess is allergic to perfume.

EATING OUT

• Sligo
The Cottage, Castle Street, ☎ 071 453 19. On the upper floor. Lunchtime vegetarian dishes, baked potatoes with varied fillings, quiches, pasta and so on, between €5-7.50. More expensive in the evening, but generous portions, from €13 upwards.
Café Cairo, Rockwood Parade, ☎ 071 505 44. Closed Sunday. On the traffic-free riverside. Pleasant setting, small meals in a wide price range, some unusual dishes including vegetarian.
Hargadon Bros, O'Connell Street. Very popular pub with traditional dishes like Irish stew (€6.50 upwards), with soups, cakes etc, served at the back of the premises.
Furey's, Bridge Street, near the public library, has the usual kinds of pub food.
Yeats River Café, near Hyde Bridge, is a good place to eat at midday (under €6.50).

• Around Sligo
Soul and Heal Café, Bridge Street, Boyle, is a pretty little building by the river, with just a few tables for eating soups, salads, sandwiches, good platefuls of the dish of the day and a range of cakes. A meal for under €6.50. Closes 6pm.
🍷 **Glebe House Restaurant**, Cooloney, ☎ 071 677 87 (see "Where to stay"). The young French chef employed here is beginning to make his mark. There is a €26 dinner menu with main courses between €13-18. Good wine list. Expensive, but food of a high standard in a very pleasant setting.
Stanford's Inn, Dromahair (southeast of Lough Gill), has traditional pub food in a bar full of character. Cheap food until 9.30pm. Restaurant open in the evening for meals between €13-25, but there's more atmosphere in the bar.
Glencar Lodge, Glencar, at the end of Glencar Lake, ☎ 071 454 75. A good place at lunchtime, with salads, sandwiches, soups, pastries for between €6.50-10. Daily 10am-6pm in summer, Friday to Sunday in May and September. €25 menu at 8.30pm Friday and Saturday.

HAVING A DRINK
🍷 **Hargadon Bros**, O'Connell Street, is full of atmosphere, with its tinted windows, wooden bar, array of objects and little snugs. There's no music, this is a place for drinking and talking.
🍷 **Shoot the Crows**, Grattan Street, easily recognisable by its violently coloured windows. Lots of atmosphere in the evenings, with a crush of clients and plenty of cigarette smoke. Music Tuesday and Thursday evenings.
Furey's Bar, opposite the County Museum, much favoured by local people.

OTHER THINGS TO DO
Seaweed baths – Celtic Seabaths, at Strandhill, has revived the ancient Mayo tradition of bathing in warm water and seaweed. With the effects enhanced by the addition of natural essences, the baths are used to treat rheumatism and are great for relieving stress.

FESTIVALS AND EVENTS
Sligo Arts Festival (late May / early June), theatre, poetry, literature, music, dance, etc.
South Sligo Summer School (mid-July), a week of traditional music of exceptional quality in Tobercurry. Dancing, courses, sessions, etc.
Literary Festival (around mid-September) keeps Sligo's literary traditions alive, with writing workshops, public readings, meetings with authors.

Making the most of Sligo and around

DONEGAL AND SLIEVE LEAGUE★★★
FROM BUNDORAN TO ARDARA
Co Donegal – Allow 3 days
Michelin map 923 F-G-H / 3-4

Not to be missed
A walk along the cliffs of Slieve League.
Malin Beg and Trabane Strand.
Maghera Falls and the walk to Port Hill.
And remember...
The sheer number of photo-opportunities means you will need more
camera film than you think.
Make sure you leave enough time to explore the scenic highlights on foot.
The wind knows how to blow in Donegal – wind-cheaters or anoraks are essential!

The Northwest

One of the historic nine counties of the province of Ulster, Donegal's profound Catholicism and deep attachment to the Gaelic language inevitably led to its inclusion in the Free State at the time of Partition. It is perhaps the most quintessentially Irish of all counties, less disfigured than most by the kind of haphazard development that has marred the beauty of other areas. There are grandiose, unspoiled landscapes aplenty here, most of all along the coast between Donegal town and Ardara.

Far-off Gaelic stronghold
Donegal earns its living from fishing, wool, tweed and tourism. In the past it was fiercely guarded by the Gaelic clans and was much influenced by Early Christian monasticism. The most famous monk of all, **Columba**, was responsible for the conversion of much of Ireland as well as Scotland. The Anglo-Irish hold on the area was less firm than elsewhere, no doubt because of its remoteness and the rigour of the climate.

From Bundoran to Donegal via the N15
50km tour

■ **Bundoran** – This seaside resort with its host of hotels and B&Bs is very popular with holidaymakers from Northern Ireland, who come here for the craic, the pubs and the amusement arcades, as well as for the superb beach to the north which is ideal for surfing *(turn left at the KFC outlet)*.

■ **Ballyshannon** – *6.3km east of Bundoran.* Ballyshannon is the home of **Donegal porcelain** *(see "Making the most of Donegal and Slieve League")* and of the equally famous **Folk and Traditional Music Festival**. Lasting three and a half days *(late-July / early August, ticket includes use of camp site)* this is a pretty steamy and well-patronised event, with huge crowds enjoying concerts, workshops and fringe activities.

A short and very worthwhile detour is to Belleek, 7km east towards Enniskillen and right on the border (see page 443). Come back to Ballyshannon and continue north on the N15. Turn left beyond Ballintra towards the golf course and continue to Mullinasole Strand.

■ **Mullinasole Strand★** – This splendid beach facing Donegal Bay and backed by woodland is ideal for swimming, surfing or simply having a picnic.

Go back to the N15.

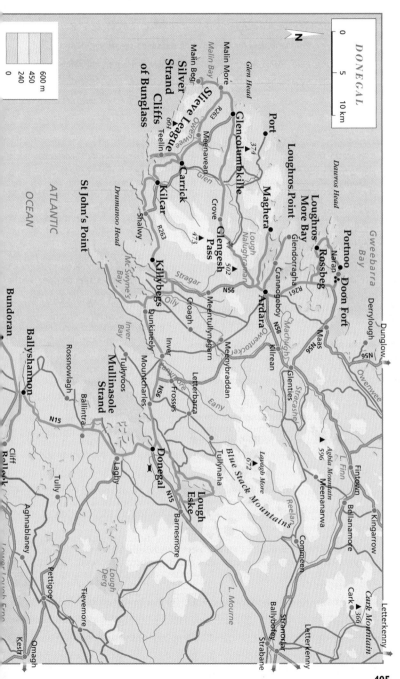

Donegal town and around

Allow 2hr

Parking to the rear of the Garda station on the way into town

Originally a Viking settlement, Donegal subsequently became the stronghold of the O'Donnell clan. In 1610, after the Flight of the Earls, it was granted to an English planter, Sir Basil Brooke, who re-planned it in an orderly manner around the central market place known as the Diamond. The town was attacked during the 1641 and 1798 rebellions but was not taken on either occasion.

The town

Despite its name, Donegal is not the county town, this honour being given to Lifford. With its castle and its distinctive market square (The Diamond), the town has a certain charm, and is a good place to stock up on tweeds and sweaters.

Donegal Castle (*mid-March-October: 9.30am-6.30pm. Admission charge. Heritage Site*) served as the headquarters of the O'Donnells. The original tower house was destroyed by Hugh Roe O'Donnell rather than let it fall into the hands of the English. The present Jacobean mansion is the work of Sir Basil Brooke, whose arms and those of Lady Brooke appear on the stone chimney-piece. The evolution of the castle is demonstrated by models.

Donegal Abbey is right by the tourist office on the south bank of the estuary of the Eske. At the time of its foundation in 1474 the abbey was very rich, but had the ill fortune to attract the attention of the English, who used it as an arsenal. In 1601, the buildings were badly damaged when some of the munitions blew up, but the remains seen against the background of Donegal Bay are very attractive.

The perils of cartography

Life was not easy for English map-makers attempting to exercise their profession in Ireland. Firm in the belief that accurate maps favoured their enemies, the Irish were very suspicious of surveyors and harassed them whenever possible. Not surprisingly, early maps of Ireland, especially those of the west, tend to be full of mistakes, as a look at the maps on show in Donegal Castle will show. Occasionally, harassment went to extreme lengths; one unfortunate attempting to carry out a survey had his head cut off!

Lough Eske★

23km tour northeast of Donegal town. The lough has a lovely setting in the shape of the Blue Stack Mountains. Look out on the way out of town towards Killybegs for a sign pointing to the **Lough Eske Drive**, a scenic route running right round the lough.

The coast road★

65km tour via the coast or 44km by the direct road

Accommodation available at Killybegs or St John's Point

Take the N56 towards Killybegs. In Dunkineely turn left towards St John's Point.

■ **St John's Point★** – The minor road hugging the shore of the narrow peninsula has a number of marvellous **viewpoints★** overlooking McSwyne's Bay and Slieve League to the north and the Sligo coast and Benbulben to the south. The road runs through a landscape of strange dark laminated rocks before ending at a delightful sheltered bay.

Go back the way you came and continue on the N56, then turn left onto the R263 to Killybegs.

Slieve League

■ **Killybegs** – The strong smells emanating from the quayside leave no doubt about how this important **fishing harbour** earns its living. Full of character, Killybegs is especially lively when the catch is landed towards the end of the day. The pubs stay open longer here than elsewhere, no doubt to allow the crews to catch up on their drinking (a good place to check this out is the Sail Inn). The town is also known for hand-woven **Donegal carpets** (the factory is on the Kilcar road).

Continue on the R263. In Shalwy, turn left onto the Kilcar Coast Road.

The **Kilcar Coast Road** is the key to the loveliest part of Donegal, with a wild and jagged coastline and wind-blasted fields bounded by drystone walls. There are fine views across the bay to the Sligo mountains.

■ **Kilcar** – Not particularly renowned for its beauty, the village of Kilcar is a centre of **tweed** production. Fine quality wool is used, and the tweed is hard-wearing and flecked with a wonderful range of subtle colours. The workshops of the **Studio Donegal** weavers are open to the public (closed Sunday). Opposite is a small factory specialising in hand-loomed woollens, often made by men, as opposed to hand-knitted work which is usually done by women.

On the way out of Kilcar, the **Coast Road** towards Glencolumbkille leads to Carrick and runs along the shore of a deep inlet of the sea. On the far shore, the tiny village of Teelin crouches at the foot of Slieve League.

Carrick is famous for its excellent **traditional music festival**, which takes place every year in late October.

Turn left on the way out of Carrick towards Bunglass and Teelin.

Slieve League★★★
Allow at least half a day for the cliff walk
On no account should the walk be attempted in fog or in wet or windy conditions

As soon as the road leaves Carrick, a vast landscape opens up, its character and colour changing constantly with the light. Fields in every shade of green undulate gently between sea and mountain, while the rivers discharging into Donegal Bay are famous for their salmon. This is the approach to Slieve League, one of the most spectacular mountains in the country. There are several routes up to the summit (601m) of this cliff dropping sheer into the sea. Whichever one is chosen, the climb is an unforgettable experience.

The Pilgrim's Path★★★
Turn right 2km beyond Carrick and follow the Slieve League signs to the end of the surfaced road. The warning bears repetition; all the cliff paths are extremely hazardous when it is wet or windy, and the cliffs have claimed many victims.
The route taken by the faithful passes the ruins of a **chapel** once frequented by a hermit who was the cousin of St Columba. Further on, at **One Man's Pass**★★★ it becomes very narrow (less than 1m wide!), at a point 500m above the waves. Definitely not for sufferers of vertigo!
From here it is possible to continue westwards *(for about 5hr)*, finally emerging at Silver Strand *(see below)*, or alternatively to go back eastwards along the coast to join the path leading to **Bunglass** and then **Teelin** before returning to the starting point of the walk *(circular walk of about 5hr)*.

The Bunglass Path★★★
If time is short, go to Teelin and take the road towards Bunglass. After 5km of hairpin bends a car park is reached.
The stunning view takes in two **watchtowers** to the southeast, the larger of them dating from the time of the Napoleonic Wars, when a French invasion was expected. The footpath leads north to a **viewpoint**★★★ commanding the 300m-high **Cliffs of**

Bunglass. Cutting into the flank of Slieve League, the cliffs are the highest in Europe. Anyone who is nervous of heights or short of time need go no further, but it is possible to continue the walk from here. Allow 1hr30min to reach One Man's Pass *(see above)*.

Go back to Carrick and continue towards Glencolumbkille. Turn left in 3.2km towards Malin Beg.

Silver Strand★★★

After the stirring sight of the Bunglass cliffs, the road now runs round the back of the mountains, through a treeless landscape studded with little lakes. From Malin Beg follow signs to Silver Strand (the local name for Trabane Strand). The road skirts a series of black cliffs grazed by agile sheep. Finally, a lovely crescent of fine sand appears in a setting of high green cliffs; this is one of the country's most beautiful beaches, reached by an extremely steep stairway. The car park marks one of the ends of the **walk★★★** along the Slieve League cliffs. It is possible to walk southeastwards along part of the path *(2hrs to the summit of Slieve League, or 45min to the flank of Mount Leahan for a fine view of the cliffs of Bunglass).*

Go back to the road and continue to Glencolumbkille.

Glencolumbkille
Allow half a day including the surrounding area

More attractive than the direct route along the R263, the approach to the village of Glencolumbkille from Malin Beg has views down a valley with cliff-like sides opening out onto a lovely sandy beach.

Glencolumbkille is named after St Colmcille or **Columba**, who founded a monastery here in the 6C. In more recent times, the parish priest Father James McDyer (d 1987)

Standing stone at Glencolumbkille

C Legrand/MICHELIN

set up a co-operative to try and improve living conditions in this poor and remote parish. Mains electricity was provided and local crafts encouraged. Out of his initiatives grew the **Glencolumbkille Folk Village★** *(Easter-September: 10am-5.30pm, guided tours every 30min. Admission charge)*. It consists of three **thatched cabins**, each furnished in the style of a different period (1700, 1800 and 1900), as well as a school, a shop, a **shebeen**, and a café. The inside of the cabins can only be seen by taking one of the guided tours.

Every year on **9 June**, St Columba's feast day, the pilgrimage called the **Turas Colmcille★** takes place. Five kilometres long, it begins at midnight from the Protestant church and follows a route

Bed-hopping lovers
The tale is told of the beautiful Gráinne, daughter of the king of Tara, who promised her to Fionn, chief of the legendary warriors known as the Fianna. But Fionn was already old, and the girl fell for the charms of one of his young followers, the handsome Dermot. Gráinne persuaded Dermot to elope with her. The enraged Fionn pursued the lovers without respite, forcing them to change their hiding place from one day to the next. Then, alas! Dermot was killed by a wild boar he encountered on the top of Benbulben. Legend has it that the burial mounds and heaps of stones littered around the countryside are the beds in which the fleeing lovers spent their fitful nights.

past 12 Stations of the Cross marked by **standing stones**, probably dating from pre-Christian times. Rather than removing these pagan symbols, St Columba diplomatically incorporated them into Christian ritual. The pilgrimage route along the valley slopes is a very attractive walk (details from the shop which does duty as a tourist information centre), revealing along its course an array of **prehistoric remains** such as cairns and burial mounds (*station n° 7 is further north*).

A walk and a drive from Glencolumbkille
The fine walk along the cliffs to the north of the village leads to **Port***** (*5hr there and back*), the ruins of a village abandoned at the time of the Famine.

Port can also be reached by car. Go towards Ardara for a little over 8km, then turn left onto a minor road leading to the spectacular cliffs near the village.

Go back the way you came, and continue towards Ardara to **Glengesh Pass****, from where there are splendid views of the glaciated valley in its steep and rugged mountain setting.

Ardara and around**
Allow half a day without the side-trips

Ardara prides itself on being the capital of homespun **tweed**. There is evidence of systematic weaving having been practised as far back as the Bronze Age, and it is known that cloth was exported from the area in medieval times. By the end of the 19C there were regular monthly fairs in the town, when merchants and weavers came together in the open air to conduct their business. In 1912 a covered market was built. Donegal owes its flourishing modern tweed industry largely to the efforts of the Englishwoman **Alice Hart**, who brought in skilled workers from England and Scotland. At that time production was carried on in the workers' own homes (homespun tweed), then, in the 20C, it was centralised in factories in Ardara and Donegal town by firms like Molloy and Magee (*see page 95*). Today, home production has virtually ceased, and the fairs have lost their original function. This has not meant the end of the annual **Weaver's Fair**, with lots of jollity and music (*1st weekend in June*).

Colourful tweed
Sheep-shearing takes place in June and July, after which the wool is washed and dyed using only natural materials. In the old days, the grey lichen growing on granite was the main source of colour, yielding a dark red tint once it had been boiled up with the wool. Nowadays, thanks to the experiments carried out by Alice Hart, the range is much more extensive. Heather gives a bright yellow, peat a brownish yellow, bramble roots a lovely chestnut. Other dyes include blackthorn (sloe), moss and gorse, and colours vary according to where the plants are harvested, the quantity used, and a host of more or less secret recipes. The colours are fixed using tannin from oaks and alders or ammonia from urine.

Loughros Point**
Leave Ardara on the Killybegs road and turn right almost immediately towards Loughros Point. The best time to walk here is towards the end of the afternoon,

when the ruddy-coloured cliffs are bathed in sunlight. Grassy little islands stud the surface of the sea, and meandering streams twist and turn across the sand-banks when the tide is low. To the south, on the far side of **Loughros More Bay****, the steep slopes of the hills light up in the setting sun, creating a scene of great beauty.

Maghera**

Turn right onto the Maghera road about 1km from Ardara in the Killybegs direction. An early start is essential if you want to do the walk.

The narrow road runs along the south shore of Loughros More Bay, with fine views of shining sand-banks and of the landward side of the shingle bar, lit by the morning sun. About 9km from Ardara, the **Maghera Falls*** cascade from a cleft in the rock. On the beach a little further on are the **Maghera Caves** *(20min from the car park)*, which are exposed at low tide. Dark and deep, they served as a clandestine Catholic chapel as well as a lurking place for makers of poteen.

At the far end of the village of Maghera, a signposted **footpath**** (can be cycled with difficulty by mountain bike) climbs through a rocky and lonely valley to Glengesh or Port Hill *(allow a whole day there and back)*.

North of Ardara**

Take the R261 north from Ardara to Naran. At **Naran** the road runs high above a superb semicircle of **sandy beach***, then drops down to the tiny harbour village of **Portnoo**

Continue for 1km beyond Portnoo post office and turn left just beyond the lake.

After 1.6km follow the sign to **Doon Fort****; the owner of the McHugh Farm has a boat for hire (€6.50) which is the only way to get to the perfectly preserved **Neolithic ringfort** *(invisible from the road)* on its island in the middle of the little lake. This is a delightful excursion, made all the more special by having to row oneself.

Go back to the main road and turn left.

The road now winds among hills past a number of exquisite little **lakes**, with occasional views over the sea, to **Rossbeg***, with its deep bays and its splendid **panorama*** over Loughros Bay.

COMING AND GOING

By train – The nearest stations are at Sligo and Londonderry.

By bus – *Bus Eireann*, ☎ 073 211 01 run 3 to 5 services daily to Dublin from Donegal town and the villages along the coast to the north. *O'Donnell*, ☎ 075 481 14, run daily buses between Galway, Sligo, Donegal and the coastal villages (6hr Galway-Bunbeg for example). *McGeehan*, ☎ 075 461 50 has a bus to Dublin starting at Dungloe and calling at Ardara, Glenties and other places. **John McGinley**, ☎ 074 352 01, has a Donegal-Dublin service.

ADDRESS BOOK

Tourist information – *Tourist Office*, Quay Street, Donegal, ☎ 073 211 48, open Easter-October. Out of season: 9am-5pm, except weekends (open also Saturday June-September); July-August: daily 9am-8pm. Information is very thin on the ground further north, so find out all you need to know here.

Banks / Currency exchange – Banks and cash machines at Bundoran, Ballyshannon, Donegal, Killybegs, Ardara and Glenties.

Medical service – Chemists at Bundoran, Donegal, Killybegs and Ardara (films processed in 1hr).

Internet – *The Blueberry Cyber Café*, Donegal, ☎ 073 236 63. 11am-11pm weekdays, 4pm-11pm Sunday.

WHERE TO STAY

● **Bundoran**

Between €45-50

Bay View Guesthouse, Main Street, ☎ 072 412 96 – 25rm ♨ ♬ TV CC Hotel-sized Victorian house on the seafront. Rooms facing the sea suffer from Saturday night noise. It's better to take a room on the 2nd floor. Sauna (extra charge) and billiards.

Ceol na Mara, Tullan Strand, ☎ 072 412 87 – 5rm ♨ Turn left at the KFC on the way out of town on the Donegal road. This establishment is right at the end of the road close to the beach among the sand-dunes. There is good surfing, and a riding school is right next door. Very comfortable, but note that the bedroom doors have frosted glass.

● **Ballyshannon**

Between €45-50

Carrigdún B&B, Portnason, ☎ 072 514 17 – 4rm ♨ CC Set back a little from the N15 and half-hidden behind a hedge, 800m from the way into Ballyshannon. Well-kept and comfortable, and the least expensive in this category. The cheapest room is the one with the bathroom on the landing.

Rockville House, Station Road, ☎ 072 511 06 – 5rm ♨ CC First right after the big roundabout on the Dublin road. Imposing house with comfortable rooms.

Cavangarden House, on the Donegal road, ☎ 072 513 06 – 5rm ♨ TV ✗ CC On the left 4km outside Ballyshannon towards Donegal. Lovely old farmhouse set back from the road at the end of a long avenue. Perfect peace and quiet in the middle of the countryside. Evening meal by arrangement.

● **Donegal town and around**

More than €13

Cliff View House, Coast Road, ☎ 073 216 84 – 30 beds in dormitories and 11 smaller rooms. Brand-new establishment on the way out of town towards Killybegs. Very well-kept, rather dark rooms. Breakfast extra.

Ball Hill Hostel, Ball Hill, ☎ 073 211 74 – 66 beds. Turn left 2km from Donegal towards Killybegs and continue to the end of the road. Ideal location overlooking the sea, superb walks in the surrounding area.

Between €40-50

Diamond Lodgings, The Diamond Centre, ☎ 073 220 27 – 10rm ♨ TV ✗ CC On the 2nd floor of a building in the shopping centre right in the middle of town. Very well-kept, spacious and comfortable and not expensive rooms. No breakfast, but tea and coffee-making equipment in the rooms. An even better bargain out of season. Parking to the rear, locked at night.

Drumcliffe House, Coast Road, ☎ 073 212 00 – 7rm ⌂ TV Pretty house sheltering behind trees on the way out of town towards Killybegs. The less expensive rooms are on the 1st floor. Attractively decorated and comfortable. Rather impersonal reception.

😊 **Ardeevin B&B**, Lough Eske, Barnesmore, Donegal, ☎ 073 217 90 – 6rm ⌂ TV CC On the north shore of Lough Eske 8km from Donegal, this is a pretty and attractively decorated house. Warm welcome. Superb lake views. Varied breakfast. The "Benbulben Room" is the best.

The Arches, Lough Eske, Barnesmore, Donegal, ☎ 073 220 29 – 6rm ⌂ TV Next door to the previous establishment in the same splendid setting. Some guests find it difficult to tear themselves away from this lovely house.

- **St John's Point**
Around €45

😊 **Seaview House**, St John's Point, Dunkineely, ☎ 073 372 52 – 3rm ⌂ CC 6km along the road from Dunkineely to St John's Point. Overlooking the bay and facing Slieve League, this is a brand-new bungalow with gaily decorated and inexpensive rooms (the blue room is the prettiest). For anyone who likes the sea and a sense of space and freedom.

Harbour Lights, St John's Point, Dunkineely, ☎ 073 372 91 – 4rm ⌂ CC A bit further on from the previous establishment, but the same superb surroundings and a friendly landlady.

Between €65-75

Castle Murray, St John's Point, Dunkineely, ☎ 073 370 22 – 10rm ⌂ ♟ TV ✗ CC Two minutes from Dunkineely on the road to St John's Point. This little hotel is run by a French couple. Lovely view of the bay with its black rocks. Very comfortable, modern rooms.

- **Killybegs and Slieve League**
Between €30-40

Don Ross, Scenic Road, Kilcar, ☎ 073 381 25 – 3rm CC Straightforward accommodation facing the sea on the road between Killybegs and Kilcar. Well-kept. Shared bathroom.

Dún Ulun House, Coast Road to Glencolumbkille, Kilcar, ☎ 073 381 37 – 10rm ⌂ CC Take the coast road on the way out of Kilcar towards Slieve League. Friendly establishment with owners keen on traditional culture. Rates negotiable; B&B at standard prices, but much cheaper "hostel accommodation" is also available, though it still uses the B&B rooms! Guests then have use of a kitchen for making their own breakfast. Camping possible on the far side of the road by the sea (€5 per person).

Between €45-50

Cornton House, Killybegs, ☎ 073 315 88 – 4rm ⌂ TV CC Clearly signposted on the right 1.5km from Killybegs on the Glencolumbkille road. Very quiet location well away from the main road. Warm welcome.

Lismolin, Killybegs, ☎ 073 310 35 – 5rm ⌂ TV CC On the left 1.5km from Killybegs on the road towards Glencolumbkille. Very friendly welcome and lots of tips on what to do in the area.

😊 **Credo House**, Benroe, Killybegs, ☎ 073 313 64 – 3rm ⌂ ✗ Clearly signposted on the right 3km from Killybegs on the Donegal road. Lovely view of Killybegs harbour on the far side of the bay. Evening meal by arrangement.

😊 **Tullycullion House**, Tullaghcullion, Killybegs, ☎ 073 318 42 – 4rm ⌂ CC Well-signposted on the right 2km from Killybegs on the Donegal road. Deep in the hills, lovely views and splendid walks. Very well-kept and efficiently run. Attractive rooms.

- **Glencolumbkille**
Between €30-45

Sunset Heights, Doonalt, ☎ 073 300 48 – 2rm ⌂ Just beyond the Folk Village towards Malin Beg. Straightforward accommodation in a plain house on rising ground with fine sea views. Inexpensive.

Trade Winds, Lower Dooey, ☎ 073 300 56 – 6rm ⌂ Directly opposite the Folk Village. Small but comfortable rooms. Inexpensive, and even cheaper with shared bathroom.

Strand House, Lower Dooey, ☎ 073 300 32 – 3rm ⌂ Very plain but well-kept. Only one room has private facilities. Next door to the above establishment and same rates.

Between €65-75
Glencolumcille Hotel, ☎ 073 300 03
– 37rm ⚐ ♪ TV ✗ CC Beyond the
Folk Village on the Malin Beg road. Impersonal but comfortable and in a good
location. Bar meals between 12.30pm-
9.30pm (€5-10) and restaurant meals in
the evening (individual dishes €13-15,
full menu €21).

● **Ardara and around**
Between €6-20
Drumbarron Hostel, The Diamond,
Ardara, ☎ 075 412 00 – 16 beds,
1 room. Good location right in the mid-
dle of town. The double room is plain
but well-kept.
Between €35-45
🌰**Holly Brook**, Killybegs Road, Ar-
dara, ☎ 075 415 96 – 5rm ⚐ TV CC
1km from Ardara on the Killybegs road.
Very good value, extremely well-kept.
Modern house, attractively decorated.
Between €45-50
🌰**Rosewood House**, Killybegs Road,
Ardara, ☎ 075 411 68 – 6rm ⚐ CC
Charming hosts, prices negotiable for
longer stays.
Bay View Country House, Portnoo
Road, Ardara, ☎ 075 411 45 – 6rm ⚐
CC Less than 1km from Ardara on the
way to Portnoo. Flower-loving, amiable
and efficient landlady.
🌰**An Geata Glas** (The Green Gate),
Ardvally, Ardara, ☎ 075 415 46 – 4rm
⚐ Take the first turning on the right on
the way out of Ardara towards Donegal.
Little wooden signs mark the way up to
the top of the hill, where there are three
little cottages and a breathtaking view.
Here you can live under a thatched roof,
splash around in a panelled bathroom,
and enjoy the aroma of a peat fire, and
take breakfast whenever you feel like it.
The French landlord has fallen in love
with Ireland and is full of good advice
on hidden places.
Thalassa Country House, Naran, Portnoo, ☎ 075 451 51 – 4rm ⚐ CC Lovely
view from the lounge over Naran beach
and a little lake. Quite plain rooms,
friendly landlady who can give useful
tips on where to walk.
Ceol na Mara, Naran, Portnoo,
☎ 075 451 79 – 3rm ⚐ TV Opposite
the previous establishment and a little
bit more expensive. Very comfortable.

Lisdanar, Mill Road, Glenties,
☎ 075 518 00 – 4rm ⚐ TV CC Imposing house on the way into Glenties
from Aradara. Spacious and comfortable
rooms with mosquito-proof windows.
Good choice at breakfast-time, including
vegetarian.

EATING OUT

● **Bundoran**
The Kitchen Bake, Castle Street,
☎ 071 453 19. Easy to find in the main
street, this converted chapel has straightforward dishes for between €4-9.

● **Donegal town**
The Blueberry, Castle Street. Right by
the castle, good for the usual snacks including baked potatoes, between €3-
6.50.
🌰**The Mill Court Antique & Coffee
Shop**, Mill Court, The Diamond. On the
2nd floor of the courtyard, this is a combined antique shop and café with tasty
snacks served in a quiet and tasteful setting. Quiches, baked potatoes, soups,
good range of sandwiches, breakfast
served till 11.30am, plus an excellent
choice of coffee. 9am-5pm, closed Sunday.
Just William's, Central Hotel, The Diamond. In the basement of the hotel, this
bar has excellent carvery lunches for
around €6.50-7.
McGrorarty's Pub, The Diamond. On
the far side of The Diamond from the
Central Hotel, this is a cheerful pub with
bar food during the day. Good too for a
drink in the evening.
🌰**The Olde Bar**, next to the castle.
Reasonably priced at lunch-time, but
more expensive in the evening (reckon
on €20). Pleasantly old-fashioned and
friendly atmosphere. French chef.

● **Along the coast**
Castle Murray, St John's Point, Dunkineely, ☎ 073 370 22. Generally reckoned to be one of the best restaurants in
the area. Cuisine based on ultra-fresh local produce. Design your own meal from
the extensive menu. Not cheap though
(between €25-35 for dinner).
🌰**Kitty Kelly's Restaurant**, Largy,
Killybegs, ☎ 073 319 25. About 5km
from Killybegs towards Glencolumbkille, this little red house is located on a

curve in the road and has a whole series of little rooms on two floors. Interesting menu, mostly based on seafood. Dishes between €12-24. Evenings only.

Teach Barnaí, Kilcar. For evening meals and Sunday lunch. Reckon on between €20-25 for dinner. Much in favour among local people.

• Ardara and around

Lake House Hotel, Naran, Portnoo, ☎ 075 451 23. Bar food for €5-10 until 6pm, then dinner. Traditional dishes for between €13-20, high quality and generous portions.

HAVING A DRINK

• Bundoran

Old Bridge Bar. One of the rare bars in this area to have traditional music as opposed to rock.

• Donegal town

Zack's Bar, Main Street. Down a passageway, lively and cheerful atmosphere with old barrels used as tables. Varied clientele, music every evening in summer and at weekends the rest of the year. Another place to try is the particularly lively **Olde Bar**.

The Scotsman, Bridge Street. Special atmosphere in this pub, where a fiddler may strike up a tune at any moment and the landlady join in on the spoons.

• Ardara

Nancy's, in the main street beyond the Heritage Centre. Traditional decor and convivial atmosphere. Food available in the daytime, inexpensive and good portions.

Patrick's Bar, in the main street. This is a rather special place, unchanged since the 1950s, with dim lighting, no draught beer, and opening times depending on the whim of the landlord. But quite an experience...

SHOPPING

Tweeds and woollens – Magee, The Diamond, Donegal, is easily the best place to buy traditional tweeds (among the very last still being made on hand looms) as well as immaculately cut clothes. Expensive, but guaranteed to last a lifetime. Reckon on €25 per metre and between €225-315 for a suit

(man or woman). Caps, hats, and scarves correspondingly less expensive. It's sheer pleasure to handle material of this quality.

John Molloy, Donegal, Glencolumbkille and Ardara, is another local producer. The quality is not quite as good, but is still of a high standard. Kilts and skirts, jackets, hand- or machine-knitted sweaters. Prices are more or less the same in all three shops, though the Glencolumbkille shop is supposed to be a factory outlet.

McGinty's Sweater Shop, Main Street, Donegal, has a good range of traditional sweaters, often in more unusual styles and patterns than elsewhere.

Cyndi Graham Weaving Studio, St John's Point. This charming individual weaver makes scarves, shawls and plaids using Kilcar wools and Belfast linen. Her workshop is in a delightful thatched cabin facing Slieve League.

Studio Donegal, Kilcar, has slightly different tweeds from those offered by Magee and Molloy, and stocks a few clothes, plaids, scarves and headgear.

Michael Byrne Knits & Tweeds, Carrick, on the coast road towards Kilcar. Local hand-knitted items. Good range of patterns and colours. The individual responsible is named on the label.

W McNelis & Sons, Main Street, Ardara, belongs to one of the last weavers to make tweed on a hand loom. Production has unfortunately stopped, but rolls of material are still available as well as hand-knitted items.

Liam & Brid McGinley, Glencolumbkille. In the upper part of the village to the east, this couple sell machine-knitted items. The coarse-knit sweaters are particularly good (€25-35).

Porcelain – This is a local speciality, with factories open to visitors and factory outlets. The products are elaborately decorated with lots of floral ornamentation. **Donegal Parian China**, Ballyshannon, on the Bundoran road (closed weekends between October-April). **Celtic Weave China**, Cloghore, Ballyshannon, on the Belleek road, make basketweave-ware. See "Making the most of Fermanagh" for the Belleek factory in Northern Ireland (7km from Ballyshannon).

NORTHERN PENINSULAS★★

Co Donegal – Allow 3 or 4 days
Michelin map 923 G-H-I-J-K / 2-3 and map page 418

Not to be missed
Inland Donegal, no less lovely than the coast.
Errigal Mountain and the Glenveagh National Park.
Horn Head and the Atlantic Drive.
The pre-Christian fort of Grianan of Ailigh.

And remember...
Letterkenny traffic is a nightmare best avoided.
Accommodation is thin on the ground on the Inishowen Peninsula
and needs to be booked well in advance.
Take some warm clothes – there's almost always a chill in the air.

The thin northern light falls on the vastness of the Atlantic, a scattering of islands, and a highly indented coastline, protected by many a rocky reef. Inland are the Derryveagh Mountains, set in a landscape of lakes and peat bogs which is a paradise for anglers and walkers. The country may be less dramatic than that of southern Donegal, but this misty stronghold of Gaelic language and culture has an austere allure of its own.

On Inishowen

B Kaufmann/MICHELIN

Islands and peninsulas
95km tour along coast roads – allow half a day

From Ardara (see page 410) take the R261 towards Naran and at Maas continue on the N56 towards Dungloe.

The road reaches the estuary of the **Gweebarra River**, a subtle landscape of rocky shoreline, shifting sandbanks, dunes and grassy islands. To the northwest rise the Derryveagh Mountains.

Anyone with a little time to spare should turn left after crossing the Gweebarra onto the **Scenic Route***, which bumps along through the wind-blown grasslands. The almost flat countryside is studded with ruined cabins, a few inhabited houses, and heaps of seaweed waiting to be spread on the thin soils. The road then reaches the sandy shore of a pale green lagoon.

The Rosses*

The last place to stock up before exploring the Rosses, the bustling little town of **Dungloe** comes as something of a surprise. It is the gateway to a strange landscape of low and stony **hill country**, bounded by beaches and **dunes**, with the occasional conifer plantation and a scattering of hundreds of little **lakes** with water of the deepest black.

To the west of Dungloe, the R259 first runs along the shore of a rocky bay to the fishing village of **Burtonport** *(6km from Dungloe)* sheltered by a string of little islands. Local specialities include oysters, mussels and lobster.

Boats make the crossing from Burtonport to **Arranmore Island**** *(3 to 8 times daily, 20min, €7.50 there and back)*. With only about 500 inhabitants, the island is almost completely unspoiled; it can explored by walking the **Arranmore Way**, a signposted

footpath going right round the island and taking in the rugged 150m **cliffs** on its western shore *(reckon on 6hr)*.

Continue along the R259 and watch out for the signpost on the left pointing to **Cruit Island**. Linked to the mainland by a bridge, the island has lovely beaches of pinkish sand and an inland landscape of equally pink granite rocks. The road runs across a golf course and terminates with a view seaward of Owey Island.

Continue along the R259 to Crolly, and from here go north on the N56, turning off almost at once on the R257 towards Bunbeg. To carry on into the mountains and to Dunlewy, continue towards Gweedore and turn right on to the R251 (see below).

Gweedore

To the east are the Derryveagh Mountains with their lines of tall white wind turbines. The road joins the coast again at **Bunbeg**, the gateway to the Gweedore Peninsula, a stronghold of the Gaelic language. In Bunbeg, a road to the left signposted **The Pier*** leads to the lovely little harbour, well-sheltered from the stormy Atlantic in its rocky bay. With trawlers and a shipyard, it is full of atmosphere, unlike Bunbeg beach, which is attractive in itself but which has been spoiled by modern development.

Northern peninsulas

Beyond the resort area the road approaches the headland known as **Bloody Foreland****. One explanation of its name refers to the blood-stained waters following a shipwreck, another to the effects of the setting sun. From the road, drystone-walled and boulder-strewn fields slope down to the pebbly shore.

Far out to sea to the north is **Tory Island**, a harsh and wind-swept place, notorious as a lurking-place for pirates and smugglers. Its legendary first inhabitants were the fierce **Formorians**, led by the Celtic god of darkness, one-eyed Balor. The Gaelic-speaking islanders are still something of a law unto themselves, with their own "king". The island has a "cursing stone", supposedly called into action in 1884, when a British gunboat attempting to collect unpaid taxes suddenly sank

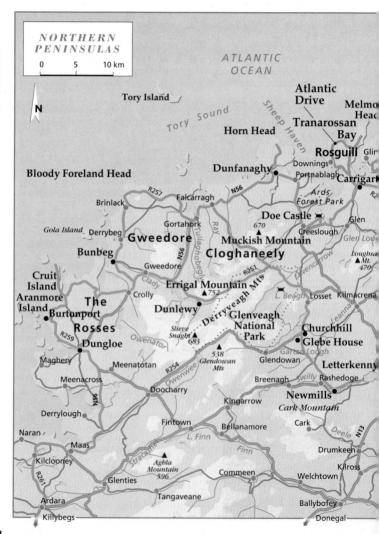

with much loss of life in calm conditions. *Access to the island: Turasmara Cruises,* ☎ 075 313 20, *ferry from Bunbeg all year; from Magheroarty and Portnablagh in summer, €20.*

Beyond Bloody Foreland the road runs through great expanses of bogland. The distinctive conical outline of Errigal Mountain is visible in the distance, while to seaward, the mouth of the bay is almost closed by a sandbar.

The N56 is reached again at Gortahork. Continue to the little town of Falcarragh if there is any shopping to be done. Otherwise go south in the direction of Donegal, turning left in 9km onto the R251 towards Dunlewy. The road runs along the flank of Errigal Mountain.

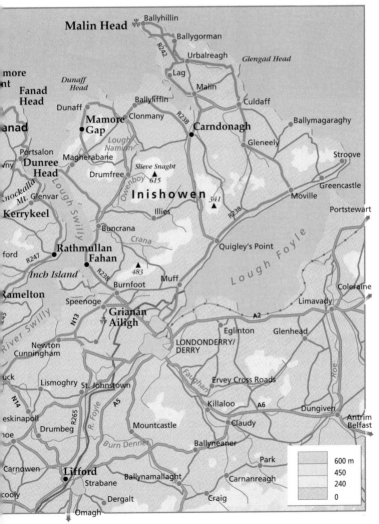

Cruit Island dwelling

Derryveagh Mountains★★
Allow a day

■ **Errigal Mountain**★★ – *Reckon on a tiring but not difficult 4hr climb.* Errigal is Donegal's highest mountain (752m), easily identifiable by its almost perfectly conical shape. It is possible to get a fairly close look at it by driving along the road from the pub opposite the church on the way into the village of **Dunlewy**. To do the actual climb, continue along the R251 beyond the youth hostel to a car park. The effort of getting to the top is rewarded by a **view** over the whole of the range and the north coast.

The **Dunlewy Lakeside Centre** *(10.30am-6pm; 11am-7pm Sunday. Admission charge)* is a family-oriented visitor centre, with a children's zoo, a weaver's workshop, souvenirs, a café, and the chance of a boat trip on the lake *(see "Making the most of the Northern Peninsulas")*.

Continue eastwards around Errigal on the R251 towards the Glenveagh National Park.

■ **Glenveagh National Park**★★ – The approach to the park is magnificent, a desert of undulating peatland where the crests of the hills break the skyline like the spikes on the back of some dinosaur.

The National Park covers an area of 9 667 hectares and includes **Glenveagh Castle and Gardens**★★ *(mid-March-mid-November: 10am-6.30pm; closed Friday in October. Admission charge to park and castle. Heritage Site. Bear in mind that there are limits on the number of people visiting the castle; make a reservation on arrival).* The **Visitor Centre** has displays on the flora and fauna of the estate. From here visitors are taken by minibus to the castle, passing a pretty mountain lake on the way. The luxuriant gardens are in total contrast to the wild nature all around. There are a number of walks, one of which leads along the lakeside, another to an elevated **viewpoint** giving a panorama over the surrounding area.

Rising over the trees is the castle's **battlemented tower**, built of granite quarried from the mountainside. The magnificent Victorian residence was erected in 1870 by John George Adair, notorious for his ruthless eviction of hapless tenants. In the

1930s, it passed into the hands of the Irish-American millionaire Henry McIlhenny, who bequeathed it to the nation in 1983 together with its rich furnishings.

Turn right on leaving the park and continue on the R251 towards Churchill and Glebe Gallery (around 12km).

■ **Churchill and around** – Once the National Park is left behind the landscape becomes more verdant. Rising over a little lake is the romantic silhouette of **Glebe House & Gallery*** *(Easter and mid-May-September: 11am-6.30pm; closed Friday. Admission charge. Heritage Site)*. The house was bought in 1953 by the English artist Derek Hill, and contains his collection of modern Irish and European paintings as well as Japanese prints, William Morris textiles, and ceramics. There are also works by Hill himself and naïve paintings by the Tory Islanders who were his protégés.

About 10km further along the N251 towards Letterkenny are the restored **Newmills Corn and Flax Mills** *(mid-June-September: 10am-6.30pm; closed Friday. Admission charge. Heritage Site)*, with explanations of how these water-powered mills functioned.

From here it is possible to continue to Letterkenny (5km), or alternatively return to Falcarragh (35km) by going back along the R251 past the National Park, and shortly afterwards turning towards Muckish Gap.

■ **Muckish Mountain**** – *4km climb up a steep path.* Easily recognised by its flattened peak topped by a cairn, this stony mountain can be climbed via the austere defile of **Muckish Gap**.

Go northeast from Falcarragh on the N56 to Dunfanaghy.

The northwestern headlands**
170km via the coast road from Falcarragh to Letterkenny –
Allow at least a day

Horn Head**
The pretty seaside resort of **Dunfanaghy** is flanked by lovely beaches. On the way into town is the **Dunfanaghy Workhouse** *(March-October: 10am-5pm weekdays, 12pm-5pm weekends. Admission charge)*, now converted to house an exhibition on the Famine and its ravages in the region.

Beyond the isthmus at the head of the bay is the beginning of the **Horn Head Drive*****, the area's star excursion *(turn left at the fork and drive round in a clockwise direction)*. There are a number of little detours from the drive, all of which are worth taking in order to enjoy the splendid **views** along the coast. Bloody Foreland can be seen to the west, then, once past the headland, Rosguill Peninsula appears to the east, plus, in clear weather, far-off Fanad Head and beyond it Malin Head. On the way back, the flat summit of Muckish reappears together with the cone of Errigal.

Leave Dunfanaghy on the N56 towards Letterkenny. Turn left in Cresslough towards Doe Castle, 1km further on. If time is short, continue through Cresslough and turn left on to the R245 towards Carrigart. Doe Castle soon comes into view.

Doe Castle* *(closed for reconstruction)* stands in a serene setting on a headland overlooking a deep bay. The castle has a 16C four-storey **keep**, and is protected by the sea and by a moat, now dry.

Rosguill Peninsula**
To the northwest of the village of **Carrigart**, with its banks and shops, is the 14.5km **Atlantic Drive*****. The road passes through Rosapenna and Downings, the latter a centre of traditional tweed production.

The first section of the drive is the least spectacular, but the road rises steadily towards the heights of the headland before reaching **Tranarossan Bay*****, its lovely sandy beach set among high cliffs. Beyond the beach, the hills stretch all the way to

Melmore Head. Inland, the landscape becomes greener and less harsh, overlooking an anchorage favoured by fishing vessels. This is **Mulroy Bay**, an inlet of the sea running far inland between the Rosguill and Fanad peninsulas. A good place to linger awhile along the last bit of the drive is the cheerful **Singing Pub**.

From Carrigart, follow the R245 along the shore of Mulroy Bay to Millford (14.5km), then turn left towards Kerrykeel.

Fanad★★
Almost surrounded by the sea, this peninsula contains even more contrasts than the others. On the way to **Kerrykeel**, the road follows the green and well-wooded shore of the inlet.

Beyond Kerrykeel, take the R246 Portsalon road, then turn left on to the minor road leading to Tawney, Kildrum, and Tulaigh na Dála.

The landscape is one of gently undulating hills, quite different from the coast and countryside experienced so far. At the tip of the peninsula a long beach backed by dunes separates **Rinmore Point★** and its pretty little bays to the west from the austere cliffs of **Fanad Head★★** to the east. The road now runs back down the eastern side of the peninsula towards **Portsalon**, with views across **Lough Swilly** to the heights of Inishhowen.

From Portsalon follow the road to the golf course by the beach and continue along the coast on minor roads to Rathmullan.

Rathmullan is an attractive place laid out along the sea wall. It was from here in 1607 that Hugh O'Neill and Rory O'Donnell sailed in the incident that came to be known as The Flight of the Earls.

Continue on the R247 to Ramelton.

Surrounded by typically Irish countryside, **Ramelton★★** is a very English-looking place, a typical 17C plantation town. It prospered greatly thanks to the linen trade and the tanning industry, and is graced by numerous Georgian houses built in grey stone. The quayside is particularly fascinating, with a number of fine old commercial and storage buildings; it's pleasant to linger here at the end of the day. By **Fish House**, the arches can still be seen through which goods were loaded and unloaded before the quay was built. Close by is the Victorian **weighbridge**. At the end of the quayside are a number of large 18C warehouses with red doors and beyond them the old building of **Kelly's Grain Store**. The whole group of buildings and their setting still evoke the atmosphere Ramelton must have had in its glory days.

The R245 continues to **Letterkenny**, 14km away, It is a rather charmless place, but a useful base for exploring the coast and countryside around.

Leave Letterkenny to the east on the N13 towards Londonderry. After 23km turn right by the modern round church towards Grianán Ailigh.

The Inishowen Peninsula★
About 160km – Allow a day

■ **Grianán Ailigh★★** – *Free admission.* This enormous **circular fort** has a superb **panorama★★** over much of Northern Ireland and Donegal, including Errigal and Muckish. It is one of the most spectacular structures of its kind in the country, 23m in diameter and with stone walls 4m thick on three sides. Dating from the

Ramelton

pre-Christian era, it was sufficiently important to have featured in Ptolemy's map of the world, where it is identified as a royal residence. Later it served as the headquarters of the O'Neill rulers for five hundred years, before being destroyed in the 5C.

A footpath to the rear of the fort leads down to a **well**, where St Patrick is supposed to have baptised the founder of the O'Neill dynasty.

Return to the N13 and turn almost immediately onto the R238 towards Buncrana.

■ **Fahan** – This village is not particularly attractive in itself, but has a ruined Protestant church with a rare example of a 7C **Celtic cross-slab**. The slab stands in the neglected graveyard of what was a monastery founded by St Columba; it is decorated on each face with a cross formed of interlaced bands, plus, on one face, two flanking figures. *(Poorly signposted. Enquire at the modern church with a square tower next to the old chapel).*

Go through the popular resort of Buncrana and continue to Dunree Head.

■ **Dunree Head** – The rather desolate headland is crowned with a fortress and offers a fine view across Lough Swilly to Fanad.

The road continues over a little pass from Dunree Head to an attractive sheltered **beach** which makes a good picnic spot before beginning the climb up to Mamore Gap.

■ **Mamore Gap**★★ – The road climbs up in a series of hairpin bends to the saddle which guards the approach to the northern part of the peninsula. At the top, a white figure of the Virgin Mary blesses all who pass by. Beyond, the road descends giving splendid **views**★ over the sea.

Continue to Carndonagh.

■ **Carndonagh** – The village has an 8C **high cross**★★, the oldest in the country *(on the way into the village on the R238 from Ballyliffin)*. Decorated with interlace, it has a Crucifixion and is flanked by two pillars representing David dressed as a warrior and playing the harp. The crude canopy protecting the cross hardly adds to its allure.

■ **Malin Head**★★ – The local name for this northernmost point in the country is **Banba's Crown**. Banba is supposed to be the name of a Celtic queen representing Ireland, making Malin Head the head of the country. The wind-blasted road running round the headland has spectacular **views**★★★ of the peninsulas to the west.

Beyond the weather station and radio masts look out for the sign to the **Wee House of Malin**. A path leads down the slope to a ruined church and the Wee House itself, a cave in the cliff which once housed a hermit and which is now an important place of pilgrimage. The cliffs are broken by a succession of little bays, and strangely shaped rocks stand out northward.

Take the road through a bleak landscape to Glengad, then on to the coast and the Londonderry road via Culdaff and Moville.

COMING AND GOING

By bus – In terms of efficiency and price, the best services in the area are run by private firms. **O'Donnell**, ☎ 075 481 14, has a daily service to Sligo and Galway (southward in the morning, return in the evening). **John McGinley**, ☎ 074 352 01, has a daily service to and from Dublin (3 buses from Dublin on Friday, 2 to Dublin on Sunday). Buses to Inishowen depart from Letterkenny, but this part of the Republic is mostly served by buses to and from Londonderry: **Lough Swilly Buses**, ☎ 077 613 40 offers "Rambler" tickets which are valid for a week's travel, and **Northwest**, ☎ 077 826 19 has services linking Inishowen to Buncrana as well as Derry.

By car – From the Dublin area and the midlands, road access to Inishowen is via Londonderry. The route is clearly signposted. From the west or elsewhere in Donegal, take the Derry road from Letterkenny.

ADDRESS BOOK

Banks / Currency exchange – There are banks and cash machines in Dungloe, Bunbeg, Falcarragh, Buncrana, Carndonagh and Moville. Bear in mind that Irish punts are not accepted in the North, though sterling can be used in the Republic.

Medical service – There are chemists at Dungloe, Bunbeg, Falcarragh, Buncrana, Carndonagh and Moville.

Internet – Celtic Internet Services, Main Street, Dungloe, ☎ 075 222 02.

WHERE TO STAY

• The Rosses
Between €40-45
Ardcrone House, Menmore, Dungloe, ☎ 075 211 153 – 4rm ⌐ TV On the way out of Dungloe to the north coast. Well-kept rooms, all with coastal views.
Inismil House, Dungloe, ☎ 075 420 87 – 5rm ⌐ TV Turn left down a minor road about 3km beyond Dungloe towards the Rosses. Green-painted, very comfortable house in a dreary setting.

Smoked salmon can be purchased right next door.
Erin House, Burtonport, ☎ 075 420 79 – 5rm ⌐ TV CC Facing the sea between Dungloe and Burtonport, this lovely, traditionally furnished house is run by a friendly landlady who is also a fine pastry-cook. Good choice at breakfast. The rooms sharing a bathroom are less expensive.
Teac Hughie Bán, Burtonport, ☎ 075 421 04 – 4rm ⌐ TV CC Clearly signposted off the road coming into Burtonport. Pleasant views of the surrounding area. Rooms sharing a bathroom are less expensive.

Around €65
⌐ **Danny Minnie's**, Teach Killindarragh, Annagry, ☎ 075 482 01 – 7rm ⌐ TV ✕ CC Almost buried beneath its Virginia creeper, this house has a cosy lounge with an open fire, an elegant and refined dining room, and very tastefully decorated rooms. In the restaurant, individual dishes are between €20-25. A charming place to stay. Flexible rates out of season.

Cottages to rent
Donegal Thatched Cottages, ☎ 071 771 97 or 075 432 55. ⌐ TV CC A group of delightful thatched cottages tucked away among great boulders in the wildest part of Cruit Island. Between €230-830 per week for 7 people according to season.

• Gweedore Peninsula
Between €13-25
⌐ **Tír na nÓg**, The Harbour, Bunbeg, Gweedore, ☎ 075 312 32 – 15rm ⌐ Large establishment by the little harbour in Bunbeg, all mod cons and a huge kitchen for use of guests.

Between €35-45
Ocean Lodge, Bloody Foreland, ☎ 075 320 84 – 4rm ⌐ CC Modern bungalow on the Gweedore Peninsula just short of Bloody Foreland. Pretty views.
Cuan na Mara, Ballyness, Falcarragh, ☎ 074 353 27 – 4rm ⌐ Clearly signposted on the beach road in Falcaragh. Plain but well-kept rooms.

Between €45-50

*☺**Atlantic View**, Strand Road, Bunbeg, Gweedore, ☎ 075 315 50 – 4rm ⌂ TV A homely establishment almost on the beach. Rooms 1 and 6 have sea views. Lovely garden with a barbecue and tables and chairs. The owners also have cottages to rent next door (6 beds, €550 per week in July-August).

Teach Campbell, Bunbeg, Gweedore, ☎ 075 315 45 – 23rm ⌂ ✎ TV CC Long low building in the middle of the village. Rather impersonal roooms. Meals by arrangement in the pleasant dining room.

More than €50

Bunbeg House, The Harbour, Bunbeg, ☎ 075 313 05 – 14rm ⌂ TV ✗ CC Spacious and very comfortable accommodation overlooking the little harbour. Somewhat more expensive than the other establishments. Basic restaurant with individual dishes from €6.50.

- **Derryveagh Mountains**
Between €45-50

Dunlewey Lodge, Moneymore, Dunlewey, ☎ 075 327 74 – 3rm ⌂ TV Signposted to the right on the way out of the village towards Glenveagh. Modern stone cottage, overlooking Dunlewey Lough.

Radharc an Ghleanna, Moneymore, Dunlewey, ☎ 075 318 35 – 3rm ⌂ TV Just before the previous establishment, with plain but well-kept accommodation. Two of the rooms have a view down to the lough.

St Jude B&B, Tullybeg, Churchill, ☎ 074 371 38 – 4rm ⌂ Fine view of Gartan Lake from the lounge. Straightforward accommodation, two rooms with shared facilities. Very pleasant elderly landlord and landlady.

- **Horn Head**
Between €9-20

Corcreggan Mill Hostel, Dunfanaghy, ☎ 074 365 07 – 22 beds and 8rm 3km west of Dunfanaghy, this youth hostel occupies a lovely old mill building. Some of the accommodation is in the buildings, the rest of it in an old railway coach. Basic comforts but loads of character. The rooms in the new cottage have their own facilities.

Between €35-45

Swan Nest B&B, Purt, Dunfanaghy, ☎ 074 365 60 – 4rm ⌂ 1km from Dunfanaghy by New Lake, this is a new and very well-kept bungalow. Two of the rooms have lake views. The rooms with shared facilities are slightly less expensive.

Carrigan House, Kill, Dunfanaghy, ☎ 074 362 76 – 4rm ⌂ TV CC Facing the golf club and the sea. Big new and brightly decorated house. Varied breakfast menu, including vegetarian.

The Links, Kill, Dunfanaghy, ☎ 074 366 83 – 4rm ⌂ TV A little further on from the previous establishment. Very comfortable but somewhat more expensive. Rates negotiable out of season.

*☺**The Whins**, Kill, Dunfanaghy, ☎ 074 364 81 – 5rm ⌂ TV CC On the same road as the two previous establishments, nestling in its attractive garden. Fine views of Horn Head from the lounge and dining room. Good library with lots of local information. Imaginatively decorated rooms. Friendly landlady. Varied breakfast menu, generous portions. A great place to stay.

- **Rossguill, Fanad and Letterkenny**
Between €35-45

*☺**Lennon Lodge***, Ramelton, ☎ 074 512 27 – 42 beds in 2, 4 and 5-bed rooms. ⌂ TV By the church, well-kept and comfortable accommodation, ideal for couples and families. Half the rooms have their own facilities. Rates vary according to the facilities provided. Breakfast extra. Good communal kitchen.

*☺**Mandalay House***, Drumreen, Carrigart, ☎ 074 556 00 – 3rm ⌂ Turn right at the church on the way out of Carrigart towards Millford, then immediately right again (almost doubling back) and continue for 3km. Lost among the hills, this house has superb views along the whole of the coast. But its main attraction is its unusual décor put in place by the owner, a world traveller who has brought back mementoes from every corner of the globe. A great place to stay, and it's not expensive either.

Baymount, Downings, ☎ 074 553 95 – 6rm Plain but very well-kept establishment, overlooking the start of the Atlantic Drive beyond the village of Downings. One room with own bathroom. Otherwise ask for one with a view. Indifferent reception.

Rinmore Cottage, Fanad Head, Ballylar, Fanad, ☎ 074 592 18 – 3rm Pale yellow modern bungalow behind the dunes just short of Fanad Head. Only one room with own bathroom.

🐚 **The Knoll**, Rathmullan, ☎ 074 582 41 – 4rm ⌂ TV Old house in a delightful garden, lots of charm and character, set back from the quayside in Rathmullan. The ground-floor bedroom has its own pretty lounge.

🐚 **Killererin House**, Ballyderg, Mountain Top, Letterkenny, ☎ 074 245 63 – 5rm ⌂ CC Leave Letterkenny on the N56 towards Kilmacrennan and continue for 3km. Clearly signposted to the left. Luxury at low cost in this big new house. Two of the rooms share facilities and have no TV, and the price is correspondingly lower. Lower still if you take the continental breakfast!

Riverview, Drumnahoagh, Letterkenny, ☎ 074 249 07 – 5rm ⌂ TV CC Look out for signs on the right on the way out of town towards Londonderry just before the Holiday Inn. Big house and a friendly welcome. Billiard table. Very quiet. When full, try the following establishment.

Larkfield, Drumnahoagh, Letterkenny, ☎ 074 214 78 – 3rm ⌂ Next door to Riverview, well-kept rooms, slightly more expensive.

Between €45-50

Sheephaven Lodge, Church Road, Carrigart, ☎ 074 556 85 – 4rm ⌂ Turn right by the church on the way out of Carrigart towards Millford. Well-kept and conveniently close to the village.

Sonas, Upper Carrick, Carrigart, ☎ 074 554 01 – 5rm ⌂ 🏌 TV CC Well-signposted on the right 5km from Carrigart on the Millford road. Very well-kept establishment set back from the road.

🐚 **An Crosóg**, Downings, ☎ 074 554 98 – 4rm ⌂ CC Beyond Downings on the Atlantic Drive, this is an attractively decorated farmhouse with

a pleasant conservatory for breakfast (good choice of breakfast dishes and generous helpings). Canny guests ask for the room with separate bathroom – it's attractive and less expensive. If possible, ask for a room with a view.

Waters Edge, Rathmullan, ☎ 074 581 82 – 11rm ⌂ TV ✗ CC This little hotel lives up to its name. Lovely views from the dining room and bedrooms (otherwise a bit dark). Evening meal (see "Eating out").

Ardeen House, Ramelton, ☎ 074 512 43 – 5rm ⌂ CC In the road running off behind the quayside warehouses, this is a large and characterful house. The well-kept rooms are attractively decorated and there is a warm welcome. Generous breakfast. The only room without its own facilities is slightly cheaper.

Grammond House, Market Street, Ramelton, ☎ 074 510 55 – 6rm ⌂ In the middle of town in the street climbing at an angle from opposite Fish House. Plain rooms, a bit old-fashioned but well-kept. Two share a bathroom and are less expensive.

Green Gables, 41 Orchard Grove, Letterkenny, ☎ 074 263 62 – 4rm ⌂ TV CC In a road running off the Ramelton road opposite the Pitch & Putt pub. Quiet location, 15mins on foot from the town centre.

🐚 **Glencairn House**, Ramelton Road, Letterkenny, ☎ 074 243 93 – 6rm ⌂ TV CC 2km from the town centre, this house is run by a flower-loving landlady who looks after her guests with great care. Good variety of breakfast dishes.

Between €65-140

🐚 **Rathmullan House**, Lough Swilly, Rathmullan, ☎ 074 581 88 – 25rm ⌂ 🏌 TV ✗ 🏊 CC Less than 1km north on the R247. Lovely residence in the middle of parkland going down to the lough. Victorian conservatory, loads of charm. Covered pool, sauna, hammam. Reasonably-priced restaurant.

● **Inishowen Peninsula**

Between €40-45

Oaklawn, Fahan, ☎ 077 602 99 – 3rm ⌂ CC Under 1km from the main road on a narrow road behind the village church. Very quiet, pretty garden.

🍴 **Ennerdale House**, Fahan, ☎ 077 602 49 – 4rm To the right on the R238 in Fahan. Delightful house with a pretty conservatory in a charming garden. Thoughtful and efficient landlady. Only 50m from the beach for anyone bold enough to take a dip!

Brookvale House, Chapel Glen, Clonmany, ☎ 077 763 60 – 4rm 📺 TV Pink and white roadside bungalow on the way out of Clonmany towards Malin. Decent but impersonal accommodation.

McEleny's B&B, Ballyliffin, ☎ 077 765 41 – 6rm 📺 TV CC Under 1km from the village in the Clonmany direction. Friendly landlady who does everything in her power to make her guests feel at home. Normal rates in season, reductions the rest of the year.

🍴 **Druim Doo**, Umgal, Malin Head, ☎ 077 702 87 – 3rm Clearly signposted halfway along the road between Malin and Malin Head. Simple little cottage with the warmest of welcomes. Plain but well-kept rooms, one particularly charming room beneath the eaves of the barn. The owners' dogs are very much part of the family.

Highview, Ballygorman, Malin Head, Inishowen, ☎ 077 702 83 – 4rm 📺 Lovely views, especially from the upper rooms. Reduced rates for continental breakfast.

Barraicín, Malin Head, Inishowen, ☎ 077 701 84 – 3rm TV Run by a charming landlady who makes her guests feel part of the family. Traditional Irish interior.

Most Northerly B&B, Ard Malin, Malin Head, Inishowen, ☎ 077 702 49 – 2rm When everywhere else is full.

Carraig Garbh House, Moville, ☎ 077 825 27 – 3rm 📺 Big pink house on the way out towards Greencastle. Well-kept and comfortable. The large bedroom is the most expensive.

Admiralty House, Carronaffe, Moville, ☎ 077 825 25 – 3rm TV CC Lovely pale yellow painted house overlooking the sea on the Londonderry road. Shared bathroom.

Between €45-50

The Hall Greene Farm, Porthall, Lifford, ☎ 074 413 18 – 4rm 📺 CC Big traditional farmhouse painted red. Guests wake up to the sound of farmyard noises announcing (the very generous) breakfast. Very friendly family, with a landlady who is an expert pastrycook.

🍴 **Mount Royal**, Carrigans, ☎ 074 401 63 – 4rm 📺 TV CC On the way out of the village towards Londonderry (8km away), a lovely, cosy and welcoming establishment. Bedrooms are colour-themed, and full of pretty knickknacks. Guests' every wish is taken care of (toiletries, hot-water bottle, etc) and breakfast is a real surprise. You'll be as snug as a bug in a rug.

Glen House, Strais, Clonmany, ☎ 077 767 45 – 2rm 📺 CC 18C house with an American owner in love with this part of Ireland. Rather expensive. Lovely walks in the surrounding area.

Carrickabraghey House, Shore Road, Ballyliffin, ☎ 077 769 77 – 4rm 📺 TV CC On the road to Pollan Bay. Very spacious and comfortable rooms. Higher rates in July and August.

The Manor House, Greencastle, ☎ 077 810 11 – 8rm Clearly signposted on the road to the golf course, this old house at the end of an avenue by the waterside could have come from the pages of a Daphne du Maurier novel. Given the price, the décor is rather tatty, but the views make up for this.

Around €55

Rossaor House, Ballyliffin, ☎ 077 764 98 – 4rm 📺 ✂ TV CC Large garden, attractive lounge overlooking beach and sea. Luxurious furnishings including lovely antique pieces. Good choice of breakfast dishes. The owner also has cottages to rent in the village (6 beds, between €390-€520 according to the time of year).

EATING OUT

● **The Rosses**

The Lobster Pot, Burtonport. Stone-tiled house on the way down into town. Between €5-10 until 6pm, then €13-19 for main dishes. The oysters and mussels served with wholemeal bread and butter are not expensive and well worth trying.

Iggy's Bar, Kincasslagh, is a traditional pub serving food between 12pm-6pm. Prices in the range €4-11.50, with most dishes costing €6.50-7.50. Seafood specialities. Useful place to know in an area where restaurants are thin on the ground.

Danny Minnie's Restaurant, Annagry, is an establishment of some refinement. Classic cuisine of a high standard served in a particularly elegant setting. Expensive: individual dishes between €20-25.

● **Gweedore Peninsula**

The Cottage Restaurant, Bunbeg, in the main street. Dinner served 6.30pm-9.30pm, lunch also at weekends. Classic dishes, limited choice, but pleasant setting. Between €11-16.

● **Derryveagh Mountains**

Dunlewy Lakeside Centre, Dunlewy. Cafeteria with astonishingly inexpensive food, served in generous portions. Salads, grills, cakes and pastries, and sandwiches for under €6.50. Pleasant setting, open fire. Closes 6pm.

● **Horn Head**

An Chistin, Dunfanaghy, in the main street. Straightforward dishes, good portions, eat in or take away. Salads, quiches, chicken around €6.50 at mid-day and in the evening.

Rossguill and Fanad

🍺 **The Singing Pub**, Atlantic Drive, Rossguill, is a long low thatched building on the second part of the Atlantic Drive. Peat fire, exposed beams and straightforward food: chicken, home-made burgers, and seafood including salmon and scallops, between €5-10. 1pm-9pm.

Waters Edge, Rathmullan does lunches for €6.50-7.50 and candlelit dinners with starters between €3-7 and main courses €13-20.

Rathmullan House, Lough Swilly (see "Where to stay").

Mirabeau Steak House, Ramelton, in the Mall, despite its imposing entrance has very reasonably priced food. Meals from €7.50 including vegetarian.

The Bridge Bar, Ramelton, on the way up from the bridge. Seafood specialities.

HAVING A DRINK

The Singing Pub, Atlantic Drive, Rossguill. Music every evening in summer, great atmosphere (after 9.30pm).

OTHER THINGS TO DO

Freshwater fishing – C Bonner & Sons, The Bridge, Dungloe, sell all kinds of angling gear, and can arrange all necessary licences and hire of boat. Useful tips too.

Rosses Angling Association: contact Charlie Bonner, ☎ 075 211 63. Day licence €6.50, boat €13, year card €20.

Sea angling – Information on the best places to fish from: **MV Loinnir**, Bunbeg or Burtonport, ☎ 075 484 03; **The Cricket Charters**, Dunfanaghy, ☎ 074 362 90; **Inishowen Boating**, Malin, ☎ 077 706 05.

Sailing – Bunbeg Sailing Centre, The Harbour, Bunbeg, ☎ 075 313 05. €25 per half-day.

Golf – Dunfanaghy Golf Club, ☎ 074 363 35. 18-hole course.

Making the most of the northern peninsulas

Northern Ireland

Official name: Northern Ireland (province of the United
Kingdom)
Area: 14 139sqkm
Population: around 1 700 000
Capital: Belfast
Currency: pound sterling (£)

THE OTHER IRELAND

Northern Ireland consists of six of the traditional nine counties of the ancient province of Ulster, namely Antrim, Armagh, Down, Fermanagh, Londonderry / Derry and Tyrone, the remaining three counties of Donegal, Cavan and Monaghan with their Catholic majorities having been assigned to the Free State at the time of Partition. The majority of the population consists of descendants of the Scots and English settled here at the time of the 17th century Plantation (*see page 18*).

The religious divide

Most Northern Irish – about 60 % of the population – are Protestants, the remaining 40 % nearly all Catholics. Though the eastern parts of the province tend to be Protestant and the western areas Catholic, in broad terms the population is thoroughly mixed. Belfast and Derry have substantial Catholic and Protestant minorities respectively, while to the west of the central and largely Catholic Co Tyrone there is a solid Protestant presence in Co Fermanagh. Unlike the Catholics, the Protestant population is far from homogenous; most are Presbyterians, but in addition there are Anglicans, Methodists, Baptists and others. Religious allegiance remains the basis of identity as well as a potent source of division.

A troubled province

The province of Northern Ireland was formally established by the **Government of Ireland Act** of 1921, when the Six Counties were given an autonomous administration. The shape and extent of the province was determined to some extent by political and economic factors, as it would have been impossible in any case to draw a coherent boundary separating the Catholic and Protestant populations. A frontier tightly drawn around the overwhelmingly Protestant districts would have yielded a small and hardly viable statelet, while a boundary taking in the three other counties of ancient Ulster with their substantial Protestant minorities would have included too large a Catholic population. This situation was accepted – in the hope that Partition would be temporary – by the southern Irish negotiators who signed the Treaty of London later that year (*for earlier history see page 15*). It left the Catholics of the North in an invidious position; from being part of the majority population of the island as a whole, they now became a minority, regarded by their neighbours as an element likely to subvert the very existence of the new province. Many refused co-operation with the new authorities, thereby accelerating the Protestant hold on power. A Council of Ireland, intended to promote cross-border understanding, remained a dead-letter, as did a commission intended to fine-tune the actual alignment of the frontier.

"A Protestant state for a Protestant people"

Second-class citizens – During the half-century following the Treaty of London, many of the fears of the Catholic population were realised. The government of the province remained entirely in the hands of Unionists, who set out – largely unsupervised by Britain – to create in the words of one of their leaders "a Protestant state for a Protestant people". Catholics were under-represented in the Parliament at Stormont by a systematic process of electoral gerrymandering, and never more than a few joined the successor to the Royal Irish Constabulary, the **Royal Ulster Constabulary**, regarded by most Catholics as a Protestant militia. Employers who might have been even-handed in distributing jobs were often dissuaded from doing so by their Protestant work-force; the most notorious case was that of the Belfast shipyards, where by 1970 only 400 out of a total of 10 000 employees were Catholic.

"One man, one vote" – In the improved economic situation of the 1960s, cautious hopes arose of reconciliation between the two communities. Tentative contacts were made between the governments of North and South, and Prime Minister Terence

O'Neill made unprecedented visits to Catholic institutions such as schools. Inspired by liberation movements such as the anti-discrimination struggle of Blacks in the United States, the Civil Rights Association was founded in 1967 under the slogan "one man, one vote". Its demands were regarded as provocative by many Protestants, and some of its demonstrations were broken up, the province's "B-Specials" (auxiliary police) playing a notably brutal role.

Escalating violence

By 1969, communal violence had reached such a pitch that the British government decided to deploy troops. In Belfast, the soldiers were at first welcomed by a Catholic population fearful of being firebombed from their homes, and some of the most serious confrontations were between the army and Protestant rioters. But, inevitably, the army was identified with the civil power, still the Protestant-dominated Stormont government. Despite the forcing through of anti-discriminatory measures in employment and housing, the climate soon worsened. The imposition of curfews and the introduction of internment of suspects alienated Catholic sympathies and led to a revival of activity on the part of the **Irish Republican Army** (IRA), now split into two factions: the Official IRA, content to let its socialist programme mature slowly, and the Provisional IRA, devoted to the armed struggle in pursuit of nationalist aims. As the Officials faded into the background, the Provisionals developed a strategy and tactics modelled on Third World independence movements, notably radical Palestinians. The terrorist violence they unleashed was all the more incomprehensible to most people, including Catholics, because most of the demands of the Civil Rights movement had by now been met. The use of violence to achieve reunification had long been condemned by the government of the Republic, and Sinn Féin, the political wing of the IRA, only succeeded in capturing a small share of the Nationalist vote at elections. At this time most of the Catholic vote went to the moderate Social Democratic and Labour Party led by Gerry Fitt.

Violence was far from being a monopoly of the IRA and other armed nationalist organisations like the Irish National Liberation Army. Protestant extremists formed paramilitary groups such as the **Ulster Defence Association** (UDA), the **Ulster Volunteer Force** (UVF) and the **Ulster Freedom Fighters** (UFF) which practised ruthless terror tactics against their opponents and the nationalist community as a whole.

Direct rule

A spiral of violence culminated in 1972 with an orgy of bombings and shootings. January 30, 1972, has gone down in history as **"Bloody Sunday"**; an initially peaceful civil rights march degenerated into rioting and led to an attack on unarmed civilians by soldiers of the Parachute Regiment in which thirteen were shot dead (*see page 454*). The Stormont Parliament was suspended and direct rule from London imposed.

Carnage in the streets – There now began almost a quarter of a century of uninterrupted violence, with killings not only across the sectarian divide, but within it, as competing factions eliminated rivals and opponents. A total of 3 280 people lost their lives, 900 of them soldiers or police officers, while 36 000 were wounded. Outside Northern Ireland, only high-profile deaths caught the headlines. In 1979, Lord Mountbatten and his grandson were assassinated by the IRA while on a sailing holiday, and Prime Minister Thatcher's special adviser Airey Neave was blown up in his car within the precincts of Westminster. In 1981, Provisional commander **Bobby Sands** was elected to Parliament while on hunger strike in the Maze prison, and subsequently died, along with several of his comrades. In 1984, Prime Minister Margaret Thatcher herself narrowly escaped injury or death when a bomb was exploded at Brighton's Grand Hotel during a Conservative Party conference.

The search for a political solution – The British Government had thought of Direct Rule as a strictly temporary measure and made various attempts to find a political and constitutional settlement acceptable – or at least tolerable – to the two commu-

The other Ireland

nities, as well as to the government of the Republic. The **Sunningdale Agreement** providing a power-sharing executive came into force in 1974, but was immediately rendered ineffective by a general strike organised by the Protestant Ulster Workers Council. In 1985, the **Anglo-Irish Agreement** introducing an array of cross-border cooperative measures met with outrage on the part of Protestants. However, six years of negotiations between the different parties finally paid off in 1993, permitting Prime Minister John Major and Taoisach Albert Reynolds to sign the **Downing Street Declaration**. This envisaged no change to the constitutional status of Northern Ireland without the consent of the majority of the population as well as negotiations with all organisations prepared to renounce violence.

A rocky road to peace – The first decisive move towards peace followed eight months after the signing of the Declaration. On 31 August 1994, the IRA announced a unilateral **ceasefire**, followed in October by a similar announcement on the part of the Protestant paramilitaries. In 1996, the IRA suspended its ceasefire, giving as its reason the exclusion of Sinn Féin from negotiations. There were more bombings and assassinations, as well as continuing confrontations between Orange marchers, Catholic residents, police and army at **Drumcree**. But a fresh ceasefire eventually emerged, and all-party negotiations, including Sinn Féin, began in earnest. American encouragement in rallying support for peace was constant, President Clinton involving himself personally, and making several visits to Ireland.

The Good Friday Agreement

A crucial step forward was taken when Tony Blair met the Sinn Féin leader Gerry Adams in December 1997. Despite strong disapproval on the part of Unionists, this removed an important psychological obstacle and helped open the way to the **Good Friday Agreement** signed in Belfast on 10 April 1998.

Provisions of the Agreement – The Agreement included a guarantee that Northern Ireland would remain a part of the United Kingdom as long as a majority of its inhabitants wished it to. At the same time the province was given a considerable degree of autonomy, with a Northern Ireland Assembly consisting of 108 members elected by proportional representation. A North-South Council was created for resolving issues of common interest in areas such as agriculture, fisheries, tourism, transport and education. For its part, the Republic undertook to amend that part of its constitution claiming jurisdiction over the whole island. Lastly, the Agreement envisaged the withdrawal of most British forces from the province, the decommissioning of all paramilitary weapons, and the release of people imprisoned for "scheduled offences", including terrorist crimes. A referendum held in both parts of Ireland in May 1998 showed the Agreement to be approved by 71.1% of Northerners and 94.4% of people in the Republic. Elements within and outside the IRA remained violently opposed to what they regarded as a betrayal of nationalist ideals, and on 15 August 1998 the "Real IRA" showed its disapproval by exploding a car bomb in Omagh which killed 29 people.

New institutional arrangements – Despite everything, the new devolved Assembly was elected on 25 June 1998. **David Trimble**, leader of the Ulster Unionist Party, and **Seamus Mallon**, leader of the moderate nationalist Social Democratic and Labour Party were selected as First and Deputy First Minister respectively. Later in the year, David Trimble and John Hume, the former SDLP leader, jointly received the Nobel Peace Prize for their role in furthering the peace process.

Power was due to be devolved to the new executive on 10 March 1999, but since the IRA had failed to decommission any of its arms, the Unionist parties withdrew from government, making the Assembly unworkable. Strenuous intervention on the part of US Senator George Mitchell and others led eventually to the reconvening of the Assembly and the election of an Executive, which met for the first time on 2 December. A commission on policing chaired by the British former Governor of Hong Kong, Chris Patten, proposed reforms to the Royal Ulster Constabulary which would make it acceptable to the nationalist community and attract young Catholic recruits. Army activity was scaled down, with many troops leaving the province and a number of bases and observation posts abandoned. The prisoner release scheme came to an end, with a total of 433 being freed from gaol (193 loyalist, 229 republican, 11 others) by the autumn of 2000. Because of the lack of progress on arms decommissioning, the Assembly was suspended by the Northern Ireland Secretary, Peter Mandelson, and direct rule re-introduced in early 2000, but the impasse was resolved after IRA arms dumps were inspected by Martti Ahtisaari and Cyril Ramaphosa. For the first time in several years, the marching season produced no major incidents, though there was an outbreak of killings among feuding loyalist factions. Peace, however precarious, seemed to have finally arrived, perhaps helped by the increasing prosperity of both parts of the island.

The economy

Northern Ireland's economic life was seriously affected by 30 years of Troubles as well as by Thatcherite liberalism which left its traditional industries, in particular Belfast's shipyards, exposed to world competition. Unemployment levels were high, with joblessness affecting up to half the population of the poorer Catholic areas of Belfast at certain times.

Religious disparities
Religion has fashioned distinct cultural identities and approaches to work and economic life. Even though the situation is changing rapidly, income per head is much higher among Protestants than Catholics, and 25 % more than in the Republic. In 1998, 38 % of Catholic households were dependent on unemployment benefit compared with a Protestant figure of 18 %. Like the British, the Protestants of Northern Ireland have historically had a more open attitude to the world, and were quick to exploit the country's natural resources and develop manufacturing, notably linen. With its shipyards, Belfast participated fully in the 19C Industrial Revolution at a time when Catholic Ireland remained almost entirely rural, and even today it is still possible to explain economic inequalities by reference to the historic contrast between a liberal, urbane and culturally individualistic Protestant Ireland, and a rural, Catholic Ireland long dominated by the Church and treated as a colony.

Geographical inequalities
Northern Ireland has no important mineral resources, though for many years iron ore was extracted from the Antrim Glens. Peat is still dug and used for domestic heating and in power stations. The relative **agricultural wealth** and broad **range of crops** cultivated in the 19C meant that the North was much less affected than the rest of the country by the Famine. There are many areas of good soil, notably in the Ards Peninsula, the province's granary. The most important crops today include potatoes, oats, barley, hay, turnips, apples and pears, while the excellent grazing supports large numbers of sheep and cattle. Even though farms are smaller and methods more traditional than in the rest of the United Kingdom, Northern Ireland did not escape the effects of BSE, with 1 787 cases reported since 1991.

Outside aid
As part of the United Kingdom, Northern Ireland has benefited from massive subsidies from central government, as is obvious from its relatively high standard of infrastructure and public services, and an unusually high proportion of the economically active population are employed in the public sector. Since 1973, when the UK joined the European Economic Community, further subsidies have flowed from Brussels. In the last few years, wary foreign investors have been encouraged by the apparent outbreak of peace, and investment in landscaping and pedestrianisation schemes is improving the appearance of many towns. The traditional manufacturing activities may still be in decline, but hi-tech industry and the service sector are flourishing. And the enthusiasm many of the province's inhabitants show for the Internet is surely a sign of their interest in modernity and progress.

The other Ireland

Exploring Northern Ireland

The Giant's
Causeway

The colourful Antrim coast

THE NORTH
AND THE WEST

A wonderful coastline stretches all the way from bustling Belfast to Donegal in the far north of the Republic, its highlight the legendary Giant's Causeway. A giant could indeed step from Antrim to the coast of Scotland, and much of Ireland's history has had its origin in the crossing of these narrow waters. As the glaciers receded at the end of the Ice Age, the country's first inhabitants came this way, followed in the 17C by settlers lured by the tempting prospect presented by the Jacobean Plantation. Taking possession of much of Ulster's best land, their arrival heralded the beginning of conflicts which have still to reach a final resolution. Despite everything, ancient Irish traditions were upheld in the fastness of the Sperrin Mountains. Still wild, these hills retain the memory of rebel peasants who lived from smuggling and the distillation of clandestine liquor. Hardly affected by industrialisation, the area has preserved much of its natural heritage, as has Fermanagh, which with its limpid lakes and wooded hills is one of Ireland's most unspoiled counties. Back on the main tourist trail, the Giant's Causeway has kept its magical allure despite the crowds of visitors marvelling at its uncanny basalt columns. There are many other delights along the coast, but nothing can match the beauties of the Antrim glens, where rivers have cut deep and narrow valleys into the windswept, heather-clad uplands.

COUNTY FERMANAGH★★
AROUND LOUGH ERNE
On the border between Northern Ireland and the Republic
County Fermanagh – Michelin map n° 923 I-J / 4-5

Not to be missed
A walk in the park at Castle Coole.
Devenish Island as seen from Lough Erne.
The panorama from the Cliffs of Magho.

And remember...
The countryside is Fermanagh's main attraction, and is at its best in summer.

Well away from the tourist trail and with a wealth of lakes, forests and hill country, Fermanagh stretches out towards the boundary with the Republic. Its "capital" is the pretty little Enniskillen, a historic town occupying a strategic site between the two parts of Lough Erne. Eighty kilometres long, this is one of the country's most glorious lakes, fed by the River Erne and studded with 154 wooded islands. The Fermanagh landscape is a paradise for nature-lovers of all kinds, from ramblers to anglers and people who simply enjoy messing about in boats. There is little mass tourism, and most visitors come here simply in order to enjoy fresh air and exercise.

Enniskillen and around★
133km west of Belfast – pop 14 000
Allow half a day including Castle Coole

The administrative and commercial centre of County Fermanagh is an attractive place that has kept much of its traditional character. The historic core of the town was built on an island, and its name is derived from *Inis Ceithleann* (Kathleen's island), the lady in question being the spouse of a Celtic chieftain. Enniskillen is a Plantation

Castle Coole

F Baume/MICHELIN

town (see "History", page 18), its formidable castle built to protect the interests of the English Crown, two of whose most famous regiments (the Royal Inniskilling Fusiliers and the Inniskilling Dragoons) subsequently bore its name, albeit with a somewhat eccentric spelling.

Enniskillen's main street

Most of the town's attractions are around the main thoroughfare (called Church Street to start with, then Main Street) which runs east-west from East Bridge to the Castle. At the beginning of the street, the **Courthouse** has a Classical portico erected early in the 19C. A little further on, on the right, is the **Town Hall** of 1896, its corner tower graced by a neo-Renaissance clock.

Turn right into Church Street to reach the **Buttermarket**. Laid out around a court-yard, its restored early 19C buildings now house boutiques and craft studios.

Continuing along the main street, you will see on your left **St Michael's Church**, an imposing Roman Catholic edifice erected towards the end of the 19C. Opposite is the somewhat earlier **St Macartin's**, the town's Anglican cathedral.

Further along the street on the same side as St Michael's are the Corinthian columns of the Methodist church, beyond which a left turn leads to the **Castle**★(May to September: 10am-5pm, 2pm-5pm Monday and Saturday; closed Sunday (except July and August); October to April: 10am-5pm, 2pm-5pm Monday; closed week-ends. Admission charge). Built in the 15C by the powerful lords of Fermanagh, the Maguire family, the original stronghold was extended and strengthened when it passed into the hands of the English at the beginning of the 17C. The picturesque **Watergate** with its twin turrets rising over the lake dates from this later period. The castle interiors overlooking the courtyard contain exhibits relating to the history of the area, while the **keep** is mostly given over to the displays of the **Regimental Museum of the Royal Inniskilling Fusiliers**. Uniforms, weapons, and much other military paraphernalia testify to the colourful history of this most prestigious regiment.

Castle Coole★★★

2.5km southeast of Enniskillen on the A4. April and September: 1pm-6pm, weekends only; May to August: 1pm-6pm daily except Thursday. Admission charge. Guided tour 1hr. Park open without charge all year.

This superb neo-Classical mansion stands proudly on its elevated site overlooking its lake. It was completed in 1798 to designs by James Wyatt, and until its acqui-sition by the National Trust in 1951 was the residence of the Corrys, Counts of Belmore, one of the great fam-ilies of the Ascendancy. The building consists of a central block flanked by two colonnaded wings, a wonderfully harmonious composition further enhanced by the brilliant white stonework, at its spectacular best when seen in sunlight against the deep green background of lawns and trees. A thoroughgoing restoration programme has returned the interiors to their original Regency glory. Elaborate plasterwork, precious veneers, and rich furnishings give the **library**★, the **State Bedroom**★, and above all, the **Oval Saloon**★★, an elegance which combines opulence and delicacy.

As well as magnificent beech trees, the **park** has the remains of the **ice-house**, a kind of pre-industrial refrigerator in which food was kept cool by means of ice collected from the frozen surface of the lake in winter.

Fermanagh

Around Lower Lough Erne★★
Tour of 106km – allow a day

Most of the area's attractions are to be found around Lower Lough Erne to the north of Enniskillen. Upper Lough Erne is less accessible and has fewer point of interest.

■ **Devenish Island★** – *Ferry landing stage 6km north of Enniskillen. Take the B82 towards Kesh and turn left towards Trory Point. 1 April-30 September: ferries at 10am, 11am, 1pm, 3pm and 5pm; 3pm and 4pm Sunday (times may change because of weather conditions). Other trips from Round O'Jetty, Brook Park, on the way out of Enniskillen towards Belfast, with MV Kestrel Tours,* ☎ 028 6632 2882.

The **round tower** rising over this little island forms part of the remains of the monastery founded here in the 6C by St Molaise and later sacked by the Vikings. The site was subsequently used by other religious orders, who built the **Lower Church** and **St Mary's Priory**, both now ruined. Steps lead to the top of the round tower, but the view from it is rather restricted and in any case does not bear comparison with the romantic outline of the ruins when seen from the lake.

Continue on the B82 for 12km as far as Lisnarrick and follow signs.

■ **Castle Archdale Country Park** – *April-June: 2pm-6pm at weekends; July-September: 11am-7pm except Monday. Admission charge.* Of the great house which once stood at the entrance to the estate there remain only ruins, though the former outbuildings now house a **museum**. As well as a fascinating collection of old agricultural implements, there are exhibits on the wildlife of Lough Erne and on the flying-boat base established here in the Second World War.

In addition there is an **arboretum**, a **butterfly garden**, a **kitchen garden**, as well as a marina, a tea-room, a youth hostel and a camp-site *(see "Making the most of Lough Erne")*.

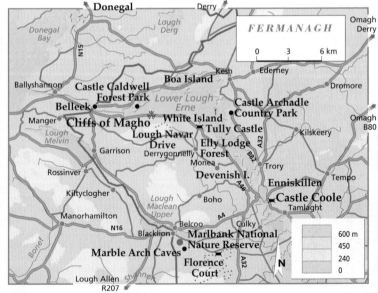

The North and the West

■ **White Island★** – *Hourly ferries 11am-6pm from the marina at Castle Archdale Country Park in July and August; weekends and public holidays Easter-June and September.* This little island is an ancient religious site. It has a strange collection of eight enigmatic **stone figures★**, of pagan inspiration, set in the wall of a 12C **monastery**.

Continue towards Belleek, but instead of taking the B82, follow the Scenic Road which runs along the lakeshore for 7km before rejoining the main road at Kesh.

Boa Island – This 8km long island is joined to the mainland at either end by the main road between Enniskillen and Belleek. It is the site of a famous **Janus figure** *(private property, no access)* dating from the Iron Age and one of the symbols of Fermanagh.

Carry on for 10km along the A47 to-wards Belleek.

B Kaufmann/MICHELIN

■ **Castle Caldwell Forest** – At the far western end of Lough Erne this vast forest park and bird reserve contains the ruins of a 17C **castle** overlooking the lake shore. The **Fiddler's Stone** recalls the legendary figure of a violinist who is supposed to have drowned after falling into the lake from his boat.

Continue on the A47 to Belleek.

■ **Belleek** – With its main street lined by colourful buildings, the village of Belleek is only separated from Donegal *(see page 404)* in the Republic by its bridge. Craftspeople can be seen at work in a number of places along the street making glassware and fashioning tin, but Belleek is famous above all for its pottery *(at the lower end of the village by the bridge)*. Even if you don't find the style of its products particularly attractive, you should not miss out on a visit to the **Belleek Pottery and Visitor Centre★**

Janus figure on Boa Island

(30min guided tour – fee payable – every 20min daily Monday-Friday, last tour 3.30pm Friday. Visitor Centre and shop daily except Sunday morning March-June and September-October; closed at weekends November-February. Audio-visual presentation, cafeteria and shop. ☎ 028 6865 8501).

For 150 years, the pottery founded by John Caldwell has been making **Parian ware**, a kind of pottery inspired by the marble of the Greek island of Paros. The area around Belleek provides all the necessary ingredients, from clay and kaolin to peat for firing the kilns and even hydroelectric power. An alternative to the guided tour is provided by the free **film** demonstrating the skills deployed by the pottery's employees, who show amazing dexterity in fashioning the raw material into delicate basketwork decorated with fanciful flowers. Some of the more elaborate pieces are on show in the little museum.

On the left on leaving the village, Belleek Island is the site of **ExplorErne**, *(mid-May-end October: 10am-6pm; interactive audiovisual presentation. Admission charge)* gives a very complete account of the ecology, history and man-made environment of Lough Erne.

Take the A46 towards Enniskillen and follow the lakeside for 16km.

Fermanagh

■ **Tully Castle and Gardens** ★ – *April-September: 10am-7pm; closed Sunday morning and Monday. Admission charge.*
The evocative ruins of this 17C fortified planter's house are surrounded by gardens laid out in the style of the time. An outbuilding contains a small **exhibition** dealing with local history.

Return to the A46 and almost immediately take the B81 to the right and follow signs to Lough Navar for 5km.

The **Lough Navar Forest Drive** ★ winds for 11km through a vast forest inhabited by deer, wild goats and squirrels. There are numerous places to stop and picnic as well as plenty of opportunities to stroll along well-signposted paths leading to fine viewpoints. The most spectacular viewpoint is at the **Cliffs of Magho** ★★★, where the superb panorama takes in Boa Island and the whole of the northern part of Lower Lough Erne.

Return by the same route to the A46 and continue for another 8km towards Enniskillen.

Elly Lodge Forest – This lakeside woodland has attractively designed picnic areas and the splendid lookout of **Carrickreagh View** ★, a promontory reached on foot some 800m from the car park.

South of Enniskillen
Allow half a day

Florence Court ★★
8km south of Enniskillen by the A4 and A32. April and September: 1pm-6pm, Saturday, Sunday and public holidays; Good Friday to Tuesday after Easter: 1pm-6pm; May-August: 1pm-6pm; closed Tuesday. Admission charge (guided tour), free access to park all year.
Designed by an architect whose name has been lost, this splendid Palladian **mansion** was built between 1756 and 1771 for the Cole family, Counts of Enniskillen. The interior, damaged by a fire in 1954, has been restored, but contains little original furniture. However, there are some fine **family portraits**, a number of erotic **Japanese prints**, and gloriously exuberant **plasterwork** ★★ on the main staircase. In the basement are the gloomy **servants' quarters**, which give an idea of the lack of consideration extended to the house's domestics who were expected to work from 6.30 in the morning until 11 at night.
The vast wooded estate of **Florence Court Forest Park** extends outward from the house, offering signposted walks, one of which leads to the famous **Florence Court Yew**, a unique specimen which can only be reproduced by cuttings. Energetic walkers might want to attempt the conquest of **Mount Cuilcagh** *(8hr return)*, a flat-topped limestone outcrop rising to 668m on the border between Northern Ireland and the Republic.

Marble Arch Caves ★
5km west of Florence Court towards Belcoo. Mid-March-late September: 10am-4.30pm; admission charge. Stout footwear and warm clothing recommended.
These vast underground spaces carved out by a network of subterranean rivers were explored at the end of the 19C by the famous French cave scientist Edouard Martel. Only some of the system is open to the public. Part of the visit is made aboard a boat. Artificial lighting increases the spectacular appearance of the **stalactites**, which are further enhanced by being reflected in the underground lake. A visit here is really worth a detour, but for anyone suffering from claustrophobia, there is the alternative of a film show in the visitor centre.

The road to the right on leaving the Marble Arch Caves leads in 2km to the **Marlbank National Nature Reserve**, a tract of wild limestone country not unlike the Burren in County Clare. The map available at the cottage which serves as a visitor centre gives details of the waymarked footpath leading through this rocky wilderness with its peat deposits and **megalithic remains**.

Making the most of Enniskillen

COMING AND GOING

By bus – The coach station is on Wellington Road close to the Tourist Information Centre. Route 261 runs 12 times daily to Belfast (2hr15min), 4 times on Sunday. Route 94 runs 7 times daily to Londonderry (3hr), 4 times at the weekend, and there is one bus a day to Londonderry on Route 296 (not weekends).

GETTING AROUND

Bicycle hire – *Lakeland Canoe Centre*, Castle Island, ☎ 028 6632 4250.

ADDRESS BOOK

Tourist Information – *Fermanagh Tourist Information Centre*, Wellington Road, ☎ 028 6632 3110, Fax 028 6632 5511. July and August: 9am-7pm, 10am-6pm Saturday and 11am-5pm Sunday (Easter to September); rest of the year: 9am-5.30pm, 10am-5pm Monday and public holidays. Lots of useful information on Enniskillen and the rest of the county.

Banks / Currency exchange – Cash machines by East Bridge and on the main street.

Post office / Telephone – East Bridge Street, 9am-5.30pm; closed Sunday. Sub-post office in Ann Street.

WHERE TO STAY

Between £10-£15 per person
Lakeland Canoe Centre, Castle Island, ☎ 028 6632 4250 – 40 beds. Follow the avenue leading from the rear of the Tourist Information Centre. Access by ferry (no charge). With a wide range of sporting and recreational activities, the Centre has accommodation in comfortable dormitories as well as in a limited number of smaller rooms. There is a cafeteria and a small camp site.

Rossole Guest House, 85 Sligo Road, ☎ 028 6632 3462 – 5rm Decently furnished rooms with showers on the landing in a modern house outside the town centre by the lake.

Dromard House, Tamlaght, ☎ 028 6638 7250 – 4rm ⌗ TV CC On the right 3.5km outside Enniskillen on the Belfast road. Attractive, tastefully decorated rooms in the annexes to a fine 19C rural residence built on a hilltop only 500m from the lake.

Fort Lodge Hotel, 72 Forthill Street, ☎ 028 6632 3275, Fax 028 6632 0275 – 35rm ⌗ Traditional hotel with exceptionally comfortable rooms.

EATING OUT

Under £10
Rebecca's Place, Buttermarket. Café with good salads and pasta dishes.
Franco's, Queen Elizabeth Road, ☎ 028 6632 4424, Open 12pm-10pm. Quality pizzas and generous platefuls of pasta in an attractive setting.
Leslie's Home Bakery, 10 Church Street, ☎ 028 6632 4902. Pleasant tearoom with home-made cakes and self-service lunches.

Between £10-15
Oscar's, Belmore Street, ☎ 028 6632 7037. Open 12pm-10pm. The Oscar celebrated here is Oscar Wilde, who spent some of his schooldays at Enniskillen's Portora Royal School. Good international dishes served in an intimate setting.

HAVING A DRINK

Bush Bar, Townhall Street. Traditional music on Monday evening.
Charlie's Bar, George Street. Huge Victorian pub, a good place for a pint.
The Crow's Nest, High Street. Traditional or country music several nights a week plus disco at the weekend.
Mulligan's, Darling Street, offers good pub food plus music on Wednesday, Friday and Saturday evenings.
Blakes, Church Street. Enniskillen's oldest pub, with musical evenings every Tuesday and Thursday.

OTHER THINGS TO DO

Theatre – *Ardhowen Theatre*, Dublin Road, on the banks of the lake, ☎ 028 663 254 40. A fine auditorium for summer concerts and other events.

Bingo – *Zodiac Bingo*, Sligo Road, ☎ 028 6632 0006. Evening sessions Monday, Wednesday, Thursday and Saturday from 6.30pm. The jackpot can amount to as much as £8 000.

Fishing – Lough Erne holds a world record with 140 kilos of fish caught in 5hr. Bream, perch, salmon and trout are present in abundance, but fishing for them is subject to strict regulation. Apply to the Tourist Information Centre for a licence, as well as a permit which authorises one rod only per person. **Home, Field and Stream**, Church Street, sells equipment and is a useful source of information.

Boat hire – Erne Tours, Round' O'Jetty, Brook Park, Belleek Road, ☎ 028 6632 2882. Day hire of boats for 4 to 5 people. Reckon on £40-55.

Golf – Castle Coole Golf Club, ☎ 028 6632 5250, 18 hole course, part of the Castle Coole estate. Green fee £15 weekdays, £18 at the weekend.

SHOPPING

Fishing flies – The Classic Salmon, Buttermarket Craft Centre, ☎ 028 6632 3047. Frankie McPhilips has a world-wide reputation for his superb hand-made flies.

Making the most of Lough Erne

WHERE TO STAY

• Castle Archdale
Under £10
Castle Archdale Youth Hostel, in the grounds of the Country Park, ☎ 028 6662 8118 – 30 beds. Open March to October. Comfortable establishment in an attractive natural setting. Good range of recreational activities including riding, mountain bike hire, canoeing, etc.
Castle Archdale Caravan Park, ☎ 028 6662 1888. Open 1 April to 30 October. Well equipped site with pitches for 60 caravans and 50 tents.

• Kesh (near Boa Island)
Under £10
Lakeland Caravan Park, 3km from Kesh on the A47 towards Belleek, ☎ 028 6663 1578 / 6663 1025. Open all year. Caters mostly for caravans but also has a number of pitches for tents as well as rooms in the adjoining guesthouse.

Between £25-35
Muckross Lodge, ☎ 028 6863 1887 – 5rm ⬛ 📺 Signposted on the way out of the village towards Belleek. Modern house on rising ground with a good view of the lake. Decently furnished rooms.

Between £35-50
Clareview House, 85a Crevenish Road, ☎ 028 6663 1455 – 3rm ⬛ 📺 CC 4km south of Kesh on the Scenic Road. A substantial old residence on a hilltop

site with an unbeatable view over the lough. Impeccable rooms and a friendly welcome.

🏠 **Ardress House**, ☎ 028 6663 1267 – 6rm ⬛ CC Signposted 2km beyond the village. Dorothy and William Pendry use their old rectory not only to receive visitors but also for weaving and spinning courses, using the wool from their own flock of Jacob's sheep.

• Belleek
The Fiddlestone Guesthouse, 15 Main Street, ☎ 028 6665 8008 – 5rm ⬛ 📺 CC Charming village pub with delightful, well-lit rooms. The excellent breakfast is served amid an incredible array of antiques of all kinds.

• Around Tully Castle
Between £30-35
Navar Guest House, Derryvarey, ☎ 028 6654 1384 – 5rm ⬛ Go 5km south of Tully Castle on the B81 as far as Derrygonnelly, then follow signs on the way out of the village. Comfortable rooms, nearly all with bathroom, in a restored house on rising ground in the middle of the countryside. Fishing rights (trout) are available. Dinner if booked in advance.

• Belcoo
Between £35-40
🏠 **Corralea Forest Lodge**, ☎ 028 6638 6325 – 4rm ⬛ 📺 CC Go 4.5km towards Garrison on the B52, then turn

left along an avenue. Open March to the end of October. Perfect parkland setting on the edge of Lough MacNean Upper, complete with its own herd of deer. All rooms have a view over the lake and breakfast is served on the terrace in summer.

EATING OUT

• **Boa Island**

Between £10-15

Lusty Beg, Lusty Beg Island, ☎ 028 6663 1342. Signposted on the left by Ardshankill. A little ferry (foot passengers only) takes you to this holiday island with its very pleasant restaurant specialising in fish dishes. 12noon-9.30pm.

• **Florence Court**

Between £10-15

Tullyohona House, Marble Arch Road, ☎ 028 6624 3452. Non-residents welcome Easter to September. Flexible opening hours. Reserve in advance for dinner. Rosemary Armstrong's home cooking is mostly intended for the guests staying in Tullyohona House's 7 comfortable rooms, but she will also cater for passing travellers. What is on the menu depends on the hostess's whim.

• **Blacklion (in the Republic)**

Between £20-25

🕲 *MacNean Bistro*, ☎ 072 530 22, Fax 072 534 04. On the far side of the bridge at Belcoo. Evening meal only, open Sunday midday; closed Monday. Reservation necessary. Nevan Maguire is one of the rising stars of the new Irish cuisine, and people come here from far and wide to enjoy dishes based on fresh local ingredients prepared with a touch of Mediterranean and Oriental flair.

OTHER THINGS TO DO

Bike hire – *Cycle Ops*, 26 Main Street, Kesh, ☎ 028 6663 1850.

Cruising – *Belleek Charter Cruising*, Erne Gateway Marina, Belleek, ☎ 028 6634 8267, Fax 028 6634 8866. Boats for 4 to 8 people for hire for between £730-£1 200 per week according to category.

SHOPPING

Porcelain – *Belleek Pottery*, Belleek, produces perfect examples of a kind of pottery which may not be to everyone's taste, but which nevertheless commands admiration for the level of skill and craftsmanship involved. The pottery also has an attractive café serving drinks and light meals at reasonable prices.

Making the most of Lough Erne

SPERRIN MOUNTAINS★
Co Londonderry and Co Tyrone
Allow 2 days
Michelin map 923 K-L / 2-3-4

Not to be missed
The spectacular views along the Sawel Mountain Drive.
The waterfall in Ness Wood Country Park.
The beetling machines in operation at Wellbrook Beetling Mill.

And remember...
You can only really get to know the area by car.

The Sperrin Mountains run east-west for a distance of about 60 km to the south of Londonderry and to the west of Lough Neagh. Made up of ancient rocks, they reach their highest point in Sawel Mountain (678m). Sharp ridges of schist rise over the heather and blanket bog of the uplands, which are interrupted by deep and wonderfully wooded gorges carved by rivers rich in fish. Economic progress mostly left the Sperrins untouched, but more recently the area has begun to develop its tourist potential. This is based more on its fine landscape, wildlife and natural environment than on towns like Omagh, Limavady, Strabane and Cookstown, which are of limited interest, certainly compared with the appeal of forest and country parks or attractions like the Ulster History Park and the Ulster American Folk Park. Visitors can now appreciate more fully the appeal of a region which, over the centuries, made the most of its frugal natural resources to become more or less self-sufficient.

The northern foothills

Ness Wood Country Park★
At Ervey Cross Roads, 11km southeast of Londonderry via the A6 towards Belfast, then follow signs to the left. This vast forest is crossed by the River Burntollet, whose peaty waters have hollowed out a series of deep ravines. A track leads from the car park

In the Sperrins

to Northern Ireland's highest **waterfall***. Amid greenery of extravagant luxuriance, the river roars down a deep gorge lined with lichens, mosses and bracken. *The sides of the gorge are unfenced and visitors should not let children wander unattended.*

Roe Valley Country Park

3km south of Limavady via the B68. The **River Roe** flows for 5km through a landscape of woodlands and meadows threaded by attractive pathways. In the 19C the river was lined with a whole series of mills, most of them used for beetling linen. In 1896 a hydroelectric plant was built, which supplied the town of Limavady with its electricity until 1946. Its metal wheel still intact, one of the old mills has been adapted recently to house the **Green Lane Heritage Centre** *(opening hours not yet available)* with exhibits on the area's pre-industrial history.

A hundred metres away, the **Dogleap Countryside Centre** *(June-August: 10am-8pm; September-May: 10am-5pm; closed weekends)* has displays on the valley's history and natural environment.

Dungiven Priory

15km south of Limavady via the B68, the priory is at the end of a minor road on the right on the way out of Dungiven village towards Belfast.

The ruins of this 13C Augustinian priory stand atop a high point overlooking the Roe. The priory's cemetery has a number of fascinating but damaged **tombs**. Opposite the cemetery you will notice rags tied to the bushes; they are evidence of a continuing belief in the healing properties of an ancient stone once used for grinding grain, since rainwater collecting in a hollow in the stone is believed to cure warts.

The hound of the O'Cahans

Until the coming of the Normans, the fierce O'Cahan clan ruled over the River Roe and the surrounding area. Legend has it that in the course of a battle, one of the clan's dogs was given a message to carry summoning help from nearby Dungiven. The brave creature cleared the Roe in a single bound, a feat which instantly passed into folk memory and is commemorated to this day in the place-name of Dogleap on the banks of the river. Even the name of Limavady recalls the exploit (Gaelic "léim an mhadaidh" = leap of the dog).

C Boisvieux

Sperrin Mountains

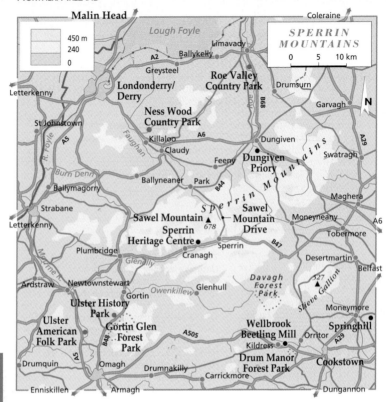

The central heights

Between the hamlet of Park on the B44 and and Sperrin on the B47, the narrow **Sawel Mountain Drive★** winds for a dozen or so kilometres through the austere uplands at the foot of **Sawel Mountain**, offering a number of spectacular **viewpoints★★**.

Sperrin Heritage Centre
On the B47 between Sperrin and Cranagh. April-October: 11am-6pm; 11.30am-6pm Saturday; 2pm-5pm Sunday. Admission charge.
The centre has a number of reconstructions of traditional domestic interiors, giving a good idea of life as lived in the region in the past. The Sperrins once had a reputation as a hide-out for clandestine distillers of **poteen** *(see page 77)*.

The southern foothills

Ulster History Park★
7.5km north of Omagh via the B48. April-September: 10.30am-6.30pm; 11.30am-7pm Sunday; October-March: 10.30am-5pm; closed weekends.
In a delightful setting of wooded hills and verdant clearings, the park is devoted to the history of settlement in Ireland. There are full-size and strikingly realistic reconstructions of many types of human habitat, from prehistoric encampments to

houses built in the course of the 17C Plantation, and, in addition, an audio-visual presentation and an exhibition help visitors retrace the principal phases in the country's evolution.

Gortin Glen Forest Park

Access 1km north of the History Park. 10am to dusk all year. Admission charge. Information about the park and its wildlife available from the little visitor centre.

A one-way scenic road runs for 8km through this vast and lovely coniferous forest. Vistors who follow the carefully waymarked **Lady's View Walk** *(2hr on foot)* may be rewarded by a close encounter with a rare **Japanese deer**.

Ulster-American Folk Park★

Near Mountjoy, 9km north of Omagh on the A5 towards Strabane. Easter-September: 11am-6.30pm; 11.30am-7pm Sunday and public holidays; October-Easter: 10.30am-5pm; closed weekends. Allow 2hr.

This theme park evokes the fate of the 250 000 Ulster Scots who emigrated to America at the end of the 18C and the beginning of the 19C. A visit to the **Emigration Gallery** gives a good idea of the reasons for emigration and of how the migrants fared in their new country. The **park** itself is divided into two sections, the Old World and the New World. Thatched cottages, a blacksmith's forge, a weaver's dwelling, a school and a post office give a vivid impression of life as lived in Ulster by the would-be migrants, not least because of the presence of authentically costumed guides engaged in the trades and occupations of the time. The new life on the far shore of the Atlantic is recreated by means of log cabins, a corn silo, a smokehouse and a barn. There is even a dock with a **sailing ship★**, and a quayside bustling with activity as the emigrants prepare to depart.

The Park is the lively setting for a whole series of summer events, outstanding among which is the **Blue Grass Music Festival**, held annually at the beginning of September *(Information and booking: ☎ 028 8225 6330).*

Cookstown and around

County Tyrone – Allow half a day

Stretching out interminably along both sides of its main street, this little town is chiefly remarkable for its busy **Saturday market**. But its proximity to Lough Neagh as well as to the Sperrins makes Cookstown a good base for exploring the whole area.

Springhill★

Close to Moneymore, 6.5km north of Cookstown via the A29 and the B18. April, May and September: 2pm-6pm weekends and public holidays only; Good Friday-Tuesday after Easter: 2pm-6pm; June-August: 2pm-6pm except Thursday. Admission charge.

This splendid Plantation farmhouse was for three centuries the home of the Lenox-Conyngham family who came to Ulster from Scotland in the 17C. The house has retained all its intimate charm, and there is even a ghost, whose haunting of one of the upstairs bedrooms is recounted to visitors in all seriousness. A particularly fascinating feature is the blue **wallpaper** in the ground floor Gun Room; dating from the 18C, it is the only wallpaper of its kind in the United Kingdom to have survived. Much of the house's fine Georgian furniture was fashioned from timber harvested on the estate.

The **costume collection★** housed in a wing of the building has a fine array of aristocratic clothes from the 18C and 19C. The embroidery of some of the waistcoats is of astonishingly meticulous workmanship.

Wellbrook Beetling Mill★

Near Kildress, 6km west of Cookstown towards Omagh via the A505. April-June and September: 2pm-6pm at weekends and public holidays; Good Friday-Tuesday after Easter: 2pm-6pm; July-August: 2pm-6pm except Tuesday. Admission charge.

Sperrin Mountains

This is the last survivor of the many mills which prepared linen by "beetling". This apparently brutal process involved battering the raw **linen** with wooden hammers activated by a water-wheel, thereby giving it the required sheen and suppleness.

The din produced by beetling was appalling, and visitors treated to a demonstration soon appreciate why the majority of workers in such a mill suffered deafness towards the end of their lives. On the upper floor of the mill, a fascinating **exhibition** gives a comprehensive account of the whole range of complex processes necessary to produce fine linen.

Drum Manor Forest Park

Near Kildress, 6km west of Cookstown towards Omagh via the A505. 8am-dusk; charge for vehicles. Campsite on the edge of the park (See "Making the most of the Sperrin Mountains").

The old country house here is now in ruins, but its lovely parkland is home to all sorts of wildlife, including otters, herons and wild cats. But visitors are more likely to see the **butterflies** which, in summer, fly freely in the enclosed garden, the walls of which have been specially designed to facilitate their breeding.

Making the most of the Sperrin Mountains

COMING AND GOING

By bus – Service n° 210 runs between Cookstown and Belfast (90min) 4 times daily during the week, twice on Saturday and once on Sunday.

ADDRESS BOOK

Tourist information – *Tourist Information Centre*, 49 Molesworth Street, Cookstown, ☎ 028 8676 6727. April-October: 9am-5pm except weekends; May and September: 9am-5pm; 10am-4pm Saturday; closed Sunday; June-August: 9am-5pm; 12pm-5pm Sunday; 10am-4pm public holidays. Friendly staff and good range of information on local attractions and activities.

Tourist Information, Cornell Street, Limavady, ☎ 028 7776 0307. September-May: 9am-5pm; closed weekends; June-August: 9am-5.45pm; closed Sunday. Local information for Limavady and the Roe Valley.

Sperrin Centre, 1 Market Street, Omagh, ☎ 028 8224 7831. 9am-5pm, open Saturday April-September; closed Sunday.

Banks / Currency exchange – Cash machines in Cookstown, Limavady and Omagh.

Post office / Telephone – 7 High Street, Omagh.

GETTING AROUND

The area can only really be explored with a car, though a possible alternative would be a tour by bicycle.

Bicycle hire – In Omagh: ***Conway Cycles***, Old Market Place, ☎ 028 8224 6195. Open 9am-5.30pm;

closed Sunday; **Glenhordial Hostel** (see below).

• Omagh
Under £10
Glenhordial Hostel, 9a Waterworks Road, ☎ 028 8224 1973 – 22rm Four kilometres north via the B48 towards Gortin, then turn right into Killybrack Road. 6-bed dormitories and 2 double rooms in a delightful house whose attractiveness is enhanced by a profusion of flowers. Well-equipped kitchen, washing machine for use of visitors. Bicycle hire. Camping.

Between £30-40
Clanabogan House, 58 Clanabogan Road, ☎ 028 8224 1171 – 8rm ☏ TV CC Three and a half kilometres towards Enniskillen via the A32. Most of the rooms in this vast restored Georgian house have own facilities. Peaceful location, excellent breakfast and attractive natural surroundings. Evening meal must be ordered in advance.

• Cookstown
Under £10
Drum Manor Forest Park, ☎ 028 8676 2774. Attractive camp and caravan site in the pleasant surroundings of this forest park.

Between £30-40
Edergole B&B, ☎ 028 8676 2924 – 5rm 🐎 Outside the town on the road to Moneymore. Ms Short offers unpretentious but comfortable and spotlessly clean accommodation. Family atmosphere and horses to ride (See "Other things to do").

• Gortin
Under £10
Gortin Glen Caravan Park, ☎ 028 8264 8108, between the Ulster History Park and Gortin Glen Forest Park. Lovely surroundings for tents and caravans. Bicycle hire.

• Dungiven
Under £10
🏠 **Flax Mill Hostel**, ☎ 028 7774 2655 – 16 beds. 3km from Dungiven, take the A6 towards Londonderry, turn right on to the B192 beyond the bridge, then take the third turning on the left and follow signs. Deep in the countryside, this is a thatched house which has been turned into a kind of hostel by a German couple. Trendy atmosphere, rustic comfort, bicycles to ride, and traditional music several times a week, all help make this one of the best places to stay in the North for those on limited budgets.

• Dungiven
Under £10
Castle Inn, Upper Main Street, ☎ 028 7774 1369. Daily 12noon-9.30pm. Good pub food and lively atmosphere.

• Cookstown
Under £10
Courtyard, 56 William Street, ☎ 028 8676 5070. Daily 8am-5.15pm; closed Sunday. Pleasant café with rustic décor. No drinks licence.

• Omagh
Between £10-15
Grant's, 29 George Street, ☎ 028 8225 0900. Daily 12pm-9pm. Good range of meat and pasta dishes, generous portions, particularly good for lunch as evening meals are more expensive.

• Dungiven
Murphy's, Main Street. Traditional music evenings on Thursday, rock or folk Friday to Sunday.

Riding – Edergole Equestrian Centre, Cookstown (See "Where to stay"), organises trekking in the Sperrins all year round except Sundays. Hunting parties between November and March.

Golf – Killymoon Golf Club, 200 Killymoon Road, Cookstown, ☎ 028 8676 3762. 18 hole course in a countryside setting. Green fee £21-25. **Omagh Golf Club**, Omagh, ☎ 028 8224 3160. 18-hole course in an attractive valley setting. Green fee £10-15.

Making the most of the Sperrin Mountains

LONDONDERRY / DERRY★

Co Londonderry / Derry – pop 72 000
The second largest city in Northern Ireland

Not to be missed
A stroll around the city walls.
Live music in the pubs along Waterloo Street.

And remember...
The city has to be explored on foot.
Cars can be parked in the Foyleside Commercial Centre,
but make a note of closing time.

Unchallenged capital of the western part of Ulster, Northern Ireland's second city is also a place of great interest to visitors. The town has undergone something of a renaissance, and has succeeded in putting behind it at least some of the dark memories of the thirty years when it was the focus of much inter-communal conflict. A degree of economic vitality has returned, evidence of which can be seen in the shopping malls which now grace the city centre, while a burgeoning night-life fills streets and pubs with young people to whom religious affiliations seem less important than the determination to have a good time. The vexed question of whether the city should be called Derry (favoured by Catholics) or Londonderry (the choice of Protestants) has been solved by calling it both ie Londonderry / Derry (or, more neatly, "Stroke City", an inspired invention by a local DJ).

From Doire to Londonderry

In the 5C St Columba founded a monastery on an island "planted with oak-trees" (*doire* in Gaelic) in the River Foyle. It was not until 1613 that the English rechristened Doire **Londonderry**, James I having granted the town and its surroundings to "The Honourable the Irish Society", composed of members of the livery companies of the City of London, whose task it was to finance the Plantation. The walls which still encircle the old city date from this time. When the Catholic army of James II besieged the city in 1668-89, the defenders held out for 105 days. The unsuccessful siege became a seminal event, the symbol of the city's Protestant identity, commemorated annually by a march recalling the shutting of the town gate in the face of a detachment of Catholic troops by the city's Apprentice Boys.

Bloody confrontations

Immigration from the surrounding countryside during the course of the Industrial Revolution meant that Roman Catholics became the majority population in the city. However, systematic gerrymandering meant that this was not reflected in the way the city was run, the council remaining for long the preserve of the Protestant minority. Catholics endured discrimination and a high rate of unemployment, and the unlovely **Bogside** area to the northwest of the old city became notorious as a place of multiple social deprivation, and, later, as an IRA stronghold.
Rioting broke out on the occasion of a civil rights demonstration in October 1968, and again in August 1969, when the Protestant Apprentice Boys march took place. But in the history of the Troubles, Derry is chiefly remembered for the 30 January 1972, known ever since as **Bloody Sunday**, when 13 unarmed civilians were shot dead by British paratroopers. The subsequent report on the event by Lord Widgery was widely regarded as a whitewash, even though the troops claimed they had been fired on from the Bogside. A further inquiry initiated in 1998 may yet elicit the truth about these horrific events, one outcome of which was the consolidation of the IRA's position as the defenders of the Catholic population.

The North and the West

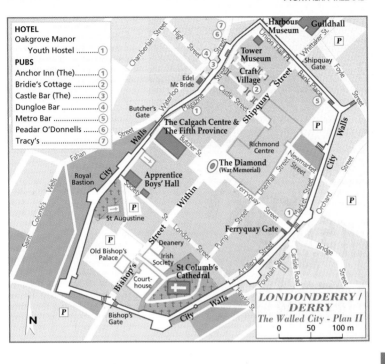

HOTEL
Oakgrove Manor
    Youth Hostel .... ①

PUBS
Anchor Inn (The).......... ①
Bridie's Cottage .... ②
Castle Bar (The) .... ③
Dungloe Bar .... ④
Metro Bar .... ⑤
Peadar O'Donnells .... ⑥
Tracy's .... ⑦

*LONDONDERRY /
DERRY*
The Walled City - Plan II
0   50   100 m

Derry has moved on since those dark days. Civil rights have been claimed and exercised, and an SDLP-dominated council has beautified and regenerated much of the city's physical fabric. Nevertheless an insidious form of ethnic cleansing has taken place; Protestants have felt obliged to quit the city centre which they controlled for so long, and many have resettled in the **Waterside** area on the right (east) bank of the Foyle.

The walled city (Plan II)
Allow 2hr30min

A walk along the walls★
Almost uniquely in the British Isles, Derry has retained its city walls in their entirety. 1.6km long, the ramparts have encircled the town since they were completed in 1613 on the orders of **The Honourable the Irish Society**. Of their three main gateways, the most famous is the **Ferryquay Gate**, whose doors were slammed in the face of James II's soldiery by the Protestant Apprentice Boys in 1688. To the right of the gate on the outside of the walls is a detailed plan of the city at the time of the siege.

From Artillery Street to the left of the gate, a stairway rises up to the top of the ramparts. From here there is a view over the **Fountain** area, the last Protestant enclave on the left bank of the Foyle, readily identifiable by the usual red, white and blue kerbstones, Union flags, as well as flamboyant murals painted to counter those adorning the Bogside.

Walk to the Cathedral graveyard.

The North and the West

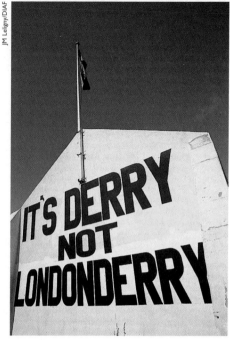

JM Leligny/DIAF

What's in a name?

From St Columb's Cathedral to the Tower Museum

Towers and a full set of battlements give **St Columb's Cathedral**★ *(summer: 9am-5pm; winter: 9am-1pm / 2pm-5pm; open only for services on Sunday; donation welcome)* something of the look of a fortress. Derry's Anglican cathedral was built between 1628 and 1633 in Gothic style. During the siege of 1688-89 the bell-tower was used as a gun emplacement. The cannon shell fired into the city bearing the terms of surrender is preserved in the porch. There are more cannon balls in the **Chapter House**, added to the Cathedral in 1910 and now housing a fascinating little **museum**. Among the other historical exhibits are the huge original padlocks from the city gates. The spacious nave has a superb timber roof, supported on corbels with **carved heads** depicting former bishops of Derry. The kneelers ranged along the pews are worth a glance for the extraordinary diversity of their embroidered motifs.

On leaving the Cathedral, turn right into Bishop's Street, then left into Society Street.

On the right, just before the walls at the end of Society Street is the **Apprentice Boys' Hall**.

The ramparts close to the Apprentice Boys' Hall offer a panoramic view over the **Bogside** with its numerous **murals**, among them the famous "You are now entering Free Derry" painted in 1969 at a particularly tense time in the Troubles. Not far away is the **Bloody Sunday Monument**.

Continue along the walls to Butcher Street.

Anyone with the slightest interest in history or Ireland's Celtic past will be enthused by **The Fifth Province** *(10am-4.30pm; closed weekends. Admission charge)*. This is a hi-tech, interactive journey through the country's heritage, evidence that the Irish are just as much at home with modernity as with their ancient roots. The multi-media show is housed in the **Calgach Centre**, devoted to genealogy.

Butcher Street leads to **The Diamond**, the walled city's central square, each side of which was once defended by a cannon.

On the far side of the square Shipquay Street leads to the Craft Village (on the left).

The **Craft Village** is a group of old buildings and alleyways which was completely rebuilt in 1996. It has a number of souvenir shops, cafés and restaurants, but is somewhat disappointing as a tourist attraction, with little in the way of real craftsmanship on show. **Bridie's Cottage**, a thatched cabin brought here from

Donegal, has information on traditional music, and concerts are staged here in summer. One of the souvenir shops, the **Irish Shop**, gives onto a little courtyard with direct access to the Tower Museum, the main entrance to which is on Union Hall Place.

Tower Museum★ *(September-June: 10am-5pm; closed Sunday and Monday; July-August: 10am-5pm; 2pm-5pm Sunday. Admission charge).* This well-designed museum is housed in a modern structure built in medieval style. It is entered along a **brick tunnel** paved with cobblestones, similar to the innumerable underground passageways built beneath the city in the 17C. Beyond are displays evoking the story of Derry from prehistory to modern times. There are audio-visual presentations, historic items of all kinds, and wax figures. The cut-off date is the 1960s, but the **documentary film** shown in the museum's cinema attempts to explain causes and consequences of the Troubles.

Bold apprentice boys and cowardly colonel
As rumours spread in 1688 that King James II was everywhere replacing Protestant officials and administrators by Catholics and that massacres of Protestants had begun, a mood akin to panic began to seize the city, its population swelled by thousands of frightened refugees from the surrounding countryside. Nevertheless, when a detachment of royal troops – all Catholics – arrived to replace the existing garrison, the Protestant authorities were inclined to bow to the royal will and allow them into the city. It was at this point, on 7 December 1688, that 13 young apprentices seized the initiative, stealing the keys to the city gates and slamming them firmly in the face of the would-be garrison, thereby stirring the population to resistance.

The siege began in earnest several months later, in April 1689. The governor, Colonel Robert Lundy, considered opposition to be futile and advocated surrender, not least because British ships bringing reinforcements up the Foyle had shown themselves too timid to break through the boom stretched across the river by the besiegers. But Lundy misjudged the city's mood; he was deposed, and fled, disguised as a common soldier. Citizens and soldiers held out, despite a diet of cats, mice, candles and leather, and the siege was broken at the end of July. Lundy's name lives on among Northern Ireland's Protestants as a synonym for treachery; his effigy is burnt during the Apprentice Boys' parade every August.

On leaving the Tower Museum, turn right and go out of the walled city through the Shipquay Gate.

Beyond the ramparts
Allow 2hr

North of the walls (Plan I B3)
The Shipquay Gate faces the splendid **Guildhall★** *(9am-5pm; closed weekends; guided tours in July and August).* The seat of the city council is built in neo-Gothic style in red sandstone and has a **tower** based on London's Big Ben. The **council chamber** has a set of fine stained-glass windows with symbolic designs, restored after being damaged in a bomb explosion in 1972. A **modern stained-glass window**, close to the entrance to the Guildhall, evokes the events of Bloody Sunday.

On leaving the Guildhall, go round the block of buildings on the right to reach the **Harbour Museum** *(10am-1pm, 2pm-4.30pm; closed weekends)*, with its collection of items recalling the city's maritime history.

Return to the walls, and turn right immediately into **Waterloo Place** in the heart of the pedestrian area. A group of contemporary sculptures occupies the centre of the square, from which **Waterloo Street** with its array of lively pubs runs along the edge of the Bogside.

Towards Waterside
Railway enthusiasts will find plenty to interest them on the Foyle Road just upstream from the modern two-level **Craigavon Bridge**; the **Foyle Valley Railway Centre** (Plan I B4) *(April-September: 10am-4.30pm; closed Sunday and Monday. Admission charge)*

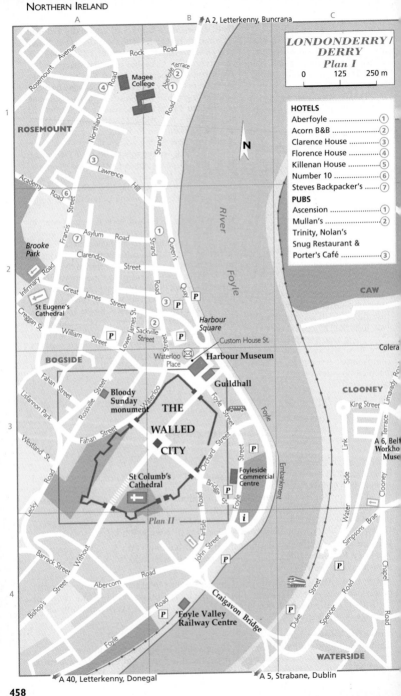

A 2, Letterkenny, Buncrana

LONDONDERRY / DERRY
Plan I

0   125   250 m

HOTELS

Aberfoyle .... ①
Acorn B&B .... ②
Clarence House .... ③
Florence House .... ④
Killenan House .... ⑤
Number 10 .... ⑥
Steves Backpacker's ..... ⑦

PUBS

Ascension .... ①
Mullan's .... ②
Trinity, Nolan's
Snug Restaurant &
Porter's Café .... ③

ROSEMOUNT

Rosemount Avenue

Rock Road

Aberfoyle Terrace

Magee College

Northland Road

Strand Road

Lawrence Hill

Academy Road

Brooke Park

Francis Street

Asylum Road

Clarendon Street

St Eugene's Cathedral

Infirmary Road

Great James Street

William Street

Creggan St.

BOGSIDE

Fahan Street

Lisfannon Park

Rossville Street

Waterloo Street

Bloody Sunday monument

THE WALLED CITY

St Columb's Cathedral

Westland St.

Lecky Road

Plan II

Barrack Street

Bishop's Street

Without Street

Abercorn Road

Foyle Road

Foyle Valley Railway Centre

Queen's Quay

Strand Road

Sackville Street

Lower James St.

Harbour Square

Custom House St.

Waterloo Place

Harbour Museum

Guildhall

Foyle Street

Orchard Street

Foyleside Commercial Centre

Carlisle Road

John Street

Craigavon Bridge

River Foyle

CAW

Colera

CLOONEY

King Street

A 6, Belf Workho Muse

Link

Side

Water

Clooney

Simpsons Brae

Embankment

Duke Street

Spencer Road

Chapel Road

WATERSIDE

A 40, Letterkenny, Donegal

A 5, Strabane, Dublin

458

has a fascinating collection of locomotives and rolling stock and in addition offers trips along a section of restored narrow-gauge line beside the Foyle *(trains depart at 2.30pm)*.

The Waterside area spreads out on the far side of the Craigavon Bridge. It is now Derry's main Protestant district, but despite having received an influx of Protestants from other parts of the city still retains a Catholic majority. For visitors, its chief interest lies in the **Workhouse Museum** *(10am-4.30pm; closed Sunday; in summer: Sunday opening 2pm-4pm)* at 23 Glendermot Road (Plan I towards C3). The museum is housed in the building of the 19C city workhouse; as well as an important **library** it has well-presented displays on 19C living conditions and the Famine. Also evoked is Derry's role in the Second World War, when considerable Allied forces were stationed here and the city served as an important base of operations in the Battle of the Atlantic.

Making the most of Londonderry / Derry

COMING AND GOING

By train – *Waterside Railway Station*, Duke Street (Plan I C4), in the Waterside area on the right bank of the Foyle. 6 trains daily to Belfast (2hr30min) via Coleraine, 5 trains Saturday and 3 Sunday. A shuttle bus links the railway station to the bus station.

By bus – *Ulsterbus* services use the Foyle Street bus station (Plan I B3). 15 coaches daily to Belfast (1hr30min to 3hr), 14 Saturday and 5 Sunday. Change at Portrush for the Giants' Causeway. 5 coaches daily to Dublin (4hr30min), 3 Sunday (service n° 274).

GETTING AROUND

The city is best explored on foot as most of the places of interest are within easy walking distance of each other. Drivers should leave their vehicle in one of several public car parks, the most convenient being the one forming part of the Foyleside Commercial Centre.

By bus – There is a bus stop on Foyle Street.

By taxi – Taxi rank at the upper end of Foyle Street.

Car hire – *Desmond Motors*, 173 Strand Road, ☎ 028 7136 0420. Minimum age 25.

Bicycle hire – *Oakgrove Manor Youth Hostel* (See "Where to stay")

ADDRESS BOOK

Tourist information – *Tourist Information Centre*, 44 Foyle Street (Plan I B4), ☎ 028 7126 7284. July-September: 9am-7pm; 10am-6pm Saturday; 10am-5pm Sunday; October-Easter: 9am-5.15pm, 9am-5pm Friday; closed weekends; Easter-June: 9am-5.15pm; 9am-5pm Friday; 10am-5pm Saturday; closed Sunday. Efficient staff and copious information. Ask for a free copy of the "Derry Tourist Guide". Between June and September there are guided tours of the walled city on weekdays (not Saturday) at 10.30am and 2.30pm.

Post office / Telephone – Custom House Street (Plan I B3). 9am-5.30pm; Monday 8.30am-5.30pm; closed Saturday afternoon and Sunday.

Banks / Currency exchange – There is a bureau de change at the tourist office and another at the Foyleside Shopping Centre. Cash machines by the Guildhall and elsewhere in the city centre.

Medical service – *Altnagelvin Hospital*, Glenshane Road, ☎ 028 7134 5171.

WHERE TO STAY

Under £10

***Oakgrove Manor Youth Hostel*,** 6 Magazine Street, ☎ 028 7128 4100, Fax 028 7128 4101 – 120 beds and 8 rooms. Youth hostel in a fine old 18C building in the city walls. The dormitories are a bit basic but reasonably comfortable. Bicycle hire.

Steve's Backpackers, 4 Asylum Road, ☎ 028 7137 7989 – 16 beds. Comfort and cleanliness not outstanding, but good for young people and plenty of atmosphere.

Between £35-40

Florence House, 16 Northland Road, ☎ 028 7126 8093 – 4rm 🏠 TV Small B&B establishment with plain but well-kept rooms and parking to the rear of the building. Family atmosphere with a musical touch: the daughter of the house is a concert pianist.

Aberfoyle B&B, 33 Aberfoyle Terrace, ☎ 028 7128 3333, Fax 028 7128 3334 – 12rm 🏠 TV CC Half of the rooms in this brick-built house from around 1900 have their own facilities. Reasonable accommodation, but nothing special.

Acorn B&B, 17 Aberfoyle Terrace, ☎ 028 7127 1156, Fax 028 7137 7262 – 3rm 🏠 TV Next door to the above. Friendly landlady and plain but bright and cheerfully decorated little rooms.

No 10, 10 Crawford Square, ☎ 028 7126 5000 – 3rm 🏠 TV The main attraction of this little B&B is its location just a short distance from the city centre. Otherwise the level of comfort leaves something to be desired.

Killenan House, Killennan Road, Drumahoe, ☎ 028 7130 1710 – 3rm 🏠 TV Signposted on the right, 7km from Derry on the Belfast road. This pleasant farmhouse has quiet and spacious rooms with views over open countryside. Excellent breakfast.

Clarence House, 15 Northland Road, ☎ 028 7126 5342 – 9rm 🏠 ✐ TV CC Pretty B&B with comfortable rooms in pastel shades. Two of the rooms have facilities on the landing. 6% surcharge for payment by credit card.

EATING OUT

Under £10

Annie's Hot Bread Shop, 8 William Street (Plan I B3), ☎ 028 7126 9236. The main attraction of this establishment is that it serves cheap meals late in the evening. Otherwise it leaves a lot to be desired in terms of quality and cleanliness.

Badgers, 16-18 Orchard Street (Plan II), ☎ 028 7136 0763. Friday and Saturday, 11.30am-1am, 12pm-9.30pm, 12pm-5pm Sunday. To the east of the walls, a comfortable place with pub decor and atmosphere. Generous portions and good value for money.

Passport, The Diamond (Plan II), ☎ 028 7126 1817. Cafeteria on the 3rd floor of the pleasantly old-fashioned Austin's Department Store with a fine view over the city. A good place for a quick bite during the day.

The Strand, 35-38 Strand Road (Plan I B2), open until late in the evening, this establishment occupies the upper floor of a neo-Gothic pub and provides meals with an international or Tex-Mex flavour.

Thra'n Maggies, Craft Village (Plan II), ☎ 028 7126 4267. Traditional décor in a good place to lunch off a pie or pork stewed in beer.

Between £15-20

The Nolan's Snug, 22-24 Strand Road (Plan I B2), ☎ 028 7127 1271, evenings only 6pm-10pm. This is the restaurant of the grand Trinity Hotel, offering Italian-style cuisine in an appropriate setting.

Café Nosh, 20 Foyle Street (Plan I B3), ☎ 028 7130 8273, open 6pm-10pm. Brightly decorated little restaurant with carefully prepared Mediterranean food.

HAVING A DRINK

Ascension, 64 Strand Road, ☎ 028 7137 4002. The city's only gay bar is open to all comers until 6am, and from Thursday to Saturday becomes a night-club between 11pm and 3am.

Metro Bar, Bank Place, in the walled city. Young, fairly raucous atmosphere to a background of films projected onto the walls.

Mullan's, Sackville Street. Classic pub with a varied programme of music in the evenings.

Peadar O'Donnells, 59 Waterloo Street. With a bright yellow façade and whole hams hanging over the bar, this is one of the most characterful pubs in town. Traditional music every evening from 10.30.

The North and the West

The Anchor Inn, 38 Market Street. Popular establishment with a red and green façade and a maritime theme to its décor. Live music Thursday evening and snacks available daily.

The Dungloe Bar, 41-43 Waterloo Street has Victorian décor and hosts rock bands in its upstairs room on Tuesday, Thursday, Friday and Saturday.

The Castle Bar, 26 Waterloo Street, opposite the above establishment, has traditional music in an authentic atmosphere every evening.

Porter's Café, 22-24 Strand Road. This is the bar of the Trinity Hotel, attracting a fairly upmarket and trendy young crowd, but with good rock bands every evening except Tuesday. Disco from 10pm-1am Monday, Thursday, Friday and Saturday.

Bridie's Cottage, Craft Village. Thatched Donegal cabin transported to the middle of town, with traditional music evenings in summer.

OTHER THINGS TO DO

Golf – City of Derry Golf Club, Prehen, 3.5km south of town, ☎ 028 7134 6369. 18-hole course. Green fee: £20 during the week, £26 at the weekend (book in advance). **Foyle International Golf Centre**, 2km north of town on the banks of the Foyle. 18 holes and 9-hole, par 3. Green fee: £11-14.

Fishing – Both the estuary of the Foyle and the rivers in the surrounding area have salmon and trout in abundance. **Angling Safaris Ireland**, 10 Rossodowney Park, ☎ 028 7131 3880, organises trips to places where a good catch is likely.

Riding – Culmore Road Riding Centre, 3km north via the R238, ☎ 028 7135 9248. Closed Monday, otherwise open all year.

SHOPPING

Shopping centre – Foleyside Commercial Centre, Foyle Street (Plan I B3). Vast shopping centre completed in 1996 and a symbol of the city's economic revival.

Woollens – Edel McBride, 2 Castlegate (Plan II), ☎ 028 7126 6166. Good range of unusual designs in women's woollens from Donegal.

Derry street scene

B Kaufmann/MICHELIN

Making the most of Derry

CAUSEWAY COAST★
Co Antrim
Michelin map 923 L-M-N/2

Not to be missed
A walk along the Giant's Causeway Coastal Path.
Whiskey tasting at Bushmills.
Crossing the Carrick-a-rede rope bridge.
The spectacular viewpoint at Kinbane Castle.

And remember...
The clifftop path can be dangerously slippery in places;
keep children well under control.

Looking over the sea towards Scotland, Ulster's northern coastline is the site of one of the world's most visited natural attractions, the famous Giant's Causeway. But this extraordinary geological curiosity made up of countless basalt columns is far from being the only reason to come to the area, which has much else to offer its visitors. To the west is Lough Foyle, the broad estuary whose far shore is bounded by Donegal, while to the east are the glorious Glens of Antrim. For some of its length, the coastal road runs along high cliffs, while elsewhere it passes superb sandy beaches and characterful fishing villages.

From Magilligan Strand to the Giant's Causeway
46km drive - allow half a day

■ **Magilligan Strand** – At the northern extremity of Lough Foyle, a long sandy beach stretches for almost 10km between Magilligan Point and Downhill *(Access via the B202, a narrow road which runs past a military training ground and a prison)*. Facing the Inishowen Peninsula in the Republic, Magilligan Point is disappointingly polluted and not really very inviting. But there are wonderful walks to be had among the extensive sand dunes which are a designated nature reserve. Close by is the seaside recreational centre of Benone, which gets very crowded in summer.

Return to the hamlet of Magilligan and continue for 10km on the A2 to Downhill

■ **Downhill** – The late 18C gardens and Classical buildings of this estate over-looking the ocean were the work of **Frederick Hervey**, Bishop of Derry and Earl of Bristol. Little remains of past glories, but the **Bishop's Gate** gives some idea of what this eccentric nobleman had in mind. His residence is now a ruin, burnt down in a great fire of 1851. A passionate collector of antiquities, the Earl-Bishop also built the **Lion's Gate** which rises close to a walled garden. Dominating the shore from the cliff-top, the **Mussenden Temple★** *(July-August: 12pm-6pm; April-June and September: 2pm-5pm weekends and public holidays; Good Friday-Tuesday after Easter: 12pm-6pm. Admission free)* is the principal survivor from Hervey's ambitious schemes. A copy of the Temple of Vesta at Tivoli, the building housed a library; from it there is a superb **view★** over the sandy beach, a favourite spot for surfers.

Return to the A2, turning towards Coleraine. Continue for 3km past Castlerock.

■ **Hezlett House** – *April-June and September: 1pm-6pm weekends and public holidays; July-August: 12pm-5pm except Tuesday. Admission charge.*
This unusually large thatched cottage dating from 1691 served as a residence for the archdeacons of Londonderry for 70 years, before passing into the hands of the Hezlett family. A tour of the building gives an idea of domestic conditions in the 18C and 19C as well as of the construction techniques used in the building. The **Victorian furnishings** of the house and the little **museum of farming implements** in an out-building fill out the picture of life as once lived here.

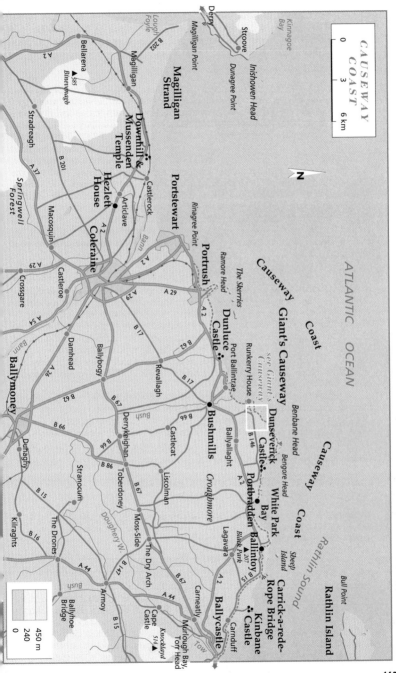

The A2 leads into **Coleraine**, a place of some importance but of limited tourist interest. The road then continues to the seaside resorts of **Portstewart** and **Portrush**, both very popular in summer and useful bases for exploring the coast because of their numerous restaurants and places to stay.

From Portrush follow the A2 for 7km to Dunluce Castle.

■ **Dunluce Castle**★★ – *April-October: 10am-6pm; 12pm-6pm Sunday; closed Monday; November-March: 10am-4pm; 2pm-4pm Sunday; closed Monday. Admission charge.*
The jagged outline of this 16C **fortress** seems suspended between sea and sky, rising as it does high above the waves atop a hundred-foot cliff. Its solitary and mysterious air makes it one of the most striking places in all of Northern Ireland. The castle was originally built by the Scottish clan of MacDonnell, who fought with the Irish against the English. With improvements in artillery, the fortifications lost their importance, and in the 17C the castle became a luxurious and lavishly furnished residence, the home of the Duchess of Buckingham who had married a MacDonnell. It was at this time that a terrible incident occurred: one evening in 1635, part of the cliff beneath the kitchens crashed into the sea, taking with it pots and pans, cooks and scullions. The duchess quit the castle, leaving it to crumble slowly away. From various points around the stronghold there are spectacular **views** over sea and coast. It is fascinating to note that part of the castle was constructed using blocks of **stone** quarried from the Giant's Causeway.

Return to the A2 and continue for 4km to Bushmills.

■ **Old Bushmills Distillery**★ – *April-October: 9.30am-5.30pm; 12pm-5.30pm Sunday, last guided tour 4pm; November-March: Monday-Friday guided tours promptly at 10.30am, 11.30am, 1.30pm, 2.30pm and 3.30pm. Admission charge includes a tasting.*
The distillery is recognisable from far off by the distinctive shape of its **kilns**, shaped like pagodas and used to dry the germinating barley. The establishment is supposed to be one of the oldest in the world, its stills having produced whiskey ever since the 13C. What is beyond dispute is that in 1608 King James I gave the then owners a distilling licence. Today the distillery belongs to Irish Distillers, a company forming part of the French Pernod-Ricard group.
A tour reveals the various stages in the production of whiskey, from malting onwards. Blends include **Bushmills** and **Blackbush**, made by mixing malt whiskey with grain alcohol, as well as single malts aged 10, 12 and 16 years made entirely in the distillery. A tasting can be followed by a meal in the cafeteria and, naturally enough, the products of the distillery can be purchased, though not at especially favourable prices.

Continue for 3.5km along the A2 to the Giant's Causeway.

The Giant's Causeway★★★
Allow 3hr

The source of many a legend, this extraordinary geological phenomenon is Northern Ireland's outstanding visitor attraction. It was only in the 19C that the origin of its basalt columns was understood; they were the end-product of lava flows from deep in the Earth's core some 60 million years ago. Polygonal in shape, the tops of the columns resemble a gigantic paved area. Similar formations can be seen along other parts of the Antrim coast, as well as in Scotland and Iceland.
Visitors should not limit themselves to a trip in the shuttle bus between the **visitor centre** and the Causeway, but should search out the various inlets, caves and viewpoints along the **Giant's Causeway Coastal Path**. In addition, there are shorter walks leading to the other strange formations known by various nicknames.
In the late 18C and early 19C, these and other stories were exploited for all they were worth by the "guides" who showed early tourists around and sold them all kinds of tools and other fantastic items supposedly used by Finn and his fellow-giants.

The North and the West

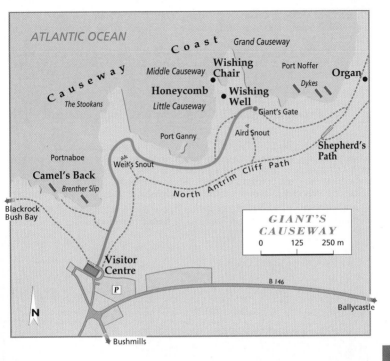

Visitor Centre – *July-August: 10am-7pm; June: 10am-6pm; May, September and October: 10am-5.30pm; March-April: 10am-5pm, 5.30pm weekends; November-February: 10am-4.30pm. Admission free. Charge for car park.* The centre has displays showing how the Giant's Causeway evolved over time into one of Ireland's foremost tourist sights and there is a video presentation as well. A useful purchase is the National Trust brochure with a detailed map of the Causeway.

Access to the site – It is possible to walk from the Visitor Centre to the Causeway (800m) or to take the shuttle bus which departs from below the building every 15min. Once at the Causeway, most people clamber over the columns and take photographs. Warning signs remind visitors of the danger from sudden waves which can break even during the calmest conditions, and it is advisable to keep well away from the water.

In the footsteps of the Giants

A number of signposted footpaths help visitors appreciate more fully the geological complexities of the Causeway, formed from different kinds of basalt which support a rich birdlife as well as a varied flora. The **Shepherd's Path**★ runs along the cliff, giving good views of features with fanciful names like the **Camel's Back**, the

Giant legends and tall tales

According to one old legend, the Causeway was built by the giant Finn McCool so that his Scottish rival Benandonner could cross the sea for a trial of strength. Defeated, the Scotsman set off for home, but Finn cast a spell on the causeway, making it sink beneath the surface of the sea. An alternative version has the Scottish titan arriving in Ireland, only to find his opponent tucked up in a cot in infant's apparel. The thought of encountering the parent of such a massive baby struck such panic in Benandonner's breast that he fled back across the sea, tearing up the causeway as he went.

Causeway Coast

465

Organ★, the **Wishing Chair**, the **Wishing Well**, and the **Honeycomb★★**. A stairway with 149 steps climbs up the cliff-face, from which a 3km walk loops back to the Causeway.

More adventurous walkers may want to try the **Causeway Coastal Path★★**, which leads 8km eastward to the ruins of **Dunseverick Castle**. Walking shoes or boots and rainproof clothing are strongly advised, as the path is steep and slippery in places.

Return to the A2 and continue eastwards for 5km to Portbradden.

From the Giant's Causeway to Ballycastle
21km – allow 2hr30min

■ **White Park Bay★** – The little harbour village of **Portbradden** stands at the western end of a splendid white sandy **beach** stretching for 3km at the foot of a collapsed chalk terrace. There is a striking contrast in colours, with the pale sand standing out against the green of the dunes rising gently towards the cliff. The area is rich in fossils and archeological remains. Bathing is inadvisable because of the strong currents.

The A2, then the B15 follow the shore for 3km as far as the tiny port of **Ballintoy**, nestling at the foot of a cliff and bordered by **basalt rocks** resembling those at the Giant's Causeway.

Stormy scene on the Giant's Causeway

The North and the West

Leave Ballintoy on the B15 and after 2km leave the vehicle in the Carrick-a-rede car park and continue on foot to the bridge.

■ **Carrick-a-rede**** – *April-June and September: 10am-6pm; June-August: 10am-8pm. Admission charge. Allow 45min to cross the bridge and return.*

Carrick-a-rede means "Rock-in-the-road", and this is a place where salmon are deflected from returning to their spawning grounds by a rocky island, a phenomenon taken advantage of by the fishermen who have set up their nets here for more than 400 years.

The **Rope Bridge**** linking the rock to the mainland was first installed about 250 years ago, and has obviously been renewed several times since. It is reached by a track about 800m long which runs along the clifftop, giving superb **views**** of the coast and Rathlin Island. Here too there are **basalt columns** like those at the Giant's Causeway. The bridge can only be crossed when there is little or no wind. The crossing, 25m above the foaming waves, is not for the faint-hearted! Anyone suffering from even a trace of vertigo is strongly advised not to chance their luck. People have more than once succeeded in making the crossing, only to find that their nerve has failed them for the return trip! However, a guide is on site to help deal with such eventualities.

C Boisvieux

Follow the B15 for 5km, then turn left and continue to the Kinbane Castle car park.

■ **Kinbane Castle*** – *Free admission.* Little remains of the castle built in the 16C by Colla Dubh MacDonnell. But there is a wonderful **view*** from the cliff edge towards Rathlin Island and the promontory of Fair Head to the east. A narrow pathway descends to a rocky outcrop from which rise the ruins of the castle. But beware of falling rocks!

Continue on the B15 for 3km as far as Ballycastle.

■ **Ballycastle** – This pleasant little resort is a useful stopping place along the route between the Giant's Causeway and the Glens of Antrim (*see page 472*). Boats leave here for Rathlin Island and there is a good range of places to stay as well as restaurants, cheerful pubs, and various visitor facilities. Ballycastle is a popular destination for Scottish holidaymakers coming over on the ferry from Campbeltown on the Mull of Kintyre (*see "Making the most of the Causeway Coast"*).

At the western end of the harbour stands the **Marconi Memorial**, commemorating the great Italian's

Causeway Coast

467

Carrick-a-rede rope bridge

success in setting up a wireless link between Ballycastle and Rathlin island. The resort's main square, **The Diamond**, is lined with lively pubs and is also the site of the fine 18C **Holy Trinity Church**.

Ballycastle gets very busy on Monday and Tuesday of the first week in August, when the **Ould Lammas Fair** takes place. This is a traditional event, going back for more than 400 years, which attracts not just Northern Irish but many people from Scotland and the Islands. It is the occasion for eating "dulse", dried seaweed, which is supposed to have beneficial properties, as well as "yellow man", a kind of toffee.

■ **A trip to Rathlin Island*** – *Boats are operated by Caledonian MacBrayne,* ☎ *028 2076 2024. Departures from Ballycastle 1 June-30 September: 9.30am, 11.30am, 4pm, and 6pm, returning 8.30am, 10.30am, 3pm and 5pm; remainder of year: one return trip per day depending on weather conditions. Crossing of 45min.*

Nature-lovers and those attracted by the simple life will appreciate this little L-shaped island 8km off the coast of Ireland and 20km away from Scotland. Its strategic location has not always been of great benefit to the island's inhabitants, of whom only about a hundred remain today. The traditional activities of farming, fishing and smuggling, have been progressively abandoned in favour of the tourist trade. There is in truth not all that much to do on tree-less Rathlin, apart from taking long walks across the fields bounded by stone walls, where rusting wrecks of cars sometimes seem to be the only crop. But fishermen and divers will find plenty to keep them happy (*see "Making the most of the Causeway Coast"*).

If moving on by car from Ballycastle to the Glens of Antrim (*see page 472*) via the A2, visitors should not miss the **Ballypatrick Forest Drive**, a 12km scenic route through a lovely coniferous forest bordered by peat bogs and with many an interesting walk to enjoy.

Making the most of the Causeway Coast

COMING AND GOING

By bus – Ulsterbus services nos 172 and 252 run 6 times daily (4 on Sunday) between Portrush and Ballycastle via the Giant's Causeway and Bushmills. In July-August, open-top bus n° 177 runs 4 times daily to Bushmills and the Giant's Causeway from Portrush.

Service n° 252, the **Antrim Coaster**, runs twice daily 24 May-25 September Monday to Saturday (and Sunday from 4 July): this is a particularly useful service for anyone without a car, stopping at all places along the Antrim Coast between Belfast and Coleraine, including the Giant's Causeway.

By boat – Ballycastle-Campbeltown ferry run by the **Argyll and Antrim Steam Packet Co**, ☎ 084 5752 3523.

ADDRESS BOOK

Tourist information – Tourist Information Centre, Sheksburn House, 7 Mary Street, Ballycastle, ☎ 028 2076 2024. July-August: 9.30am-7pm; 10am-5pm Saturday; 2pm-4pm Sunday; remainder of year: 9.30am-5pm, closed weekends. Good range of information on the coast, Rathlin Island and the Glens of Antrim.
Dunluce Centre, Portrush, ☎ 028 2082 3333. July-September: 9am-7pm; April-June: 9am-5pm; 12pm-5pm weekends.
Town Hall, Portstewart, ☎ 028 2083 2286. July-August only: 10am-1pm / 1.30pm-4pm; closed Sunday.

Banks / currency exchange – Cash machine in Ann Street, near the Diamond, Ballycastle.
Cash machines in Main Street and Eglington Street, Portrush.
Cash machines on the Promenade, Portstewart.

Post office / Telephone – Ann Street, Ballycastle. 9am-1pm / 2pm-5.30pm; 9am-1pm Wednesday; 9am-12.30pm Saturday; closed Sunday.
Same hours for post offices at 23 Eglington Street, Portrush, and 90 Promenade, Portstewart.

Bicycle hire – Ballycastle: **Northern Auto Factors**, Castle Street, close to the Diamond, ☎ 028 2076 3748. **Stewart Sport & Leisure**, ☎ 028 2076 3548. Portrush: **Bicycle Doctor**, 104 Lower Main Street, ☎ 028 2082 4340. Open 9am-6pm.

WHERE TO STAY

• Downhill
Under £10
Downhill Hostel, ☎ 028 7084 9077 – 32 beds. Near the beach, 3km west of Castlerock. A renovated old house needing further attention, with sea views, decent dormitories and a few double rooms.

• Bushmills
Between £50-55
Craig Park, 24 Carnbore Road, ☎ 028 2073 2479 – 3rm ⌁ TV CC From Bushmills, take the B17 towards Ballycastle, turn right into How Road past the Citroen garage, then after 1.5km turn left, continuing for 400m to the 4th house on the left. A pretty Georgian-style house with extremely comfortable rooms.

• Portrush
Under £10
Portrush Youth Hostel, 5 Causeway View Terrace, ☎ 028 2082 4845 – 24 beds. 4 and 6-bed dormitories in an old building currently undergoing restoration. Friendly welcome and lots of useful information about the area.

Between £50-55
Maddybenny Farm, Longuestown Road, ☎ / Fax 028 2082 3394 – 3rm ⌁ ♫ TV ✕ CC Outside the town, look for signs on the A29. Spacious, comfortable rooms with country-style furnishings in a renovated 17C farmhouse. Excellent breakfast with home-produced ingredients. Riding available.

• White Park Bay
Under £10
White Park Bay Youth Hostel, Portbradden, ☎ 028 2073 1745 – 54 beds, 4 double rooms. Open May-October. This recently built hostel has sea views and a fine location close to the

White Park sands. Good range of facilities. Bicycle hire.

Sheep Island View Campsite, 42 Main Street, Ballintoy, ☎ 028 2076 9391. Good all-year camping ground.

Between £30-35

Ballintoy House B&B, ☎ 028 2076 2317 – 3rm 🏊 TV On the left leaving Ballintoy on the way to Carrick-a-rede. Restored 18C house with attractively furnished and well-kept rooms.

👁***White Park House***, close to White Park beach, ☎ 028 2073 1482 – 3rm 🏊 This opulent little chateau-like residence has oriental décor and an extraordinary array of antique furniture. Extremely comfortable. Excellent breakfast.

• **Ballycastle**

Under £10

Castle Hostel, 62 Quay Road, ☎ 028 2076 2337 or 2076 9822 – 45 beds and 3 rooms. This yellow-painted early 20C building has double rooms and dormitories with 4-8 beds, all rather small, with showers and toilets on the landings, and breakfast is not included. Given the price, no-one complains.

Watertop Open Farm, 188 Cushendall Road, ☎ 028 2076 2576. Extensive caravan and camp site, opposite the entrance to Ballypatrick Forest. Good range of facilities. Fishing available.

Between £35-40

Cúchulainn House, 56 Quay Road, ☎ 028 2076 2252 – 3rm TV CC Overlooking the sea, an early 20C house with a loggia and plain but well-kept rooms. Attractive dining-room with nice china and silver at breakfast-time.

👁***Colliers Hall***, 50 Cushendall Road, ☎ 028 2076 2531 – 3rm 🏊 TV CC Around 1.5km outside town. Open April-October. Very amiable landlady who welcomes guests to her knick-knack crammed residence, with huge bedrooms furnished in country style and looking out over the fields. Excellent breakfast with pancakes. A hostel with dormitories is due to open next door.

Kenmara House, 45 North Street, ☎ 028 2076 2600 – 5rm TV On the right on the way out of town towards the Giant's Causeway. The bedrooms may be somewhat lacking in charm, but this delightful white-painted house on the clifftop has a wonderful view over the bay. Note that the view is only visible from two of the rooms.

• **Rathlin Island**

Under £10

Soenorg View Hostel, ☎ 028 2076 3954 – 12 beds. 10min on foot from the ferry landing, but you can arrange to be picked up. The establishment is clean and the rooms have their own facilities. Advance reservation essential.

Between £30-35

Rathlin Guest House, The Quay, ☎ 028 2076 3917 – 4rm Open April-September. Family atmosphere and decent rooms in a house by the harbour.

EATING OUT

• **Portrush**

Between £10-15

👁***The Harbour***, ☎ 028 2082 2430, open 12.15pm-2.15pm / 5.30pm-10pm, -3pm and -9pm Sunday. This is an annexe to the famous Ramore establishment next door, offering oriental-influenced seafood in a bistro-type setting. Considerably cheaper than the main restaurant but comparable quality.

Ramore Wine Bar, next door to the above and with the same style of cuisine. Extensive and reasonably priced wine list.

• **Bushmills**

Under £10

Old Bushmills Distillery Cafeteria. Classic lunch menu in one of the old buildings of the distillery.

• **Giant's Causeway**

Under £10

Pub in the Causeway Hotel. This is a good alternative to the rather impersonal cafeteria in the Visitor Centre, with solid pub grub served all day.

• **Ballintoy**

Under £10

Fullerton Arms, Main Street. Open 12.30pm-8.30pm. Classic dishes served in an authentic inn.

• **Ballycastle**

Under £10

Wysner's, 16 Ann Street, in the town centre. ☎ 028 2076 2373. Open 8am-5pm; closed Wednesday and Sunday; 7pm-9pm Friday and Saturday. This establishment makes an attempt to provide light dishes based on fresh local produce.

The Strand, by the harbour, ☎ 028 2076 2349. Open 11am-9pm. Unpretentious modern décor and decent food. Try the fish cakes made from haddock or the leek and Stilton flan.

Between £10-15

Kimark, 52 Quay Road, ☎ 028 2076 2888. Open 5pm-9.30pm Wednesday to Saturday. Slightly dearer that the places listed above, but worth it for dishes like the baked salmon in fennel sauce or sausages on a bed of mushrooms.

HAVING A DRINK

• **Ballycastle**

There are plenty of pubs with live music. The Angler's Arms on the quayside has traditional music on Tuesday evenings in the summer.

Central Bar, Main Street, is full of fiddlers on Wednesday evenings.

MacCarroll's has Celtic sounds on Thursdays.

The House of MacDonnell, Castle Street, also has traditional music on Friday evenings.

Boyd Arms, close to the above establishment, hosts folk groups on Fridays.

• **Ballintoy**

Traditional music Thursday and Sunday evenings in the **Carrick-a-Rede**, and on Tuesday and Thursday at the **Fullerton Arms**.

OTHER THINGS TO DO

Golf – **Ballycastle Golf Club**, Cushendall Road, Ballycastle, ☎ 028 2076 2536. 18-hole course overlooking the sea between two rivers. Green fee: £18-25.

Riding – **Hillmount Riding Centre**, 6a Straid Road, Ballycastle, ☎ 028 2076 3313.

Diving – **Tommy Cecil**, Rathlin Island, ☎ 028 2076 3915, can arrange dives around the numerous wrecks in the waters surrounding the island.

Fishing – The River Bush is famous for its salmon. Licences, information and day permits can be obtained from the River Bush Salmon Station, 21 Church Street, Bushmills, ☎ 028 2073 1435, Fax 028 2073 2130.

Making the most of the Causeway Coast

ANTRIM GLENS★★
THE COAST ROAD FROM BALLYCASTLE TO LARNE

Co Antrim – Michelin map 923 N-O / 2-3
113km drive – Allow 2 days

Not to be missed
The cliffs at Murlough Bay.
The coast road and its numerous viewpoints.
The waterfalls in Glenariff Forest Park

And remember...
The coast road between Murlough Bay and Cushendun
is at its best at sunrise or sunset.

Divided inland by deep and narrow glens running down from the uplands, this spectacular coastline is among the most loved regions in all Ireland. It has an almost infinite variety of landscapes, each a self-contained little world, revealed in turn as the traveller rounds the successive headlands. The nine glens – **Glentaisie**, **Glenshesk**, **Glendun**, **Glencorp**, **Glenaan**, **Glenballyemon**, **Glenariff**, **Glencloy** and **Glenarm**, occupy a special place in Irish hearts, standing as they do for a sense of an authentic way of life lived in a wonderfully well-preserved landscape.

The whole area in general, and the individual glens in particular, remained cut off from the rest of the country right up until the end of the 19C, the moment when the railway made its appearance, and it was only in the middle of the 20C that the coast road was made more or less suitable for motor traffic. This is a place to linger in, not only to discover landscapes that take the breath away, but to get to know something of the local people, known for their warmth and hospitality and their strong sense of identity.

Between sea and mountain

■ **Murlough Bay★★** *From Ballycastle (see page 468) drive east on the A2. At Ballyvoy the A2 continues towards Ballypatrick Forest (see page 468), while the coast road turns off to the left.*

Spectacular sea views, a rich, almost luxuriant vegetation cladding the cliffs, and with luck, a glimpse of a herd of deer, make Murlough Bay one of the most enchanting places in Northern Ireland.

There are two ways of exploring this superb spot. On the left of the upper car park, a grassy footpath marked with yellow posts leads into a mass of fallen rocks before continuing along the clifftop to **Fair Head**. From this wind-blown headland there is a spectacular **view★★** encompassing Rathlin Island, the Causeway Coast, and, in the distance, the Mull of Kintyre. The middle car park is reached by a track bordered by fine beech, birch and rowan trees. An information panel explains the unusual ecology of the area and also helps identify the various islands off the Scottish coast.

From the lower car park, a footpath on the right runs parallel to the shore towards a **woodland** with an extraordinarily diverse vegetation, including eucalyptus. The path goes past an old **lime-kiln** and a **miner's cottage**. The area around the bay was mined for coal, but extraction came to an end at the beginning of the 1940s. More relics of this era can be seen along the path to the left of the car park.

Return to the coast road and continue for 4km.

A track on the left leads to a car park close to an old observation post atop the promontory of **Torr Head**. This is the nearest point in Ireland to Scotland, a mere 19km away.

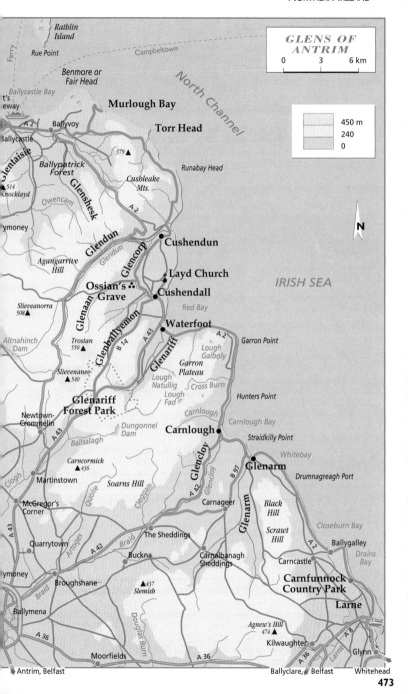

GLENS OF
ANTRIM

0   3   6 km

450 m
240
0

Rathlin
Island

Rue Point

Campbeltown

Ferry

North Channel

Benmore or
Fair Head

Ballycastle Bay

t's
eway

A 2   Ballyvoy

Murlough Bay

Torr Head

A

allycastle

Glentaisie

379 ▲

Runabay Head

514 ▲
Knocklayd

Ballypatrick
Forest

Cushleake
Mts.

ymoney

Owencam

Glenshesk

A 2

North Channel

Glendun

Agangarrive
Hill

Glendun

Glencorp

Cushendun

Slieveanorra
508 ▲

Ossian's
Grave

Glenaan

Layd Church

Cushendall

Altnahinch
Dam

Trostan
550 ▲

Glenballyemon

B 14

A 43

Waterfoot

A 2

Red Bay

IRISH SEA

Garron Point

Slievenanee
▲ 540

Glenariff

Lough
Galboly

Garron
Plateau

Lough
Natullig

Cross Brun

Hunters Point

Glenariff
Forest Park

Lough
Fad

Carnlough

Newtown-
Crommelin

A 43

Dungonnel
Dam

Ballsalagh

Carnlough

Carnlough Bay

Carnlough

Straidkilly Point

Whitebay

Carncormick
▲ 436

Soarns Hill

Glencloy

Glenarm

Drumnagreagh Port

Martinstown

Quoile

Cleggan

A 42

Glendoy

B 97

Clogh

Carnageer

Glenarm

Black
Hill

Closeburn Bay

McGregor's
Corner

The Sheddings

Scrawt
Hill

A 2

Ballygalley

A 43

Braid

Quarrytown

Buckna

A 42

Arloges

Carnalbanagh
Sheddings

Carncastle

Drains
Bay

ymoney

Broughshane

Braid

▲ 437
Slemish

Carnfunnock
Country Park

Larne

Ballymena

A 36

Douglas Burn

Agnew's Hill
474 ▲

Kilwaughter

A 36

Larne

A 8

Glynn

Moorfields

A 36

Antrim, Belfast

Ballyclare, Belfast

Whitehead

473

Carry on along the narrow **coast road****. A number of cliff-top **viewpoints** give superb prospects over the sea as far as the Scottish coast. On summer evenings, there can be extraordinary visual effects when the setting sun illuminates the violet of the fuchsias against the dark green background of the other vegetation.

The road continues through **Cushendun**, a tiny township with attractive houses and cottages lining the pretty bay.

Beyond Cushendun, the coast road rejoins the A2. About 3km before reaching Cushendall, turn right and follow signs to Ossian's Grave which is reached along a rough track.

■ **Ossian's grave** – Like many other Megalithic monuments, this stone circle has become the focus of later legends which have little to do with prehistory. Ossian appears in Irish myth and legend in a number of guises, as an associate of St Patrick, as a bard, or as the son of the giant Finn McCool from the Giant's Causeway. Each story has its own appeal, as does the attractive landscape around the circle, with its **views** of the surrounding hills.

■ **Cushendall** – This little summer resort offers a good choice of accommodation as well as a number of cheerful pubs. Its principal sight is the **Curfew Tower**, built in red sandstone in the 19C as a gaol. A minor road leads along the coast to the north of the town to the 13C **Layd Church**, now in ruins and romantically surrounded by a graveyard overlooking the sea.

From Cushendall, Waterfoot can be reached directly via the A2 or by taking a detour through Glenariff Forest Park.

From Cushendall, the B14 runs for 10km up **Glenballyemon** through a landscape of heath, bogland and conifer plantations.

On joining the A43, go towards Waterfoot for 3km as far as the entrance of the Forest Park.

■ **Glenariff Forest Park*** – *10am-dusk. Admission charge.* This 1 185-hectare park consists mostly of conifer plantations alternating with peat bogs and rocky outcrops. The best places to enjoy a picnic are the official sites, especially the one by the main entrance to the park. From here there is a fine **view** over the uplands, their mantle of vegetation showing every possible tint of green. In the distance is the sea and the far-off coast of Scotland.

Exploring the park is far more rewarding once a visit has been made to the excellent **Information Centre**, with its informative displays on the flora and fauna of the park and on the area's mining heritage.

Among the four waymarked footpaths leading through the park, the 2.5km **Waterfall Trail** leads to the **Ess na Larach*** falls. The river's peaty waters foam and swirl beneath a canopy of luxuriant vegetation where giant pines and majestic beeches shade a lush growth of ferns (*the falls can also be reached by car; drive towards Waterford and turn right to the car park of the Manor Lodge inn*).

Return to the coast road via the A43.

Minerals from the Glens

Between 1865 and 1927 iron ore was extracted from the Glenariff area. The ore, 13 000 tonnes of it in 1877, was transported to the harbours on the coast and shipped from there to steelworks in Bristol. When it was no longer profitable to exploit the ore, bauxite was extracted, following the same route to England. This activity came to an end in the late 1920s, but resumed during the Second World War to help satisfy the needs of war production and reduce Britain's reliance on imported minerals.

■ **Waterfoot**** – Nestling between the imposing uplands of the Garron plateau to the south and the Lurig heights to the north, this coastal village is sited at the entrance to **Glenariff**, known as the king – or queen – of the Antrim Glens. The rich grasslands cloaking the Lurig slopes are grazed, not by sheep but by cattle, and have an uncanny resemblance to Swiss mountain pastures, hence the local name of "Little Switzerland" for this delightful

The North and the West

spot. During the last week of June and the first week in July the **Feis na nGleann** is held here. As well as hurling, this festival of Celtic games includes a whole range of other sports and musical events.

Continue along the coast on the A2.

■ **Carnlough** – A pleasant stopping-place comfortably sited on its fine sandy bay, this village owes its name to **La**, a disciple of St Patrick. Frustrated by his lack of success in converting the local people to Christianity, La is supposed to have torn off his hand and buried it beneath a cairn. Hence the name Carnlough, a deformation of *Cairn of La*.

In the middle of the 19C, the village became an important centre for the quarrying of limestone, which was brought down to the harbour by narrow-gauge railway line and shipped to Scotland. The old railway line now forms part of the **Ulster Way**,

Glenariff Forest Park

B Kaufmann/MICHELIN

The Glens of Antrim

and leads to the worked-out **Gortin Quarry**, now a nature reserve with a waterfall known as the **Cranny Falls**. Determined walkers may want to continue along the Ulster Way for 14km across the wild and lonely **Garron plateau** before descending to the coast again.

At Doonan, about 3km south of Carnlough before reaching the A42, there is a very pleasant picnic site, with a viewpoint close to a **waterfall**.

Turn right onto the A42, which winds up Glencloy. After 10km, turn left onto B97 which leads back down to the coast, a loop of about 20km.

The road leads through a fine landscape of patchwork fields divided by low dry-stone walls. At one point, a bend reveals a magnificent **view**★ of the basalt cliffs along the coast to Larne.

■ **Glenarm** – At the point where the southernmost of the Antrim Glens meets the sea, this little port is one of the most charming villages along the coast. Seat of the Earls of Antrim, the **castle** is still inhabited, but as a private residence is only open to the public once a year. However, it is possible to stroll in the gardens which are guarded by a **barbican**. The main street runs up to **Glenarm Forest Park**, with attractive riverside footpaths and fine stands of oak, beech, and elm as well as conifers.

Return to the A2 and continue south for 15km.

■ **Carnfunnock Country Park** – *July-August: 10am-8pm; closed 6pm the rest of the year. Parking charge.* With its **maze**, **walled garden**, and **sundials**, a golf course and caravan site, this Country Park combines natural beauty and visitor facilities in a fine setting of green hills dropping down to the sea.

Continue on the A2 for a further 5km.

■ **Larne** – Larne is an important harbour for freight as well as for the ferries linking Northern Ireland with Cairnryan and Stranraer in Scotland (*see "Making the most of the Glens of Antrim"*). It's not a particularly attractive town, its only interest to tourists being its choice of places to stay. In 1914, the port was the scene of the "Larne Gun-Running", when 25 000 rifles and 3 million rounds of ammunition purchased in Germany were clandestinely unloaded, then distributed among Unionists determined to resist Home Rule by whatever force was necessary.

To the south of the harbour, the peninsula known as **Island Magee** can be reached by a ferry for foot passengers (*hourly 7am-5.30pm, ☎ 028 2827 4085*) or by road via Whitehead, 15km to the south. The far side of the peninsula has splendid sandy beaches, but the presence of a huge power station and its transmission lines do not enhance the area's attractiveness.

The North and the West

Making the most of the Glens of Antrim

COMING AND GOING

By bus – Service n° 252, also known as the **Antrim Coaster**, runs in summer between all the places along the coast between Belfast and Coleraine (see "Making the most of the Causeway Coast"). During the rest of the year, connections are less frequent. Service no 162 runs between Cushendun and Larne (90min) 5 times daily, twice Saturday and 3 times Sunday. No 162A links Cushendun with Ballycastle (50min) once daily. From Belfast, n° 150 runs to Cushendun (2hr40min) via Waterfoot 5 times daily from Monday to Friday and 3 times Saturday.

By boat – The ferry service between Larne and Cairnryan is operated by **P&O**, ☎ 028 2827 4321, while **Stena Line**, ☎ 028 2827 3616, run the service to Stranraer.

ADDRESS BOOK

Tourist information – Tourist Information Centre, 25 Mill Street, Cushendall, ☎ 028 2171 180. July-September: 10am-1pm / 2.30pm-5pm, 10am-1pm Saturday; closed Sunday; October-mid-December and March-June: 10am-1pm Tuesday-Saturday. Good range of information on walking in the area.

McKillop's, close to the Londonderry Arms in Carnlough, has a limited range of tourist information.

Tourist Information near the harbour at Glenarm, ☎ 028 2884 1307. Variable hours in summer; closed the rest of the year.

Tourist Information Centre, Narrow Gauge Road, Larne, south of the town going towards Belfast, ☎ 028 2826 0088. Open 9am-5pm; closed weekends; Easter-September: open also Saturday at these times and 10am-4pm public holidays. Closes later July-August. Small exhibition on the region and good range of other information.

Banks / Currency exchange – Several banks and cash machines in Main Street, Larne. Cash machine in Shore Street, Cushendall.

Post office / Telephone – Glenarm Post Office, 39 Toberwine Street, open 9am-1pm / 2pm-5.30pm Monday, Tuesday, Thursday, Friday; 9am-12.30pm Wednesday, Saturday. **Larne Post Office**, 98 Main Street. Same hours as above.

Bicycle hire – In Cushendall, **Cushendall Youth Hostel** (see "Where to 3stay"); **Ardclinis Activity Centre**, 11 High Street, ☎ 028 2177 1340, offers a range of sporting and recreational activities as well as bike hire. Also at the Tourist Office in Larne and **Carnfunnock Country Park**, ☎ 028 2827 8465.

WHERE TO STAY

• **Cushendun**

Between £35-40

🏠 **The Villa Farmhouse**, ☎ 028 2176 1252 – 3rm 🍴 TV Signposted on the left on the coast road leaving Cushendun. Delightful detached house of around 1900 nicely sited on rising ground with a superb view over the bay. Spacious and comfortable rooms with antique furnishings. Visitors can lunch with the family for a very reasonable sum. Reservations necessary for evening meal.

• **Cushendall**

Under £10

Cushendall Youth Hostel, 42 Layde Road, ☎ 028 2177 1344 – 44rm One kilometre to the north of the town, well signposted. A fine example of a youth hostel in a restored old house, a few steps from the sea. Cooking facilities, bike hire and a good range of other facilities.

Cushendall Caravan Park, 62 Coast Road, near Red Bay, ☎ 028 2177 1699. Reasonable facilities but unattractive setting.

Between £30-35

Glendale, 46 Coast Road, ☎ 028 2177 1495 – 5rm 🍴 TV Modern house well located on the way into the town. Comfortable rooms and exceptionally friendly welcome.

Making the most of the Glens of Antrim

• **Waterfoot**

Under £10

Glenariff Forest Park, ☎ 028 2175 8232. A campsite with basic facilities, but the surroundings are lovely and peace and quiet is guaranteed.

Between £25-30

Wilmar House, 26 Kilmore Road, on the road towards Glenariff Forest Park, ☎ 028 2177 1653 – 2rm Open March-September. Plain but decent rooms in an exceptionally fine setting.

Between £30-35

Sanda B&B, 29 Kilmore Road, ☎ 028 2177 1785 – 2rm ⌐ Open March-October. Opposite the establishment above but more comfortable. Rooms in traditional style in a modern house with a fine view of the glen. Lots of useful information available about the area.

• **Carnlough**

Between £30-35

Harbour View, 50 Harbour Road, ☎ 028 2888 5335 – 2rm ⌐ As its name suggests, this small family B&B has a fine view over harbour and cliffs. One large and one rather smaller room, shared but attractive bathroom.

• **Glenarm**

Between £30-35

Nine Glens B&B, 18 Toberwine Street, ☎ 028 2884 1590 – 3rm ⌐ TV CC Small well-located B&B with charming and comfortable rooms decorated in pastel colours.

Riverside House, 13 Toberwine Street, ☎ 028 2884 1474 – 4rm ⌐ TV Open March-September. Small, very well-kept rooms, family atmosphere.

• **Larne**

Between £25-30

The Harbour Inn, 25 Olderfleet Road, ☎ 028 2827 2386 – 5rm TV ✕ A few steps from the ferry terminal, this Victorian house with its loggia has rooms which are not particularly luxurious but are priced accordingly. Value-for-money meals until 9.30pm.

Between £30-35

Seaview House, 156 Curran Road, not far from the harbour, ☎ 028 2827 2438 – 8rm ⌐ TV Old-fashioned pension-style establishment not entirely lacking in charm. Most rooms have own facilities, breakfast is good, and there is a wide selection of information on things to do in the area.

Killyneedan B&B, 52 Bay Road, ☎ 028 2827 9442 – 3rm TV Small, nicely kept B&B in a quiet street near the harbour.

Between £50-60

Magheramorne House Hotel, 59 Shore Road, ☎ 028 2827 9444 – 40rm ⌐ ♪ TV ✕ CC Three kilometres south of Larne on the road to Carrickfergus. Scottish Baronial-style hotel with bags of old-fashioned charm, surrounded by luxuriant vegetation. The rooms in the older building have very attractive views, but those in the modern annex are less interesting.

Between £60-85

Ballygalley Castle Hotel, Ballygalley, ☎ 028 2858 3212, Fax 028 2858 3681 – 31rm ⌐ ♪ TV ✕ CC Five kilometres north of Larne on the A2. This fine old castle has been turned into a luxury hotel, and even has a ghost, one Mrs Nixon, an elegant 18C lady who is reputed to knock at residents' doors at night.

EATING OUT

• **Cushendun**

Under £10

The Villa Farmhouse, (see "Where to stay") – 12pm-2.30pm / 6pm-10pm. Lunchtime snacks and home cooking in the evening (reservation advised) in an attractive setting.

• **Cushendall**

Between £10-15

Harry's, 10 Mill Street, ☎ 028 2177 2022. Monday-Saturday, 11.30am-9pm; 12.30pm-2.30pm / 7pm-10pm Sunday. This charming village inn makes a real effort to serve fresh and inventive cuisine. The mackerel mousse and leg of lamb is worth making a detour for. Straightforward lunchtime menu.

• **Waterfoot**

Under £10

Angela's Restaurant, 33 Main Street, ☎ 028 2177 1700. Open 9am-5pm;

12.30pm-2.30pm Sunday. Friendly café / snack bar with a pleasant courtyard for fine days. Good home-made cakes and a whole range of appetising dishes.

The Manor Lodge, Glen Road, ☎ 028 2175 8221. Daily 11am-11pm. On the road to Glenariff Forest Park, signposted on the left. People come from far and wide to enjoy the garish but nevertheless charming décor of this woodland inn on the edge of the Glenariff Forest Park. Straightforward food at lunchtime, copious grills at slightly higher prices in the evening.

• **Carnlough**
Between £10-15
Londonderry Arms Hotel, 20 Harbour Road, ☎ 028 2888 5255. This is the restaurant of Carnlough's leading hotel. Meat and seafood dishes tend to be on the elaborate side in the evening. Sandwiches and *plats du jour* served all day in the bar.

• **Glenarm**
Under £10
Drumnagreagh Hotel, ☎ 028 2884 1651. Open 12.30pm-8pm. On the left on the road in from Larne, 2km before Glenarm. The rooms in this old hillside property now converted into a hotel may not be up to much, but the food served in the restaurant is fine and there is a good view too.
Poacher's Pocket, 1 New Row. Friendly pub with a varied menu.

• **Larne**
Under £10
Chekkers Wine Bar, 31 Lower Cross Street, ☎ 028 2827 5305. Monday-Saturday 12pm-9pm; 1pm-8pm Sunday. Straightforward meals served on the ground floor at midday, or in a lively atmosphere on the first floor in the evening.

Bengal Cuisine, 6 High Street, ☎ 028 2826 0000. From midday until late evening. Tasty Bangladesh cuisine, but service is not the quickest.
Magheramorne House Hotel, (see "Where to stay"). Good self-service lunches in a very pleasant setting.
Ballygalley Castle. Traditional menu in this castle converted into a hotel.

HAVING A DRINK

• **Cushendall**
Jo McCollan, fiddlers liven up this place every evening in summer and at the weekend in winter.
The Luric Bar has disco music every Friday and Saturday evening.

• **Waterfoot**
The Mariners Bar, Main Street, is one of the town's liveliest pubs. At the weekend, try **Chekkers Wine Bar** (see "Eating out").

OTHER THINGS TO DO

Golf – Cairndu Golf Club, 192 Coast Road, Ballygalley, 5km north of Larne on the A2, ☎ 028 2858 3324. 18-hole course in a splendid setting at the foot of hills overlooking the sea. Green fee: £15 weekdays, £20-24 weekends. Nearby is the **Carnfunnock Golf Club**, in the Carnfunnock Country Park, ☎ 028 2827 8465. A 9-hole course in wooded surroundings. Green fee: £3.50.

SHOPPING

Smoked salmon – Glenarm Salmon, on the right on the way into the village from Larne, ☎ 028 2884 1691. Mid-July-late September: 12pm-6pm; 1pm-7pm Sunday. The fish raised in this salmon farm located at sea are sent to England for smoking and returned for sale here.

Making the most of the Glens of Antrim

The Mourne Mountains

BELFAST
AND THE SOUTH

Lough Neagh, shallow but vast in extent, fills much of central Ulster, forming a natural obstacle which has made Belfast and its region look more to the sea than to the interior. With a distinctive maritime, industrial and farming heritage, the area has sometimes seemed more British than Britain, and Belfast itself once had the rather austere look of many another Victorian city on the far side of the water. The city has suffered more than its share of the sectarian horrors of the 20C, but cease-fire and peace process have brought significant changes; Belfast has undergone a revival not unlike that enjoyed by its sister Dublin to the south, and its population now seems to be enthusiastically making up for lost time.

Beyond the city, the Ards Peninsula resembles a jewel set splendidly in the Irish Sea, while the Mourne Mountains are the heartland of the country's most venerable legends. The hills of County Down saw St Patrick's first sermons, his tomb is at Downpatrick and Armagh is Ireland's most sacred city. Quintessential Ireland, revered by all its diverse Christian traditions, awaits the traveller here.

BELFAST AND AROUND★★

Co Antrim – Pop 380 000
Capital of Northern Ireland
Michelin map 923 N-O / 3-4

Not to be missed
The city's pubs.
The Spanish Armada treasure in the Ulster Museum.
The Ulster Folk and Transport Museum at Cultra.
The Irish Linen Centre at Lisburn.

And remember...
Keep away from the Belfast area at the height of the Orange marching season
around 12 July as many hotels, restaurants and tourist attractions are closed.

The capital city of Northern Ireland is an important port and industrial centre, now undergoing rapid change. The combined effect of the peace process and an astonishing level of economic growth has renewed Belfast's confidence in itself and the city now presents an image almost wholly at variance with the clichés of the last thirty years. The gable walls of houses in some of the diehard districts of the inner city may still be adorned with sectarian murals and slogans, but their paint is losing its freshness. The strictures of History seem to have been overcome finally by the demands of Economy, the most obvious signs of revival being the ultramodern office blocks, shops and banks which have mushroomed in many parts of the centre. But there are other symptoms of rebirth too. If the centre itself empties in the evening and still wears something of its severe old Victorian face, it is because night-life has moved to the adjacent Golden Mile, the area stretching from near City Hall to the University, which has filled up over the last few years with pubs, restaurants and night-spots. Revelry continues until the small hours, but there is no need for visitors to feel at all unsafe; paradoxical though it may seem, Belfast is one of the safest cities in the world, not least because of the formidable but discreet police presence. Nightlife has indeed become one of the city's principal attractions, while the conventional tourist sights like museums and monuments are unlikely to detain the average visitor for more than a day or two. By contrast, the surrounding area has some of the country's outstanding attractions, among them Carrickfergus Castle and the Ulster Folk and Transport Museum, all helping to justify a longer stay in Ulster's capital.

Trials of history

Harbour town – The city is strategically located at the point where the River Lagan flows into the long arm of the sea known as Belfast Lough. The name Belfast itself comes from the Gaelic *Béal Feirsde* meaning the mouth of, or approach to, a sandbank. The site had never been settled by the native Irish when, in the 12C, the Norman Jean de Courcy ordered a castle built here, but it was the construction of a quay for merchant ships which really stimulated the growth of the town in the 17C. At this time too, the immigration of Scottish Presbyterians anchored the place firmly in the Protestant tradition of hard work and industry, and this character was reinforced by the arrival of a number of French Huguenots, whose particular contribution was to the development of the linen industry in the hinterland. Harbour improvements in the course of the 18C and 19C helped Belfast become one of the United Kingdom's most important ports and the country's leading ship-building centre. It was from the city's famous Harland and Wolff shipyard that the *Titanic* steamed off towards her tragic encounter with the iceberg.

Cradle of nationalism – Towards the end of the 18C, the city prospered, favouring the development of a liberal-minded Protestant middle class desirous of throwing off the constraints imposed by rule from London. In 1791, the Protestant

Wolfe Tone, inspired by the ideas of the French Revolution, helped found the Society of United Irishmen, an event which led directly to the revolt of 1798. However, over the following decades, Belfast's wealth and prosperity was in flagrant contrast to the famine and suffering of much of the rest of the country, and the city which had been at the forefront of Irish nationalism became, for Catholics, a symbol of injustice and oppression.

This duality, further nourished during the Industrial Revolution by the emergence of a disenfranchised Catholic working class, contributed to the build-up of bitter resentments which were accentuated by Partition in 1922, and thereafter Belfast was always at the centre of the murderous sectarian clashes which shook the country until the 1994 cease-fire.

Hopes for peace

Good Friday and beyond – The Good Friday agreement of 10 April 1998 led to a considerable calming of the atmosphere in the streets of Belfast. In the course of the summer of 1999, the armoured vehicles of the RUC were replaced by ordinary police cars, and apart from the more or less constant presence of surveillance helicopters, there is little evidence of tension in areas likely to be of interest to visitors. Nevertheless, despite the desire of the overwhelming majority of the population on both sides of the religious divide for peace, the situation is still unpredictable, and it will doubtless be many years before yesterday's enemies are able to coexist amiably in a prosperity shared by all.

Sectarian strongholds – The decades of the Troubles led to a reinforcement of the sectarian character of Belfast's inner suburbs, as people felt safer living with their co-religionists, and moved – sometimes with brutal encouragement – away from areas where they felt themselves to be an exposed minority. The names of these districts featured regularly and sombrely in news bulletins. The city's Protestant working-class is concentrated in the area between the Shankill and Crumlin Roads, with other

Shankill scene

C. Legrand/MICHELIN

Belfast and around

communities in North Belfast, in Sandy Row to the southeast of the city centre, as well as in East Belfast, close to the shipyards which were traditionally a source of Protestant employment. Catholics live overwhelmingly in the Falls, the area to the west of the city centre to which they flocked in large numbers as the Industrial Revolution sucked in cheap labour from the countryside. The Ardoyne and New Lodge are other Catholic enclaves. Flags, painted kerbstones, and **murals** fiercely proclaim an area's identity and allegiance. The murals themselves have become something of a tourist attraction, though it should never be forgotten that, for many local people, their iconography is charged with intense significance; they have certainly not been created as works of art for voyeuristic admiration by outsiders.

Visitor's Belfast

The main areas of interest for anyone making a short stay in Belfast include the areas around **City Hall**, in the north, and **Queen's University** in the south. About 1km apart, they are at either end of the axis formed by University Road and Victoria Street. City Hall dominates **Donegall Square**, the focus of a number of pedestrianised shopping streets. Teeming with life in the daytime, by the early evening the area has been almost completely depopulated, though a number of pubs remain lively enough.

By contrast, it is now that the **Golden Mile** comes to life, along University Road, Bradbury Place, Dublin Road and around the University. It is here too that the majority of bed and breakfast establishments are concentrated, and that most visitors will begin their exploration of the city.

The Queen's University area
Allow half a day, including a visit to the museum

With its imposing red-brick façade, turrets and bell-towers, **Queen's University**∗ consists of a fine group of buildings in 19C neo-Tudor style, their architecture inspired by Oxford's Magdalen College. To the right of the main entrance, the **Visitor Centre** *(Monday-Friday 10am-4pm; May-September Saturday only. Free admission)* has information on the history of the university as well as on its programme of cultural, musical and other events. These culminate during the **Queen's University Festival**, lasting for three weeks, with concerts and other events of the highest quality which take place over the whole of the university quarter.

The University's fine lawns run into those belonging to the **Botanic Gardens**∗ *(Greenhouses: 10am-12pm / 2pm-5pm – 4pm in winter. Free admission)*. At the entrance to the gardens stands the statue of the physician William Thompson, **Lord Kelvin** (1824-1907), a native of Belfast, whose name has forever been linked to the calculation and measurement of temperatures. Covering 11 hectares, the gardens slope gently down to the River Lagan, and in summer the grass is covered with the bodies of sunbathing students.

The **Tropical Ravine House** has a permanent temperature of 35 degrees Celsius and contains fine specimens of exotic plants. Close by is the **Palm House**∗, its elegant architecture topped by a cupola; it is one of the oldest greenhouses of its kind in Europe.

To the south of the Botanic Gardens, the **Ulster Museum**∗ *(10am-5pm; Saturday 1pm-5pm; Sunday 2pm-5pm. Free admission)* is devoted to a wide range of subjects, from fine art to history and natural science. It is best to start a visit by taking the lift to the top floor, where there are 18C-20C paintings by leading British and Irish artists like **Turner**, **Reynolds** and **Roderic O'Connor**, as well as works by 17C Flemish painters.

The floor below is devoted to arts and crafts, with fine examples of stained glass, jewellery, and glass and silver ware, mostly from the 17C. There is also a natural history collection, as well as a pleasant cafeteria with a view of the Botanic Gardens.

Belfast and the South

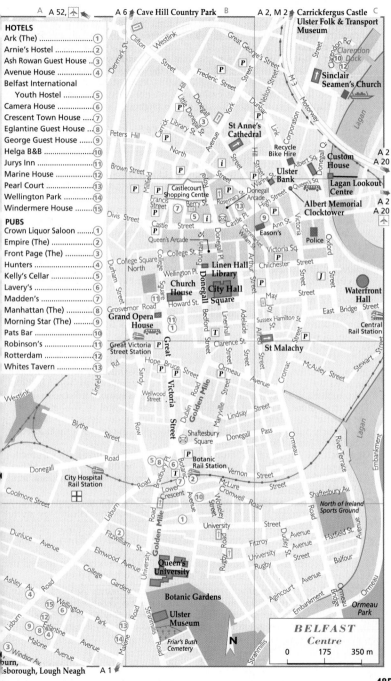

HOTELS

Ark (The) ....①
Arnie's Hostel ....②
Ash Rowan Guest House ..③
Avenue House ....④
Belfast International
    Youth Hostel ....⑤
Camera House ....⑥
Crescent Town House ....⑦
Eglantine Guest House ..⑧
George Guest House ......⑨
Helga B&B ....⑩
Jurys Inn ....⑪
Marine House ....⑫
Pearl Court ....⑬
Wellington Park ....⑭
Windermere House ....⑮

PUBS

Crown Liquor Saloon .....①
Empire (The) ....②
Front Page (The) ....③
Hunters ....④
Kelly's Cellar ....⑤
Lavery's ....⑥
Madden's ....⑦
Manhattan (The) ....⑧
Morning Star (The) ....⑨
Pats Bar ....⑩
Robinson's ....⑪
Rotterdam ....⑫
Whites Tavern ....⑬

BELFAST
Centre

0   175   350 m

485

Levels I and II trace the evolution of Ireland from prehistory to the present. Items include the skeleton of an Ice Age **giant reindeer** and, above all, the **Spanish Armada treasure★★**, a collection of gold and silver coins as well as of precious stones and jewellery, including a magnificent golden **salamander★** encrusted with rubies. This booty was recovered by divers from the wrecks of Spanish galleons sunk along the Irish coast.

The ground floor deals with the evolution of science and technology. Occupying pride of place is an enormous stationary **steam engine**.

The city centre★
Allow half a day

Along Great Victoria Street (B2-B3)

Opposite the bus station is the famous **Crown Liquor Saloon★**, which began life as a station buffet. Its incredible all-over decoration owes something to Hindu temples and Moorish palaces as well as to Gothic cathedrals.

A right turn on leaving the pub soon leads to a point opposite the **Grand Opera**, an over-the-top example of Victorian architectural exuberance which looks like nothing so much as a huge wedding cake with lashings of cream. Seriously damaged by bomb blasts in 1991 and 1993, it has now been meticulously restored at great expense.

On the corner of Howard Street, on the right, is **Church House**. This strange building in Renaissance style was once the headquarters of the Presbyterian Church in Ireland, but now houses a shopping arcade, **Spires Mall**.

Around Donegall Square (B2)

Howard Street leads into this spacious square with its lawns and formal gardens. There is a statue of Queen Victoria, and, in Donegall Square East, a **Titanic memorial** commemorating those who perished when the huge Belfast-built liner went down.

In the centre of the square rises the impressive bulk of **City Hall★** (*guided tours June-September: 10.30am, 11.30am, 2.30pm weekdays; 2.30pm Saturday; October-May: 2.30pm except Sunday. Free admission*). Construction of the great building was begun in 1898 and completed in 1906. It is in neo-Classical style, with a number of Rococo touches. The copper dome, supported on columns, recalls the Capitol in Washington DC. The décor of the pompous and grandiloquent interior evokes the history of Belfast. An especially noteworthy item, in the Reception Hall, is the original charter granted to Belfast by James I in 1613.

Opposite City Hall, Donegall Square North has been pedestrianised. To either side of Donegall Place are fine old buildings, among them, on the right, a corner edifice which was once a linen warehouse, a splendid 19C structure in pink sandstone with sculptural decoration.

To the left is the **Linen Hall Library**, founded in 1788, the city's oldest public library, worth looking into for its old-fashioned charm and studious atmosphere, very much in contrast to its busy city centre surroundings.

Donegall Place, the continuation of Royal Avenue, is a fairly ordinary pedestrian street lined with shops and banks and leading to the city's tourist information centre. The Tesco supermarket, opposite the Castle Place Post Office occupies what used to be a bank, whose exuberant neo-Gothic character has been well preserved.

In Donegall Street, beyond the tourist information centre, stands the city's Anglican **St Anne's Cathedral★** (B1) (*9am-5pm except during services; donation welcome*), begun in 1899 in Irish Romanesque style on the site of a church dedicated to St Anne built by the Marquess of Donegall in 1776. After a construction history dogged by unstable

Belfast City Hall

subsoil as much as by the hazards of history and problems of finance, the building was only finally completed in 1981, which explains the variety of architectural styles encountered in it.

The sober interior has a **military chapel**, as well as an **ecumenical chapel** dedicated to the reconciliation of the various Christian traditions. The capitals of the south transept and the nave evoke an extraordinary range of subjects, among them temperance, theology, femininity, ship-building, wisdom, art and free-masonry.

The cathedral is the resting-place of Lord Edward Carson (1854-1935), the Dublin-born politician who led Protestant opposition to the Third Home Rule Bill in the years preceding the First World War.

Along the Lagan (C1-C2)

The **Lagan Lookout Centre**★ (April-September: 11am-5pm; Saturday 12pm-5pm; Sunday 2pm-5pm; October-March 11am-3.30pm; Saturday 1pm-4.30pm; Sunday 2pm-4.30pm. Admission charge) by the Custom House at the end of the bridge is an old observation post with fascinating displays on Belfast's maritime past. The city's role as a port has been intimately linked with the River Lagan, whose tides are regulated by the **Lagan Weir**, a modern barrage with a walkway on top.

For several years, the area around the Lagan has been the subject of an ambitious regeneration project, and has become a huge building site criss-crossed by major roads, hardly a particularly inviting environment for a quiet stroll. The first fruit of the scheme can be seen in the shape of the **Waterfront Hall**, a vast circular structure in glass in postmodern style intended as a concert venue and conference centre (see "Making the most of Belfast").

Standing amid the confusion of construction sites and the din of traffic are the old **Custom House** and the **Albert Memorial Clock**, dusty relics of another age altogether. Because of subsidence, the 35m-high clock tower tilts slightly, and now has something of the appearance of Big Ben crossed with the Leaning Tower of Pisa.

Anyone wanting to explore this area more thoroughly should make a detour along Waring Street, the continuation of Albert Square, and look into the **Ulster Bank**, a fine example of a prestige building in an exuberant variant of Rococo style. Another unusual building is the **Sinclair Seamen's Church**★ (Sunday 11am-1pm / 6.30pm-8.30pm; 2pm-5pm Wednesday March-October). As its name implies, the church was intended for mariners of all kinds, and its fascinating decoration is entirely inspired by the sea and ships. The poor-boxes, for example, are boat-shaped.

The area around Belfast

Cave Hill Country Park

6.5km north of Belfast via the A6 or M2. Pierced by several caves, the great black cliff of basalt overlooking the city and Belfast Lough is nicknamed "Napoleon's hat" because of its prominent outline. A number of attractive footpaths lead to the summit of the hill, where in clear weather there are splendid **views**★★ over the city, the sea and as far as the Sperrin Mountains and the Mountains of Mourne. At the foot of the hill stands the late-19C **Belfast Castle**, splendidly sited among formal gardens. Once an aristocratic residence, it now houses a prestigious restaurant, though visitors in a hurry may be more interested in the bar. The Cave Hill footpaths are also accessible from the car park at the **Belfast Zoological Gardens**★ (April-September: 10am-5pm; October-March: closed 3.30pm and 2.30 Friday. Admission charge). The zoo is a model of its kind, which shows off its exotic animals in a well-landscaped setting.

Carrickfergus Castle★★

15km north of Belfast via the M5 and A2, or by Ulsterbus service no 163 from Laganside Bus Centre. April-September: 10am-6pm; 2pm-6pm Sunday; closed 16 November-March. Admission charge.

Crown Liquor Saloon

The fishing boats and pleasure craft in the harbour of the pretty little town of Carrickfergus are overlooked by the great grey mass of Ireland's best-preserved Norman castle. Rising from a basalt outcrop protruding into the sea, this formidable stronghold was built at the end of the 12C by Jean de Courcy to control access to Belfast Lough. It was attacked on many an occasion by Scots and Irish, but always remained in the hands of the English. A tour of the castle reveals the vast extent and complexity of its defences. In the **keep**, a video presentation evokes the atmosphere of medieval festivals, while waxwork figures placed here and there give the otherwise austere interiors some semblance of life.

Ulster Folk and Transport Museum★★

At Cultra, near Holywood 13km east of Belfast via the A2 towards Bangor. The train from Belfast to Bangor stops at Cultra station, just by the Transport Museum. April-June and September: 9.30am-5pm; 10.30am-6pm Saturday; 2pm-6pm Sunday; July-August: 10.30am-6pm; 12pm-6pm Sunday; October-March: 9.30am-4pm; 12.30pm-4.30pm weekends. Admission charge. Allow half a day.

The vast park laid out around Cultra Manor is the home of two extremely well-thought-out museums, which together make up one of the most important visitor attractions in the whole of Ireland.

The **Transport Museum★★** consists of a series of galleries and sheds in which are gathered examples of more or less everything in Ireland which ever moved on one, two, three, four or more wheels since the early years of the Industrial Revolution. The collections have all the more appeal because of the emphasis laid on the social and human environment of the different means of locomotion and on their effect on Irish society. The reconstructions of a station booking-office and a country garage are compelling in their realism.

Belfast and around

Ups and downs of an Amphicar
The very first amphibious motor-car was designed in the Bugatti factory in France during the Second World War. Production was resumed in Germany in the 1960s, using Triumph engines. 2 800 examples were manufactured, most of them sold to buyers in America. The amphicar on show in the museum has a number of records to its credit, including the crossing from Scotland to Ballycastle on the Antrim coast and a journey across Belfast Lough from Carrickfergus to Bangor. But in the end the amphicar turned out to be neither a good car nor a good boat, and production stopped at the end of the 1960s, not least because of the unreliability of the engine.

The **Folk Museum**★★ consists of the **Folk Galleries**★ with thematic displays illustrating the evolution of Irish society, and **The Town**★★, a full-scale reconstruction of a traditional Irish village with churches, a school, shops, post office, etc. All the buildings were removed from their original site and rebuilt here stone by stone and brick by brick. Interiors have been recreated with striking accuracy, notably in the case of a thatched-roof cottage, where a peat fire burns in the grate and a grandfather clock ticks away the time of days gone by.

Lisburn and around
14km southwest of Belfast via the M1

Now part of the continuous built-up area of Greater Belfast, this town of 40 000 inhabitants was once the world capital of linen manufacture, made from the flax grown in the surrounding countryside. The spinning begun here in 1698 under the direction of Louis Crommelin, a French Huguenot, brought prosperity to Ulster for more than three hundred years and helped this part of Ireland escape the consequences of the great famines of the 19C.

Irish Linen Centre★★
In the town centre, 9.30am-5pm; closed Sunday (except April-September: 2pm-5pm). Admission charge.
This excellent museum occupies the old **Linen Hall** to which workers brought the cloth woven in their homes. The fascinating displays illustrate the history of linen manufacture from Ancient Egypt to the present, with full explanations of the various processes which turn flax into cloth. Former mill employees give demonstrations of spinning, weaving and use of a Jaquard loom to produce elaborate designs, and there are reconstructions of a number of interiors including a weaver's cottage and a mill.

Hilden Brewery
Signposted on the right on the way out of Lisburn towards Belfast. 10am-5pm; closed Sunday and Monday, brewery tours at 11.30am and 2.30pm. Free admission.
The thirst brought on by watching weavers at work can be slaked at this brewery, one of the last real-ale establishments in Ireland. All the brewer's secrets are revealed during the tour, at the end of which there is a tasting of the brewery's products as well as the possibility of a meal in the pleasant restaurant.

The Lagan towpath
4-5hr walk from Hilden. The Linen Centre has pamphlets describing the various stages of this path which runs for about 15km.

The Lambeg drum
The pretty village of Lambeg has a church and a suspension bridge, but the place is more famous for the drum which bears its name. William III's army brought huge and terrifyingly loud drums with them from Holland to help intimidate their enemies. The brightly painted drums, almost as large as the drummers carrying them, feature prominently in today's Orange parades, their deep beat keeping marchers in step and announcing the approach of the parade from far away.

If there is time to spare, this is an interesting walk laid out along the banks of the Lagan. Linking Lisburn and Belfast, the pathway takes walkers through **Belvoir Park Forest** and the picturesque villages of **Lambeg** and **Drumbeg**.

One and a half kilometres south of **Shaw's Bridge**, on the northern section of the path, is the **Giant's Ring★**, a vast stone circle of Neolithic date, in the centre of which stands a dolmen *(accessible by car from Lisburn via the B23 towards Newtownbreda)*.

Hillsborough★
Co Down – 4km south of Lisburn via the A1
From Belfast, take the n° 38 bus from the Europa Bus Centre

An enchanting village with Georgian houses lining its sloping main street, Hillsborough is worth visiting for its sense of the past, its attractive park and its fine restaurants. Its **International Oyster Festival** *(second week in September)* combines gastronomy with a varied programme of cultural events.

The town
Hillsborough's **tourist information centre** *(see "Making the most of Belfast and around")* is housed in the old linen market building, which was turned into a courtroom in the 19C. It contains a fascinating exhibition *(free admission)* on law and justice. The harsh penalties imposed in the past are calculated to shock the modern visitor, among them the transportation to Australia of a 14-year old for the theft of a couple of bottles of beer, or the wearing of a scold's bridle for a woman given to too much gossip.

Beyond the courthouse rises **Hillsborough Castle★**, a fine neo-Classical red-brick edifice from the late 18C with imposing wrought-iron gateways. Between 1924 and 1973 the castle was the official residence of the Governor of Northern Ireland and is now occupied by administrative offices and used for official functions.

At the bottom of the main street, a majestic avenue leads towards the imposing **St Malachy's Church**, a harmonious 18C structure dominated by its tall spire.

To the right of the church, a drive leads to **Hillsborough Fort★** *(April-September: 10am-7pm; 2pm-7pm Sunday; remainder of year: 10am-4pm; closed Sunday. Free admission)*. One hectare in extent, the square-shaped stronghold was built at the beginning of the 17C by Colonel Arthur Hill, hence the name Hillsborough. The fort was intended to control the route between Belfast and County Down. Later, in the Georgian era, the guardhouse was converted into a fanciful residence in Gothic style. The fort's sentry-walk gives views over the attractive parkland of **Hillsborough Forest**, with a lake and picnic area. It can be reached through a gap in the wall of the fort or along a footpath on the left on the way out of Hillsborough to the south.

Around Lough Neagh
Co Antrim, Armagh, Tyrone and Londonderry

Vast (400sqkm) but shallow (12-15m), the largest lake in the British Isles is a major nature reserve, well-preserved since most of its banks are inaccessible. It is of the first importance for migratory birds, which from September to January are attracted by its fish-rich waters. The lough is famous for its pike, carp, bream and above all, eels.

For the time being, the only boat trips are aboard the *Master McGra* from **Kinnego Marina** at Oxford Island on the southern shore of the lake *(April-October according to weather conditions. Contact Paddy Prunty, ☎ 028 3832 7573 or mobile: 0374 811 248)*.

Oxford Island
37km west of Belfast via the M1. Leave the motorway at Junction 10 and follow signs. This peninsula is the only place around the lough where there is woodland, and is the best, in fact almost the only point where there is access to the waterside. The **Lough Neagh Discovery Centre** *(April-September: 10am-7pm; October-March: 10am-5pm*

Eels in abundance

Archaeological evidence proves that eels have been fished in Lough Neagh for 4 000 years. The elvers are born in the Sargasso Sea, then swim north, turning into the River Bann at its mouth at Coleraine and making their way upstream to the lough. Those that avoid being caught live in the lake for between 12 and 14 years before returning to their birthplace to breed and die. Few local people eat eel, smoked or unsmoked, and the catch is exported almost in its entirety. However, eel can be bought from the co-operative eel fishery at Toome on the north shore of the lake *(see "Making the most of the area around Belfast").*

Wednesday-Sunday only. Admission charge) has hi-tech interactive displays explaining the ecology of the lake and its surroundings. There is also a 6C oak **dugout** which was recovered from the bed of the lough. Visitors can enjoy more direct experience of nature by walking some of the 7km of **footpaths** laid out around the peninsula, among the reedbeds, alder and poplar groves. A number of hides offer the chance of observing ducks, geese and swans, particularly interesting at migration time.

Peatlands Park★

At Maghery, 17km west of Oxford Island via the M1. Leave the motorway at Junction 13 and follow signs. 9am-dusk all year. Admission free, charge for train ride.

The park consists of 250 hectares of woodland and peat bogs. A visit here is a good way to get to know about the importance of the Irish boglands, the cutting of peat and its use as a fuel. A **narrow-gauge railway** once used for peat extraction takes visitors around the park and its unusual landscapes.

Ardboe Cross★

17km east of Cookstown via the B73 (see page 451). This is one of the most evocative spots around Lough Neagh. Close to a romantic old cemetery, the high cross rises over the site where an abbey once stood. It is one of the finest such crosses in the whole of Ireland, carved with Biblical scenes on both faces. A walk to the point of the promontory gives a superb **view★** over the lough with, in the distance, the outline of the Sperrin Mountains to the north and the Mountains of Mourne to the south.

Belfast and the South

Making the most of Belfast

COMING AND GOING

By plane – Belfast International Airport (from A1), 31km west of the city, ☎ 028 9442 2888, has flights to cities in Britain and to a limited number of destinations in Europe and North America. Shuttle bus from the airport to the Europa Bus Centre.

Belfast City Airport (from C2), Sydenham, 5km east of the city centre, ☎ 028 9045 7745, has flights to Dublin and a number of airports in Britain. Access by Belfast-Bangor trains.

By train – Visitors are warned that stations have no left-luggage facilities. **General information**, ☎ 028 9089 9411.

Belfast Central Station, Eastbridge Street (C2). Trains to Bangor and Larne. Bangor (30min): services every 30min, less frequently Sunday; these trains call at the Folk and Transport Museum. Larne (50min): 16 services daily, 6 Sunday; Larne trains stop at Carrickfergus. **Great Victoria Street Station** (B2). Trains to Londonderry, Dublin and Portadown.

Derry (2hr20min): 6 trains daily via Lisburn and Coleraine, 5 Saturday, 3 Sunday.

Dublin Connolly Station (1hr50min and 2hr): 8 trains daily, 5 Sunday via Portadown and Dundalk.

By bus – Europa Bus Centre, Great Victoria Street (B2). Buses to destinations in Co Armagh, Tyrone, Londonderry, Fermanagh, West Down and the Republic.

Laganside Bus Centre, Oxford Street (C2), close to the Albert Memorial Clock. Buses to Co Antrim, East Down and the Cookstown area. **Ulsterbus Information**, ☎ 028 9033 3000.

By boat – To Stranraer: **Seacat** catamaran, Donegall Quay, ☎ 0345 523 523, or **Stena Line** ferry, Ballast Quay, ☎ 028 9074 7747. To the Isle of Man: **Steam Packet Co**, Donegall Quay, ☎ 028 9035 1009. To Liverpool: **Norse Irish Ferries**, West Bank Road, ☎ 028 9077 9090.

GETTING AROUND

Belfast may give itself the airs and graces of a big city, but distances are never very great and it is easy to find your way around. It is best to get around on foot and with occasional use of local buses. Bringing a car into town can lead to all sorts of difficulties; places to park are few and far between and none are free, and police and traffic wardens are quite pitiless. If you must bring your vehicle into the city centre, you should leave it in a car park as soon as possible.

By bus – Ulsterbus information, ☎ 028 9033 3000. Service nos 69, 70 and 71 for the Ulster Museum and Botanic Gardens and Queen's University. Services 45 to 51 all go to Belfast Zoo and Cave Hill. Services nos 1 and 2 from Laganside Bus Centre for the Folk and Transport Museum. **Nightline** night-time services (B3) leave from Shaftesbury Square to the suburbs until 2am.

By taxi – There is a distinction between ordinary taxis and the black, London-style cabs which travel to and from the outlying Protestant and Catholic districts. The main taxi rank is in Donegall Square, or taxis can be ordered by phone from **City Cab**, ☎ 028 9024 2000.

Car hire – Budget, 96-102 Great Victoria Street (B3). Minimum age 23.

Bicycle hire – Recycle, 1-5 Albert Square (C1), ☎ 028 9031 3113. Open normal hours Monday-Saturday.

ADDRESS BOOK

Tourist information – Northern Ireland Tourist Board, St Anne's Court, 59 North Street (B1), ☎ 028 9023 1221, September-June: 9.30am-5.15pm Monday, 9am-5.15pm Tuesday-Saturday; July-August: 9am-7pm, 12pm-4pm Sunday. Also **Belfast Welcome Centre**, 47 Donegall Square ☎ 028 9024 6609, with full documentation on Northern Ireland in general and Belfast in particular, bureau de change, hotel booking and souvenir shop.

Other tourist information centres at both airports.

Bord Fáilte, the tourist information service of the Republic of Ireland, is at 53 Castle Street near Donegall Square (B2), ☎ 028 9032 7888. Open 9am-5pm Monday-Friday and 9am-12.30pm Saturday March-September. Useful range of information, some publications for sale only.

Banks / Currency exchange – Numerous banks with cash machines in the city centre. Bureau de change at the **Tourist Board** and the **General Post Office**, Shaftesbury Square.

Post Office – The city centre Post Office is on Castle Square (B2). 9am-5.30pm, 9am-7pm Saturday; closed Sunday. Another main Post Office on Shaftesbury Square in the Queen's University area. 9am-5.30pm, 8.45am-Monday; 9am-12.30pm Saturday.

Emergencies – ☎ 999.

Medical service – The most centrally-located hospital is **Shaftesbury Square Hospital** (B3), ☎ 028 9032 9808.

WHERE TO STAY

Under £10

😊 **Belfast International Youth Hostel**, 22-32 Donegall Road, next to Shaftesbury Square, ☎ 028 9031 5435, Fax 028 9043 9699 – 124 beds ✗ Easily the best place to stay for budget travellers. Some double rooms and dormitories with 4-6 beds, all very well-kept. No cooking, but good value for money in the hostel cafeteria. Exchange office, tourist information, organised trips to the Giant's Causeway and around Belfast. Close to the Sandy Row Protestant district and thus handy for anyone interested in murals.

Arnie's Hostel, 63 Fitzwilliam Street, ☎ 028 9024 2867 – 22 beds. Small private hostel open to all, with four 4-bed dormitories and one 6-bed. Comfort not outstanding but very central and not expensive for Belfast.

The Ark, 18 University Street, ☎ 028 9032 9626 – 30 beds. Similar to the above, but marginally inferior in terms of cleanliness and comfort. For emergency use only.

Between £30-40

Windermere House, 60 Wellington Place, ☎ 028 9066 2693 / 9066 5165 – 11rm TV Bright rooms, quiet and well-kept, but not outstanding otherwise apart from the below-average price.

Eglantine Guest House, 27 Eglantine Avenue, ☎ 028 9066 7585 – 7rm TV Small B&B with friendly reception and reasonable rates. Bathrooms with bathtubs on landing.

Between £40-50

Avenue House, 23 Eglantine Avenue, ☎ 028 9066 5904, Fax 028 9029 1810 – 6rm ⌚ ✐ TV Modern guesthouse conversion with spacious and comfortable rooms with good facilities.

😊 **Camera House**, 44 Wellington Park, ☎ 028 9066 0026, Fax 028 9066 7856 – 13rm TV CC Attractive and very well kept rooms in a Victorian house. Breakfast served in the conservatory at the rear of the building.

Helga B&B, 7 Cromwell Road, ☎ 028 9032 4820, Fax 028 9032 0653 – 31rm TV CC Attractive outside appearance, but level of comfort leaves something to be desired. Useful when all else fails. 5% surcharge for payment by credit card.

😊 **The George Guest House**, 9 Eglantine Avenue, ☎ 028 9068 3212 – 6rm ⌚ One of the best places to stay on this street. Most rooms have their own, small bathroom, and are attractively decorated. Friendly reception and good breakfast.

Marine House, 30 Eglantine Avenue, ☎ / Fax 028 9066 2828 / 9038 1922 – 11rm ⌚ TV For emergency use. Huge brick edifice from around 1900. Six rooms have their own facilities, but the overall level of comfort is far from outstanding.

Pearl Court, 11 Malone Road, ☎ 028 9066 6145, Fax 028 9020 0212 – 10rm ⌚ 1900 building with pretty garden. Six of the rooms have their own bathroom. Fairly basic.

Between £50-60

Jurys Inn, Fisherwick Place, Great Victoria Street, ☎ 028 9053 3500, Fax 028 9053 3511 – 190rm ⌚ ✐ TV ✗ CC Vast modern hotel in an excellent location, but otherwise its only advantage is that rates are calculated by room rather than number of occupants.

Between £70-80

Ash Rowan Guest House, 12 Windsor Avenue, ☎ 028 9066 1758, Fax 028 9066 3227 – 5rm 📶 🖉 TV CC
Little seems to have changed in this establishment since Victorian times. Full of antiques and bric-a-brac, its luxurious rooms have been decorated with great care and are all different from one another. Breakfast is one of the most sumptuous to be had in Belfast.

Between £80-100

Wellington Park Hotel, 21 Malone Road, ☎ 028 9038 1111, Fax 028 9066 5410 – 75rm 📶 🖉 TV ✕ CC
Prestigious but charmless modern hotel although well located in the Queen's University area.

The Crescent Town House, 13 Lower Crescent, ☎ 028 9032 3349, Fax 028 9032 0646 – 11rm 📶 🖉 TV ✕ CC
Excellent location in a restored historic building in the heart of the Golden Mile. Luxurious but rather impersonal rooms.

EATING OUT

• **Queen's University area**

Under £10

Connor Café Bar, 11a Stranmillis Road (B4), ☎ 028 9066 3266. Open 9am-11pm. Pleasant and restful café-restaurant in what was once an artist's studio. Solid fare in the form of all-day Irish breakfasts or excellent open sandwiches.

Jaca Mellis, 3-5 Malone Road (B4), ☎ 028 9068 2005. Open 9am-5pm; closed weekend. Pretty little café in a good location in a Georgian house. A good place for a quick salad or a baked potato with a variety of fillings. No drinks licence.

Café Clementine, 245 Lisburn Road (A4), ☎ 028 9038 2211. Open 9.30am-4.30pm Sunday-Tuesday, 9.30am-10.30pm Wednesday-Saturday. This strikingly individual place with its yellow walls and brightly coloured tablecloths has value-for-money food, including copious salads, sweet or savoury flans, and a good range of desserts. No drinks licence.

International Youth Hostel cafeteria (see "Where to stay"), ☎ 028 9032 3349.

Botanic Inn, 23 Malone Road (A4), ☎ 028 9066 0460. Open 12pm-3pm, 12.30pm-2pm Sunday. Very popular with students from Queen's. Lively atmosphere guaranteed, with good plain cuisine at reasonable prices and an interesting selection of *tapas* in the evening (4pm-11pm except Sunday).

• **Golden Mile** (B3)

Under £15

Metro Brasserie, the restaurant of the Crescent Town House (see "Where to stay"). Open 12pm-3pm / 6pm-9.30pm weekdays (-10pm Friday and Saturday); *tapas* Sunday between 12pm-5pm. One of the best places to eat in Belfast, with modern, tasteful décor. A taste of the leek and potato soup with lardons and a smidgeon of lavender or cod steak and fresh tomatoes on a bed of new potatoes will convince any gourmand of the prodigious inventiveness of the new Irish cuisine.

Benedicts, 7-21 Bradbury Place, ☎ 028 9059 1999. Open 12pm-11pm, with variable menu. In the heart of the Golden Mile, this huge establishment with its Gothic-cum-Baroque architecture has equally improbable offerings ranging from confit of goose with ginger to chicken with pineapple and red mullet and mango in crème de chorizo.

La Belle Epoque, 61 Dublin Road, ☎ 028 9032 3244. Open 12pm-11pm, from 6pm Saturday; closed Sunday. Talented re-creation of Parisian brasserie décor and cuisine. A fine example of Irish openness to the world and ability to reinterpret traditional food in contemporary terms. Good value for money. Excellent wine list.

Roscoff, 7 Leslie House, Shaftesbury Square, ☎ 028 9033 1532. Closed Saturday midday and Sunday. With its sober, modern décor, this is one of Belfast's most reputable restaurants, serving fresh, delicate international cuisine with an Italian or Oriental flavour.

• **City centre** (B2)

Under £10

Flannigan's Eaterie, 19 Amelia Street (above the Crown Liquor Saloon). Open 12pm-9pm; 12.30pm-7pm Sunday. Despite the raucous disco music,

Making the most of Belfast

this is a good place to sample a real Irish stew or a beef and Guinness pie and other Irish specialities.

Bewleys Oriental Café, Donegall Arcade, ☎ 028 9023 4955. Open 8am-5.30pm Monday-Saturday; -8.30pm Thursday. A branch of the famous Dublin establishment with coffee as good as its cakes and pastries and freshly made open sandwiches.

Marshall's Café, 11 Donegall Square West. Open 7.15am-5.15pm. Its appearance notwithstanding, this well-located snack bar has an impressive choice of sandwiches, cakes and salads, enough to satisfy most appetites for a mere £3-£4.

YMCA Coffee Shop, 12 Wellington Square. Open 10am-3.30pm (9am-2.30pm Monday); closed weekends. Small, quiet and inexpensive cafeteria, ideal for a quick bite, with flans, quiches and salads.

Roscoff Café, Fountain Street or Arthur Street. Open 7.30am-5.30pm, -9pm Monday-Wednesday and Saturday, -8.30pm Friday. These are offshoots of the famous Roscoff Restaurant, offering a copious breakfast as well as a good range of sandwiches, salads and dishes of the day, all of excellent quality.

Alto's, 6 Fountain Street, ☎ 028 9032 3087. Open 10am-5pm Monday and Tuesday, -6pm Wednesday, 10am-10.30pm Thursday-Saturday. Tasty Italian cuisine at rates varying according to the time of day.

Queen's, 4 Queen's Arcade. Open 12pm-6pm (-8pm Thursday); closed Sunday. Very popular with city centre office workers at lunchtime, this pub in a turn-of-the-century shopping arcade has a good reputation for its fine home cooking.

Between £10-15

Café Society, 3 Donegall Square East, ☎ 028 9043 9525. Open 7.30am-11am/12pm-9pm; closed Sunday. Restaurant: 12pm-3pm Monday-Friday, 6pm-10pm Wednesday-Saturday. Housed in a fine red sandstone structure in neo-Gothic style, this recently opened restaurant makes every effort to serve fine food. But it is a little on the expensive side, especially in the evening.

Between £15-20

Downstairs at Deane's, 38-40 Howard Street, ☎ 028 9056 0000. Open 12pm-3pm / 5pm-11pm; closed Sunday. The standard of food in this rather starchy establishment is equivalent to that served in the city's most famous restaurant, which occupies the upper floor of the building and to which it belongs. The menu features a whole array of flavours from around the world, and there is an excellent wine list.

HAVING A DRINK

One way of getting to know a few of Belfast's watering holes in a short time is to go on the **Historical Pub Tour**. This guided tour departs from **Flanagan's** restaurant above the **Crown Liquor Saloon**, ☎ 028 9068 1278, at 4pm on Saturday between April and the end of September, with additional tours at 5.30pm on Friday between May and September and 7pm on Tuesday in June and August. Price: £5, drinks not included.

• Queen's University area

The Empire, Bradbury Place. Now a pub and disco, this old church is one of the coolest places in town, with live rock in the bar in the evening from Wednesday to Sunday, and all kinds of other sounds on the upper floors, which are haunted by a ghost called Abraham. There may be a charge for admission.

The Manhattan, 23-31 Bradbury Place, is one of the city's newest and trendiest hang-outs. People come here for the sport-themed bar, where matches are shown on a big screen, or for the night-club, the **Mclub**, open 9pm-1.30am Wednesday-Saturday.

Hunters, 149 Lisburn Road, is a classic pub with a mixed clientele including students, Good pub grub at midday and DJ evenings Thursday-Saturday.

Lavery's, Bradbury Place, is one of the liveliest places in this area, with a traditional pub and two upstairs discotheques every evening.

• City centre

Kelly's Cellar, Bank Street, to the rear of Tesco, ☎ 028 9032 4835. Down the end of an alleyway in the heart of the business district, this quintessential Belfast tavern has valiantly held out against the city's growing modernisation and Americanisation. It is as if a preservation order had been put on its cracked concrete floor, its tobacco-stained ceiling, and the ruddy features of its vociferous regulars. Traditional music Friday and Saturday, restaurant on the upper floor.

Crown Liquor Saloon, 46 Great Victoria Street, ☎ 028 9024 9476. A city institution, protected as a historical monument, an outstanding example of a florid High Victorian pub in mixed Italian and Oriental style. It has its own beer, Belfast Crown, with a characteristic well-hopped taste. Traditional music Tuesday, Thursday and Saturday evening, and pub grub Monday-Saturday from midday.

Robinson's, next door to the above, and also worth a detour for its Victorian bar and especially for its back room with its country grocery décor, the venue for musical sessions every evening (folk and traditional).

The Morning Star, 17 Pottinger Entry, between High Street and Ann Street, ☎ 028 9023 2976. A rarity in the business district, an old-fashioned pub with splendid Victorian panelling and décor.

White's Tavern, Winecellar Entry, ☎ 028 9024 3080. A city centre institution with venerable exposed beams, probably the oldest pub in town. People come here for good pub grub and for evening sessions of traditional and folk music.

Madden's, Berry Street, ☎ 028 9024 4114. This is one of the most characterful pubs in the city centre, with a cheerful atmosphere and musical instruments hung all over the place. Good traditional music Friday and Saturday evening.

The Front Page, 108 Donegall Street, ☎ 028 9032 4924. Specimens of the front pages of newspapers dominate the décor of this establishment, a good place to eat at lunch-time or to listen to music until late most evenings.

• **Waterfront area**

Rotterdam, 54 Pilot Street, close to Clarendon Dock, ☎ 028 9074 6021.

Tucked away some distance from the centre, this pub is a haven of tranquillity during the day, when a peat fire burns away within its whitewashed walls. It is a different story in the evening and at weekends, when it becomes one of the liveliest places in town because of its proximity to the concert area recently laid out in nearby Clarendon Park. Blues and salsa Friday and Saturday, and Irish traditional Sunday and Tuesday.

Pats Bar, 19-22 Prince's Dock, right next door to the above, also has music on Friday and Saturday evening amid a striking décor of antique weaponry.

OTHER THINGS TO DO

Cinema – Virgin Cinemas, 14 Dublin Road (B3), Belfast's biggest multiplex, shows all the latest blockbusters. Discriminating film-goers may find things more to their liking at **Queen's Film Theatre**, in a passageway giving onto Botanic Avenue, which screens avant-garde and foreign productions.

Concerts – The **Grand Opera House** (B2) (see page 486) not only stages opera but also dance, drama and classical concerts. Information and reservations opposite, 8.30am-8pm Monday-Wednesday, -8.30pm Thursday, -6.30pm Friday and -5.30pm Saturday. ☎ 028 9024 1919.

Waterfront Hall (C2), the city's big new concert and congress hall (see page 488) has a varied programme of performances and concerts of all kinds.

SHOPPING

Belfast is far from being an ideal shopping city, at least as far as tourists are concerned. Clothes are marginally more expensive than elsewhere, and the brands are no different from anywhere else. There is virtually nothing in the way of crafts, and things like linen and crystal are expensive. Salmon and whiskey are no cheaper than elsewhere.

Traditional jewellery – Catherine Shaw, 25-27 Queen's Arcade (B2), ☎ 028 9032 6053, is a good place for excellent recreations of traditional Celtic jewellery.

Making the most of Belfast

Making the most of the area around Belfast

ADDRESS BOOK

Tourist information – *Lisburn Tourist Information Centre*, Market Square, ☎ 028 9266 3377, April-September: 9.30am-5.30pm; 2pm-5.30pm Sunday, closes 30mins earlier rest of the year. In the same building as the Irish Linen Centre. Souvenir shop. ***Hillsborough Tourist Information***, The Square, ☎ 028 9268 9717. 9am-5.30pm, open Sunday only July-August, 2pm-6pm.

WHERE TO STAY

• Near Belfast Zoological Gardens
Under £10
Jordanstown Lough Shore Park, Shore Road, Newtownabbey, ☎ 028 9086 8751. 8km north of Belfast via the A2. Pleasant camp site overlooking Belfast Lough in a woodland setting, mostly for caravans but with some pitches for tents.

• Near the Ulster Folk and Transport Museum
Between £55-60
🏨 ***Beech Hill***, 23 Ballymoney Road, Craigantlet, ☎ 028 9042 5892 – 2rm 🛏 ✒ 📺 🆑 On the Bangor road, 2.5km from the museum, turn right towards Craigantlet and continue for a further 3km. A charming Georgian house in the middle of the countryside with very comfortable rooms furnished in Victorian style.

EATING OUT

• Hillsborough
Between £10-15
🍴 ***The Plough Inn***, The Square, ☎ 028 9268 2985. Open 12.30pm-2.30pm / 5pm-9.30pm. Inventive, refined cuisine in the rustic setting of a traditional pub. Very reasonable prices at lunch-time, more expensive in the evening.

The Grand Opera House, Belfast

Consortium Photographers/DIAF

Belfast and the south

The Hillside, 21 Main Street, ☎ 028 9268 2765. Daily 12pm-2.30pm/ 5pm-9pm. This well-reputed restaurant offers excellent pub grub in the modern Refectory at lunch-time. In the evening, the elegant, country-style dining room on the upper floor has a variety of internationally-flavoured dishes based on fresh local ingredients.

OTHER THINGS TO DO

Golf – There are a dozen or so golf courses in the immediate surroundings of Belfast. Most are sited close to the Lagan or Belfast Lough, and most are quite expensive. The most affordable is the **Mount Ober Golf Club**, ☎ 028 9079 5666. 18 holes, about 6km southeast of the city on the banks of the Lagan. Green fee: £11 weekdays. Members only Saturday.

Carrickfergus Golf Club, 35 North Road, Carrickfergus, ☎ 028 9336 3713. A fine 18-hole course overlooking Belfast Lough, members only Thursday, Saturday and Sunday. Green fee: £14.

Riding – **Burn Equestrian Club**, Knockbracken Health Care Park, Sainfield Road, ☎ 028 9040 2384. 9km to the south of Belfast via the A24, classic riding centre open all year round.

Fishing – Fishing in Lough Neagh is difficult without one's own boat. But the rivers running into the lake are popular for fly-fishing from mid-July onwards because of the Dollaghan, a kind of trout unique to the region. For further information and permits apply to the **Fisheries Conservancy Board**, 1 Mahon Road, Portadown, ☎ 028 3833 4666, or to **Paddy Punty**, Craigavon Borough Council, Kinnego Marina, Oxford Island, ☎ 028 3832 7573.

SHOPPING

Smoked eels – The co-operative fishery at **Toome Bridge** at the northern end of Lough Neagh has smoked eels for sale at around £10 per kilo, 9am-5pm (-4pm Friday); closed weekends.

ARDS PENINSULA ★★
STRANGFORD LOUGH
Co Down
Michelin map 923 P / 4

Not to be missed
Doing the rounds of the pubs in Bangor.
A walk in the gardens of Mount Stewart.
The Exploris Aquarium at Portaferry.
The view from Scrabo Tower at Newtownards.

And remember...
The best place to stay in the area is Bangor,
where there is a good choice of things to do in the evening.

Less than an hour's drive from Belfast, the Ards Peninsula offers charming landscapes and lovely country houses. About 40km long and only 5 or 6km across, the peninsula runs north-south between the Irish Sea to the east and Strangford Lough to the west. The exposed east coast is wilder and consists of a succession of bays and little fishing ports. The more sheltered western coast faces the shallow lough, which is linked to the sea by a narrow channel through which exceptionally strong tides surge several times a day.

Although the area was subject to early colonisation by the Vikings, no traces remain of this era. By contrast, links with Britain are prominent, not least in the shape of the Union flag fluttering over most of the villages.

The area's main attraction is the splendid country house and estate of Mount Stewart, which brings in visitors in large numbers. But everywhere the lovely landscapes of the Ards peninsula invite exploration; one of the best ways of getting to know them is by bike.

A tour of the peninsula
90km starting from Bangor – Allow half a day

■ **Bangor** – Every day many of the inhabitants of seaside Bangor (pop 50 000) quit the town and travel 20km to work in Belfast, either along the dual carriageway or aboard one of the frequent commuter trains.

There are few traces of Bangor's important religious past to be seen today. Founded in the 6C, it was a major monastic centre before being pillaged by the Vikings. In the 17C, Scottish settlers founded today's town, developing its harbour and textile industry. While there may be little of historic interest here today, Bangor is nevertheless an attractive and busy resort town, with a marina, the sandy beach of **Ballyholme**, and grand old Victorian residences stacked side by side on the slopes overlooking the sea. The town is full of friendly pubs and delightful bed and breakfast establishments, making it a good place to stay when exploring the Ards Peninsula.

Anyone with a little time to spare should look in at the **North Down Heritage Centre** (*10.30am-4.30pm; Sunday 2pm-4.30pm; closed Monday; July-August: closes 1hr later. Free admission*) to the south of the marina. Housed in part of what used to be Bangor's castle and is now the town hall, this little museum tells the story of Bangor from prehistoric times to the present, and also has a fine collection of items from the Far East.

■ **Donaghadee** – *10km southeast of Bangor via the A2.* The houses of this pretty little town nestle around its well-sheltered harbour, which until the mid-19C was the main port for traffic between Northern Ireland and Scotland. Overtaken by Larne

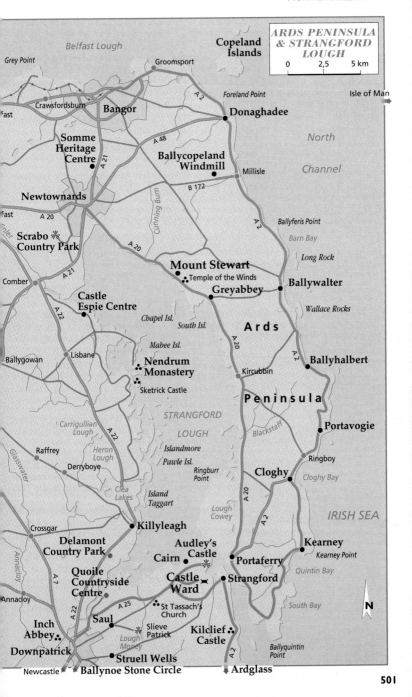

ARDS PENINSULA & STRANGFORD LOUGH

0   2,5   5 km

Belfast Lough

Grey Point

Copeland Islands

Groomsport

Foreland Point

Isle of Man

Crawfordsburn

Bangor

Donaghadee

North

'ast

Channel

A 48

Somme Heritage Centre

Ballycopeland Windmill

Millisle

Newtownards

B 172

Ballyferis Point

'ast   A 20

A 2

Barn Bay

Cunning Burn

Long Rock

Scrabo Country Park

A 20

Mount Stewart

Temple of the Winds

Ballywalter

Comber

A 21

Greyabbey

Wallace Rocks

Castle Espie Centre

Chapel Isl.

South Isl.

A r d s

Ballygowan

Lisbane

Mahee Isl.

Nendrum Monastery

Kircubbin

A 20

Ballyhalbert

A 2

Sketrick Castle

P e n i n s u l a

Carrigullian Lough

A 22

STRANGFORD

LOUGH

Blackstaff

Portavogie

Raffrey

Heron Lough

Islandmore

Ringboy

Derryboye

Pawle Isl.

Cloghy

Cloghy Bay

Ringburr Point

Clea Lakes

Island Taggart

Lough Cowey

A 20

IRISH SEA

Crossgar

Killyleagh

A 2

Kearney

Delamont Country Park

Audley's Castle

Cairn

Portaferry

Kearney Point

Quintin Bay

Quoile Countryside Centre

Castle Ward

Strangford

St Tassach's Church

A 25

South Bay

N

Inch Abbey

Saul

Slieve Patrick

Kilclief Castle

Downpatrick

Lough Money

Ballyquintin Point

Newcastle

Struell Wells

Ballynoe Stone Circle

Ardglass

(see page 472), Donaghadee is now used by numerous pleasure craft. The Norman **motte** dominating the town stands on the site of a Bronze Age fortification; in the 19C it was here that the explosives were stored which were used when the harbour was being improved and extended. The surrounding area has been laid out as public gardens. From the top of the motte there are fine views which on clear days extend as far as Scotland and the Isle of Man. The islands just off the coast are the **Copeland Islands**, the biggest of which no longer has a permanent population, only sheep and the summer residences of a fortunate few. **Lighthouse Island** is a bird sanctuary, and seals can sometimes be seen here too *(daily trips in July-August and on application May-October. Nelson's Boat, 146 Killaughy Road, ☎ 028 9188 3403)*.

Leave Donaghadee on the A2 towards Portaferry and continue as far as Millisle, then turn right on to the B172 and carry on for 1.5km.

■ **Ballycopeland Windmill** – *1 May-30 September: 10am-7pm; Sunday 2pm-7pm; closed Monday. Admission charge.* Dating from the 18C, this is the oldest **windmill** in Northern Ireland, its sails only ceasing to turn in 1915. Well-restored and in full working order, it is however not open to the public, unlike the **miller's house** with its little museum, where there is a fine model of the mill's machinery.

Go back to Millisle, then along the coast on the A2 towards Portaferry.

The coast road runs past a number of sandy beaches before reaching **Ballywalter**, a sleepy little port. **Ballywalter Park** consists of a group of Victorian buildings surrounded by fine gardens with a good collection of rhododendrons. The admission charge is a bit steep, but in summer visitors can stop here to buy strawberries (PYO possible too).

4km further on is the village of **Ballyhalbert**, with the remains of a Norman castle and church. Next comes the working port of **Portavogie**, where the fishing fleet specialising in crabs and herring, and where part of the catch is put on sale at the quayside.

The road runs alongside the fine sandy beach of **Cloghy**, near which there is a famous golf course *(see "Making the most of the Ards Peninsula")*. Further on is **Kearney**, a tiny fishing hamlet where the fishermen's cottages have been meticulously restored. Then the tip of the peninsula is crossed before reaching Portaferry.

■ **Portaferry** – *Ferry to Strangford every 30min 7.45am-10.45pm weekdays; 8.15am-11.15pm Saturday and 9.45am-10.45am Sunday. From Strangford to Portaferry every 30min 7.30am-10.30pm weekdays; 8am-11pm Saturday, 9.30am-10.30pm Sunday.*
This charming harbour town is where the ferry leaves to cross the mouth of Strangford Lough to the village of **Strangford** *(see page 511)* on the Co Down shore. The best view of Portaferry is in fact from Strangford; above the little town's brightly painted houses and Georgian residences rises the battlemented outline of the 16C **Portaferry Castle**.
Portaferry is a popular spot with visitors mainly because of the presence here of **Exploris★** *(March-August: 10am-6pm; Saturday 11am-6pm; Sunday 1pm-6pm; September-February: closed daily 5pm)*. This is an exceptionally fascinating aquarium and marine centre, with a variety of displays and interactive exhibits to help in the appreciation of the complex aquatic life of the Irish Sea and Strangford Lough, where marine life is adapted to the ebb and flow of massive tides measuring up to 400 million litres a day. The main attraction is the **Open Sea Tank**, where visitors can observe sea life from an underwater cave.

Drive 20km towards Bangor on the A20 along the eastern shore of Strangford Lough as far as Greyabbey.

■ **Greyabbey** – Known for its antique shops, the village owes its name to the **Cistercian abbey★** *(1 April-30 September: 10am-7pm; Sunday 2pm-7pm; closed Monday. Admission charge)* located on the road towards Ballywalter. The abbey was founded by Affreca, the wife of the Norman John de Courcy, and is the oldest example of Gothic building in Ireland. Most of its buildings were destroyed during the Reformation. Of the **abbey church**, there remain the **portal**, the **cloisters**, and the **chapter house**, all built in pink sandstone. The visitor centre has an interesting exhibition on monastic life and a **herb garden** has been laid out using the medicinal plants which would have been grown by the monks.

Return to the A20 and go 4.5km towards Bangor as far as Mount Stewart.

Bending the rule

The Cistercian rule as formulated by St Bernard envisaged a return to the former austerity of monastic life, but the inhabitants of Grey Abbey seem to have interpreted it fairly liberally. The medieval accounts of the abbey show that the monks were quite well-off, able to live comfortably from stock-raising and from their fisheries in Strangford Lough. Their meals were washed down with the beer they brewed themselves, and which sometimes also served to pay their employees in liquid form; an abbey servant might for example receive 80 litres of beer a week to sustain himself and his family.

■ **Mount Stewart***** *The estate comprises house, gardens, and the Temple of the Winds. House: April-October: 1pm-6pm weekends; May-September: 1pm-6pm (last admission 5pm); closed Monday. Gardens: March: Sunday only 2pm-5pm; April-end September: daily 11am-6pm; October: weekends 11am-6pm. Temple of the Winds: April-October: weekends 2pm-5pm. Admission charge.*

This splendidly aristocratic residence and the gardens around it make up one of Ireland's most popular visitor attractions. The estate owes its name to the Stewarts, one of the Scottish families who took part in the Plantation of Ulster in the 17C. Two centuries later, in 1816, a descendant was given the title of Marquess of Londonderry. The present house dates from this time, and is mainly the work of the London architect George Dance, another of whose achievements was the seduction of the Marquess's sister-in-law.

The **Temple of the Winds**** *(accessible on foot along an avenue to the right of the main entrance)* was part of an extensive landscaping scheme, most of which remained on the drawing board. It is based on the Temple of Aeolus in Athens and was intended as a pleasure pavilion and banqueting hall. Its elegant outline rises over a promontory in an idyllic spot opposite Strangford Lough. The inlaid wooden **floor*** is made from different kinds of bog-fir (petrified pine) retrieved from the peat deposits around the estate. In the basement, the dark and cramped **servants' quarters** give a good idea of the social contrasts prevailing at the time.

The **mansion***** consists of a main block flanked by two wings. Still lived in occasionally by its proprietors, it has numerous **family portraits**, fine **porcelain**, and English and Irish furniture of great sumptuousness. One of the ground-floor rooms is dedicated to **Lord Castelreagh**, son of the first Marquess of Londonderry. A prominent figure in British politics, he presided over the creation of the United Kingdom of Great Britain and Ireland in 1800 and, as Foreign Secretary, attended the Congress of Vienna in 1815. Some of the furniture here was used at the Congress, and a set of miniatures depicts a number of the chief delegates.

The **gardens**** were created from 1920 onwards by Edith, **Lady Londonderry**, wife of the 7th Marquess. They include trees and shrubs from all parts of the world, which flourish in the mild microclimate of Strangford Lough. There are avenues of yew, a profusion of sculpture, lakes and ponds, and a whole series of theme gardens, among them an Italian **garden**, a **Spanish garden**, a **Lily wood**, a **sunken garden**, and a **shamrock garden**. The **Dodo terrace** has sculptures of animals which recall the not always complimentary nicknames given by Lady Londonderry to members of her London set. The extraordinarily varied nature of the planting means that something is always in flower, making a visit here a pleasure at any time of the year between early Spring and late Autumn.

Continue on the A2 for 8km to Newtownards.

Ards Peninsula

Mount Stewart Gardens

■ Newtownards – This busy town is an important shopping centre with a splendid Georgian **town hall**, but is otherwise really only interesting from a practical point of view.

Anyone with an interest in the history of the First World War should visit the **Somme Heritage Centre**, 233 Bangor Road, 2km north of the town on the A21 (*October-March: Monday-Thursday 10am-4pm; April-June and September: Monday-Thursday 10am-4pm; weekends 12pm-4pm; closed Friday; July-August: closes 1hr later. Admission charge*). The Centre offers an audio-tour around its displays, which pay tribute to the fighting men from all over Ireland who took a prominent part in this bloodiest of battles and who were slaughtered in their thousands.

A less demanding way of spending time would be a visit to **Scrabo Country Park** (*free admission*), to the south of Newtownards towards Comber. Scrabo Hill is of volcanic origin, the black stone from its quarries having being used, among other purposes, for the construction of Mount Stewart. Rising from the summit is **Scrabo Tower**, also built of black lava. Completed in 1857, it commemorates the actions of the 3rd Marquess of Londonderry in bringing relief to the victims of the Great Famine. There is an exceptional **view★★** from the country park, extending over Strangford Lough and the Mourne Mountains to the south, and to Belfast far away to the north. There is a small **exhibition** (*June-September: 11am-6.30pm. Free admission*) in the tower devoted to the history of Strangford Lough and its natural environment.

Western shore of Strangford Lough

Wilder and less accessible than the eastern shore, this side of Strangford Lough has an archipelago of little islands rich in bird life.

Castle Espie Centre

4km southeast of Comber. The Visitor Centre is open May-end September: 10am-7pm; Sunday 2pm-7pm; closed Monday. Admission charge.

This **nature reserve** belonging to the Wildfowl and Wetlands Trust harbours migratory birds, and consists of lakes formed from old clay and limestone workings along the shore of the lough. The sanctuary is at its most interesting in autumn and winter, when birds pass through on their way south from the Arctic, but in summer the centre has plentiful displays on bird life in general and the phenomenon of migration in particular.

Drive east for 2km along a minor road which leads to a peninsula.

Belfast and the South

504

Nendrum Monastery

April-September: 10am-7pm; Sunday 2pm-7pm; closed Monday. Admission charge.

This early Christian site on the peninsula known as **Mahee Island** is connected to the mainland by a causeway. A monastery is supposed to have been founded here in the 7C by St Mochaio. Destroyed by the Vikings, it was succeeded in the 12C by a Benedictine convent. Excavations have revealed the outline of the early monastery and some of the monks' cells. The remains of a medieval **church** and a **round tower** enhance the romantic atmosphere of this peaceful spot.

The A22, 7km to the south, leads in 15km to Downpatrick (see page 508).

Making the most of the Ards Peninsula

COMING AND GOING

By train – Bangor station is in Abbey Street in the town centre. Trains leave for Belfast Central Station every 30min Monday-Saturday, less frequently Sunday. Journey time 30min.

By bus – The bus station is next to the railway station. Service n° 3 runs to Ballywalter via Millisle and Donaghadee 8 times daily Monday-Friday. Open-top bus to Ballywalter 4 times daily Tuesday-Saturday in July-August.

From the Laganside Bus Centre in Belfast, service n° 7 runs to Newtownards and Donaghadee 22 times daily Monday-Friday, slightly less frequently weekends. Services 9, 9A and 10 run to Portaferry via Portavogie, Ballyhalbert, Ballywalter, Greuabbey and Newtownards 14 times daily, and nos. 9 and 10 also stop at Mount Stewart.

USEFUL ADDRESSES

Tourist information – *Tower House*, Quay Street, Bangor, ☎ 028 9127 0069. January-May and October-December: 9am-5pm; Saturday 10am-4pm; closed Sunday; June and September: Saturday 10.30am-4.30pm, Sunday 12pm-5pm; July-August: 9am-7pm; Saturday 10am-7pm, Sunday 12pm-6pm. Ample information on the area as well as hotel bookings.

Tourist Information, 31 Regent Street, Newtownards, ☎ 028 9182 6846. July-August: 9am-5.15pm; Friday and Saturday 9am-5.30pm; Sunday 2pm-6pm; rest of year 9.15am-5pm; Saturday 9.30am-5pm; closed Sunday. Copious information on the Ards Peninsula and Strangford Lough.

The Stables, ☎ 028 9172 9882, Castle Street, Portaferry. Easter-September: 10am-5pm; Sunday 2pm-6pm; closes 5.30pm Monday-Saturday in July and August. Information on the Ards Peninsula and Strangford Lough.

Banks / Currency exchange – Cash machines in the centre of Bangor and Newtownards. Bureaux de change in the tourist offices at Bangor, Newtownards and Portaferry.

Post office – The Post Office in Bangor is at 143 Main Street. 9am-2.30pm; Saturday 9am-12.30pm; closed Sunday.

In Newtownards, the ***Post Office*** is in the Ards Shopping Centre. 9am-9pm Monday, Tuesday, Thursday, Friday, 9am-5.30pm Wednesday and Saturday. Post offices at Ballyhalbert, Ballywalter, Donaghadee, Greyabbey and Portaferry.

Making the most of the Ards Peninsula

Bicycle hire – Bangor: *Sampson's Cycles*, 70-71 Balloolink, ☎ 028 9146 2929, and *On Your Bike*, 128 High Street, ☎ 028 9127 0288.
Newtownards: for mountain bikes and touring machines, *Mike the Bike*, 53 Frances Street, ☎ 028 9181 1311.

WHERE TO STAY

• Bangor
Between £40-45
Hebron House, 59 Queen's Parade, near the harbour, ☎ 028 9146 3126, Fax 028 9127 4178 – 3rm ⌶ ℰ TV Warm welcome by the Maddock family in their Victorian home close to the sea front. Pleasant rooms. Evening meal available if booked in advance.
Tara Guest House, 51 Princetown Road, ☎ 028 9146 8924, Fax 028 9146 9870 – 10rm ⌶ ℰ TV The bright, spacious rooms in this quiet house all have excellent facilities.

Between £50-60
Cairn Bay Lodge, 278 Seacliff Road, ☎ 028 9146 7636, Fax 028 914 577 28 – 3rm ⌶ ℰ TV This charming house has a garden and its rooms are tastefully furnished and enjoy sea views. All have a variety of facilities including tea-making equipment, hair-dryers, etc.

• Greyabbey
Between £25-30
Woodview B&B, 8 Ballywalter Road, ☎ 028 4278 8242 – 2rm Signposted off the Ballywalter road. Small farmhouse run by retired farming couple. Plain but quiet rooms with country views.

• Newtownards
Between £40-50
⌂ **Ballycastle House**, Mount Stewart Road, ☎ 028 4278 8357 – 3rm ⌶ CC Signposted on the left 6km south of Newtownards on the A20. Attractive country house buried in vegetation and lavishly furnished with antiques. Charming rooms and sumptuous breakfast served at a communal table in the Victorian dining-room.
⌂ **Edenvale House**, 130 Portaferry Road, ☎ 028 9181 4881, Fax 028 9182 6192 – 3rm ⌶ TV CC Set well back on the right of the road coming from Newtownards and before Mount Stewart. Fine old house with views of Strangford Lough. Full of character, with Victorian furniture and spacious rooms with four-poster beds.

• Millisle
Under £10
Ballywhiskin Caravan & Camping Park, 216 Ballywalter Road, between Millisle and Ballywalter. Pleasant site close to the sea, one of the few which has a number of pitches for tents.

• Portaferry
Under £10
Portaferry Youth Hostel, Barholm, 11 The Strand, ☎ 028 4272 9598 – 38 beds. Very attractive hostel with a number of double rooms in an old building with a view of Strangford Lough. Cooking and laundry facilities.

EATING OUT

• Bangor
Under £10
Heatherlea Tea Rooms, 94 Main Street, ☎ 028 9145 3157. Open 9am-5.30pm, except Sunday. No drinks licence. Part of a family bakery, this café is a good place for freshly made sandwiches and tasty home-made cakes and pastries.
Imperial, 4 Central Avenue. Open 12pm-5pm; 12.30pm-2.30pm; 7pm-10pm Sunday. Popular spot for solid, tasty dishes.

Between £10-15
Marine Court Hotel, 18 Quay Street, ☎ 028 9145 1100. Open 12pm-10pm. Hotel restaurant with harbour views with a good choice of dishes mostly featuring roasts.

Between £20-30
⌂ **Shanks**, Crawfordsburn Road, ☎ 028 9185 3313, Fax 028 9184 2493. Open 12pm-2pm / 7pm-9.30pm; 12pm-2pm Sunday, 12.30pm-4pm Monday. One of the best places in Northern Ireland for refined and innovative cuisine. Gourmets will find much to please them in dishes such as the lobster fricassee with mushrooms, potatoes and truffle gnocchi, or the mille-feuilles meringue with poached pear and chocolate mousse. The bill reflects the quality.

- **Donaghadee**
Between £15-20
🦪 **Grace Neill's Bistro**, 33 High Street, ☎ 028 9188 2553. Open Tuesday-Friday 12pm-2.30pm / 5pm-9.30pm; Sunday brunch 12.30pm-3.30pm. This is the gastronomic annexe of Ireland's oldest pub (one of many such claims, it has to be said!), offering contemporary Irish cuisine with a mixture of influences in an elegant setting, The langoustine and smoked haddock risotto and the venison hamburger in onion sauce will leave no true gourmet indifferent. The meals served in the pub are less expensive, but obviously more ordinary.

- **Newtownards**
Under £10
Old Cross Inn, 4 Castle Place. Open 12pm-3pm / 5.30pm-8.45pm. Traditional inn with rustic but respectable cooking.

- **Portaferry**
Between £10-15
🦪 **The Narrows**, 8 Shore Road, ☎ 028 4272 8148. Open Monday-Thursday 12pm-2.30pm / 6pm-9pm; Friday-Saturday 12pm-2.30pm / 6pm-9.30pm; Sunday 12pm-8pm. This establishment is well-known for its home cooking with an international and contemporary touch to it. Delicious seafood and good wine list. Advance booking advisable. Rooms are available, but are expensive.

HAVING A DRINK

- **Bangor**
The area around the harbour is busy every evening, even more so at the weekend.
Ceol has a huge Art Deco ballroom where a variety of groups perform.
Penny Whistle, next door to the above. Busy, noisy establishment, with rock and ballads Friday-Sunday in a setting supposedly resembling a pirates' tavern.
Steamer Bar, live music guaranteed on Friday and Saturday evenings.
Calico Jacks, live music Tuesday-Thursday.

- **Portaferry**
The Quiet Man, in the centre of the village. Décor inspired by the John Wayne film of that name.

Making the most of the Ards Peninsula

DOWNPATRICK AND AROUND★
LECALE PENINSULA
Co Down
37km southeast of Belfast
See maps page 509 and page 523 – Michelin map 923 O-P / 4-5

Not to be missed
The park at Castle Ward.
Ballynoe stone circle.
The panorama from Audley's Castle.
A musical evening in Mullan's pub at Downpatrick.

And remember...
This lovely area demands at least a day of your time.

According to his chroniclers, when **St Patrick** sailed back to the place where he had already spent six years as a slave, his ship was wrecked near Saul on the shore of Strangford Lough, close to present-day Downpatrick. Their accounts maintain that, once his mission in life was accomplished, he returned here to die and was buried close to Downpatrick's cathedral. In this undulating countryside rich in vestiges of the past, this is one of the high places of Irish Christianity, for centuries a destination for Protestant and Catholic pilgrims alike.

A walk around Downpatrick
Allow 2hr30min

Once the county town of Co Down, Downpatrick acts as a shopping and commercial centre for the surrounding countryside, and has kept a certain quiet charm best savoured by a gentle stroll through its picturesque streets. The town centre is defined by English Street, Irish Street and Church Street, which form a triangular square dominated by the **Down Civic Arts Centre**. The Centre is housed in a brick-built Victorian edifice which once served as the town hall, but is now a home for art exhibitions, concerts and other performances, and in addition has a pleasant cafeteria (*see "Eating out"*).

Around the Cathedral
Opposite the Arts Centre, **English Street★**, the town's finest thoroughfare, rises to the Cathedral. It is lined with elegant **Georgian residences** with pillared porticoes. A particularly splendid example, on the right-hand side of the street, is the **Court House**, comprehensively and expensively restored after a bomb explosion in 1971.

The street widens out to become the Mall, bordered on a lower level to the left by the brick buildings of the **Southwell Foundation**. Now converted into housing, they were erected in 1733 to house schools and a hospice.

On the other side of the Mall stands the old County Jail, an imposing 18C stone structure. It was here in 1803 that **Thomas Russell**, one of the leaders of the 1798 rebellion, was hanged. The building now houses the **Down County Museum** (*June-August: Tuesday-Friday 10am-5pm; weekends and public holiday Mondays 2pm-5pm; September-May: Tuesday-Friday and public holiday Mondays 10am-5pm; Saturday 2pm-5pm. Free admission*). The museum has a **St Patrick Heritage Centre** featuring an audio-visual presentation in the former guard-house. The main building has collections telling the story of County Down from prehistory to the present, and in the cells there are lifelike figures illustrating the conditions under which prisoners lived in days gone by.

The Mall is dominated by the imposing bulk of the Anglican **Down Cathedral*** *(9.15am-1pm / 2pm-5pm; weekend 2pm-5pm. Free admission; donation welcome)*. Damaged by an earthquake, ransacked by the Vikings, burned down by the Scots then pillaged again by the English, the original buildings erected over the supposed place of St Patrick's burial have completely disappeared. Dating from the beginning of the 19C, the present cathedral nevertheless incorporates some of the fabric of its predecessor. The interior has a fine 18C **organ**, a **bishop's throne** and a **font** made from a medieval watering trough.

Contentious remains

In the 12C, the Norman lord John de Courcy founded a Benedictine abbey on the site of the cathedral, and it is said that he brought the remains of St Patrick here for reburial, as well as the remains of two other favourite Irish saints: St Brigid and St Columba. The Book of Armagh, now on show in Trinity College, Dublin, states that St Patrick was buried on the Mound of Down, but other writings maintain that the he was laid to rest at Saul. Whatever the truth of the matter, the fact remains that the "official" site at Downpatrick has been for centuries a place of pilgrimage for the devout, Catholic and Protestant alike.

Outside the Cathedral stands a stone **high cross** sculpted with bas-reliefs which are difficult to interpret. The faithful still gather in the graveyard by the granite slab placed in the early 20C over the supposed site of **St Patrick's grave**.

The cathedral precinct offers fine **views*** over the surrounding countryside and River Quoile. From the marshy levels around the town rises the **Mound of Down**, one of Ulster's most important Neolithic monuments.

Around Downpatrick

Saul

3km east of Downpatrick. Follow signposted route. The landscape around the area where St Patrick is held to have made his landfall exudes a quiet charm. A Celtic Revival **church**, accompanied by a round tower, was built here in 1932 to mark the place where the saint supposedly made his first converts to Christianity. The graveyard has a number of ancient **tombstones**.

Struell Wells

3km to the south towards Ardglass. Free admission. Pleasant picnic area nearby. Nestling in a rocky hollow are several **stone buildings** and a little **chapel**. Traditionally linked to accounts of St Patrick's mission, they formed **public baths**, fed by a fast-flowing stream and endowed with healing powers. As was the case with other similar sacred sites, their veneration by the ancient Celts seems to have passed seamlessly into Christian tradition.

Inch Abbey

Go 3.5km north on the A2, then turn left and follow signs. April-September: 10am-7pm; closed Sunday and Monday. Admission charge.
The romantic ruins rising over what was once an island in the River Quoile belong to a Cistercian abbey founded in 1180 by John de Courcy. The most substantial remains are those of the abbey **church** built in Early English style, with a characteristic triple-lancet window at its eastern end.

Ballynoe Stone Circle*

5km south via a minor road. Take a poorly signposted track on the right on the way into Ballynoe village and walk about 500m.
This is one of Northern Ireland's finest prehistoric monuments, a 4 000-year old **double stone circle** enclosing a small **tumulus** from which human remains have been recovered.

Downpatrick and around

Delamont Country Park

Go 8km north on the A22, then before reaching Killileagh follow signs to the right. 9am-10pm in summer, 9am-5pm in winter. Parking fee. Cafeteria, play and picnic areas. This serene spot has been laid out as a country park and **bird sanctuary** on the shores of Strangford Lough.

Two kilometres to the north, the Renaissance turrets of the highly picturesque **Killileagh Castle*** dominate the village of the same name. The castle itself is unfortunately not open to the public.

Around the Lecale Peninsula

26km drive
Allow half a day including a visit to Castle Ward

A lovely area, with a number of fascinating places to visit, the Lecale Peninsula is defined to the north by Strangford Lough and to the east by the Irish Sea.

■ **Quoile Countryside Centre** – *From Downpatrick, take the A25 towards Strangford for 2km, then follow signs. 1 April-30 September: 11am-5pm; weekends 1pm-5pm. Rest of year: weekends only. Free admission.*

Closed off by a barrage, the estuary of the River Quoile forms a vast body of water bordered by marshlands on which a luxuriant vegetation thrives in summer, a paradise for birds as well as for animals such as otters and foxes.

Return to the A25 and continue for 2.5km towards Strangford as far as Castle Ward.

■ **Castle Ward***** – *April, September and October: weekends and Easter Week 1pm-6pm; May-August: 1pm-6pm except Thursday. Admission charge. Gardens open all year dawn to dusk.*

This superb mansion in its lovely park is built on rising ground overlooking Strangford Lough. It is unique in having one façade in neo-Classical style, the other in Strawberry Hill Gothic. It was built between 1760 and 1775 by the Ward family from England, their ancestors having acquired the estate from the Fitzgeralds of Kildare (*see page 17*) in the 16C. The Wards remained in residence until the 1950s, and the luxurious interior retains something of its domestic atmosphere. The entrance hall, once the music room, has exuberant **stuccowork**. The state rooms, the dining room and the bedrooms on the first floor have fine Victorian furnishings, and every room in the place is decorated with 19C **paintings** of the English school.

Outbuildings now house a cafeteria as well as a playroom, where children can dress up in Victorian clothes and play with toys from the same era.

In the old laundry there is a **lingerie museum** where the secrets of Victorian underwear are revealed in all their glory.

Castle Ward is famous for its **gardens** and its vast informal **park**. At some distance from the mansion is the lake known as **Temple Water**, named for the **Temple*** rising over it, a delightful summerhouse in Classical style with a Doric portico.

In the lower part of the park, close to Strangford Lough, a trackway leads to **Old Castle Ward**, a 19C farmstead erected on the site of the original 17C castle, of which a battlemented tower remains. Part of the buildings are given over to a **museum of rural life**, with demonstrations of saw-milling and grain-milling. Other parts are occupied by the **Strangford Lough Wildlife Centre** (*April-June and September: weekends and public holidays 2pm-6pm. Open daily at the same times July-August*). The centre has informative displays on the 2 000-plus species of wildlife which inhabit the area of the lough.

From Old Castle Ward follow signs for about 800m to Audley's Castle.

■ **Audley's Castle** – *Free admission.* In a ruinous state, this fortified dwelling dating from the 15C has an exceptionally fine **view*** over the channel linking Strangford Lough with the sea. A track leads across the fields to a **cairn**, a small Neolithic tomb with a surrounding stone wall.

Castle Ward

Return to the A25 and continue for 3km to Strangford.

There is little to detain visitors in the little port of **Strangford**, unless they are unlucky enough to get caught up in the queue of vehicles waiting for the ferry to cross to Portaferry on the far side of the entrance to the lough *(for ferry times see page 502)*.

From Strangford take the A2 towards Ardglass.

The attractive coast road gives striking views of the rocks which emerge dramatically from the water at low tide. On the right-hand side of the road, 4km from Strangford, **Kilclief Castle** faces an inlet with a beach of white sand. It is a fortified house *(not open to visitors)* built to guard the entrance to Strangford Lough.

Just before the road reaches Ardglass, a lane turns off to the left towards **St Patrick's Well**, a water-filled hole at the foot of a crucifix. It is said to mark the spot where the saint made his first converts to the Christian faith. The rocky shoreline has a wild beauty all of its own.

■ **Ardglass** – Ardglass is a working port, a natural harbour with a fishing fleet further protected by a string of little islands. There are several good B&Bs as well as a friendly pub *(see "Making the most of Downpatrick and around")*. Dominating the place is a well-preserved 15C fortified house, **Jordan's Castle** *(opening times and admission charges not yet available)*, next to it a number of more recent crenellated constructions at the entrance to a golf course.

Downpatrick and around

Making the most of Downpatrick and around

COMING AND GOING

By bus – The bus station is in Market Street in the town centre. Services n° 215, 15 and 15A run 25 times to Belfast (45min) on weekdays, 15 on Saturday and 6 on Sunday. Service n° 16 runs to Strangford (25min) 9 times Monday-Friday and 4 on Saturday, and services nos 17 and 240 link Downpatrick with Newcastle 19 times Monday-Friday, 11 on Saturday and 6 Sunday.

ADDRESS BOOK

Tourist information – *Tourist Information Centre*, 74 Market Street, ☎ 028 4461 2233. 9am-5pm; closed Saturday 1pm-2pm; closed Sunday; mid-June to end September: 9am-6pm; Sunday 2pm-6pm. Plentiful information on County Down and the Mourne Mountains.

Bank / Currency exchange – Bureau de change in the tourist information centre and cash machines in Market Street nearby.

Post office / Telephone – Post office in ***Supervalu***, 65 Market Street, close to the tourist information centre. 9am-5.30pm; Saturday 9am-12.30pm; closed Sunday.

WHERE TO STAY

• Downpatrick
Under £10
Castle Ward Caravan Park, ☎ 028 4488 1680. Caravan and camp site with good facilities in the wonderful setting of the castle grounds.

Between £35-40
Hillcrest, 157 Strangford Road, ☎ 028 4461 2583 – 3 rooms ⌖ Warm welcome from Jennie Fitzsimons in her plain but comfortable little B&B in open countryside on the road to Strangford.
Havine, 51 Ballydonnell Road, ☎ 028 4485 1242 – 3 rooms ⌖ Eight kilometres from Downpatrick. Go 6km on the A25 towards Clough, then turn left towards Tyrella and follow signs for a further 3km. Modest farmhouse in open countryside with simply furnished

rooms. Genuine family atmosphere, guests welcomed with a cup of tea and cakes. Piano available.

Between £40-50
Denvir's Hotel, English Street, ☎ 028 4461 2012 – 8 rooms ⌖ 🖉 TV ✕ CC Traditional, comfortable hotel in a Georgian building close to the cathedral. It also has a pub and restaurant (see "Eating out").

• Ardglass
Between £35-40
Burford Lodge, 30 Quay Street, ☎ 028 4484 1141 – 6 rooms ⌖ TV Plain but comfortable rooms in a Georgian guesthouse with a conservatory overlooking the harbour. Evening meal available if required.
The Cottage, 9 Castle Place, ☎ 028 4484 1080 – 4 rooms ⌖ TV Very pleasant B&B on rising ground overlooking the harbour. Attractive rooms (two of them share facilities), good value for money, friendly reception and unbeatable breakfast.

EATING OUT

• Downpatrick
Under £10
Down Civic Arts Centre, Irish Street (see main text). Open from midday during the week. Inexpensive little cafeteria with salads and dishes of the day in a building of Victorian date.

Courtside Bistro, 19 English Street, next to Court House, ☎ 028 4461 7886. 12pm-2.30pm / 5pm-9pm. Good traditional cooking in the modernised interior of a fine Georgian building. More refined dishes in the evening at a higher price. At the weekend, dinner is served upstairs amid the Victorian décor of what used to be the clubroom of the local hunting fraternity.

Denvir's (see "Where to stay"). 12pm-2.30pm / 6pm-8pm; Friday and Saturday 5.30pm-9pm. Good pub food in the historic setting of an old inn where Jonathan Swift once lodged and where the United Irishmen held their meetings. The Denvir family emigrated to America, where they gave a version of their name to the capital of Colorado.

- **Strangford**

From £10-15

Cuan, 6 The Square, ☎ 028 4488 1222. 11.30am-9.30pm; from 12.30pm Sunday. Pleasant village restaurant offering tasty seafood and other dishes based on local ingredients. Good wine list.

- **Ardglass**

Under £10

The Moorings, 8 Kildare Street. Daily 12pm-2.30pm / 5.30pm-9.30pm. Little pub-type establishment serving a number of fish dishes and traditional roasts.

HAVING A DRINK

- **Downpatrick**

McGivern's, 21 Irish Street, has good rock groups Tuesday, Friday, Saturday and Sunday.

The Hoote, the night-club next door to the above has live music on Saturday evening from 9.30pm-1.30am.

Russell Bar, 7-9 Church Street. Traditional music Thursday evening and pop at the weekend from 10pm-1pm.

Mullan's, 48 Church Street, better known as **Speedy's**, is another good place for traditional music, Sunday evening from 6pm.

OTHER THINGS TO DO

Golf – Downpatrick Golf Course, 43 Saul Road, ☎ 028 4461 5947, is an 18-hole course in a classic countryside setting 2km north of town. Green fee: £15 weekdays, £20 weekends.

Ardglass Golf Club, ☎ 028 4484 1219, is unusual in that it is in the middle of the village, on a hilltop close to Jordan Castle. Green fee: £15 weekdays, £21 weekends.

Fishing – The mouth of the River Quoile by the **Quoile Countryside Centre** (see above) is a good place to tempt onto your line fish like perch, bream and eel. These may be caught all year round, brown trout only from 1 March-31 October. Permit compulsory.

Riding – Tullymurry Equestrian Centre, 24 Ballydugan Road, 6km from Downpatrick towards Clough, ☎ 028 4481 1880. Good riding through woodland or along the coast.

Making the most of Downpatrick and around

MOURNE MOUNTAINS★

Co Down
Michelin map 923 N-O / 5

Not to be missed
A climb up Slieve Donard.
Tollymore and Castlewellan Forest Park.
The Slieve Gullion scenic road.

And remember...
You will need at least two days in the area if you want to do some mountain walking.

Rising from the Irish Sea in the southernmost part of Northern Ireland, this ancient and compact range stretches east-west from the seaside resort of Newcastle to Carlingford Lough on the frontier with the Republic. Dominated by Slieve Donard, at 850m the highest summit in Ulster, the Mourne Mountains are a paradise for walkers and hikers, who can experience them by using the **Ulster Way** *(see page 93)*. Small rectangular fields bounded by drystone walls contrast with dark forests of conifers; tumbled masses of rock are speckled with the bright violet colour of heather in bloom, while in the valleys, reservoirs reflect the constant procession of clouds driven by ocean winds. The mountains are fringed by a number of lovely forest parks, but there are few historic remains in what was always a poor and remote region.

Newcastle and around
Allow a day

Making the most of its location between sea and mountain, Newcastle (pop 7 300) is an attractive and popular resort which gets very crowded in summer. Above it rises the imposing mass of Slieve Donard, its summit often veiled in mist. The town stretches out along its busy main street which runs parallel to the fine sandy beach. It makes an excellent base for exploring the mountains and their fringe of forest parks.

Visitors who lack the courage to tackle the peaks can content themselves with a walk in **Donard Park**, on the banks of the Glen River to the south of the town. Pilgrims gather in this attractive public park here every year on 25 July before setting off in procession to the summit of Slieve Donard, named after a follower of St Patrick.

Tollymore Forest Park★
2.5km to the northwest via the B180. 10am-dusk. Admission charge. The **Shimna River**, one of the finest salmon streams in the North, flows through this vast 500 hectare estate. Laid out as parkland in the 18C around a now demolished mansion, the area was declared a Forest Park in 1955, the first of its kind in the province. Beyond a barbican gate is a fine avenue lined with majestic deodar cedars. The park is threaded with well-signposted footpaths which lead to an **arboretum**, a **lake** well-stocked with waterfowl, and to a variety of old buildings, among them the **Clanbrassil Barn**, now housing a visitor centre. There is also a cafeteria, as well as picnic areas and a caravan and camp site, all helping to make the park very popular with visitors.

Murlough National Nature Reserve
3km to the north via the A2. Access on foot along the coastal section of the Ulster Way. Dawn-dusk. Parking charge.
Between the Carrigs River and Dundrum Bay, the reserve is an important sanctuary for migratory birds. The sparse vegetation growing on the sand dunes harbours a surprisingly wide range of species.

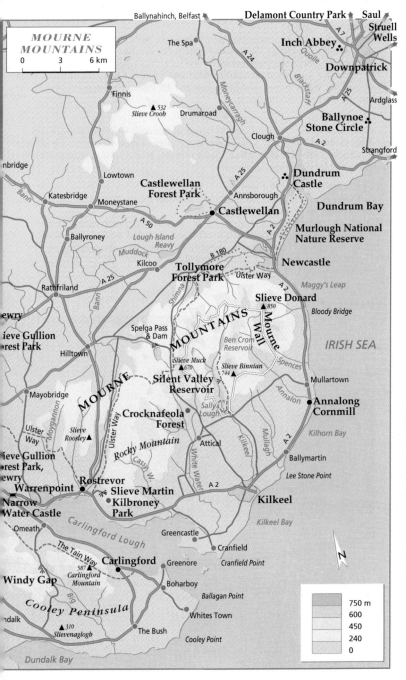

Dundrum Castle*

6.5km north via the A2. 10am-7pm; Sunday 2pm-7pm; public holidays 10am-7pm; closed Monday. Admission charge. On its rocky hilltop, this Norman stronghold was built to observe and control shipping making for the Lecale Peninsula and Strangford Lough. The attractive ruins are dominated by what remains of the **keep**, from which there are striking **views**** over Dundrum Bay and its lagoon to the north and to the Mourne Mountains to the south.

Castlewellan

6.5km north via the A50. The Georgian houses of this quiet little township are laid out along its broad and shady main street. It is a place of great charm, with a number of friendly pubs. The **post office** shares premises with a tobacconists and a shop selling children's clothes.

Castlewellan Forest Park**

1km north of Castlewellan. 10am-nightfall. Admission charge. Picnic sites and camp site (see "Making the most of the Mourne Mountains")
This is an enchanting spot, with an imposing **castle** *(a conference centre not open to the public)* in Scottish Baronial style overlooking a vast and well-stocked fishing lake. In the ownership of the Ministry of Agriculture, the estate extends over an area of 450 hectares; it includes a lovely **arboretum**, protected by the walls enclosing **Annesley Garden**

The Mourne Mountains

Belfast and the South

The 5km-long **Sculpture Trail** leads around the lake; at intervals along it are examples of the work of contemporary sculptors who have used natural materials found on site. Guarded by a brace of Napoleonic eagles, the buildings of a 19C **farmstead** have been converted to house a cafeteria and an information centre.

On foot up hill and down dale

There are plenty of walks starting at Newcastle which present no special difficulty. Given the right equipment, most of them can be done in a day or less and at any time of the year. For details of tourist information centres (see "Making the most of the Mourne Mountains").

The summit of Slieve Donard

Starting from Donard Park *(see above)* to the south of the town. Allow half a day. Go along the left bank of the Glen River, then cross to the other bank before returning to the left bank which is followed for about 3km on a stony path through the forest. The route then veers slightly left to reach the **Mourne Wall**, a drystone structure completed in 1922 to mark the boundary of the **Silent Valley** *(see below)*. From here there is a fine view seawards. Then the climb really begins, following the wall which leads right up to the summit. In clear weather, there is a marvellous **panorama★★** extending over Newcastle, the sea and the hills all around. Return by the same route.

B Kaufmann/MICHELIN

Mourne Mountains

Dundrum Coastal Path

2km north of Dundrum (see above), turn right off the A2 to the coast. Allow an hour. For those more comfortable with flat country than with mountains, this is an ideal walk. The path runs along **Dundrum Bay** with its abundant bird life, before rejoining the A2 near the village of Clough.

The coast from Newcastle to Newry
52km drive – Allow a day

■ **Annalong Cornmill** – *From Newcastle, follow the A2 southwards for 10km along the foot of Slieve Donard as far as Annalong, then turn left towards the sea. Tuesday-Saturday 11am-5pm; closed December-January. Admission charge.*
Powered by the waters of the Annalong River, this restored **watermill** is the last of about twenty mills in this area which were used to grind grain or scutch linen. Inside, the millstones and the gear-wheels of the mechanism show how the mill functioned in the 18C. A **marine park** has been laid out near the harbour of the little seaside town.

Return to the A2 and continue for 8km, then turn right before reaching Kilkeel towards the Silent Valley. Carry on for 5km to the car park.

■ **Silent Valley Reservoir★** – *Three buses daily from Newcastle bus station (service n° 34A). May-September: 10am-6.30pm; October-April: 10am-4pm. Admission charge.*
The reservoir and dam across the Kilkeel River were completed in 1933 after a construction period which lasted 10 years and employed up to 2000 workers. The reservoir holds 136 million cu.m of water, and supplies Co Down and Belfast. Another reservoir further to the north, the Ben Crom reservoir, completed this mammoth engineering project. The catchment area is bounded by the **Mourne Wall**, 26km long and built entirely by hand at the beginning of the 1920s.
This is a fine area to walk in, with lovely **views★** over the lake in its deep and austere valley setting. The permanent **exhibition** in the visitor centre at the entrance to the area tells the story of the dam and reservoir.

Return to the A2, drive through the fishing port of Kilkeel and continue for 15km. Before reaching Rostrevor, turn right and follow signs to Kilbroney Park.

■ **Kilbroney Park** – *Free admission. Restaurant and picnic sites.* A pleasant forest park has been laid out on the slopes of **Slieve Martin**, the southernmost peak of the Mourne Mountains. Footpaths lead to a fine **viewpoint★** giving a panorama over Carlingford Lough and the Cooley Peninsula *(see page 162).*

Return to the A2 and carry on to Warrenpoint.

■ **Warrenpoint** – *A ferry crosses from Warrenpoint to Omeath in the Republic. June-September: every 20min, 1pm-6pm.* This lively harbour town at the northern end of Carlingford Lough makes a good stopping point, with pubs and restaurants grouped around its main square. The Victorian edifices lining the seafront look out over the somewhat murky waters of the lough, though their state does not seem to deter the more daring kind of swimmer.

■ **Narrow Water Castle** – *3km beyond Warrenpoint towards Newry. 10am-6pm; Sunday 2pm-6pm; closed Monday; public holidays 10am-6pm. Admission charge.*
This battlemented tower house rising over the muddy waters of the Newry River was built in the mid-17C to house the English garrison responsible for controlling access by water to Newry. More than three centuries later, on 18 August 1979, the same day that the Queen's cousin Lord Mountbatten was assassinated in Co Sligo, an IRA bomb was exploded here, killing 18 British soldiers. Known subsequently as the Warrenpoint massacre, this was one of the worst setbacks suffered by the army in the whole course of the Troubles.

Return to the A2 and continue for 11km to **Newry** (pop 22 000), a cathedral town and an important industrial and commercial centre with a foot in both Co Down and Co Armagh and only a short distance from the Republic. However, it's a rather austere place with little to detain the visitor.

■ **Slieve Gullion Forest Park**★★ – *13km south of Newry via the B113 towards Forkhill. 10am-sunset in summer; may be closed during the rest of the year. Parking charge.* Visitors are more likely to be tempted to stay a while in the enchanting surroundings of this forest park than in Newry. At the entrance to the park, former farm buildings now house a **visitor centre** with an exhibition about the work of woodsmen and foresters. Close to the buildings is a **walled garden**, a delightful place to linger in.

Rising to a peak of 573m, **Slieve Gullion** is surrounded by a chain of lesser hills of volcanic origin, the Ring of Gullion. They can be viewed from the **Scenic Drive**★★ which winds its way up through forest and rocky outcrops. Dramatic effects of the light can be experienced at sunset, as the last rays of the sun enhance the contrast between the mauve of the underlying granite and the vivid green of the bracken. This may also have appealed to Neolithic people, who built two **cairns** at the summit of the mountain. The summit can be reached on foot by a signposted footpath which leads off to the right about half-way along the Scenic Drive. Those making the effort are rewarded by a breathtaking **view**★★.

Making the most of the Mourne Mountains

COMING AND GOING

By bus – Newcastle bus station is in the eastern part of the town at the beginning of the main street. Service n° 17 links Newcastle and Downpatrick (35min) 16 times weekdays, 10 Saturday and 6 Sunday. Buses nos 18 and 20 run to Belfast (75min) via Dundrum and occasionally via Castlewellan 17 to 20 times weekdays and Saturday and 6 times Sunday.

Newry bus station on Edward Street. Goldline service n° 240 links Newry and Downpatrick (1hr) 4 times daily weekdays and Saturday and twice Sunday via Newcastle. Service n° 238 runs to Belfast (75min) 17 times daily weekdays, 14 Saturday and 5 Sunday. Bus n° 29 leaves the Mall once an hour for Kilkeel via Warrenpoint.

By train – Dublin trains from Belfast's Great Victoria Street station stop at Newry's Carnlough Road station 2km north of the town. 8 trains daily weekdays, 7 on Saturday, 4 on Sunday. Journey time to Newry 60min, and another 1hr20 to Dublin.

ADDRESS BOOK

Tourist information – *Newcastle Tourist Information Centre*, 10-14 Central Promenade, ☎ 028 4372 2222, Fax 028 4372 2400. 10am-5pm; Sunday 2pm-6pm. Plentiful information on the Mourne Mountains. Souvenir shop. ***Newry Tourist Information***, Town Hall, ☎ 028 3026 8877. June-September: 9am-5pm; Saturday 10am-4pm; closed Sunday; rest of year: 9am-1pm / 2pm-5pm, apart from weekends. Some useful information on the town and the area around.

Belfast and the South

Kilkeel Tourist Information, 6 Newcastle Street, ☎ 028 4176 2525. April-September: Monday-Saturday 9am-5.30pm; closed Saturday rest of year. Friendly staff and useful information on the Mourne Mountains.

Bank / Currency exchange – Several cash machines on the Promenade in Newcastle and bureau de change at the tourist information centre. Cash machines near the Town Hall in Newry.

Post office / Telephone – 35 Central Promenade, Newcastle, near the bus station. Monday-Wednesday 9am-5.30pm; Thursday and Saturday 9am-12.30pm. Main post office 50-52 Hill Street, Newry.

Bicycle hire – Wiki Wiki Wheels, 10 Donard Street, Newcastle, ☎ 028 4372 3973.

WHERE TO STAY

• **Newcastle and around**

Under £10

Newcastle Youth Hostel, 30 Downs Road, ☎ 028 4372 2133 – 30 beds. Closed 24 December-1 March. Very useful for budget travellers, in a good position in the town centre, close to the seafront and near the post office. Friendly staff. The usual facilities, but no double rooms.

Tollymore Forest Park, 176 Tullybranigan Road, ☎ 028 4372 2428. Pitches for both caravans and tents in the magnificent setting of this Forest Park.

Castlewellan Forest Park, The Grange, Castlewellan, ☎ 028 2377 8664. Good facilities for campers in a natural environment of great beauty.

Between £30-35

Drumrawn House, 139 Central Promenade, ☎ 028 4372 6847 – 3rm 🛏 TV The Kelly family make guests welcome in their comfortable Georgian house with its sea view.

⌖ **Hill View**, 18 Bog Road, Attical, ☎ 028 4176 4269 – 4rm 🛏 TV CC From Kilkeel (to the south of Newcastle via the A2), take the B27 for 5km, then turn left and follow signs. Warm welcome from Marie Trainor to her home in the middle of the countryside, with comfortable rooms looking out over fields and mountains. She can supply maps for walking trips and show you good places to tickle trout, as well as providing an excellent breakfast. She also has accommodation for up to 6 people to rent by the week for £200.

Arundel Guest House, 23 Bryansford Road, ☎ 028 4272 2232 – 4rm 🛏 TV CC Spacious rooms in a house on the edge of town, opposite Donard Park and facing the mountains. Evening meal on request.

⌖ **Briers Country House**, Middle Tollymore Road, ☎ 028 4372 4347, Fax 028 4372 6633 – 9rm 🛏 TV CC Go towards Tollymore Forest Park and follow signs. Restored by the present owners, this is an 18C farmhouse with most of its comfortable guest rooms in a newly built annexe. Rustic furnishings, excellent breakfast and evening meal on request.

Hylliard House, 1-5 Castle Avenue, Castlewellan, ☎ 028 4377 0141, Fax 028 4377 0011 – 9rm 🛏 TV CC Anyone wanting to stay overnight in this charming township could try this establishment in what was the old post office and is now a conference centre. Functional but quite adequate rooms.

• **Newry**

Between £30-35

Black Gap Farm, 26 Divernagh Road, Bessbrook, ☎ 028 3083 0358 – 3rm 🛏 TV CC Four kilometres northeast of Newry on the A25, turn right towards Bessbrook and follow signs. Restored farmhouse with plain but comfortable rooms with views of Slieve Gullion.

EATING OUT

• **Newcastle**

Under £10

It is possible to eat quite adequately and inexpensively in the pleasant setting of the cafeterias at Castlewellan and Tollymore Forest Parks.

Anchor Bar, 9 Bryandsford Road. Open 12pm-2.30pm weekdays and until 6pm on Saturday. Copious pub food in a lively bar.

Maple Leaf Cottage, 149 Bryandsford Road, on the way to Tollymore Forest Park. Open Tuesday-Saturday 11am-

6pm; Sunday 12pm-7pm. Closed December, open weekends only September-Easter. Delightful café and craft shop with chocolate-box decor with tasty sweet and savoury specialities. No drinks licence.

🦀 **The Harbour Inn**, 4 South Promenade, ☎ 028 4372 3445. Daily 12.30pm-9.30pm. On the left on the road out of Newcastle by the seashore. Cosy inn with maritime décor serving mussels, oysters and other sorts of seafood depending on the catch of the day. Fresh ingredients guaranteed, as is the friendly welcome. Rooms available with sea views.

• **Newry**
Under £10
The Brass Monkey, 1 Sandy Street, opposite the law courts. This pub is a local institution, with a lively atmosphere on weekend evenings and a good choice of steak, chicken and seafood dishes. More expensive in the evening.

HAVING A DRINK

• **Newcastle and around**
The town has plenty of pubs with a good atmosphere in the evenings, especially in summer.
Quinn's, 62 Main Street, has different kinds of live music Thursday-Saturday.
Central Park Nite Club, South Central Promenade. Discotheque with live groups every weekend.
The Salvage's, 17 Main Street, Castlewellan, has rock and pop groups Saturday evening and traditional music on Friday evening.
Magin's, next door to the above, is the local temple to rock music on Thursday evening, and has karaoke upstairs on Saturday.

• **Warrenpoint**
The pubs around the main square are lively places to go most evenings.
Jack Ryan's has blues or jazz Thursday to Sunday.
Cearnog's specialises in rock the same evenings as the above.
Corner House, Rostrevor, on the way out towards Newcastle is a good place to hear traditional music.

OTHER THINGS TO DO

Walking – Many useful walking tips from the Newcastle Tourist Information Centre (see above), as well as from the Mourne Countryside Centre, 91 Central Promenade, Newcastle, ☎ 028 4372 4059. June-September: weekends 9am-5pm. During the rest of the year, the Mourne Heritage Trust, 87 Central Promenade, can provide the same information Monday-Friday at the same time. Both offer a wide choice of maps and of leaflets with details of the various routes for exploring the mountains.

Golf – **Royal County Down Golf Club**, 36 Golf Links Road, Newcastle, ☎ 028 4372 3314. This club has an 18-hole and a 9-hole course beautifully located between sea and mountain. Green fee: £4-17 according to course and time of week. **Kilkeel Golf Club**, 4km towards Newry, ☎ 028 4176 2296. Guest players welcome Monday and Wednesday-Friday. 18-hole course with sea views. Green fee: £16.

Fishing – For a salmon or trout permit for the Shimna River in Tollymore Park, apply to **Four Seasons**, 47 Main Street, Newcastle, ☎ 028 4372 5078. For permits for the lake in the park at Castlewellan, apply to the **Fisheries Office** at the park administration, ☎ 028 4377 8937.

Riding – **The Mourne Riding Trail Centre**, 96 Castlewellan Road, Newcastle, ☎ 028 4372 4351, arranges rides through Tollymore Forest Park or along the shore. **The Mount Pleasant Riding & Trekking Centre**, 15 Bannonstown Road, Castlewellan, ☎ 028 4377 8651, arranges treks in the Mourne Mountains as well as rides through the Forest Parks.

SHOPPING

Jewellery – **The Celtic Crafts Gallery**, 45 Dromara Road, Dundrum. 10am-5pm; 2pm-5pm Sunday. Wide choice of Celtic-style jewellery in precious and non-precious metals, plus a pleasant café.

Making the most of the Mourne Mountains

ARMAGH AND AROUND★
Co Armagh – Pop 14 300
65km southwest of Belfast

Not to be missed
The Neolithic site at Navan.
The Argory and its lovely interior.

And remember...
Armagh doesn't stay up late in the evening; diners should make sure they eat early.

In the midst of lovely countryside famous for its apple orchards, Armagh is a place of the greatest importance in the history of Christianity in Ireland.

In AD 445, the old Celtic stronghold of *Ard Mhacha* (meaning the "Hill of Mhacha", a legendary Celtic queen) was chosen by St Patrick as the capital city of the new religion. In the Middle Ages, Armagh became the most important scholastic and theological centre of the country, and it was here that the celebrated **Book of Armagh** *(now in Trinity College, Dublin, page 112)*, relating the confession of St Patrick, was written.

Armagh is the seat of both a Catholic and a Protestant bishopric, and each denomination has its own cathedral. The little town is proud of its status as the "Irish Rome", but it has not escaped its share of the Troubles; there is a sharp demarcation between Unionist and Nationalist parts of the town.

The town
Allow half a day

A good way to start a tour of the town is to call at the **Tourist Information Centre** (B3) and visit **St Patrick's Trian** *(April-September: 10am-5.30pm; October-March: 10am-5pm; Sunday 2pm-5pm; Admission charge)*. This is an exhibition giving an overview of the city's religious past illustrated with lifelike tableaux. Another exhibition (same opening times), intended mainly for children, is based on Jonathan Swift's Gulliver's Travels, and features a giant figure of Gulliver himself; Swift was a frequent visitor to the Armagh area.

Turn left out of the tourist information centre into Abbey Street, then right along Dawson Street as far as Cathedral Street.

Monumental steps lead up the hilltop to **St Patrick's Cathedral** (A1-2). The city's Catholic cathedral is an austere neo-Gothic edifice with twin spires. Its construction, begun in 1840, was not completed until 1873. The nave vaults are painted with lovely **frescoes** depicting the life of St Patrick, while the walls have **mosaics** representing the patron saints of Ireland's 20 dioceses.

Go back down the steps, turn left into the avenue where a market is held several times a week, then right into Dawson Street.

Queen's University of Armagh (A3), part of Queen's Belfast *(see page 484)*, is housed in what used to be an old hospital.

Swift and the carpenter
In the course of a visit to Armagh in 1722, Swift noticed a carpenter working on the site of the Presbyterian church: "How much do you earn?" asked the writer, who at the time was Dean of St Patrick's Cathedral in Dublin. "Fifteen pence a day, Your Honour" replied the workman. "Fifteen pence! Why, in Dublin you pay a carpenter who is perfectly happy with ten pence". "Well, Your Honour, I can introduce you to a clergyman who gives excellent sermons for £40 a year, compared with the Dean of St Patrick's £700!". Always ready to laugh at his own failings as much as at others', Swift rewarded the man with half-a-crown.

Opposite the University, the corner building is the home of the **Robinson Public Library** *(10am-1pm / 2pm-4pm; closed weekends)*, founded in 1771. Among its greatest treasures are **manuscript letters** written by Jonathan Swift and a **first edition** of *Gulliver's Travels*.

Close by, a path leads up to the Anglican **St Patrick's Cathedral*** (A3) *(April-October: 10am-5pm; November-March: 10am-4pm. Guided tours at 1.30pm and 2.30pm June-August, not Sunday)*. Like its Catholic counterpart, Armagh's Protestant cathedral dominates the town from its hilltop site. It was here in the 5C that St Patrick is supposed to have built Armagh's first church. Later, in 1014, the Celtic king Brian Ború and his sons were buried here after the Battle of Clontarf against the Danes *(see page 17)*. The plans of the present building date from 1268, and though destroyed 17 times, the cathedral was always rebuilt. Inside, the white marble 17C and 18C **funerary monuments** are particularly striking.

Around the Mall

The Mall, a vast open space in the lower part of the town, is bordered on the north by the elegant Georgian **Court House** with its peristyle, and to the south, by the **Gaol**, an austere edifice which once served as a barracks.

Military history buffs will find much to interest them in the **Royal Irish Fusiliers Museum** *(10am-12.30pm / 1.30pm-4pm; closed weekends; Admission charge)* opposite the Court House at the corner of the Mall and College Hill. The museum has a fine array of uniforms and other items telling the story of this illustrious regiment founded in 1793 to fight the French.

A climb back up College Hill leads in about 200m to an avenue which in turn leads to the **Planetarium** *(September-March: 10am-4.45pm weekdays, show every hour 12pm-4pm; 1.15pm-4.45pm Saturday and Sunday, no show at 1pm and 2pm; rest of year: one show only at 3pm Monday-Friday. Admission charge)*. The Planetarium is housed beneath a dome 15m in diameter. It was built in 1968 close to the **Observatory** dating from 1789. The show consists of a guided tour of the universe using strikingly effective audio-visual techniques.

St Patrick's Catholic Cathedral

B. Kaufmann/MICHELIN

Armagh and around

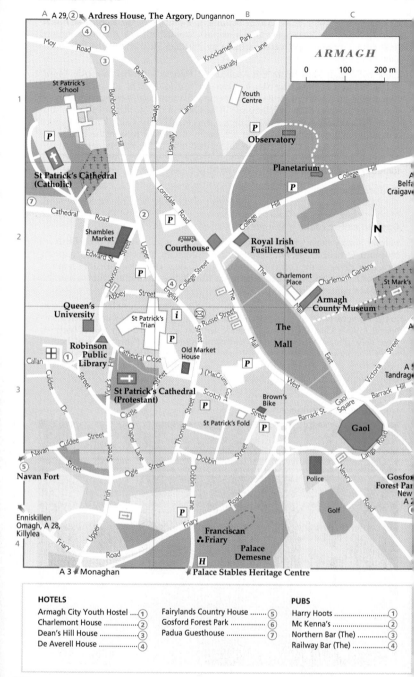

ARMAGH

0   100   200 m

A 29, Ardress House, The Argory, Dungannon

Moy Road

Railway Street

Knockamell Park Lane

Lisanally Lane

St Patrick's School

Barbrook Hill

Youth Centre

Observatory

Planetarium

College Hill

Belfast Craigavon

St Patrick's Cathedral (Catholic)

Cathedral Road

Lisanally Lane

Lonsdale Road

College Hill

N

Shambles Market

Upper

Courthouse

College Street

Royal Irish Fusiliers Museum

Charlemont Place

Charlemont Gardens

St Mark's

Edward St.

Dawson

Abbey Street

English Street

Russel Street

The Mall

Armagh County Museum

Queen's University

Robinson Public Library

St Patrick's Trian

i

Old Market House

Callan

Cathedral Close

Vicar's Street

MacCrum's Court

The Mall

East Street

Victoria Street

A Tandragee

Culdee Dr.

St Patrick's Cathedral (Protestant)

Castle Street

Scotch Street

Brown's Bike

Barrack St.

West

Gaol Square

Barrack Hill

Gaol

Navan

Culdee Street

Chapel Lane

Thomas Street

St Patrick's Fold

Dobbin Street

Police

Langar Road

Navan Fort

Ogle Street

Dobbin Street

Dobbin Lane

Gosford Forest Park New A

Enniskillen Omagh, A 28, Killylea

Friary

Upper

Friary Road

Friary Road

Franciscan Friary

H

Palace Demesne

Golf

A 3 Monaghan

Palace Stables Heritage Centre

HOTELS		PUBS
Armagh City Youth Hostel ....①	Fairylands Country House ....⑤	Harry Hoots ....①
Charlemont House ....②	Gosford Forest Park ....⑥	Mc Kenna's ....②
Dean's Hill House ....③	Padua Guesthouse ....⑦	Northern Bar (The) ....③
De Averell House ....④		Railway Bar (The) ....④

Among the fine Georgian buildings on the eastern side of the Mall is the **Armagh County Museum** (*10am-5pm; closed 1pm-2pm Saturday; closed Sunday. Free admission*). In its Grecian temple, this is a fascinating little museum, with a range of local history collections. Among the items are domestic utensils, uniforms, 19C fashions and jewellery, including an amusing necklace made from watch-cases.

Palace Demesne* (B4)

On Friary Road in the southern part of the town, what was once the residence of the Anglican Archbishop of Ireland nowadays houses the council offices. The Demesne is reached via an avenue bordered on the left by the ruins of a **Franciscan monastery**.

The **Palace Stables Heritage Centre** (*September-June: 10am-5pm; Sunday 2pm-5pm; July-August: 10am-5.30pm; Sunday 2pm-6pm. Admission charge for the exhibition*) occupies some of the outbuildings of the palace. On two floors, the exhibition tells the story of a day in the life of the palace in 1776. Visitors are guided round by costumed interpreters who play their allotted roles with great conviction. The gardens too are well worth a visit, as is the **Primate's Chapel**, the archbishop's private place of worship, a fine example of Georgian neo-Classical architecture. Play areas, picnic sites and a **garden of the senses** all help make this a popular spot much appreciated by local people.

Around Armagh

Navan*

3km to the west via the A28 towards Killylea. According to historians, this is the site of *Emain Mhacha*, the ancient Celtic capital described in the legendary tales of the *Ulster Cycle*. But archeological investigation of the surrounding area has shown that Navan was inhabited by Mesolithic hunter-gatherers long before the time of the Celts.

The **fort*** was built around 1100 BC, both as a sacred place and as a stronghold surrounded by a defensive ditch. Its tumulus dominates the countryside around. The **Visitor Centre*** (*July-August 10am-7pm; Sunday 11am-7pm; closes 6pm April-June and September, 5pm rest of year. Last admission 75min before closing time. Admission charge*) has a video presentation on the archaeological work carried out here, and on display are a number of objects found on site. The most surprising discovery was that of the skull of a monkey from North Africa, whose arrival here some 2 000 years ago has so far defied explanation.

Gosford Forest Park

At Markethill, 11km southeast via the A28. 8am-dusk. Admission charge. Caravan and camp site (see "Making the most of Armagh and around").

This is one of the most attractive forest parks in the North, laid out in a 240 hectare estate which belonged to the Earls of Gosford. The original castle was destroyed by fire and was replaced at the start of the 19C by the present edifice in pseudo-Norman style *(private residence)*.

In the park are numerous **rare trees** from all over the world including majestic deodar cedars from the Himalayas. Swift spent time as a guest at Gosford, and a semi-circular hollow hedged with yew is known as Dean Swift's Chair.

Ardress House*

At Annaghmore, 11km northeast of Armagh via the B77. April, May and September: Sunday and public holidays 2pm-6pm; June-August: 2pm-6pm except Tuesday. The farmyard is open at the same times and also May and September 12pm-4pm except Tuesday. Admission charge.

In a setting of lovely wooded countryside, this elegant **country house** was the property of the Dublin architect George Ensor, who acquired it by marriage in 1760 and transformed what had been a modest farmhouse into a residence worthy of a

Armagh and around

gentleman. The well-preserved interior has kept its decoration and its opulent Chippendale furniture. The **stuccowork** of the drawing room and the superb collection of **Irish glassware** are particularly fine.

The cobbled **farmyard**, bounded by outbuildings containing all kinds of traditional agricultural implements, is a lively place, with a population of pigs and chickens, ducks, goats and ponies who seem quite unfazed by visitors.

The Argory★

Signposted 3km from Ardress House, or 16km north of Armagh via the A29, then follow signs to the right on the way into Moy. Same opening times as Ardress House.

This lovely **country house** built in pale stone and dating from 1824 is beautifully set in extensive well-wooded parkland on the banks of the River Blackwater. For several generations it was in the ownership of the wealthy Bond family, who decorated it with loving care and attention to detail. The interior has not been changed since the early years of the 20C. The kitchen, the living rooms and the library all show that mixture of refinement, comfort and rustic elegance so typical of the Anglo-Irish Ascendancy of the 19C. The most fascinating single object is the **barrel organ★** on the first floor, still in full working order.

Outside, the **gardens** are a pleasant place for a summer stroll, with a particularly fine collection of **roses★**.

Making the most of Armagh and around

COMING AND GOING

By bus – Bus station on Lonsdale Road, north of the Mall, near Court House (B2). 20 buses daily to Belfast (1hr15min to 2hr10min), 15 Saturday and 8 Sunday.

ADDRESS BOOK

Tourist information – *Armagh Tourist Information Centre*, 40 English Street (B3), ☎ 028 375 218 00. September-June: 9am-5pm; Sunday 2pm-5pm; July-August: 9am-5.30pm; Monday 1pm-5.30pm; closed Sunday. Very professional service with abundant information about the area. The Centre also houses the St Patrick's Trian exhibition, a souvenir shop and a cafeteria.

Banks / Currency exchange – Cash machine opposite the tourist information centre and another in Scotch Street.

Post office – At the back of a grocer cum newsagent's, 31 English Street (B3). 9am-5.30pm; Saturday 9am-12.30pm; closed Sunday. Poste restante is at n° 46 in the same street.

Bicycle hire – *Brown's Bikes*, Scotch Street (B3), ☎ 028 375 227 82. *Armagh City Youth Hostel* (see "Where to stay").

WHERE TO STAY

Under £10

Armagh City Youth Hostel, 39 Abbey Street, ☎ 028 375 118 00, Fax 028 375 118 01 – 62 beds. Between October and March the hostel is closed during the daytime from 11am to 5pm. Comfortable accommodation in a modern building close to the town centre. Cooking and laundry facilities, bicycle hire, etc.

Gosford Forest Park, Markethill, ☎ 028 375 512 77. Eleven kilometres southeast via the A28, caravan and camp site with good facilities in the attractive setting of this Forest Park.

Between £25-30
Padua Guesthouse, 63 Cathedral Road, ☎ 028 375 220 39, Fax 028 375 235 84 – 2rm Basic accommodation in a small family B&B, the main attraction of which (apart from the price) is the amazing collection of dolls adorning the stairs.

Between £40-50
Fairylands Country House, 25 Navan Fort Road, ☎ 028 375 103 15 – 5rm ⌂ TV Modern house in neo-Georgian style with bright, spacious and very well-kept rooms, albeit of no particular charm.

De Averill House, 46 Upper English Street, ☎ 028 375 112 13, Fax 028 375 112 21 – 5rm ⌂ ℘ TV ✕ CC Comfortable hotel in a building dating from the 18C, with spacious rooms decorated simply and tastefully.

Dean's Hill House, College Hill, ☎ 028 375 248 23 – 3rm ⌂ TV Very spacious rooms, most with own facilities, in an 18C vicarage nestling in greenery.

☺ **Charlemont House**, Moy, ☎ 028 877 847 55 – 9rm TV CC Eleven kilometres north of Armagh via the A29. Huge old village house. Bedrooms and the other rooms for the use of guests are furnished with all kinds of antiques and have a charm all their own. One of the very best places to stay in the North.

EATING OUT

Under £10
Shambles, 9 Lower English Street (A2), ☎ 028 375 241 07. Daily 12pm-2.30pm/Friday-Sunday 6.30pm-9.30pm. Traditional pub food in the big main room on the ground floor or in a smaller but quieter room upstairs.

Calvert's Tavern, 3 Scotch Street (B3). Open 12pm-2.30pm / 6pm-10pm except Sunday. Good, inexpensive pub grub. Lively lunchtime atmosphere.

Between £10-15
Jodie's, 37a Scotch Street (B3), ☎ 028 375 275 77. Open Monday-Saturday 12pm-3pm / Wednesday-Sunday 5.30pm-10pm. More or less the only restaurant really worthy of the name in the town centre. Reasonable food but nothing special.

Mandarin House, 30 Scotch Street (B3), ☎ 028 375 222 28. Open 12pm-2pm / 5pm-11pm Tuesday-Saturday and Sunday evening. Chinese restaurant with the advantage of relatively late evening opening, on the upper floor of an old building.

Palace Stables, Palace Demesne (B4), ☎ 028 375 296 29. Open Thursday-Sunday 6pm-10pm. Armagh's best restaurant, especially for anyone wanting to enjoy their evening meal in an historic setting. Cafeteria open at lunchtime.

HAVING A DRINK

Armagh has a good dozen or so pubs with music and a lively atmosphere at the weekend.

Harry Hoots, in the area by the old station, attracts a young crowd and is the coolest spot in town, with live music at the bar and a DJ at the weekend in the upstairs section.

McKenna's, in Lower English Street doesn't have a set programme but there is always a group here on Saturday evenings.

The Northern Bar has traditional music on Tuesday and Sunday evenings, pop on Thursdays and there's an upstairs night-club at the weekend.

The Railway Bar, opposite Harry Hoots. Totally traditional, both in terms of ambience and music, Monday evenings.

OTHER THINGS TO DO

Golf – Armagh County Golf Club, Newry Road, ☎ 028 375 225 01. 18-hole course in a classic woodland setting. Green fee: £12 weekdays, £18 at weekends.

Riding – Moy Riding School, Moy, eleven kilometres north via the A29, ☎ 028 877 844 40. Classic riding school specialising in jumping. Demonstration evenings open to all comers on Fridays.

Making the most of Armagh and around

Index

Shannon Valley: place or attraction described in the text
Joyce, James: individual
Turf: term explained in the text or practical information

MAPS AND PLANS

Manufacture Française des Pneumatiques Michelin

Société en commandite par actions au capital de 2 000 000 000 de francs
Place des Carmes-Déchaux – 63000 Clermont-Ferrand (France)
R.C.S. Clermont-Fd B 855 200 507

© Michelin et Cie, Propriétaires-éditeurs, 2001
Dépôt légal Juillet 2001 – ISBN 2-06-100058-4– ISSN 0763-1383
No part of this publication may be reproduced in any form without
the prior permission of the publisher.

Printed in France 06/01/1.1
Compograveur : Nord Compo – Villeneuve d'Ascq
Imprimeur : IME – Baume-les-Dames

Cover photography:
Traditional farm Meenlaragh, Co Donegal (Pratt-Pries/DIAF)
Young Irish girl (Ch. Boisvieux)
Local shop Clifden, Co Connemara (E. Quéméré/DIAF)

Your opinion matters!

In order to make sure that this collection satisfies the needs of our readers, please help us by completing the following questionnaire with your comments and suggestions and return to:

Michelin Travel Publications   or
The Edward Hyde Building
38 Clarendon Road
Watford, WD1 1SX UK

Michelin Travel Publications
P.O. Box 19008
Greenville, SC 29602-9008
USA

■ YOUR HOLIDAYS/VACATIONS:

I. In general, when you go on holiday or vacation, do you tend to travel... (Choose one)

☐ Independently, on your own
☐ Independently, as a couple
☐ With 1 or 2 friends

☐ With your family
☐ With a group of friends
☐ On organised trips

2. How many international holidays or vacations of I week or more have you taken in the last 3 years? _____

Last 3 destinations: Month/Year:

_____   _____

_____   _____

_____   _____

3. What do you look for most when planning a holiday or vacation?

	Not at all	Sometimes	Essential
Somewhere new and exotic	☐	☐	☐
Real experience/meeting people	☐	☐	☐
Experiencing the wildlife/scenery	☐	☐	☐
Cultural insight	☐	☐	☐
Rest & relaxation	☐	☐	☐
Comfort & well-being	☐	☐	☐
Adventure & the unexpected	☐	☐	☐

4. When travelling, do you take a travel guide with you?

☐ Always   ☐ Usually   ☐ Sometimes   ☐ Never

■ You and the Michelin NEOS guides

5. About your purchase of a NEOS Guide

How long was your holiday where you used the NEOS guide?
How many days? _____
For which country or countries? _____
How long before your departure did you buy it? How many days? _____

6.What made you choose a NEOS Guide?

Highlight everything that applies.

☐ Something new and interesting
☐ The layout
☐ Easy to read format
☐ Cultural details

☐ Quality of the text
☐ Quality of the mapping
☐ Practical Information
☐ Michelin quality

7. Which sections did you use most during your holiday or vacation?

Score 1-4   *(1 = least used)*   *(4 = most used)*

"Setting the Scene"	☐ 1	☐ 2	☐ 3	☐ 4
"Meeting the People"	☐ 1	☐ 2	☐ 3	☐ 4
"Practical Information"	☐ 1	☐ 2	☐ 3	☐ 4
"Exploring …"	☐ 1	☐ 2	☐ 3	☐ 4

8. How would you rate the following aspects of your NEOS guide?

Score 1-4   *(1 = Poor)*   *(4 = Excellent)*

Cover design	☐ 1	☐ 2	☐ 3	☐ 4
Chapter Order	☐ 1	☐ 2	☐ 3	☐ 4
Layout (photos, diagrams)	☐ 1	☐ 2	☐ 3	☐ 4
Ease of reading (typeface)	☐ 1	☐ 2	☐ 3	☐ 4
Style of writing	☐ 1	☐ 2	☐ 3	☐ 4
Text boxes and stories	☐ 1	☐ 2	☐ 3	☐ 4
Plans & Maps	☐ 1	☐ 2	☐ 3	☐ 4
Star ratings system	☐ 1	☐ 2	☐ 3	☐ 4
Format	☐ 1	☐ 2	☐ 3	☐ 4
Weight	☐ 1	☐ 2	☐ 3	☐ 4
Durability	☐ 1	☐ 2	☐ 3	☐ 4
Price	☐ 1	☐ 2	☐ 3	☐ 4

9. Did you use other travel guides during your trip?   ☐ Yes   ☐ No
If yes, which ones? _____

10. Please give your NEOS guide a rating out of 20: ____/20 (with 20 as top rating)
Would you use a NEOS guide for your next trip?   ☐ Yes   ☐ No
If no, why not? _____
Which other destinations would you like NEOS to cover? _____

11. Any other comments or suggestions: _____

_____

_____

_____

_____

_____

_____

Surname/Last Name: _____ First Name: _____

Address: _____

Age: _____ Sex: ☐ M ☐ F

Profession: _____

Where did you purchase your NEOS Guide: What type of store?
                                         Which country?